Reference

Rev. Greg Crocker

WILLMINGTON'S
SURVEY OF THE OLD TESTAMENT

WILLMINGTON'S SURVEY OF THE OLD TESTAMENT

AN OVERVIEW OF THE SCRIPTURES FROM CREATION TO CHRIST

Harold L. Willmington

Copyright

All Scripture quotations are from the *King James Version*.

Recommended Dewey Decimal Classification: 221
Suggested Subject Headings: BIBLE, OLD TESTAMENT

Library of Congress Catalog Card Number: 86-63141
ISBN: 0-88207-824-0

VICTOR BOOKS
A division of SP Publications
Wheaton, Illinois 60187

Art Acknowledgments

National Aeronautics and Space Administration: Page 22.
Victor Handbook of Bible Knowledge, © V. Gilbert Beers, 1981: Pages 60, 82, 160, 166, 174, 180, 234, 252, 298, 348, 379, 383, 564.
Willmington's Guide to the Bible, © 1981, Tyndale House: Page 340.
Visualized Study Bible, © 1981, Hugh Claycombe: Page 363.
Bettman Archives: Pages 26, 47, 56, 80, 93, 112, 116, 140, 154, 190, 280, 286, 500.
Culver Pictures: Pages 106, 111, 332.
Art Resources: Pages 32, 52, 220, 228, 529.
The Doré Bible Illustrations: Pages 24, 28, 33, 34, 38, 48, 67, 98, 170, 182, 186, 189, 212, 259, 293, 307, 310, 354, 421, 457, 478, 489, 496, 507, 514, 521, 537, 569, 591, 607, 613.
The Oriental Institute of the University of Chicago: Page 457.

ACKNOWLEDGMENTS

The following scholars have contributed greatly to this volume:

JERRY H. COMBEE, B.A., M.A., Ph.D.
Dean, School of Business and Government,
Professor of Political Science
Liberty University

PAUL R. FINK, B.A., Th.M., Adv. M.Ed., Th.D.
Professor of Pastoral Ministries
Liberty University

F. GERALD KROLL, B.A., M.Div., D. Min.
Associate Professor of Pastoral Ministries
Liberty University

NEAL D. WILLIAMS, B.A., Th.M., Th.D.
Associate Professor of Biblical Studies
Liberty University

TABLE OF CONTENTS

DEDICATION

This Old Testament volume is dedicated to the more than 20,000 faithful students presently enrolled in the Liberty Home Bible Institute. They can be found in every state in the United States and in over 40 foreign countries. All share, however, a common love for the wonderful Word of God!

PREFACE

GO FOR THE GOLD! This book summarizes the entire Old Testament in 96 lessons. Its supreme goal is to offer the most pointed and practical overview of the Old Testament ever made available in a single textbook. Each of the 96 lessons is presented through a unique, unified, and useful 4-phased teaching plan.

Phase One:
This features *ORIENTATION,* and answers the question, "What are the main features of this lesson?" The orientation consists of both a paragraph preview and a charted overview.

Phase Two:
This features *INFORMATION,* and answers the question, "What does this lesson say?" Phase One is, in essence, a printed chronological and analytical outline arrangement of those key bottom-line verses which, by themselves, relate in concise fashion the scriptural account.

Phase Three:
This features *INTERPRETATION,* and answers the question, "What does this lesson mean?" The printed scriptural account of each lesson is followed by one or more commentary sections which aptly explain the meaning of the verses.

Phase Four:
This features *ILLUSTRATION,* and answers the question, "How can this lesson be best visualized and clarified?" Many graphs, charts, maps, and photos can be found among the 96 lessons.

The Creation Stage

Genesis 1–11

I. The Creation of All Things (Gen. 1–2)
   A. First day: the creation of light (1:2-5)
   B. Second day: the separating of the waters (1:6-8)
   C. Third day: the creation of plant life (1:9-13)
   D. Fourth day: the creation of the sun, moon, and stars (1:14-19)
   E. Fifth day: the creation of fish and fowl (1:20-23)
   F. Sixth day: the creation of land creatures and man (1:24-31)
   G. Seventh day: God rests (2:1-3)

II. The Corruption of All Things (Gen. 3–5)
   A. The subtlety of Satan (3:1-5)
   B. The sin of Adam (3:6-8)
   C. The redemption of God (3:9-23)
   D. The martyrdom of Abel (Gen. 4)
   E. The ministry of Enoch (Gen. 5)

III. The Condemnation of All Things (Gen. 6–9)
   A. The conditions preceding the Flood (6:1-8)
   B. The salvation through the Flood (7:1–8:22)
   C. The tragedy following the Flood (9:20-29)

IV. The Confusion of All Things (Gen. 10–11)
   A. The arrogance of man (11:1-4)
   B. The judgment of God (11:5-7)
   C. The origin of nations (11:8-9)

The Patriarchal Stage

Genesis 12–50; Job

I. The Story of Abraham (Gen. 12–24)
   A. His conversion
   B. His calling (12:1; Josh. 24:2-3; Acts 7:2-3)
   C. His commission (Gen. 12:2-3)
   D. His caution (11:31-32)
   E. His Canaan (12:4-9)
   F. His carnality (12:10-20)
   G. His condescension (13:1-18)
   H. His courage (14:1-16)
   I. His communion (14:17-24)
   J. His covenant (15:1-21)
   K. His compromise (16:1-16)
   L. His circumcision (17:1-27)
   M. His compassion (18:1-33)
   N. His corrupted kin (19:1-14)
   O. His carnality—second time (20:1-18)
   P. His celebration (21:1-34)
   Q. His calvary (22:1-24)
   R. His cave (23:1-20)
   S. His command (24:1-67)
   T. His Keturah (25:1-6)
   U. His city (25:7-10; Heb. 11:8-10)

II. The Story of Isaac (Gen. 25–27)
   A. On a Jerusalem mountain—the submissive son (22:1-14)
   B. By a Hebron field—the gentle groom (24:61-67)
   C. In a Philistine apartment—the copycat (26:1-11)
   D. Alongside some desert wells—the well digger (26:15-22)
   E. At a supper table—the frustrated father (27:1-46)

III. The Story of Jacob (Gen. 28–35)
   A. The devising brother (25:27-34)
   B. The deceitful son (27:11-29)
   C. The dreaming pilgrim (28:1-22)
   D. The love-struck suitor (29:1-20)
   E. The frustrated family man (29:21–30:24)
   F. The enterprising employee (30:25–31:55)
   G. The determined wrestler (Gen. 32–33)
   H. The enraged father (Gen. 34)
   I. The obedient patriarch (35:1-7)
   J. The sorrowing saint (35:8-29)

IV. The Story of Joseph (Gen. 37; 39–50)
   A. The favored son (Gen. 37)
   B. The faithful steward (Gen. 39)
   C. The forgotten servant (Gen. 40)
   D. The famed statesman (Gen. 41–44)
   E. The forgiving saint (Gen. 45–48)
   F. The fruitful shade tree (Gen. 49–50)
   G. The foreshadow of the Saviour

V. The Story of Job (Job 1–42)
   A. His terrible trials (Job 1–2)
   B. His whimpering wife (2:9-10)
   C. His fickle friends (2:11-13; 3–37)
   D. His glorious God (Job 38–41)
   E. His bountiful blessings (42:7-17)

The Exodus Stage

Exodus; Leviticus; Numbers; Deuteronomy

I. Israel, Enslaved in Egypt (Ex. 1:1–12:36)
   A. God's people (Ex. 1)
   B. God's grace (2:23-25)
   C. God's man—Moses! (Ex. 3–4)
   D. God's enemy—Pharaoh! (Ex. 5–10)
   E. God's plagues (Ex. 7–11)
   F. God's salvation
   G. God's selection

II. Israel, En Route to Mount Sinai (Ex. 12:37–18:27)
   A. Round one
   B. Round two
   C. Round three
   D. Round four
   E. Round five
   F. Round six

III. Israel, Settled Down at Sinai (Ex. 19:1–Num. 10:10)
   A. An introduction to the action at Mount Sinai
   B. A consideration of the action at Mount Sinai
      1. *The commandment of the Law*
      2. *The corruption of the golden calf (Ex. 32:1)*
      3. *The construction of the tabernacle (Ex. 25–31; 35–40)*

IV. Israel, from Sinai to Kadesh-barnea (Num. 10:11–12:16)
   A. Mobilizing for the march (10:11-28)
   B. A balking brother-in-law (10:29-32)
   C. The cloud of the covenant (10:33-36)
   D. A fiery judgment (11:1-3)
   E. A malicious mixed multitude (11:4-9)
   F. A provoked prophet (11:10-30)
   G. A deadly diet (11:31-35)
   H. A suffering sister (Num. 12)

V. Israel, at Kadesh-barnea (Num. 13–14)
   A. The penetration by the spies (13:1-25)
   B. The lamentation by the people (13:26–14:10)
   C. The condemnation by the Lord (14:11-45)

VI. Israel, from Kadesh-barnea to the Eastern Bank of Jordan (Num. 15–36)
   A. The stoning of a Sabbath-breaker (15:32-36)
   B. The rebellion and destruction of Korah (Num. 16)
   C. The budding of Aaron's rod (Num. 17)
   D. The death of Miriam, Moses' sister (20:1)
   E. The sin of Moses (20:1-13)
   F. The animosity of the Edomites (20:14-22)
   G. The death of Aaron (20:23-29)
   H. The serpent of brass (21:5-9)
   I. A perverted prophet named Balaam (Num. 22–24)
   J. A zealous priest (Num. 25)
   K. The second census (Num. 26)
   L. A change in commanders (27:12-23)
   M. The destruction of Midian (Num. 31)
   N. Some worldly warriors (Num. 32)
   O. Six cities of salvation (Num. 35)

VII. Israel, on the Eastern Side of the Jordan River (Deut.). Final Acts of Moses
   A. His three sermons
      1. *First sermon* (Deut. 1–4)
      2. *Second sermon* (Deut. 5–26)
      3. *Third sermon* (Deut. 27–30)
   B. His challenges to Joshua (Deut. 31)
   C. His song (Deut. 32)
   D. His blessings on the individual tribes (Deut. 33)
   E. His departure for heaven (31:2, 14-18; 32:48-52; 34:1-12)

The Conquest Stage

Joshua

I. The Invasion of the Land—Israel Claims Its Possessions (Josh. 1–5)
   A. The preparation (Josh. 1)
   B. The penetration (Josh. 2)
   C. The promise (Josh. 3)
   D. The passage (Josh. 3)
   E. The pyramid of stones (4:2, 8-9, 21)
   F. The perplexity (5:1)
   G. The purification of the people (5:3)
   H. The Passover (5:10)
   I. The palatable diet (5:11-12)
   J. The Prince from heaven (5:13-15)

II. The Subjection of the Land—Israel Conquers Its Possessions (Josh. 6–8)
   The central campaign
   A. Jericho—a city shouted down (Josh. 6)
   B. Ai—the arrogance knocked down (7:1-13)
   C. Achor—a sinner sought down (7:14-26)
   D. Gerizim and Ebal—the Law handed down (8:30-35)

   The southern campaign (Josh. 9–10)
   A. Gibeon—the wool pulled down (Josh. 9)
   B. Aijalon—the sun shone down (10:1-15)
   C. Makkedah—the enemy trampled down (10:16-43)

   The northern campaign (Josh. 11–12)
   A. The waters of Merom—the horses slowed down (11:6, 9)
   B. Hazor—a capital burned down (11:10-13)

III. The Distribution of the Land—Israel Colonizes Its Possessions (Josh. 13–24)
   A. The land divided
   B. A warrior excited
   C. An altar indicted
   D. A final sermon recited

The Judges Stage

Judges; Ruth; 1 Samuel 1–7

I. The Angel of the Lord (Christ Himself)

II. The Spirit of God

III. An Evil Spirit

IV. Twelve Military Reformers—the Judges
   A. First judge: Othniel (Jud. 1:12-13; 3:7-11)
   B. Second judge: Ehud (3:12-30)
   C. Third judge: Shamgar (3:31)
   D. Fourth judge: Barak (as helped by Deborah, Jud. 4–5)
   E. Fifth judge: Gideon (Jud. 6–8)
   F. Sixth judge: Tola (10:1)
   G. Seventh judge: Jair (10:3-5)
   H. Eighth judge: Jephthah (10:6–12:7)
   I. Ninth judge: Ibzan (12:8-10)
   J. Tenth judge: Elon (12:11-12)
   K. Eleventh judge: Abdon (12:13-15)
   L. Twelfth judge: Samson (Jud. 13–16)

V. A Bloody Butcher—Abimelech (Jud. 9)

VI. An Idol-worshiping Son—Micah (Jud. 17–18)

VII. A Cowardly Levite (Jud. 19–21)
   A. The wickedness in Benjamin
   B. The war against Benjamin
   C. The wives for Benjamin

VIII. A Moabite Girl—Ruth (Ruth 1–4)
   A. Ruth renouncing (Ruth 1)
   B. Ruth requesting (Ruth 2)
   C. Ruth resting (Ruth 3)
   D. Ruth reaping (Ruth 4)

IX. A Dedicated Mother—Hannah (1 Sam. 1:1–2:11, 18-21)

X. An Undisciplined Priest—Eli (2:12-17, 22-36; 4:1-22)

XI. Some Frustrated Philistines (1 Sam. 5–6)

XII. A Circuit-riding Preacher—Samuel (1 Sam. 7)

The United Kingdom Stage

1 Chron.; 2 Chron. 1–9; 1 Sam. 8–31; 1 Kings 1–11; Ps.; Song; Ecc.; Prov.

THE RULERS OF THIS STAGE

I. Saul, Israel's First King (1 Sam. 8–15; 1 Chron. 10)
   A. The selection of Saul
   B. The rejection of Saul

II. David, Israel's Finest King (1 Sam. 16–2 Sam. 24; 1 Chron. 11–29)
   A. David, the shepherd (1 Sam. 16:1-13)
   B. David, the singer (16:14-23)
   C. David, the soldier (1 Sam. 17)
   D. David, the sought (1 Sam. 18–31)
   E. David, the sovereign (2 Sam. 1–10; 1 Chron. 11–19)
   F. David, the sinner (2 Sam. 11)
   G. David, the sorrowful (2 Sam. 12–19; 1 Chron. 20–21)
   H. David, the statesman (2 Sam. 21:1-14)
   I. David, the census taker (2 Sam. 24; 1 Chron. 21)
   J. David, the sponsor (1 Chron. 22–29)
   K. David, the scribe

III. Solomon, Israel's Fabulous King (1 Kings 1–11; 2 Chron. 1–9)
   A. His triumph over his enemies (1 Kings 1:1-12, 46)
   B. His talent from God (3:4-28; 2 Chron. 1:3-12)
   C. His total and tranquil reign over all Israel (1 Kings 4:1-34)
   D. His temple of worship (1 Kings 5–8; 2 Chron. 2–7)
   E. His treasury of riches
   F. His testimony throughout the land (1 Kings 4:29-34; 10:1-13)
   G. His transgressions against God

THE WRITINGS OF THIS STAGE

I. The Psalms
   There are (at least) five ways one may study the Psalms.
   A. By book division (each division ends with a doxology)
   B. By authorship
   C. By subject matter
   D. By messianic content
   E. By suggested chapter titles

II. Proverbs
   It is impossible to construct a chronological outline of this book. At least 11 main subjects are discussed.
   A. A good name
   B. Youth and discipline
   C. Business matters
   D. Marriage
   E. Immorality
   F. Evil companions
   G. Wisdom
   H. Self-control
   I. Strong drink
   J. Friendship
   K. Words and the tongue

III. Ecclesiastes
   A. The quest—man's problems stated (Ecc. 1–2)
   B. The digest—man's problems studied (Ecc. 3–10)
   C. The best—man's problems solved (Ecc. 11–12)

IV. Song of Solomon
   A. Act 1—the shulamite cinderella
   B. Act 2—the shepherd stranger
   C. Act 3—the mighty monarch

The Chaotic Kingdom Stage

1 Kings 12–22; 2 Kings; 2 Chron. 10–36; Obad.; Joel; Jonah; Amos; Hosea; Micah; Isa.; Nahum; Zeph.; Hab.; Jer.; (Lam.)

I. An Introduction to the Chaotic Kingdom Stage
   A. The Northern Kingdom
   B. The Southern Kingdom

II. The Rulers of the Chaotic Kingdom Stage

Northern Rulers
   A. Jeroboam
   B. Nadab
   C. Baasha
   D. Elah
   E. Zimri
   F. Omri
   G. Ahab
   H. Ahaziah
   I. Jehoram
   J. Jehu
   K. Jehoahaz
   L. Jehoash
   M. Jeroboam II
   N. Zechariah
   O. Shallum
   P. Menahem
   Q. Pekahiah
   R. Pekah
   S. Hoshea

Southern Rulers
   A. Rehoboam
   B. Abijam
   C. Asa
   D. Jehoshaphat
   E. Joram
   F. Ahaziah
   G. Athaliah
   H. Joash
   I. Amaziah
   J. Uzziah
   K. Jotham
   L. Ahaz
   M. Hezekiah
   N. Manasseh
   O. Amon
   P. Josiah
   Q. Jehoahaz
   R. Jehoiakim
   S. Jehoiachin
   T. Zedekiah

III. The Prophets of the Chaotic Kingdom Stage
   A. The Nature of the Prophets
   B. The Names of the Prophets
   C. The Important Oral Prophets
      1. Elijah
      2. Elisha

IV. The Old Testament Books Written during the Chaotic Kingdom Stage

Obadiah (Destination Edom)
   A. The house of Edom—to be reviled by God (vv. 1-16)
   B. The house of Jacob—to be revived by God (vv. 17-21)

Jonah (Destination Nineveh)
   A. Jonah protesting—a demonstration of God's patience (Jonah 1)
   B. Jonah praying—a demonstration of God's pardon (Jonah 2)
   C. Jonah preaching—a demonstration of God's power (Jonah 3)
   D. Jonah pouting—a demonstration of God's pity (Jonah 4)

Joel (Destination Southern Kingdom)
   A. Israel and God's judgment—a review of the past (1:1-20)
   B. Israel and God's judgment—a preview of the future (Joel 2–3)

Amos (Destination Northern Kingdom)
   A. Eight nations denounced (Amos 1–6)
   B. Five visions announced (Amos 7–9)

Hosea (Destination Northern Kingdom)
   A. A grieving husband and his grievous wife (Hosea 1–3); Hosea and Gomer
   B. A grieving Husband and His grievous wife (Hosea 4–14); God and Israel

Isaiah (Destination Southern Kingdom)
   A. A general outline of Isaiah
   B. A summary of Isaiah's prophecies
   C. The Gentile nations in Isaiah

D. The nation Israel in Isaiah
E. The fall of Satan in Isaiah
F. The greatness of God in Isaiah
G. The Son of God in Isaiah
H. The Tribulation in Isaiah
I. The Millennium in Isaiah

Zephaniah (Destination Southern Kingdom)

A. A bad day—the prophet pronounces judgment (1:1–3:8)
B. A glad day—the prophet announces justice (3:9–20)

Habakkuk (Destination Southern Kingdom)

A. The doubts (Hab. 1–2)
B. The shouts (Hab. 3)

Jeremiah (Destination Southern Kingdom)

A. A personal history of Jeremiah
B. The rulers that Jeremiah ministered under
C. The threefold ministry of Jeremiah
D. The prophecies of Jeremiah
E. The New Covenant of Jeremiah
F. The sufferings of Jeremiah
G. Classic passages in Jeremiah

Micah (Destination Southern Kingdom)

A. The outward look—Micah's public sermons (Micah 1–6)
B. The inward look—Micah's personal contemplations (7:1-6)
C. The upward look—Micah's prayerful petitions (7:7-20)

Nahum (Destination Nineveh)

A. The patience of God (1:1-8)
B. The pride of Sennacherib (1:9-14)
C. The promise to Judah (1:15)
D. The punishment of Nineveh (Nahum 2–3)

Lamentations (Destination Southern Kingdom)

A. The provocation against God (Lam. 1)
B. The punishment from God (Lam. 2)
C. The prophet of God (Lam. 3)
D. The people of God (Lam. 4)
E. The prayer to God (Lam. 5)

The Captivity Stage

Ezekiel; Daniel

Daniel

I. A Divine Diet (Dan. 1)

II. A Statue and a Stone (Dan. 2)

III. A Fiery Furnace (Dan. 3)

IV. A Tree in Turmoil (Dan. 4)

V. A Heavenly Hand (Dan. 5)

VI. The Lions and the Lionhearted (Dan. 6)

VII. Godless Kingdoms and the Kingdom of God (Dan. 7)

VIII. The Horns of the Heathen (Dan. 7–8)

IX. The Secret of the Seventy Sevens (9:20-27)

X. The Conflict above the Clouds (Dan. 10)

XI. A Chronology of Christless Kings (Dan. 11)

XII. Closing Conditions (Dan. 12)

Ezekiel

I. The Sanctification of the Man of God—Ezekiel (Ezek. 1–3; 33)

II. The Desolation of the City of God—Jerusalem (Ezek. 4–24)

III. The Condemnation of the Enemies of God (Ezek. 25–32; 35)

IV. The Presentation of the Shepherd of God—Jesus Christ (Ezek. 34)

V. The Restoration of the Nation of God—Israel (Ezek. 36–37)

VI. The Demonstration of the Wrath of God—Russia (Ezek. 38–39)

VII. The Manifestation of the Glory of God—the Temple (Ezek. 40–48)

The Return Stage

Ezra; Esther; Nehemiah; Haggai; Zechariah; Malachi

Ezra

I. The Return to Jerusalem under Zerubbabel (Ezra 1–6)

II. The Return to Jerusalem under Ezra (Ezra 7–10)

Esther

I. The Rise of Esther (Es. 1–2)
II. The Lies of Haman (Es. 3–5)
III. The Prize of Faith (Es. 6–10)

Nehemiah

I. The News concerning the Wall (Neh. 1)

II. The Request to Build the Wall (2:1-8)

III. The Necessity for the Wall (2:9-20)

IV. The Gates in the Wall (Neh. 3)

V. The Opposition to the Wall (Neh. 4; 6:1-14)

VI. The Builder of the Wall—Nehemiah

VII. Blessings of the (Completed) Wall (6:15-19)

Zechariah

I. The Visions of the Prophet (Zech. 1–6)

II. The Vanities of the People (Zech. 7–8)

III. The Victories of the Greeks and Jews

IV. The Visitations of the Prince (Zech. 9–14)

A. The first coming of the Prince
B. The second coming of the Prince

Haggai

I. A September Message, Directed to the Hands of the People. It said, *perform* (Hag. 1)

II. An October Message, Directed to the Hearts of the People. It said, *patience* (2:1-9)

III. A December Message, Directed to the Head of the People. It said, *ponder* (2:10-23)

Malachi

I. The Love of God Stated (1:1-5)
II. The Love of God Scorned
III. The Love of God Shown

Preview of the Old Testament

In the councils of eternity past the divine decision was made. Even today angels and mortals are prone to gasp in amazement as they ponder the implications of that mind-boggling plan. Here was the decision. In the fullness of time, the sinless Son of God would visit a cursed planet and shed His blood for its sinful inhabitants. Could anything more unexpected and undeserved be imagined?

But many things must first precede and prepare for that glorious journey from heaven to earth. To begin with, man and his universe would be created. Then, among the many, a particular nation would be selected to serve as a divine channel. Finally, all those events, places, and personalities playing a part in that glorious tale consummated at Bethlehem had to be carefully and accurately recorded. God's schedule called for 30 human authors to describe that sovereign story in some detail. Moses was the first and Malachi the final writer. However, God was in no hurry to complete His marvelous manuscript. A thousand years would transpire between the first and last Old Testament books. Then an additional four centuries passed before the beginning of the New Testament. But that is another story.

Overview of the Old Testament

<table>
<tr><td>SCRIPTURE</td><td colspan="4">The Entire Old Testament</td></tr>
<tr><td rowspan="2">SUBJECT</td><td rowspan="2">Creating the planets</td><td rowspan="2">Choosing a people</td><td colspan="2">To serve as a channel for the Scriptures</td></tr>
<tr><td colspan="2">To serve as a channel for the Saviour</td></tr>
<tr><td rowspan="3">SPECIFICS</td><td rowspan="3">NINE BASIC STAGES</td><td>1 The Creation Stage</td><td>2 The Patriarchal Stage</td><td>3 The Exodus Stage</td></tr>
<tr><td>4 The Conquest Stage</td><td>5 The Judges Stage</td><td>6 The United Kingdom Stage</td></tr>
<tr><td>7 The Divided Kingdom Stage</td><td>8 The Babylonian Captivity Stage</td><td>9 The Return Stage</td></tr>
<tr><td>SAINTS AND SINNERS</td><td colspan="4">Adam, Noah, Abraham, Moses, Joshua, David</td></tr>
<tr><td rowspan="2">SENTENCE SUMMARIES</td><td>O.T. Verses</td><td colspan="3">"The statutes of the LORD are right, rejoicing the heart; the commandment of the LORD is pure, enlightening the eyes. . . . More to be desired are they than gold, yea, than much fine gold. Sweeter also than honey and the honeycomb" (Ps. 19:8, 10).</td></tr>
<tr><td>N.T. Verses</td><td colspan="3">"Verily I say unto you, 'Till heaven and earth pass, one jot or one tittle shall in no wise pass from the Law, till all be fulfilled' " (Matt. 5:18).
"For the prophecy came not in old time by the will of man; but holy men of God spake as they were moved by the Holy Ghost" (2 Peter 1:21).</td></tr>
</table>

Creation

There are 1,189 chapters in God's Word, the Bible. Undoubtedly, the most important among all these are the first 11 for they effectively serve as sturdy foundations on which the remaining 1,178 chapters firmly rest. If one rightly understands the divine information presented here, then a clear and concise picture appears, showing in some detail the origin, purpose, and future of all things.

The necessity for accepting these early chapters in a literal, factual, normal, and historical manner cannot be overstated if one is to correctly ponder his past, and please his God! Note the pointed words of Jesus and the writer to the Hebrews:

"If I have told you earthly things, and ye believe not, how shall ye believe, if I tell you heavenly things?" (John 3:12)

"Through faith we understand that the worlds were framed by the word of God, so that things which are seen were not made of things which do appear. . . . But without faith it is impossible to please Him; for he that cometh to God must believe that He is, and that He is a rewarder of them that diligently seek Him" (Heb. 11:3, 6).

Four stupendous events transpire during this original stage. Each is mind-staggering. The final three would forever and radically change the course of history. These four are:

1. The origin of all things
2. The Fall of man
3. The universal Flood
4. The Tower of Babel

One may well experience confusion and depression at the completion of this stage. How could a story which began with such majesty end at Babel with such idolatry?

But this is only the first stage in the story. One must read on for the answer.

Preview

God's Wonderful Work Week

GENESIS 1–2

"In the beginning God created the heaven and the earth" (Gen. 1:1). Of the 23,214 Old Testament verses, this is without doubt the most important. *First* of all, it serves as a factual summary verse. In 10 short, simple, but sublime words we are informed concerning the WHEN, WHO, HOW, and WHAT of all things.

"In the beginning." That's the WHEN!

"God." That's the WHO!

"Created." That's the HOW!

All things, "the heaven and the earth." That's the WHAT!

The only question not answered in this first verse is the WHY of all things. David would later answer that question:

"The heavens declare the glory of God, and the firmament showeth His handiwork" (Ps. 19:1).

Secondly, Genesis 1:1 is a corrective verse, for it refutes many false isms today. It denies both polytheism (the belief in many gods) and atheism (the belief in no god). The grievous errors of pantheism, evolutionism, materialism, and fatalism are also soundly condemned.

Thus, the very first verse in Genesis gives us the *theology* of Creation, while the remaining 30 verses provide us with the *chronology* of Creation. In a nutshell we are clearly informed that in six days the Almighty God created all things, from electrons to galaxies, from dandelions to dinosaurs, and from apples to Adam!

But mighty Creation was not the end, only the means to something even more wonderful. God's workday schedule now gives way to His wedding-day schedule. Watch carefully, for here comes the bride!

Overview

<table>
<tr><td>SCRIPTURE</td><td colspan="5">Genesis 1–2</td></tr>
<tr><td>SUBJECT</td><td colspan="5">Creation of all things and the first marriage</td></tr>
<tr><td rowspan="8">SPECIFICS</td><td colspan="3">God's work schedule</td><td colspan="2">God's wedding schedule</td></tr>
<tr><td rowspan="7">The work week</td><td>1</td><td>Light</td><td rowspan="4">Step 1</td><td rowspan="4">Eve is removed from the side of Adam</td></tr>
<tr><td>2</td><td>Space & water</td></tr>
<tr><td>3</td><td>Plant life</td></tr>
<tr><td>4</td><td>Sun, moon, stars</td></tr>
<tr><td>5</td><td>Fish & fowl</td><td rowspan="3">Step 2</td><td rowspan="3">Eve is returned to the side of Adam</td></tr>
<tr><td>6</td><td>Animals & man</td></tr>
<tr><td>7</td><td>God rests</td></tr>
<tr><td>SAINTS AND SINNERS</td><td colspan="5">Adam and his wife Eve</td></tr>
<tr><td rowspan="2">SENTENCE SUMMARIES</td><td>O.T. Verse</td><td colspan="4">"Know ye that the LORD He is God; it is He that hath made us, and not we ourselves; we are His people, and the sheep of His pasture" (Ps. 100:3).</td></tr>
<tr><td>N.T. Verse</td><td colspan="4">"Thou art worthy, O LORD, to receive glory and honor and power; for Thou hast created all things, and for Thy pleasure they are and were created" (Rev. 4:11).</td></tr>
</table>

THE CREATION OF ALL THINGS

FIRST DAY

God created light. *"And God said, 'Let there be light' "* (Gen. 1:3).

SECOND DAY

God separated the waters. *"And God said, 'Let there be a firmament in the midst of the waters, and let it divide the waters from the waters' "* (v. 6).

THIRD DAY

God created plant life. *"And God said, 'Let the earth bring forth grass, the herb yielding seed, and the fruit tree yielding fruit after his kind, whose seed is in itself, upon the earth'; and it was so"* (v.11).

FOURTH DAY

God created the sun, moon, and stars. *"And God made two great lights; the greater light to rule the day, and the lesser light to rule the night; He made the stars also"* (v. 16).

FIFTH DAY

God created the fish and fowl. *"And God created great whales, and every living creature that moveth, which the waters brought forth abundantly, after their kind, and every winged foul after his kind; and God saw that it was good"* (v. 21).

SIXTH DAY

God created land creatures and man. *"And God made the beast of the earth after his kind, and cattle after their kind, and everything that creepeth upon the earth after his kind; and God saw that it was good"* (v. 25).

Man was made in the image of God. *"And God said, 'Let Us make man in Our image, after Our likeness; and let them have dominion over the fish of the sea, and over the fowl of the air, and over the cattle, and over all the earth, and over every creeping thing that creepeth upon the earth' "* (v. 26).

Man was to subdue the earth and fill it. *"And God blessed them, and God said unto them, 'Be fruitful, and multiply, and replenish the earth, and subdue it; and have dominion over the fish of the sea, and over the fowl of the air, and over every living thing that moveth upon the earth' "* (v. 28).

He was to enjoy the tree of life and all other trees of Creation except one. *"And out of the ground made the LORD God to grow every tree that is pleasant to the sight, and good for food; the tree of life also in the midst of the Garden, and the tree of knowledge of good and evil. . . . And the LORD God commanded the man, saying, 'Of every tree of the garden thou mayest freely eat' "* (2:9, 16).

He was forbidden to eat of the tree of the knowledge of good and evil. *"But of the tree of the knowledge of good and evil, thou shalt not eat of it; for in the day that thou eatest thereof thou shalt surely die"* (v. 17).

He was to name all the animals. *"And out of the ground the LORD God formed every beast of the field, and every fowl of the air; and brought them unto Adam to see what he would call them; and whatsoever Adam called every living creature, that was the name thereof. And Adam gave names to all cattle, and to every beast of the field; but for Adam there was not found an helpmeet for him"* (vv. 19-20).

Then he was given a wife. *"And the LORD God said, 'It is not good that the man should be alone; I will make him an helpmeet for him.' . . .*

"And the LORD God caused a deep sleep to fall upon Adam, and he slept. And He took one of his ribs, and closed up the flesh instead thereof. And the rib, which the LORD God had taken from man, made He a woman, and brought her unto the man.

"And Adam said, 'This is now bone of my bones, and flesh of my flesh; she shall be called Woman, because she was taken out of Man.'

"Therefore shall a man leave his father and his mother, and shall cleave unto his wife; and they shall be one flesh.

"And they were both naked, the man and his wife, and were not ashamed" (vv. 18, 21-25).

SEVENTH DAY

God rested. *"Thus the heavens and the earth were finished, and all the host of them. And on the seventh day God ended His work which He had made; and He rested on the seventh day from all His work which He had made.*

"And God blessed the seventh day, and sanctified it; because that in it He had rested from all His work which God created and made" (vv. 1-3).

The Days of Creation

COMMENTS

No amount of evolutionary supposition can destroy the simple statement, "In the beginning God created the heaven and the earth." After the smoke of conflict clears, the statement stands, head unbowed.

In the Hebrew, the opening verse of the Bible contains a grammatical discord—a plural subject with a singular verb: "In the beginning God [*Elohim,* a plural noun meaning 'Gods'] created [*bara,* a singular verb meaning 'creates'] the heaven and the earth." This grammatical discord refutes two heresies:

(1) Unitarianism, which denies the Trinity, and

(2) Polytheism, which denies the unity of the Godhead.

The doctrine of the Trinity is confirmed—the truth of the *unity* (there is only one true God) and *tri-unity* (one God eternally coexisting in three Persons: God the Father, God the Son, and God the Holy Spirit).

How are we to understand the "days" of Creation? Four views are commonly held:

(1) *The Pictorial Day View:* The days of Genesis have nothing to do with what was created during them. Rather, they deal with truths God revealed to Moses on six successive days.

(2) *The Day-Age View:* The days of Genesis are not necessarily 24-hour periods. They are indefinite periods of time (as in the phrase—"the Day of the Lord," used elsewhere in the Bible).

(3) *The Gap or Reconstruction View:* Verse 1 of Genesis 1 presents the *original* creation of the heavens and earth. Verse 2 describes how the earth *became* "without form, and void" as the result of God's judgment (probably of Satan); God's "reconstruction" of His Creation followed. A "gap" or long period of time—possibly millions or even billions of years—occurred between verses 1 and 2.

(4) *The Extreme Literal View:* There is no "gap" between verses 1 and 2 and the date of Adam's creation was about 4004 B.C.

None of these views fits the facts. Let us suggest a modification of the fourth view. We may call it simply the Literal View. We cannot dogmatically proclaim 4004 B.C. as the date of Creation. But we can confidently state that there is no gap in Genesis 1.

The language used clearly indicates that the days of Genesis were literal 24-hour days, each occasioned by one rotation of the earth on its own axis. Each day had an evening and a morning, which ages do not. Each day is denoted by a numerical adjective (first, second, third, etc.).

Moses could have selected no clearer language to present the concept of 24-hour days!

Some have seen a discrepancy between the fact that God created light on the first day (vv. 2-5) but did not create the sun, moon, and stars until the fourth day (vv. 14-19). The nature of the light created on the first day is not given. It is a scientific fact that man sees only a small part of the full spectrum of light—he is virtually blind! The lights which God created on the fourth day are particularly suited to that range of the light spectrum in which man's vision is designed to function. The purpose of the sun, moon, and stars is to provide light that is compatible with man—not to determine time or the length of a day. It was possible to have evenings and mornings defined by the rotation of the earth on its axis before the sun, moon, and stars were created.

The first five days of Creation have two functions:

(1) To bring the earth to final form and to fill it with life, thus rectifying the "without form and void" of verse 2.

(2) To prepare all of the support systems necessary for the crown jewel of God's Creation on the sixth day—man.

Man: in the Image of God

COMMENTS

The determination of the inter-Trinity council of Genesis 1:26 ("Let Us make man in Our image") is realized in verse 27 ("So God created man in His own image"). The plural pronouns (Us, Our) in verse 26 show that there is plurality in the Godhead—Father, Son, and Holy Spirit.

Certainly the "image of God" in man is seen in his immaterial part, the fact that he (in distinction from the animals) has intellect, sensibility, and will. However, the parallelism in verse 27 ("in the image of God created He him; male and female created He them") suggests that plurality is also a part of "the image of God." Just as with God it takes three Persons—Father, Son, and Holy Spirit—to make one God, so with man it takes three—male, female, and God—to make a single and complete unit. Both husband and wife should find their centers in God. The closer each draws to God, the closer each draws to the other.

Verse 27 lets us know that sex was God's idea. It was He who created mankind male and female. It was God who gave the command, "Be fruitful, and multiply, and replenish [fill] the earth" (v. 28). This command is unique: it is the only command that God gave to man which man has always willingly tried to obey!

Man was also given the responsibility of subduing the earth and having dominion over all of God's Creation. If the Fall had never taken place, God's perfect will would still have had to be tended. Man's dominion over the rest of Creation is demonstrated by the fact that he assigned names to the animals "and whatsoever Adam called every living creature, that was the name thereof" (2:19).

As the result of his naming of the beasts and fowls, Adam learned what God knew all along—that he was alone and that was not good! Evolution cannot account for the origin of woman—Eve. God made (literally, "built") her from the material He took from Adam's side. Adam recognized her as his equal ("bone of my bones, and flesh of my flesh" [v. 23]). He named her "Woman" ("Mrs. Man"), indicating that from the beginning, man is to be the head of the union between man and woman, and that woman takes her name from man.

Adam's words end in verse 23, and Moses' reflection is recorded in verse 24 in what has been called the Universal Law of Marriage. Three important truths concerning marriage are evident:

(1) The responsibility for a marriage is on the man's shoulders. He is to leave his father and mother and set up a separate economic unit with his wife, independent of both fathers and mothers.

(2) Man is responsible for maintaining the marriage. He is to cleave ("stick to") his wife. If the marriage breaks up it is his responsibility, for he did not cleave to her.

(3) Divorce is not an option for solving marital problems. Husband and wife constitute "one flesh." They are a separate unit comprised of two individuals who cannot be broken apart and still constitute wholes.

In their original state, Adam and Eve "were both naked . . . and were not ashamed" (v. 25). There is no shame in nudity when it takes place in the proper circumstances within the bonds of marriage.

God's sabbatical rest is not an indication that He was weary because of His creative activity. That He "rested on the seventh day from all His work" simply indicates that He ceased any further direct creative activity. God's rest became the pattern for man. Like God, man should cease his activity on the Sabbath. He should devote the day to the worship of his Creator.

Preview

The Agony of Adam in the Garden

GENESIS 3

What a difference a day can bring! Genesis chapter 2 ended so beautifully and blissfully. Earth's first bride and groom were seen with hands and hearts perfectly knit together, strolling toward Eden's magnificent sunset. What a place for a honeymoon! The sights, sounds, and sensations of that glorious hour can scarcely be imagined by their present-day sons and daughters. Perhaps they were serenaded by the music of angels. Certainly they knew the majesty of an unfallen Creation. All the splendor and serenity of that past paradise, however, would soon end, for two hateful and horrible events took place which immediately and eternally changed things, both for the Creator and for His creatures.

The first evil action may have occurred between Genesis 2 and 3, while the second definitely transpired in the middle of chapter 3. What was the nature of these twin tragedies? Both have to do with one word, the worst of all words—SIN! The very sound carries with it the hiss of the serpent.

In Isaiah 14 and Ezekiel 28 we read of an unholy and unsuccessful attempt by a powerful angelic being to take over God's throne. Lucifer was that angel who then became the devil. This was the heinous crime which may have happened between the second and third chapters of Genesis. He is thus seen at the beginning of Genesis 3 enticing Adam and Eve to do what he had previously done—disobey God!

A final thought. Everything that God has ever done, or is doing today, or ever will do, can be placed in one of two categories. These are His work in *Creation,* and His work in *redemption.* Genesis 1 and 3 provide the account of His work in Creation. But with the advent of man's sin in Genesis 3, God rolled up His spiritual sleeves and began His second—and greatest—work, that of redemption! That work still goes on today!

Overview

SCRIPTURE	Genesis 3		
SUBJECT	The Fall of man		
SPECIFICS	The treachery	Satan	The body of the serpent
	The tragedy	Sin	The fruit of the tree
	The triumph	Salvation	The seed of the woman
SAINTS AND SINNERS	Adam, Eve, the serpent, Satan		
SENTENCE SUMMARIES	O.T. Verse	"All we like sheep have gone astray; we have turned every one to his own way; and the LORD hath laid on Him the iniquity of us all" (Isa. 53:6).	
	N.T. Verse	"For as in Adam all die, even so in Christ shall all be made alive" (1 Cor. 15:22).	

THE CORRUPTION OF ALL THINGS

THE SUBTLETY OF SATAN

Speaking through the serpent, Satan began by doubting God's Word. *"Yea, hath God said, 'Ye shall not eat of every tree of the garden'?" (Gen. 3:1)*

Satan ended by denying God's Word. *"And the serpent said. . . . 'Ye shall not surely die. For God doth know that in the day ye eat thereof, then your eyes shall be opened, and ye shall be as gods, knowing good and evil' " (vv. 4-5).*

THE SIN OF ADAM

His foolish act. Eve and Adam became the first human sinners (v. 6; Rom. 5:12; 2 Cor. 11:3; 1 Tim. 2:14). *"And when the woman saw that the tree was good for food, and that it was pleasant to the eyes, and a tree to be desired to make one wise, she took of the fruit thereof, and did eat, and gave also unto her husband with her; and he did eat" (Gen. 3:6).*

His futile attempts. Adam attempted (at first) to hide his nakedness before God. *"And the eyes of them both were opened, and they knew that they were naked; and they sewed fig leaves together, and made themselves aprons" (v. 7).*

Adam attempted (at last) to hide himself from God. *"And they heard the voice of the LORD God walking in the Garden in the cool of the day; and Adam and his wife hid themselves from the presence of the LORD God amongst the trees of the garden" (v. 8).*

The Darkest Chapter in the Bible

COMMENTS

Genesis 3 is the darkest chapter in the Bible. It records how sin entered the world and how people became sinners.

It is a chapter that man, left to himself, would not include in the Bible. Its inclusion is a proof of the Bible's divine inspiration. In the time between the creation of Adam and Moses' writing of this account, man had forgotten this dreadful event. But God had it recorded in His Word so that man would be reminded from whence he had fallen.

The events recorded in this chapter are not a myth. This story is not a fairy tale, nor is it simply a record of what the people of Israel believed. These events are historical, as the New Testament writers understood them to be (see, for example, Rom. 5:12-14; 1 Cor. 15:22; 2 Cor. 11:3; 1 Tim. 2:13-14). Exactly when these events took place is not given. But since it happened before Eve became pregnant, it must have been shortly after the Creation.

Every person born into the world (except Jesus, of course) is related to Adam and Eve and is born a sinner. We are not sinners because we do acts of sin—we do acts of sin because we are sinners. We do not *become* sinners—we *are* sinners. No descendant of Adam is able to do anything to make himself pleasing or presentable to God.

The instrument through which the temptation was presented to Eve was the serpent. The fact that he spoke to Eve and did not startle her indicates that Eve did not regard the serpent's speaking as unusual. It may be that not only the serpent, but other animals in the Garden had the capability of speech and that Adam and Eve could communicate with them. It is an anatomical fact that many animals (canines, for example) have larynges similar to man's. Given the proper kind of tongue and pharyngeal structure, they would be physically and mechanically capable of speech.

In Genesis 2:17, God had said that Adam should not eat of the tree of the knowledge of good and evil. In 3:1, Satan asks through the serpent, "Yea, hath God said. . . ?" One of Satan's favorite attacks is to put a question mark where God puts a period!

Satan's question caused Eve to add to what God had said. She stated that God had not only said that they should not eat of the tree, but also that they should not touch it. God had never said anything about not touching the tree or its fruit. Getting Eve first to question God's Word, then to add to it, prepared Eve for the final step—the serpent's direct denial of God's Word; "Ye shall not surely die."

Eve capitulated and convinced Adam to join her. The result was threefold:

(1) Their eyes were opened. They knew they were naked and attempted to cover themselves.

(2) They died spiritually. Their souls were separated from God, and they sought to hide from Him.

(3) They began to die physically. They did not realize it immediately, but ultimately their bodies would die.

Temptation came to Eve through three channels:

(1) The eye gate—"it was pleasant to the eyes."

(2) The flesh—"good for food."

(3) The pride of life—"to be desired to make one wise."

These are the same three channels through which temptations come to us (cf. 1 John 2:16).

THE REDEMPTION OF GOD

Until now we have seen only those attributes of God—His power and wisdom, for example—directly involved in His *creative* acts.

In Genesis 3, however, after man's sin, we are introduced to God's *redemptive* attributes, those of His holiness and grace.

God's holiness, as He deals with sin. God pronounced a fivefold judgment sentence:

(1) Upon the man: to exert hard labor for his bread. *"And unto Adam He said, 'Because thou hast hearkened unto the voice of thy wife, and hast eaten of the tree, of which I commanded thee, saying, "Thou shalt not eat of it"; cursed is the ground for thy sake; in sorrow shalt thou eat of it all the days of thy life. . . .*

" 'In the sweat of thy face shalt thou eat bread, till thou return unto the ground; for out of it wast thou taken; for dust thou art, and unto dust shalt thou return' " (vv. 17, 19).

(2) Upon the woman: to be in subjection to her husband and to experience pain in childbearing. *"Unto the woman He said, 'I will greatly multiply thy sorrow and thy conception; in sorrow thou shalt bring forth children; and thy desire shall be to thy husband, and he shall rule over thee' " (v. 16).*

(3) Upon all nature: to be infested by thorns, drought, etc. *"Thorns also and thistles shall it bring forth to thee; and thou shalt eat of the herb of the field" (v. 18).*

(4) Upon the serpent: to crawl upon its belly. *"And the LORD God said unto the serpent, 'Because thou hast done this, thou art cursed above all cattle, and above every beast of the field; upon thy belly shalt thou go, and dust shalt thou eat all the days of thy life' " (v. 14).*

(5) Upon the devil: someday to be utterly crushed by the Saviour.

God's grace, as He deals with sinners. God sought out Adam. *"And the LORD God called unto Adam, and said unto him, 'Where art thou?'*

"And he said, 'I heard Thy voice in the Garden, and I was afraid, because I was naked; and I hid myself.'

"And He said, 'Who told thee that thou wast naked? Hast thou eaten of the tree, whereof I commanded thee that thou shouldest not eat?'

"And the man said, 'The woman whom Thou gavest to be with me, she gave me of the tree, and I did eat.'

"And the LORD God said unto the woman,

'What is this that thou hast done?' And the woman said, 'The serpent beguiled me, and I did eat' " (vv. 9-13).

God promised them a Saviour. *"And I will put enmity between thee and the woman, and between thy seed and her seed; it shall bruise thy head, and thou shalt bruise His heel" (v. 15).*

This all-important verse is knows as the *proto-evangel*—the first (*proto*) Gospel (*evangel*) promise in the Bible.

God clothed them. *"Unto Adam also and to his wife did the LORD God make coats of skins, and clothed them"* (v. 21).

God removed them from Eden. *"And the LORD God said, 'Behold, the man is become as one of Us, to know good and evil; and now, lest he put forth his hand, and take also of the tree of life, and eat, and live forever'; therefore the LORD God sent him forth from the Garden of Eden, to till the ground from whence he was taken.*

"So He drove out the man, and He placed at the east of the Garden of Eden cherubims, and a flaming sword which turned every way, to keep the way of the tree of life" (vv. 22-24).

Driving Adam and Eve from the Garden was an act of mercy. God did not want them to eat of the tree of life and thus be forced to live forever in their sin.

Angels (the cherubim) now began their ministry to men.

The Fall

COMMENTS

God's question, "Where art thou?" (v. 9) is pedagogic. God knew full well where Adam was. Adam, however, needed to realize that something was drastically wrong when creatures whose chief delight had been to fellowship with God suddenly began to run away and try to hide from Him.

The first words from fallen man were half-truths, evasions, and attempted deceptions.

(1) "I heard Thy voice (sound) in the Garden."

(2) "I was afraid."

(3) "I was naked."

(4) "I hid myself" (v. 10).

God's first question in verse 11—"Who told thee that thou wast naked?"—was designed to arouse guilt. Adam must have done something to make him realize that he was naked.

God's next question—"Hast thou eaten of the tree, whereof I commanded thee that thou shouldest not eat?"—was designed to drive Adam to admit his guilt. But notice Adam's threefold response to God's interrogation.

(1) He refused to admit guilt.

(2) He blamed the woman directly.

(3) He blamed God indirectly.

Adam had aspired to Godlikeness. But he now stood before God shamefaced and guilty. He had no defense. He was convicted, and his excuses were not worth refuting.

As God turned to interrogate Eve, His question pointed to the enormity of her deed. Eve also refused to admit guilt and blamed the serpent. She too was convicted, and her excuses were likewise not worth refuting.

Tremendous anatomical changes occurred as the result of man's sin and God's judgment.

(1) The serpent had apparently walked on legs before the Fall, for now God condemned him to go on his belly and to eat dust. Many speculations have been made as to the exact identity of the serpent in the Garden of Eden. Ancient Jewish commentators suggested that the serpent may have been what we know as the dinosaur, and that the curse accounts for its extinction. However, one would have to admit that a legless dinosaur would make a rather large snake! In any event, God not only judged the serpent as the instrument of temptation, but also Satan as the instigator of the temptation. In verse 15 God gave the first prophecy in the Bible (spoken to Satan), announcing "the conflict of the ages." As a general principle, God gives a prophecy after man has broken down in sin. The conflict between Satan and Christ will result in Satan's winning a temporary victory ("thou shalt bruise His heel"). But it will terminate in Christ's seed of woman ultimately defeating Satan completely ("it shall bruise thy head").

(2) Adam's and Eve's lives were also changed as a result of sin. Women would experience pain in childbirth. To insure woman's willingness to conceive, God gave her a heightened sexual desire ("thy desire shall be to thy husband"). She was also made subject to her husband ("he shall rule over thee").

Because of the Fall, man, perspiring freely, would have to earn his living from a cursed ground that brings forth thorns and thistles. Creation was cursed because of man's sin. Sinful man could not exist in a perfect environment. The environment had to be cursed so its condition would match man's. The whole creation earnestly looks forward to the time when the curse will be lifted (cf. Rom. 8:19-21).

In spite of the darkness of the moments after the Fall, Adam manifested faith by calling his wife Eve, "mother of all living" (Gen. 3:20). They accepted the garments provided by God.

For man's own good, God drove Adam and Eve from the perfect environment of the Garden of Eden.

The Story of Two Sons

GENESIS 4

"And Adam knew Eve his wife; and she conceived, and bore Cain" (Gen. 4:1). What a family they were! There would never be another like it. Each member had come to live on this earth by a different method. The husband suddenly appeared without father or mother. The wife had no mother. But then came their son, history's first baby to be born through the union of both father and mother. Centuries later the Creator would choose His fourth and final method of bringing an individual to this planet. This time a Babe would be born without a human father!

But the unity of Adam's unique family would not last. Soon a fourth member was added, another baby boy. Before the story ended the oldest son would, without reason or remorse, brutally murder his younger brother!

A previous passage (Gen. 2) recorded the blessing of the world's original wedding. This pasage (Gen. 4) relates the bitterness of earth's first funeral. From this point on, the second ceremony would be conducted by the sons and daughters of Adam far more often than the first ceremony.

Overview

SCRIPTURE	Genesis 4			
SUBJECT	The lives of Cain and Abel			
SPECIFICS	Abel the martyr		Cain the murderer	
	Demonstrating the right way to God—a flock offering	God accepted Abel God avenged Abel	Demonstrating the wrong way to God—a field offering	He was an apostate He was an assassin He was an architect
SAINTS AND SINNERS	Cain, Abel, Seth			
SENTENCE SUMMARIES	O.T. Verse	"The LORD knoweth the way of the righteous; but the way of the ungodly shall perish" (Ps. 1:6).		
	N.T. Verses	"Cain . . . was of that wicked one, and slew his brother. And wherefore slew he him? Because his own works were evil, and his brother's righteous" (1 John 3:12). "By faith Abel offered unto God a more excellent sacrifice than Cain, by which he obtained witness that he was righteous, God testifying of his gifts; and by it he being dead yet speaketh" (Heb. 11:4).		

THE MARTYRDOM OF ABEL

Eve gave birth to Cain and Abel. *"And Adam knew Eve his wife; and she conceived, and bare Cain, and said, 'I have gotten a man from the Lord.'*

"And she again bare his brother Abel. And Abel was a keeper of sheep, but Cain was a tiller of the ground" (Gen. 4:1-2).

God rejected Cain's bloodless offering. *"And in process of time it came to pass, that Cain brought of the fruit of the ground an offering unto the Lord. . . . But unto Cain and to his offering He had not respect. And Cain was very wroth, and his countenance fell.*

"And the Lord said unto Cain, 'Why art thou wroth? And why is thy countenance fallen? If thou doest well, shalt thou not be accepted? And if thou doest not well, sin lieth at the door. And unto thee shall be his desire, and thou shalt rule over him' " (vv. 3, 5-7).

God accepted Abel's blood offering, a lamb. *"And Abel, he also brought of the firstlings of his flock and of the fat thereof. And the Lord had respect unto Abel and to his offering" (v. 4).*

Then Cain murdered his brother. *"And Cain talked with Abel his brother; and it came to pass, when they were in the field, that Cain rose up against Abel his brother, and slew him" (v. 8).*

God drove Cain from His presence. *" 'Behold, Thou hast driven me out this day from the face of the earth; and from Thy face shall I be hid; and I shall be a fugitive and a vagabond in the earth; and it shall come to pass, that everyone that findeth me shall slay me.'*

"And the Lord said unto him, 'Therefore whosoever slayeth Cain, vengeance shall be taken on him sevenfold.' And the Lord set a mark upon Cain, lest any finding him should kill him" (vv. 14-15).

Cain established the first civilization. *"And Cain went out from the presence of the Lord, and dwelt in the Land of Nod, on the east of Eden.*

"And Cain knew his wife, and she conceived, and bare Enoch; and he builded a city, and called the name of the city, after the name of his son, Enoch" (vv. 16-17).

Eve gave birth to Seth, who took Abel's place.

Cain and Abel

COMMENTS

Genesis 4 contains important historical evidence concerning the inroads sin made into the human race and the degradation it caused. Yet this information is almost entirely overlooked by students of history and anthropology.

Man did not start on a low simian or anthropoid level and evolve to his present high state. On the contrary, man began on a very high social and intellectual level, was brought low by the Fall, and then degenerated.

History and archeology record the fact that man once lived in caves. The biblical record rells us *why* he lived in caves. Man did not start there. His "primitive" existence is ample testimony to the devastating effect of sin.

The question is often asked, "Where did Cain get his wife?" Those who attempt to hold to both the Bible and to evolution conclude that Cain must have married one of the women who were evolving at the same time that Adam and Eve were created, but there is a better explanation. Genesis 4:16 records the fact that Cain went out from God's presence and dwelt in the land of Nod. How old Cain was at this time is not stated. He may have been 60 or 100 years old or even older. Sufficient time had passed for many women to have been born. Cain obviously married either his sister or a close relative. Because the effect of sin had not fully developed, such a union did not have the same genetic peril it would have today.

The difference between Cain and Abel did not stem from their different occupations. Without doubt, Adam was already engaged in both keeping sheep and tilling the ground. Cain merely specialized in one of those occupations and Abel specialized in the other.

The difference between Cain and Abel was one of heart relationship toward God. What each man did revealed his heart relationship toward God. Cain's offering was one of pure formalism, though his intent was to please Jehovah. Abel's offering was one of pure worship, offering "the firstlings of the flock" with the same intent.

Neither Cain's nor Abel's offering should be confused with the offerings which would come later with the Mosaic system. They may not have even used an altar, for none is mentioned until after the Flood.

The problem was that Cain insisted on worshiping God in his own way (vain, ritualistic, formalistic), whereas Abel worshiped God in the way that God had prescribed, probably when he made coats for Adam and Eve (3:21). God gave Cain a second chance, which he refused.

God's rejection of Cain's offering had three results:

1. Malice (4:5-7).
2. Murder (v. 8).
3. Punishment (vv. 9-15).

Cain did not thank God for His warning, did not repent of his jealousy, and did not mend his ways. He murdered Abel, and murder must always be punished.

After His investigation, God pronounced a curse on Cain. This was the first time that a divine curse was directly inflicted on man; previously the curse had been placed on the beasts and the ground. The curse on Cain was not a curse of damnation, but rather a curse designed to bring Cain to repentance.

Cain ceased being a farmer and became a bedouin. He did not repent, but was sorry that he had gotten himself into such difficulty and cringed at the judgment he had to bear.

In grace, God gave Seth to replace the slain Abel. With the advent of Seth's son, Enos, came the first revival (4:25-26).

Preview

The Day before Destruction

GENESIS 5:1–6:8

"This is the book of the generations of Adam" (Gen. 5:1).

The world's oldest and most unusual obituary column is recorded in Genesis 5. Ten names appear on the list. The column is unique because of the ages of the nine and the agelessness of the tenth. The average life span of the nine was 912 years. But the tenth never died!

"By faith Enoch was translated that he should not see death" (Heb. 11:5). As the obituary record closes we read of the birth of Enoch's great-grandson, who later became even more famous than his great-grandfather. The boys' name was Noah. In 1983 ABC televised a controversial moved titled, *The Day After,* a fictitious account of events after a nuclear holocaust. Genesis 6 could rightfully be titled, *The Day Before,* for it provides a factual account of human activities just prior to the great Flood. "And God saw that the wickedness of man was great in the earth, and that every imagination of the thoughts of his heart was only evil continually" (Gen. 6:5).

So the divine decision that had to be made, was made: the earth would be destroyed by a worldwide flood! But would all mankind perish? Could anyone possibly survive? No, and yes! No, all mankind would not perish. Yes, one man and his family would be saved.

"But Noah found grace in the eyes of the Lord" (v. 8).

Overview

<table>
<tr><td>SCRIPTURE</td><td colspan="3">Genesis 5:1–6:8</td></tr>
<tr><td>SUBJECT</td><td colspan="3">The pre-Flood testimonies of Enoch and Noah</td></tr>
<tr><td rowspan="2">SPECIFICS</td><td colspan="3">The grace of God
1 Spared Enoch from the Flood
2 Prepared Noah for the Flood</td></tr>
<tr><td colspan="2">Enoch walked with God
Enoch witnessed for God
Enoch was taken by God</td><td>The need for divine judgment—universal sin

The method of divine judgment—universal Flood</td></tr>
<tr><td>SAINTS AND SINNERS</td><td colspan="3">Enoch, Methuselah, Noah</td></tr>
<tr><td rowspan="2">SENTENCE SUMMARIES</td><td>O.T. Verse</td><td colspan="2">"Blessed is the man that walketh not in the counsel of the ungodly, nor standeth in the way of sinners, nor sitteth in the seat of the scornful" (Ps. 1:1).</td></tr>
<tr><td>N.T. Verses</td><td colspan="2">"By faith Enoch was translated that he should not see death, and was not found, because God had translated him; for before his translation he had this testimony, that he pleased God" (Heb. 11:5).
"The long-suffering of God waited in the days of Noah, while the ark was a-preparing, wherein few, that is, eight souls, were saved by water" (1 Peter 3:20).</td></tr>
</table>

THE MINISTRY OF ENOCH

Enoch was the first recorded preacher, and he preached on the coming judgment. *"And Enoch also, the seventh from Adam, prophesied of these, saying, 'Behold, the Lord cometh with ten thousands of His saints, to execute judgment upon all, and to convince all that are ungodly among them of all their ungodly deeds which they have ungodly committed, and of all their hard speeches which ungodly sinners have spoken against Him' " (Jude 14-15).*

Enoch was a man of great faith (see Heb. 11:5; Gen. 5:22), and the father of Methuselah. *"And Enoch walked with God after he begat Methuselah 300 years, and begat sons and daughters; and all the days of Enoch were 365 years" (vv. 22-23).*

Enoch departed from the earth without dying. *"And Enoch walked with God; and he was not; for God took him" (v. 24).*

CONDITIONS PRECEDING THE FLOOD

In the days before the Flood, a great population explosion took place. *"And it came to pass, when men began to multiply on the face of the earth, and daughters were born unto them" (6:1).*

There was an outpouring of satanic activity. *"That the sons of God saw the daughters of men that they were fair; and they took them wives of all which they chose" (v. 2).*

"There were giants in the earth in those days; and also after that, when the sons of God came in unto the daughters of men, and bare children to them, the same became mighty men which were of old, men of renown" (v. 4).

All humanity (except eight individuals) became totally depraved. *"And God saw that the wickedness of man was great in the earth, and that every imagination of the thoughts of his heart was only evil continually" (v. 5).*

God was ready to destroy all flesh. *"And the LORD said, 'My spirit shall not always strive with man, for that he also is flesh: yet his days shall be 120 years' " (v. 3).*

"And it repented the LORD that He had made man on the earth, and it grieved Him at His heart. And the LORD said, 'I will destroy man whom I have created from the face of the earth; both man, and beast, and the creeping thing, and the fowls of the air; for it repenteth Me that I have made them' " (vv. 6-7).

But Noah and his family found grace in God's sight. *"But Noah found grace in the eyes of the LORD. These are the generations of Noah: Noah was a just man and perfect in his generations, and Noah walked with God" (vv. 8-9).*

Between the Fall and the Flood

COMMENTS

The main purpose of Genesis 5 is to provide a connecting link between two universal events: the Fall and the Flood. It is a genealogy of the men who lived between the time of Seth and the time of Noah.

All of the men in the line of Seth were godly, but it is specifically stated of Enoch that he "walked with God" (v. 22). Enoch enjoyed an intimate relationship with God throughout the 365 years of his life. A children's chorus stated, "He walked so far with God one day that he walked right into heaven!" In a similar manner, one day Jesus will return in the air and take every believer home to heaven with Him (cf. 1 Cor. 15:51-52; 1 Thes. 4:14-18).

The identity of "the sons of God" in Genesis 6:2 has been much discussed. Many have concluded that they were angels because that expression is used of angels (cf. Job 1:6; 2:1; 38:7). However, angels are not previously mentioned in Genesis. It would seem strange to introduce them in this context without previous mention. Further, we know from our Lord's teaching (cf. Matt. 22:30) that angels do not marry or cohabit even among themselves, much less with lower orders of beings such as humans.

It seems best to view the question in light of its overall context. In Genesis 4:16-22, Moses recorded the genealogy of the godless line of Cain. In 5:6-32, Moses recorded the genealogy of the godly line of Seth. In Genesis 6, men of Seth's line intermarried with women of Cain's godless line. The "giants" of verse 4 were not the result of the unions in verse 2. Indeed, there is no grammatical connection between them. The Septuagint (LXX) translates the Hebrew word *nephalim* ("robbers, attackers, bandits") with *gigantes* from which the English word "giants" is derived. These violent men were already in the land when the union between the godly line of Seth and the ungodly line of Cain took place. Because of the corruption of the Sethites with the Cainites, their offspring took on the characteristics of Cain. Consequently, the whole earth was filled with violence and the thoughts of man became only evil continually. Sin had to be judged, and God determined to destroy man.

Competent conservative scholars estimate the world's population in Noah's day to have been about 2½ billion. Noah preached righteousness (cf. 2 Peter 2:5) to them for 120 years, but only had seven converts: his wife, his three sons, and their wives. We would not consider him a successful evangelist by today's standards. Yet he successfully reached a group that many evangelists entirely overlook—his own family. Noah is the perfect example of one who did his preaching by answering questions of those who asked him of the hope that was within him (cf. 1 Peter 3:15, 20).

The effect of man's sin and degradation on God caused Him to repent and be grieved. These are anthropomorphisms in which human characteristics are ascribed to the eternal God. God did not repent in the sense of changing His mind. Rather, God acted in a manner consistent with the changed situation. Man had sinned, and sin had made increasing inroads into all the population. God had to bring judgment, or He would not have been God. From man's point of view, it appears that God changed in mid-course. To communicate in terms that man could understand, God said that He repented ("had an afterthought").

God, of course, is not finite. He does not grieve in the same sense that human beings do. It is touching, however, to see that even so wonderful a Being as the infinite God is touched by man's failures. Thus, it is revealed to us that God is indeed a Person.

Preview

A Family and a Flood

GENESIS 6:9–9:29

"And the Lord said unto Noah, 'Come thou and all thy house into the ark' " (Gen. 7:1).

How simple the solution back then. Physical salvation from the Flood judgment came about through a ship. How simple the solution today. Eternal salvation from the fire judgment comes about through a cross.

In the midst of the Flood we are told: *"And God remembered Noah and every living thing, and all the cattle that was with him in the ark" (8:1).*

How wonderful the little phrase, "God remembered." As He did for this dedicated patriarch, He would later do for a dying thief: *"And he said unto Jesus, 'Lord, remember me when Thou comest into Thy kingdom.' And Jesus said unto him, 'Verily I say unto thee, Today shalt thou be with Me in paradise' " (Luke 23:42-43).*

One final thought about the Great Flood. There are 774,745 words in the Bible. God spoke two particular words to Noah at that time which, by themselves, summarize the remaining 774,743. One word was spoken before, and the other following the Flood. The one before: "And the LORD said unto Noah, '*Come* thou and all thy house into the ark' " (Gen. 7:1). The one after: "And God spake unto Noah, saying, '*Go* forth of the ark' " (8:15-16).

Here it is—the Scriptures summarized by two words! To the *sinner,* the word is *Come*—"*Come* into the ark of safety."

To the saint, the word is *Go*—"*Go* ye into all the world."

Overview

<table>
<tr><td>SCRIPTURE</td><td colspan="6">Genesis 6:9–9:29</td></tr>
<tr><td>SUBJECT</td><td colspan="6">The faithfulness of God and the foolishness of Noah</td></tr>
<tr><td rowspan="2">SPECIFICS</td><td rowspan="2">God's faithfulness</td><td>A ship in the water</td><td>→ The provision through the Flood</td><td rowspan="2">Noah's foolishness</td><td>His folly</td><td>Noah, the pathetic sot
• the failure</td></tr>
<tr><td>A sign in the sky</td><td>→ The promise after the Flood</td><td>His family</td><td>Noah, the prophetic seer
• the future</td></tr>
<tr><td>SAINTS AND SINNERS</td><td colspan="6">Noah, Ham, Shem, Japheth, Canaan</td></tr>
<tr><td rowspan="2">SENTENCE SUMMARIES</td><td>O.T. Verses</td><td colspan="5">"God is our refuge and strength, a very present help in trouble. Therefore will not we fear, though the earth be removed, and though the mountains be carried into the midst of the sea" (Ps. 46:1-2).</td></tr>
<tr><td>N.T. Verse</td><td colspan="5">"By faith Noah, being warned of God of things not seen as yet, moved with fear, prepared an ark to the saving of his house; by the which he condemned the world, and became heir of the righteousness which is by faith" (Heb. 11:7).</td></tr>
</table>

SALVATION THROUGH THE FLOOD

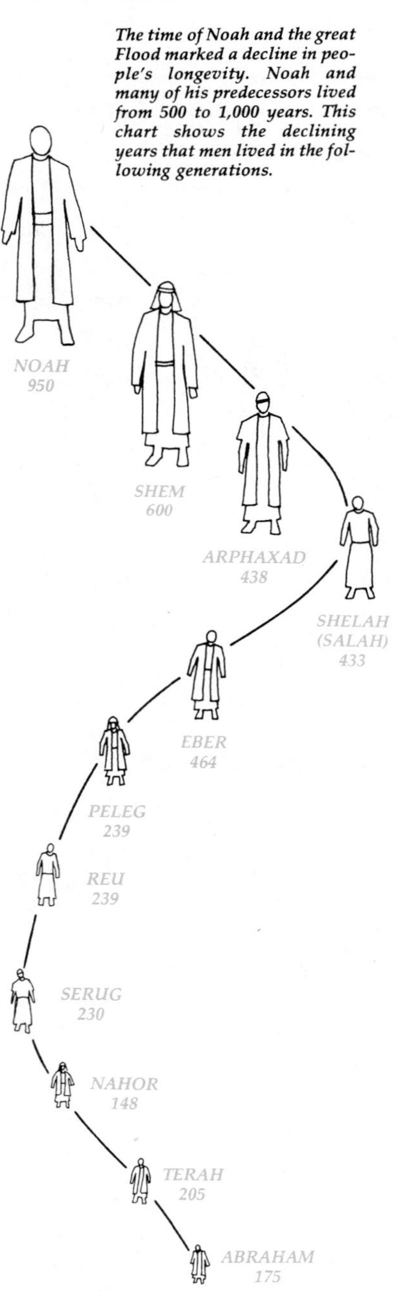

The Patriarchs—
Noah to Abraham

The time of Noah and the great Flood marked a decline in people's longevity. Noah and many of his predecessors lived from 500 to 1,000 years. This chart shows the declining years that men lived in the following generations.

God commanded Noah to build a 450 x 75 x 45-foot floating barge—the ark. *"Make thee an ark of gopher wood; rooms shalt thou make in the ark, and shalt pitch it within and without with pitch. . . . And, behold, I, even I, do bring a flood of waters upon the earth, to destroy all flesh, wherein is the breath of life, from under heaven; and everything that is in the earth shall die.*

"But with thee I will establish My covenant; and thou shalt come into the ark, thou, and thy sons, and thy wife, and thy sons' wives with thee" (Gen. 6:14; 17-18).

Noah and his family were joined in the ark by a male and female of all the earth's animals, including seven pairs of the "clean" animals. *"And the LORD said unto Noah, 'Come thou and all thy house into the ark; for thee have I seen righteous before Me in this generation.' . . . And Noah did according unto all that the LORD commanded him. And Noah was 600 years old when the flood of waters was upon the earth.*

"And Noah went in, and his sons, and his wife, and his sons' wives with him, into the ark, because of the waters of the Flood. . . . And it came to pass after seven days, that the waters of the Flood were upon the earth.

"In the six-hundredth year of Noah's life, in the second month, the seventeenth day of the month, the same day were all the fountains of the great deep broken up, and the windows of heaven were opened. And the rain was upon the earth forty days and forty nights" (7:1, 5-7, 10-12).

The ark successfully survived the 371-day flood. It came to rest on the mountains of Ararat. *"And God remembered Noah and every living thing, and all the cattle that was with him in the ark; and God made a wind to pass over the earth, and the waters assuaged. . . . And the ark rested in the seventh month, on the seventeenth day of the month, upon the mountains of Ararat. . . . And God spake unto Noah, saying, 'Go forth of the ark, thou, and thy wife, and thy sons, and thy sons' wives with thee.' . . .*

"And Noah went forth, and his sons, and his wife, and his sons' wives with him. . . . And Noah builded an altar unto the LORD; and took of every clean beast, and of every clean fowl, and offered burnt offerings on the altar.

"And the LORD smelled a sweet savor; and the

LORD said in His heart, I will not again curse the ground anymore for man's sake; for the imagination of man's heart is evil from his youth; neither will I again smite anymore everything living, as I have done. While the earth remaineth, seedtime and harvest, and cold and heat, and summer and winter, and day and night shall not cease" (8:1, 4, 15-16, 18, 20-22).

God established a rainbow covenant with Noah, consisting of:

1. A command: that Noah's three sons replenish the earth.
2. An institution: human government and capital punishment were ordained.
3. A promise: that God would never again destroy the world by a great flood.

"And God said, 'This is the token of the covenant which I make between Me and you and every living creature that is with you, for perpetual generations. I do set My bow in the cloud, and it shall be for a token of a covenant between Me and the earth' " (9:12-13).

THE TRAGEDY FOLLOWING THE FLOOD

Noah the sot. Noah became drunk from his own vineyard and exposed himself within his tent. His son Ham and grandson Canaan viewed Noah's nakedness. For some unspecified reason, Canaan especially incurred the wrath of his grandfather.

Noah the seer. Noah predicted the future physical and spiritual lifestyles of his three sons and their descendants:

(1) Concerning Canaan: that his seed would be in servitude to the seed of his brethren (fulfilled in Josh. 9:27).

(2) Concerning Shem: that from his seed would come the Messiah (fulfilled in Matt. 1:1).

(3) Concerning Japheth: that his seed would "dwell in the tents of Shem" (fulfilled in Rom. 11:13-25).

Noah's Ark

COMMENTS

It took Noah and his sons 120 years to build the ark. It was 300 cubits (450 ft.) long, 50 cubits (75 ft.) wide, and 30 cubits (45 ft.) high. The ark was as long as a 45-story building is high, as wide as a 7- to 8-story building is high, and as high (from keel to top) as a 4- to 5-story building!

Probably resembling a barge, the ark apparently was squared on the ends. It only had to withstand the force of the flood waters, not make headway in them. the ark was perfectly suited for its purpose—to preserve the lives of Noah and the people and animals with him.

Noah and his sons did not have to round up the animals and lead them into the ark. When the time came to load the ark, Noah and his family boarded first. God then brought the animals into the ark. What a sight that must have been as the animals, gathered by God, marched on His command into the ark!

The biblical account of the ark introduces the distinction between clean and unclean beasts. Many years later, the Mosaic Law recognized and gave definition to that distinction. How it originated is not known. Of clean animals Noah was to take "by sevens" (seven each: three pairs plus one), and of unclean "by twos" (one pair). Apparently the seventh clean animal was taken along to be offered in a sacrifice after the Flood.

That Noah was commanded to take the fowls of the air proves that the Flood was universal. The earth would be covered with water, leaving nowhere for the birds to land. Further, the Bible states that God determined to destroy "every living thing" on the face of the earth. Nothing would escape that was not safely aboard the ark, except sea creatures.

Once Noah and the animals were inside, God shut the door. No person or animal could get in or get out.

Noah, his family, and the animals were in the ark seven days before the first drop of water fell. The waters came from two sources:

(1) Water captured in the crust of the earth
(2) Water in the atmosphere

Massive geological activity took place as God broke up the earth's crust and released the water contained there since the Creation. The early earth also was enveloped with a vapor canopy which God broke up and showered on the earth.

There must have been earthquakes, thunder, and lightning the likes of which the earth had never seen and will never see again! The water built up on the earth for 40 days. It reached a depth of 15 cubits (22-23 feet) above the highest mountains, a depth sufficient to permit the heavily laden ark to clear them.

God's purpose in sending the Flood was that all flesh on the earth would die. Conservative scholars estimate that the earth's population in Noah's, day was approximately 2½ billion people—almost half of what it is today. All but 8 died and are cited in the Bible as examples of judgment. It was the largest segment of earth's population ever to experience the judgment of God at one time (cf. 1 Peter 3:20).

The Flood lasted a little over a year (371) days. When it was over, Noah offered sacrifices to God, who promised never to destroy the earth again by water. He set His rainbow in the sky as a guarantee.

God's promise stands as long as there are rainbows! The earth will be destroyed again, but the agent will be fire (2 Peter 3:10-12).

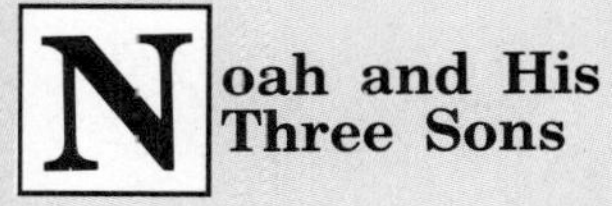

Noah and His Three Sons

COMMENTS

After the Flood, Noah apparently took to farming, as Cain had done (Gen. 4:2). The idea that man took a long time to advance to farming skills is foreign to Scripture.

Noah probably was not ignorant of the potency of the wine he had prepared. His problem was that he had neglected to use proper caution. Since mankind had been in agriculture before, it is unlikely that no one had ever had wine before.

Noah became drunk and lay uncovered (the Heb. verb is reflexive—literally, "he uncovered himself"). It was not a young and untried Noah who sinned but rather the seasoned Noah, who had stood alone against the entire world. Now, in a moment of comparative safety, he sinned.

The attitudes of Noah's sons toward their father indicated their attitudes toward God. Shem and Japheth were respectful and reverent. Walking backward, they covered their father's nakedness. Their silent action spoke loudly as a rebuke to Ham, Canaan's father, who was disrespectful and derogatory. Ham not only "saw" his father's nakedness, but literally "gazed upon it with satisfaction." He not only "told" Shem and Japheth about their father, but "told it with delight."

When Noah awoke, he noticed something unusual—probably the way his robe was laid upon him. After inquiring, he learned what his youngest (lit., "younger") son had done to him (an act of homosexuality?). Noah then pronounced the curse on Canaan.

It should be noted that Noah's statement (9:25-27) is really a prophecy in which predictions are made concerning each of Noah's sons and their descendants. It should also be noted that Ham was without specific blessing, and that the curse of verse 25 was only on Canaan. Ham had three other sons—Cush, Mizraim, and Phut—who were not included.

Both Shem and Japheth were the recipients of a positive blessing, and Canaan was to be their servant. Noah actually blessed Jehovah, the God of Shem, for the blessings He will shower on Shem in making his line the primary means of fulfilling the messianic promise made in Genesis 3:15.

Japheth received positive blessing primarily of a territorial nature. Japheth would "dwell in the tents of Shem," predicted Noah. This expression indicated that Japheth would not conquer or displace Shem, but rather that the blessings he received would be because of his relationship to Shem.

Paul expressed a similar thought when he pointed out that the blessings to the Gentiles have come because of God's blessing on Israel (Rom. 11:18ff.). God will break some of the branches off and graft in the Gentile church (v. 17), which will not replace Israel but will share in Israel's blessing. When God is finished with the church, He will remove the olive branch and graft back the natural branches again.

Why did Noah curse Canaan and not Ham? Two reasons can be suggested.

(1) Because of Noah's prophetic knowledge of Canaan's wickedness. Noah's prophecy was a call to Canaan and his descendants to repent. From Canaan, of course, came the Canaanites, who were some of the most degraded people ever to live on the earth.

(2) Because Noah wished to punish Ham more intensely. Ham probably would have rather had the curse on himself than on his son.

The curse on Canaan has absolutely no relationship to black people today. Black people descended from Phut, not from Canaan.

The curse was partially fulfilled when Joshua conquered the land of Canaan. It was further fulfilled in David's expansion of his kingdom and his conquest of Canaanite territories.

Phoenicia was a large Canaanite colony which, on its destruction, moved to Carthage in North Africa and carried on extensive warfare against Rome. The curse on Canaan was ultimately fulfilled in the Third Punic War. Rome went to Carthage, defeated it, killed all the inhabitants, literally scraped it off the face of the earth, and dumped it into the sea (149-146 B.C.).

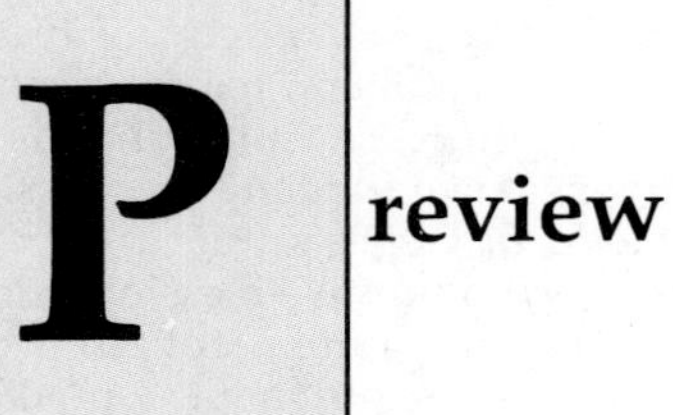

review

The Tragedy of a Tower

GENESIS 10–11

So many different kinds of language, spoken by so many different kinds of people! That's the way it is today. But this was not always the case. People once enjoyed a common oral unity which would amaze us today. What happened to change this? It all began sometime after the great Flood. A fabulous and feverish religious project was begun at the plain of Shinar on the banks of the Euphrates River, near where ancient Babylon would later be built. The Shinar project included both a city and a tower. The rebel architect behind all this was Nimrod, a religious apostate, who was a grandson of Noah himself. So much concerning the WHAT and WHO. But now for the WHY of the project. Archeological findings strongly indicate the Tower of Babel was in reality a temple given over to the worship of the stars. Listen to the actual words as taken from that dedication address.

"And they said, 'Go to, let us build us a city and a tower, whose top may reach unto heaven; and let us make us a name, lest we be scattered abroad upon the face of the whole earth' " (Gen. 11:4).

Note the pronouns "we" and "us" appear five times in this one sentence. This was nothing less than an arrogant and unholy attempt to exclude the Creator and exalt the creature. But it didn't work. God separated the Babel workers in small groups by altering the structure of their common language. This divine action directly answers the question of present-day language differences. The Babel judgment also indirectly answers a second question, for as human beings began to marry in smaller groups, the genetic variations leading to the distinctive characteristics of skin color, height, hair texture, facial features, etc. would develop swiftly.

Overview

SCRIPTURE	Genesis 10–11		
SUBJECT	The Tower of Babel and the table of nations		
SPECIFICS	UNION	DISUNION	REUNION
	Man attempts to unite apart from God at Babel	God defeats this attempt by confusing man's language at Babel	Small language groups then resettle the ancient world after Babel
	The sin	The sentence	The settlements
SAINTS AND SINNERS	Ham, Shem, Japheth, Nimrod		
SENTENCE SUMMARIES	O.T. Verses	"The wicked, through the pride of his countenance, will not seek after God: God is not in all his thoughts. . . . The LORD is King forever and ever; the heathen are perished out of His land" (Ps. 10:4, 16).	
	N.T. Verses	"God made the world and all things therein, seeing that He is Lord of heaven and earth, dwelleth not in temples made with hands. . . . and hath made of one blood all nations of men for to dwell on all the face of the earth, and hath determined the times before appointed, and the bounds of their habitation" (Acts 17:24, 26).	

THE CONFUSION OF ALL THINGS

THE ARROGANCE OF MAN

A rebel named Nimrod (a grandson of Ham) instigated a religious building program. The planned structure consisted of an astrological tower and a city on the plains of Shinar, near Babylon.

"And Cush begat Nimrod; he began to be a mighty one in the earth. He was a mighty hunter before the LORD; wherefore it is said, 'Even as Nimrod the mighty hunter before the LORD.'

"And the beginning of his kingdom was Babel, and Erech, and Accad, and Calneh, in the land of Shinar" (Gen. 10:8-10).

"And the whole earth was of one language, and of one speech. And it came to pass as they journeyed from the east, that they found a plain in the land of Shinar; and they dwelt there.

"And they said one to another, 'Go to, let us make brick, and burn them thoroughly.' And they had brick for stone, and slime had they for mortar. And they said, 'Go to, let us build us a city and a tower, whose top may reach unto heaven; and let us make us a name, lest we be scattered abroad upon the face of the whole earth' " (11:1-4).

THE JUDGMENT OF GOD

God punished this evil ecumenical attempt. He separated mankind into small ethnic groups by confusing their once-universal language into many dialects.

"And the LORD came down to see the city and the tower, which the children of men builded. And the LORD said, 'Behold, the people is one, and they have all one language; and this they begin to do; and now nothing will be restrained from them, which they have imagined to do. Go to, let Us go down, and there confound their language, so that they may not understand one another's speech.'

"So the LORD scattered them abroad from thence upon the face of all the earth; and they left off to build the city. Therefore is the name of it called Babel; because the LORD did there confound the language of all the earth; and from thence did the LORD scatter them abroad upon the face of all the earth" (vv. 5-9).

The Tower of Babel

COMMENTS

Genealogical tables make dry reading. The names are unfamiliar and difficult to pronounce. But occasionally, tucked away in the middle of a genealogical table, is a wonderful gem. Such is Genesis 10:25, which provides the key to the relationship between chapters 10 and 11.

Genesis 11 deals with the last item in the general history of all mankind—the Tower of Babel and the origin of the different human languages. Genesis 10:25 tells us that the division of the earth's languages took place in the days of Peleg. Comparing 11:10-16 with 10:25 and adding up the years involved, we calculate that Peleg lived 100 years after the Flood. Peleg (whose name means "division") was given his name in memory of the division of human languages, which happened either just before his birth or during his infancy. Chronologically, the events of 11:1-9 precede the events described in chapter 10. Chapter 11 tells us *why* the peoples of the world were scattered and *why* they speak different languages. Chapter 10 tells us *how* they were scattered after their languages were confused.

Genesis 10:8-12 introduces us to Nimrod, Cush's son, who was a mighty empire-builder. Nimrod's name means "let us revolt." The skill attributed to him (10:9) may give us a clue as to his character.

Nimrod was a "mighty one"—a tyrant or despot—and a "mighty hunter"—apparently one who hunted men to enslave them. His name became a byword for evil in the society of his day, much as Hitler's name is a byword for evil and cruelty in our century.

Nimrod's kingdom was the first known empire. Apparently he took over Babel, Erech, Accad, and Calneh in the land of Shinar, and made them the beginning of his kingdom. From Babel he went forth and built Nineveh, Rehoboth, Calah, and Resen. Nineveh was a great city even in Moses' day. It continued to grow until, in Jonah's day, it was a great city "of three days' journey" (Jonah 3:3). Following the character of its founder, Nineveh was noted for its ruthlessness and warfare.

Some have thought that the purpose of the Tower of Babel was to build an alternate way into heaven. But the intent of constructing the tower was not to reach heaven; the language of the Bible is simply a description of the tower—it was to be a skyscraper! If the builders had wanted the tower to help them get into heaven, they would have built it on a mountain rather than on a plain.

Actually, the purpose of the tower was to provide a common religious center as a rallying point, lest the people be scattered. The builders of the tower were in open defiance of God's command (Gen. 9:1).

Until this time, everyone had spoken the same language. Communication had been simple. But God came down to look at the tower which was the rallying point for man's rebellion. It was simple for God to defeat man's grandest plans of rebellion.

That night all mankind went to bed using the same language. When they awoke in the morning their thought patterns, vocabularies, and articulation practices were completely changed. Men and women, who had easily communicated a few hours before, could not understand one another. And each, of course, thought the other was the one who had changed.

Those who spoke the same language gathered together and departed to a geographical area where they could freely communicate with one another. Thus the people were scattered abroad on the face of the earth, as God had originally intended.

Today, whenever we hear someone speaking a different language, it is a reminder of the fact that in response to man's rebellion, God confused the languages of mankind.

THE ORIGIN OF NATIONS

The ancient world was settled by the descendants of Noah's three sons.

The descendants of Japheth, and the peoples they founded, included:

(1) Gomer (Germany; see Ezek. 38:6)

(2) Magog, Tubal, and Meshech (Russia; see Ezek. 38:1-3)

(3) Javan (Greece; see Gen. 10:2)

(4) Madai (Persia)

(5) Tiras (Italy)

(6) Togarmah (Armenia)

(7) Tarshish (Spain)

(8) Kittim (Cyprus)

The descendants of Ham, and the peoples they founded, included:

(1) Cush (Ethiopia)

(2) Mizraim (Egypt)

(3) Phut (Africa)

(4) Canaan (the Canaanites of Palestine; see Gen. 10:19; 13:12-13; 18:20-21; 19:1-11; 1 Kings 14:24)

(5) Nimrod (Babylon and Assyria; see Gen. 10:8-10)

(6) Sidon (Phoenicia)

(7) Heth (Hittites)

(8) Jebus (the Jebusites, the occupants of Jerusalem prior to David's reign; see 2 Sam. 5:6-9)

(9) Philistim (the Philistines; see Gen. 10:14)

(10) Sin (possible founder of oriental peoples: China, Japan, India, etc.)

The descendants of Shem, and the peoples they founded, included:

(1) Through Abraham, Isaac, and Jacob: the nation Israel

(2) Through Abraham, Ishmael, and Esau: the Middle Eastern Arab countries

Above: one reconstruction of the Tower of Babel as it may have appeared.

From the Three Sons of Noah

COMMENTS

If it were not for Genesis 10, we would not have a reliable record of the unity of the human race or a record of its development from the three sons of Noah. Critics, of course, find fault with this chapter, for it contains claims not supported by any other historical document. But none of the information given in chapter 10 has ever been disproved.

From Japheth came those peoples we call Indo-Europeans. They settled pretty much in a straight line from east to west, from Asia Minor to Spain.

From Ham came the negroid peoples who settled on the continent of Africa and around the coastal areas of the Mediterranean Sea, eastward and northward to Sidon.

From Shem came the Oriental peoples who settled in the areas of Arabia eastward. With Abram, the Shemites would move west and ultimately drive the Canaanites (descendants of Ham) from their dwelling places in the coastal areas at the western end of the Mediterranean Sea.

The main purpose of the genealogy in chapter 10 is to give us the origin and general areas of settlement of all the three sons of Noah. The genealogy in 11:10-32 moves the Genesis account from Shem to Abram, the next individual with whom Moses wished to deal. Previously Moses had been dealing with the entire human race. Now he begins to deal exclusively with a single nation, Israel.

Thousands of years had passed since Creation. Moses devoted only 11 chapters to the four universal events: the Creation, the Fall, the Flood, and the Tower of Babel. The remaining 39 chapters of Genesis cover only about 200 years, and deal with the four patriarchs of Israel: Abraham, Isaac, Jacob, and Joseph.

In considering the genealogy of chapter 10, it is important to see how God was preparing Israel for its future. Nimrod was the founder of the great Assyrian and Babylonian Empires. Thus Israel would know from whence these empires sprang. This information is not found anywhere else among the records of antiquity. Later, Israel would be threatened by both of these empires. Assyria carried the 10 Northern Tribes off into captivity in 722 B.C.; they never returned. In 606 B.C., Babylon carried Judah off into Captivity for 70 years. Both the major and minor prophets were concerned in their prophecies with the rise and threat of these two empires. Assyria and Babylon forgot their Noahic-Hamitic origin and served false gods, thinking that they themselves had sprung from gods. Israel not only knew her Noahic-Shemetic origin, but also the true origin of these powerful nations which would bring it so much suffering.

Verses 15-18 give the genealogy of the sons of Canaan. This genealogy is repeated in 1 Chronicles 1:13-16. In view of Israel's future, it was important for that nation to know definitely who were and who were not Canaanites. Only in this way would they definitely be able to know exactly whom they were to drive out of the land of Canaan (cf. Deut. 20:17).

The genealogy in Genesis 11:10ff. documents another startling fact: at the time of Peleg the span of human life dropped almost to half of what it had been. The confusion of man's languages took place in Peleg's day. The sharp drop in the human life span shows the seriousness and far-reaching effects of God's judgment on man at the Tower of Babel.

Patriarchal

A founding father and his three descendants. A suffering saint and his three friends. Their lives make up the Patriarchal Stage.

Abraham is the founding father. His three descendants are Isaac (son), Jacob (grandson), and Joseph (great-grandson).

Job is the suffering saint. Eliphaz, Bildad, and Zophar are his three "friends."

Here are some facts about the founding father. Abraham's life may be summarized by two words—seed and soil. In a special promise known as the Abrahamic Covenant, God assured Abraham that he would father a great nation (seed) and that a particular land (soil) would be given to them forever. That nation would later become Israel, and the land, Canaan. Two of Abraham's three descendants would serve as spiritual types, foreshadowing the New Testament person and work of Christ. Isaac the son became a type by his supernatural birth and sacrificial role. Joseph the great-grandson became a type by his manifold sufferings. And now for the suffering saint.

Question: Why does a loving and sovereign God allow pain and persecution to fall on His people? Though the complete answer will only be revealed in heaven, the Book of Job does suggest at least three reasons. First, to *glorify* the person of God, second, to *purify* the lives of saints, and third to *nullify* the lies of Satan.

Abraham, Isaac, Jacob, Joseph, and Job. What are the spiritual lessons to be learned from this "quality quintet"? Abraham demonstrates faith; Isaac, submission; Jacob, self-mastery; Joseph, character; and Job, patience!

Preview

Father of the Faithful (Part One)

GENESIS 12–16

Whatever could have happened to one of Ur's leading citizens? Not only had he forsaken the worship of the moon goddess for that of an invisible monotheistic Being, but he was actually planning to leave this famous, fruitful city for a forsaken, far-off country. Had Abram taken leave of his senses? More than one eyebrow must have raised as the future father of the faithful started his pilgrimage toward Canaan. He was 75 years old at the time. Marvelous and mysterious things would befall him during the next 100 years before his death. He would win a war with a small band of servants, father a child through a barren wife, entertain angels unaware, and be visited by God Himself.

The importance of Abraham's life cannot be overestimated. In fact, the very relationship between heaven and earth changed drastically with the advent of Abraham. Prior to this, as seen in Genesis 1–11, God had used, as it were, the shotgun method in His approach to the world, dealing in a general way with nations, peoples, and entire civilizations. But beginning in chapter 12, He laid down the shotgun and employed a rifle, training the sight in on one man and his immediate descendants. Or, to use another analogy, with Abraham, heaven's floodlight gave way to a brilliant spotlight!

Overview

<table>
<tr><td>SCRIPTURE</td><td colspan="3">Genesis 12–16</td></tr>
<tr><td>SUBJECT</td><td colspan="3">Life of Abraham: part 1</td></tr>
<tr><td rowspan="7">SPECIFICS</td><td>The sinner</td><td colspan="2">The saint</td></tr>
<tr><td rowspan="3">His mission to Egypt</td><td>Location</td><td>Dedication</td></tr>
<tr><td>Leaves Ur for Canaan</td><td>His obedience to God</td></tr>
<tr><td>Builds altar at Bethel</td><td>His worship of God</td></tr>
<tr><td rowspan="3">His marriage to Hagar</td><td>Rescues Lot at Dan</td><td>His service for God</td></tr>
<tr><td>Meets Melchizedek at Salem</td><td>His communion with God</td></tr>
<tr><td>Receives covenant at Hebron</td><td>His belief in God</td></tr>
<tr><td>SAINTS AND SINNERS</td><td colspan="3">Abraham, Sarah, Pharaoh, Lot, Melchizedek, Hagar, Ishmael</td></tr>
<tr><td rowspan="2">SENTENCE SUMMARIES</td><td>O.T. Verses</td><td colspan="2">"Joshua said unto all the people, 'Thus saith the LORD God of Israel, "Your fathers dwelt on the other side of the Flood in old time, even Terah, the father of Abraham, and the father of Nachor; and they served other gods. And I took your father Abraham from the other side of the Flood, and led him throughout all the land of Canaan, and multiplied his seed, and gave him Isaac" ' " (Josh. 24:2-3).</td></tr>
<tr><td>N.T. Verse</td><td colspan="2">"By faith Abraham, when he was called to go out into a place which he should after receive for an inheritance, obeyed; and he went out, not knowing whither he went" (Heb. 11:8).</td></tr>
</table>

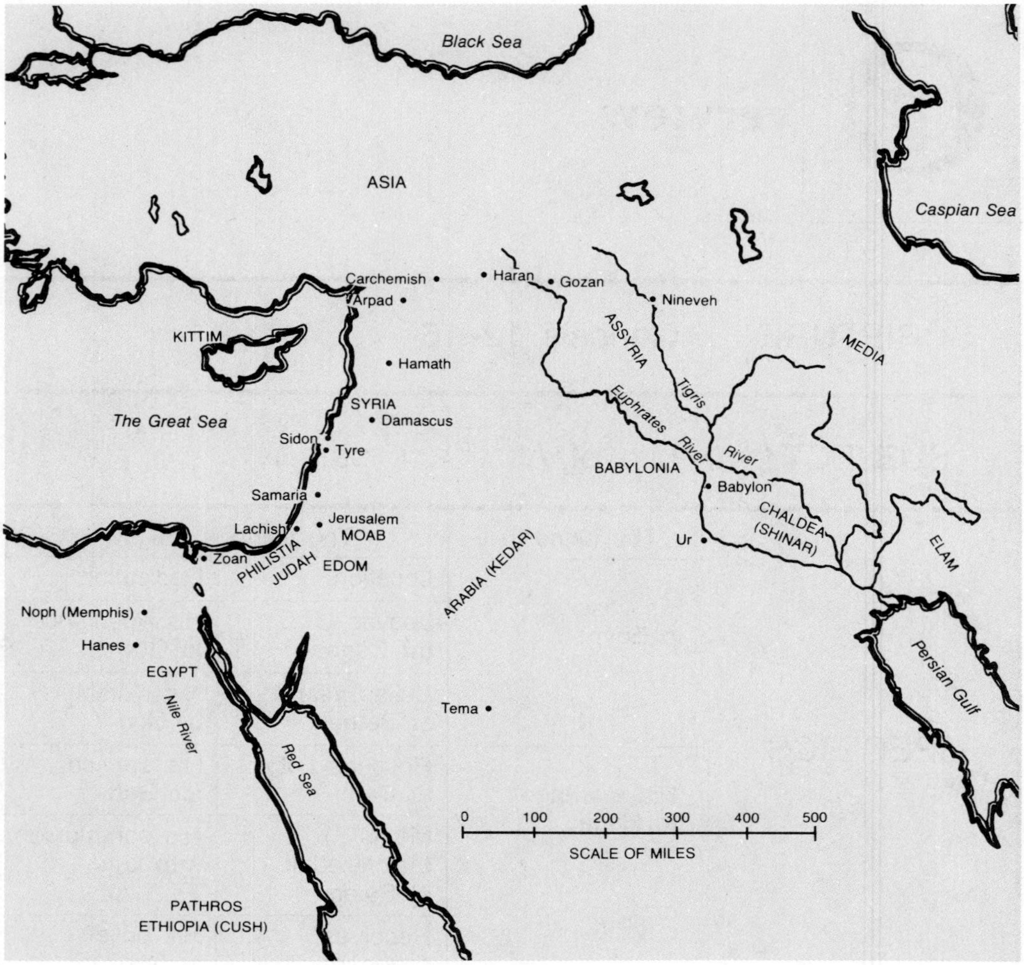

ABRAHAM OBEYS GOD

HIS CONVERSION

Abraham became a believer around 2100 B.C. while living in the city of Ur of the Chaldees.

"Then said the high priest, 'Are these things so?'

"And he said, 'Men, brethren, and fathers, hearken: The God of glory appeared unto our father Abraham, when he was in Mesopotamia, before he dwelt in Haran, and said unto him, "Get thee out of thy country, and from thy kindred, and come into the land which I shall show thee."

" 'Then came he out of the land of the Chaldeans, and dwelt in Haran; and from thence, when his father was dead, he removed him into this land, wherein ye now dwell' " (Acts 7:1-4).

HIS CALLING

Abraham, then Abram, was told to leave Ur and his father's house for a land that God would show him.

"And Joshua said unto all the people, 'Thus saith the Lord God of Israel, "Your fathers dwelt on the other side of the Flood in old time, even Terah, the father of Abraham, and the father of Nachor; and they served other gods.

" ' "And I took your father Abraham from the other side of the Flood, and led him throughout all the land of Canaan, and multiplied his seed, and gave him Isaac" ' " (Josh. 24:2-3).

HIS COMMISSION

No less than seven precious and powerful promises were involved in this divine commission (Gen. 12:1-3):

(1) I will make of thee a great nation.
(2) I will bless thee.
(3) I will make thy name great.
(4) Thou shalt be a blessing.
(5) I will bless them that bless thee.
(6) I will curse him that curseth thee.
(7) In thee shall all the families of the earth be blessed.

HIS CAUTION

God told Abram to leave his father's house and head for Canaan.

But Abram was disobedient (for a while) concerning both matters. He took his father with him and allowed himself to become bogged down in a place called Haran.

HIS CANAAN

Abram entered Canaan and set up camp near Shechem, some 30 miles north of Jerusalem. God now promised to give him the land.

He then moved to Bethel, a place meaning "house of God," and built an altar.

HIS CARNALITY

In a time of famine Abram backslid and went down to Egypt.

Fearing for his life, he led Pharaoh to believe that Sarai was his sister. On discovery of this deceit, Pharaoh soundly rebuked Abram and sent him back to Canaan.

HIS CONDESCENSION

An argument over grazing rights developed between Abram's herdsmen and those of Lot, his nephew. Unwilling to argue, Abram graciously allowed Lot to choose his section of land.

The young man foolishly picked that area near Sodom, the ancient world's most wicked city.

After Lot left, God appeared, promising Abram both soil (the land of Palestine) and seed (that he would father a great nation).

"And the LORD said unto Abram, after that Lot was separated from him, 'Lift up now thine eyes, and look from the place where thou art northward, and southward, and eastward, and westward.

" 'For all the land which thou seest, to thee will I give it, and to thy seed forever.

" 'And I will make thy seed as the dust of the earth; so that if a man can number the dust of the earth, then shall thy seed also be numbered' " (13:14-16).

HIS COURAGE

A pagan king captured Sodom and carried its citizens, including Lot, into captivity.

After a night march, Abram and his army of 318 trained servants defeated this pagan king in a surprise attack. Abram freed Lot just north of Damascus.

HIS COMMUNION

After returning from this battle (the first war mentioned in the Bible), Abram was met by the priest-king of Jerusalem, whose name was Melchizedek.

Abram paid tithes to Melchizedek. In a bread and wine ceremony, Abraham received God's blessings from him.

"And Melchizedek king of Salem brought forth bread and wine; and he was the priest of the Most High God.

"And he blessed him, and said, 'Blessed be Abram of the Most High God, possessor of heaven and earth. And blessed be the Most High God, which hath delivered thine enemies into thy hand.' And he gave him tithes of all" (14:18-20).

HIS COVENANT

Abram asked God to let him adopt a favorite servant lad named Eliezer, that he might consider him as his physical heir.

God refused, promising Abram that Sarai herself would later give birth to the promised heir. Abram would thus, through his son, be the founder of a mighty nation.

"And He brought him forth abroad, and said, 'Look now toward heaven, and tell the stars, if thou be able to number them.' And He said unto him, 'So shall thy seed be.'

"And he believed in the LORD; and He counted it to him for righteousness" (Gen. 15:5-6).

God now ratified His threefold promise to believing Abram (concerning soil, seed, and salvation) through a blood covenant. *"And he said, 'Lord GOD, whereby shall I know that I shall inherit it?'*

"And He said unto him, 'Take Me a heifer of

three years old, and a she goat of three years old, and a ram of three years old, and a turtledove, and a young pigeon.'

"And he took unto Him all these, and divided them in the midst, and laid each piece one against another; but the birds divided he not.

"And when the fowls came down upon the carcasses, Abram drove them away.

"And when the sun was going down, a deep sleep fell upon Abram; and, lo, a horror of great darkness fell upon him" (vv. 8-12).

"And it came to pass, that, when the sun went down, and it was dark, behold a smoking furnace, and a burning lamp that passed between those pieces" (v. 17).

Abram was given a sevenfold prophecy by God:

(1) His descendants would be strangers in a foreign land (see Gen. 46:2-4).

(2) They would be servants in that land (see Ex. 1:7-14).

(3) This slavery would last 400 years (see 12:40).

(4) God would later judge that nation (see chaps 7–12).

(5) Abram would be spared all this (see Gen. 25:7-8).

(6) His descendants would eventually return to Canaan (see the Book of Josh.).

(7) They would come out of their slavery with great substance (see Ex. 12:35-36; Ps. 105:37).

HIS COMPROMISE

Sarai persuaded Abram to father a child through her Egyptian maiden girl Hagar, that they might adopt this child.

Hagar became pregnant and her arrogant attitude caused trouble, causing her dismissal from Abraham's household by Sarai.

Hagar was found by the Angel of the Lord beside a desert spring and commanded to return to Sarai. This angel prophesied the sex (a boy) and name (Ishmael) of her unborn child.

This is the first official mention of the Angel of the Lord in the Old Testament. It is believed that He was Christ Himself. This Angel appears at least four times in Genesis. (See Gen. 16:7; 21:17; 22:11; 31:11).

When Ishmael was born, Abraham was 86.

The Abrahamic Covenant

COMMENTS

Some of the most important words in all the Bible are found in Genesis 12:2-3. These words are the words of the Abrahamic Covenant.

The most important words within the covenant are, "I will." This covenant is unconditional, depending only on God.

These words explain all that God has done in the past, continues to do in the present, and will do in the future. They have never yet been completely fulfilled.

The blessings promised in this covenant embrace three aspects:

(1) National—this is amplified in the Palestinian Covenant (Deut. 30:1-9).

(2) Personal—these are amplified in the Davidic Covenant (2 Sam. 7:10-17).

(3) Universal—these are amplified in the New Covenant (Jer. 31:31-34).

Two main views are held concerning the Abrahamic Covenant.

The first view holds that God gave this covenant to Abram conditioned on his obedience. Abram (and Israel following) disobeyed God and thus were disqualified from realizing any benefits of the covenant. Instead, God is fulfilling them spiritually in another people, the church.

The second view holds that since God has not yet fulfilled the provisions of the covenant completely, there yet must be a time when He will do so. That time will be when Jesus returns to the earth, sets up His kingdom, and reigns over Israel and all the world for 1,000 years (the Millennium).

The former view is that of reformed theology, and the latter is the view of dispensational premillennial theology. In favor of the latter, note that this covenant is unconditional—only God is obligated to bring it to pass. If God cannot keep His word to Abraham (and He will), then He cannot keep His word to us either (but He will).

On his arrival in the land of Canaan, Abram found a severe famine and went on down into Egypt. Fearing for his own life, he told the Egyptians that Sarai was his sister. She was his half-sister, but this half-truth was a whole lie.

Sarai was taken to become a part of Pharaoh's harem. Abram was 75 or 76 at this time. Sarai was 10 years younger, so she was 65 or 66. Sarai must truly have been beautiful to be considered "harem material"!

God protected Sarai by bringing plagues on Pharaoh's house.

In this event the great Abram is seen to be a frail human being, beset by fear and lying. The heathen Pharaoh is more righteous in the matter than is the man of God. After summoning Abram into his presence, Pharaoh restored Sarai to him and expelled them from Egypt.

Having failed to trust the Lord earlier and lapsing in Egypt, Abram returned to Bethel ("the house of God"), built an altar, and called on God. He was restored to fellowship with God.

His faith was again tested by the difficulty that arose between his and Lot's herdsmen. Separation became imperative. This time Abraham left his future in God's hands and let Lot have his choice of land. Lot, of course, chose the best land. God came to Abram, promised him all the land forever, and that his descendants would be as numerous as the dust of the earth.

Lot settled down on the well-watered plain, became entangled with the sinful life of Sodom (from which we get the word *sodomy*), and had to be rescued by Abram.

Abram gave testimony to his dependence on God by giving a tithe to Melchizedek and refusing to take any reward from the King of Sodom.

bram's Faith

COMMENTS

Genesis 15:1-7 records the reaffirmation of the covenant given to Abram in 12:1-3.

Abram's name means "honored father," and God had promised to make of him a great nation. But 10 years had passed and "the honored father" had no children. No wonder he was concerned and thought God intended his servant Eliezer to be his heir.

God responded by telling Abram that he would sire his own heir. God challenged Abram's faith further by taking him out to survey the stars. God promised Abram that he would truly be an "honored father," with progeny as numerous as the stars.

Abram's response is noteworthy: he believed God. His faith had no intrinsic value, but God attributed to it the value of His own righteousness. In commenting on this many centuries later, Paul pointed out that Abram received God's righteousness not by working for it, but by simply believing God's revelation (Rom. 4:1-5). God's salvation has always been by the grace of God and appropriated through belief in the revelation of God—and so it is today.

There were three kinds of covenants in early Israel: (1) the shoe covenant—enacted when the covenanting parties exchanged shoes (cf. Ruth 4:1-12); (2) the salt covenant—enacted when the covenanting parties exchanged pinches of salt from their individual salt pouches (cf. 2 Chron. 13:5); and (3) the blood covenant—enacted when the covenanting parties walked together between the halves of a slain animal (Gen. 15:9ff.). Each of these covenants was more binding than the preceding one. One could get his shoe back and one conceivably could get his own salt crystals back, but it was impossible to put the halves of an animal back together and have it live. One animal was sufficient to enact a blood covenant. The more important the covenant, the more animals would be used.

Abram knew exactly what God was proposing. He and Abram were going to ratify the covenant, each agreeing to keep his part of it. But when it came time for the covenanting parties to walk between the halves of the animals, Abram was asleep. In a vision he saw a burning lamp, symbolic of the presence of God, pass between the halves of the animals. Abram never did walk between the animal halves. God thus obligated solely Himself to keep His covenant with Abram. It is an *unconditional* covenant, dependent solely on God.

But great moments with God are no guarantee of one's future stability. Shortly after the momentous events of Genesis 15, Sarai, who now was 75, came to Abram. Realizing that she was past normal childbearing years, she proposed that Abram take Hagar, her bond servant, and have a child by her. That way the child would truly be Abram's son, though not hers. Abram agreed.

Hagar conceived by Abram. This caused domestic strife, for Hagar despised her mistress. Sarai responded by treating Hagar so harshly that her servant ran away. The Angel of the Lord (the preincarnate Jesus) apprehended Hagar, directed her to return to Sarai, and told her that a great multitude of people would come from her son, whom He named Ishmael ("man from God").

The Arabs are descendants of Ishmael. The domestic discord occasioned by Abram's heeding Sarai's advice continues to the present day. What a harvest can be occasioned by an act in an unguarded moment.

Preview

Father of the Faithful
(Part Two)

GENESIS 17–25

His parents first named him at birth in the city of Ur. God renamed him at age 99 in the land of Canaan. From Abram ("honored father") to Abraham ("founder of nations"). Quite a difference! His wife also was renamed. No longer would she be known as Sarai (contentious) but now, Sarah (a princess). The divine timing was perfect, for in less than a year the founder of nations and the barren princess would conceive and bear their first child—Isaac.

Wonder of wonders! God's promise had come true. There awaited, however, one final test for Abraham. It took place on Mount Moriah, right outside ancient Jerusalem. Here, obeying the command of God, Abraham prepared to offer up His only son. But the scheduled execution was stayed at the last moment. A substitute was found. God, who had previously changed Abraham's and Sarah's names, chose this occasion to give His obedient servant a new name for Himself: *Jehovah-jireh,* "the Lord will provide!" So He did with Abraham. So He will with us, if we obey Him.

Twenty centuries later, another Father led His only Son up similar mountain slopes for the identical purpose. This time, however, there was no last-minute reprieve.

"For God so loved the world, that He gave His only begotten Son, that whosoever believeth in Him should not perish, but have everlasting life" (John 3:16).

Overview

<table>
<tr><td>SCRIPTURE</td><td colspan="5">Genesis 17–25</td></tr>
<tr><td>SUBJECT</td><td colspan="5">Life of Abraham: part 2</td></tr>
<tr><td rowspan="4">SPECIFICS</td><td>A special seal</td><td colspan="4">Circumcision</td></tr>
<tr><td>A special name</td><td colspan="2">Abram becomes Abraham</td><td colspan="2">Sarai becomes Sarah</td></tr>
<tr><td rowspan="2">A special son</td><td colspan="4">Isaac</td></tr>
<tr><td>The birth of Isaac</td><td colspan="2">The binding of Isaac</td><td>The bride of Isaac</td></tr>
<tr><td>SAINTS AND SINNERS</td><td colspan="5">Abraham, Sarah, Lot, Abimelech, Isaac, Abraham's servant, Rebekah</td></tr>
<tr><td rowspan="2">SENTENCE SUMMARIES</td><td>O.T. Verse</td><td colspan="4">"Thou art the LORD the God, who didst choose Abram, and broughtest him forth out of Ur of the Chaldees, and gavest him the name of Abraham" (Neh. 9:7).</td></tr>
<tr><td>N.T. Verses</td><td colspan="4">"For what saith the Scripture? Abraham believed God, and it was counted unto him for righteousness. . . . He staggered not at the promise of God through unbelief, but was strong in faith, giving glory to God" (Rom. 4:3, 20).</td></tr>
</table>

GOD FULFILLS HIS PROMISE

When Abram was 99 years of age, God again appeared to him.

God changed his name from Abram ("exalted father") to Abraham ("father of nations"), and his wife's name from Sarai ("contentious") to Sarah ("princess").

The religious ceremony of circumcision was instituted as a seal and sign of the promised threefold covenant (concerning the soil, seed, and salvation) already given in Genesis 15.

"This is My covenant, which ye shall keep, between Me and you and thy seed after thee. Every man child among you shall be circumcised" (Gen. 17:10).

God again gave the promise of an heir, causing Abraham to laugh for joy. At Abraham's request God promised to bless Ishmael.

HIS COMPASSION

God again appeared to Abraham, this time accompanied by two angels. God had some good news and some bad news.

The good news was that Sarah would give birth to the long-promised heir in the following spring. This caused Sarah to laugh in unbelief.

The bad news was that Sodom (Lot's home city) was to be destroyed because of its wickedness. Abraham (who began by asking for 50) received God's promise that Sodom would be spared if only 10 righteous people could be found in the city.

HIS CORRUPTED KIN

The two angels informed Lot of Sodom's impending doom, but first had to blind some threatening sexual degenerates. Lot attempted (unsuccessfully) to persuade his married daughters and their husbands to leave with him.

At daybreak Lot and his family were physically removed from Sodom by the angel. Sodom was totally destroyed by fire. Lot's wife, who looked back, died.

In a cave outside the city, Lot's two unmarried daughters, fearing that they would never marry, got their father drunk and had sexual relations with him. Both became pregnant and bore him children. The oldest named her son Moab ("father of the Moabites")— and the younger called her boy Benammi ("father of the Ammonites").

Note the steps of Lot's downfall:

(1) He looked longingly at Sodom.
(2) He chose the area of land near Sodom.
(3) He pitched his tent toward Sodom.
(4) He moved into the city of Sodom.
(5) He returned to Sodom in spite of a severe warning by God.
(6) He gave both his daughters and his energies to Sodom.

HIS CARNALITY (The Second Time)

Abraham fell into the same pattern he once had in Egypt. He moved into the land of the Philistines and lied to Abimelech concerning Sarah, as he had to Pharaoh.

God warned Abimelech in a dream not to touch her. Abimelech, as Pharaoh had done, rebuked Abraham for lying to him. Then Abraham prayed for God's blessings to fall on Abimelech.

HIS CELEBRATION

A son was born to Abraham (now 100) and Sarah (now 90). They named him Isaac, meaning "laughter."

A great feast was held to mark his weaning. Both Hagar and her 14-year-old son Ishmael were sent away from Abraham's household for mocking Isaac during this happy occasion.

The Angel of the Lord again ministered to this Egyptian mother. Ishmael later married an Egyptian girl and became an expert archer.

Abraham's fame grew, causing Abimelech to seek a truce with him.

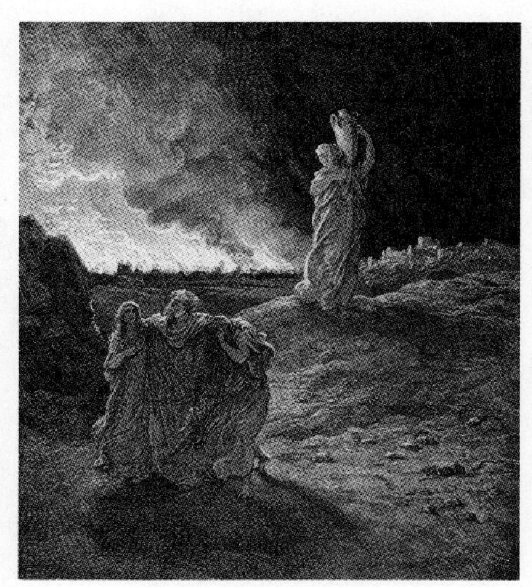

Abraham and the Promises of God

COMMENTS

The Abrahamic Covenant, first given to Abram (Gen. 12:1-3), ratified 10 years later (15:1-8), was reconfirmed nearly 13 years later (17:1-14). In addition, Abram's name was changed from Abram ("exalted father") to Abraham ("father of multitudes"), though he still had no children. At this time Abraham was 99; Sarai was 89. Her name was likewise changed from Sarai to Sarah ("princess").

God promised to give Abraham many children and that Sarah herself would bear him a son. This news caused Abraham joyful wonder, for it would mean that a 90-year-old woman would give birth to a son whose father was 100. The thought caused him to wish that Ishmael ("man from God") could be given a place of recognition in God's sight. God promised Ishmael prominence, but guaranteed that the covenant given to Abraham would be passed on to the son to be born and to his succeeding generations in perpetuity. This further confirms the unconditional nature of the Abrahamic Covenant. None of its beneficiaries is in any way responsible to assist in its realization. It depends solely on God.

As a token (sign) of the covenant, Abraham was given the rite of circumcision. Every male child born to Abraham and his descendants was to be circumcised on the eighth day. In obedience, Abraham circumcised every male in his house, including Ishmael (age 13) and himself (age 99). Even today, Jews circumcise their sons at eight days of age and Arabs circumcise their sons at age 13.

Circumcision was a testimony of the father's faith in God's promise to Abraham. The father, in circumcising his son, was saying in effect: "I believe the promises God gave to Father Abraham, that He will fulfill them—if not in my day, then in the day of my son." Jewish boys bore on their bodies visible testimony of their father's belief (or unbelief) in God's covenant with Abraham.

A short time later, God (in the person of the Angel of the Lord and accompanied by two angels) came to Abraham and Sarah. They accepted Abraham's hospitality and confirmed that Sarah indeed would have a son. Sarah, knowing that her menstrual cycle had ceased, understandably laughed when she overheard the news. The Angel of the Lord heard her laugh and confirmed that indeed she would have a son and specified that it would be within a year. This was realized, just as the Angel of the Lord promised.

With the birth of Isaac, human beings have been brought into the human race in four ways thus far in the Book of Genesis:

(1) by direct creation—Adam.

(2) from a rib taken out of man—Eve.

(3) from the union of male and female—most of the population.

(4) from parents who have passed fertility—Isaac.

(5) There is one other way remaining—from a virgin by the Holy Spirit—Jesus. God is able to do the impossible whenever He chooses to do so.

After confirming the birth of Isaac, the Angel of the Lord revealed to Abraham His intended destruction of Sodom. Abraham, knowing that Lot had become a resident of that city, interceded with God and secured the promise from God that if there were as few as 10 righteous persons He would not destroy it.

The depth of Sodom's degradation is shown by the angels' visit to Lot's house in Sodom. Sexually degenerate men surrounded the house, desiring a homosexual relationship with Lot's visitors. Lot offered them his virgin daughters.

In spite of the degradation and filth in which he lived, Lot was still righteous in God's sight. God delivered him from Sodom's destruction. Lot was out of Sodom, but Sodom was not completely out of Lot, as was evidenced by the fact that his daughters got him drunk and conceived children by him.

HIS CALVARY

God tested Abraham by ordering him to offer up Isaac as a burnt offering on Mount Moriah. *"And it came to pass after these things, that God did tempt Abraham, and said unto him, 'Abraham.' And he said, 'Behold, here I am' " (22:1).*

Upon arriving three days later, Isaac, not knowing he was to be the sacrifice, asked: *"Behold, the fire and the wood; but where is the lamb for a burnt offering?" (v. 7)*

With breaking heart, Abraham answered: *"My son, God will provide Himself a lamb . . ." (v. 8).*

Abraham built an altar and bound his beloved son to it. At the last moment God stopped him, showing him a nearby substitute ram.

Abraham named this place *Jehovah-Jireh* ("the LORD will provide"). The Angel of the Lord again assured him of the features of the Abrahamic Covenant. *"And the Angel of the LORD called unto Abraham out of heaven the second time, and said, 'By Myself have I sworn,' saith the LORD, 'for because thou hast done this thing, and hast not withheld thy son, thine only son; that in blessing I will bless thee, and in multiplying I will multiply thy seed as the stars of the heaven, and as the sand which is upon the seashores and thy seed shall possess the gate of his enemies. And in thy seed shall all the nations of the earth be blessed; because thou hast obeyed My voice' " (vv. 15-18).*

HIS CAVE

Sarah died at age 127. Abraham bought the cave at Machpelah for 400 pieces of silver and buried her.

HIS COMMAND

Abraham ordered his servant Eliezer to go to Haran and find a wife for Isaac. On arriving at Haran, Eliezer asked God for a sign concerning the right choice for Isaac. Rebekah's action and kindness fulfilled this prayer.

"And he said, 'O LORD God of my master Abraham, I pray then, send me good speed this day, and show kindness unto my master Abraham. Behold, I stand here by the well of water; and the daughters of the men of the city come out to draw water. And let it come to pass, that the damsel to whom I shall say, "Let down thy pitcher, I pray thee, that I may drink"; and she shall say, "Drink, and I will give thy camels drink also"; let the same be she that Thou has appointed for Thy servant Isaac; and thereby shall I know that Thou has showed kindness unto my master.'

"And it came to pass, before he had done speaking, that, behold, Rebekah came out, who was born to Bethuel, son of Milcah, the wife of Nahor, Abraham's brother, with her pitcher upon her shoulder" (24:12-15).

She agreed to go with him to marry Isaac. Isaac awaited her arrival and they became husband and wife.

This is one of Scripture's greatest typical chapters:

(1) Abraham is a type of the Father. (See Matt. 22:2)

(2) Isaac is a type of the Son. (Compare Gen. 24:67 with Eph. 5:25)

(3) Eliezer is a type of the Holy Spirit. (Compare Gen. 24:4 with Acts 2:1-4; Eph. 1:10-14.)

(4) Rebekah is a type of the church.

HIS KETURAH

Abraham married a woman named Keturah, who bore him six sons. The most important was the fourth, who was named Midian, the father of the Midianites.

HIS CITY

Abraham died at 175 and was buried alongside Sarah in the Machpelah cave.

"By faith Abraham, when he was called to go out into a place which he should after receive for an inheritance, obeyed; and he went out, not knowing whither he went.

"By faith he sojourned in the land of promise, as in a strange country, dwelling in tabernacles with Isaac and Jacob, the heirs with him of the same promise. For he looked for a city which had foundations, whose builder and maker is God" (Heb. 11:8-10).

Abraham's Faith in God

COMMENTS

Genesis 22 records the supreme test of Abraham's faith and the supreme victory accomplished by faith.

One well could wonder how God could demand a human sacrifice in view of His unalterable opposition to such sacrifices (cf. Lev. 18:21; Deut. 12:31; 18:10). The best answer is that God actually wanted Abraham to give up his son as a spiritual sacrifice. Without this, even a bloody sacrifice would be fruitless and meaningless. What one does proves what he believes.

That Abraham was willing to give up Isaac physically demonstrates beyond question that he had already given him up to God in a spiritual sacrifice (cf. James. 2:21-24). Though God's instructions seemed contrary to His revealed will concerning Isaac, Abraham was willing to do what God wanted him to do and let the consequences rest in God's hands.

Some have suggested that Abraham was willing to slay Isaac because he thought that God would give him another offspring (as God gave Adam and Eve Seth in place of Abel). This cannot be true, because God had said that Abraham's progeny would be realized through Isaac (cf. Gen. 21:12), and Abraham had promised his servants that he and Isaac would return to them (22:5). Therefore, it is best to understand that Abraham fully expected to put Isaac to death and fully expected God to raise him up from the dead again (cf. Heb. 11:17-19).

It has been said, "Like father; like son." Abraham's simple faith in God is reflected in Isaac's simple faith in his father. He likely could have overpowered his father and escaped. If it were not for his faith in God and in his father, Isaac might have reasoned that his father had indeed gone mad. This event caused Isaac always to know that God was more precious to his father than he was. The Angel of the Lord who spoke to Abraham was the preincarnate Jesus. Abraham was just as quick to obey and refrain from slaying Isaac as he had been to obey God's previous command to offer him as a sacrifice. As the result of Abraham's obedience, the Angel of the Lord called to him a second time and reconfirmed the Abrahamic Covenant to him again.

Abraham died, never fully realizing the things God had promised. There must yet be a day when he will realize the fulfillment of everything God promised. That day will indeed come when Jesus returns to the earth to set up His kingdom and reign over it for a thousand years.

The death and burial of Sarah could have been covered in a couple of verses, but God devotes the entire twenty-third chapter of Genesis to it because it is such an outstanding act of faith. It is a common event—the burial of a loved one—but the greatest faith is often displayed in the ordinary events of life. In faith, Abraham wanted his wife's remains to rest in the land that had been promised to him and to his descendants after him. The presence of Sarah's sepulcher in the land was a silent witness to later generations that Abraham indeed believed in God and was sure of the validity of the promises God had made to him.

Abraham's faith is reflected in another common event—the marriage of his son. Sarah had died (no more progeny would come from her); Isaac was near 40; Abraham was 140. Abraham sent his servant because of his advanced age and because of the custom of the day (cf. Gen. 23:8). Abraham did not want his son to marry an unbelieving Hamitic Canaanite. Abraham's servant went about the whole procedure in a faith that was characteristic of his master. God honored the faith of Abraham, Isaac, and the servant, and gave them Rebekah, who responded with faith like Abraham's.

Preview

The Child of the Covenant (Isaac)

GENESIS 25–27

In 1990 B.C., Abraham died. The man of God was gone but the mission of God would go on. The torch would pass on to his son Isaac, then to his grandson Jacob, and finally to his 12 great-grandsons, particularly to Joseph.

In addition to death and taxes, a third thing is certain. The message and mission of God will be heard and experienced as long as the world stands. One of the primary purposes for the writing of the Old Testament was to prepare the way for the coming Messiah.

The life of Isaac serves to illustrate three factors that would be fulfilled by the prophesied Saviour.

The first was Isaac's supernatural birth. He was conceived by an old barren woman. Jesus was conceived by a young virgin girl.

The second factor was Isaac's obedience. He agreed to be offered up by his father. Two thousand years later Christ would demonstrate that same obedience to His Heavenly Father.

The third factor was Isaac's marriage. He was content to await the coming of his bride from a foreign land, as Christ in heaven awaits His bride, the church.

Overview

<table>
<tr><td>SCRIPTURE</td><td colspan="5">Genesis 25–27</td></tr>
<tr><td>SUBJECT</td><td colspan="5">Life of Isaac</td></tr>
<tr><td rowspan="4">SPECIFICS</td><td rowspan="4">Isaac and his spouse</td><td rowspan="2">He lies about Rebekah</td><td rowspan="4">Isaac and his sons</td><td colspan="2">Jacob</td></tr>
<tr><td>Obtaining the birthright</td><td>Obtaining the blessing</td></tr>
<tr><td>He prays for Rebekah</td><td colspan="2">Esau</td></tr>
<tr><td>He is deceived by Rebekah</td><td>His ungodly malice</td><td>His unwise marriage</td></tr>
<tr><td>SAINTS AND SINNERS</td><td colspan="5">Isaac, Rebekah, Jacob, Esau, Abimelech</td></tr>
<tr><td rowspan="2">SENTENCE SUMMARIES</td><td>O.T. Verse</td><td colspan="4">“The LORD said unto Moses, ‘Depart, and go up thence, thou and the people which thou hast brought up out of the land of Egypt, unto the land which I sware unto Abraham, to Isaac, and to Jacob, saying, “Unto thy seed will I give it” ’ ” (Ex. 33:1).</td></tr>
<tr><td>N.T. Verse</td><td colspan="4">“By faith Isaac blessed Jacob and Esau concerning things to come” (Heb. 11:20).</td></tr>
</table>

HE STORY OF ISAAC

Isaac has been described as a mediocre son of a great father (Abraham) and the mediocre father of a great son (Jacob).

The main action of Isaac's life occurs in five key places.

ON A JERUSALEM MOUNTAIN

The submissive son.

We have already noted his willingness to be offered up by his father.

BY A HEBRON FIELD

The gentle groom.

It was here, as previously seen, where he first met Rebekah.

After 20 years of a childless marriage, Isaac entreated God for children. Rebekah gave birth to twin boys, Esau and Jacob.

IN A PHILISTINE APARTMENT

The imitator.

During a famine Isaac repeated the sin of his father Abraham. He moved to a foreign land (Philistia) and lied about his wife Rebekah, claiming that she was his sister.

On discovery of this deceit, the Philistine king Abimelech rebuked Isaac. In spite of Isaac's carnality, however, God reaffirmed the Abrahamic Covenant to Isaac and blessed him.

ALONGSIDE SOME DESERT WELLS

The well-digger.

The Philistines, jealous of Isaac's great prosperity, filled up some old wells his father had once dug. Isaac spent much time clearing the debris from those clogged water holes.

God reappeared to Isaac, assuring him of divine blessing.

Both Isaac and Rebekah were grieved over the marriage of Esau, who at 40 picked a pagan girl for his wife.

AT A SUPPER TABLE

The frustrated father.

Isaac instructed Esau to kill a deer and prepare him a venison meal so that he might eat and give Esau the blessing before he died.

Rebekah overheard the conversation and arranged to have Jacob play the part of Esau before his half-blinded father so he would receive the blessing instead. The ruse worked, and Jacob was blessed.

On his return from the field, Esau learned of this deceit. Esau vowed to murder Jacob after their father died.

Isaac and Rebekah sent Jacob away to Haran to escape the hand of Esau and also to get himself a bride.

At this point Isaac drops from the biblical record. He lived another 43 years, dying at the age of 180 (35:28).

Isaac, the Connecting Link

COMMENTS

Probably the most significant role Isaac played in God's plan was to be a "connecting link" between Abraham, his father, and Jacob, his son.

Abraham made a sharp distinction between Isaac and his other sons. Isaac alone was the child of promise. He alone was the child of Sarah, and thus Abraham gave nearly everything he had to Isaac. To his other sons he gave gifts sufficient to get them started in life. But he sent them away from Isaac so that they would not interfere with Isaac and the messianic line. Isaac's unique relationship was also recognized by God, who blessed him and recognized him as Abraham's successor.

Realizing that he was the successor to Abraham ("father of multitudes"), that he was the only one born who was to produce the nation promised to Abraham (cf. 12:1-3), and that he had no children, Isaac entreated God for Rebekah, so she might bring forth children in fulfillment of the promises to Abraham. God graciously answered and Rebekah conceived. God gave Isaac and Rebekah twins.

Before they were born, their fetuses struggled within Rebekah in an unusual way, causing her to inquire of Jehovah. She was told that the two infants within her would be progenitors of two distinct nations which would have nothing to do with each other. Contrary to custom, the elder, Esau, would serve the younger, Jacob. The boys were entirely different, and the hint of problems to come was indicated by the fact that Isaac loved Esau, but Rebekah loved Jacob.

In the incident of the selling of the birthright, most interpreters assume that Esau was all right and Jacob was all wrong. The biblical account, however, holds Esau primarily responsible, for he despised his birthright. To his credit, Jacob was spiritually minded and valued the benefits of the birthright. Esau, on the other hand, did not value his birthright. He felt that he would die before his father and that the birthright would be useless. He did not realize that the very terms of God's covenant including the birthright demanded that its recipient be preserved alive at least until he brought forth an offspring.

Isaac fell into the same trap of unbelief that his father Abraham had fallen into twice. Like father like son; Isaac reacted in the same way Abraham did—with deceit. The deceit went on for a long time and was discovered only when Abimelech observed Isaac fondling and caressing Rebekah in a manner in which one treats his wife, not his sister. The discovery brought about inquiry and a well-deserved rebuke. Once again the heathen king appeared in a much better light than this man of God who ceased to walk by faith.

Two conspiracies are revealed in Genesis 27: The conspiracy of Isaac and Esau and the conspiracy of Rebekah and Jacob. These conspiracies were made in spite of the clear revelation that God had given (25:23). Isaac and Esau's conspiracy was a deliberate attempt to circumvent the Word of God. Rebekah and Jacob's conspiracy was a deliberate attempt to shortcut the will of God.

In spite of the scheming and deceit, Isaac blessed Jacob as God intended. This event shows how God overrules in the affairs of men and sometimes controls a sinful man so that he does God's will even though he attempts to do what he knows is not God's will. For his part in the deception, Jacob received just retribution:

(1) He never saw his dear mother again.

(2) He was more cruelly deceived by his own sons, concerning Joseph.

(3) He performed hard and rigorous service for 20 years.

(4) He was deceived by Laban and given Leah after he had bargained for Rachel.

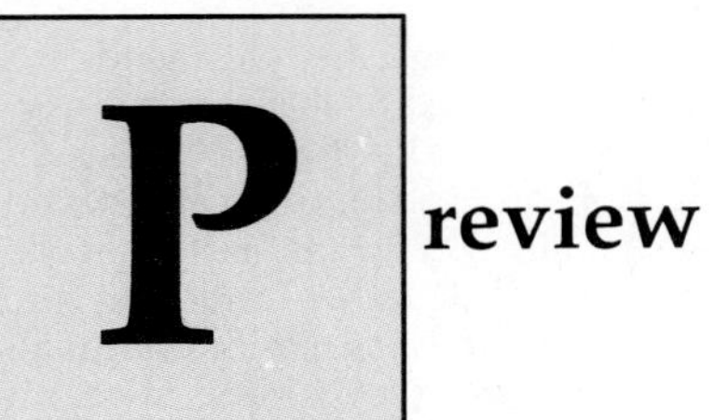

Preview

The Journeys of Jacob (Part One)

GENESIS 25; 27–31

The younger son definitely had a spiritual edge over his slightly older twin brother. Both parents could easily see that. But there was a deceitful trait about him that troubled them. Oh, well, perhaps he would grow out of it. After all, God Himself had predicted the older would serve the younger. But as the years went by, the father apparently forgot about this promise and attempted to give the family blessing (a spiritual responsibility) to his eldest son. This only triggered more deceit in the family, as both mother and younger son successfully tricked the father, resulting in an angry vow from the older to murder his younger twin! Few soap operas could design a more twisted plot. The parents in this true story of course were Isaac and Rebekah. Their two sons were Esau and Jacob. To say the least, this was not the happiest of families.

When corrective action was finally taken by the father it proved too late, for Esau married an unbeliever and became a desert wanderer. Jacob would eventually fare much better, but not before experiencing many painful trials, the majority of which were self-inflicted.

Overview

<table>
<tr><td>SCRIPTURE</td><td colspan="6">Genesis 25; 27–31</td></tr>
<tr><td>SUBJECT</td><td colspan="6">Life of Jacob: part 1</td></tr>
<tr><td rowspan="9">SPECIFICS</td><td>Obtaining</td><td colspan="3">The birthright from his brother</td><td colspan="2">The blessing from his father</td></tr>
<tr><td>Receiving</td><td colspan="5">The Abrahamic Covenant from God</td></tr>
<tr><td rowspan="6">Gathering</td><td rowspan="6">His family</td><td>Wives</td><td colspan="3">Leah, Rachel, Bilhah, Zilpah</td></tr>
<tr><td rowspan="4">Sons</td><td>1 Reuben</td><td>2 Simeon</td><td>3 Levi</td></tr>
<tr><td>4 Judah</td><td>5 Dan</td><td>6 Naphtali</td></tr>
<tr><td>7 Gad</td><td>8 Asher</td><td>9 Issachar</td></tr>
<tr><td>10 Zebulun</td><td>11 Joseph</td><td>12 Benjamin</td></tr>
<tr><td>Daughter</td><td>Dinah</td><td></td><td></td></tr>
<tr><td>Negotiating</td><td colspan="5"></td></tr>
<tr><td>SAINTS AND SINNERS</td><td colspan="6">Isaac, Rebekah, Jacob, Esau, Laban, Rachel, Leah</td></tr>
<tr><td rowspan="2">SENTENCE SUMMARIES</td><td>O.T. Verse</td><td colspan="5">" 'I have loved you,' saith the LORD. 'Yet ye say, "Wherein hast Thou loved us?" Was not Esau Jacob's brother?' saith the LORD; 'yet I loved Jacob' "(Mal. 1:2).</td></tr>
<tr><td>N.T. Verses</td><td colspan="5">"Not only this, but when Rebekah also had conceived by one, even by our father Isaac . . . it was said unto her, 'The elder shall serve the younger' " (Rom. 9:10, 12).</td></tr>
</table>

HE STORY OF JACOB

THE DEVISING BROTHER

As a boy Jacob took advantage of his famished brother and obtained from him the birthright which normally went to the eldest child. This Esau carelessly sold for a mess of pottage.

THE DECEITFUL SON

It has already been observed how Jacob deceived his father into giving him the blessing meant for Esau.

THE DREAMING PILGRIM

Jacob left Beersheba for Haran. His first stop that night was Bethel, some 40 miles away.

As he slept he saw a ladder from earth to heaven with angels ascending and descending on it. Above the ladder stood God Himself, who now reaffirmed to Jacob the provisions of the Abrahamic Covenant.

"And he lighted upon a certain place, and tarried there all night, because the sun was set; and he took of the stones of that place, and put them for his pillows, and lay down in that place to sleep.

"And he dreamed, and behold a ladder set up on the earth, and the top of it reached to heaven; and behold the angels of God ascending and descending on it. And, behold, the LORD stood above it, and said, 'I am the LORD God of Abraham thy father, and the God of Isaac. The land whereon thou liest, to thee will I give it, and to thy seed. And thy seed shall be as the dust of the earth, and thou shalt spread abroad to the west, and to the east, and to the north, and to the south; and in thee and in thy seed shall all the families of the earth be blessed.

" 'And, behold, I am with thee, and will keep thee in all places whither thou goest, and will bring thee again into this land; for I will not leave thee, until I have done that which I have spoken to thee of' " (28:11-15).

On awakening, Jacob anointed with oil the rock he had used for a pillow and vowed to serve God.

THE LOVE-STRUCK SUITOR

Jacob arrived in Haran and met Rachel, his cousin. He fell deeply in love with her and promised Laban (his uncle and her father) to work seven years for her hand in marriage. *"And Jacob served seven years for Rachel; and they seemed unto him but a few days, for the love he had to her" (29:20).*

THE FRUSTRATED FAMILY MAN

Jacob (the deceiver) was himself deceived on his wedding night by a crafty Laban who secretly substituted his oldest girl named Leah in place of Rachel his youngest.

Jacob was furious, but agreed to work another seven years for Rachel without pay. However, he was permitted to marry her within a week.

Jacob now had two wives and soon gathered two more, as Leah and Rachel each presented him their personal handmaidens for childbearing purposes. These four women would bear Jacob 12 sons and one recorded daughter.

From Leah:
(1) Reuben—his first son
(2) Simeon—his second son
(3) Levi—his third son
(4) Judah—his fourth son
(5) Issachar—his ninth son
(6) Zebulon—his tenth son (Note: Leah also bare him Dinah, his only recorded daughter [30:21].)

From Bilhah (Rachel's handmaiden):
(1) Dan—his fifth son
(2) Naphtali—his sixth son

From Zilpah (Leah's handmaiden):
(1) Gad—his seventh son
(2) Asher—his eighth son

From Rachel:
(1) Joseph—his eleventh son
(2) Benjamin—his twelfth son

THE ENTERPRISING EMPLOYEE

After the birth of his sons (with the exception of Benjamin, who would be born later in Bethlehem), Jacob desired to return home but was persuaded by Laban to remain. *"And Laban said unto him, 'I pray thee, if I have found favor in thine eyes, tarry: for I have learned by experience that the LORD hath blessed me for thy sake' " (v. 27).*

During the next six years Jacob became a wealthy man and was commanded by God to return to Palestine. *"And the Lord said unto Jacob, 'Return unto the land of thy fathers, and to thy kindred; and I will be with thee' " (31:3).*

"I am the God of Bethel, where thou anointedst the pillar, and where thou vowedst a vow unto Me. Now arise, get thee out from this land, and return unto the land of thy kindred" (v. 13).

Jacob quickly broke camp and left for home without bothering to inform Laban.

Learning of this, an angry Laban caught up with him at Mount Gilead after a week's journey. Warned by God not to harm him, Laban rebuked Jacob for sneaking off and accused him of stealing his household gods. Unaware that Rachel had taken them, Jacob angrily denied this.

At Laban's suggestion, the two men marked a boundary line by a pile of stones over which both agreed not to cross onto the other man's side. *"And Laban said, 'This heap is a witness between me and thee this day.' Therefore was the name of it called Galeed, and Mizpah, for he said, 'The LORD watch between me and thee, when we are absent one from another' " (vv. 48-49).*

Jacob's Dream

COMMENTS

Jacob's dream at Bethel was the first of seven recorded theophanies that he witnessed. They are recorded in Genesis 31:11-13; 32:1-2, 24-30; 35:1; 9-13; 46:1-4.

In 28:4, Isaac had bestowed on Jacob "the blessing of Abraham." He could only "wish" it on Jacob. At Bethel, God appeared to Jacob and confirmed the blessing which Isaac had "wished" upon him.

When Jacob said, "Surely the LORD is in this place; and I knew it not" (v. 16), he was not indicating an inferior knowledge of the nature of God. He knew that Jehovah was not limited to any one geographical spot. This was Jacob's first venture away from home. At this point he was an exile from his home, where he had enjoyed a fellowship with God. His dream caused him to realize that such rich and personal fellowship with God could be his anywhere!

The names that Jacob gave to this location are significant. "House of God" indicated that this was a place where God met man. "Gate of heaven" indicated that this was the place where man met God. "Gate of heaven" indicated that Jacob regarded it not only as a gate leading into heaven, but also a gate from heaven through which God stepped to reveal Himself to man when it pleased Him to do so.

The second mention of the voluntary tithe is recorded in verse 22 (the first mention is in 14:20). In 35:1-7 Jacob carried out the vow made here, though no mention was made of his giving the tenth. The omission may be because giving the tenth to God was Jacob's lifelong practice rather than something fulfilled in a single instance.

It might be asked how Jacob could roll the stone away from the well's mouth unaided. It is not likely that he was so enamored with Rachel's beauty that he was showing off to impress her. Jacob was 77 at this time. Three suggestions are in order:

(1) He was a naturally strong man.

(2) This was a very emotional time for Jacob. Perhaps he received extra strength from seeing the fulfillment of much he had heard from his mother for many years.

(3) The other shepherds were girls or young boys who needed their combined strength to accomplish what one strong adult man could do.

Jacob found out what it was like to be deceived when after fulfilling his part of the contract faithfully he was given Leah as his wife rather than Rachel. It is difficult to understand how Jacob could have been deceived, but it must be remembered that his wife was brought to him under the cover of darkness and was, no doubt, veiled. Except for her facial features she may have had a physical appearance similar to her sister Rachel's. Leah's part in the deception is not fully known and certainly not fully excusable on the grounds of her unquestioning obedience to her father's wishes.

Jacob could not cast off Leah without making her a laughingstock and without becoming such himself. So he negotiated another contract with Laban and was given Rachel without waiting for the second period of seven years to be fulfilled.

The words of 31:49 are often mistakenly used as a benediction in churches today. These words were originally uttered by Laban, who had taken advantage of Jacob in every way possible for more than 20 years.

After Jacob left Laban to return to his homeland, Laban overtook him and accused him of stealing his household gods. After Laban's search failed to turn up the gods which Rachel had indeed stolen (unknown to Jacob, vv. 32-35), Laban proposed a covenant. The witness to the covenant was a pile of stones which each man named "heap of testimony / witness" in his own language. With the words of verse 49 Laban indicated that it was Jacob who needed to be watched, when in reality the record showed that the opposite was true!

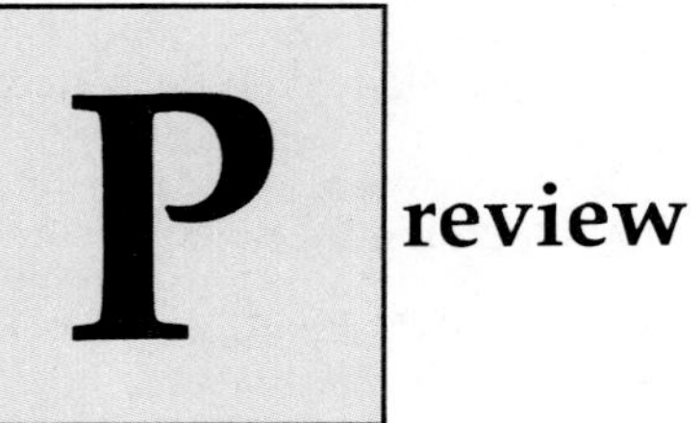

The Journeys of Jacob (Part Two)

GENESIS 32–35; 38

There was no doubt about it. The aging patriarch was walking differently. His wives, children, and servants all agreed. What they could not agree on was just how his walk had changed. Perhaps it could be best described as a confident limp. But was that possible? How could he possess any confidence whatever? Had he forgotten that an angry Esau and his 400 men would catch up with their little camp today and get even for past injustices? Would anyone in Jacob's group live to see another sunset? They would indeed—every one of them. Esau's attitude would be drastically altered from that of fierce revenge to friendly reunion.

None of the frightened people in that early morning camp could know any of this, or that their survival that day was directly connected to Jacob's limp. It all began at the Brook Jabbok where Jacob and God engaged in an all-night wrestling match. The results? Both a new walk and a new name. Jacob now would be known as Israel and the one who wrestled with God.

Overview

<table>
<tr><td>SCRIPTURE</td><td colspan="5">Genesis 32–35; 38</td></tr>
<tr><td>SUBJECT</td><td colspan="5">Life of Jacob: part 2</td></tr>
<tr><td rowspan="5">SPECIFICS</td><td rowspan="5">The surrender of Jacob</td><td rowspan="2">He surrenders himself at Jabbok</td><td rowspan="5">The sorrow of Jacob</td><td rowspan="2">Over the sins of his family</td><td>Levi & Simeon committed murder</td></tr>
<tr><td>Judah & Reuben committed adultery</td></tr>
<tr><td rowspan="3">He surrenders his idols at Shechem</td><td rowspan="3">Over deaths in his family</td><td>Deborah, his nurse</td></tr>
<tr><td>Rachel, his wife</td></tr>
<tr><td>Isaac, his father</td></tr>
<tr><td>SAINTS AND SINNERS</td><td colspan="5">Jacob, Esau, Dinah, Shechem, Simeon, Levi, Rachel, Judah, Tamar</td></tr>
<tr><td rowspan="2">SENTENCE SUMMARIES</td><td>O.T. Verse</td><td colspan="4">"And I gave unto Isaac Jacob and Esau; and I gave unto Esau Mount Seir, to possess it; but Jacob and his children went down into Egypt" (Josh. 24:4).</td></tr>
<tr><td>N.T. Verse</td><td colspan="4">"By faith Jacob, when he was a-dying blessed both the sons of Joseph; and worshiped, leaning upon the top of his staff" (Heb. 11:21).</td></tr>
</table>

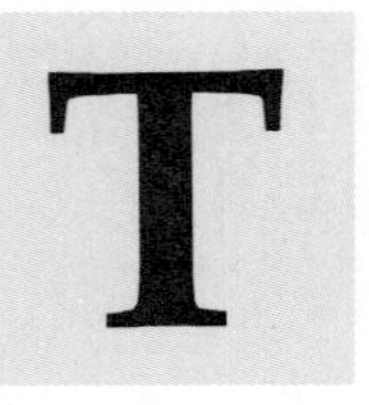

HE DETERMINED WRESTLER

Jacob was again ministered to by angels on the way home. He now learned the terrifying news that Esau was en route to meet him with 400 men.

After dividing his household in two groups and sending a bribe gift of 550 animals to Esau, a desperate Jacob spent the night by the Brook Jabbok, wrestling with God in prayer. *"And Jacob said, 'O God of my father Abraham, and God of my father Isaac, the* L*ORD which saidst unto me, "Return unto thy country, and to thy kindred, and I will deal well with thee."*

" 'I am not worthy of the least of all the mercies, and of all the truth, which Thou hast showed unto Thy servant; for with my staff I passed over this Jordan; and now I am become two bands.

" 'Deliver me, I pray Thee, from the hand of my brother, from the hand of Esau; for I fear him, lest he will come and smite me, and the mother with the children.

" 'And Thou saidst, "I will surely do thee good, and make thy seed as the seed of the sea, which cannot be numbered for multitude" ' " (Gen. 32:9-12).

"And Jacob was left alone; and there wrestled a Man with him until the breaking of the day. And when He saw that He prevailed not against him, He touched the hollow of his thigh; and the hollow of Jacob's thigh was out of joint, as he wrestled with Him.

"And He said, 'Let me go, for the day breaketh.' And he said, 'I will not let Thee go, except Thou bless me.'

"And He said unto him, 'What is thy name?' And he said, 'Jacob.'

"And He said, 'Thy name shall be called no more Jacob, but Israel; for as a prince hast thou power with God and with men, and hast prevailed.' And Jacob asked Him, and said, 'Tell me, I pray Thee, Thy name.' And He said 'Wherefore is it that thou dost ask after My name?' And He blessed him there.

And Jacob called the name of the place Peniel, 'for I have seen God face to face and my life is preserved' " (vv. 24-30).

Jacob and Esau met. To Jacob's immense relief the reunion was a happy one. Esau had forgotten all past wrongs.

Jacob entered Palestine, settled at Shechem, and built an altar there.

THE ENRAGED FATHER

Jacob's children were guilty of the sins of murder and adultery.

The sin of murder committed by Levi and Simeon. Jacob allowed his daughter Dinah to run loose, resulting in her being seduced by Shechem, the son of King Hamor of the Hivites. Shechem determined to marry Dinah and asked Jacob for the necessary permission.

Dinah's brothers, inwardly boiling with rage, but too weak to attack the Hivites, cruelly deceived Shechem by agreeing to his request with the stipulation that all male Hivites be circumcised.

On the third day, when the Hivites' wounds were sore and sensitive to every movement, Levi and Simeon walked into the camp and slaughtered every male there.

Furious, Jacob soundly rebuked his two murderous sons, saying, *"Ye have troubled me to make me to stink among the inhabitants of the land" (34:30).*

The sin of adultery, committed by Judah. Though Jacob's name does not occur in chapter 38, we may assume he was well aware of its tragic facts and disapproved of them.

Judah, Jacob's fourth son, married a Canaanite girl, who bore him three sons: Er, Onan, and Shelah. His oldest son, Er, married a girl named Tamar, but God soon killed him for an unrecorded act of wickedness. Judah then commanded his second son, Onan to marry her. He was soon slain for wickedness. Judah promised Tamar to give her his youngest son Shelah in due time, though he secretly had no intention of doing this.

After a while Tamar realized this and, disguising herself as a common harlot, enticed Judah into her tent for sexual purposes. For a pledge of payment she demanded and received his signet, bracelets, and staff. Tamar became pregnant from this relationship.

Some three months later an indignant Judah ordered her to be burned to death. Tamar then showed him his own signet, bracelets, and staff. A remorseful and doubtless red-faced Judah immediately set her free.

"And Judah acknowledged them, and said, 'She hath been more righteous than I; because that I gave her not to Shelah my son.' And he knew her again no more" (v. 26).

Tamar had twins and called them Pharez and Zerah. Both this Canaanite prostitute woman and her illegitimate firstborn son would later be included, through the amazing grace of God, in the sacred genealogy of the Lord Jesus Christ (Matt. 1:3).

THE OBEDIENT PATRIARCH

God again reminded Jacob of His previous command to return to Bethel. *"And God said unto Jacob, 'Arise, go up to Bethel, and dwell there; and make there an altar unto God, that appeared unto thee when thou fleddest from the face of Esau thy brother' " (Gen. 35:1).*

Jacob ordered his entire household to destroy their idols, to wash themselves, and to put on fresh clothing in preparation for the trip to Bethel. Their idols were then collected and buried under an oak tree near Shechem.

Jacob arrived at Bethel and built an altar there, naming it El-Bethel, meaning "the God of the house of God."

THE SORROWING SAINT

Jacob lost, in rapid succession, three loved ones:

(1) His old nurse, Deborah, first mentioned here, apparently came to live with Jacob after the death of her boss (and Jacob's mother) Rebekah.

(2) His beloved wife, Rachel, died giving birth to her second (and Jacob's twelfth) son, who was named Benjamin. She was buried in Bethlehem.

This is the first mention of Bethlehem in the Bible.

(3) Jacob's father, Isaac, died at age 180 and was buried by Jacob and Esau alongside Abraham and Sarah in the cave of Machpelah, at Hebron.

J**acob Wrestles God**

COMMENTS

As angels had ministered to Jacob on his departure from Canaan (cf. chap. 28), they met and comforted him on his return. No sooner had he gotten rid of the danger of Laban than the greater danger of Esau threatened him. But the appearance of the angels gave Jacob reassurance.

How did he see them? Nothing suggests a vision or a dream. Jacob seems to have been the only one to have seen them. Perhaps God worked a special miracle to enable him to see the unseen (cf. 2 Kings 6:17). He recognized the angelic host as God's host (army) and named the place Mahanaim ("two camps" or "two hosts") to commemorate the two hosts—God's and his.

Jacob no longer felt unprotected. He knew he was home.

Having sent his family, preceded by a generous 550-animal present to appease Esau's wrath, Jacob remained behind and wrestled a Man until daybreak.

Who was his Opponent? Jacob recognized Him as God, so he must have wrestled with the Angel of the Lord, the preincarnate Christ!

What was the nature of the conflict? Whatever the physical effort, the conflict certainly involved prayer. Jacob learned what it meant to agonize in prayer. The Angel demonstrated that though Jacob could persevere in prayer, God was still the Master. With a simple touch of His hand, He put the ball and socket joint of Jacob's hip out of place.

The once-proud Jacob would hereafter hobble. This experience was to Jacob what offering up Isaac on Mount Moriah was to Abraham. He learned he could no longer depend on his own cleverness and ingenuity. He came to the end of himself and had to cast himself on God completely.

Jacob was never the same again. In recognition of this fact the Angel changed his name from Jacob ("supplanter") to Israel ("prince with God") and blessed him.

The tragedy of Genesis 34 was occasioned by Dinah's going out to get acquainted with the girls of the land of Canaan. Whether she did so without consulting her parents or contrary to their wishes is not known. She should have known that Egyptians and Canaanites regarded unmarried women as legitimate prey (cf. 12:15; 20:2; 26:7) and should not have gone out unattended. Shechem saw her, seduced her, and raped her.

Jacob reacted admirably in holding his peace until he could discuss the matter with Shechem's father. Lengthy negotiations were entered into with a view to securing Dinah as Shechem's wife.

But Jacob's sons opposed the negotiations because of the wrong done to their sister. They feigned forgiveness on the condition that Hamor's men be circumcised. Simeon and Levi felt it their responsibility to avenge their sister, since they were full brothers (as were also Reuben, Judah, Isaachar, and Zebulon). While the Hivite men were disabled, Simeon and Levi entered with their servants into the city and slew all the incapacitated males.

Jacob rebuked his sons for their treachery, but they were indifferent. It may be that this whole event was occasioned by a young teen-age girl's romantic fantasies. If so, these fantasies brought about tragic results.

The custom by which a man married his brother's widow when he died and left no offspring was known as levirate marriage. The understanding was that the firstborn son would carry on the line of the deceased brother, but all other children born to the union would be accounted as his own. Moses, under the direction of the Holy Spirit, later made this custom into a provision of the Mosaic Law (cf. Deut. 25:5ff.). It is also referred to in the New Testament (cf. Matt. 22:24ff.). The measure was designed to assure that a widowed woman would have someone to care for her when she was old.

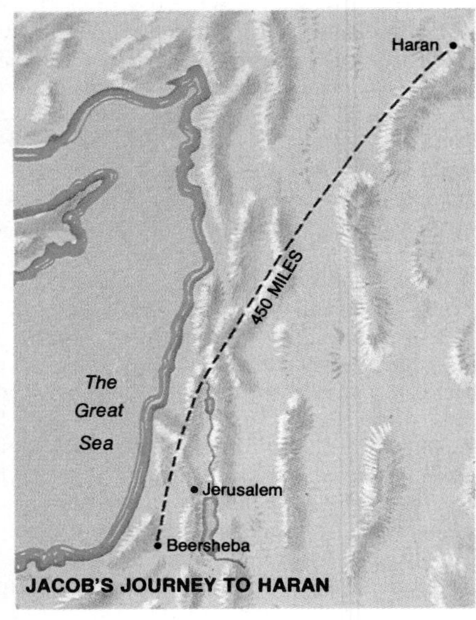

JACOB'S JOURNEY TO HARAN

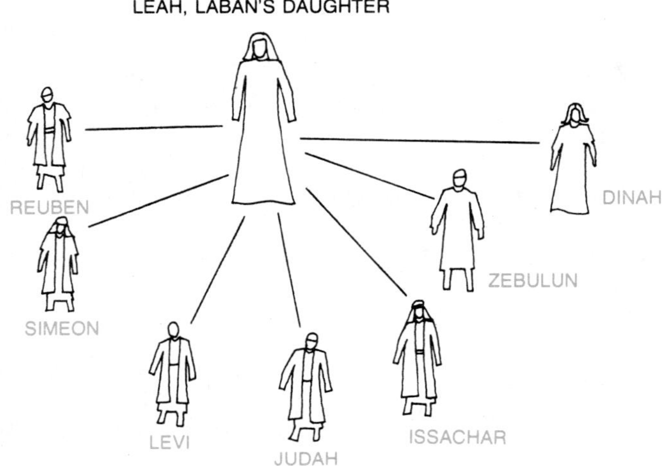
LEAH, LABAN'S DAUGHTER
REUBEN
SIMEON
LEVI
JUDAH
ISSACHAR
ZEBULUN
DINAH

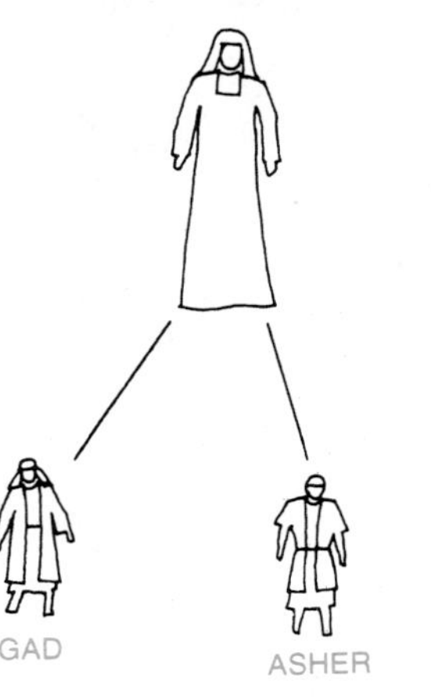
ZILPAH, LEAH'S SERVANT
GAD
ASHER

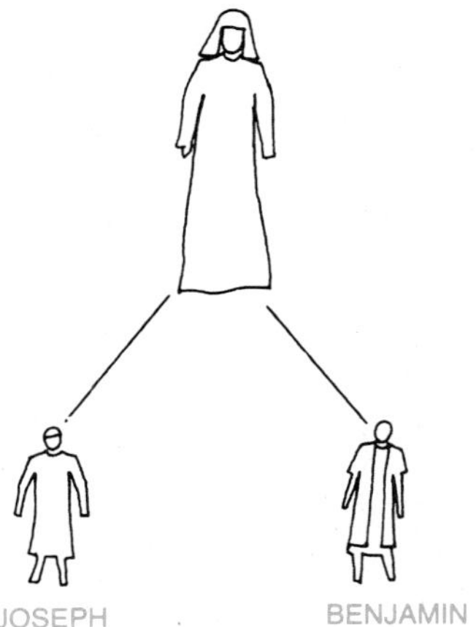
RACHEL, LABAN'S DAUGHTER
JOSEPH
BENJAMIN

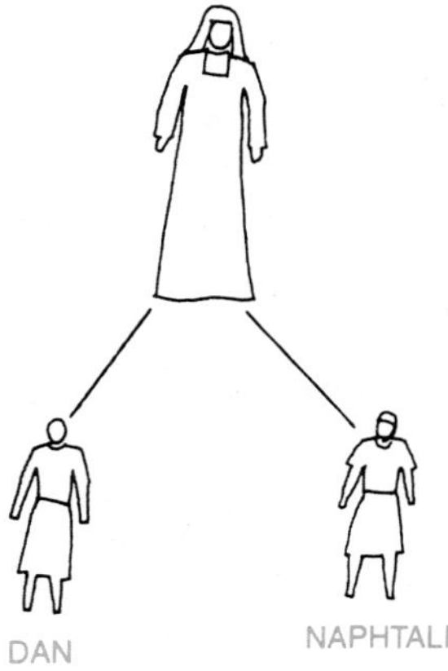
BILHAH, RACHEL'S SERVANT
DAN
NAPHTALI

Joseph: The First Years

GENESIS 37; 39–44

Just how long their consciences troubled them is not known. But surely the 10 brothers spent more than one sleepless night, tortured by memories of the past. Selling their younger brother into cruel Egyptian slavery was bad enough. That crime, however, had been compounded by lying to their father. The old man was led to believe that a wild animal had attacked and killed his beloved son, Joseph.

Could that evil event in the past ever be forgotten? This would prove impossible, for in the near future all 10 brothers would be confronted with their crime in a totally unexpected and unpleasant manner. Be sure your sin will find you out!

This, in a nutshell, is the story of Joseph and his 10 brothers. No other Old Testament character in matters of personal purity and unjust sufferings so foreshadows the person of Christ as does Joseph. But his sufferings, like those of Christ, served merely to prepare him for "the glory that should follow" (1 Peter 1:11). In one simple day Joseph was promoted from a prisoner in Egypt to the Prime Minister over Egypt.

Overview

<table>
<tr><td>SCRIPTURE</td><td colspan="4">Genesis 37; 39–44</td></tr>
<tr><td>SUBJECT</td><td colspan="4">Life of Joseph: part 1</td></tr>
<tr><td rowspan="3">SPECIFICS</td><td colspan="2">The evil</td><td rowspan="3">“Ye thought evil against me; but God meant it unto good.”</td><td>The good</td></tr>
<tr><td colspan="2">He is sold into slavery because of his prophecies</td><td>His elevation in jail by the prison keeper</td></tr>
<tr><td colspan="2">He is cast into prison because of his purity</td><td>His exaltation in Egypt by the Pharaoh</td></tr>
<tr><td>SAINTS AND SINNERS</td><td colspan="4">Jacob, Joseph, Reuben, Judah, Simeon, Benjamin, Potiphar, Potiphar’s wife, a butler & baker, Pharaoh</td></tr>
<tr><td rowspan="2">SENTENCE SUMMARIES</td><td>O.T. Verses</td><td colspan="3">“He sent a man before them, even Joseph, who was sold for a servant; whose feet they hurt with fetters; he was laid in iron; until the time that his word came. The word of the LORD tried him. The king sent and loosed him, even the ruler of the people, and let him go free. He made him lord of his house, and ruler of all his substance” (Ps. 105:17-21).</td></tr>
<tr><td>N.T. Verses</td><td colspan="3">“The patriarchs, moved with envy, sold Joseph into Egypt, but God was with him. And delivered him out of all his afflictions, and gave him favor and wisdom in the sight of Pharaoh, King of Egypt; and he made him governor over Egypt; and all his house” (Acts 7:9-10).</td></tr>
</table>

HE FAVORED SON

The dreams of Joseph. The remaining chapters in Genesis describe the life of Joseph, Jacob's second-youngest son, born to him of his beloved Rachel.

Joseph had brought down on himself the wrath of his 10 half brothers. Three factors had led to this sad situation:

(1) He had reported to his father some of the bad things the 10 were doing: *"These are the generations of Jacob. Joseph, being seventeen years old, was feeding the flock with his brethren; and the lad was with the sons of Bilhah, and with the sons of Zilpah, his father's wives; and Joseph brought unto his father their evil report" (Gen. 37:2).*

(2) He had become Jacob's favorite son. To show this special affection, the old man gave Joseph a long-sleeved brightly colored tunic.

(3) Joseph had had strange dreams.

In one of Joseph's dreams his whole family was in the field binding sheaves, when suddenly his sheaf stood up and their sheaves all gathered around it and bowed low before it.

During his second dream he saw the sun, moon, and 11 stars bow low before him.

One day Joseph was sent from his home in Hebron to Shechem to check on his half brothers and their grazing flocks.

The deceit of his brothers. Joseph's 10 brothers saw him in the distance and determined to kill him. However, Reuben, Jacob's firstborn (29:32) apparently had second thoughts, for he suggested that they simply throw Joseph in a pit and let him die.

Joseph was stripped of his coat and cast into a pit. Ignoring his pitiful cries, his cruel brothers sat down to eat.

Suddenly a slave caravan of Ishmaelites and Midianites, en route to Egypt, came into view. The nine brothers made a hasty and heartless decision to sell Joseph as a slave. Joseph was sold for 20 pieces of silver (the going price of a slave) and carried into Egypt.

The despair of his father. To conceal their horrible crime, Joseph's brothers took Joseph's coat, smeared it with goat's blood, and deceived Jacob into believing that his beloved son had been slain and eaten by a wild animal.

"And he knew it, and said, 'It is my son's coat; an evil beast hath devoured him; Joseph is without doubt rent in pieces.' And Jacob rent his clothes, and put sackcloth upon his loins, and mourned for his son many days.

"And all his sons and all his daughters rose up to comfort him; but he refused to be comforted; and he said, 'For I will go down into the grave unto my son mourning.' Thus his father wept for him" (37:33-35).

THE FAITHFUL STEWARD

His service. Joseph was sold as a slave to Potiphar, an officer in Pharaoh's Egyptian palace guard.

Under the blessing of God, he was quickly entrusted with the entire administration of Potiphar's household.

His self-control. Joseph was enticed by the wife of Potiphar to commit immorality, but refused her continued advances: *"How then can I do this great wickedness, and sin against God?" (39:9)*

In an act of revenge, she accused Joseph of rape.

His sufferings. Joseph was thrown into prison.

THE FORGOTTEN SERVANT

The jailer, like Potiphar, soon recognized Joseph's beautiful and talented character and put him in charge of the entire prison administration.

For some reason, Pharaoh's anger was aroused against both his chief baker and chief butler, and he sent them to Joseph's prison.

While in prison both of these men had mysterious dreams. God gave Joseph the ability to correctly interpret each dream. He predicted that within three days the king would free the butler, but execute the baker.

Three days later, on Pharaoh's birthday, he dealt with the butler and baker exactly as Joseph had predicted. But the butler forgot to mention anything about Joseph.

Jacob and Joseph

COMMENTS

Jacob made a tragic mistake in loving Joseph more than all of his other children.

Two reasons account for his partiality:

(1) Joseph was a son of Jacob's old age—younger children commonly enjoy privileges and favoritism older children never experience.

(2) Joseph was the only one of Jacob's sons who shared his spiritual values.

Jacob compounded his (and Joseph's) problems by openly expressing his favoritism by making a special coat for Joseph. The translation "coat of many colors" is unfortunate, for it conveys the wrong idea. The thing that was different about Joseph's coat was not its color, but rather that it had long sleeves which reached to his wrists and the length extended to his ankles—it was a long-sleeved cloak (Heb., *ketho'neth passim,* better translated, "a long garment with sleeves"). Such a garment was not suitable for physical labor. It was a garment such as a foreman, supervisor, or superintendent would wear.

The fact that Joseph had such a coat indicated that his father desired that Joseph have preeminence over the other sons. Both Joseph and his brothers knew the significance well.

Thanks to Reuben's intercession, the brothers' fiendish intention to kill Joseph was modified, to selling him into slavery. They sold him for "20 pieces of silver."

The word "pieces" does not occur in the Hebrew text. They literally sold Joseph for "20 of silver," which represents the weight of the silver paid. They did not receive coins because no coined money had circulated yet. Later, Moses designated this amount of silver as being the value of a young boy between 5 and 25 years of age (Lev. 27:5). Joseph was 17 (37:2), so this was a fair price. Thirty shekels of silver was the average price paid for a slave who was fully mature physically (cf. Ex. 21:32).

The events recorded in Genesis 39 fulfill several purposes. First, Joseph was prepared for his later exaltation in two ways:

(1) He learned Egyptian culture and got valuable administrative experience in Potiphar's house.

(2) His prison experience humbled him so that he could be exalted by God later without being puffed up.

Second, these years of humiliation and hardship refined Joseph's character. Without them he would have been unsuitable and proud (cf. his attitude about his dreams, Gen. 37:5-11). With his character refined, he could be used by God to refine his brothers.

Third, chapter 39 stands in sharp contrast to chapter 38. There an unfaithful Judah at home fell before the morals of the Canaanites. Here, Joseph, far from home, stood where Judah had fallen.

Fourth, this chapter shows that living a righteous life is no guarantee that one will not have difficulty. In fact, it may be the occasion for receiving unrighteous judgment and punishment. Joseph learned this lesson early in his life.

The events of chapter 39 can be outlined as follows:

(1) Joseph established in Potiphar's house (vv. 1-6).
(2) Joseph seduced in Potiphar's house (vv. 7-18).
(3) Joseph removed from Potiphar's house (vv. 19-23).

The events of chapter 40 prepared Joseph for his deliverance from prison. He may have thought that God had forgotten him, but God was with him all the time and was working to bring him to a place of exaltation, though his advancement was over two years in coming after the events of the last chapter were completed.

There was nothing unusual about either the butler's or baker's dream. Both dreams denoted things that each man commonly did. God gave Joseph the ability to discern the distinctive features of each dream and to give the interpretations immediately, with definiteness and accuracy.

THE FAMED STATESMAN

The revelation of Joseph. One night two years later Pharaoh experienced two mysterious dreams.

In the first dream he was standing on the bank of the Nile River when suddenly seven sleek, fat cows came up out of the river and began grazing in the grass. Then seven other cows came up, but they were skinny and all their ribs stood out. Suddenly, the skinny cows ate the fat cows.

In his second dream Pharaoh saw seven heads of grain on one stalk, with every kernel well-formed and plump. Suddenly, seven more heads appeared on the stalk, but these were shriveled and withered by the east wind. The dream ended as the thin heads devoured the plump ones.

Pharaoh consulted his magicians about these dreams the next morning, but they were unable to interpret them. Then the butler suddenly remembered the amazing talent of Joseph and related to the Pharaoh those events which had occurred in prison two years back.

Joseph cleaned up, shaved, and was brought before Pharaoh. After hearing the contents of the dreams, Joseph immediately interpreted them, giving God the glory.

According to Joseph, both dreams meant the same thing. The seven fat cows and the seven plump heads of grain meant that there were seven years of prosperity ahead. The seven skinny cows and the lean heads of grain meant that a seven-year famine period would follow the years of plenty.

Joseph then advised Pharaoh to appoint a capable administrator over a nationwide farm program, and to divide Egypt into five districts. The officials of these districts should then gather into the royal storehouses all the excess crops of the next seven years.

The elevation of Joseph. Pharaoh appointed Joseph to this high office on the spot, and gave him a wife. *"And Pharaoh said unto his servants, 'Can we find such a one as this is, a man in whom the spirit of God is?'*

"And Pharaoh said unto Joseph, 'Forasmuch as God hath showed thee all this, there is none so discreet and wise as thou art. Thou shalt be over my house, and according unto thy word shall all my people be ruled; only in the throne will I be greater than thou.'

"And Pharaoh said unto Joseph, 'See, I have set thee over all the land of Egypt.'

"And Pharaoh took off his ring from his hand, and put it upon Joseph's hand, and arrayed him in vestures of fine linen, and put a gold chain about his neck: and he made him to ride in the second chariot which he had; and they cried before him, 'Bow the knee.' And he made him ruler over all the land of Egypt" (41:38-43).

Joseph was now 30 years of age. In time Joseph's wife presented him with two boys. The first was named Manasseh ("made to forget"), and the younger, Ephraim ("fruitful").

As Joseph had predicted, the seven fat years were followed by lean ones, causing people from many lands to buy their food in Egypt.

The consternation of Joseph's brothers. Jacob sent his 10 oldest sons into Egypt from Hebron to buy food. They arrived in Egypt and bowed low before Joseph, but did not recognize him, thus fulfilling his dream of some 20 years before.

Joseph threw them into jail for three days and then released them, but kept Simeon as a hostage until they would return with Benjamin, whom he demanded they bring to him.

The famine intensified in Hebron, so Jacob was forced to allow Benjamin to go with Joseph's other brothers back into Egypt for food. Judah attempted to guarantee the safety of Benjamin.

They again presented themselves to Joseph, who took them to his palace for a feast. For the first time in 20 years all 12 brothers were together, but only one was aware of it.

The brothers were fed at a separate table from that of Joseph. But to their amazement he seated them in the order of their ages, giving Benjamin five times as much food as the others.

Before they left the next morning, Joseph once again secretly had the payment money put in each man's sack, along with Joseph's own silver cup at the top of Benjamin's sack. Soon after the brothers had left the city they were arrested (at Joseph's command) and accused of stealing his silver cup. They quickly denied the charge and agreed to serve as slaves if any stolen loot should be found on them. A search quickly revealed the cup in Benjamin's sack.

Standing before Joseph for the third time, Judah stepped forward and begged Joseph to accept his life in place of Benjamin. Tearfully Judah reminded Joseph that their old father Jacob would simply die if anything happened to Benjamin.

Joseph and Pharaoh

COMMENTS

Genesis 41 records the third time that dreams figured prominently in Joseph's life. The first dreams were his own and were interpreted by others—his brothers and father (chap. 37). The last two occurrences (chaps. 40–41) were the dreams of others which he interpreted. The dreams that Joseph interpreted were given for the benefit of others. God used them to reveal to the dreamers what He would do in the near future.

The "magicians" and "wise men" of Egypt had probably been called on to interpret Pharaoh's dreams before. They could have fabricated some kind of meanings but did not. Their honesty in this circumstance is admirable.

The butler related to Pharaoh how Joseph had interpreted his dream two years earlier. Pharaoh summoned Joseph, who went through preparations before coming into Pharaoh's presence.

Joseph's honesty is likewise admirable. He did not seek personal gain or attempt to bargain with Pharaoh in any way. He set the record straight—there was no innate ability in him; the ability belonged to God alone. By this time Joseph had suffered more than 12 years of injustices, and yet he still had the proper perspective. His first concern was not for his own personal deliverance, but that his relationship with God be right and that God's honor be in no way impugned. Nor did Joseph seek to build himself up at the expense of the court magicians and wise men who had failed to interpret the dreams.

After listening to Pharaoh's telling of his dream, Joseph gave the interpretation just as clearly and certainly as he had for the butler and baker two years earlier. Joseph set forth two important interpretive principles.

(1) The two dreams were in reality one.

(2) The dream was vitally related to what God was about to do.

Failure to recognize these principles would result in a wrong interpretation. The dreams indicated that seven years were coming when plenty would be experienced. These would be followed by another seven years of a famine so severe that the plenty of the first seven years would be forgotten.

Under inspiration Joseph spoke directly and immediately, whereas the Egyptian magicians and wise men had been completely stumped. Just as clearly, Joseph set forth the divine recommendation.

Pharaoh recognized that the man who could give the interpretation and the recommendation was the man who should be elevated to the position of second highest in the land. Joseph was elevated immediately and invested with the outward symbols of authority: a signet ring, fine clothes, a gold chain, and elaborate chariot, and a public salute.

Joseph enacted the preparations he had recommended. When the famine came, only Egypt was prepared. Pharaoh referred everyone to Joseph, including Joseph's brothers! His confidence in Joseph was not misplaced.

The interrogation of Joseph's brothers begins in Genesis 42, continues in chapter 43, and concludes in chapter 44. The final phase of God's work of conviction in the hearts of Joseph's brothers was brought to completion. They resigned themselves completely to their fate. Having come to the end of themselves, God had them in the precise place where He could manifest Himself to them in a glorious way which they themselves never had dreamed possible.

They were tested to see whether they would abandon their younger and more-favored brother, Benjamin, and leave him to an uncertain fate in preference of their own safety—as they had abandoned Joseph about 20 years earlier.

The words of Judah revealed that he was a transformed man. The other brothers probably exhibited a similar change in their attitudes and manners. Judah probably expressed all of their thoughts and heart-attitudes toward their father, as well as their attitudes toward his dearly loved son, Benjamin.

They passed Joseph's test successfully and indicated they were truly transformed men. The effect on Joseph was greater than Judah or the brothers could have ever imagined. It resulted in Joseph's self-revelation (chap. 45).

Preview

Joseph: The Final Years

GENESIS 45–50

Joseph could scarcely believe his eyes. But how could he deny what he saw? There they stood, all 10 of them. How long had it been? His mind quickly flashed back some 23 years to the small Canaanite town of Dothan. That was the day they sold him into slavery. Watching them now, he felt absolutely no anger, but awe, as he thought of a mysterious dream he experienced as a boy. It had probably been a mistake telling them about it.

"And he said unto them, 'Hear, I pray you, this dream which I have dreamed. For behold, we were binding sheaves in the field, and lo, my sheaf arose, and also stood upright; and behold, your sheaves stood round about, and made obeisance to my sheaf' " (Gen. 37:6-7).

Who would have thought the dream would be fulfilled under the present circumstances? But here they were, subdued and, no doubt, somewhat hungry, requesting food in a foreign land. The irony of course was they did not recognize him. But then, how could they? In their minds he was either dead by this time, or was serving as a slave somewhere.

Yes, he would reveal himself to them, but not yet. The following few weeks became a nightmare for Joseph's 10 brothers, as they were made to sweat, fret, and regret their past crime. Finally, the agony was over and the announcement was made: "Don't you recognize me? I am Joseph, your younger brother!" Never one to harbor a grudge, Joseph would on two occasions reassure his brothers, still plagued by guilt:

"Now therefore, be not grieved, nor angry with yourselves, that ye sold me hither; for God did send me before you to preserve life" (45:5).

"But as for you, ye thought evil against me; but God meant it unto good, to bring to pass, as it is this day, to save much people alive" (50:20).

Overview

<table>
<tr><td>SCRIPTURE</td><td colspan="2">Genesis 45–50</td></tr>
<tr><td>SUBJECT</td><td colspan="2">Life of Joseph: part 2</td></tr>
<tr><td rowspan="5">SPECIFICS</td><td colspan="2">Joseph and his brothers</td></tr>
<tr><td colspan="2">The revealing—"I am your forgotten brother."
The reassuring—"I am your forgiving brother."</td></tr>
<tr><td colspan="2">Joseph and his father</td></tr>
<tr><td>Jacob predicts the future of Joseph's sons</td><td>They would be famous</td></tr>
<tr><td>Jacob predicts the future of Joseph himself</td><td>He would be fruitful</td></tr>
<tr><td>SAINTS AND SINNERS</td><td colspan="2">Joseph, Jacob, Pharaoh, Ephraim, Manasseh</td></tr>
<tr><td rowspan="2">SENTENCE SUMMARIES</td><td>O.T. Verses</td><td>"The king sent and loosed him, even the ruler of the people, and let him go free. He made him lord of his house, and ruler of all his substance; to bind his princes at his pleasure, and teach his senators wisdom. Israel also came into Egypt; and Jacob sojourned in the land of Ham. And He increased His people greatly, and made them stronger than their enemies" (Ps. 105:20-24).</td></tr>
<tr><td>N.T. Verses</td><td>"By faith Jacob, when he was a-dying, blessed both the sons of Joseph; and worshiped, leaning upon the top of his staff. By faith Joseph, when he died, made mention of the departing of the Children of Israel; and gave commandment concerning his bones" (Heb. 11:21-22).</td></tr>
</table>

THE FORGIVING SAINT

Jospeh and his brothers. Joseph, unable to contain himself any longer, revealed his identity to his brothers.

After a time of tearful reuniting, Joseph informed them that the two-year drought they had already experienced would continue another five years. He urged that they bring Jacob back with them and all make plans to live in Egypt.

Joseph reassured his brothers (still in shock) that he had no hard feelings, but felt God had overruled their evil plot in a manner to guarantee that Israel would be a great nation.

Pharaoh rejoiced along with Joseph over his restored brethren and also invited the entire clan to live in Egypt.

Joseph and his father. At first the old patriarch Jacob could not comprehend the thrilling news concerning Joseph, but then he believed the report and planned his trip to Egypt.

En route, at Beer-sheba, God reassured Jacob that He would still bless him, even in Egypt. Jacob was told that he was to die there, but that God would someday bring his descendants back to Palestine.

"And God spake unto Israel in the visions of the night, and said, 'Jacob, Jacob.' And he said, 'Here am I.'

"And He said, 'I am God, the God of thy father. Fear not to go down into Egypt; for I will there make of thee a great nation. I will go down with thee into Egypt; and I will also surely bring thee up again; and Joseph shall put his hand upon thine eyes' " (46:2-4).

Jacob entered Egypt with his entire household. *"And Joseph made ready his chariot, and went up to meet Israel his father, to Goshen, and presented himself unto him; and he fell on his neck, and wept on his neck a good while.*

"And Israel said unto Joseph, 'Now let me die, since I have seen thy face, because thou art yet alive' " (vv. 29-30).

The population of Israel in Goshen expanded rapidly in spite of the famine everywhere else.

At the age of 147 Jacob realized his time was near and called for his beloved son Joseph and his favorite grandsons, Ephraim and Manasseh.

Joseph promised his father that he would not be buried in Egypt.

Jospeh and his sons. Joseph's two sons stood before their grandfather, waiting to be blessed. The old man adopted them as his own sons and assured them of an equal inheritance.

THE FRUITFUL SHADE TREE

Then Joseph received his father's blessing (see also Heb. 11:21). *"Joseph is a fruitful bough, even a fruitful bough by a well; whose branches run over the wall" (Gen. 49:22).*

"And he blessed Joseph, and said, 'God, before whom my fathers Abraham and Isaac did walk, the God which fed me all my life long unto this day, the Angel which redeemed me from all evil, bless the lads; and let my name be named on them, and the name of my fathers Abraham and Isaac; and let them grow into a multitude in the midst of the earth' " (48:15-16).

Jacob gathered his 12 sons around his bedside just before his death, *"that I may tell you that which shall befall you in the last days" (49:1).* Jacob then predicted the future of each of the 12 sons. Especially interesting is his prophecy concerning Judah and his tribe (vv. 8-12).

"The scepter shall not depart from Judah, nor a lawgiver from between his feet, until Shiloh come; and unto Him shall the gathering of the people be" (v. 10).

The other brothers were to praise Judah and bow before him. Judah would destroy his enemies, and would be left undisturbed, like a young lion. The scepter would not depart from Judah until Shiloh (Christ) came (see Num. 24:17; Rev. 5:50).

Joseph returns his father's body. Jacob died at age 147. His body was embalmed in Egypt during a 40-day preparation period. All Egypt mourned over him for 70 days. He was carried by his sons into Palestine and buried alongside Abraham and Isaac in the cave of Machpelah.

Joseph reassured his troubled brothers that favorable conditions would remain as before the funeral. He gently reminded them: *"Ye thought evil against me; but God*

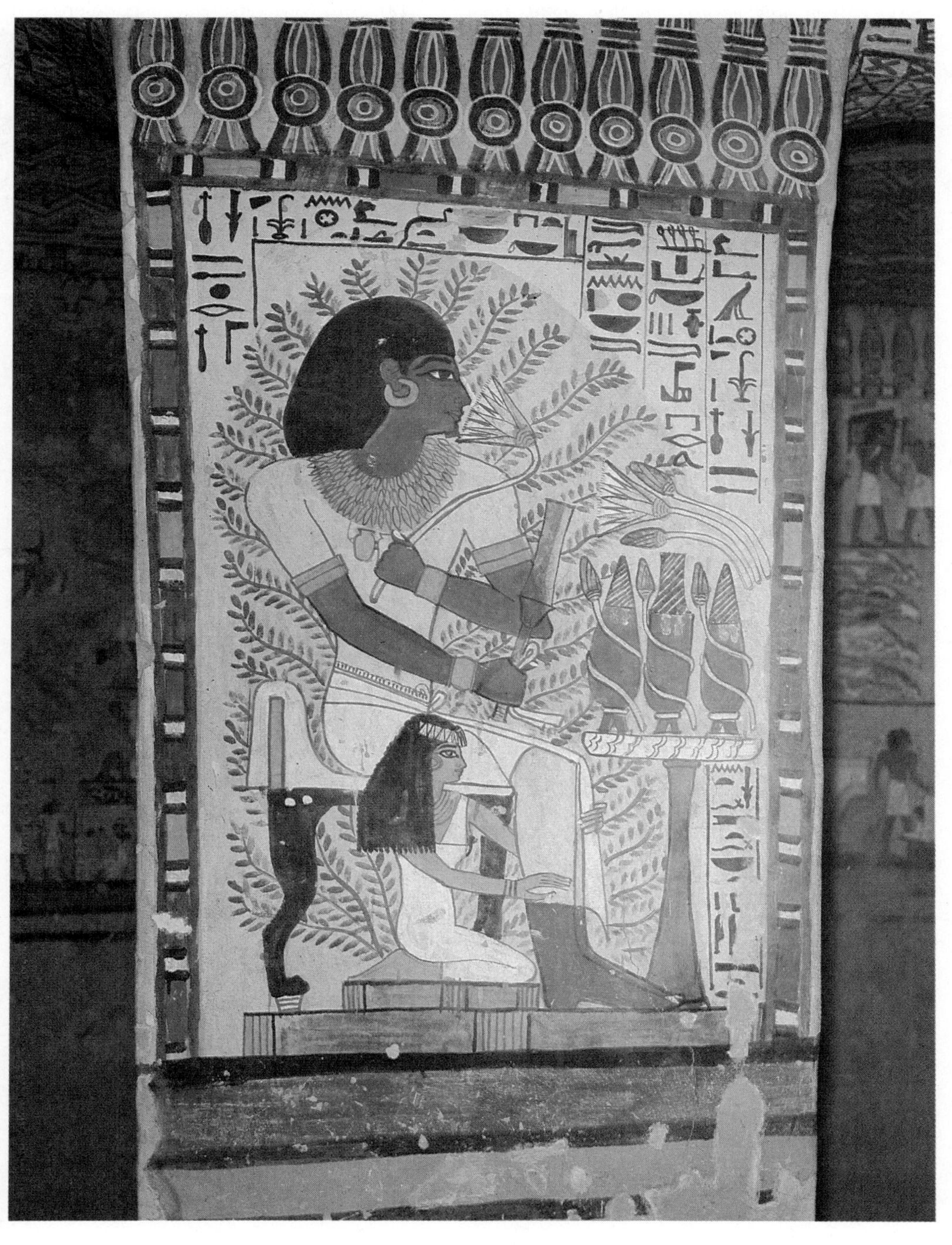

meant it unto good, to bring to pass, as it is this day, to save much people alive" (Gen. 50:20).

Joseph died at age 110. *"And Joseph said unto his brethren, 'I die; and God will surely visit you, and bring you out of this land unto the land which He sware to Abraham, to Isaac, and to Jacob.' And Joseph took an oath of the Children of Israel, saying, 'God will surely visit you, and ye shall carry up my bones from hence.'*

"So Joseph died, being 110 years old. And they embalmed him, and he was put in a coffin in Egypt" (vv. 24-26).

THE FORESHADOW OF THE SAVIOUR

Joseph is the most complete type of Christ in all the Bible. Note the amazing similarities between these two:

(1) Both were beloved by their fathers (37:3; Matt. 3:17).

(2) Both regarded themselves as shepherds (Gen. 37:2; John 10:11-14).

(3) Both were sent to their brethren by their fathers (Gen. 37:13-14; Luke 20:13; John 3:17; Heb. 10:7, 19).

(4) Both were hated by their brethren without a cause (Gen. 37:4-5, 8; John 1:11; 7:5; 15:25).

(5) Both were plotted against by their brethren (Gen. 37:20; John 11:53).

(6) Both were severely tempted (Gen. 39:7; Matt. 4:1).

(7) Both were taken to Egypt (Gen. 37:28; Matt. 2:14-15).

(8) Both were stripped of their robes (Gen. 37:23; John 19:23-24).

(9) Both were sold for the price of a slave (Gen. 37:28; Matt. 26:15).

(10) Both were bound (Gen. 39:20; Matt. 27:2).

(11) Both remained silent and offered no defense (Gen. 39:20; Isa. 53:7).

(12) Both were falsely accused (Gen. 39:1-18; Matt. 26:59-60).

(13) Both experienced God's presence through everything (Gen. 39:2, 21, 23; John 1:32).

(14) Both were respected by their captors (Gen. 39:21; Luke 23:47).

(15) Both were placed with two prisoners, one of which was later lost, and the other saved (Gen. 40:2-3, 21-22; Luke 23:32, 39-43).

(16) Both were about 30 when their ministries began (Gen. 41:46; Luke 3:23).

(17) Both were highly exalted after their sufferings (Gen. 41:41; Phil. 2:9-11).

(18) Both took Gentile brides (Gen. 41:45; Eph. 3:1-12).

(19) Both were lost to their brothers for a while (Gen. 42:7-8; Rom. 10:1-3; 11:7-8).

(20) Both forgave and restored their repentant brothers (Gen. 45:1-15; Micah 7:18-20; Zech. 12:10-12).

(21) Both were visited and honored by all earthly nations (Gen. 41:57; Isa. 2:2-3; 49:6).

Jacob in Egypt

COMMENTS

Why did God have Jacob and his family move to Egypt? The immediate reason was to preserve them during a period of intense famine. Four further reasons can be suggested:

(1) They had been prone to forget their individuality in Canaan. For example, Judah had married a Canaanite woman. In Egypt they would be isolated because Egyptians disdained all foreigners—especially shepherds.

(2) They would be removed from the idolatry of Canaan, and their isolation from the Egyptians would guard them from the idolatry of Egypt.

(3) The move would remove them from Canaanite culture and put them in touch with the great Egyptian culture, though not make them an intimate part of it.

(4) The people's faith would be quickened as they looked forward to the fulfillment of God's promises to Abraham, Isaac, and Jacob concerning their possession in the land of Canaan.

The difference in sums of the numbers of people making the journey in Genesis 46:26 (66) and 27 (70) is that the number in 46:26 is exclusive of Jacob, Joseph, and Joseph's two sons whereas the number in verse 27 includes them. Luke says that 75 made the trip (cf. Acts 7:14) because, in writing Acts, he apparently followed the Septuagint translation which includes Joseph's five grandsons in the list of descendants.

Joseph presented his father and brothers to Pharaoh and "Jacob blessed Pharaoh" (Gen. 47:7). The greater always blesses the lesser, yet Pharaoh was the king and Jacob was his guest. Jacob realized that he had more to offer than Pharaoh did.

If Pharaoh were a believer (which he well could have been had he believed God's revelation given to him), then he would be relatively new in his walk with God, and Jacob would have been his senior. If Pharaoh were not a believer, then all he could offer was wealth and a temporary haven, whereas Jacob could offer the knowledge of the true God. In a real sense, Egypt had been singularly blessed because of Jacob and the work that God wanted to do through him. The blessings of God on His people usually "spill over" to ungodly people around them.

Jacob formally adopted Joseph's two sons who were probably 18-20 years of age (48:5; cf. 47:28; 41:50). Because of Laban's trickery, Rachel was not Jacob's only wife and Joseph was not his firstborn; though he was his firstborn by Rachel. Jacob could have no more sons through Rachel because she was dead. Therefore, the only way he could have sons descended from Rachel would be to adopt Joseph's sons as his and give them prominent positions (cf. 1 Chron. 5:2-6). By this means, Joseph also received a double portion of his father's inheritance that normally would have gone to the firstborn son. This is precisely what Jacob had intended to show earlier when he gave Joseph a long-sleeved cloak (cf. Gen. 37). This is also what God had intended, as was shown by the dreams given Joseph (cf. chap. 37). Jacob's mistake had been to attempt to "shortcut" the will of God in exalting Joseph without testing and proving him first in the furnace of affliction.

In blessing his grandsons, Jacob crossed his hands, giving the primary blessing to the younger, much to Joseph's dislike (48:10-20). Once again the fact is established that the blessing of God is transmitted not through chronological age, but spiritual qualifications. It is not bestowed because of personal merit, but because of God's sovereign grace.

Jacob and Joseph are the only two Israelites whom the Scripture records were embalmed (50:2, 26). In the case of Jacob it was a necessary measure for transporting his remains from Egypt to Canaan, in keeping with his dying wish (49:29-31). In the case of Joseph it was in keeping with his station as a high Egyptian official.

Preview

A Sovereign God and a Suffering Saint (Part One)

JOB 1–2

"Oh, for the good old days!" Only eternity will reveal the countless times human beings have sighed those words in time of trouble. In truth, for the majority, the good old days were probably not that good. But this was not the case for a certain rich man from the land of Uz, living in the early days of human history. His desire to turn back the clock was understandable, for in a matter of hours he lost his friends, fortune, and family. But there was more to come. Soon a fearful and loathsome disease would befall him, causing the suffering victim to despair of life itself. But by far the most unbearable agony was heaven's deafening silence to his pitiful cry—"Why is all this happening to me? Where is God? Does He care? Will He hear?"

Forget the good old days, Job. Your sobbing today will be turned into singing tomorrow. This is true for all who love God, and Job, you qualify. So endure the pain, that you might enjoy the prize. One final word of advice: Don't put too much stock in either your friends or your feelings, for both can let you down! Better still, Job, just remember your own words:

"For I know that my Redeemer liveth, and that He shall stand at the latter day upon the earth" (Job 19:25).

Overview

<table>
<tr><td>SCRIPTURE</td><td colspan="6">Job 1–2</td></tr>
<tr><td>SUBJECT</td><td colspan="6">Life of Job: part 1</td></tr>
<tr><td rowspan="4">SPECIFICS</td><td rowspan="4">The adversary—Satan</td><td rowspan="4">The attack—four areas</td><td>1</td><td>Job's fortune</td><td>2</td><td>Job's family</td></tr>
<tr><td colspan="2">His animals are stolen
His servants are slaughtered</td><td colspan="2">The destruction of his children
The derision of his wife</td></tr>
<tr><td>3</td><td>Job's flesh</td><td>4</td><td>Job's friends</td></tr>
<tr><td colspan="2">The agony involved: "Satan . . . smote Job with sore boils."
The area involved: "From the sole of his foot unto his crown."</td><td colspan="2">Their assumptions were wrong

Their advice was wrong</td></tr>
<tr><td>SAINTS AND SINNERS</td><td colspan="6">Job, Job's wife, Eliphaz, Bildad, Zophar</td></tr>
<tr><td rowspan="2">SENTENCE SUMMARIES</td><td>O.T. Verse</td><td colspan="5">"Many are the afflictions of the righteous, but the Lord delivereth him out of them all" (Ps. 34:19).</td></tr>
<tr><td>N.T. Verse</td><td colspan="5">"Behold, we count them happy which endure. Ye have heard of the patience of Job, and have seen the end of the Lord; that the Lord is very pitiful, and of tender mercy" (James 5:11).</td></tr>
</table>

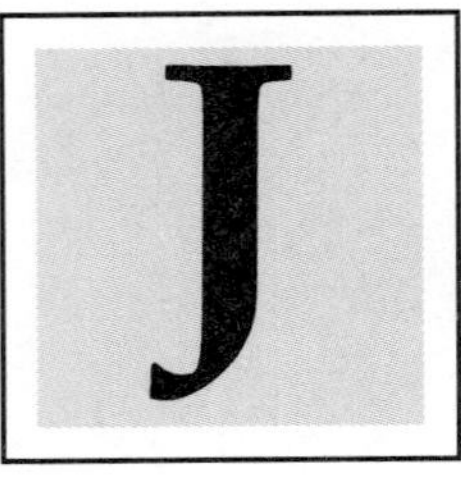

JOB'S TERRIBLE TROUBLES

The nature of these trials. In Job's first trial, his oxen and donkeys were stolen and his farmhands killed by a Sabean raid.

In his second trial, his sheep and herdsmen were burned up by fire.

In his third trial, his camels were stolen and his servants killed by a Chaldean raid.

In his fourth trial, his sons and daughters perished in a mighty wind.

In his fifth trial, Job himself was struck with a terrible case of boils.

The reason for these trials. A conversation between God and Satan concerning Job took place in heaven. The devil sneeringly charged that Job only worshiped God because of two selfish benefits.

(1) God had given His servant much wealth:

"Hast not Thou made a hedge about him, and about his house, and about all that he hath on every side? Thou hast blessed the work of his hands and his substance is increased in the land" (Job 1:10).

(2) God had given His servant good health.

Satan argued that if he could remove these two elements, that Job would curse God to His face. To shut the devil's mouth, God gave him permission to remove both Job's wealth and health.

It should be noted here that Satan cannot tempt a believer apart from God's specific permission.

THE FAITH SHOWN THROUGH THESE TRIALS

"Then Job arose, and rent his mantle, and shaved his head, and fell down upon the ground, and worshiped, and said, 'Naked came I out of my mother's womb, and naked shall I return thither. The LORD gave, and the LORD hath taken away; blessed be the name of the LORD.'

"In all this Job sinned not, nor charged God foolishly" (vv. 20-22).

HIS WIMPERING WIFE

"Then said his wife unto him, 'Dost thou still retain thine integrity? Curse God, and die.'

"But he said unto her, 'Thou speakest as one of the foolish women speaketh. What? Shall we receive good at the hand of God, and shall we not receive evil?' In all this did not Job sin with his lips" (2:9-10).

HIS FICKLE FRIENDS

It has been pointed out that Job's friends came to sympathize, but stayed on to sermonize. At any rate, Job's three "friends" delivered eight full-blown messages, all with three points and a poem, to the long-suffering patriarch.

Eliphaz preached three of these (chaps. 4–5; 15; 22); Bildad, three (chaps. 8; 18; 25); and Zophar, being less-winded, came up with two (11; 20).

No sooner had this tiresome trio finished than the filibuster began again by a young "preacher boy" named Elihu who droned on for six chapters (32–37). Perhaps at no other Bible conference in history did so many preachers preach to so few in attendance where the congregation enjoyed it less.

Each of Job's three "friends" based their advice to Job on the same foolish and wicked conclusion still held by all modern faith-healers, namely that his suffering was due to sin.

God, Satan, and Job

COMMENTS

In Job 1:6 a sharp distinction is made between "the sons of God" and "Satan." The "sons of God" in this context are unfallen angels who have been confirmed in righteousness. Satan, on the other hand, because he has fallen, is no longer considered to be one of them. He stands forever as a testimony to the eternal effect of sin. He had been Lucifer, the "son of the morning" (cf. Isa. 14:12), and the "anointed cherub that covereth" (i.e., protects the throne of God; cf. vv. 13-14; Ezek. 28:13-18). But the "son of the morning" became Satan ("adversary, hater, accuser, slanderer") and since then has been opposed to God, his Creator. Satan's name reveals both his character and his mission.

The question directed to Satan, "Whence comest thou?" (Job 1:7) was designed so that Satan would know that God knew about his activities and that he was accountable to God for his actions. Undoubtedly Satan had contemplated making Job the target of his evil schemes but had discarded the idea, thinking that Job was unassailable because of God's favor.

Job knew nothing of this exchange between God and Satan. He was unaware of the excellent standing that he had in the sight of God. He was totally unaware either of the fact that God had given him over into Satan's power, or of the restraint put on that power.

Four lightning-swift tragedies came on Job without warning. He lost everything dear to him, his wife, and his own life.

Job did not know what God had done or that Satan was responsible, but he knew God and "sinned not, nor charged God foolishly" (v. 22). Without knowing it, Job demonstrated beyond question that God had been right and Satan was wrong.

How much time elapsed between the time the sons of God and Satan appeared before God in the first and second chapters of Job is not known. It may be that God regularly summoned them for "staff meetings" to hold them accountable for their individual responsibilities.

Satan would have loved to have been absent, but God required him to report his defeat. Satan wanted to salvage his pride and have more freedom in his attack on Job. God granted Satan's wish, again giving Job into Satan's power with the single restriction not to take his life.

Job still knew nothing of the exchange between God and Satan, or that he had passed his first test with flying colors. Three more tragedies befell him in rapid succession. His comforters turned out to be his greatest affliction! Job still did not know what God had done or that Satan was responsible, but he knew God and "In all this did not Job sin with his lips" (2:10).

These chapters reveal a number of interesting facts pertaining to Satan.

(1) Though Satan is powerful, he is not all-powerful—he can do nothing without God's permission.

(2) Though Satan is intelligent, he is not omniscient—he thought that God would not permit him to attack Job so he made no effort to do so until God gave him permission.

(3) Though Satan has great power, he is accountable to God—God always knows where he is and what he is doing and calls him to account.

(4) Though Satan is mobile, he is not omnipresent—he could not be in God's presence and on earth at the same time.

(5) Though Satan will be cast out of heaven, at present he has access to God and his main activity is to try to get permission to bring trials to God's children.

The Book of Job lets us know that Satan still has access to heaven and that he is no friend of God's children. The Book of 1 John, however, lets us know that Someone Else has access to the Father—Jesus Christ the righteous—and He is our Advocate to meet Satan's attack (cf. 2:1-2).

When Satan attacks, Christ defends!

P review

A Sovereign God and a Suffering Saint (Part Two)

JOB 4–5; 8; 11; 15; 18; 20; 22; 25; 32–37

Some friends. Job's children were dead, his wealth was gone, and his body was wracked with disease and pain. His own wife had advised him to curse God and die. But now his friends had come. did ever a man so desperately need his friends as did this man?

Some friends. More like foes. They would condemn rather than comfort, adding to instead of taking from his grief. No tender touch they offered; only pointing fingers. He would be quickly judged and condemned without trial or defense. His pitiful protests fell on deaf ears. "Face it, Job," they said, "you're a terrible sinner, for the Almighty simply does not allow righteous people to suffer." The greater the sin, the greater the suffering.

For a while, Job seemed able to cope with this heaped-on hostility. But eventually fallen flesh displayed itself and he heard himself lash out against these fake friends, and, worse still, against his very God. This was Job's ultimate low. Could things possibly get any worse? Would his troubles never end? Patience, Job, patience. James tells us you still possessed it. True, your travail seems so pointless and endless. But in reality it is neither. Patience. The storm will pass. The light will shine.

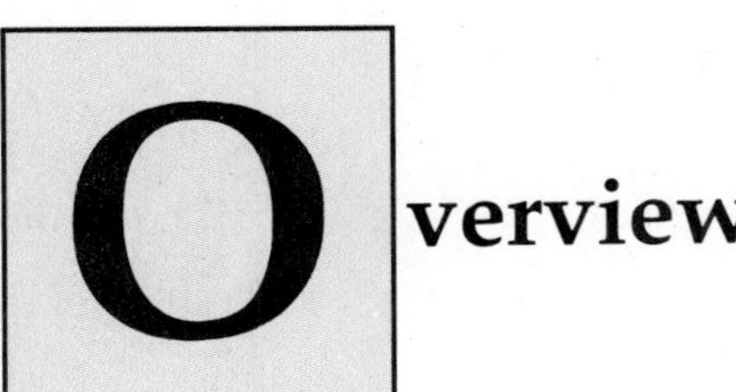

Overview

SCRIPTURE	Job 4–5; 8; 11; 15; 18; 20; 22; 25; 32–37
SUBJECT	Life of Job: part 2

<table>
<tr><td rowspan="3">SPECIFICS</td><td rowspan="3">Source for their criticism</td><td>Eliphaz</td><td>Personal experience</td><td rowspan="3">Summary of their criticism</td><td rowspan="3">"God does not permit the righteous to suffer. . . . Therefore, you are suffering for your sin!"</td></tr>
<tr><td>Bildad</td><td>Tradition</td></tr>
<tr><td>Zophar</td><td>Dogmatism</td></tr>
</table>

SAINTS AND SINNERS	Job, Eliphaz, Bildad, Zophar, Elihu

<table>
<tr><td rowspan="2">SENTENCE SUMMARIES</td><td>O.T. Verse</td><td>"Trust ye not in a friend; put ye not confidence in a guide; keep the doors of thy mouth from her that lieth in thy bosom" (Micah 7:5).</td></tr>
<tr><td>N.T. Verses</td><td>"My brethren, count it all joy when ye fall into divers temptations; knowing this, that the trying of your faith worketh patience" (James 1:2-3).</td></tr>
</table>

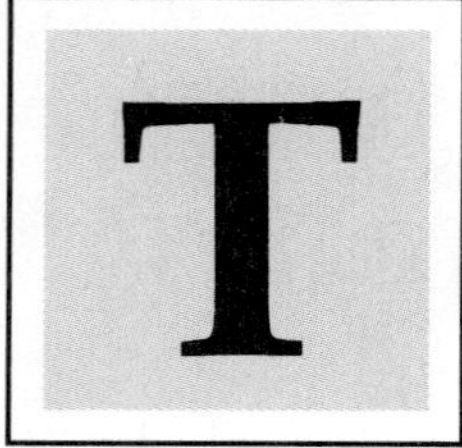

HE COMFORT OF FRIENDS

THE SPEECHES OF ELIPHAZ

Eliphaz claimed that Job was suffering for his sins. *"Remember, I pray thee, whoever perished, being innocent? Or where were the righteous cut off? Even as I have seen, they that plow iniquity, and sow wickedness, reap the same" (Job 4:7-8).*

"Thine own mouth condemneth thee, and not I; yea, thine own lips testify against thee" (15:6).

Eliphaz then accused Job of the following:

(1) He had cheated the poor.

(2) He had withheld bread from the hungry.

(3) He had mistreated widows and orphans.

(4) He was a windbag!

Eliphaz based his conclusions on personal experiences (4:8; 12-16; 5:3, 27; 15:17).

He related his night vision "ghost story." *"Now a thing was secretly brought to me, and mine ear received a little thereof. In thoughts from the visions of the night, when deep sleep falleth on men, fear came upon me, and trembling, which made all my bones to shake. Then a spirit passed before my face; the hair of my flesh stood up; it stood still, but I could not discern the form thereof. An image was before mine eyes, there was silence, and I heard a voice, saying, 'Shall moral man be more just than God? Shall a man be more pure than his Maker?' " (4:12-17)*

He urged Job to repent and turn back to God. *"If thou return to the Almighty, thou shalt be built up; thou shalt put away iniquity very far from thy tabernacles [tents]" (22:23).*

THE SPEECHES OF BILDAD

Bildad (a descendant of Shuah) claimed Job was suffering for his sins. *"Behold, God will not cast away a perfect man, neither will He help the evildoers" (8:20).*

Bildad based his conclusions on tradition. *"Inquire, I pray thee, of the former age, and prepare thyself to the search of their fathers" (v. 8).*

He urged Job to repent and turn back to God. *"If thou wouldest seek unto God betimes [early], and make thy supplication to the Almighty; if thou were pure and upright, surely now He would awake for thee, and make the habitation of thy righteousness prosperous" (vv. 5-6).*

THE SPEECHES OF ZOPHAR

Zophar claimed that Job was suffering for his sins. *"For thou hast said, 'My doctrine is pure, and I am clean in thine eyes.' But O that God would speak, and open His lips against thee. . . . Know, therefore, that God exacteth of thee less than thine iniquity deserveth" (11:4-6).*

Zophar based his conclusions on sheer dogmatism (v. 6; 20:4).

He urged Job to repent and turn back to God. *"If thou prepare thine heart, and stretch out thine hands toward Him; if iniquity be in thine hand, put it far away, and let not wickedness dwell in thy tabernacles [tents]. For then shalt thou lift up thy face without spots; yea, thou shalt be steadfast, and shalt not fear" (11:13-15).*

THE SPEECH OF ELIHU

Elihu waited awhile before speaking because of his youth. However, once begun, he felt as confident and qualified to straighten out Job as the former three did. In fact, he actually suggested that he was the one whom Job had sought. *"Behold, I am according to thy wish in God's stead. I also am formed out of the clay" (33:6).*

Elihu was angry at all four—at Job because of his self-righteousness, and at the three friends because, "they had found no answer, and yet had condemned Job" (32:3).

He accused Job of both foolish speaking and false righteousness. He exhorted Job to consider God's glory and His greatness.

Job's Counselors

COMMENTS

Job's counselors, Eliphaz, Bildad, Zophar, and Elihu, represent the spectrum of human counselors in their attempts to account for the tragedies that befall people. All of them agreed on one point: Job's problems had overtaken him because, whether he was aware of it or not, he had sinned.

Each counselor, beginning with this premise, approached the task of bringing Job to the realization of his sin from a different perspective.

Eliphaz approached Job from the perspective of personal experience—things he had observed which related to sin and calamity. To him, it was unthinkable that tragedy could come into one's life for any reason other than his personal sin.

Bildad approached Job from the philosophical perspective of tradition—Job's problems would be solved if only he would look to the past and act on the principles he could learn from history. To Bildad, all of man's problems had their roots in the past (cf. 8:8ff.).

Zophar approached Job from the perspective of dogmatism—he had observed Job's situation and made a diagnosis. Job only needed to own up to his sin and take the corrective measures Zophar prescribed. With Zophar, Job's problem and its solution was all cut and dried (cf. 11:2-6; 20:2-5).

Eliphaz and Bildad spoke three times and Zophar spoke twice. Job answered each suggestion and seems to have interrupted Bildad (as he was just getting started with his third speech) with a rather lengthy defense.

Through all of this the younger Elihu remained silent. He may have been a student of the other three and have come along on this "ministerial visit" as an observer or trainee. He heard the speeches of his three elders and their sound defeats by Job's defenses. Elihu became angry with Job because he staunchly maintained his innocence. He also became angry with his three colleagues because they condemned Job but were not able to bring about any resolution to Job's problem.

Elihu approached Job from the perspective of the self-appointed counselor who has the answers to everyone's problems. Elihu felt that he was the only one, in spite of his youth, who saw things clearly. He gave his opinion, which he equated with God's. Elihu's opinion was quite lengthy. He viewed himself as being God's spokesman.

Job's four counselors had one thing in common: they were all wrong. They were simplistic in their approaches to tragedy. In their minds the only cause of tragedy had to be punishment from God because of one's personal sin. Like Job, they knew nothing of the exchange between God and Satan. Their counseling strategies were rigid, allowing only their own presuppositions and convictions. They knew nothing of the warfare between Satan and God. They knew nothing of God's using man in that conflict to defeat Satan. They thought that if a man were really righteous he would have no big problems. They did not realize that if a man were righteous he may have more problems than he ever thought possible. They illustrate a danger in counseling, when a counselor seeks to make the one being counseled come to the counselor's own predetermined conclusions. They also illustrate the danger of ignoring or discounting the testimony and explanations of the person being counseled.

Job's counselors were not totally wrong, however. They should be given credit for realizing that the final answer to Job's plight was to be found with God. Their error, however, was that they themselves did not know enough about God to realize that God was capable of working in ways beyond their knowledge or experience.

A Sovereign God and a Suffering Saint (Part Three)

JOB 3; 6–7; 9–10; 12–14; 16–17; 19; 21; 23–24; 26–31; 38–42

Was he dead? Was he dreaming? One thing was sure. Never before had he seen such a glorious light or heard such a majestic sound. And the wind—who could withstand the force of that wind? Yet he was not blown about, but stood there as if frozen in his tracks. Then the moment of realization. Job was neither dead nor dreaming, but rather stood awestruck in the very presence of Almighty God Himself. Oh, what a moment. He was like an insect facing the power of the noonday sun. Now came the questions. Heavenly questions with no earthly answers. How strange it had all become. Job remembered the numerous times during his terrible trials how he had longed (and even demanded) an audience with God that he might ask God a few questions. Now the opportunity had come, but his lips could not form a word. He experienced no despair, however, for somehow it seemed no questions were needed from him. For God was here.

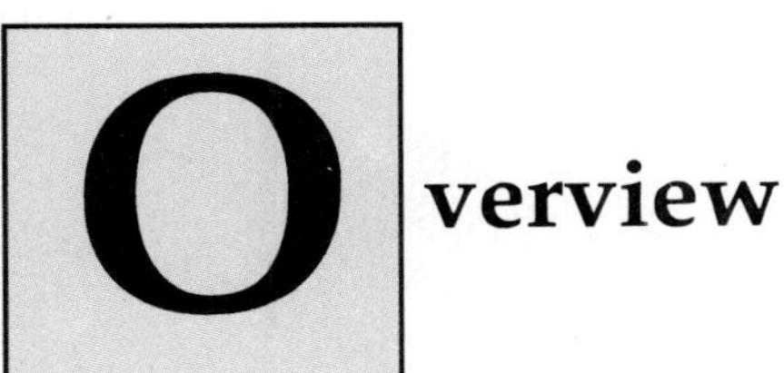

verview

<table>
<tr><td>SCRIPTURE</td><td colspan="4">Job 3; 6–7; 9–10; 12–14; 16–17; 19; 21; 23–24; 26–31; 38–42</td></tr>
<tr><td>SUBJECT</td><td colspan="4">Life of Job: part 3</td></tr>
<tr><td rowspan="4">SPECIFICS</td><td colspan="4">Job and his grief</td></tr>
<tr><td>His defense: "I am innocent."</td><td>His despair: "I wish I had never been born."</td><td colspan="2">His declaration: "I know that my Redeemer liveth."</td></tr>
<tr><td colspan="4">Job and his God</td></tr>
<tr><td>He is confronted by God</td><td>He is corrected by God</td><td>He is championed by God</td><td>He is comforted by God</td></tr>
<tr><td>SAINTS AND SINNERS</td><td colspan="4">Job</td></tr>
<tr><td rowspan="2">SENTENCE SUMMARIES</td><td>O.T. Verse</td><td colspan="3">"He hath not despised nor abhorred the affliction of the afflicted; neither hath He hid His face from him; but when he cried unto Him, He heard" (Ps. 22:24).</td></tr>
<tr><td>N.T. Verse</td><td colspan="3">"But the God of all grace, who hath called us unto His eternal glory by Christ Jesus, after that ye have suffered awhile, make you perfect, stablish, strengthen, settle you" (1 Peter 5:10).</td></tr>
</table>

THE DEFENSES AND DIALOGUES OF JOB

The suffering patriarch responded to his accusers in nine separate speeches. During these nine speeches Job discussed 14 topics. These are:

(1) I am righteous, and therefore not suffering for my sin. *"My righteousness I hold fast, and will not let it go; my heart shall not reproach me so long as I live"* (Job 27:6).

(2) In the past I have performed many good works.

I have helped the poor and fatherless.
I have aided the blind and lame.
I have wept with the sorrowing.

(3) Oh, for those good old days when I enjoyed health, wealth, and respect.

(4) But now I am being unfairly punished by God. *"For He breaketh me with a tempest, and multiplieth my wounds without cause"* (9:17).

"I will say unto God, 'Do not condemn me; show me wherefore Thou contendest with me. . . . Thou knowest that I am not wicked; and there is none that can deliver out of Thine hand. Thine hands have made me and fashioned me together round about; yet Thou dost destroy me' " (10:2, 7-8).

"Know now that God hath overthrown me, and hath compassed me with His net. . . . He hath fenced up my way that I cannot pass, and He hath set darkness in my paths. . . . He hath destroyed me on every side, and I am gone; and mine hope hath He removed like a tree. He hath also kindled His wrath against me, and He counteth me unto Him as one of His enemies" (19:6, 8, 10-11).

"I cry unto Thee, and Thou dost not hear me. I stand up, and Thou regardest me not" (30:20).

(5) My three so-called friends are miser-

able comforters. *"No doubt but ye are the people, and wisdom shall die with you"* (12:2).

"I have heard many such things; miserable comforters are ye all" (16:2).

(6) If they were in my place I would help them and not unjustly accuse them. *"I also could speak as ye do: if your soul were in my soul's stead, I could heap up words against you, and shake mine head at you. But I would strengthen you with my mouth, and the moving of my lips should assuage your grief"* (16:4-5).

(7) Even my neighbors, associates, and servants have turned against me. *"He hath put my brethren far from me, and mine acquaintance are verily estranged from me. . . . They that dwell in mine house, and my maids, count me for a stranger: I am an alien in their sight. . . . Yea, young children despised me. . . . and they whom I loved are turned against me. . . . O that my words were not written! O that they were printed in a book!"* (19:13, 15, 18-19, 23).

"But now they that are younger than I have me in derision, whose fathers I would have disdained to have set with the dogs of my flock. . . . And now am I their song, yea, I am their byword. They abhor me, they flee far from me, and spare not to spit in my face" (30:1, 9-10).

(8) I wish I could find the answers for all this.

(9) I wish I could find God. *"O that I knew where I might find Him! That I might come even to His seat! . . . Behold, I go forward, but He is not there; and backward, but I cannot perceive Him; on the left hand, where He doth work, but I cannot behold Him. He hideth Himself on the right hand, that I cannot see Him"* (23:3, 8-9).

(10) My flesh is clothed with worms, etc. (7:5, 13-14; 30:17-18, 30).

(11) I wish I had never been born. *"Let the day perish wherein I was born, and the night in which it was said, 'There is a man child conceived.' Let that day be darkness; let not God regard it from above; neither let the light shine upon it. . . . Because it shut not up the doors of my mother's womb, nor hid sorrow from mine eyes.*

"Why died I not from the womb? Why did I not give up the ghost when I came out of the belly? . . . Or as an hidden untimely birth I had not been; as infants which never saw light" (3:3-4, 10-11, 16).

(12) I wish I were dead. *"O that I might have my request; and that God would grant me the thing that I long for! Even that it would please God to destroy me; that He would let loose His hand, and cut me off!"* (6:8-9)

(13) I have no hope. *"Are not my days few? Cease then, and let me alone, that I may take comfort a little, before I go whence I shall not return, even to the land of darkness and the shadow of death. A land of darkness, as darkness itself; and of the shadow of death, without any order, and where the light is as darkness"* (10:20-22).

(14) In spite of all, I shall trust God. *"Though He slay me, yet will I trust in Him: but I will maintain mine own ways before Him"* (13:15).

"Also now, behold, my witness is in heaven, and my record is on high" (16:19).

"But He knoweth the way that I take; when He hath tried me, I shall come forth as gold" (23:10).

HIS GLORIOUS GOD

Suddenly from out of a whirlwind came the mighty voice of God.

The sullen Job was then subjected to a 60-question quiz.

God's first set of questions:

"Where wast thou when I laid the foundations of the earth? Declare, if thou hast understanding" (38:4).

"Hast thou perceived the breadth of the earth? Declare if thou knowest it all" (v. 18).

"Where is the way where light dwelleth? And as for darkness, where is the place thereof. . . ? (v. 19)

"By what way is the light parted, which scattereth the east wind upon the earth?" (v. 24)

"Hath the rain a father? Or who hath begotten the drops of dew?" (v. 28)

"Shall he that contendeth with the Almighty instruct Him? He that reproveth God, let him answer it" (40:2).

Job's reply:

"Behold, I am vile. What shall I answer Thee? I will lay mine hand upon my mouth. Once have I spoken; but I will not answer; yea, twice; but I will proceed no further" (vv. 4-5).

God's second series of questions:

Behold now behemoth, which I made with thee; he eateth grass as an ox" (v. 15).

"Canst thou draw out leviathan with an hook? Or his tongue with a cord which thou lettest down?" (41:1)

(Note: These two creatures may well refer to a land dinosaur and a sea dinosaur.)

Job's reply:

"Then Job answered the LORD*, and said, 'I know that Thou canst do everything, and that no thought can be withholden from Thee. Who is he that hideth counsel without knowledge? Therefore have I uttered that I understood not; things too wonderful for me, which I knew not. Hear, I beseech Thee, and I will speak: I will demand of Thee, and declare Thou unto me. I have heard of Thee by the hearing of the ear; but now mine eye seeth Thee: Wherefore I abhor myself, and repent in dust and ashes' "* (42:1-6).

Job and His Trials

COMMENTS

Job's various responses to his "friends" reveal the humanness of this man whom God said was perfect and upright (1:8).

He suffered tremendous multiple tragedies in a very short time. In the first cycle of testing he suffered in the area of his possessions—he lost everything. While he was still "down" from that tragedy, he was overtaken by the second cycle of testing, sufferings in the area of his person. Not only did he endure tremendous personal suffering, but he also lost the support and encouragement of his wife. Added to this, when his "friends" heard of the tragedies, they came "to mourn with him and to comfort him" (2:11). For seven whole days they sat silently by and said nothing (v. 13).

With the loss of all his possessions, his health, his wife's support and encouragement, and with three "friends" sitting closely by in silence, it is understandable why Job had a bad case of the "poor me's."

Being in total ignorance of what had preceded in the exchange between God and Satan (chaps. 1–2) and not having the benefit of the comfort of the Scriptures, it is amazing that Job did not feel sorry for himself sooner.

His friends did not help the matter, for they all argued from the same basic premises: tragedy overtakes those who have sinned; and thus sought to convince Job of his sin, which he knew he had not committed. No wonder he became self-righteous as he sought without result to find the sin for which God was punishing him. Probably not one of us would have done as well as Job under the same circumstances.

It would be good to reflect on why God permitted such material and personal tragedies to overtake Job. Paul tells us, "Now all these things happened unto them for examples [i.e., typically, or by way of example]" (1 Cor. 10:11).

Thus, from the events that overtook Job we can learn at least eight reasons why Job (and we) are sometimes overtaken by trials and tragedies:

(1) To cause us to trust fully in God. Job did not know why he was suffering, but he never lost sight of God and trusted Him implicitly.

(2) To cause us to know ourselves better. Job came to realize that though he was not being punished for sin, he did have a problem with self-righteousness.

(3) To cause us to develop grace to cope with tragedies. Only in trials and tragedies can we learn that God's grace is sufficient for us.

(4) To cause us to hate sin more. Tragedy drives us closer to God and enables us to see things from God's perspective. The closer we draw to God the more we hate anything that is inconsistent with His character.

(5) To cause us to realize that we are in a spiritual warfare. Job's problems were not occasioned by his own sin, but because of the continual warfare between Satan and God. We become aware of that conflict when we become casualties in it.

(6) To cause us to hold the things of this life loosely. All the blessings of this life are temporal and can be lost in a moment. Therefore, we should learn to realize, as Job did, that "the LORD gave and the LORD hath taken away" (Job 1:21).

(7) To cause us to appreciate the future glory we will enjoy with God. Paul said it best: "For I reckon that the sufferings of this present time are not worthy to be compared with the glory which shall be revealed in us" (Rom. 8:18).

(8) To cause glory to abound to God. All that happened to Job in the final analysis demonstrated what a great God Job's God is. Without those tragedies the greatness of God would not have been realized.

When such trials and tragedies overtake us in the warfare with the powers of darkness, we need to respond as Job did, "Blessed be the name of the LORD" (Job 1:21).

HIS BOUNTIFUL BLESSINGS

Job had been subjected to five fiery trials and had participated in five painful debates, but now he received at the hand of God a tenfold blessing.

(1) He was allowed to see the glory of God.

(2) He saw himself as God saw him. (This is always a blessing.)

(3) He was vindicated by God before the eyes of his three critical friends.

(4) He discovered the joy of praying for these three friends.

(5) His former health was fully restored.

(6) He was comforted by his brothers and sisters.

(7) He was given money and double his former wealth.

(8) He was given seven more sons and

three more daughters.

(9) He lived to enjoy his grandchildren and great-grandchildren.

(10) He was given an additional 140 years—twice the number normally accorded a man (Ps. 90:10).

CLASSIC STATEMENTS IN JOB

"He taketh the wise in their own craftiness" (Job 5:13), quoted by Paul (1 Cor. 3:19).

"Behold, happy is the man whom God *correcteth; therefore, despise not thou the chastening of the Almighty" (Job 5:17),* quoted in Hebrews 12:5-6.

"Neither is there any daysman betwixt us, that might lay his hand upon us both" (Job 9:33). "Daysman" refers to a mediator. In the New Testament, of course, all this changed (1 Tim. 2:5).

"Man that is born of a woman is of few days, and full of trouble. He cometh forth like a flower, and is cut down; he fleeth also as a shadow, and continueth not" (Job 14:1-2).

"They have gaped upon me with their mouth; they have smitten me upon the cheek reproachfully; they have gathered themselves together against me. God hath delivered me to the ungodly, and turned me over into the hands of the wicked" (16:10-11). These words are repeated (in paraphrase fashion) in Psalms 22:13; 35:21, which refer to the sufferings of Christ on the cross.

"Also now, behold, my witness is in heaven, and my record is on high" (Job 16:19).

"But He knoweth the way that I take; when He hath tried me, I shall come forth as gold" (23:10).

"He stretcheth out the north over the empty place, and hangeth the earth upon nothing" (26:7).

"O that I knew where I might find Him, that I might come even to His seat" (23:3). This problem was solved through the incarnation of Christ. (See John 1:1, 45.)

"How then can man be justified with God? Or how can he be clean that is born of a woman?" (Job 25:4) This problem is solved through the death of Christ! (See Rom. 4:24-25; 5:1.)

"If a man die, shall he live again? (Job 14:14) This problem is solved through the resurrection of Christ.

"For I know that my Redeemer liveth, and that He shall stand at the latter day upon the earth; and though after my skin worms destroy this body, yet in my flesh shall I see God" (19:25-26).

SOME REASONS FOR JOB'S SUFFERINGS

(1) That Satan might be silenced. *"Then Satan answered the* LORD *and said, 'Doth Job fear God for nought? Hast not Thou made an hedge about him, and about his house, and about all that he hath on every side? Thou hast blessed the work of his hands, and his substance is increased in the land. But put forth Thine hand now, and touch all that he hath, and he will curse Thee to Thy face' " (1:9-11).*

"And Satan answered the LORD *and said, 'Skin for skin, yea, all that a man hath will he give for his life. But put forth Thine hand now, and touch his bone and his flesh, and he will curse Thee to Thy face' " (2:4-5).*

(2) That Job might see God. *"I have heard of Thee by the hearing of the ear; but now mine eye seeth Thee" (42:5).*

(3) That Job might see himself. *"Behold, I am vile; what shall I answer Thee? I will lay mine hand upon my mouth" (4:4).*

"Wherefore I abhor myself, and repent in dust and ashes" (42:6).

(4) That Job's friends might learn not to judge. *"And it was so, that after the* LORD *had spoken these words unto Job, the* LORD *said to Eliphaz the Temanite, 'My wrath is kindled against thee, and against thy two friends; for ye have not spoken of Me the thing that is right, as My servant Job hath' " (v. 7).*

(5) That Job might learn to pray for, rather than to lash out against, his critics. *"And the* LORD *turned the captivity of Job, when he prayed for his friends: also the* LORD *gave Job twice as much as he had before" (v. 10).*

(6) That all God's plans for His own might eventually have happy endings.

The Blessings of Job

COMMENTS

The Book of Job opens with Job overtaken by multiple tragedies in the areas of his possessions and person and with his "friends" coming to mourn with and comfort him. It ends with Job praying for his "friends," being healed, and being given twice as much as he had before of sheep, camels, oxen, and donkeys.

When it came to children, however, he was given seven sons and three daughters, the same number that he had at the beginning (cf. 1:2). Why did not God give Job and his wife twice as many children as he had before?

The answer is probably found in the character of Job. He functioned as the priest of his own household (cf. v. 5), even after his children had left his home to establish their own homes. Undoubtedly he had brought them up "in the nurture and admonition of the Lord" and they had responded to God in faith. His first 10 children, then, were "believers" and upon their untimely deaths went into the presence of God.

Job's second 10 children would be reared with similar values. If anything, they would have been even more carefully reared because of the trials and tragedies through which Job passed during the course of his testing. They, like the first 10 children, likewise were "believers" in the God of their father. Today, in heaven, Job is basking in the presence of God with his 20 children—twice as many as he had in the beginning of the book!

Another interesting observation can be made concerning Job's children. Material possessions are only of value and use in this present life—you cannot take them with you. However, there is one possession that you can take with you—your children! How important it is to see to it that your children are surrounded from birth with God's truth and that they respond to God in faith while young. An investment in children is of eternal value—you can take them with you and enjoy them for all eternity.

Probably the most famous single passage from the Book of Job is his statement, "For I know that my Redeemer liveth, and that He shall stand at the latter day upon the earth; and though after my skin worms destroy this body, yet in my flesh shall I see God" (19:25-26). Is Job speaking of the Lord's return and his beholding Him in a resurrected body?

It may be that Job, in fact, did believe that personally, but to conclude this from Job's statement is more than his language will permit. In the context of his statement Job made a plea for pity (vv. 21-22) and a record of his innocence (vv. 23-24). The "Redeemer" for which Job looked is a "vindicator, defender, or rescuer"—One who will plead the cause of the downtrodden and unjustly oppressed. His view is of Jehovah as the Kinsman-Redeemer who would redress his wrongs, avenge his enemies, and deliver him out of bondage. This Redeemer "lives": He presently exists, He is a living witness and defender, He has power, and will act with real and substantial effort on Job's behalf. The "latter day" is literally "at last"—his friends have spoken first; Jehovah will have His last word. The Redeemer will stand "upon the earth" (lit., "upon the dust")—the dust in which Job is soon to be laid.

Job thought that he would die, but that after his death he would be vindicated. His expression is best understood literally as "without my flesh" or "free from my flesh"—in the sense of death. Putting the verses together, Job thought that he was going to die and that his body would be buried in the earth. He was confident that in the final analysis his Vindicator would arise, place himself over the dust in which his body had decayed, pronounce his cause just, and vindicate him fully before his friends and family. His soul, however, would go immediately into the presence of God. His earthly reputation would be safe in God's hands. Being thus released from his sufferings he would be safely "home."

Exodus

"What are nice people like you doing in a nasty place like this?" As the Book of Genesis ends, Jacob and his entire family clan had moved from Canaan to Egypt. This stage now tells us just how God will bring His people out of the land of bondage.

It begins with the persecution by Pharaoh and ends with the proclamation by Moses. Between these two key events, separated by 80 years and 800 miles, a breathtaking history transpires. Both God's faithfulness and Israel's fickleness are clearly seen. Examples of the first include the pouring out of 10 plagues, the rolling back of the Red Sea, the bringing forth of water from a rock, the handing down of the Law, and the raising up of the tabernacle. Examples of the second include the idolatry at Sinai and the rebellion at Kadesh.

During this stage Israel received a special diet directly from God (the manna) and a special day (the Sabbath).

This stage is actually the tale of three trips. The first trip was from Egypt to Mount Sinai, the second, from Mount Sinai to Kadesh-barnea, and the third from Kadesh to the east bank of the Jordan.

Two of Scripture's most famous and capable men were divinely appointed to direct these journeys—Moses, the Lawgiver, and Joshua, the rest-giver!

Observe the confusion of Moses concerning the person of God at the beginning of this stage:

"And Moses said unto God, 'Behold, when I come unto the Children of Israel, and shall say unto them, "The God of your fathers hath sent me unto you"; and they shall say to me, "What is His name?" What shall I say unto them?' " (Ex. 3:13)

Observe the confidence of Moses concerning the person of God at the end of this stage:

"I will publish the name of the LORD; ascribe ye greatness unto our God. He is the Rock; His work is perfect; for all His ways are judgment. A God of truth and without iniquity, just and right is He" (Deut. 32:3-4).

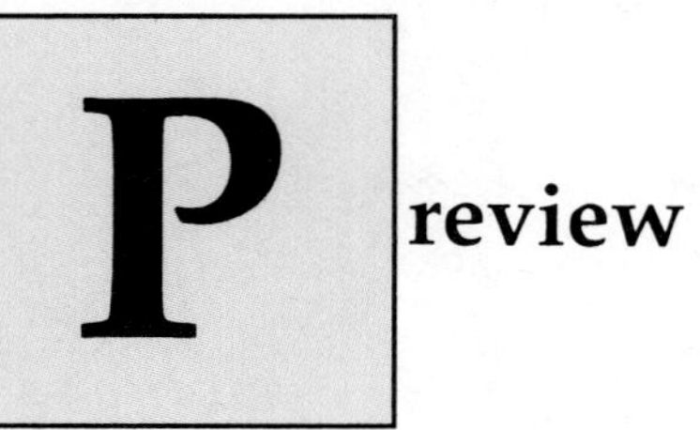

The Making of a Man

EXODUS 1–6

He stood there quietly, taking it all in. How little things seemed to have changed since he left on that fateful night. The pyramids still stood, bold and proud, glistening in the brilliant sun, beside the mighty Nile River. The noise of the merchants, the dust of the streets, and the clatter of the chariots was exactly as he had remembered. He then saw and heard another familiar sight and sound. This experience, however, not only triggered his memory, but grieved his soul—the pitiful cries of his own people bogged down in cruel slavery. No, things had not changed in Egypt.

But he had changed. Forty years back he had left here, an unmarried, well-to-do, rising young political figure. Now, he was 80, a family man, and a shepherd. Why was he here? The answer was simple. The same God who once saved him from the watery Nile and later met him by a burning bush had ordered him back here to denounce Pharaoh and deliver the enslaved people! Moses was his name. This was why he had come. This is what he would do.

Overview

<table>
<tr><td>SCRIPTURE</td><td colspan="6">Exodus 1–6</td></tr>
<tr><td>SUBJECT</td><td colspan="6">Moses: his first 40 years</td></tr>
<tr><td rowspan="4">SPECIFICS</td><td rowspan="4">The preparation</td><td>In Egypt</td><td rowspan="4">The revelation</td><td>At Sinai</td><td rowspan="4">The agitation</td><td>In Egypt</td></tr>
<tr><td rowspan="2">Israel's misery</td><td>The miracle of the bush</td><td rowspan="2">Coming from the Pharaoh of Egypt</td></tr>
<tr><td>The mission of God</td></tr>
<tr><td>God's mercy preserving Moses preparing Moses</td><td>The misgivings of Moses</td><td>Coming from the people of God</td></tr>
<tr><td>SAINTS AND SINNERS</td><td colspan="6">Pharaoh #1, Moses' parents, Moses' sister, Moses, Pharaoh's daughter, Pharaoh #2, Jethro, Zipporah, Aaron, Pharaoh #3</td></tr>
<tr><td rowspan="2">SENTENCE SUMMARIES</td><td colspan="2">O.T. Verses</td><td colspan="4">"Therefore He lifted up His hand against them, to overthrow them in the wilderness; to overthrow their seed also among the nations, and to scatter them in the lands" (Ps. 106:26-27).</td></tr>
<tr><td colspan="2">N.T. Verse</td><td colspan="4">"By faith Moses, when he was born, was hid three months of his parents, because they saw he was a proper child; and they were not afraid of the king's commandment" (Heb. 11:23).</td></tr>
</table>

I SRAEL ENSLAVED IN EGYPT

GOD'S PEOPLE

Some 75 years after Joseph's death the people of Israel living in Egypt began to be cruelly oppressed by a suspicious Pharaoh.

GOD'S GRACE

God heard their cries of anguish and began a plan to deliver them.

"And it came to pass in process of time, that the king of Egypt died: and the Children of Israel sighed by reason of the bondage, and they cried, and their cry came up unto God by reason of the bondage. And God heard their groaning, and God remembered His covenant with Abraham, with Isaac, and with Jacob" (Ex. 2:23-24).

GOD'S MAN MOSES

The prince of Egypt. Moses was born (1525 B.C.).

*The baby on the Nile: *"And there went a man of the house of Levi, and took to wife a daughter of Levi. And the woman conceived, and bare a son: and when she saw him that he was a goodly child, she hid him three months. And when she could not longer hide him, she took for him an ark of bulrushes, and daubed it with slime and with pitch, and put the child therein: and she laid it in the flags by the river's brink. . . .*

"And the daughter of Pharaoh came down to wash herself at the river; and her maidens walked along by the river's side; and when she saw the ark among the flags, she sent her maid to fetch it. And when she had opened it, she saw the child; and, behold, the babe wept. And she had compassion on him, and said 'This is one of the Hebrews' children' " (vv. 1-3, 5-6).

*The boy in the court: *"And the child grew, and she brought him unto Pharaoh's daughter, and he became her son. And she called his name Moses: and she said, 'Because I drew him out of the water' " (v. 10).*

*The body in the sand: At age 40 Moses left Egypt for the Sinai Peninsula. Two reasons prompted him.

(1) Because of a manslaughter charge (2:11-15).

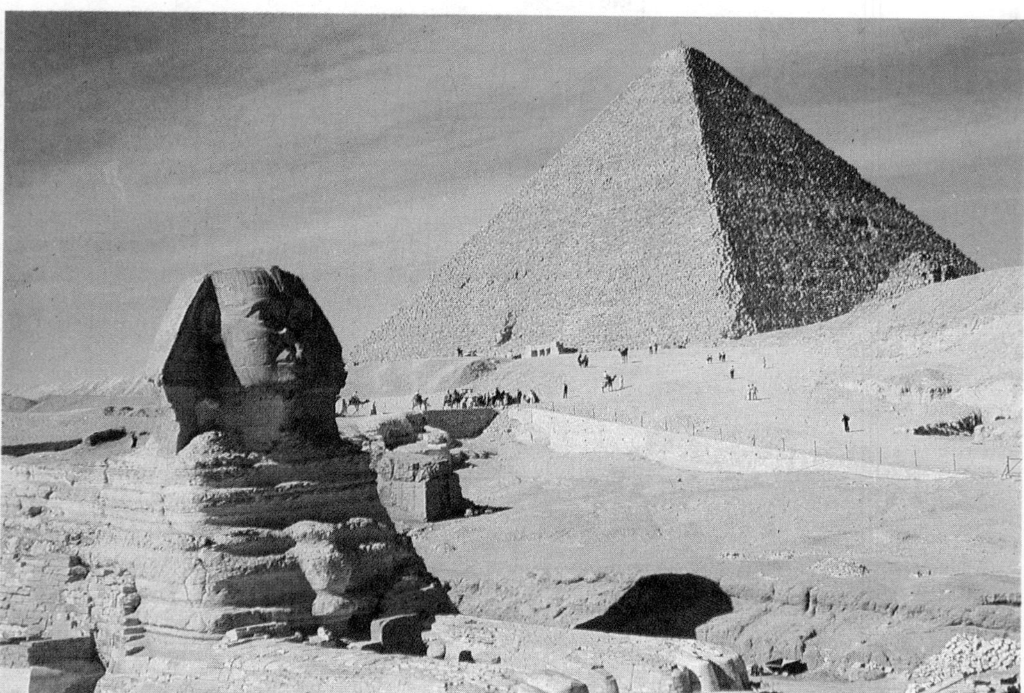

(2) Because of a messianic conviction (Heb. 11:23-26).

"By faith Moses, when he was come to years, refused to be called the son of Pharaoh's daughter; choosing rather to suffer affliction with the people of God, than to enjoy the pleasures of sin for a season; esteeming the reproach of Christ greater riches than the treasures in Egypt: for he had respect unto the recompense of the reward" (vv. 24-26).

The shepherd of Midian. He found refuge in the Sinai desert and married Zipporah, a Midianite girl. She gave birth to two sons, Gershom and Eliezer (Ex. 2:22; 18:4). When Moses was 80, God appeared to him from a burning bush.

"Now Moses kept the flock . . . to the backside of the desert, and came to the mountain of God, even to Horeb. And the Angel of the LORD appeared unto him in a flame of fire out of the midst of a bush; and he looked, and, behold, the bush burned with fire, and the bush was not consumed.

"And Moses said, 'I will now turn aside, and see this great sight, why the bush is not burnt.'

"And when the LORD saw that he turned aside to see, God called unto him out of the midst of the bush, and said, 'Moses, Moses.'

"And he said, 'Here am I.'

"And He said, 'Draw not nigh hither; put off thy shoes from off thy feet, for the place whereon thou standest is holy ground. . . . Now therefore, behold, the cry of the Children of Israel is come unto Me; and I have also seen the oppression wherewith the Egyptians oppress them. Come now therefore, and I will send thee unto Pharaoh, that thou mayest bring forth My people the Children of Israel out of Egypt" (3:1-5, 9-10).

At first Moses argued with God, listing five lame excuses why he could not perform God's command. Each excuse is answered, both here and in the New Testament.

*No ability (see Phil. 4:13): *"And Moses said unto God, 'Who am I, that I should go unto Pharaoh, and that I should bring forth the Children of Israel out of Egypt?' " (Ex. 3:11)*

*No message (see 1 Cor. 15:3-4): *"And Moses said unto God, 'Behold, when I come unto the Children of Israel, and shall say unto them, "The God of your fathers hath sent me unto you"; and they shall say to me, "What is His name?" What shall I say unto them?'*

"And God said unto Moses, 'I AM THAT I AM'; and He said, 'Thus shalt thou say unto the Children of Israel, "I AM hath sent me unto you" ' " (Ex. 3:13-14).

*No authority (see Matt. 28:18-20): *"And Moses answered and said, 'But, behold, they will not believe me, nor hearken unto my voice: for they will say, "The LORD hath not appeared unto thee." '*

"And the LORD said unto him, 'What is that in thine hand?' And he said, 'A rod.'

"And He said, 'Cast it on the ground.' And he cast it on the ground, and it became a serpent; and Moses fled from before it. . . . And the LORD said furthermore unto him, 'Put now thine hand into thy bosom.' And he put his hand into his bosom; and when he took it out, behold, his hand was leprous as snow" (Ex. 4:1-3, 6).

*No eloquence: *"And Moses said unto the LORD, 'O my LORD, I am not eloquent, neither heretofore, nor since Thou hast spoken unto Thy servant; but I am slow of speech, and of a slow tongue.' And the LORD said unto him, 'Who hath made man's mouth? or who maketh the dumb, or deaf, or the seeing, or the blind? Have not I the LORD?*

" 'Now therefore go, and I will be with thy mouth, and teach thee what thou shalt say' " (vv. 10-12).

*No inclination: The devil nearly succeeded in preventing Moses from going. *"And it came to pass by the way in the inn, that the LORD met him, and sought to kill him.*

"Then Zipporah took a sharp stone, and cut off the foreskin of her son, and cast it at his feet, and said, 'Surely a bloody husband art thou to me.'

"So He let him go; then she said, 'A bloody husband thou art, because of the circumcision' " (vv. 24-26).

GOD'S ENEMY PHARAOH

"And the LORD said unto Moses, 'When thou goest to return into Egypt, see that thou do all those wonders before Pharaoh, which I have put in thine hand; but I will harden his heart, that he shall not let the people go' " (v. 21).

Pharaoh (Amenhotep II) refused Moses' demands.

Reviled by the Pharaoh. "And Pharaoh said, 'Who is the LORD, that I should obey His voice to let Israel go? I know not the LORD, neither will I let Israel go.' . . .

"And Pharaoh commanded the same day the taskmasters of the people, and their officers, saying, 'Ye shall no more give the people straw to make brick, as heretofore; let them go and gather straw for themselves. And the tale of the bricks, which they did make heretofore, ye shall lay upon them; ye shall not diminish aught thereof; for they be idle. Therefore they cry, saying, "Let us go and sacrifice to our God" ' " (5:2, 6-8).

Rebuked by the people. "And the officers of the Children of Israel did see that they were in evil case, after it was said, 'Ye shall not minish aught from your bricks of your daily task.'

"And they said unto them, 'The LORD look upon you, and judge; because ye have made our savour to be abhorred in the eyes of Pharaoh and in the eyes of his servants, to put a sword in their hand to slay us' " (vv. 19-21).

I Am that I Am

COMMENTS

In response to Moses' desire for authentication God reveals for the first time His unique name—I AM THAT I AM (Ex. 3:14). It would be sufficient for Moses to announce simply that "I AM" had sent him to go to Pharaoh and bring the Children of Israel out of their Egyptian captivity (v. 11).

I AM THAT I AM should be understood causally, "I AM *because* I AM." It is omnitemporal in its import: "I AM THE ONE WHO IS, I AM THE ONE WHO WAS, I AM THE ONE WHO WILL BE." In his translation of the Old Testament, Moffatt rightly translates the name as "The Eternal." Jesus used this name of Himself in John 8:58, "Before Abraham was, I am." The Jews understood what Jesus was saying and took up stones to kill Him for the claim was blasphemy if it were not true—which it was. Jesus again used the name of Himself in 18:5-6, 8 (note that the "He" is in italics indicating it was supplied by the translators). No wonder the men who came to arrest Him fell backward helplessly to the ground (cf. v. 6). John used the name of Jesus and gave it the full omnitemporal import as he said that the Alpha and Omega is "the Lord, which is, and which was, and which is to come" (Rev. 1:8).

Grammatically speaking, the name is the first person singular of the verb "to be." Man, however, does not address God by this name. Man's name for God is given in Exodus 3:15, "The LORD." In most English Bibles, whenever the name for God is written "LORD" the name in the Hebrew manuscript is YHWH ("Yahweh," commonly rendered "Jehovah" as in the *American Standard Version*). Grammatically, this is the third person singular of the verb "to be" and could be simply translated, "He is." Thus man's name for God, Yahweh/Jehovah ("He is") merely confirms what God has revealed in His name for Himself, EHYH (Ehyeh = "I AM").

Why, then, is man's name for God, YHWH ("He is"), rendered LORD in our English Bible? The English translators simply adopted the Jewish custom as relates to the name for God. The four letters comprising God's name, YHWH, are the sacred tetragrammaton (the sacred four letters). They are so sacred that the Jews would not even pronounce them. Each time the manuscript copiers wrote them, they took a complete bath, had a complete change of clothing, and broke the pen with which they had written the letters. Whenever readers saw those sacred four letters in the text, they pronounced the name Adonai ("Lord") in their place. Sometimes Adonai ("Lord, Master") is used as God's name. To distinguish when the Hebrew text uses Adonai from the times when the Hebrew text uses YHWH (Yahweh/Jehovah) the English translators render the name Adonai as "Lord" and Yahweh as "LORD." Thus, the English reader can always tell from the English rendering which name occurs in the Hebrew Scriptures.

There is yet another primary name used for God in the Hebrew Scriptures. In the singular it is "El" and in the plural it is "Elohim." This name emphasizes the might or power of God and is uniformly rendered in the English texts as "God."

The three primary Hebrew names for God, then, reveal different aspects of the character of God. Yahweh/Jehovah emphasizes His eternality or immutability. Adonai emphasizes His sovereignty. Elohim emphasizes His mighty power.

Preview

Godly Power in a Godless Land

EXODUS 7–15

Egypt's Pharaoh was both awed and angered. Awed at the mighty power of the Hebrew God. Angered at the utter helplessness of his own gods. Why could not Egypt's revered and ancient deities stop those horrible plagues? Bloody waters, invading frogs, lice, and flies. These were bad, but only the beginning. As the judgment continued, his land filled with dead cattle and greedy locusts. His own people began suffering from an epidemic of painful and putrid boils. In fact, nature itself had turned against him. A destructive hail had fallen, mingled with fire. This was followed by a fear-filled three-day darkness, so thick it could actually be felt.

Pharaoh had never seen anything like all this! What would happen next? Could it possibly get worse? Well, whatever the case, Pharaoh once again set his mind—Israel under no circumstances would be allowed to leave Egypt.

But oh, how wrong he would be. Things did get worse, and Israel would leave, for not even his sinful and stubborn will could withstand the onslaught of God's tenth and final plague, the slaying of the firstborn. Nor would Pharaoh's trouble end at the departure of the Hebrew slaves. Because of his utter inability to comprehend both the person and power of God, he made one final and foolish effort to recapture the Lord's people. The attempt proved disastrous. Soon the Red Sea would be choked with the floating bodies of his drowned soldiers.

Overview

<table>
<tr><td>SCRIPTURE</td><td colspan="8">Exodus 7–15</td></tr>
<tr><td>SUBJECT</td><td colspan="8">Ten plagues and the Red Sea crossing</td></tr>
<tr><td rowspan="7">SPECIFICS</td><td colspan="8">The power of God</td></tr>
<tr><td rowspan="6">Liberating His people</td><td colspan="2">The ten plagues</td><td rowspan="6">Leading His people</td><td colspan="2">By the cloud</td><td colspan="2">Through the sea</td></tr>
<tr><td>1 Water into blood</td><td>2 Frog invasion</td><td rowspan="2">To Israel</td><td rowspan="2">The brightness of the cloud</td><td rowspan="2">West Bank</td><td rowspan="2">The separation of the sea</td></tr>
<tr><td>3 Lice</td><td>4 Flies</td></tr>
<tr><td>5 Cattle disease</td><td>6 Boils</td><td rowspan="3">To Egypt</td><td rowspan="3">The blackness of the cloud</td><td rowspan="3">East Bank</td><td rowspan="3">The celebration of the saints</td></tr>
<tr><td>7 Hail and fire</td><td>8 Locusts</td></tr>
<tr><td>9 Three-day darkness</td><td>10 Slaying of first-born</td></tr>
<tr><td>SAINTS AND SINNERS</td><td colspan="8">Moses, Aaron, Pharaoh #3, Egyptian magicians</td></tr>
<tr><td rowspan="2">SENTENCE SUMMARIES</td><td>O.T. Verses</td><td colspan="7">"He divided the sea, and caused them to pass through; and He made the waters to stand as a heap. In the daytime also He led them with a cloud, and all the night with a light of fire" (Ps. 78:13-14).</td></tr>
<tr><td>N.T. Verses</td><td colspan="7">"Through faith he kept the Passover, and the sprinkling of blood, lest he that destroyed the firstborn should touch them. By faith they passed through the Red Sea as by dry land, which the Egyptians assaying to do were drowned" (Heb. 11:28-29).</td></tr>
</table>

OD'S PLAGUES

"And Moses and Aaron went in unto Pharaoh, and they did so as the LORD had commanded. And Aaron cast down his rod before Pharaoh, and before his servants, and it became a serpent.

"Then Pharaoh also called the wise men and the sorcerers. Now the magicians of Egypt, they also did in like manner with their enchantments" (Ex. 7:10-11).

Water into blood (v. 20).
A frog invasion (8:16).
Lice (v. 17).
Flies (v. 24).
Cattle disease (9:6).
Boils (v. 10).
Hail mingled with fire (v. 24).

"And the LORD said unto Moses, 'Rise up early in the morning, and stand before Pharaoh, and say unto him, "Thus saith the LORD God of the Hebrews, 'Let My people go, that they may serve Me. For I will at this time send all My plagues upon thine heart, and upon thy servants, and upon thy people, that thou mayest know that there is none like Me in all the earth.

" ' " 'For now I will stretch out My hand, that I may smite thee and thy people with pestilence; and thou shalt be cut off from the earth. And in very deed for this cause have I raised thee up, for to show in thee My power; and that My name may be declared throughout all the earth' " ' " (vv. 13-16).

"He that feared the word of the LORD among the servants of Pharaoh made his servants and his cattle flee into the houses" (v. 20).

"And Pharaoh sent, and called for Moses and Aaron, and said unto them, 'I have sinned this time. The LORD is righteous, and I and my people are wicked' " (v. 27).

Locusts (10:13).

A three-day darkness (v. 22).

Pharaoh offered Moses four compromises during these plagues, but all were refused.

(1) Don't leave, but do your thing here in Egypt (8:25).

(2) Leave, but don't go too far (v. 28).

(3) Leave, but allow your children to remain here (10:10).

(4) Leave, but without your flocks and herds (v. 24).

The slaying of the firstborn (12:29).

GOD'S SALVATION

The final plague was so severe that even the Israelite homes needed protection. Thus, they were to sprinkle the blood of a sacrificed lamb on their doors. All such homes would then be spared (11:4-5; 12:12-13, 21-23).

"And the LORD spake unto Moses and Aaron in the land of Egypt, saying, 'This month shall be unto you the beginning of months; it shall be the first month of the year to you.

" 'Speak ye unto all the congregation of Israel, saying, "In the tenth day of this month they shall take to them every man a lamb . . . for a house" ' " (vv. 1-3).

"And ye shall keep it up until the fourteenth day of the same month; and the whole assembly of the congregation of Israel shall kill it in the evening.

"And they shall take of the blood, and strike it on the two side posts and on the upper door post of the houses, wherein they shall eat it" (vv. 6-7).

"For I will pass through the land of Egypt this night, and will smite all the firstborn in the land of Egypt, both man and beast; and against all the gods of Egypt I will execute judgment; I am the LORD.

"And the blood shall be to you for a token upon the houses where ye are; and when I see the blood, I will pass over you, and the plague shall not be upon you to destroy you, when I smite the land of Egypt" (vv. 12-13).

On April 15, 1445 B.C. at midnight all this happened, resulting in Pharaoh (whose son was killed) allowing Israel to leave Egypt (vv. 29-36).

GOD'S SELECTION

The sanctification of the firstborn. (Compare with Num. 8:16.)

"Sanctify unto Me all the firstborn, whatsoever openeth the womb among the Children of Israel, both of man and of beast; it is Mine" (Ex. 13:2).

The choice of the safer route. Had they gone the regular route, Israel would have been attacked by the Philistines.

"And it came to pass, when Pharaoh had let the people go, that God led them not through the way of the land of the Philistines, although that was near; for God said, 'Lest peradventure the people repent when they see war, and they return to Egypt.'

"But God led the people about, through the way of the wilderness of the Red Sea: and the Children of Israel went up harnessed out of the land of Egypt.

"And Moses took the bones of Joseph with him; for he had straitly sworn the Children of Israel, saying, 'God will surely visit you; and ye shall carry up my bones away hence with you' " (vv. 17-19).

The Ten Plagues

COMMENTS

The 10 plagues represent open warfare between God and Pharaoh. If there is significance to the number 10, it is the idea of universality. The 10 plagues can be viewed in three ways: (1) as evidence of God's lordship over all nature—water, land, air, animals, and man; (2) as a righteous judgment against all the false gods of Egypt (cf. 12:12); and (3) as a visitation against Egypt for the affliction they had inflicted on Israel. The 10 plagues can be divided into triplets with the tenth one striking the final blow. The first, fourth, and seventh plagues are introduced by the words "in the morning" (cf. 7:15; 8:20; 9:15). After the second plague the magicians could no longer compete (8:18-19); after the sixth plague the magicians could no longer stand before Moses (9:11); after the ninth plague there was a complete break between Pharaoh and Moses and Aaron (10:27-29). The first three plagues were particularly loathsome. The second three plagues were particularly painful. The third three plagues were predominately plagues of nature. Progression is shown in the plagues in at least two ways: (1) from external to internal and (2) from a mediate to an immediate display of God's power. The 10 plagues took place over the space of about a year. The first plague took place when the Nile River was rising in the middle of the year (June). The seventh plague came in February. The tenth plague came in April (Abib or Nisan). The 10 plagues are the model of all later or future warfare between God and man. They were meant for universal instruction.

Each of the plagues was directed against a different Egyptian god. In each instance the people's religion added to their problem and their religion was a detriment rather than a help to them. The 10 plagues may be summarized as follows: (1) Nile River turned to blood—the pride of Egypt into which Israelite babies had been cast was turned against them. (2) Frogs—associated with the frog-headed god. Frogs were especially disgusting to the Egyptians for they made a special effort to be clean. Their priests had to shave their entire bodies every day. They bathed twice at night and twice a day. Every effort at cleanliness confronted them with frogs. (3) Lice—disgusting to the Egyptians because of the uncleanliness and filth they represented. The magicians could not duplicate this miracle. They recognized it as supernatural (8:19), but they did not necessarily confess the true God. (4) Flies—literally a plague of beetles, the emblem of their sun god, Ra. (5) Murrain on cattle—When man sins, lower creation is always affected (cf. Jonah 3:8). Sometimes man will pay greater heed when his property is affected. It was a great call to repentance. (6) Boils—the first plague that was life-threatening. (7) Hail in Egypt but not in Goshen (9:25-26)—God knows how to judge His enemies and protect His own. (8) Locusts—so great in number that they darkened the sky and land. The people began to question Pharaoh (10:7). They had their own interest at heart, not Israel's. (9) Darkness in Egypt but not in the Israelites' homes. To the Egyptians the darkness was equivalent to death. This was God's last warning before death came fulfilling 4:22-23. (10) Death of firstborn—not through nature, but with the direct hand of God, Israel was immune (11:7).

We know these plagues were from God because of: (1) their intensity—more intense than anything before or afterward; (2) their extent—involved so many different realms—air, sun, water, insects, cattle; (3) their succession—they increased in intensity; (4) their inauguration—they began at Moses' command; (5) their cessation—they stopped at Moses' command; (6) their selectivity—they affected Egypt but not Israel. For God's commentary on the 10 plague judgments see Psalm 105:26-36.

SRAEL, EN ROUTE TO MOUNT SINAI

The following rounds of action took place between Rameses, their departure city in Egypt, and the arrival at the base of Mount Sinai, a distance of 150 miles.

ROUND ONE

The decision of Pharaoh—to follow up. "And it was told the king of Egypt that the people fled. And the heart of Pharaoh and of his servants was turned against the people, and they said, 'Why have we done this, that we have let Israel go from serving us?'

"And he made ready his chariot, and took his people with him. And he took 600 chosen chariots, and all the chariots of Egypt, and captains over every one of them" (Ex. 14:5-7).

The despair of the people—to give up. "And when Pharaoh drew nigh, the Children of Israel lifted up their eyes, and, behold, the Egyptians marched after them, and they were sore afraid; and the Children of Israel cried out unto the LORD.

"And they said unto Moses, 'Because there were no graves in Egypt, hast thou taken us away to die in the wilderness? Wherefore hast thou dealt with us, to carry us forth out of Egypt?

" 'Is this not the word that we did tell thee in Egypt, saying, "Let us alone, that we may serve the Egyptians? For it had been better for us to serve the Egyptians, than that we should die in the wilderness" ' " (vv. 10-12).

The declaration of the prophet—to look up. "And Moses said unto the people, 'Fear ye not, stand still, and see the salvation of the LORD, which He will show to you today. For the Egyptians whom ye have seen today, ye shall see them again no more forever. The LORD shall fight for you, and ye shall hold your peace' " (vv. 13-14).

ROUND TWO

The cloudy pillar—protecting. "And the LORD went before them by day in a pillar of a cloud, to lead them the way; and by night in a pillar of fire, to give them light; to go by day and night. He took not away the pillar of the cloud by day, nor the pillar of fire by night, from before the people" (13:21-22).

"And the Angel of God, which went before the camp of Israel, removed and went behind them; and the pillar of the cloud went from before their face, and stood behind them.

"And it came between the camp of the Egyptians and the camp of Israel; and it was a cloud and darkness to them, but it gave light by night to these; so that the one came not near the other all the night" (14:19-20).

The Red Sea—parting. "And Moses stretched out his hand over the sea; and the LORD caused the sea to go back by a strong east wind all that night, and made the sea dry land, and the waters were divided.

And the Children of Israel went into the midst of the sea upon the dry ground and the waters were a wall unto them on their right hand, and on their left" (vv. 21-22).

The Egyptian army—perishing. "And Moses stretched forth his hand over the sea, and the sea returned to his strength when the morning appeared; and the Egyptians fled against it; and the LORD overthrew the Egyptians in the midst of the sea.

"And the waters returned, and covered the chariots, and the horsemen, and all the host of Pharaoh that came into the sea after them; there remained not so much as one of them" (vv. 27-28).

The LORD's people—praising. "Then sang Moses and the Children of Israel this song unto the LORD, and spake, saying, 'I will sing unto the LORD, for He hath triumphed gloriously: the horse and his rider hath He thrown into the sea.

" 'The LORD is my strength and song, and He is become my salvation. He is my God, and I will prepare Him a habitation; my father's God, and I will exalt Him. . . .

" 'Thy right hand, O LORD, is become glorious in power; Thy right hand, O LORD, hath dashed in pieces the enemy. . . . Who is like unto Thee, O LORD, among the gods? Who is like Thee, glorious in holiness, fearful in praises, doing wonders? Thou stretchedst out Thy right hand, the earth swallowed them.

" 'Thou shalt bring them in, and plant them in the mountain of Thine inheritance, in the place, O LORD, which Thou hast made for Thee to dwell in, in the sanctuary, O LORD, which Thy hands have established. The LORD shall reign forever and ever.

" 'For the horse of Pharaoh went in with his chariots and with his horsemen into the sea, and the LORD brought again the waters of the sea upon them; but the Children of Israel went on dry land in the midst of the sea.'

"And Miriam the prophetess, the sister of Aaron, took a timbrel in her hand; and all the women went out after her with timbrels and with dances" (15:1-2, 6, 11-12, 17-20).

Pharaoh's Final Lesson

COMMENTS

Exodus 14 records God's final lesson for a hardened Pharaoh (vv. 4, 8) and God's first lesson for a redeemed Israel. God's purpose for Egypt was that they might learn that He is the LORD (Jehovah, The Eternal). God's purpose for Israel was that they might realize that their LORD (Jehovah) was their Deliverer and Defender (vv. 13-14). Both objectives were realized—the Egyptians realized who Jehovah is (v. 25) and Israel believed (v. 31). Israel had believed earlier (or they wouldn't have been out there in the wilderness) but needed new assurance which God graciously provided.

When they departed from Egypt Israel had experienced for the first time divine leadership day and night (13:21-22). Never in history had this been done. Israel should have realized that the God who would provide such leadership would also provide protection. However, when they realized that the Egyptians were after them they were fearful. They cried to the Lord (14:10) and to His human representative, Moses (v. 11). They were not prepared to fight and feared they would die in the wilderness at the hands of the Egyptians (v. 11). What could they do to protect themselves? Nothing! The only thing they could do was to stand still and trust Jehovah. In response to their belief Jehovah would deliver them completely (vv. 13-14). It must have seemed ludicrous. With the Egyptian hordes bearing down on them they were to do nothing but wait and watch? Precisely. Why? Because God had a plan—a plan to get glory unto Himself (v. 17) and to cause the Egyptians to know Him; not in salvation, but in judgment (v. 18).

The only movement in Israel's camp was on the part of the cloud. The cloud was the Shekinah cloud which was the visible sign of the presence of God (cf. Ezek. 11) in whom they dwelt. The cloud took up a position between His people and the enemy (Ex. 14:19). To the Israelites the cloud's position meant life; to the Egyptians it meant death. A similar situation is experienced today by the believer. To those who believe he is a "savour of life unto life" and to the unbelievers he is "the savour of death unto death" (cf. 2 Cor. 2:15-16).

The deliverance of God's people and the destruction of the Egyptians is recorded in Exodus 14:21-31. The Israelites feared the sea ahead more than they feared the Egyptians behind. They were willing to return to Egypt and be slaves again (v. 12). The sea that they thought would mean certain death became a wall of protection and deliverance and life for them. The sea that they and the Egyptians thought was an ally to the Egyptians became complete destruction and death to the Egyptians. The sea was divided and the Israelites passed over on dry ground—some 2 ½ million strong. Not one of them was lost! The Egyptians entered into the parted sea in hot pursuit. God caused them confusion to the point of causing the wheels of the chariots to fall off. The Egyptians came to realize that Israel was not their foe but that their foe was the Lord (Jehovah) (vv. 23-25). After the last Israelite was saved, the sea closed and not one Egyptian survived (vv. 26-28). As a result, Israel was delivered and Egypt was defeated. They could not be a threat to Israel for many years to come. God's deliverance was complete and final.

Commenting on this incident, Paul (1 Cor. 10:1-2) states that in this great event Israel was "baptized unto Moses." It is interesting to observe that in the historical situation those who were baptized never got wet and those who got wet never came up. On this day a great change of identity did in fact take place. For 430 years Israel had been known as Egypt's slaves. Now they were identified with Moses as God's redeemed nation (cf. Ex. 19:5-6).

Preview

The March to the Mountain

EXODUS 15–19; 24

What a trip it had been! Seven weeks of desert marching now brought Israel from the Egyptian border to the base of Mount Sinai. Who could ever forget such a journey? Was any other nation so blessed by its God as had been Israel? First, the Red Sea had been rolled back, its mighty waters held firm as though in some invisible grip. Small wonder a joyous celebration broke out on the eastern shore of that turbulent water after all had safely crossed.

So much for past blessings. But now they were in the barren desert. Could God protect and provide in this hot and hostile place? He could and He would. Bitter water was sweetened on one occasion and made to flow from a rock on another. Then the manna fell—bread from heaven, proving God could indeed both lead and feed His own. Lest they forget all this, a special day was now officially set aside that He might be worshiped—the weekly Sabbath.

Then there was that thrilling moment when He used the prayer warrior Moses and military warrior Joshua to defeat a dangerous enemy, the Amalekites. Now, here they stood at Sinai's base, awaiting further instruction from Moses.

Overview

<table>
<tr><td>SCRIPTURE</td><td colspan="8">Exodus 15–19; 24</td></tr>
<tr><td>SUBJECT</td><td colspan="8">The journey from the Red Sea to Mount Sinai</td></tr>
<tr><td rowspan="6">SPECIFICS</td><td rowspan="6">From the Red Sea to Rephidim</td><td rowspan="2">Marah</td><td rowspan="6">From Rephidim to Mount Sinai</td><td rowspan="3">The water</td><td rowspan="3">Their thirst quenched</td><td rowspan="6">At Mount Sinai</td><td rowspan="3">3 occurrences</td><td>The Law — Israel's constitution</td></tr>
<tr><td>Golden calf — Israel's prostitution-</td></tr>
<tr><td rowspan="2">The manna</td><td>The tabernacle — Israel's restitution</td></tr>
<tr><td rowspan="3">The warfare</td><td rowspan="3">Their tormentors vanquished</td><td rowspan="3">2 appearances</td><td rowspan="3">God meets with the people
God meets with the prophet</td></tr>
<tr><td rowspan="2">The memorial</td></tr>
<tr></tr>
<tr><td>SAINTS AND SINNERS</td><td colspan="8">Moses, Aaron, Hur, Joshua, Jethro</td></tr>
<tr><td rowspan="2">SENTENCE SUMMARIES</td><td colspan="2">O.T. Verse</td><td colspan="6">"Thou gavest also Thy good Spirit to instruct them, and withheldest not Thy manna from their mouth, and gavest them water for their thirst" (Neh. 9:20).</td></tr>
<tr><td colspan="2">N.T. Verse</td><td colspan="6">"[They] did all drink the same spiritual drink; for they drank of that spiritual Rock that followed them; and that Rock was Christ" (1 Cor. 10:4).</td></tr>
</table>

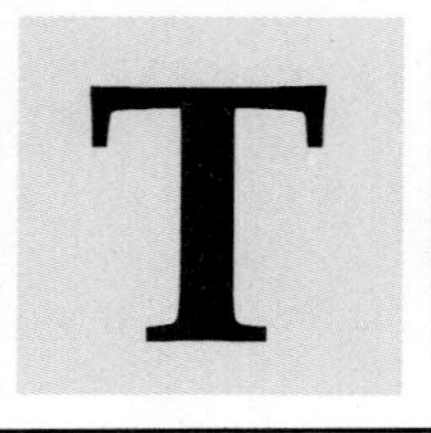

THE REBELLIOUS ISRAELITES

ROUND THREE

The galling water—the problem. "So Moses brought Israel from the Red Sea, and they went out into the wilderness of Shur; and they went three days in the wilderness, and found no water. And when they came to Marah, they could not drink of the waters of Marah, for they were bitter; therefore the name of it was called Marah" (Ex. 15:22-23).

The goodly tree—the purification. "And the people murmured against Moses, saying, 'What shall we drink?'

"And he cried unto the LORD; and the LORD shewed him a tree, which when he had cast into the waters, the waters were made sweet. There He made for them a statute and an ordinance, and there He proved them" (vv. 24-25).

The Great Physician—the promise. "And [the LORD] said, 'If thou wilt diligently hearken to the voice of the LORD thy God, and wilt do that which is right in His sight, and wilt give ear to His commandments, and keep all His statutes, I will put none of these diseases upon thee, which I have brought upon the Egyptians; for I am the LORD that healeth thee.'

"And they came to Elim, where were 12 wells of water, and threescore and ten palm trees: and they encamped there by the waters" (vv. 26-27).

ROUND FOUR

A special diet—the manna. "Then said the LORD unto Moses, 'Behold, I will rain bread from heaven for you; and the people shall go out and gather a certain rate every day, that I may prove them, whether they will walk in My law, or no.' . . . And when the dew that lay was gone up, behold, upon the face of the wilderness there lay a small round thing, as small as the hoarfrost on the ground.

"And when the Children of Israel saw it, they said one to another, 'It is manna'; for they wist not what it was.

"And Moses said unto them, 'This is the bread which the LORD hath given you to eat.' . . . And they gathered it every morning, every man according to his eating; and when the sun waxed hot, it melted. . . .

"And the Children of Israel did eat manna 40 years, until they came to a land inhabited; they did eat manna, until they came unto the borders of the land of Canaan" (16:4, 14-15, 21, 35).

A special day—the Sabbath. "And the LORD spake unto Moses, saying, 'Speak thou also unto the Children of Israel, saying, "Verily My Sabbaths ye shall keep; for it is a sign between Me and you throughout your generations; that ye may know that I am the LORD that doth sanctify you. Ye shall keep the Sabbath therefore; for it is holy unto you. Everyone that defileth it shall surely be put to death; for whosoever doeth any work therein, that soul shall be cut off from among his people.

" ' "Six days may work be done; but in the seventh is the Sabbath of rest, holy to the LORD. Whosoever doeth any work in the Sabbath Day, he shall surely be put to death. Wherefore the Children of Israel shall keep the Sabbath, to observe the Sabbath throughout their generations, for a perpetual covenant.

" ' "It is a sign between Me and the Children of Israel forever. For in six days the LORD made heaven and earth, and on the seventh day He rested, and was refreshed" ' " (31:12-17).

ROUND FIVE

A rock struck open. "And the LORD said unto Moses, 'Go on before the people, and take with thee of the elders of Israel; and thy rod, wherewith thou smotest the river, take in thine hand and go.

" 'Behold, I will stand before thee there upon the rock in Horeb; and thou shalt smite the rock, and there shall come water out of it, that the people may drink.' And Moses did so in the sight of the elders of Israel" (17:5-6).

This was done to provide water, which God supernaturally gave from the side of that rock. Nearly 40 years later Moses would strike another rock in a distant place, but at that time he was out of God's will (Num. 20:7-13).

An enemy struck down. "Then came Amalek, and fought with Israel in Rephidim" (Ex. 17:8).

Here four important "firsts" should be noted:

(1) The first mention of Joshua, who was selected by Moses to lead the armies of Israel (v. 9).

(2) The first prayer of Moses for Israel (vv. 11-12).

"And it came to pass, when Moses held up his hand, that Israel prevailed, and when he let down his hand, Amalek prevailed. But Moses' hands were heavy; and they took a stone, and put it under him, and he sat thereon; and Aaron and Hur stayed up his hands, the one on the one side, and the other on the other side; and his hands were steady until the going down of the sun" (17:11-12).

(3) The first part of the Bible to be written? (v. 14)

"And the LORD said unto Moses, 'Write this for a memorial in a book, and rehearse it in the ears of Joshua; for I will utterly put out the remembrance of Amalek from under heaven' " (v. 14).

(4) The first reference to one of God's great names—Jehovah-nissi ("the LORD is my banner") (v. 15).

The Song of Redemption & the Food of Redeemed

COMMENTS

Exodus 15:1-19 records the first song of redemption in the Bible. Others are recorded in Isaiah 12 and Revelation 15:2-3. Exodus 15:1-12 is historical while verses 13-18 are prophetical. Verses 1-3 describe what God is: "my strength," "my song," "my salvation," "my God" and "my father's God." Verses 4-12 describe what God has done to His enemies: defeated them completely. Verses 13-18 describe what God did and will do for His own: He has led them forth and will establish them in their land. Verse 13 sees things from faith's perspective; it sees God's works as accomplished before they are historically realized. This is the same view that Abraham had as recorded by Paul in Romans 4:13ff. This song of praise issued from a redeemed heart that finds its focus first, last, and always in the Lord.

The "dukes of Edom" are the chiefs of Edom. God's work in behalf of His people will strike terror into their (and all other enemies') hearts (Ex. 15:15). The song climaxes in verse 18 with looking forward to Jehovah's eternal reign. This verse contains the roots of Handel's famous "Hallelujah Chorus" which looks forward to Christ's eternal reign as King of kings and Lord of lords. This song was sung antiphonally and must have been stirring as 2 ½ million newly redeemed people sang praise to their God.

Beginning with verse 22, the song of the redeemed heart is put to the test. This is always true for the believer. God's child needs always to be careful of what follows great victories. New heights and new experiences with God are always put to the test so that the child of God might learn to walk by faith and not by sight (cf. 2 Cor. 5:7). The desert, like the world in which the believer finds himself, cannot meet the needs of God's people. Just three days after the Israelites sang God's wonderful praise, they became bitter and murmured against God's leader because they found no water (Ex. 15:22-24). The water that they did find was bitter and they named it Marah ("bitter") which was also the name that Naomi took for herself when she returned from Moab (cf. Ruth 1:20). The problem was not Moses' fault, but Moses knew what to do with the people's complaint—he took it to Jehovah (Ex. 15:25). God showed Moses a tree. When the tree was put into the bitter waters they became sweet (v. 25). God demonstrated conclusively that He is able to make the bitter and disagreeable sweet!

The promise of healing (v. 26) was to Israel, not the people of today. God promised that if they would obey Him, they would be free from the sicknesses of Egypt. They did not obey Him and hence experienced the sicknesses.

A blessed experience with God is no guarantee for the future. Israel continued its murmuring; this time for food (16:2-3). Their murmurings, while directed against their leaders, were in reality against their God (vv. 7-8). God manifested His abundant grace to Israel in supplying a miraculous substance that they had never seen before. They called it *manna* (which means, "What is it?") (v. 15). It fell every morning, and the needs of each person were met; none had too much, and no one lacked. Of course there were those who had to test God's instructions by gathering more than they needed. The surplus manna bred worms, smelled, and incurred Moses' anger (v. 20).

On the sixth day the people were to gather twice as much as on other days for it was to last over the Sabbath. What they did not eat on the sixth day did not decay on the seventh day. God had told them to gather only one day's food at a time, and God had commanded the Sabbath rest. The things God wills never contradict or confuse. What man needs to do is to obey God completely.

When he does, he will experience God's ample provisions of all of his needs.

Israel ate of the manna for 40 years; from this day until they entered the Promised Land (v. 35).

From Egypt to Sinai

COMMENTS

In summarizing Israel's journey from Egypt to Mount Sinai, three notable things happened which were directly related to God's purposes for the nation. The first notable thing was God's working physical miracles to provide for Israel's physical needs. These miracles were: (1) the sweetening of the bitter waters of Marah (15:22-26), (2) the miraculous provision of manna and quail (16:13ff.), and (3) the supply of water from out of the rock (17:1-7). These great physical provisions ought once and for all to have lain to rest any doubt about God's capability and willingness to meet any future physical needs. The second notable thing was the victory over the Amalekites (vv. 8-16). This was Israel's first warfare after leaving Egypt and it was their first victory over a heathen (Gentile) enemy. Joshua is first mentioned in this account (v. 9). Later Joshua was to lead Israel in an eight-year campaign to conquer the land of Canaan. In this battle with Amalek Joshua learned that the condition of victory is dependence on God. The battle was not won down in the valley with the Amalekites, but up on the mountaintop with God! The third notable thing that happened on this journey was the advice of Jethro to Moses and the consequent appointment of the elders to assist him in the matters of governing the people. Jethro's advice was to have a representative form of government (18:21). Moses put various ones to work in the work of the Lord so that all of the work would get done efficiently. These elders took care of the day-to-day matters and brought only the difficult cases to Moses (v. 26).

Israel camped at the foot of Mount Sinai for just about a year—11 months and five days, to be exact (cf. Num. 10:11). Approximately 59 chapters of the Bible are devoted to this period of time. It was very important to Israel's history because it was during this time that God changed His way of dealing with His people. Up to this time God's Word and will had not been written down in any form. Before they left Mount Sinai God gave them not only the Ten Commandments, but also civil, ceremonial, and health laws. They were the only nation ever to receive a culture direct from the hand and mouth of God.

During the time that Israel was encamped at the foot of Mount Sinai, God accomplished at least three things that were important for the future of the nation. (1) He gave them rest so that they were in the best possible physical shape, (2) He instructed them fully and precisely, and (3) He made them into a fledgling nation (they would not become a full-fledged nation until they were in their own land with their own king ruling over them some time later).

Shortly after their arrival at Mount Sinai, God called Moses from the mountain (Ex. 19:3) telling him to remind the people of their speedy and safe delivery out of Egypt (v. 4) and laying a unique opportunity before them. If they would but obey His voice and keep His commandments, they would be: (1) a peculiar treasure unto Him, (2) a kingdom of priests, and (3) a holy nation (vv. 5-6). What a lofty goal and noble future. When the people heard of it they were excited and determined to do all that the Lord had spoken (v. 8). Too soon they would learn that "the spirit is willing but the flesh is weak" (cf. Matt. 26:41). Peter quoted Exodus 19:5-6 with slight modification (cf. 1 Peter 2:9). Peter was writing to Gentile Christians. Some would draw the erroneous conclusion that since Peter's readers and Moses' people are equated and described in the same ways that they therefore must be equal to each other and without distinction. It is not similarity, but lack of difference that proves identity. There is one notable distinction: Israel is an earthly, political nation. Peter's readers are members of a spiritual body, the church. Each maintains its distinct identity.

ROUND SIX

The arrival of Moses' family.

The advice of Moses' family. Zipporah, Moses' wife, and his two sons, Gershom and Eliezer, met Moses at the base of Mount Sinai. Jethro, his father-in-law observed that Moses was spending most of his time settling disputes among the Israelites and offered the following advice.

"Moreover thou shalt provide . . . able men . . . to be rulers of thousands, and rulers of hundreds, rulers of fifties, and rulers of tens. And let them judge . . . and it shall be, that every great matter they shall bring unto thee, but every small matter they shall judge" (18:21-22).

ISRAEL, SETTLED DOWN AT SINAI

On June 15, 1445 B.C., Israel arrived at Mount Sinai. They would be here for 11 months and five days (Num. 10:11). Three major events took place during this time. These are:

(1) The commandment of the Law (requirement for fellowship).

(2) The corruption of the golden calf (ruin of that fellowship).

(3) The construction of the tabernacle (restoration to that fellowship). We shall now look at an introduction *to* and a consideration *of* these three events.

AN INTRODUCTION TO THE ACTION AT MOUNT SINAI

"And Moses went up unto God, and the LORD called unto him out of the mountain, saying, 'Thus shalt thou say to the house of Jacob, and tell the Children of Israel:

" ' "Ye have seen what I did unto the Egyptians, and how I bare you on eagles' wings, and brought you unto Myself. Now therefore, if ye will obey My voice indeed, and keep My covenant, then ye shall be a peculiar treasure unto Me above all people; for all the earth is Mine.

" ' "And ye shall be unto Me a kingdom of priests, and a holy nation." These are the words which thou shalt speak unto the Children of Israel' " (Ex. 19:3-6).

Soon after their arrival at Sinai, God manifested Himself to Israel by thunderings, lightning, smoke, fire, and an earthquake and spoke to them in a trumpetlike voice from out of a thick cloud (vv. 10-18). Moses ascended Mount Sinai and received in oral fashion the Law. He then descended and repeated it to the people who agreed to keep it (19:20–24:3). This was all written by Moses and ratified by the sprinkling of blood on an altar of 12 pillars (vv. 4-8).

He again ascended the mountain for 40 days. During this time he viewed God's glory for the first time and received the pattern for the tabernacle (v. 12; chaps. 25–31).

"Then went up Moses and Aaron, Nadab and Abihu, and 70 of the elders of Israel.

"And they saw the God of Israel; and there was under His feet as it were a paved work of a sapphire stone, and as it were the body of heaven in His clearness. . . .

"And the LORD said unto Moses, 'Come up to Me into the mount, and be there, and I will give thee tables of stone, and a Law, and commandments which I have written; that thou mayest teach them.' . . .

"And the glory of the LORD abode upon Mount Sinai, and the cloud covered it six days, and the seventh day He called unto Moses out of the midst of the cloud. And the sight of the glory of the LORD was like devouring fire on the top of the mount in the eyes of the Children of Israel. And Moses went into the midst of the cloud, and gat him up into the mount. And Moses was in the mount 40 days and 40 nights" (24:9-10, 12, 16-18).

He was then ordered down to deal with the golden calf idolatry taking place below by the fickle and foolish Israelites (32:1-10).

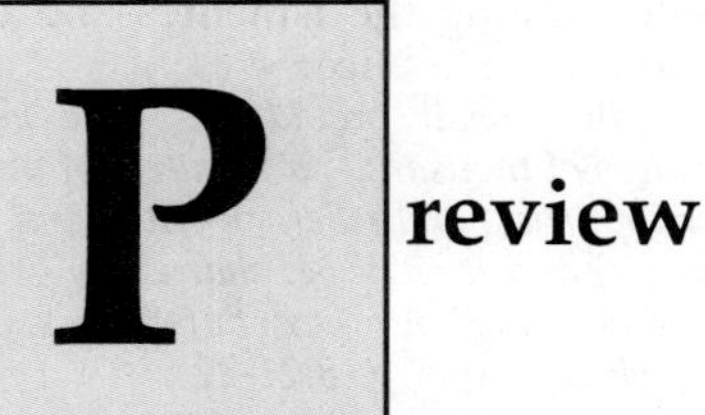

Revelation and Rebellion

EXODUS 20–23; 32–34; LEVITICUS 11–15; 17–19; 21–22; 24–27

No doubt about it. This was the biggest mountain they had ever seen. In fact, for most of them it was the *only* mountain they had ever seen! Egypt boasted of many pyramids, but not one mountain. Furthermore, they would soon discover that this was no ordinary mountain. With fear and fascination they watched as it blazed with fire and smoke, as from a furnace. Out of that inferno could be seen brilliant flashes of lightning, resulting in deafening thunderclaps. Finally there was heard the voice of God Himself, resembling a mighty trumpet.

This mount could be none other than the habitation of the Holy One. This was the mountain Moses would ascend to receive in written form from the divine hand those principles on which God's holiness was based—the Ten Commandments. Would Israel receive those heavenly precepts with willing hearts and hands? On the contrary, while Moses met with God, the people indulged in an orgy of idolatry and immorality in the valley below. But in the midst of this shameful and sorrowful hour the compassionate Creator introduced a plan whereby their wrecked fellowship could be restored. The plan was in the form of a building—the tabernacle.

Overview

<table>
<tr><td>SCRIPTURE</td><td colspan="7">Exodus 20–23; 32–34; Leviticus 11–15; 17–19; 21–22; 24–27</td></tr>
<tr><td>SUBJECTS</td><td colspan="7">At Sinai—part 1</td></tr>
<tr><td rowspan="9">SPECIFICS</td><td colspan="7">The revelation of God's Law</td></tr>
<tr><td rowspan="3">The Commandments</td><td colspan="2">Moral code</td><td rowspan="3">The Christ</td><td>Spiritual code</td><td rowspan="3">The Community</td><td>Social code</td></tr>
<tr><td>Vertical</td><td>Horizontal</td><td rowspan="2">Dealing with the sacrifices
Dealing with the suppers</td><td rowspan="2">Property
Purity
Priests
Peace and war
Personal injuries</td></tr>
<tr><td>Worship no other god
No graven image
No vain usage of God's name
Observe Sabbath Day</td><td>Honor your parents
Don't kill
Don't commit adultery
Don't steal
Don't lie
Don't covet</td></tr>
<tr><td colspan="7">The rebellion against God's Law</td></tr>
<tr><td colspan="4">Idolatry</td><td colspan="3">Immorality</td></tr>
<tr><td colspan="4">Breaking all the vertical commands</td><td colspan="3">Breaking all the horizontal commands</td></tr>
<tr><td colspan="7"></td></tr>
<tr><td colspan="7"></td></tr>
<tr><td>SAINTS AND SINNERS</td><td colspan="7">Moses, Aaron, men of Levi</td></tr>
<tr><td rowspan="2">SENTENCE SUMMARIES</td><td>O.T. Verse</td><td colspan="6">"Thou camest down also upon Mount Sinai, and spakest with them from heaven, and gavest them right judgments, and true laws, good statutes, and commandments" (Neh. 9:13).</td></tr>
<tr><td>N.T. Verse</td><td colspan="6">"Wherefore then serveth the Law? It was added because of transgressions, till the seed should come to whom the promise was made; and it was ordained by angels in the hand of a mediator" (Gal. 3:19).</td></tr>
</table>

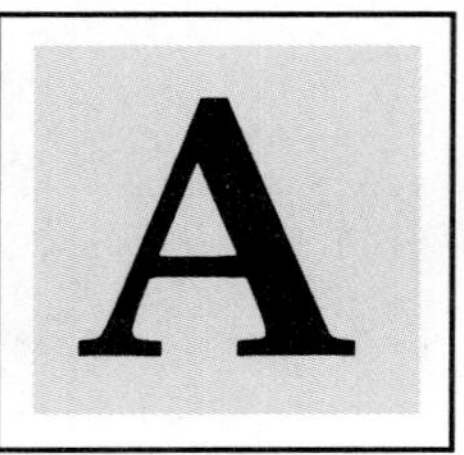

CONSIDERATION OF THE ACTION AT MOUNT SINAI

The commandment of the Law. There were three basic sections of the Mosaic Law.

*The moral code: This section is commonly known as the Ten Commandments (Ex. 20:3-17; Deut. 5:7-21).

(1) Thou shalt have no other gods before Me.
(2) Thou shalt not make unto thee any graven image.
(3) Thou shalt not take the name of the Lord thy God in vain.
(4) Remember the Sabbath Day to keep it holy.
(5) Honor thy father and thy mother.
(6) Thou shalt not kill.
(7) Thou shalt not commit adultery.
(8) Thou shalt not steal.
(9) Thou shalt not bear false witness.
(10) Thou shalt not covet.

*The spiritual code: This section dealt with the ordinances, all of which foreshadowed Christ and salvation. See Hebrews 10:1. It included the levitical feasts, offerings, etc. (Ex. 23; 35–40; Lev.). At this time God made a twofold promise.

(1) He would send His Angel (the Messiah) to bring the nation Israel into Canaan (Ex. 23:20-23).

(2) He would send His avengers (the hornets) to drive the pagan nations out of Canaan (v. 28).

*The social code: This section dealt with the judgments and divine laws of God's new establishment for Israel.

- Individuals
  - Motherhood (Lev. 12)
  - Lepers (chaps. 13–14)
  - Priests (chaps. 21–22)
  - Master-servant relationships (Ex. 21)
  - Disobedient children (Deut. 21)
  - False prophets (chaps. 13; 18)
- Personal purity
  - Regarding sex (Lev. 18; 20)
  - Regarding unclean issues (chap. 15)
  - Regarding food (Deut. 14)
  - Regarding marriage (chaps. 21–22; 24)
- Warfare (chap. 20)
- Sacrificial animals
  - Clean and unclean animals (Lev. 11)
  - Blood (chap. 17)
- The land
  - Usage of (chap. 25)
  - Prosperity in (chap. 26)
  - Results of obedience (vv. 1-13)
  - Results of disobedience (vv. 14-39)
- Personal injuries (Ex. 21)
- Property rights (chap. 22)
- Inquests (Deut. 21)
- Blasphemy (Lev. 24)
- Vows (chap. 27)

Simply stated, it can be said that the moral code acted as the REVELATION of God's Law, the social code as the REGULATION of that Law, and the spiritual code as the REALIZATION of that Law—in Christ. (See Matt. 5:17-18; Rom. 10:4.)

God's Law and Life

COMMENTS

When Israel said, "All that the LORD hath spoken we will do" (Ex. 19:8), God took them at their word. In response, God literally wrote down what He wanted them to do. We call it "the Law." The part that God wrote with His finger on tables of stone (31:18) we call the Ten Commandments. It is also known as the Decalogue (lit., the ten words, 34:28). Nine of the Ten Commandments are repeated in the New Testament under grace conditions. Only the fourth commandment (dealing with the Sabbath) is omitted. The purpose of the Law was not to enable man to do something pleasing to God. Rather, it was given to demonstrate that even when man wanted to please God (cf. 19:8) he could not. The purpose of the Law is to declare all men guilty before God (cf. Rom. 3:19). It is impossible for one to receive God's righteousness by keeping the Law because he cannot keep the Law, even when he wants to do so. The Law makes sin abound, for its purpose is to reveal the fact of sin (cf. 5:20; 7:7-13). The Law neither creates nor removes evil; it merely reveals evil (cf. vv. 7, 13). Sin is not knowable without the principle of law whether it be the law of conscience (by which the Gentiles were condemned) or the revealed Law of God (by which all men are condemned). The purpose of the Law is to function as a schoolteacher to bring us to the point where we realize that only in Christ can we be saved (cf. Gal. 3:24). It is only as we come to Christ in faith (belief) that we actually receive the righteousness of God to which the Law could only point. The Law could only point to what man should be and do. The Law could only condemn man when he did not live up to the standards it imposed. The Law reveals to us the unbreakable power of sin's grip on us and sentences us to receive the penalties it prescribes. The Law points to the necessity of righteousness but in no way provides the righteousness it demands. No one was ever saved by keeping the Law but all men are condemned because they have not kept it—whether the law of conscience or the Ten Commandments. The Christian is not saved by Law nor does he live under it (cf. Rom. 6:14; 8:4; 13:10; 1 Peter 3:18). However, whenever the believer lives and walks under the control of the Holy Spirit his conduct is consistent with the righteousness to which the Law points (cf. Rom. 3:31). No one walking under the control of the Holy Spirit will do anything that is contrary to the conduct prescribed by the Law. If one decides that he wants to live under the Law, he must realize that it is a unit—all of it goes together (cf. Gal. 5:3), the moral code (the Ten Commandments), the spiritual code (which regulated Israel's worship), and the social code (which regulated Israel's social life). One cannot limit himself simply to the observance of the Ten Commandments. If he breaks one part of the Law he is just as guilty as if he had broken it all (cf. James 2:10).

What practical purpose did the Law serve in God's economy? Paul answers that question fully in Galatians 3:15ff. Negatively, it was NOT to do away with the promise made to Abraham (the Abrahamic Covenant, Gen. 12:2-3) (Gal. 3:17). Positively, it was added alongside of the promise made to Abraham so that those who believed the promise would be able to know how they should conduct their lives in relation to God and man (v. 19). It was to serve until Messiah should come (v. 19) at which time it would be done away (vv. 21-26). It was never given for life or righteousness. God's righteousness can only be received by belief in Christ (3:26). Christ perfectly fulfilled all of the demands of the Law and paid the penalty of the Law (death) for us that we might have life and righteousness through Him (cf. 2 Cor. 5:21).

The corruption of the golden calf. During his stay on Sinai the fickle Israelites, having decided Moses would not return, demanded that Aaron make them a visible god. Aaron foolishly did this. After their "worship" service, the people celebrated by staging a sexual orgy.

"And Aaron said unto them, 'Break off the golden earrings, which are in the ears of your wives, of your sons, and of your daughters, and bring them unto me.' . . .

"And he received them at their hand, and fashioned it with a graving tool, after he had made it a molten calf: and they said, 'These be thy gods, O Israel, which brought thee up out of the land of Egypt.' . . .

"And they rose up early on the morrow, and offered burnt offerings, and brought peace offerings; and the people sat down to eat and to drink, and rose up to play" (Ex. 32:2, 4, 6).

God ordered Moses down immediately. On viewing this terrible sin, he broke the two stones containing the Ten Commandments (v. 19). He severely rebuked his brother Aaron and Israel was judged by a death plague which fell on 3,000 of the troublemaking ringleaders.

"And when Moses saw that the people were naked (for Aaron had made them naked unto their shame among their enemies), then Moses stood in the gate of the camp, and said, 'Who is on the LORD's side? Let him come unto me.' And all the sons of Levi gathered themselves together unto him.

"And he said unto them, 'Thus saith the LORD God of Israel, "Put every man his sword by his side, and go in and out from gate to gate throughout the camp, and slay every man his brother, and every man his companion, and every man his neighbor" ' " (vv. 25-27).

Moses, who had already pleaded for them while on the mountain (vv. 11-14), once again interceded for the sinning nation (vv. 30-34).

His first prayer. "And Moses besought the LORD his God, and said, 'LORD, why doth Thy wrath wax hot against Thy people, which Thou hast brought forth out of the land of Egypt with great power, and with a mighty hand?

" 'Wherefore should the Egyptians speak, and say, "For mischief did He bring them out, to slay them in the mountains, and to consume them from the face of the earth"? Turn from Thy fierce wrath, and repent of this evil against Thy people.

" 'Remember Abraham, Isaac, and Israel, Thy servants, to whom Thou swearest by Thine own self, and saidst unto them, "I will multiply your seed as the stars of heaven, and all this land that I have spoken of will I give unto your seed, and they shall inherit it for ever." '

"And the Lord repented of the evil which He thought to do unto His people" (vv. 11-14).

His second prayer. "And it came to pass on the morrow, that Moses said unto the people, 'Ye have sinned a great sin: and now I will go up unto the LORD: peradventure I shall make an atonement for your sin.'

"And Moses returned unto the LORD, and said, 'Oh, this people have sinned a great sin, and have made them gods of gold. Yet now, if Thou wilt forgive their sin; and if not, blot me, I pray Thee, out of Thy book which Thou hast written.'

"And the LORD said unto Moses, 'Whosoever hath sinned against Me, him will I blot out of My book. Therefore now go, lead the people unto the place of which I have spoken unto thee: behold, Mine Angel shall go before thee. Nevertheless in the day when I visit I will visit their sin upon them' " (vv. 30-34).

He requested and was allowed to view the glory of God while hidden in the cleft of a rock (33:18-23, 34:5-9).

"And he said, 'I beseech Thee, show me Thy glory.' And He said, 'I will make all My goodness pass before thee, and I will proclaim the name of the LORD before thee; and will be gracious to whom I will be gracious, and will show mercy on whom I will show mercy.' And He said, 'Thou canst not see My face; for there shall no man see Me, and live.'

"And the LORD said, 'Behold, there is a place by Me, and thou shalt stand upon a rock. And it shall come to pass, while My glory passeth by, that I will put thee in a cleft of the rock, and will cover thee with My hand while I pass by. And I will take away Mine hand, and thou shalt see My back parts; but My face shall not be seen" (33:18-23).

He once again ascended Mount Sinai where God rewrote the Ten Commandments and ordered Moses to construct a box and place these tablets of stone in it. This box would later be known as the ark of the covenant (34:1-4; Deut. 10:1-2).

He descended from Mount Sinai (Ex. 34:29-30, 33-35).

"And it came to pass, when Moses came down from Mount Sinai with the two tables of testimony in Moses' hand, when he came down from the Mount, that Moses wist not that the skin of his face shone while he talked with Him.

"And when Aaron and all the Children of Israel saw Moses, behold, the skin of his face shone; and they were afraid to come nigh him. . . .

"And till Moses had done speaking with them, he put a veil on his face. But when Moses went in before the LORD to speak with Him, he took the veil off, until he came out. And he came out, and spake unto the Children of Israel that which he was commanded.

"And the Children of Israel saw the face of Moses, that the skin of Moses' face shone. And Moses put the veil upon his face again, until he went in to speak with Him" (vv. 29-30, 33-35).

The Apostasy of Aaron

COMMENTS

Israel had pledged themselves to do all that God wanted them to do (cf. Ex. 19:8). All too soon they were going to realize that "the spirit is willing, but the flesh is weak" (cf. Matt. 26:41). Before they found out historically what God wanted them to do, they broke every commandment. Their sin grew out of impatience (Ex. 32:1). Tragically, Aaron, who was supposed to be the spokesman for God (cf. 4:14-15), became the leader in the apostasy. What ensued is one of the greatest contrasts in the Bible—Moses on the mountain with God (32:1) and the people in the valley worshiping the golden calf (v. 4ff.). The people never suggested substituting Aaron as their leader in place of Moses. They knew that Aaron was weak and susceptible. His weakness is seen in his reply to the people (v. 2) and in his reply to Moses (vv. 22-24). The people would rather have had a god of their own making than have no god at all. How weak was their flesh in view of their profession (19:8).

Aaron's apostasy is particularly flagrant. He not only made the molten golden calf but went along with the people's suggestion that these were the gods that brought them up from Egypt (32:4). He further encouraged the apostasy by proclaiming the next day to be a religious feast to Jehovah (v. 5) and must have officiated at the religious rituals (v. 6).

Idolatry is spiritual suicide. The consequences of idolatry and sin must be faced. While the deed was hidden from Moses' eyes, it was in God's full view (vv. 7-14). God revealed to Moses what he would encounter on his return to camp. God threatened to wipe Israel out and begin again with Moses (v. 10). Moses pled for the people on the solid ground of God's glory, name, oath, and power (vv. 11-14) and returned (v. 15).

Moses' intercession was effective for "the LORD repented of the evil which He thought to do unto His people" (v. 14). This statement should not be understood to mean that the unchangeable God (cf. James 1:17) changed. His eternal will was to move Moses to intercede for sinning Israel. This brought Israel's actual miserable condition to Moses' attention and assured that he would make Israel deal with its sin. On the basis of Israel's change God could continue His plan and promise made to Abraham. Described from man's viewpoint, it appeared as if God changed; actually it was man who changed.

Immodesty and immorality always accompany idolatry (Ex. 32:6, 19, 25). In his anger, Moses broke the tables of the Law thus visibly demonstrating what Israel had done (v. 19). Aaron was more fearful of Moses' anger than he was of God's (v. 22). Moses melted down the idol, ground it up, and made the people drink it (v. 20). What an insignificant god it must be to take this kind of treatment without retribution or protest. What a small god that one could drink. How foolish is apostasy—to forsake God for nothing. Aaron's explanation was pathetic (vv. 23-24).

Confession calls for rededication—a new stand must be taken (v. 26). Apparently, only the sons of Levi responded to the invitation. Apostasy brings death—3,000 were slain (v. 28).

God's grace extends even to apostates. Moses returned to the mountain, confessed Israel's sin—even offering to give up his own salvation (vv. 30-32). God executed judgment (vv. 33-35). But the repentant were restored (34:7). Moses rose to new heights in his personal relationship with God and was permitted to see God's back (33:18-23).

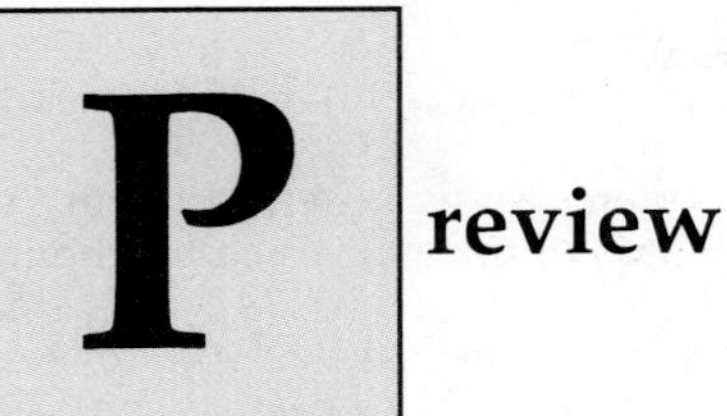

The Dwelling Place of Deity (Part One)

EXODUS 25–31; 35–40; Leviticus 1–9; 16; 23

After six months and a cost of millions, it was completed. The importance of the building was certainly not demonstrated by its size, a mere 150 feet long, 75 feet wide, and 15 feet high. Centuries before, in Noah's day, the ark had been three times the size of this building which now stood at Mount Sinai's base. Nevertheless, to Moses and his people, this simple structure was as vital to their spiritual salvation as that ship had once been to Noah's physical salvation. The name of the building was the tabernacle.

It served, in one sense of the word, as a divine halfway house, whereby the sin of Israel, both nationally and individually, could be dealt with through blood sacrifices until the advent of God's perfect and permanent Lamb—the Lord Jesus Christ. Here, in the holy of holies above the mercy seat, in blinding light, was the Shekinah glory of God Himself.

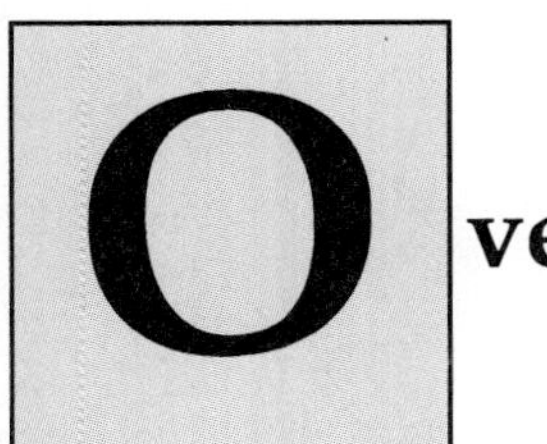

Overview

<table>
<tr><td>SCRIPTURE</td><td colspan="10">Exodus 25–31; 35–40; Leviticus 1–9; 16; 23</td></tr>
<tr><td>SUBJECTS</td><td colspan="10">At Sinai—part 2</td></tr>
<tr><td rowspan="7">SPECIFICS</td><td colspan="10">God's tabernacle</td></tr>
<tr><td colspan="4">The survey</td><td colspan="6">The sacrifices</td></tr>
<tr><td rowspan="2">Framework</td><td>3 partitions</td><td rowspan="2">Furniture</td><td>6 pieces</td><td rowspan="2">Four meat offerings</td><td rowspan="2" colspan="3">Burnt
Peace
Sin
Trespass</td><td rowspan="2">One meal offering</td><td rowspan="2">Meal</td></tr>
<tr><td>Outer court
Inner court
Holy of holies</td><td>Altar of bronze
Laver of bronze
Table of bread
Golden lampstand
Ark of incense</td></tr>
<tr><td colspan="5">The suppers</td><td colspan="5">The stewards</td></tr>
<tr><td>Depicting God's Creation</td><td>Weekly Sabbath
7-year Sabbath
50-year Sabbath</td><td>Depicting God's redemption</td><td colspan="2">Passover
Firstfruits
Pentecost
Trumpets
Day of Atonement
Tabernacles</td><td colspan="5">Their selection
Their sanctification
Their service</td></tr>
<tr><td colspan="10"></td></tr>
<tr><td>SAINTS AND SINNERS</td><td colspan="10">Moses, Aaron, Bezalel, Oholiab,</td></tr>
<tr><td rowspan="2">SENTENCE SUMMARIES</td><td>O.T. Verse</td><td colspan="9">"Lord, who shall abide in Thy tabernacle? Who shall dwell in Thy holy hill?" (Ps. 15:1)</td></tr>
<tr><td>N.T. Verse</td><td colspan="9">"Our fathers had the tabernacle of witness in the wilderness, as He had appointed, speaking unto Moses that he should make it according to the fashion that he had seen" (Acts 7:44).</td></tr>
</table>

THE TABERNACLE

The construction of the tabernacle (Ex. 25–31; 35–40).

*The compartments of the tabernacle: It consisted of three sections or divisions.

(1) The outer court. This was a picket fence arrangement, 150′ long, by 75′ wide, by 7 ½′ high.

(2) The inner court. Inside the "picket fence" was a tent, 45′ long, by 15′ wide, by 15′ high. It had two rooms, separated by a thick veil. The eastern section of the tent was known as the inner court.

(3) The holy of holies. This was the name for the western part of that tent.

*The furniture of the tabernacle: There were six main pieces.

(1) The altar of brass (Ex. 27:1-8; 38:1-7).

(2) The laver of brass (30:18; 38:8).

(3) The table of shewbread (25:23-20; 37:10-16).

(4) The golden candlestick (25:31-40; 37:17-24).

(5) The golden altar of incense (30:1-10; 37:25-28).

(6) The ark of the covenant (Ex. 25:10-22; 37:1-9).

The priesthood of the tabernacle. Aaron became the first high priest of Israel (28:1-4). From his tribe (Levi) the other priests were to be chosen (Num. 8:14-19).

"And take thou unto thee Aaron thy brother, and his sons with him, from among the Children of Israel, that he may minister unto Me in the priest's office, even Aaron, Nadab and Abihu, Eleazar and Ithamar, Aaron's sons. . . .

"And thou shalt put in the breastplate of judgment the Urim and the Thummim; and they shall be upon Aaron's heart, when he goeth in before the LORD. And Aaron shall bear the judgment of the Children of Israel upon his heart before the LORD continually" (Ex. 28:1, 30).

"Thus shalt thou separate the Levites from among the Children of Israel; and the Levites shall be Mine. And after that shall the Levites go in to do the service of the tabernacle of the congregation; and thou shalt cleanse them, and offer them for an offering. For they are wholly given unto Me from among the Children of Israel; instead of such as open every womb, even instead of the firstborn of all the Children of Israel, have I taken them unto Me" (Num. 8:14-16).

The Tabernacle, a Picture of Christ

COMMENTS

For its size, the tabernacle was the most expensive building (it was really a tent) ever built. Its total value was about 1 billion dollars—much more than that in today's dollars. The study of the tabernacle is important for at least five reasons: (1) God Himself placed great emphasis on it; (2) every aspect of the tabernacle portrays something about Christ in a way not derived, designed, or thought out by man (Heb. 9:8); (3) portions of the New Testament are largely unintelligible without it, especially Hebrews; (4) the tabernacle typically relates to practically the whole range of New Testament truth; and (5) it is an effective antidote for liberalism which is occupied with externalism—the tabernacle looks beyond the externals to the realities.

Each piece of furniture in the tabernacle stressed an important aspect of Christ's ministry for us. (1) The brazen altar—Christ our sacrifice and atonement for sin; (2) the laver—Christ our sanctification; (3) the table of shewbread—Christ our food and the center of our fellowship; (4) the golden lampstand—Christ our light and the light of the world; (5) the golden altar of incense—Christ our intercessor; (6) the veil—Christ our access into the presence of God; (7) the ark of the covenant—Christ the enthronement of God in humanity; (8) the mercy seat—Christ our propitiation (satisfaction).

All of the furniture of the outer court was bronze while all of the furniture of the holy place and the holy of holies was pure gold. All of the furniture of the tabernacle was for God first and for man second. Christ's death was for God first and for man second. All of the furniture in a straight line (east to west) represented God's provision for approach to Him. The furniture on the sides represented the privileges and responsibilities of God's children.

Each piece of furniture had a particular purpose in God's economy. The brazen altar met the righteous claims of God and sacrifice for sin through a blood sacrifice. The laver, through washing and cleansing, portrayed judicial righteousness and then personal righteousness. The table of shewbread portrayed sharing in Christ. The priests could only eat the bread after they had come by the altar and the laver of cleansing. The golden lampstand provided light before the Lord, on the table, on the altar of incense, and on itself. It manifested the grace of God worked in the lives of His children. The golden altar of incense portrayed intercessory prayers before God. It was in front of the veil as Christ is at the right hand of the Father for us. The veil portrayed the means of access into the presence of God through the body of Christ. The ark of the covenant was a golden chest which supported the mercy seat. The mercy seat presented Christ as our satisfaction before God. The blood sprinkled on the gold demonstrated Christ's death as satisfying all the demands of a righteous God.

One piece of furniture was notably absent from the tabernacle. There were no chairs. The priests were not to sit down because their work was never finished. What a contrast to our High Priest, Christ, who is seated at the right hand of God because His work is finished (Heb. 8:1; 10:12; 12:2).

Overall, the tabernacle teaches us that we are saved and sanctified in order that we might worship, serve, and enjoy God forever.

The ordination of the priests.

(1) They were washed with water (Ex. 29:4).

(2) They were clothed with garments (28:39-43; 29:5-6).

NOTE: For a description of the high priest's clothing, see 28:1-38.

(3) They were anointed with oil (29:7).

(4) They were sprinkled with blood (v. 20).

The duties of the priests.

(1) That of temple service (Num. 3:5-9).

(2) That of legal service (Deut. 17:8-9).

(3) That of personal service (Num. 6:23-27).

The offerings of the tabernacle.

(1) The burnt offering (Lev. 1).

(2) The meal offering (chap. 2).

(3) The peace offering (chap. 3).

(4) The sin offering (chap. 4).

(5) The trespass offering (chap. 5).

The first three offerings were used to maintain fellowship with God, while the last two were to restore broken fellowship.

The feasts of the tabernacle. There were nine special feasts and rest-times in Israel's calendar.

The first three were to remind the believers of God's creative work and the last six of His redemptive work.

*His creative work: (1) The weekly Sabbath (Ex. 20:8-11; Lev. 23:1-3).

(2) The seven-year Sabbath feast (Ex. 23:10-11); Lev. 25:2-7).

(3) The fiftieth-year Sabbath feast (Lev. 25:8-16).

NOTE: These three speak of God's Creation as they come in endless cycles of seven, just as God rested on the seventh day.

*His redemptive work: (1) The Feast of the Passover (Lev. 23:4-8). This speaks of Calvary (1 Cor. 5:7).

(2) The Feast of the Firstfruits (Lev. 23:9-14). This speaks of the Resurrection (1 Cor. 15:23).

(3) The Feast of Pentecost (Lev. 23:15-22). This speaks of the coming of the Holy Spirit (Acts 2).

(4) The Feast of Trumpets (Lev. 23:23-25). This speaks of the Rapture and Second Coming (1 Thes. 4:13-18).

(5) The Day of Atonement Feast (Lev. 23:26-32). This speaks of the Tribulation (Rev. 6–19). In the Hebrew this is Yom Kippur. The order of service on this all-important day is detailed for us in Leviticus 16.

The high priest would offer a bull sacrifice for himself. Preachers need to be saved and cleansed too. Lots would then be cast over two goats to determine which one would become a scapegoat, and which would be killed. The high priest would then sprinkle the blood of the slaughtered bull and goat seven times on the mercy seat. He would finally place his hands on the scapegoat, confess over it all the sins of Israel, and then appoint a man to lead the goat into the desert.

(6) The Feast of Tabernacles (23:33-44). This speaks of the Millennium (Rev. 20:1-6).

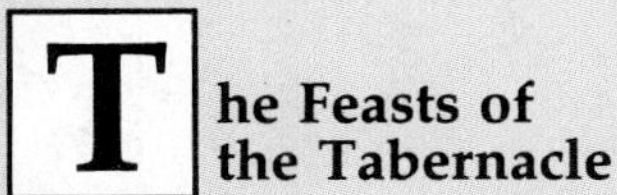

The Feasts of the Tabernacle

COMMENTS

The three Sabbath feasts were designated by God to convey to the Children of Israel different aspects of God's creative work. The weekly Sabbath reminded them that Jehovah is the Creator of all that existed. He rested on the Sabbath, not because He was tired, but because He had completed all that there was to be created. His Creation was complete. Nothing remained to be created and nothing was in the process of "evolving." On the Sabbath the Israelites were free to praise God for His creative genius. The seven-year Sabbath feast was designed by God to give the land the opportunity of replenishing itself with minerals. It was also good for the people to give their land a year's rest. They would have to depend on God to give them crops to last through this seventh year. During the Sabbath year they could give themselves completely to replenishing themselves spiritually. The fiftieth-year Sabbath feast must have been a time of special joy. The words from Leviticus 25:10, "Proclaim liberty throughout all the land," are inscribed on the Liberty Bell at Independence Hall. In this year prisoners and slaves were set free and the land reverted to its original ownership. This would remind the people that God is the Creator and Owner of all people and lands and that it is His to give to whomever He wills. Man does not really own anything. God owns everything. Man merely uses and possesses what God owns. All of these Sabbath feasts look forward to the Millennium when the final Jubilee will be realized and Jesus Christ will set up His kingdom and visibly reign over all of His world (cf. Heb. 4:9-10).

The six remaining feasts associated with the tabernacle conveyed different aspects of Christ's redemptive work. The Feasts of Passover and Firstfruits were celebrated in the spring and required the celebrants to stay in the Jerusalem vicinity for eight days. The Feast of Pentecost (also called the Feast of Weeks) was observed in the summer and required the celebrants to be in the Jerusalem vicinity at least one day. The Feast of Trumpets, the Day of Atonement, and Feast of Tabernacles were celebrated in the fall and required the celebrants to stay in the Jerusalem vicinity for at least three weeks. In the observance of these feasts the Children of Israel were perpetually being exposed to a kind of chronological confession of faith. The Passover and the unleavened bread associated with it (cf. 1 Cor. 5:7-8) looked forward to the death of Christ who was the perfect unblemished Passover Lamb. The Feast of Firstfruits looked forward to the resurrection of Christ from the dead. The Feast of Pentecost looked forward to the coming of the Holy Spirit who would complete the body of Christ (the church). The Feast of Trumpets looked forward to the gathering together of God's elect to Himself (cf. Matt. 24:31). The Day of Atonement looked forward to Israel's national suffering, repentance, and acceptance of Christ as her Messiah (cf. Rom. 11:26). The Feast of Tabernacles looked forward to the millennial reign of Christ when there would be universal peace and gladness, and Israel would be delivered from all Gentile oppressors (cf. Isa. 60–66).

Compared to American holidays, the Feast of Passover was similar to our July 4th. The Feast of Tabernacles was similar to our Thanksgiving. The Day of Atonement was similar to our Good Friday. The Feast of Firstfruits was similar to our Easter Sunday. The Feast of Pentecost was similar to our Whitsunday.

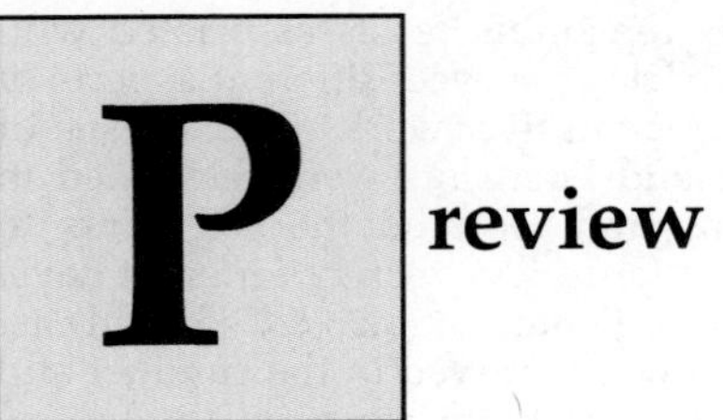

The Dwelling Place of Deity (Part Two)

EXODUS 40; LEVITICUS 10; NUMBERS 1–10

A small crowd had gathered to watch as the lifeless bodies of the high priest's two sons were quickly carried from the tabernacle. No one spoke. There was really nothing to say. One thing was certain. Israel's God might be invisible, but decidedly not indifferent or impotent. The offering of strange fire, possibly while drunk, would not be tolerated, even though the priests involved were Aaron's flesh and blood. Religious blasphemy must be punished. Divine judgment had fallen.

In light of all this, the newly announced office of a Nazarite and the accompanying threefold vow now took on new significance. The divine command to "Be ye holy for I am holy," was obviously not something to be considered lightly. But the very existence of the tabernacle itself and the ever-present glory cloud served to remind Israel of His goodness also. Though sin was hated, sinners were loved. Animal sacrifices were readily available to any and all who would seek Him for cleansing and comfort.

Overview

SCRIPTURE	Exodus 40; Leviticus 10; Numbers 1–10	
SUBJECT	At Sinai—part 3	

SPECIFICS

God's tabernacle		
The glory	The goal	The gathering
His brightness fell on the tabernacle His blessing came from the tabernacle	To review the plan of salvation To preview the person of Christ	Conducting of Israel's first census
The gifts	The gallant	The glad sound
Given by Israel's 12 leaders	Dedicated males who took the Nazarite vow	The two silver trumpets

SAINTS AND SINNERS	Moses, Aaron, Nadab, Abihu, 12 Israelite leaders

SENTENCE SUMMARIES

O.T. Verse	"In the time of trouble He shall hide me in His pavilion; in the secret of His tabernacle shall He hide me; He shall set me up upon a rock" (Ps. 27:5).
N.T. Verses	"There was a tabernacle made; the first wherein was the candlestick, and the table, and the showbread, which is called the sanctuary. And after the second veil, the tabernacle which is called the holiest of all" (Heb. 9:2-3).

ABERNACLE DEDICATION

The dedication of the tabernacle. *"And he reared up the court round about the tabernacle and the altar, and set up the hanging of the court gate. So Moses finished the work. Then a cloud covered the tent of the congregation, and the glory of the* Lord *filled the tabernacle. And Moses was not able to enter into the tent of the congregation, because the cloud abode thereon, and the glory of the* Lord *filled the tabernacle" (Ex. 40:33-35).*

Thus, was the most important building ever constructed on this earth dedicated. It took six months to complete, at a cost of millions of dollars (over 3,100 pounds of gold and some 9,600 pounds of silver alone went into its construction). It was completed around 1444 B.C. It was built by willing hands and hearts (Ex. 35:5, 21-22, 29).

"And Moses spake unto all the congregation of the Children of Israel, saying, 'This is the thing which the Lord *commanded, saying, "Take ye from among you an offering unto the* Lord*. Whosoever is of a willing heart, let him bring it, an offering of the* Lord*, gold, and silver, and brass."' . . .*

"And they came, every one whose heart stirred him up, and every one whom his spirit made willing, and they brought the Lord's offering to the work of the tabernacle of the congregation, and for all His service, and for the holy garments" (vv. 4-5, 21).

There was, however, one tragic event which marred the otherwise happy celebration, and that was the deaths of Nadab and Abihu, Aaron's two sons who were priests. They were killed by God for offering strange fire on the altar, probably while drunk (Lev. 10).

The purpose of the tabernacle. *To provide Israel with a visible center of worship: Here, in the holy of holies, God would meet with man above the blood-sprinkled mercy seat.

"And let them make Me a sanctuary: that I may dwell among them. . . . And they shall make an ark of shittim wood, two cubits and a half shall be the length thereof, and a cubit and a half the breadth thereof, and a cubit and a half the height thereof. . . . And thou shalt put the mercy seat above upon the ark; and in the ark thou shalt put the testimony that I shall give them. And there I will meet with them, and I will commune with thee from above the mercy seat, from between the two cherubim which are upon the ark of the testimony, of all things which I will give thee in commandment unto the Children of Israel" (Ex. 25:8, 10, 21-22).

*To preview the future work of Christ.

*To picture the entire program of salvation.

The census of the tabernacle. This was the first of two head counts during Israel's march from Egypt to Canaan. The second took place some 38 years later (Num. 26).

The arrangement of the tribes around the tabernacle (chap. 2). *Eastern location: Judah (Leader), Issachar, Zebulun.

*Western location: Ephraim (leader), Benjamin, Manasseh.

*Northern location: Dan (Leader), Asher, Naphtali.

*Southern location: Reuben (leader), Gad, Simeon.

The Nazarite vow of the tabernacle. There were three rules governing this religious vow.

(1) The person could not taste the fruit of the vine.

(2) He could not cut his hair.

(3) He could not come into contact with anything dead.

The great benediction of the tabernacle. *"And the* Lord *spake unto Moses, saying, 'Speak unto Aaron and unto his sons, saying, "On this wise ye shall bless the Children of Israel, saying unto them, 'The* Lord *bless thee, and keep thee; The* Lord *make His face shine upon thee, and be gracious unto thee, The* Lord *lift up His countenance upon thee, and give thee peace.'"*

"'And they shall put My name upon the Children of Israel; and I will bless them'" (6:22-27).

The offerings by the 12 tribal leaders to the tabernacle. God showed His personal interest here by recording (and repeating) each of the 12 gifts even though they were identical in nature.

The glory cloud of the tabernacle. *"And on the day that the tabernacle was reared up the cloud covered the tabernacle namely, the tent of the testimony, and at even there was upon the tabernacle as it were the appearance of fire, until the morning. So it was alway; the cloud covered it by day, and the appearance of fire by night.*

"And when the cloud was taken up from the tabernacle, then after that the Children of Israel journeyed; and in the place where the cloud abode, there the Children of Israel pitched their tents.

"At the commandment of the Lord *the Children of Israel journeyed, and at the commandment of the* Lord *they pitched; as long as the cloud abode upon the tabernacle they rested in their tents. And when the cloud tarried long upon the tabernacle many days, then the Children of Israel kept the charge of the* Lord*, and journeyed not.*

"And so it was, when the cloud was a few days

upon the tabernacle, according to the commandment of the LORD *they abode in their tents, and according to the commandment of the* LORD *they journeyed.*

"And so it was, when the cloud abode from even unto the morning, and that the cloud was taken up in the morning, then they journeyed, whether it was by day or by night that the cloud was taken up, they journeyed. Or whether it were two days, or a month, or a year, that the cloud tarried upon the tabernacle, remaining thereon, the Children of Israel abode in their tents, and journeyed not; but when it was taken up, they journeyed.

"At the commandment of the LORD *they rested in the tents, and at the commandment of the* LORD *they journeyed. They kept the charge of the* LORD*, at the commandment of the* LORD *by the hand of Moses" (9:15-23).*

The two silver trumpets of the tabernacle (Num. 10:1-9). They were to be blown on four special occasions.

(1) To gather the people for a meeting.
(2) To give warning in case of attack.
(3) When Israel itself would go to war.
(4) At Israel's appointed feasts.

Redeemed Israel Prepares to March

COMMENTS

The Book of Exodus begins with the Children of Israel in the worst bondage this world has known. God raised up a deliverer, led His people out of Egypt, gave them the Law, showed their inability to keep the Law, fed them on manna and quail, watered them with water from the rock, and finally led them to the dwelling place of God and the unlimited presence of God. Exodus ends on a note of joy because the work for God was finished, and they had done it God's way (40:16). By contrast, the best man can do was demonstrated by the debacle of the worship of the golden calf and the tragedy that it brought (cf. 32:1ff.). The Book of Exodus ends as the Bible ends—with God dwelling among men in the fullness of His glory. God longs for fellowship with man.

The Book of Numbers gets its name from the Septuagint in which it is called *arithmoi* (numbers)—after the censuses recorded in chapters 1 and 26. The Hebrew name for the book is, literally, "in the wild." The book records a journey which should have taken them about 40 days but which took them 40 years. The book is tragic, as demonstrated by the fact that they had 603,550 fighting men at the beginning (1:46) and 601,730 at the end (26:51).

The command to take the census (1:2) was something new in Israel's history. All males 20 years old and upward and able to go forth to war were to be numbered (v. 3). In Egypt they had been slaves, and God had fought their enemies for them. Now, they had been redeemed and were to do something to defend themselves. As with Israel, so it is with us. It is not until after we are saved that we can do anything for God. Prior to that time, He does it all for us.

The Nazarite (6:1ff.) was an unusual person, even in his own day. He was not a resident of Nazareth. The Nazarite vow was a voluntary vow. Some outstanding Nazarites in the Bible are Samson (cf. Jud. 13:5) and John the Baptist (cf. Luke 1:15). This explains some of the eccentricities of John the Baptist. The Nazarite's vows were three: (1) He was not to eat or drink anything from the vine. The fruit of the vine is indicative of joy. The Nazarite was to find his joy in the Lord and not in the world. (2) He was not to have his hair cut or his beard shaven. In the New Testament, long hair is a shame to a man (cf. 1 Cor. 11:14). The Nazarite was to be willing to bear shame for the Lord's sake. (3) He was not to make himself unclean at the death of members of his family. The Nazarite was willing to forsake father and mother in order to be separated unto the work and will of God (cf. Matt. 10:37).

The two silver trumpets (Num. 10:1-10) were used to call the people together for an assembly, to get them on the march, to call them to war, to announce solemn feasts, and to announce the beginning of the month. The trumpets were blown seven times to get the people on the march. The seven trumpets of Revelation (8:6) will move Israel into the place where God wants them at the beginning of the Millennium.

Preview

The Ultimate in Unbelief

NUMBERS 10–14

How long had they been there? In some ways it seemed an eternity. By actual count it was 11 months and five days. Now the Shekinah cloud of glory began moving once more. They followed as it headed north. Frankly, things had gone sour right from the very beginning. First, there was that terrible heavenly fire that fell, consuming some of them because of their constant complaining against both God and Moses. This was followed by another plague for the same sin. Would the people ever learn?

Even mighty Moses had allowed their defeatism to affect him, crying out, "I am not able to bear all this people alone, because it is too heavy for me."

Then both Aaron and Miriam got in on the act, as they suddenly turned on their own brother, Moses. Would it never end? After a march of 150 miles, the trip would end, but not the trouble.

In fact, at their destination, Kadesh-barnea, that bitter stream of unbelief which had begun its course after leaving Mount Sinai now became a surging and sullen river, completely carrying away with it an entire generation's hopes of entering Canaan's Promised Land.

Overview

<table>
<tr><td>SCRIPTURE</td><td colspan="6">Numbers 10–14</td></tr>
<tr><td>SUBJECT</td><td colspan="6">The journey from Sinai to Kadesh-barnea</td></tr>
<tr><td rowspan="3">SPECIFICS</td><td colspan="6">The death march</td></tr>
<tr><td rowspan="2">The route to Kadesh-barnea</td><td>The faithfulness of the Christ</td><td>The glory cloud directing
The glory cloud protecting</td><td rowspan="2">The rebellion at Kadesh-barnea</td><td>The sin</td><td>To reject the land of Canaan
To return to the land of Egypt</td></tr>
<tr><td>The faithlessness of the crowd</td><td>Defiance of the many
Disrespect of the two (Miriam and Aaron)
Despair of the one (Moses)</td><td>The sentence</td><td>All over 20 to dwell in the wilderness
All over 20 to die in the wilderness</td></tr>
<tr><td>SAINTS AND SINNERS</td><td colspan="6">Moses, Aaron, the mixed multitude, 70 elders, Miriam, Joshua, Caleb</td></tr>
<tr><td rowspan="2">SENTENCE SUMMARIES</td><td>O.T. Verses</td><td colspan="5">"Many times did He deliver them, but they provoked Him with their counsel, and were brought low for their iniquity. Nevertheless He regarded their affliction, when He heard their cry" (Ps. 106:43-44).</td></tr>
<tr><td>N.T. Verse</td><td colspan="5">"Harden not your hearts, as in the provocation, in the day of temptation in the wilderness" (Heb. 3:8).</td></tr>
</table>

SRAEL, FROM KADESH-BARNEA

MOBILIZING FOR THE MARCH (NUM. 10:11-28)

A balking brother-in-law (vv. 29-32). Moses unsuccessfully attempted to secure the scouting services of Hobab, his brother-in-law.

The cloud of the Covenant (vv. 33-36). "And they departed from the mount of the LORD *three days' journey. And the ark of the covenant of the* LORD *went before them in the three days' journey, to search out a resting place for them.*

"And the cloud of the LORD *was upon them by day, when they went out of the camp. And it came to pass, when the ark set forward, that Moses said, 'Rise up,* LORD, *and let Thine enemies be scattered, and let them that hate Thee flee before Thee.'*

"And when it rested, he said, 'Return, O LORD, *unto the many thousands of Israel' " (vv. 33-36).*

A fiery judgment (11:1-3). God's anger fell on them because of their sin of murmuring.

A malicious mixed multitude (vv. 4-9). "And the mixed multitude that was among them fell a lusting. And the Children of Israel also wept again, and said, 'Who shall give us flesh to eat? We remember the fish, which we did eat in Egypt freely, the cucumbers, and the melons, and the leeks, and the onions, and the garlic. But now our soul is dried away; there is nothing at all, beside this manna, before our eyes' " (vv. 4-6).

This group, consisting mainly of unsaved Egyptian band wagon jumpers caused Israel much trouble.

The complaint of Moses. "I am not able to bear all this people alone, because it is too heavy for me" (v. 14).

The grant of God. "And the LORD *came down in a cloud, and spake unto him, and took of the spirit that was upon him, and gave it unto the 70 elders" (v. 25).*

A deadly diet (vv. 31-35). Again judgment fell on those chronic complainers who spurned the manna and slaughtered quails for food.

A suffering sister (chap. 12). Both Aaron and Miriam criticized their younger brother Moses because of his wife and his strong leadership. Miriam (the ringleader) was struck with leprosy by God. At Aaron's request Moses prayed and Miriam's leprosy was cured.

THE PENETRATION BY THE SPIES AT KADESH-BARNEA

Their commission (13:1-20). Twelve men, one from each tribe, were to scout out the land of Canaan for 40 days. They were to check out the foes in the land. They were to bring back the fruit of the land.

Their mission (vv. 21-25).

THE LAMENTATION BY THE PEOPLE

The report of the 12 (vv. 26-33). The 10-man majority report (vv. 26-29, 31-33): *"We are not able to go up against the people, for they are stronger than we" (v. 31).*

The two-man minority report (v. 30; 14:6-9)—Joshua and Caleb: *"Let us go up at once, and possess it; for we are well able to overcome it" (13:30).*

The reaction of the crowd (14:1-10). "Would God that we had died in the land of Egypt!" (v. 2)

"Let us make a captain, and let us return into Egypt" (v. 4).

The crowd then threatened to stone both Joshua and Caleb.

THE CONDEMNATION BY THE LORD

Moses' prayer saved Israel from total divine judgment, but because of their constant unbelief (this episode marked the tenth time, v. 22), God pronounced the following judgment:

(1) No one over 20 (except Joshua and Caleb) would ever enter the land (v. 29).

(2) All Israel would wander 40 years in the wilderness (v. 34).

The 10 rebellions were:

(1) At the Red Sea (Ex. 14:11-12).

(2) At Marah (15:24).

(3) In the wilderness of Zin (16:2-3).

(4) At Rephidim (17:1-3).
(5) At Sinai (32:1-6).
(6) On route to Kadesh—three occasions (Num. 11:1-3, 4-9, 31-34).
(7) At Kadesh—two occasions (14:1-4, 10).

Redeemed Israel Moves Out

COMMENTS

After six months of preparation, Israel was ready to march (10:11). A typical day in the life of Israel during the 40 years of wandering went something like the following: (1) Moses and Aaron looked to see if the cloud had lifted. (2) If the cloud had lifted, Aaron went into the holy place and took down the veil which was dropped backward over the ark of the covenant. He also covered the other furniture (cf. chap. 4). (3) The sons of Kohath came to carry the tabernacle furniture. (4) Everyone packed and dismantled camp while the tabernacle was being dismantled. (5) The first trumpet sounded—Judah moved out under the standard of a lion. (6) The second trumpet sounded—Gershon moved out carrying part of the tabernacle. (7) The third trumpet sounded—Merari moved out carrying the remainder of the tabernacle. (8) The fourth trumpet sounded—Reuben moved out under the standard of a man. (9) The fifth trumpet sounded—the Kohathites moved out carrying the tabernacle furniture. (10) The sixth trumpet sounded—Ephraim moved out under the standard of an ox. (11) The seventh trumpet sounded—Dan moved out under the standard of a man. Every tribe and each man in Israel knew exactly where he belonged. It took seven trumpets to put Israel on the march. It will take seven trumpets to put Israel back into its land (cf. Rev. 8:6). (12) The mixed multitude fell in behind. They caused trouble in that day, just as they do today. They did not know where or to whom they belonged.

When Israel encamped the process was reversed. (1) The pillar of cloud stopped. (2) The ark stopped. (3) Judah moved around to the front. (5) Gershon and Merari set up the tabernacle. (6) Aaron set up the veil. (7) The Kohathites set up the furniture. (8) The Levites took off the covers. (9) The people set up camp. The whole process was well-rehearsed and could probably be done within an hour's time. They probably traveled about 10 miles a day. When the camp got ready to march, Moses pronounced the morning prayer (Num. 10:35). When Israel encamped, Moses pronounced the benediction (v. 36).

Predictably, problems beset Israel. The people complained after all God had done for them (11:11). Their problems were aggravated by the mixed multitude (v. 4) and the entire nation was affected. Three marks characterized the mixed multitude: (1) they were discontent and never satisfied, (2) they despised the manna, and (3) their destination was unknown. They never reached the Promised Land. They may have returned to Egypt or they may have died in the wilderness. The Scripture does not say what happened to them. They longed for things that grew on and under the ground. The things they wanted had little nourishment but were used to enhance other foods. They despised the perfect food of God that came down from above.

The discontent spread into Moses' family. His sister, Miriam, and brother, Aaron, were jealous of him and his strong leadership. God vindicated Moses (12:6-8), smote Miriam with leprosy (v. 10), and shut her out of camp for seven days (v. 14). Aaron was not smitten because he was the high priest, no leper could be high priest. He came to realize and confess his sin (v. 11).

At Kadesh-barnea the people had the opportunity to please God and enter into the land. They spied out the land thoroughly (13:21) and gave a factual report (vv. 27-28), but their fear caused them to look at the facts from the wrong perspective (v. 33). They were not able to enter into the land because of unbelief which grew into full-scale rebellion (14:1-10). Moses interceded for the people (vv. 13-19), in response to which God gave the prophecy concerning who would and who would not enter into the land (vv. 20-24). God sentenced the Israelites to wander in the wilderness 40 years (vv. 33-34) and slew the 10 spies who gave the false report (v. 37).

Preview

Forty Frustrating Years

NUMBERS 15–36

How to stretch a three-day trip into 40 years. These words pointedly and painfully describe Israel's aimless wanderings from Kadesh-barnea to Jordan's eastern bank. At Kadesh they stood at the very southern tip of the Promised Land. Even a few pounds of faith there would have prevented a ton of trouble during the following four decades. It began with a treacherous in-house rebellion led by Korah. Before the journey ended, both Miriam and Aaron were buried in the wilderness and Moses himself had forfeited his right to enter Canaan.

Then there were those vicious vipers. Suddenly they appeared everywhere. Never before had an entire nation faced destruction by deadly serpents. Needless to say, all these tragedies occurred because of Israel's sin. But all was not despair, darkness, and death during this time. God would keep His promise to lead the new generation into Canaan's land of milk and honey. In spite of sin, snakes, slander, and attempted seduction (at the hands of the false Prophet Balaam), Israel would prevail. Korah's rebellion was crushed, and the serpent problem solved by a brass object on a pole.

As the people neared the East Bank, light could be seen at the end of the tunnel. New opportunities lay just ahead, which required new leadership. Aaron and Moses were thus replaced by Eleazer and Joshua. The time had come. The torch was passed.

Overview

<table>
<tr><td>SCRIPTURE</td><td colspan="6">Numbers 15–36</td></tr>
<tr><td>SUBJECT</td><td colspan="6">The journey from Kadesh to the Eastern Bank of Jordan</td></tr>
<tr><td rowspan="7">SPECIFICS</td><td colspan="6">Forty fateful years</td></tr>
<tr><td colspan="3">The tragedies</td><td colspan="2">The troublemakers</td><td>The transitions</td></tr>
<tr><td>Family members who failed to enter Canaan</td><td colspan="2">Moses, Scripture's great lawgiver
Aaron, Scripture's first high priest
Miriam, Scripture's first prophetess</td><td colspan="2">A Sabbath-breaker
Korah
Some Edomites
Balaam</td><td>Phinehas succeeds Aaron
Joshua succeeds Moses</td></tr>
<tr><td colspan="2">The tabulation</td><td colspan="2">The triumph</td><td colspan="2">The types</td></tr>
<tr><td colspan="2" rowspan="2">Israel's second census</td><td colspan="2" rowspan="2">The victory over Midian</td><td colspan="2">Of carnal believers: the 2½ tribes</td></tr>
<tr><td colspan="2">Of Christ: Aaron's rod; Serpent of brass; 6 cities of salvation</td></tr>
<tr></tr>
<tr><td>SAINTS AND SINNERS</td><td colspan="6">Moses, Korah, Aaron, Miriam, Eleazar, Balaam, Balak, 2½ carnal tribes</td></tr>
<tr><td rowspan="2">SENTENCE SUMMARIES</td><td colspan="3">O.T. Verse</td><td colspan="3">"Yea, forty years didst Thou sustain them in the wilderness, so that they lacked nothing. Their clothes waxed not old, and their feet swelled not" (Neh. 9:21).</td></tr>
<tr><td colspan="3">N.T. Verse</td><td colspan="3">"But with whom was He grieved forty years? Was it not with them that had sinned, whose carcasses fell in the wilderness?" (Heb. 3:17)</td></tr>
</table>

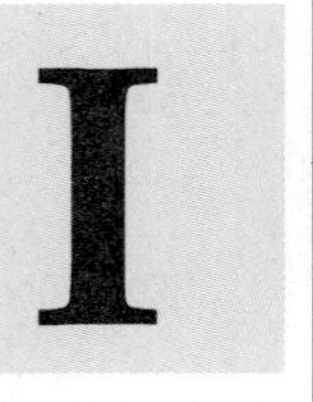

ISRAEL, FROM KADESH-BARNEA TO THE EASTERN BANK OF JORDAN

During this period of aimless wandering, the following events transpired:

THE STONING OF A SABBATH-BREAKER

This drastic action was necessary, lest absolute anarchy arise.

THE REBELLION AND DESTRUCTION OF KORAH

Korah, an influential levitical leader, instigated a revolt against the authority of Moses. This resulted in a divine judgment where the very ground opened up and swallowed Korah (Num. 16:31, 33). A later plague would kill 14,700 more of his followers (v. 49).

"And they gathered themselves together against Moses and against Aaron, and said unto them, 'Ye take too much upon you, seeing all the congregation are holy, every one of them, and the LORD is among them. Wherefore then lift ye up yourselves above the congregation of the LORD.' . . .

"And the earth opened her mouth, and swallowed them up, and their houses, and all the men that appertained unto Korah, and all their goods. They, and all that appertained to them, went down alive into the pit, and the earth closed upon them, and they perished from among the congregation" (16:3, 32-33).

THE BUDDING OF AARON'S ROD

To emphasize the authority God has invested in Aaron and Moses, He ordered the leaders from each tribe to place a rod in the tabernacle with his personal name inscribed on it. The next morning it was discovered that Aaron's rod had budded, was blossoming, and had ripe almonds hanging from it.

THE DEATH OF MIRIAM THE SIN OF MOSES

"And there was no water for the congregation; and they gathered themselves together against Moses and against Aaron. And the people chode with Moses, and spake, saying, 'Would God that we had died when our brethren died before the LORD! And why have ye brought up the congregation of the LORD into this wilderness, that we and our cattle should die there? And wherefore have ye made us to come up out of Egypt, to bring us in unto this evil place? It is no place of seed, or of figs, or of vines, or of pomegranates; neither is there any water to drink' " (20:2-5).

God instructed Moses to speak to a rock, that it might supernaturally give forth water. But instead Moses, partly due to unbelief and anger (the people were, as usual, on his back), screamed at the crowd and viciously struck the rock. The water gushed forth in spite of his unbelief, but he was told by God this sin would keep him from the Promised Land.

"And the LORD spake unto Moses and Aaron, 'Because ye believed Me not, to sanctify Me in the eyes of the Children of Israel, therefore ye shall not bring this congregation into the land which I have given them' " (v. 12).

THE ANIMOSITY OF THE EDOMITES

These people, descendants of Esau, refused to allow Israel to march through their land, thus forcing the people to trek an additional 180 miles through a hot and hostile desert.

THE DEATH OF AARON

God ordered Moses to strip Aaron of his priestly garments and place them upon his son, Eleazar. Aaron died at the age of 123 and was buried on Mount Hor.

THE SERPENT OF BRASS

God sent poisonous serpents to punish rebellious Israel. The people repented and a cure was provided by a brass serpent which was placed atop a pole where all could view it. Anyone thus bitten needed only to look on the serpent to be healed.

A PERVERTED PROPHET NAMED BALAAM

The preliminaries (Num. 22:1-14). Balak, the frightened king of Moab, offered Balaam, a pagan diviner from Mesopotamia, tempting riches if he would put a hex on the advancing Israelites and thus save Moab (vv. 1-8).

God warned Balaam not to accept this bribe (vv. 9-12). The offer was increased and Balaam agreed to go with Balak's men (22:15-21).

The prophecies (23:1–24:25). Balaam arrived in Moab and, looking down on Israel's armies in a nearby valley, attempted to curse them on four occasions. But in every case there proceeded from his mouth words of blessing, to his amazement and Balak's anger. These four blessings were as follows:

(1) First prophecy (23:1-10).

—That Israel would dwell alone and not be reckoned among the nations.

—That Israel's seed was to be as the dust of the earth.

(2) Second prophecy (vv. 11-26).

—That nothing could penetrate that divine defense which God had placed around Israel.

(3) Third prophecy (23:27–24:9).

—That Israel would be exalted as a kingdom.

—That Israel would eat up their enemies.

(4) Fourth prophecy (vv. 10-25). Concerning the Messiah Himself: *"I shall see Him, but not now: I shall behold Him, but not nigh. There shall come a Star out of Jacob, and a Scepter shall rise out of Israel" (v. 17).*

A ZEALOUS PRIEST

In spite of his failure to curse Israel, Balaam nearly succeeded in destroying that nation by craftily arranging for the Moabite women to sexually seduce the Israelite men (25:1; 31:16).

Phinehas, godly grandson of Aaron and priest of God, averted the full wrath of Almighty God by his drastic action in executing an especially brazen sexual couple, a prince from the tribe of Simeon and his harlot lover from Midian. In spite of this, 24,000 died (25:7-18).

THE SECOND CENSUS

The total of the second census was given as 601,730 (26:51). This census, about 38 years after the first (1:46) was 1,820 fewer. Not one individual was alive who was over 20 at the Kadesh rebellion except Moses, Caleb, and Joshua (26:64-65). The greatest decrease from the first census was in Simeon's tribe (37,100) and the greatest increase was in Manasseh (20,500).

A CHANGE IN COMMANDERS

Eleazar, the high priest, was instructed to lay hands on Joshua in a public ceremony, thus transferring Moses' authority over to him.

Joshua then became the new leader. Moses himself delivered the ordination address.

"Let the LORD, the God of the spirits of all flesh, set a man over the congregation, which may go out before them, and which may go in before them, and which may lead them out, and which may bring them in; that the congregation of the LORD be not as sheep which have no shepherd" (27:16-17).

THE DESTRUCTION OF MIDIAN

The attack (31:1-6).

The battle (vv. 7-18).

The purification (vv. 19-24).

The spoils (vv. 25-54). "And Moses and Eleazar the priest took the gold of the captains of thousands and of hundreds, and brought it into the tabernacle of the congregation, for a memorial for the Children of Israel before the LORD" (v. 54).

SOME WORLDLY WARRIORS

The Reubenites, Gadites, and half-tribe of Manasseh, came to Moses and asked permission to settle in Gilead, an area east of Palestine, just across the Jordan River. Moses sadly issued the requested permission providing these two and one-half tribes would cross over with the remaining tribes and help defeat the Canaanites. To this they agreed.

SIX CITIES OF SALVATION

These cities were: on the eastern side of Jordan—Bezer, Golan, and Ramoth. On the western side (in Palestine itself—Kedesh, Shechem, and Hebron (Num. 35:10-14; Deut. 4:43; Josh. 20:7-9). These 6 were part of the 48 cities given to the Levites who did not receive a regular section of land as did the other tribes when the land was later divided by Joshua. The 6 cities were designated as refuge for all accidental manslayers to avoid the dead man's avenging relatives. The manslayer was safe as long as he remained in one of these cities until the death of the high priest, at which time he could safely return home (Num. 35:25-28).

Redeemed Israel Wanders

COMMENTS

Because of its sin of unbelief and failing to enter into the Promised Land, Israel was sentenced to wander in the wilderness one year for every day the spies were in the land, or for 40 years (cf. 14:34). This was a "death sentence" for that unbelieving generation. In those years, their walking became wandering; their marching became mourning; and their witnessing became wailing. If one were to choose an occupation during those 40 years, the most profitable one he could have chosen would have been an undertaker. In those 40 years there were between 70 and 100 (and perhaps even more) funerals every day until everyone of that unbelieving generation had died off except for Caleb and Joshua. Paul used this generation of Israel as examples of what it meant to be a "castaway" (cf. 1 Cor. 9:27–10:6). Their carcasses littered the wilderness in mute testimony of their unbelief and failure—after having been redeemed by God out of Egypt. During the wilderness wanderings Israel continually committed at least three gross sins before God: (1) They did not circumcise their children (cf. Josh. 5:5-6)—further testimony of their unbelief. (2) They did not offer sacrifices at the tent of the tabernacle (cf. Jer. 7:22-26; Amos 5:25-26). They worshiped idols in the wilderness (cf. vv. 25-26; Acts 7:42).

Some notable examples of Israel's sinning are seen in Korah's rebellion (Num. 16), the jealousy over Aaron's priesthood (chap. 17), the red heifer offering which seems to have been instituted as atonement for a particularly gross sin (chap. 19), the sin of Moses in striking the rock twice (chap. 20), and the murmuring of the people and the fiery serpents (chap. 21). God dealt with Korah in kind. He had caused division in the camp; God caused him to be swallowed up by a division in the ground (16:31). God established Aaron by causing his rod alone to bud—a picture of the resurrection. The rod had no life in it, but it was raised to life again (17:8). The red heifer sacrifice was shown to be particularly severe because the priest that offered it was unclean until evening (19:20-22). This sacrifice ceased to be offered once Israel was in the land. Moses' sin was not in the fact that he smote the rock twice (20:11) but that he smote it even once. He was just to speak to the rock (v. 8). It had been smitten before when they were at this place 37 years earlier.

The severity of Moses' sin is made known to us by Paul (cf. 1 Cor. 10:4). That rock was God's picture of Christ who was to be smitten only *once* (cf. 1 Peter 3:18). God is always careful to protect that which speaks of Christ. It was the death sentence for Moses. Murder did not keep Moses out of the Promised Land; his anger did. Because of his sin he was not permitted to bring the people of Israel into their land (Num. 20:12).

The brazen serpent was the remedy for the fiery serpents which bit the people in punishment for their murmuring against Moses and God (21:4-6). To these people God for the first time revealed the message of the Cross (v. 9). Jesus, in commenting on this incident drew the parallel between Moses' lifting up the brazen serpent and His own crucifixion (cf. John 3:14-15).

With their arrival on the plains of Moab (Num. 22:1) the geographical movement of the people ceased until Joshua's day. Balaam was hired by the king of Moab to prophesy against Israel. He would have done so if he could (23:23), but God controlled him so that he gave four wonderful prophecies concerning Israel. God honors His word—never the man. Balaam had the truth, but the truth did not have him.

Chapters 26–36 are concerned with the new generation. A new census was taken. The nation suffered a net loss of 1,820 in the 40 years of wilderness wanderings. The tribes more involved in rebellion were more severely decimated than the others.

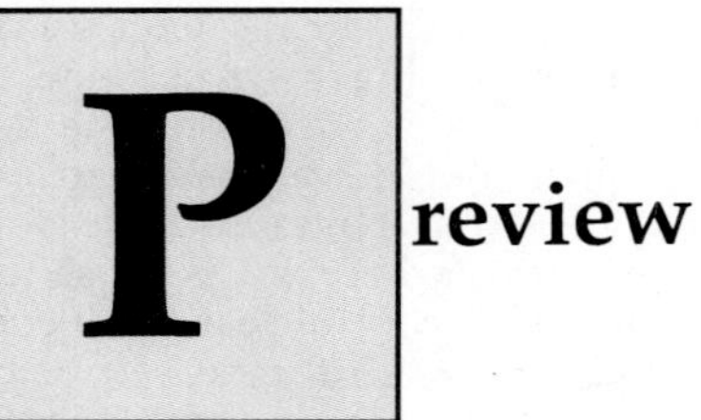

Preview

Moses Preaching to His Sheep

DEUTERONOMY 1–30

Never had they heard him speak with such unction and urgency. There he stood in their midst, the Jordan River flowing in the valley below. What a man he was. What a message he now delivered. Yet there was a note of sadness in his voice. Most in the crowd knew the reason for this. It certainly was no secret. In fact, he would mention it himself, explaining the reason behind it. Yes, it was true: Moses would not be allowed to enter the Promised Land. And the reason? A previous hour marked by anger and unbelief had caused it all. He too would soon join the old generation whose graves already dotted the desert area to the south and east of Canaan. This was the source of his sadness. But his urgency came from simply viewing his audience. There they were, a new generation, unspotted by the failures of their fathers, but also untested by their foes.

How would they fare? Were these sons and daughters made of better stuff than their parents? He could only preach to and pray for them. One thing was certain—their awareness of and obedience to the Word of God was absolutely vital to any and all future victories.

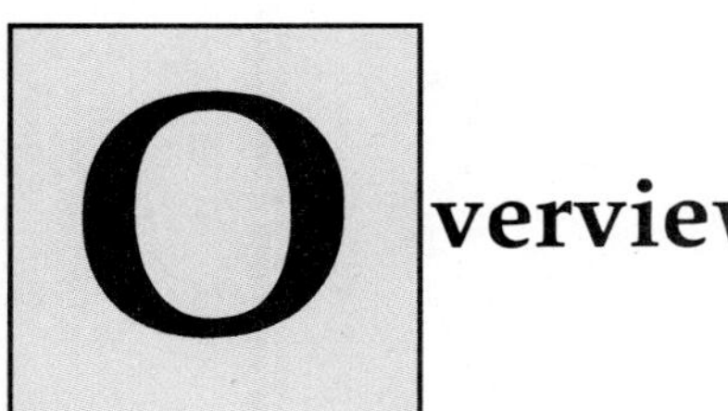verview

SCRIPTURE	Deuteronomy 1–30
SUBJECT	Moses' final days—part 1
SPECIFICS	Final messages of the man of God **First sermon** A review: Of the splendor at Sinai / Of the sin at Kadesh Israel's sin of apostasy Moses' sin of anger A resolution: To encourage Joshua / To elevate Joshua **Second sermon** Repetition: Of the Law of God Reminder: Of their giving obligations Reflection: Of His meeting with God at Sinai Restraint: Warnings against: Immorality / Idolatry / Indifference **Third sermon** A challenge Reading of the Law: Blessings to be read from Mt. Gerizin / Curses to be read from Mt. Ebal A covenant: The sevenfold Palestinian Covenant A Choice: Life or death
SAINTS AND SINNERS	Moses
SENTENCE SUMMARIES	O.T. Verse: "Thou hast commanded us to keep Thy precepts diligently" (Ps. 119:4). N.T. Verse: "Beginning at Moses and all the prophets, we expounded unto them in all the Scriptures the things concerning Himself" (Luke 24:27).

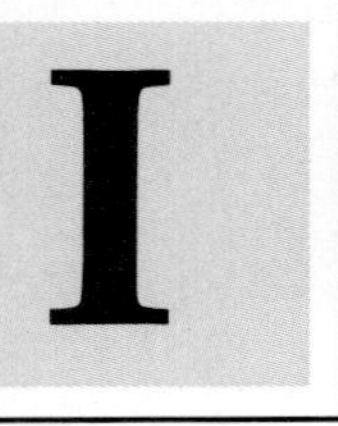

SRAEL, ON THE EASTERN SIDE OF THE RIVER JORDAN

On the banks of the Jordan Moses delivered three sermons to Israel, issued a challenge to Joshua, pronounced a blessing on the individual tribes, composed a song, and departed for heaven.

HIS THREE SERMONS

First sermon. He related the splendor of God they had experienced while at Mount Sinai (Deut. 4:10-19, 32-33).

"Did ever people hear the voice of God speaking out of the midst of the fire, as thou hast heard, and live? Or hath God assayed to go and take Him a nation from the midst of another nation, by temptations, by signs, and by wonders, and by war, and by a mighty hand, and by a stretched out arm, and by great terrors, according to all that the LORD your God did for you in Egypt before your eyes?

"Unto thee it was showed, that thou mightest know that the LORD He is God; there is none else beside Him. Out of heaven He made thee to hear His voice, that He might instruct thee; and upon earth He showed thee His great fire; and thou heardest His words out of the midst of the fire" (vv. 33-36).

He reviewed their tragic sin at Kadesh-barnea (1:27).Thus a trip that should have taken but 11 days (from Mount Sinai to Canaan) actually took some 38 years (v. 2).

He reminded them of his own sin which would keep him from the Promised Land (3:23-27; 4:21-22). See also 31:2.

He urged Israel to encourage their new leader Joshua (1:38; 3:28). See also 31:7-8, 23.

He set apart the three eastern cities of refuge (4:41-43).

Second sermon. The Ten Commandments were repeated (5:7-21). A warning was issued against immorality (23:17), compromise (7:1-5), and witchcraft (18:9-14).

Moses gave a description of Canaan.

"For the LORD thy God bringeth thee into a good land, a land of brooks of water, of fountains and depths, that spring out of the valleys and hills; a land of wheat, and barley, and vines, and fig trees, and pomegranates; a land of oil olive, and honey" (8:7-8).

He reviewed his personal experiences with God while on Mount Sinai (9:9-21).

He reminded them of their financial obligations to God (chap. 26).

"And it shall be, when thou art come in unto the land which the Lord *thy God giveth thee for an inheritance, and possessest it, and dwellest therein; that thou shalt take of the first of all the fruit of the earth, which thou shalt bring of thy land that the* Lord *thy God giveth thee, and shalt put it in a basket, and shalt go unto the place which the* Lord *thy God shall choose to place His name there. . . .*

"And the priest shall take the basket out of thine hand, and set it down before the altar of the Lord *thy God" (vv. 1-2, 4).*

Laws concerning clothing (22:5), divorce (24:1-4), women's rights (21:10-17; 22:13-20), and warfare (chap. 20) were given.

He summarized God's overall purpose and plan for that generation of Israelites.

"And He brought us out from thence [Egypt] that He might bring us in [Canaan]" (6:23).

Third sermon. He ordered the blessings and judgments (curses) of the Law to be read by the Levites on two mountains when Israel entered the Promised Land. The blessings were to be read on Mount Gerizim, and the curses on Mount Ebal. See 11:26-29; 27:1-14.

*The blessings: *"And it shall come to pass, if thou shalt hearken diligently unto the voice of the* Lord *thy God, to observe and to do all His commandments which I command thee this day, that the* Lord *thy God will set them on high above all nations of the earth. . . .*

"The Lord *shall command the blessing upon thee in thy storehouses, and in all that thou settest thine hand unto; and He shall bless thee in the land which the* Lord *thy God giveth thee. The* Lord *shall establish thee a holy people unto Himself, as He hath sworn unto thee, if thou shalt keep the commandments of the* Lord *thy God, and walk in His ways.*

"And all the people of the earth shall see that thou art called by the name of the Lord*; and they shall be afraid of thee" (vv. 1, 7-10).*

*The curses: *"But it shall come to pass, if thou wilt not hearken unto the voice of the* Lord *thy God, to observe to do all His commandments and His statutes which I command thee this day; that all these curses shall come upon thee, and overtake thee. . . .*

"The Lord *shall cause thee to be smitten before thine enemies; thou shalt go out one way against them, and flee seven ways before them; and shalt be removed into all the kingdoms of the earth. . . . And thou shalt become an astonishment, a proverb, and a byword, among all nations whither the* Lord *shall lead thee. . . .*

"And among these nations shalt thou find no ease, neither shall the sole of thy foot have rest. But the Lord *shall give thee there a trembling heart, and failing of eyes and sorrow of mind. And thy life shall hang in doubt before thee; and thou shalt fear day and night, and shalt have none assurance of thy life. In the morning thou shalt say, 'Would God it were even!' And at even thou shalt say, 'Would God it were morning!' For the fear of thine heart wherewith thou shalt fear, and for the sight of thine eyes which thou shalt see" (vv. 15, 25, 37, 65-67).*

Chapters 28–30 record the features of the Palestinian Covenant. It is in seven parts.

(1) Israel was to be dispersed for disobedience (28:36, 49-53, 63-68; 30:1). This took in the Assyrian, Babylonian, and Roman captivities, in addition to Israel's trials during the past 20 centuries. It would almost seem that Moses had Hitler's armies in mind when he wrote 28:64-67. During this time Israel would become a byword (v. 37), and be the tail instead of the head (compare v. 13 with v. 44).

(2) Israel will repent while in dispersion (30:2).

(3) The return of Christ will occur. *"That then the* Lord *thy God will turn thy captivity, and have compassion upon thee, and will return and gather thee from all the nations, whither the* Lord *thy God hath scattered thee" (v. 3).*

(4) Israel will be restored to the land. *"And the* Lord *thy God will bring thee into the land which thy fathers possessed, and thou shalt possess it; and He will do thee good, and multiply thee above thy fathers" (v. 5).*

(5) The nation will receive a new heart (v. 6).

(6) Israel's oppressors will be judged (v. 7).

(7) The nation will experience prosperity (v. 9).

(8) Moses offered his generation a choice between God's judgment or blessing (vv. 15-20). *"See, I have set before thee this day life and good, and death and evil. . . . I call heaven and earth to record this day against you, that I have set before you life and death, blessing and cursing. Therefore choose life, that both thou and thy seed may live" (vv. 15, 19).*

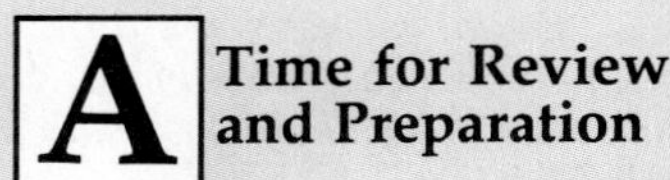

A Time for Review and Preparation

COMMENTS

Moses wrote the Book of Deuteronomy about 1451 B.C. In spite of its ancient date, the Book of Deuteronomy is amazingly up to date and even ahead of our time. Any other writing of equal age would simply be an object of scholarly scrutiny without any practical relevance for the present day.

The Book of Deuteronomy was necessitated by the facts that: (1) A new generation had arisen which did not witness the original giving of the Law at Mount Sinai. (2) The new generation was about to enter a new land which was filled with idolatry and its degenerated practices. (3) The new generation was going to assume a new role with new responsibilities in their new land—they had grown up as wandering nomads and now were going to dwell in established cities.

In the Hebrew Bible Deuteronomy is called "these are the words" (the first two words of the Hebrew text). In the English Bible, Deuteronomy gets its name from the Septuagint and means, literally "A second law," which is not technically correct. The book is really a review of the past and a preparation for the future. During the 40 years of experience with the Law since its giving at Mount Sinai, the generation that received it had died off, except for Moses, Joshua, and Caleb. Moses knew that he would soon die (4:21-22). The parents of the new generation had not taught them the Law (as indicated by the fact that the males were not circumcised, cf. Josh. 5:5-7). The events of Deuteronomy occurred one month before Israel was to enter into the Promised Land (Deut. 1:3). For this new generation, Moses reviewed the provision of the Law given 40 years earlier. The new generation needed to be taught the Law and have it applied in specific instances. For this new generation, none of whom were over 60 and the majority of whom were under 40, Moses personally gave instruction. The new generation had taken their parents' places and had assumed the burden of the Law. They needed to know the implications of that assumption. The instruction took place "on this side Jordan" (vv. 1-5)—the eastern bank in the land of Moab.

That the Book of Deuteronomy is a powerful spiritual book is seen by the fact that our Lord used it at least three times to meet the direct attacks of Satan (cf. 8:3; 6:13, 16 with Matt. 4:4, 7, 10). Jesus and the apostles quoted or alluded to it at least 90 times. The Old Testament prophets also quoted it many times.

The Book of Deuteronomy puts great emphasis on the Word of God. It is the Psalm 119 of the Pentateuch. Moses stressed obedience to the Word of God in practically every chapter. In a way, Deuteronomy is Moses' change of command ceremony. Before he gave the new generation of Israel over to Joshua's command he reviewed the Law and used Israel's deliverance from Egyptian bondage as a motive for obeying God.

The best preparation for the future is to look to the past for lessons to be learned so as not to repeat the errors of the preceding generation. The word "remember" occurs some 18 times in the course of the book. Moses caused them to remember: (1) the memorable day at Mount Sinai when God gave them the Law (Deut. 4:9-10); (2) the covenant God gave them (v. 23); (3) the past slavery from which they had been delivered (5:6); (4) God's judgment on Egypt (7:18-19); (5) God's care for His people (8:2-6); (6) their sin of rebellion (9:7); (7) the plague of leprosy (24:8-9); and (8) their call as the chosen people of God (32:7-9).

Moses never made it into the Promised Land until the New Testament at the time of the Transfiguration (cf. Matt. 17:3) and of course he, together with all Old Testament saints (cf. Heb. 11:39) will realize all of God's promises to Israel when the Old Testament saints are resurrected prior to the Millennium (cf. Dan. 12:2). True to the message of Deuteronomy, God always keeps His Word.

Moses Preparing for His Shepherd

DEUTERONOMY 28–34

Much yet remained to be done, in a little time. Joshua needed to be challenged, the tribes had to be blessed, and Moses' writings, begun some 40 years prior, had to be completed. This last task was especially important, for future generations must know God's story thus far, beginning with Adam up to the present moment. For some reason, God had selected him to write down that material. Others would no doubt add to the divine account after his death here on Mount Nebo. But above all else Moses simply had to clearly communicate the Lord's greatness and glory to that new generation. Unless they could appreciate and appropriate His person and power, then, in a real sense of the word, all the trials and triumphs of the past 40 years would be of no permanent avail.

But Moses simply could not and would not allow that to happen. In three moving sermons he expounded to the people in brief but bold phrases the majesty of God, particularly emphasizing His faithfulness, love, glory, and grace. He then warned them of God's terrible judgment that would fall on them like an angry rainstorm if they rebelled against Him. On this sober note Moses finished. His message had been favorably received. He could tell. After one final glimpse at Canaan's fair land from Pisgah's lofty heights, he was gone. God had taken him to a greener and fairer land.

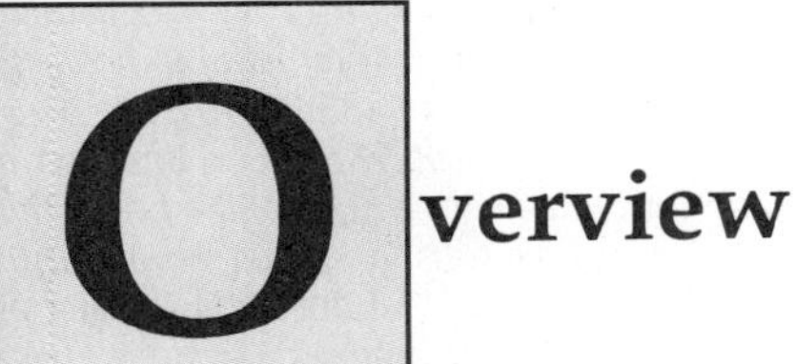

Overview

SCRIPTURE	Deuteronomy 28–34
SUBJECT	Moses' final days—part 2

SPECIFICS						
	The LORD of Israel	His person	His precepts	The lawgiver of Israel	Challenging	Composing
		Faithfulness Love Glory Grace	The Word of God		The new leader Joshua	His song of praise
		His prophecies	His plan		Completing	Conferring
		Concerning Israel's rulers Concerning Israel's Redeemer	That Israel be true to Him That Israel be gathered by Him		The Penta-teuch	A final blessing on the tribes
					"So Moses the servant of the LORD died"	

SAINTS AND SINNERS	Moses

SENTENCE SUMMARIES		
	O.T. Verse	"Thy Word is a lamp unto my feet, and a light unto my path" (Ps. 119:105).
	N.T. Verse	"Moses . . . said unto the Children of Israel, 'A prophet shall the Lord your God raise up unto you of your brethren, like unto me; him shall ye hear' " (Acts 7:37).

OSES' THREE SERMONS

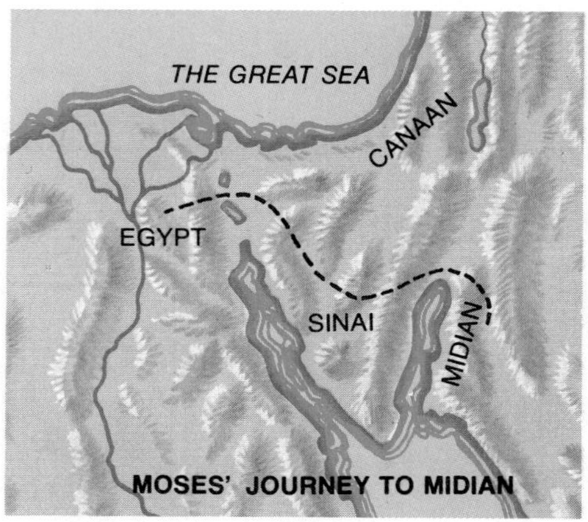

MOSES' JOURNEY TO MIDIAN

Before Israel entered the Promised Land, they gathered to hear Moses for a final time. During these sermons Moses expounded on the following great theological themes.

The faithfulness of God (Deut. 2:7; 4:33-38; 7:6-8; 8:3-4; 9:4-6; 29:5-6; 32:9-14). They had lacked nothing for 40 years (2:7); both food and clothing had been provided (8:3-4; 29:5-6); He cared for Israel as an eagle cared for its own (32:9-14). He did all this in spite of their constant sin (9:4-6).

The Word of God (4:1-2, 9; 11:18-21; 30:11-14). (1) Do not add to it or take away from it (4:1-2); (2) Teach it to your sons and daughters (v. 9; 11:19-20). *"And ye shall teach them your children, speaking of them when thou sittest in thine house, and when thou walkest by the way, when thou liest down, and when thou risest up. And thou shalt write them upon the door posts of thine house, and upon thy gates" (vv. 19-20).*

(3) Meditate on it personally. "Therefore shall ye lay up these My words in your heart and in your soul, and bind them for a sign upon your hand, that they may be as frontlets between your eyes" (v. 18).

The person of God (6:4-5; 7:9; 32:39-43). "Hear, O Israel: the LORD our God is one LORD. And thou shalt love the LORD thy God with all thine heart, and with all thy soul, and with all thy might" (6:4-5).

"See now that I, even I, am He, and there is no god with Me. I kill, and I make alive, I wound, and I heal; neither is there any that can deliver out of My hand. For I lift up My hand to heaven, and say, 'I live forever' " (32:39-40).

The love of God (7:6-8, 13). "For thou art a holy people unto the LORD thy God; the LORD thy God hath chosen thee to be a special people unto Himself, above all people that are upon the face of the earth. The LORD did not set His love upon you, nor choose you, because ye were more in number than any people; for ye were the fewest of all people.

"But because the LORD loved you, and because He would keep the oath which He had sworn unto your fathers, hath the LORD brought you out with a mighty hand, and redeemed you out of the house of bondmen, from the hand of Pharaoh king of Egypt" (vv. 6-8).

The glory of God (4:39; 10:17-18).

The grace of God (7:6-9; 9:4-6). "Speak not thou in thine heart, after that the LORD thy God hath cast them out from before thee, saying, 'For my righteousness the LORD hath brought me in to possess this land'; but for the wickedness of these nations the LORD doth drive them out from before thee.

"Not for thy righteousness, or for the uprightness of thine heart, dost thou go to possess their land; but for the wickedness of these nations the LORD thy God doth drive them out from before thee, and that he may perform the word which the Lord sware unto thy fathers, Abraham, Isaac, and Jacob.

"Understand therefore, that the LORD thy God giveth thee not this good land to possess it for thy righteousness; for thou art a stiffnecked people" (vv. 4-6).

The coming great Prophet of God (18:15-19). "The LORD thy God will raise up unto thee a Prophet from the midst of thee, of thy brethren, like unto Me; unto Him ye shall hearken. . . . And it shall come to pass, that whosoever will not hearken unto My words which He shall speak in My name, I will require it of him" (vv. 15, 19).

The will of God (10:12-16). "And now, Israel, what doth the LORD thy God require of thee, but to fear the LORD thy God, to walk in all His ways, and to love Him, and to serve the LORD thy God with all thy heart and with all thy soul. To keep the commandments of the LORD, and His statutes, which I command thee this day for thy good?" (vv. 12-13)

The kings of God (17:14-20). (1) They were not to multiply to themselves wives, gold, or horses (vv. 15-20).

(2) They were to be diligent students of God's Word (vv. 15-20).

The Israel of God (4:25-31; 11:16-17).

(1) To be scattered for unbelief.

"And the LORD shall scatter you among the nations, and ye shall be left few in number among the heathen, whither the LORD shall lead you" (4:27).

(2) To be kept nevertheless through tribulation.

(3) To repent and be gathered back into the land.

"When thou art in tribulation, and all these things are come upon thee, even in the latter days, if thou turn to the LORD *thy God, and shalt be obedient unto His voice; (For the* LORD *thy God is a merciful God) He will not forsake thee, neither destroy thee, nor forget the covenant of thy fathers which He sware unto them" (vv. 30-31).*

Israel's Shema

COMMENTS

If you were to go to a Jewish synagogue for a Sabbath Eve's service, the first item of worship would be for the congregation to stand and recite in unison and in Hebrew the words of Deuteronomy 6:4, "Hear, O Israel: The LORD our God is one LORD." The Jews refer to this verse by the first word in the Hebrew text, *Shema* (shi-mah). Israel's Shema is the most important single revelation that God ever gave concerning Himself. In this short verse God revealed three important facts about Himself.

The first fact that God revealed about Himself is *His eternality*. Note first, "The LORD." Whenever the name of God occurs in the English text written all in capital and small capital letters (LORD), the name in the Hebrew text is YHWH (Yahweh or Jehovah). To the Jews the name was so sacred that they would not even pronounce it. Instead they read another name in its place, Adonai (Lord/Master). God's name, YHWH, is actually the third person singular of the verb "to be" and properly could be translated, "The One who was, the One who is, and the One who is to come." In his translation of the Old Testament, Moffatt properly translates the name, "The Eternal." YHWH is actually man's name for God. God's name for Himself is I AM (EHYH, cf. Ex. 3:14). Man's name for God merely affirms what God's name says about Himself—He is eternal.

The second fact that God revealed about Himself is *His plurality*. If we were to translate Deuteronomy 6:4 very literally, it would read, "Hear, O Israel: The LORD our Gods is one LORD." The word "God" is actually plural, "Gods" (*Elohim*). Throughout Scripture there is a frequent grammatical disjuncture that strikes a discordant grammatical note whenever this name for God occurs—it is the use of a plural subject with a singular verb. In Genesis 1:1, for example, the text literally reads, "In the beginning Gods create. . . . " Some grammarians would explain this simply as the plural of majesty and say it should be considered grammatically as if it were a singular noun. The fact remains that the name Elohim is plural and agrees perfectly with the fact that YHWH eternally exists in three Persons, Father, Son, and Holy Spirit. Just as it takes three elements to have a fire—fuel, sufficient temperature, and adequate oxygen—so it takes three Persons to make one God. A fire can be put out in one of three ways: remove the fuel, reduce the temperature, or remove the oxygen. In a similar way, if any one of the Persons of the Godhead is removed, God ceases to exist. There is no Jehovah without the Son and the Spirit. There is no God the Son without the Father and the Spirit. Those who deny the existence of any one Person of the Godhead have no God at all.

The third fact that God reveals about Himself is *His unity*. There are two Hebrew words translated by the English word, "one." They are *echad* and *yachid*. The first word occurs in Deuteronomy 6:4, "Hear, O Israel: The LORD our God is one LORD." The second word occurs in Genesis 22:2, "Take now thy son, thine only son Isaac." *Echad* is the "one" of plurality. *Yachid* is the "one" of uniqueness. *Echad* occurs in Genesis 2:24, "Therefore shall a man leave his father and his mother, and shall cleave unto his wife: and they shall be one flesh." Here are two who are one. In the Godhead, there are three who are one—one Lord.

In Deuteronomy 6:4, then, Jehovah revealed to Israel that He is the only God eternally existing in three Persons. A Jew should have realized the truth of the Trinity for as he read the Scripture he came to know God (Gen. 1:1), the Angel of the Lord (16:7), and the Spirit of God (1:2)—these three comprising the one YHWH.

HIS CHALLENGES TO JOSHUA

"And Moses called unto Joshua, and said unto him in the sight of all Israel, 'Be strong and of a good courage, for thou must go with this people unto the land which the LORD hath sworn unto their fathers to give them; and thou shalt cause them to inherit it. And the LORD, He it is that doth go before thee; He will be with thee; He will not fail thee, neither forsake thee. Fear not, neither be dismayed' " (Deut. 31:7-8).

HIS SONG

"Give ear, O ye heavens, and I will speak; and hear, O earth, the words of my mouth. . . .

"Because I will publish the name of the LORD; ascribe ye greatness unto our God. He is the Rock, His work is perfect; for all His ways are judgment. A God of truth and without iniquity, just and right is He" (32:1, 3-4).

"For the LORD's portion is His people; Jacob is the lot of His inheritance. He found him in a desert land, and in the waste howling wilderness. He led him about, He instructed him, He kept him as the apple of His eye. As an eagle stirreth up her nest, fluttereth over her young, spreadest abroad her wings, taketh them, beareth them on her wings" (vv. 9-11).

At this time Moses also completed the Pentateuch (first five books of the Bible). (See 31:9, 24.)

HIS BLESSINGS ON THE INDIVIDUAL TRIBES

"And this is the blessing, wherewith Moses the man of God blessed the children of Israel before his death. And he said, 'The LORD came from Sinai, and rose up from Seir unto them; He shined forth from Mount Paran, and He came with ten thousands of saints. From His right hand went a fiery law for them. Yea, He loved the people; all His saints are in Thy hand; and they sat down at Thy feet; every one shall receive of Thy words" (33:1-3).

HIS DEPARTURE FOR HEAVEN

"And Moses went up from the plains of Moab unto the mountain of Nebo, to the top of Pisgah, that is over against Jericho. And the LORD showed him all the land of Gilead, unto Dan. . . .

"And the LORD said unto him, 'This is the land which I swore unto Abraham, unto Isaac, and unto Jacob, saying, "I will give it unto thy seed." I have caused thee to see it with thine eyes, but thou shalt not go over thither.'

"So Moses the servant of the LORD died there in the land of Moab, according to the word of the LORD. And He buried him in a valley in the land of Moab, over against Beth-peor: but no man knoweth of his sepulchre unto this day. . . .

"And there arose not a prophet since in Israel like unto Moses, whom the LORD knew face to face. In all the signs and the wonders, which the LORD sent him to do in the land of Egypt to Pharaoh, and to all his servants, and to all this land. And in all that mighty hand, and in all the great terror which Moses showed in the sight of all Israel" (34:1, 4-6, 10-12).

Two Covenants—Man's and God's

COMMENTS

Deuteronomy 24:1-4 is frequently cited by those who would seek scriptural support for the breaking of man's covenant—marriage. Moses, however, was not seeking to give scriptural support for dissolving the marital union but rather recognized the reality of divorce. Man would seek some way to get out of his obligation to his wife and so Moses sought to give some guidelines whereby the practice could be controlled so that divorce would not become rampant. This was the purpose of all the Mosaic Laws—to provide an orderly way by which man might conduct himself in his dealings with his fellowman.

In their controversy with Jesus, the Pharisees misused Deuteronomy 24:1 (as do most ministers and counselors today). The Pharisees had an "axe to grind" and they were seeking to trap Jesus (cf. Matt. 19:3). Jesus clearly taught that man was to cleave to his wife and that they must not be put asunder (cf. vv. 4-6). The Pharisees cited Deuteronomy 24:1 as proving that Moses taught divorce was permissible while Jesus was teaching no divorce (cf. Matt. 19:7). Jesus then explained the apparent contradiction by pointing out Moses' motive in making the provision. It was because of "the hardness of your hearts" that Moses "suffered [permitted] you to put away your wives" (v. 8). Jesus then added that "from the beginning it was not so." In other words, Moses sought to regulate divorce to keep it from getting out of hand. However, if one got a divorce—even on scriptural (Mosaic) grounds—it was because his heart was hard. There is no such thing as getting a divorce for "spiritual" reasons. The Pharisees got the point—they were defeated and departed. Deuteronomy 24:1-4, then, does not advocate divorce but rather was an accommodation to the hard-hearted Israelites so that their unspiritual practice remained the exception rather than becoming the rule.

Chapters 28–30 tell us about God's covenant with Israel which guarantees them their land forever. The Palestinian Covenant combines the characteristics of a conditional covenant and the characteristics of an unconditional covenant. It is important to see its two separate parts. Chapters 28–29 are conditional in nature. They relate to the Israel of Moses' day. Blessings are promised to Israel if they obey and cursings will come on them if they disobey. Israel disobeyed and even up to the present day is experiencing the curses and punishments that God prescribed (28:15-68). God has temporarily set the nation Israel aside and is working through the church. When His program for the church is complete, it will be removed (1 Cor. 15:51-58; 1 Thes. 4:13-18). Then, God will resume His program with Israel. After the judgments of the Great Tribulation, Jesus will return to the earth, set up His kingdom, and reign over Israel and the world for 1,000 years (cf. Rev. 20:1-7). At this time, the provisions of the Palestinian Covenant prescribed in Deuteronomy 30:1-9 will be realized. This aspect of the Palestinian Covenant is unconditional and applies to the Israel of the Millennium. It is at that time that Israel will be given forever the land for which they looked in Moses' day. In Moses' day Israel enjoyed only a partial realization of all that God had promised.

Failure to discern between these two parts of the Palestinian Covenant has caused some to conclude, erroneously, that because of Israel's disobedience God has revoked His promises to them and is fulfilling them spiritually in the church. It has also caused some to understand that the Israel of today is receiving the fulfillment of verses 1-9. The Israel of today does not figure in the Palestinian Covenant at all for it will be regathered and will experience the fulfillment of verses 1-9 (cf. Matt. 24:29-31).

Conquest

It was April 1405 B.C. Two men stood quietly beside a flowing body of water. Both were deep in thought, as they remembered a former April, standing beside a different body of water some 800 miles and 40 years removed. So much had happened since that time. In fact, of their entire generation, they alone had survived.

So far, so good. But what would happen now?

The names of these two men were Joshua and Caleb. The body of water they now stood by was the Jordan River. The former body was the Red Sea. But again the question—what of the future? Would God's faithfulness sustain the present generation as it had the previous one? It would indeed. The Jordan waters would roll back and the Jericho wall would fall down. In fact, before it ended the sun itself would stand still.

In three brilliant and brief campaigns the land was subdued. Beginning with a central attack, which separated their enemies, the victorious Israelites quickly moved south, and then completed the mopping-up exercises in the north. For the most part, the land now lay in their hands. These two April events beside two bodies of water would eventually lead to a final April scene which assured all repenting sinners of an eternal home beside the ultimate body of water. Matthew tells us of the April event and John describes the ultimate water.

"And it came to pass, when Jesus had finished all these sayings, He said unto His disciples, 'Ye know that after two days is the Feast of the Passover, and the Son of man is betrayed to be crucified' " (Matt. 26:1-2).

"And they crucified Him, and parted His garments, casting lots; that it might be fulfilled which was spoken by the prophet, 'They parted My garments among them, and upon My vesture did they cast lots' " (27:35).

"And He showed me a pure river of water of life, clear as crystal, proceeding out of the throne of God and of the Lamb. In the midst of the street of it, and on either side of the river, was there the tree of life, which bare 12 manner of fruits, and yielded her fruit every month; and the leaves of the tree were for the healing of the nations. And there shall be no more curse: but the throne of God and of the Lamb shall be in it; and His servants shall serve Him" (Rev. 22:1-3).

Preview

God's Command: Enter the Land!

JOSHUA 1–5

The news spread throughout the camp like wildfire. "The scouts are back! The scouts are back!" Sure enough, there they stood, smiling, confident, and eager to tell all. And what a story they had to tell. At Joshua's command the two men had swum the Jordan River by night to check out Jericho, that strong-walled enemy city, the first Israel must defeat to conquer the land.

But as the people listened, it soon became apparent that the real story was not so much the fortifications around the city, but rather the faith they found within the city. Rahab was her name. She had been a common harlot, but now worshiped the true God. In fact, she had saved the scouts from certain death by hiding them in her own home. Who now in that crowd could possibly doubt God's hand was in all this? Think of it—in just 72 hours they would accomplish what the previous generation could not do in 40 long years, namely, to enter the Promised Land.

To be sure, the Jordan River had yet to be crossed. This was April and it stood at flood tide, its angry current surging wide, swift, and deep. But when all was ready, this problem was solved in similar fashion to the former Red Sea crisis—the waters were supernaturally rolled back. But the best yet awaited them. When they reached the West Bank, Jesus Christ Himself stood at Jericho's gate to welcome and encourage them. What a God Joshua had. What a God we have.

Overview

SCRIPTURE	Joshua 1–5			
SUBJECT	The invasion of Canaan by Israel			
SPECIFICS	Pre-Jordan events	Crossing the Jordan River	Post-Jordan events	
	A special message —From God to Joshua —From Joshua to Israel		Constructing	A memorial rock pile
			Circumcising	All their males
			Celebrating	The Passover
	A special mission —Two men are sent, scout out Jericho		Consuming	The food of the land
			Communing	With Jesus Himself
SAINTS AND SINNERS	Joshua, the two scouts, Rahab			
SENTENCE SUMMARIES	O.T. Verses	"Trust in the LORD with all thine heart, and lean not unto thine own understanding. In all thy ways acknowledge Him, and He shall direct thy paths" (Prov. 3:5-6).		
	N.T. Verse	"Was not Rahab the harlot justified by works, when she had received the messengers, and had sent them out another way?" (James 2:25)		

THE INVASION OF THE LAND—ISRAEL CLAIMS ITS POSSESSIONS

THE PREPARATION

God spoke to Joshua: *"Moses My servant is dead; now therefore arise, go over this Jordan . . . unto the land which I do give . . . to them, even to the Children of Israel. Every place that the sole of your foot shall tread upon, that have I given unto you, as I said unto Moses. . . .*

"This Book of the Law shall not depart out of thy mouth; but thou shalt meditate therein day and night, that thou mayest observe to do according to all that is written therein; for then thou shalt make thy way prosperous, and then thou shalt have good success. Have not I commanded thee? Be strong and of a good courage; be not afraid, neither be thou dismayed, for the Lord *thy God is with thee whithersoever thou goest" (Josh. 1:2-3, 8-9).*

God spoke to the people: *"Prepare you victuals; for within three days ye shall pass over this Jordan, to go in to possess the land" (v. 11).*

THE PENETRATION

Joshua sent two men to scout out the city of Jericho. While in the city, their lives were saved by a recently converted harlot named Rahab (2:9-13). Because of this, she would later be spared when the city was destroyed.

THE PROMISE

"And the Lord *said unto Joshua, 'This day will I begin to magnify thee in the sight of all Israel,*

that they may know that, as I was with Moses, so I will be with thee' " (3:7).

THE PASSAGE

The priests were ordered to carry the ark of the covenant to the edge of Jordan, and by faith, step into that swollen body of water. When this happened, the mighty Jordan was supernaturally rolled back. Israel then crossed on dry ground.

THE PYRAMID OF STONES

After they crossed, Israel was to construct two memorial piles of 12 stones each. One pyramid was to be placed in the middle of the river and the other on the west side of Jordan. The pyramid on the western bank was there as a silent witness to future generations of God's faithfulness in rolling Jordan's waters back.

"And those 12 stones, which they took out of Jordan, did Joshua pitch in Gilgal. And he spake unto the Children of Israel, saying, 'When your children shall ask their fathers in time to come, saying, "What mean these stones?"

" 'Then ye shall let your children know, saying, "Israel came over this Jordan on dry land." For the LORD your God dried up the waters of Jordan from before you, until ye were passed over, as the LORD your God did to the Red Sea, which He dried up from before us, until we were gone over; that all the people of the earth might know the hand of the LORD, that it is mighty; that ye might fear the LORD your God forever' " (4:20-24).

THE PERPLEXITY

"And it came to pass, when all the kings of the Amorites, which were on the side of Jordan westward, and all the kings of the Canaanites, which were by the sea, heard that the LORD had dried up the waters of Jordan from before the Children of Israel, until we were passed over, that their heart melted, neither was there spirit in them any more, because of the Children of Israel" (5:1).

THE PURIFICATION OF THE PEOPLE

When they reached the western side of Palestine, God ordered the males of Israel to be circumcised. This was done, and the name of the place was called Gilgal, which means, "to roll away."

THE PASSOVER

"And they did eat of the old corn of the land on the morrow after the Passover, unleavened cakes, and parched corn in the selfsame day. And the manna ceased on the morrow after they had eaten of the old corn of the land; neither had the Children of Israel manna anymore; but they did eat of the fruit of the land of Canaan that year" (vv. 11-12).

THE PRINCE FROM HEAVEN

Joshua received a heavenly Visitor, apparently Jesus Himself on the eve of the battle against Jericho.

"And it came to pass, when Joshua was by Jericho, that he lifted up his eyes and looked, and, behold, there stood a Man over against him with His sword drawn in His hands. And Joshua went unto Him, and said unto Him, 'Art Thou for us?' " (v. 13)

Joshua was reassured of victory and told (as once was Moses, Ex. 3:5) to remove his shoes.

"And He said, 'Nay; but as Captain of the host of the LORD am I now come.' And Joshua fell on his face to the earth, and did worship, and said unto Him, 'What saith my Lord unto His servant?' " (Josh. 5:14)

Doing Things God's Way

COMMENTS

Moses had given brilliant leadership to Israel for 40 years. Compared to Moses, Joshua was plain and unpromising. He may have had self-doubts as he succeeded the multi-talented Moses. Nonetheless, he was God's choice to lead Israel. God graciously greeted His new leader with encouragement and preparation for the task that lay ahead. He began by promising to give him every piece of land that his feet should tread on (Josh. 1:3). All he needed to do was to get walking.

While Joshua was indeed a different man than Moses, he enjoyed one thing in common with him—God's presence and enablement (v. 5). God told him that he would succeed as long as he remembered and abode by God's revelation. The only Bible Joshua had was the five books penned by Moses and perhaps the Book of Job. This is why God placed emphasis on "the Book of the Law" (v. 8). The mouth is the agent by which the heart is expressed. As long as Joshua's mouth expressed the things contained in God's Law it would indicate that his heart was filled with God's revelation. Joshua would experience success because he would be doing things God's way. The only way one can be guaranteed success in all that he does is to do it God's way.

Having received strengthening and encouragement from God, Joshua assumed command of his people and prepared them to enter the land (vv. 10-15). The people recognized God's authority in God's man and responded in the only sensible way—pledging complete obedience (v. 17). Disobedience would be dealt with harshly—by death (v. 18).

Forty years earlier, Joshua had been one of the spies sent into the land to see what lay ahead (cf. Num. 13). Now that they were once again ready to enter the land it seemed that this would be a feasible strategy. This time only two spies were sent; not to spy out the entire land, but to learn about Jericho and to help plan the best strategy to take that fortified city. The spies were successful in penetrating the city, thanks to the help of Rahab who revealed to them they could have taken the land 40 years earlier (cf. Josh. 2:9-10). For 40 years, Jericho had been defeated (cf. v. 11). What a tragedy that the conquerers had themselves spent the previous 40 years defeated, wandering in the wilderness during which time 2 ½ million people died!

Rahab responded to God's revelation in belief (faith). She knew that God had given the land to Israel and that He alone was God (v. 11). The spies pledged that she and all with her in the house would be spared when Israel took the city (2:14-20). In testimony to her faith, Rahab hung the scarlet cord (by which she had let the spies down to the ground) in her window. The spies' experience with Rahab convinced them that God truly would give them victory (v. 24).

The plan for crossing the Jordan River is laid out in chapter 3. The ark of the covenant would lead the way. The people would maintain a 3,000-foot interval between them and the ark because they had "not passed this way heretofore" (v. 4). The ark would lead them. They were to follow it wherever it went. Joshua encouraged the people (v. 5) and was in turn encouraged by God (vv. 7-8). God was going to use this event to demonstrate to Israel that He was with Joshua every bit as much as He had been with Moses for the previous 40 years.

The Jordan, being at flood stage, represented an impossible barrier (v. 15). God had apparently previously revealed to Joshua the fact that He would dry up the Jordan River (v. 13). The hearts of the priests who bore the ark must have beaten fiercely as they approached the raging river. They went on in faith—no turning back. As soon as their feet were wet, the Jordan stopped, and they walked to the middle on dry ground. They did it God's way.

Three Memorials

COMMENTS

The crossing of the Jordan River at flood stage was an event that God did not want His people ever to forget. To aid their memories He had them take 12 stones—each stone representing 1 of the 12 tribes of Israel—from the middle of the riverbed (Josh. 4:3) and place them on the West Bank of the Jordan. He also set up 12 stones in the middle of the river at the point where the priests stood with the ark all during the time that the waters were stayed. These two piles of stones constituted the first memorial. They were to be memorials forever (vv. 7, 9) to remind the people of the great work God had done for them in bringing them into the land. The pile of rocks on the West Bank was visible and reminded them of the pile which they could not see beneath the river's surface. God is always pleased when His children recall the great things He has done in providing their salvation.

God's purpose in delivering Israel safely across the Jordan River when it was at flood stage was twofold: (1) to get Israel's fighting force to where it could begin its task of subduing the land (v. 13); and (2) to demonstrate that Joshua was God's man every bit as much as was Moses (v. 14). With His purpose accomplished, there was no longer reason to have the Jordan stopped. When the last priest was clear, the waters of the Jordan returned to their normal course (v. 18). Now, there was no turning back. Israel was in enemy terrritory and would have to trust the Lord in new ways—they had never gone this way before (cf. 3:4).

God quickly put His people into a situation in which they would have to trust Him in a way they had never before experienced. He directed Joshua to make sharp knives and circumcise the Children of Israel a second time (the first time was when Abraham was given the rite of circumcision as a testimony of his belief of the covenant given him, cf. Gen. 17:1-14). This was the second memorial, for it looked back to the covenant God gave to Abraham promising to make of him a great nation. Circumcision was the testimony of the *father's* belief of the Abrahamic Covenant—that God would make of Abraham a great nation (cf. 12:1-3). The fact that the males of Joshua's day were not circumcised showed that they had grown up in unbelieving homes—their fathers did not believe the promises given to Abraham (cf. Josh. 5:5-7). Now, God was about to do something new—He was going to give them the land that they refused to enter 40 years earlier. He must have people who believed in Him. If they believed, they would give testimony to that belief by circumcising every male. To do so would require faith in two things: faith in God's revelation given to Abraham and faith in God to protect them in the midst of their enemies. Circumcision was not the simple operation it is today. The man was totally incapacitated for at least three days. (v. 8). With every male incapacitated, Israel was completely unprotected and at the mercy of their enemies. To Israel's credit, they obeyed God (v. 8) and God protected them completely.

The third memorial was the Passover. Having given testimony of their belief in God's promises to Abraham, the people of Israel were in a position to remember their deliverance from Egypt with new meaning. Only Caleb and Joshua had experienced that deliverance personally. Now the people were in a proper spiritual relationship with God and could look back to the time when God redeemed them nationally and made them His people. They would do it by partaking of the memorial Passover meal. God marked this new relationship by causing the manna that had fed them for 40 years to cease and giving them the grain that had been grown in their new homeland (v. 12). God's promise to bring them into the land had been realized.

Preview

God's Command: Overcome the Land!

JOSHUA 6–12

Leaders marching, trumpets sounding, people shouting, and walls collapsing! What a moment it had been. But now it was over. Jericho was in their hands. The same glorious God who had previously provided for their fathers and mothers in the barren desert was now providing for them in the Promised Land. In light of this, could any enemy possibly defeat them? Yes, and one almost did. That threat, however, came not from outside the camp, but from within.

Achan was his name. Disobedience was his sin, causing the entire nation to suffer until he was caught and judged. That crisis had scarcely been dealt with when another arose. Israel was suddenly attacked by five fierce kings. Again, God stepped in. This time the sun itself cooperated in bringing about the victory. That was the story of the central and southern campaigns. Israel then moved north for the final mopping-up exercises. Soon the fighting was over. They had won. The land was theirs.

Overview

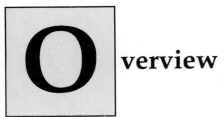

<table>
<tr><td>SCRIPTURE</td><td colspan="6">Joshua 6–12</td></tr>
<tr><td>SUBJECT</td><td colspan="6">The subjection of Canaan by Israel</td></tr>
<tr><td rowspan="4">SPECIFICS</td><td colspan="2">God's power</td><td colspan="2">God's punishment</td><td colspan="2">God's precepts</td></tr>
<tr><td rowspan="3">As seen in three great victories</td><td>Jericho</td><td rowspan="3">As seen in the valley of Achor</td><td rowspan="3">Achan is caught and executed because of his sin</td><td rowspan="3">As delivered from two mountains</td><td rowspan="3">Mt. Gerizim
The blessings of the Law are read here
Mt. Ebal
The curses of the Law are read here</td></tr>
<tr><td>Ajalon</td></tr>
<tr><td>Hazor</td></tr>
<tr><td>SAINTS AND SINNERS</td><td colspan="6">Joshua, Achan, some Gibeonites, Adonizedek</td></tr>
<tr><td rowspan="2">SENTENCE SUMMARIES</td><td>O.T. Verse</td><td colspan="5">"He cast out the heathen also before them, and divided them an inheritance by line, and made the tribes of Israel to dwell in their tents" (Ps. 78:55).</td></tr>
<tr><td>N.T. Verse</td><td colspan="5">"By faith the walls of Jericho fell down, after they were compassed about seven days" (Heb. 11:30).</td></tr>
</table>

THE SUBJECTION OF THE LAND—ISRAEL CONQUERS ITS POSSESSIONS

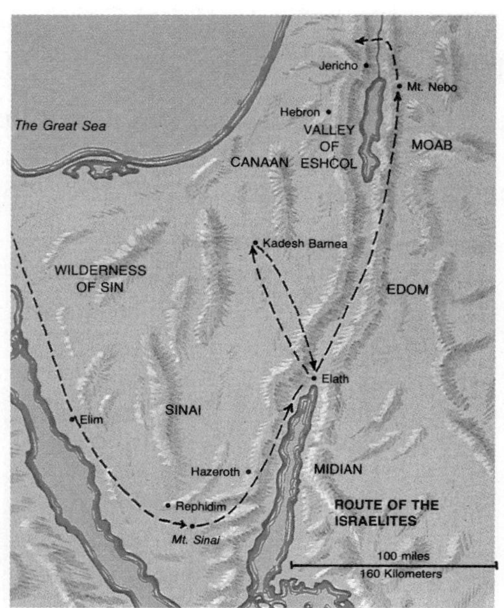

THE CENTRAL CAMPAIGN

Jericho—a city shouted down. Israel's leaders were to march around Jericho once per day for six days. On the seventh day, this was to be done seven times, followed by shouting and blowing of trumpets. God would then supernaturally cause the walls to fall down. Israel obeyed and God performed all this.

"So the people shouted when the priests blew with the trumpets. And it came to pass, when the people heard the sound of the trumpet, and the people shouted with a great shout, that the wall fell down flat, so that the people went up into the city, every man straight before him, and they took the city. . . .

"And Joshua saved Rahab the harlot alive, and her father's household, and all that she had; and she dwelleth in Israel even unto this day; because she hid the messengers, which Joshua sent to spy out Jericho. And Joshua adjured them at that time, saying, 'Cursed be the man before the L*ORD, that riseth up and buildeth this city Jericho, he shall lay the foundation thereof in his firstborn, and in his youngest son shall he set up the gates of it' " (Josh. 6:20, 25-26).*

Ai—the arrogance knocked down. After Jericho, an over-confident and arrogant Israel was soundly defeated by a small city named Ai.

"And Joshua sent men from Jericho to Ai, which is beside Beth-aven, on the east side of Bethel, and spake unto them saying, 'Go up and view the country.' And the men went up and viewed Ai.

"And they returned to Joshua, and said unto him, 'Let not all the people go up; but let about 2 or 3,000 men go up and smite Ai; and make not all the people to labor thither; for they are but few.'

"So there went up thither of the people about 3,000 men; and they fled before the men of Ai" (7:2-4).

Achan—a sinner sought down. God informed Joshua the reason for their defeat was due to sin in the camp. An Israelite had stolen and hidden some forbidden Babylonian loot.

"But the Children of Israel committed a trespass in the accursed thing. For Achan, the son of Carmi, the son of Zabdi, the son of Zerah, of the tribe of Judah, took of the accursed thing; and the anger of the L*ORD was kindled against the Children of Israel. . . .*

"And Joshua rent his clothes, and fell to the earth upon his face before the ark of the L*ORD until the eventide, he and the elders of Israel, and put dust upon their heads. And Joshua said, 'Alas, O* L*ORD God, wherefore hast Thou at all brought this people over Jordan, to deliver us into the hand of the Amorites, to destroy us? Would to God we had been content, and dwelt on the other side Jordan!' . . .*

"And the L*ORD said unto Joshua, 'Get thee up; wherefore liest thou thus upon thy face? Israel hath sinned, and they have also transgressed My covenant which I commanded them. For they have even taken of the accursed thing, and have also stolen, and dissembled also, and they have put it even among their own stuff.*

" 'Therefore the Children of Israel could not stand before their enemies, but turned their backs before their enemies, because they were accursed; neither will I be with you anymore, except ye destroy the accursed from among you' " (vv. 1, 6-7, 10-12).

A divinely conducted manhunt began which pointed to Achan, a man from the tribe of Judah. He confessed and was executed in the Valley of Achor. After this, Ai was taken by ambush.

"And the Lord *said unto Joshua, 'Fear not, neither be thou dismayed; take all the people of war with thee, and arise, go up to Ai. See, I have given into thy hand the king of Ai, and his people, and his city, and his land' " (8:1).*

Gerizim and Ebal—the Law handed down. As Moses had previously commanded, the blessings and curses of the Law were read from Mount Ebal.

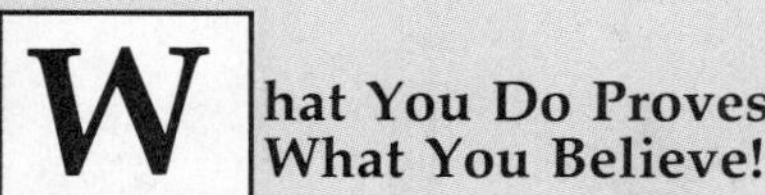

What You Do Proves What You Believe!

COMMENTS

Never before or since in history had a city been conquered like Jericho. Not a rock was thrown; not an arrow was shot; not a spear was hurled. Not a word was spoken by the conquerors. Not an Israelite life was lost in the Conquest of Jericho. The city had been at "battle stations" for 40 years. All the years Israel was wandering in the wilderness, Jericho trembled anticipating their coming (cf. 2:9-11). What great strategy was used in this amazing conquest? Israel's armed men marched before seven priests blowing seven rams'-horn trumpets and followed by the ark of the Lord and the people marching without a word behind. Once a day for six days the procession circled Jericho. On the seventh day it was "business as usual"—Israel was beginning its now-familiar routine. However, this day was different. After the first circuit, they made a second, then a third, a fourth, fifth, sixth, and seventh. At the end of the seventh circuit, the priests blew their trumpets, the people shouted, and the walls fell down *flat*—except for the section where Rahab lived. (The stones of the walls are not lying out flat today for all to see because those who rebuilt the city in subsequent days used the stones that were already there, rather than to carry in new stones.)

In the days between the time that the spies had visited Jericho and the time that Israel took the city, Rahab had been busy. When the spies went to Rahab's house, they found not only Rahab, but also her father, mother, brothers, sisters, and all her relatives. All were saved because all believed that God would deliver the city to Israel. All other people of Jericho, as well as their livestock, were put to death (6:21). Rahab and all her family were brought to Israel's camp and they became citizens of Israel. Rahab the harlot was brought right into the line of Christ. Rahab married a man named Salmon and gave birth to a son, Boaz, who married Ruth, who gave birth to Obed, who was the father of Jesse, who was the father of David the ancestor of Jesus the Messiah (cf. Matt. 1:7-16). What an illustration of the grace of God, that one who had been a harlot should become a great-grandmother many generations removed of our Saviour.

How is it that Rahab was given this privilege? Obviously, it was not because of her great spiritual heritage. Joshua tells us twice that it was "because she hid the messengers" (cf. Josh. 6:17, 25). Why did she hide the messengers? Because she believed the only message of God that she had heard—that God had given the land to Israel (cf. 2:9). The New Testament tells us that "Rahab the harlot was justified by works" (cf. James 2:25)—she received God's righteousness because of what she did in receiving the spies. What she did, proved that she believed God's revelation. So it is with us today. What we do proves what we believe. We can lie with our lips, but we cannot lie with our lives.

THE SOUTHERN CAMPAIGN

Gibeon—the wool pulled down. Joshua was tricked into signing a nonaggressive peace treaty with the city of Gibeon.

*The nature of the deceit: Some Gibeonites dressed up in worn-out clothing and arrived at Israel's camp, leading Joshua to believe they were from a far off country. Assuming they were not the enemy of Israel, he signed a peace treaty with them.

*The reason for the deceit: *"And the men took of their victuals, and asked not counsel at the mouth of the LORD" (Josh. 9:14).*

Ajalon—the sun shone down. Joshua was forced to do battle with the king of Jerusalem and his allies who had attacked Gibeon for cooperating with Israel. During the battle, God (at Joshua's request) supernaturally prolonged the duration of the light coming from the sun and thus allowed Israel the necessary time to defeat their enemies.

"And the LORD said unto Joshua, 'Fear them not; for I have delivered them into thine hand; there shall not a man of them stand before thee.' . . .

"Then spake Joshua to the LORD in the day when the LORD delivered up the Amorites before the Children of Israel, and he said in the sight of Israel, 'Sun, stand thou still upon Gibeon; and thou, Moon, in the Valley of Ajalon.'

"And the sun stood still, and the moon stayed, until the people had avenged themselves upon their enemies. Is not this written in the book of Jasher? So the sun stood still in the midst of heaven, and hasted not to go down about a whole day.

"And there was no day like that before it or after it, that the LORD hearkened unto the voice of a man; for the LORD fought for Israel" (10:8, 12-14).

Makkedah—the enemy trampled down. The king of Jerusalem and his four allied kings were captured in a cave called Makkedah. After a victory celebration which featured Israelite soldiers putting their feet on the

necks of the kings, the five were hanged from a tree.

THE NORTHERN CAMPAIGN

The waters of Merom—the horses slowed down. At this place (north of the Galilean Sea) Joshua hamstrung some horses belonging to an enemy named Jabin, thus rendering them useful for farm work but useless for warfare.

Hazor—a capital burned down. Jabin, king of Hazor, organized and led the northern attack against Israel. He was soundly defeated and had his capital burned to the ground.

"So Joshua took the whole land, according to all that the LORD said unto Moses; and Joshua gave it for an inheritance unto Israel according to their divisions by their tribes. And the land rested from war" (11:23).

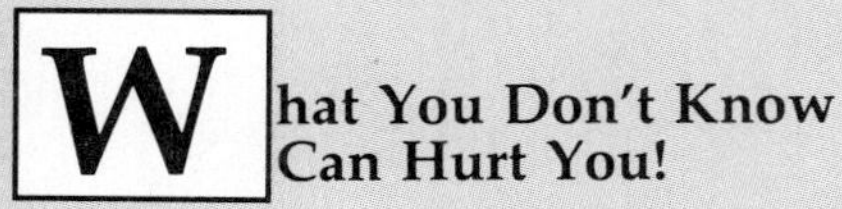

What You Don't Know Can Hurt You!

COMMENTS

The glorious victory at Jericho caused Israel to become proud and self-sufficient. They thought that they had done a mighty thing in conquering Jericho and forgot completely that it was because of God's strategy and God's undertaking that the battle was won. By comparison, Ai, a small city to the north and west of Jericho, was a pushover. After scouting out the city, the spies returned to give their report and recommended that they not bother to take all of the people but simply a task force of 3,000 men (Josh. 7:3-4). Further, they need not bother to take the ark or the priests. Ai was not significant enough to be worth the effort.

Joshua followed their ill-advised recommendations and dispatched a task force of 3,000 men to take Ai. Something untoward happened. Israel sustained 36 casualties—the only casualties suffered in all the campaign to take the land—at the hands of Ai and retreated in ignominy. The defeat was disheartening to the people (v. 5) and was totally perplexing to Joshua. He complained to Jehovah (v. 7) only to learn that the fault was with Israel for "Israel hath sinned" (vv. 10-11). Neither Joshua nor Israel knew that at Jericho Achan had taken a beautiful Babylonian garment, 200 shekels of silver and a 50-shekel weight wedge of gold and kept it for himself. Of course, his family knew, for he had hidden them in the earth in the middle of his tent in plain view of them all. What Joshua and Israel did not know hurt them—36 men died and the rest of the people were defeated and disheartened.

The wrong had to be made right. God revealed the plan for its discovery to Joshua (v. 14). All Israel was to march before Joshua so the culprit could be found. Achan could have confessed his sin at that point but thought that what Joshua didn't know couldn't hurt him, so he remained silent. All Israel passed before Joshua and the tribe of Judah was indicated as harboring the guilty person. Achan could have confessed then, but must have thought that Joshua was merely lucky in his choice. The tribe of Judah marched before Joshua and the family of the Zarhites was selected as harboring the guilty person. Achan could have owned up to his sin, but didn't. The family of the Zarhites went before Joshua and the household of Zabdi was chosen as the one being the source of the problem. Still no confession from Achan. The household of Zabdi stood before Joshua this fourth time; and Achan was pointed out as the culprit. What Israel did not know had hurt them and what Achan did not know now hurt him. Some credit does need to be given Achan, for he uttered three words men have such a hard time admitting, "I have sinned" (v. 20). In judgment, Achan, his family, and his animals were stoned to death and all that he had was burned together with their corpses in the Valley of Achor (vv. 24-25).

With the cancer of sin cut out, the nation was ready to return to the Conquest. God was pleased and gave the promise of victory (8:1) and the strategy for the conflict (v. 2). This time they were victorious and without casualty as they slew 12,000 inhabitants of Ai (v. 25). To remind them of this incident and to fix indelibly on their minds the fact that obedience brings God's blessing and disobedience brings God's cursing, Joshua built an altar, wrote the Law on the stones of it, offered burnt and peace offerings on it, and divided the people into two companies putting half of them against Mount Gerizim and half of them against Mount Ebal and read the blessings and cursings of the Law to them. Thus Israel was reminded of two lessons: (1) what you don't know can hurt you; and (2) God's battles must be fought in God's way. To obey brings blessing; to disobey brings cursing.

God's Command: Occupy the Land!

JOSHUA 13–24

The testimony of an 85-year-old man. And the testament of a 110-year-old man. Caleb gave the testimony, while Joshua would later offer his final will and testament to Israel's leaders. What a dynamic duet the two had been. The theme of their testimony was challenge, while that of their testament spoke of choice. "Give me this mountain," was the request of Caleb. "Choose you this day," was the reminder of Joshua.

The life of each man aptly demonstrated the validity of his words. Caleb conquered his mountain and Joshua faithfully served his God. But now both were growing old. Soon the time of their earthly departure would be at hand. Note their passing carefully, for a full five centuries would pass before another similar team—Elijah and Elisha—appeared on the horizon.

Overview

<table>
<tr><td>SCRIPTURE</td><td colspan="5">Joshua 13–24</td></tr>
<tr><td>SUBJECT</td><td colspan="5">The division of Canaan by Israel</td></tr>
<tr><td rowspan="4">SPECIFICS</td><td rowspan="4">God's 12 tribes</td><td>The allocation of the 12</td><td rowspan="4">God's 2 trustees</td><td rowspan="2">Caleb</td><td rowspan="2">His advice: "Thank God for the past."</td></tr>
<tr><td>2½ tribes settled east of the Jordan
9½ tribes settled west of the Jordan</td></tr>
<tr><td>The alienation of the 12</td><td rowspan="2">Joshua</td><td rowspan="2">His advice: "Trust God for the future."</td></tr>
<tr><td>The 2½ tribes built a hallowed altar of remembrance

The 9½ tribes believed it to be a heathen altar of rebellion</td></tr>
<tr><td>SAINTS AND SINNERS</td><td colspan="5">Joshua, Caleb, Phinehas</td></tr>
<tr><td rowspan="2">SENTENCE SUMMARIES</td><td>O.T. Verses</td><td colspan="4">"The children went in and possessed the land, and Thou subduest before them the inhabitants . . . the Canaanites . . . with their kings . . . that they might do with them as they would. And they took strong cities, and a fat land, and possessed houses full of all goods, wells digged, vineyards, and olive yards, and fruit trees in abundance. So they did eat . . . and became fat, and delighted themselves in Thy great goodness" (Neh. 9:24-25).</td></tr>
<tr><td>N.T. Verses</td><td colspan="4">"Our fathers had the tabernacle of witness in the wilderness, as He had appointed, speaking unto Moses, that he should make it according to the fashion that he had seen. Which also our fathers that came after brought in with Jesus into the possession of the Gentiles, whom God drave out before the face of our fathers, unto the days of David" (Acts 7:44-45).</td></tr>
</table>

HE DISTRIBUTION OF THE LAND— ISRAEL COLONIZES ITS POSSESSIONS

THE LAND DIVIDED

The land was now partitioned under the supervision of Joshua, Eleazar, and the key tribal leaders by the casting of lots.

(1) The land east of Jordan: Reuben, Gad, and one-half tribe of Manasseh.

(2) The land west of Jordan: Judah, Ephraim, one-half tribe of Manasseh, Benjamin, Simeon, Zebulun, Issachar, Asher, Naphtali, Dan.

(3) The land for Levi: Levi was given no land, as God Himself would be their portion (Josh. 13:33). However, they were given 48 special cities from the remaining tribes.

"These are the inheritances, which Eleazar the priest, and Joshua the son of Nun, and the heads of the fathers of the tribes of the Children of Israel, divided for an inheritance by lot in Shiloh before the LORD, at the door of the tabernacle of the congregation. So they made an end of dividing the country" (19:51).

A WARRIOR EXCITED

Caleb visited Joshua and gave one of the most thrilling testimonies in the Bible. Note his challenging words.

"Forty years old was I when Moses the servant of the LORD sent me from Kadesh-barnea to espy out the land; and I brought him word again as it was in mine heart.

"Nevertheless my brethren that went up with me made the heart of the people melt; but I wholly followed the LORD my God.

"And Moses sware on that day, saying, 'Surely the land whereon thy feet have trodden shall be thine inheritance, and thy children's forever, because thou hast wholly followed the LORD my God.'

"And now, behold, the LORD hath kept me alive, as He said, these forty and five years, even since the LORD spake this word unto Moses, while the Children of Israel wandered in the wilderness: and now, lo, I am this day fourscore and five years old.

"As yet I am as strong this day as I was in the day that Moses sent me; as my strength was then even so is my strength now, for war, both to go out, and to come in.

"Now therefore give me this mountain, whereof the LORD spake in that day; for thou heardest in that day how the Anakims were there, and that the cities were great and fenced. If so be the LORD will be with me, then I shall be able to drive them out, as the LORD said" (14:7-12).

AN ALTAR INDICTED

After the land was divided, Israel set up the tabernacle at Shiloh. Joshua called together the armies of the two-and-one-half tribes of Shiloh, blessed them, and sent them to their chosen home on the east side of Jordan.

Before crossing the river, these two-and-one-half tribes erected a large monument in the shape of an altar to remind them and their unborn children of their common heritage with the tribes on the west side of Jordan. This was misinterpreted by the nine-and-one-half tribes as an act of rebellion and an ugly civil war threatened. The misunderstanding was cleared up just in time by an 11-man delegation from the nine-and-one-half tribes led by Aaron's grandson, Phinehas.

A FINAL SERMON RECITED

Joshua's last words to Israel. *"And Joshua called for all Israel, and for their elders, and for their heads, and for their judges, and for their officers, and said unto them, 'I am old and stricken in age'"* (23:2).

He reminded them of God's goodness. *"And ye have seen all that the LORD your God hath done unto all these nations because of you; for the LORD your God is He that hath fought for you. . . .*

"And, behold, this day I am going the way of all the earth; and ye know in all your hearts and in all your souls, that not one thing hath failed of all the good things which the LORD your God spake concerning you; all are come to pass unto you, and not one thing hath failed thereof" (23:3, 14).

He warned them concerning disobedience, and reviewed Israel's history (24:1-13). *"And I took your father Abraham from the other side of the flood, and led him throughout all the land of Canaan, and multiplied his seed, and gave him Isaac. . . .*

"I sent Moses also and Aaron, and I plagued Egypt, according to that which I did among them; and afterward I brought you out. . . .

"And I have given you a land for which ye did not labor, and cities which ye built not, and ye dwell in them; of the vineyards and oliveyards which ye planted not do ye eat" (vv. 3, 5, 13).

He challenged them to serve God. *"Now therefore fear the LORD, and serve Him in sincerity and in truth; and put away the gods which your fathers served on the other side of the flood, and in Egypt; and serve ye the LORD. And if it seem evil unto you to serve the LORD, choose you this day whom ye will serve; whether the gods which your fathers served that were on the other side of the flood, or the gods of the Amorites, in whose land ye dwell; but as for me and my house, we will serve the LORD"* (vv. 14-15).

God had already greatly blessed His people Israel. They were thus to love and obey Him. If they obeyed, one Israelite warrior would chase a thousand pagans. If they disobeyed, God Himself would drive Israel from the land.

Joshua reviewed Israel's history from Abraham to the present moment. God had once brought Abraham their father out of Ur into Canaan. He had then brought Israel out of Egypt. He had finally brought Israel into Canaan. In light of all the above, each Israelite must choose whom he would serve, God or pagan idols.

Joshua completed the book that bears his name.

"And Joshua wrote these words in the Book of the Law of God, and took a great stone, and set it up there under an oak, that was by the sanctuary of the LORD" (v. 26).

He died and departed for heaven. *"And it came to pass after these things, that Joshua the son of Nun, the servant of the LORD, died, being a hundred and ten years old"* (v. 29).

God Rewards Individuals Individually

COMMENTS

With the completion of the Conquest of the land, the time had come to reward the victors. To the tribes of Reuben, Gad, and half of the tribe of Manasseh was given the land on the East Bank (Josh. 13). Among the remaining nine tribes and the remaining half of the tribe of Manasseh Joshua divided the land on the west bank of the Jordan River (chaps. 14–22). In this otherwise routine division, four notable examples of God's rewards of individuals for faithfulness can be noted: Caleb, the tribes of Ephraim and Manasseh, the Levites, and Joshua. God rewarded each one differently.

Caleb, a descendant of Judah, was 40 years old when he was commissioned by Moses along with Joshua and 10 others to go and spy out the land of Canaan (cf. 14:7). He faithfully served Jehovah all the days of his life (cf. v. 10). At the age of 85 he was given the mountain in the midst of Judah's inheritance on which the city of Hebron stood (cf. vv. 13-14). The area was not secure so Caleb had to liberate it from the Canaanites, which he did in spite of his advanced age. God not only rewarded him with a possession but also with the ability to acquire it.

The tribes of Ephraim and Manasseh descended from Joseph, who received no inheritance in the land. If it had not been for Joseph's faithfulness in Egypt, Israel would not have survived to become a nation and conquer the land. God rewarded Joseph by giving him a double portion of the land of Israel. He was the only son of Jacob to inherit two portions of the land (cf. chaps. 16–17). His bones, which the Children of Israel had carried with them all through the wilderness wanderings and Conquest of the land, were at last buried in Shechem located in the land occupied by the tribe of Ephraim and half the tribe of Manasseh (cf. 24:32).

The Levites were not given a separate inheritance in the land (cf. 13:33; 18:7). They faithfully served the Lord in leading the people in the worship of Jehovah. They were not to have their attention diverted to the things that an earthly inheritance would demand. They were rewarded with the privilege of serving Jehovah exclusively. They had the privilege of representing God to the people and the people to God.

Joshua faithfully served Jehovah all the days of his life. As a young man he was chosen by Moses to lead Israel's armies into battle (cf. Ex. 17:9). He was a descendant of Joseph and a member of the tribe of Ephraim. He was older than Caleb when he was chosen to be 1 of the 12 spies to enter the land to search it out. To Joshua no particular piece of real estate was given. His reward was more lasting than that, for at the age of 110 he was able to give direction to his descendants in their service of Jehovah. One is left with the impression that Joshua was rewarded with a line of godly descendants who would exert a godly influence on Israel's future generations (cf. Josh. 24:16).

These four examples illustrate one point—God individually rewards individuals who serve Him faithfully. Each was rewarded differently in keeping with his own place in God's economy. Each was given a reward in keeping with the service he performed. The record of each is left to challenge each of us to give attention to his own particular and peculiar place in God's economy with the confidence that in due time He will bestow the fitting reward. God rewards His followers individually.

Passing the Baton

COMMENTS

Joshua, having come to the end of his race, passed the baton on to the generation of Israel that would succeed him. He carefully reminded them that the victories accomplished under his leadership were because Jehovah fought for Israel (23:3). He was merely the instrument in God's hands to assign the inheritances (v. 4) but the inheritance was given by God and would be realized with God's intervention (v. 5). God would do the work; their part was simply obedience.

Israel's task was not impossible. All that they were to do, Moses had written down. They only had to obey it (v. 6). If they obeyed Jehovah, they would be invincible (vv. 8-10). They also needed to know that disobedience would carry a penalty—they would suffer defeat and be driven out of the land (vv. 13-16).

To fix in Israel's mind the significance of what he wanted them to know and do, Joshua recapitulated Israel's history (chap. 24). Only he and Caleb now remained of those who had lived during the time of Israel's deliverance from Egypt and wandering in the wilderness. He began his recital with Abraham (v. 3) and quickly brought them up to the Egyptian bondage and deliverance (vv. 4-7), the wilderness wanderings (vv. 8-10) and the conquering of the land (vv. 11-13). All of this was accomplished because of the uniqueness of Israel's God who had given them the land (v. 13). Such faithfulness on God's part brought an obligation on Israel's—faithful service and devotion to Him (v. 14).

Joshua knew that the time of his death was near (23:14) and wanted to do all he could to ensure that the Israel of the future would be true to the God that he had served so long and so faithfully. He wanted them to go on record in a way that they would remember and could be held to. Personal example is the best motivator and so he went on record concerning not only himself, but also concerning his descendants, "As for me and my house, we will serve the Lord." Israel accepted the challenge (24:16, 18, 24) and entered into a covenant with Joshua (v. 25). As a permanent reminder to recall these things to Israel's mind when he had passed away, Joshua wrote these things in the Book of the Law and designated a stone as a symbol of the covenant (v. 27). When the people saw the stone, they would be reminded of their commitment to Jehovah.

With these things completed, the baton was passed to the new generation. The people were dismissed to enjoy their inheritance (v. 28) and Joshua died at the age of 110 (v. 29). The influence of Joshua on Israel is summarized in the testimony "and Israel served the LORD all the days of Joshua" (v. 31). Joshua stands as the example of the godly influence that one man can have on an entire nation all the days of his life if he but gives willing obedience to the Lord.

Judges

"Kill the ump! Kill the ump!" How often has that cry been heard in the bleachers, from overzealous baseball fans who felt a wrong decision was made by an official.

Can you imagine, however, two professional National or American League teams actually attempting to conduct a game without an umpire? A game where both pitcher and batter would lovingly and logically decide what was a ball and what was a strike? Or, after the dust had settled resulting from an attempt to steal second base in the bottom of the ninth, can we picture the second baseman and the runner calmly and cheerfully determining whether the player was safe or out?

On second thought, "Long live the ump! Long live the ump!"

In essence, the Judges Stage is similar to that impossible ball game without an umpire. No less than four times do we read the following phrase: "In those days there was no king in Israel, but every man did that which was right in his own eyes" (Jud. 17:6; 18:1; 19:1; 21:25).

This sad and sordid stage, perhaps as no other, vividly illustrates the fact that sinful man not only needs a referee to arbitrate, but also a Redeemer to propitiate.

Preview

The Messiah's Military Men (Part One)

JUDGES 1–5

To tell the truth, he was quite uneasy at first. Not that he doubted Deborah had heard from the Lord. Her reputation as God's spokesperson was well established. No, the correctness of the message was not the problem, but rather the command in the message. According to Deborah, God had selected him to mobilize an army and defeat the Northern Canaanites who had oppressed the Galilean area for two long decades. Finally, he agreed. But only if she would help him.

In spite of his nagging doubts, Barak could not help but marvel at the preciseness of God's command. The number of his army (10,000), the identity of the troops (coming from the tribes of Naphtali and Zebulun), and even the place of battle (Mount Tabor) were all given. Surely the Lord had thought of everything. But there was one aspect of the prophecy he did not understand, that part about the enemy's General Sisera being done in by a woman. Apparently Deborah was not speaking of herself.

Well, the army did mobilize, the attack was made, and victory was his. Now, here he stood by the waters of Megiddo, joining Deborah in a duet of praise to Almighty God! What reassurance and rejoicing he felt as they sang the final words of their victory song: *"So let all Thine enemies perish, O Lord; but let them that love Him be as the sun when he goeth forth in his might" (Jud. 5:31).*

Overview

<table>
<tr><td>SCRIPTURE</td><td colspan="4">Judges 1–5</td></tr>
<tr><td>SUBJECT</td><td colspan="4">Ministry of the first four judges</td></tr>
<tr><td rowspan="2">SPECIFICS</td><td rowspan="2">The personal warfare of two Israelite guerrillas</td><td>Othniel and the Canaanites</td><td rowspan="2">The public warfare of two Israelite generals</td><td>The army of Ehud</td></tr>
<tr><td>Shamgar and the Philistines</td><td>The army of Barak</td></tr>
<tr><td>SAINTS AND SINNERS</td><td colspan="4">Othniel, Shamgar, Ehud, Eglon, Barak, Deborah, Jael, Sisera</td></tr>
<tr><td rowspan="2">SENTENCE SUMMARIES</td><td>O.T. Verses</td><td colspan="3">"They were disobedient and rebelled against Thee, and cast Thy Law behind their backs, and slew Thy prophets. . . . Therefore Thou deliveredst them into the hand of their enemies, who vexed them; and in the time of their trouble, when they cried unto Thee, Thou heardest them from heaven, and according to Thy manifold mercies Thou gavest them saviors, who saved them out of the hand of their enemies" (Neh. 9:26-27).</td></tr>
<tr><td>N.T. Verses</td><td colspan="3">"He gave unto them judges about the space of 450 years, until Samuel the prophet" (Acts 13:20).</td></tr>
</table>

FOUR JUDGES

THE ANGEL OF THE LORD (CHRIST HIMSELF)

He spoke to Israel (Jud. 2:1-5). *"And an Angel of the LORD came up from Gilgal to Bochim, and said, 'I made you to go up out of Egypt, and have brought you unto the land which I sware unto your fathers; and I said, "I will never break my covenant with you.*

" ' "And ye shall make no league with the inhabitants of this land; ye shall throw down their altars." But ye have not obeyed My voice; why have ye done this?

" 'Wherefore I also said, "I will not drive them out from before you; but they shall be as thorns in your sides, and their gods shall be a snare unto you." '

"And it came to pass, when the Angel of the LORD spake these words unto all the Children of Israel, that the people lifted up their voice, and wept" (vv. 1-4).

He spoke to Gideon (6:12, 20, 22), and He spoke to Samson's parents (13:3, 6, 9, 13, 15-18, 20-21).

THE SPIRIT OF GOD

He came on Othniel (3:10), Gideon (6:34), Jephthah (11:29), and Samson (13:25; 14:6, 19; 15:14, 19).

AN EVIL SPIRIT (9:3)

TWELVE MILITARY REFORMERS—THE JUDGES

First judge: Othniel

He was both the son-in-law and nephew of Caleb.

* Oppressing nation: Mesopotamia
* Length of oppression: 8 years
* Years of peace he gave: 40
* Accomplishments: He captured a strong Canaanite city, and drove out the Mesopotamian invaders.

Second judge: Ehud

* Oppressing nation: Moab
* Length of oppression: 18 years
* Years of peace: 80 years
* Accomplishments: This left-handed Benjamite warrior, after carrying Israel's annual tax tribute to Jericho (the Moabite capital) managed to kill Eglon, the fat Moabite king. He then gathered an army, slaughtered 10,000 enemy soldiers, and ushered in a long reign of peace.

Third judge: Shamgar

* Oppressing nation: Philistia
* Length of oppression: unrecorded
* Years of peace: unrecorded
* Accomplishments: With an oxgoad this soldier killed 600 Philistines.

Fourth judge: Barak (as helped by Deborah)

* Oppressing nation: Northern Canaanites
* Length of oppression: 20 years
* Years of peace: 40 years
* Accomplishments: The king of Hazor had cruelly oppressed Israel by the hand of Sisera (his five-star general) who commanded 900 iron chariots. At the encouragement of Deborah, an Israelite prophetess, freedom fighter Barak mobilized an army of 10,000 and attacked the enemy from the heights of Mount Tabor. Sisera's armies were totally routed. Sisera himself was later killed while hiding in the tent of a woman named Jael. Lulling him to sleep, she drove a tent peg into his forehead!

Deborah and Barak composed and sang a duet of praise to celebrate the victory.

"Then sang Deborah and Barak the son of Abinoam on that day saying, 'Praise ye the LORD for the avenging of Israel, when the people willingly offered themselves. Hear, O ye kings; give ear, O ye princes; I, even I, will sing unto the LORD; I will sing praise to the LORD God of Israel. . . .

" *'So let all thine enemies perish, O Lord; but let them that love Him be as the sun when he goeth forth in his might.'*

"And the land had rest 40 years" (vv. 1-3, 31).

We should note the following.

The grace involved in this battle. Because of Israel's idolatry, they found themselves unarmed on the eve of battle. In spite of this, God stepped in to help them.

The location of this battle. "By the waters of Megiddo."

The participants in this battle. (1) Those tribes who fought: Issachar, Zebulun, Naphtali (vv. 15, 18). *"Zebulun and Naphtali were a people that jeopardized their lives unto the death" (v. 18).*

(2) Those tribes who refused to fight: Reuben, two-and-one-half tribes in Gilead, Dan, Asher (vv. 15-17).

The supernatural intervention in this battle. (1) The Kishon River flooded, drowning many of the enemy troops (v. 21).

(2) The angels in heaven were used. *"They fought from heaven; the stars in their courses fought against Sisera" (v. 20).*

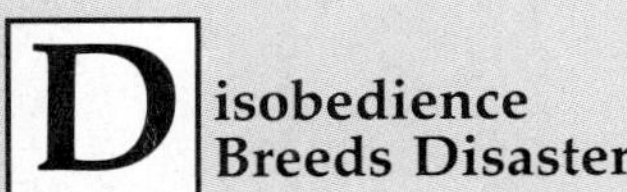

Disobedience Breeds Disaster

COMMENTS

In the Book of Joshua the people of Israel experienced victory after victory (with the notable exception of the first attempt to take Ai); in the Book of Judges they experienced defeat after defeat. In the Book of Judges, there are seven cycles of: (1) sin—defection from Jehovah, (2) servitude—deliverance into the hands of one of the enemies whom they failed to drive out of the land, (3) suffering—suffering at the hands of their enemies, (4) supplication—the people cry to Jehovah for deliverance, (5) savior—a judge delivers the people from their enemies, (6) salvation—the judge effects deliverance and the people are true to Jehovah during the lifetime of the judge, and (7) silence—Jehovah gives the people rest from abuse at the hands of their enemies. The reason for this is explained in the last verse of the book, "In those days there was no king in Israel; every man did that which was right in his own eyes" (21:25).

The nations which were left in the land "to prove Israel" are listed in 3:3. The disobedience in failing to drive these peoples out of the land led to the disasters of intermarriage with the heathen peoples (v. 6) and spiritual defection (v. 7). Jehovah delivered Israel to the king of Mesopotamia for 8 years. When the people prayed to God, God raised up Othniel, Caleb's nephew, to be the first judge/deliverer of Israel (v. 9). After 40 years (v. 11) the people sinned again and God delivered them to the king of Moab for 18 years (v. 14). When the people of Israel repented and cried to Jehovah, He raised up the second judge, Ehud, who was able to get into the presence of the king of Moab feigning the offer of a secret errand (v. 19). Most swordsmen were right-handed, carrying their swords or daggers on their left sides. Of Ehud, however, it is recorded that he was "a man left-handed" (v. 15). Being left-handed, Ehud concealed his dagger on his right side (vv. 16, 21). His move to reach for his dagger was not suspected, hence he was able to draw his dagger, plunge it into the excessively fat body of the king of Moab, and kill him. God gave Israel 80 years of rest under Ehud (v. 30). During the next 20 years the people of Israel were oppressed by the king of Canaan who had "900 chariots of iron" (4:3)—an advanced and invincible weapon for the day. This time, God raised up a woman, Deborah, to deliver Israel (v. 4). Sisera was the general of the army for the king of Canaan and Barak was Israel's general. Israel soundly defeated Sisera because God fought for Israel against Sisera (v. 15). Sisera's army was wiped out, but Sisera escaped on foot and fled to the house of Jael, which, by covenant should have been friendly to him (v. 17). Jael, however, slew Sisera by driving a tent peg through his temples while he slept (vv. 21-22). Deborah and Barak composed a song rehearsing the whole event so that Israel would have a vehicle for calling to mind the great deliverance that God had worked for Israel on that day (chap. 5).

As wonderful as it was of God to deliver His people by repeatedly raising up judges who would not only effect a political and military deliverance but, more importantly, a spiritual deliverance, one must not forget that the ministries of the judges and the miseries of suffering experienced under the hands of enemies would not have happened if Israel had obeyed God's original instructions to drive the Canaanites utterly out of the land. Their disobedience in this matter led to the disasters and sufferings experienced in subsequent history. One can bring about disaster by disobeying God.

Preview

Messiah's Military Men (Part Two)

JUDGES 6–8; 10–12

Some reflections of the fifth judge: who would have thought it would come to this? There he was, a freeborn son of God living in the Promised Land of God. And what was he doing? Attempting to thresh wheat behind a winepress, to hide it from the hated Midianites who now occupied his area. Well, it could be worse. At least he still had his home. Many of his friends, however, had been driven from theirs, and sought refuge in dark caves and smelly animal dens.

But why were he and Israel reduced to such degradation and desperation? The answer was painfully simple—because of sin! Human rebellion had brought divine retribution. But heaven was neither unaware nor unconcerned over the agony of Abraham's seed, regardless of the sin factor. Suddenly the Angel of the Lord appeared and commissioned this timid wheat-thresher to raise an army and deliver God's people. This Gideon would do, but not before his fighting force shrank from 32,000 to 10,000 to 300 men. These 300 gallant soldiers, by holding torches, breaking pitchers, and blowing trumpets would utterly route a vastly superior enemy!

Some reflections of the eighth judge: He stood there, almost transfixed, totally oblivious to the noise of the singing, shouting, and celebrating all around him. What did he have to rejoice about? If only he could take back those fateful words uttered so carelessly on the eve of battle. But he could not. A vow was a vow. His daughter would be given over as a burnt offering. His success as a soldier was meaningless. Jephthah had failed as a father.

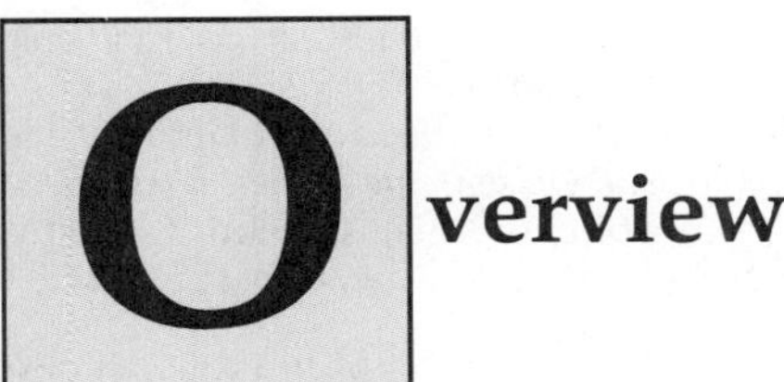

Overview

<table>
<tr><td>SCRIPTURE</td><td colspan="2">Judges 6–8; 10–12</td></tr>
<tr><td>SUBJECT</td><td colspan="2">Ministry of seven judges</td></tr>
<tr><td>SPECIFICS</td><td colspan="2">
<table>
<tr><td colspan="2">Seven soldiers</td></tr>
<tr><td>
<table>
<tr><td rowspan="5">The five anonymous</td><td>Tola</td></tr>
<tr><td>Jair</td></tr>
<tr><td>Ibzan</td></tr>
<tr><td>Elon</td></tr>
<tr><td>Abdon</td></tr>
</table>
</td><td>
<table>
<tr><td rowspan="6">The two famous</td><td rowspan="3">Gideon</td><td>Before the battle</td><td>The selection</td></tr>
<tr><td>During the battle</td><td>The shout</td></tr>
<tr><td>After the battle</td><td>The snare</td></tr>
<tr><td rowspan="3">Jephthah</td><td>Before the battle</td><td>His promise</td></tr>
<tr><td>During the battle</td><td>His proficiency</td></tr>
<tr><td>After the battle</td><td>His pain</td></tr>
</table>
</td></tr>
</table>
</td></tr>
<tr><td>SAINTS AND SINNERS</td><td colspan="2">Tola, Jair, Ibzan, Elon, Abdon, Gideon, Jephthah, Jephthah's daughter</td></tr>
<tr><td rowspan="2">SENTENCE SUMMARIES</td><td>O.T. Verse</td><td>"But after they had rest, they did evil again before Thee; therefore leftest Thou them in the hand of their enemies, so that they had the dominion over them. Yet when they returned, and cried unto Thee, Thou heardest them from heaven; and many times didst Thou deliver them according to Thy mercies" (Neh. 9:28).</td></tr>
<tr><td>N.T. Verses</td><td>"Finally, my brethren, be strong in the Lord, and in the power of His might. Put on the whole armor of God, that ye may be able to stand against the wiles of the devil" (Eph. 6:10-11).</td></tr>
</table>

MINISTRY OF SEVEN JUDGES

Fifth judge: Gideon

* Oppressing nation: Midian. Note Israel's terrible plight at this time.

"And the hand of Midian prevailed against Israel; and because of the Midianites the Children of Israel made them the dens which are in the mountains, and caves, and strongholds. And so it was, when Israel had sown, that the Midianites came up, and the Amalekites, and the children of the east, even they came up against them" (Jud. 6:2-3).

* Length of oppression: 7 years
* Years of peace: 40 years
* Accomplishments: Delivered Israel from Midianite oppression with only 300 men.

Gideon and the Angel. As he threshed wheat behind a winepress, Gideon was commissioned by the Angel of God to raise an army and defeat the Midianites.

"And the Angel of the LORD appeared unto him, and said unto him, 'The LORD is with thee, thou mighty man of valor.'

"And Gideon said unto him, 'O my LORD, if the LORD be with us, why then is all this befallen us? And where be all His miracles which our fathers told us of, saying, "Did not the LORD bring us up from Egypt?" But now the LORD hath forsaken us, and delivered us into the hands of the Midianites.' And the LORD looked upon him, and said, 'Go in this thy might, and thou shalt save Israel from the hand of the Midianites; have not I sent thee?' " (vv. 12-14)

Gideon and the altar. Gideon obeyed by building an altar to Jehovah-Shalom ("the LORD send peace") and by destroying the Baal god-idol his family had been guilty of worshiping.

"And it came to pass the same night, that the LORD said unto him, 'Take thy father's young bullock, even the second bullock of seven years old, and throw down the altar of Baal that thy father hath, and cut down the grove that is by it; and build an altar unto the LORD thy God upon the top of this rock, in the ordered place, and take the second bullock, and offer a burnt sacrifice with the wood of the grove which thou shalt cut down.'

"Then Gideon took 10 men of his servants, and did as the LORD had said unto him; and so it was, because he feared his father's household, and the men of the city, that he could not do it by day, that he did it by night" (vv. 25-27).

Gideon and the anointing. "The Spirit of the LORD came upon Gideon, and he blew a trumpet" (v. 34). In spite of this, Gideon was still doubtful until God gave him special reassurance.

"And Gideon said unto God, 'If Thou wilt save Israel by mine hand, as Thou hast said, behold, I will put a fleece of wool in the floor; and if the dew be on the fleece only, and it be dry upon all the earth beside, then shall I know that Thou wilt save Israel by mine hand, as Thou hast said.'

"And it was so; for he rose up early on the morrow, and thrust the fleece together, and wringed the dew out of the fleece, a bowl full of water.

"And Gideon said unto God, 'Let not Thine anger be hot against me, and I will speak but this once; let me prove, I pray Thee, but this once with the fleece; let it now be dry only upon the fleece, and upon all the ground let there be dew.'

"And God did so that night; for it was dry upon the fleece only, and there was dew on all the ground" (vv. 36-40).

Gideon and his army. After the twofold casting of the fleece (vv. 36-40), he raised an army of 32,000 only to see it drop down to 10,000, and finally to 300. With these 300 he would face 135,000 enemy troops (7:1-7; 8:10).

"And the LORD said unto Gideon, 'By the 300 men . . . will I save you, and deliver the Midianites into thine hand' " (7:7).

On the eve of battle, he was reassured of victory by overhearing a frightened conversation between two enemy soldiers (vv. 9-15).

"And when Gideon was come, behold, there was a man that told a dream unto his fellow, and said, 'Behold, I dreamed a dream, and, lo, a cake of barley bread tumbled into the host of Midian, and came unto a tent, and smote it that it fell, and overturned it, that the tent lay along.'

"And his fellow answered and said, 'This is nothing else save the sword of Gideon the son of Joash, a man of Israel; for into his hand hath God delivered Midian, and all the host' " (vv. 13-14).

He then divided his army into three companies, and, at the given signal during a night attack, each man blew a trumpet, broke a clay jar, raised up a blazing torch, and shouted in unison, *"The sword of the LORD and of Gideon" (vv. 16-22).*

The Midianite army was thrown into panic and completely routed. During the battle, Gideon was forced to appease the anger of the jealous tribe of Ephraim. He then punished several Transjordan cities which had refused to aid him in pursuing the enemy.

Gideon and the apostasy. After the victory,

he refused an offer by Israel to become king, but may have had aspirations for the priestly office, as he asked for a golden ephod. An ephod was part of the apparel worn by a high priest. This later proved to be a snare for Israel, as they began worshiping it.

"And Gideon made an ephod thereof, and put it in his city, even in Ophrah; and all Israel went thither a-whoring after it; which thing became a snare unto Gideon and to his house" (8:27).

Sixth judge: Tola

* Oppressing nation: unrecorded
* Length of oppression: unrecorded
* Years of peace: 23
* Accomplishments: unrecorded

Seventh judge: Jair

* Oppressing nation: unrecorded
* Length of oppression: unrecorded
* Years of peace: 22
* Accomplishments: He and his 30 sons delivered 30 Israelite cities from oppression.

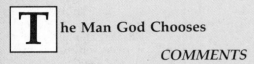

The Man God Chooses

COMMENTS

Gideon was the fifth judge whom God raised up to deliver His people. This time the enemy was Midian, who oppressed Israel for seven years. During these seven years the Midianites ranged throughout the land at will stealing and destroying crops and herds. In desperation, Israel cried to Jehovah for deliverance (6:6). Through an unnamed prophet God sent a message of promised deliverance (v. 8). God would raise up a mighty deliverer from a most unlikely place in the form of a most unlikely person, Gideon. Consider the following evidences of Gideon's cowardice that make him a most unlikely candidate to be the hero who would deliver Israel: (1) Gideon sought to hide from the Midianites by getting down inside of the winepress to thresh grain (v. 11). The KJV states that he was "by the winepress" but the RV, RSV, NASB, and NIV all translate the same expression as "in a winepress." Gideon feared the Midianites would come and take his grain so he sought to carry on his threshing in the cramped confines of a winepress so that he wouldn't be seen. (2) Gideon did not take the Angel's salutation seriously (v.13). When the Angel saw Gideon *in* the winepress and greeted him with the salutation, "The LORD is with thee, thou mighty man of valor," Gideon did not take that salutation seriously and acted as if the Angel were either speaking in jest or talking about someone else. (3) Gideon did not really believe that God could use him to save Israel (v. 15). He made every excuse he could think of to show that he was unqualified and unable to be Israel's deliverer. (4) Gideon asked for a sign so that he could be sure that he had truly spoken to God's Angel (v. 17). He prepared an offering of a kid, cakes made from an ephah (1.1 bushels—quite a sizable offering in times of deprivation) of flour, and some broth which the Angel directed him to put on the makeshift altar of a rock (v. 20). The Angel touched the offering with His staff and it was consumed with fire, indicating that it had been received as a burnt offering by God Himself. (5) Gideon thought that he would die because he had seen an Angel (v. 22). It was common Jewish tradition that at death one would see an angel. (6) Gideon was afraid to tear down the altar to Baal that his father had built and erect in its place an altar to Jehovah (vv. 25-26). To his credit, he did it, but at night when no one would be able to stop him (v. 27). (7) Gideon had to put out a fleece twice—once to have it soaked and the ground dry and a second time to have it dry and the ground soaked—to be sure that God had in fact called him (vv. 36-40). (8) Gideon took 31,700 more men then he needed into battle (7:1-7). God cut his force down to 300 by whom He promised to save Israel (v. 7). (9) Gideon feared to go down into the Midianites' camp and took Phurah along with him (v. 10). Gideon was anything but a candidate for "hero" or "deliverer."

Now, let us consider what God did to take this most unlikely candidate and make him into His champion. (1) At the winepress the Angel of the Lord encouraged him by calling him a "mighty man of valor" and assured him of His presence (6:12, 14, 16). (2) The Angel of the Lord accepted Gideon's offering as an act of worship (v. 21). (3) The Angel of the Lord assured Gideon that he would not die (v. 23). (4) God used Gideon's obedience in tearing down his father's altar to Baal to cause his father to give up Baal worship (vv. 31-32). (5) God did not rebuke Gideon but patiently complied with his tests in putting out the fleece (vv. 36-40). (6) God assured Gideon that the 300 men were adequate for His purpose of delivering Israel from the Midianites (v. 7). (7) God let Gideon and Phurah hear the interpretation of the Midianite soldier's dream which let Gideon know that the Midianites were more afraid of him than he was of them (vv. 13-15).

With such an unlikely man and 300 others like him, the mighty army of Midian consisting of 135,000 men was defeated and 120,000 slain (8:10). The man whom God chooses is one who has no confidence in himself and is willing simply to do what God tells him to do; even in fear. Such a man was Gideon, not by design, but by default.

Eighth judge: Jephthah

* Oppressing nation: Ammon
* Length of oppression: 18 years
* Years of peace: 6 years
* Accomplishments: Delivered Israel from the Ammonites; fought the Ephraimites.

The vow of Jephthah. At this time God once again severely rebuked Israel for their horrible sin of forsaking Him. He had already done this on two previous occasions. See 2:1-5, 11-23; 6:8-10.

" 'Yet ye have forsaken Me, and served other gods; wherefore I will deliver you no more. Go and cry unto the gods which ye have chosen; let them deliver you in the time of your tribulation.'

"And the Children of Israel said unto the LORD, *'We have sinned; do Thou unto us whatsoever seemeth good unto Thee; deliver us only, we pray Thee, this day.'*

"And they put away the strange gods from among them, and served the LORD; *and His soul was grieved for the misery of Israel" (10:13-16).*

A looked-down-upon harlot's son named Jephthah was now raised up by God to deliver Israel, this time from the Ammonites. On the eve of battle, however, Jephthah made a rash vow he would soon bitterly regret.

"And Jephthah vowed a vow unto the LORD, *and said, 'If Thou shalt without fail deliver the children of Ammon into mine hands, then it shall be, that whatsoever cometh forth of the doors of my house to meet me, when I return in peace from the children of Ammon, shall surely be the* LORD'S, *and I will offer it up for a burnt offering" (11:30-31).*

The virgin of Jephthah. The next day a confident and courageous Jephthah totally routed the enemy. But his victory celebration was short-lived, for when he rode into Mizpeh (his hometown), the first person to greet him from his house was his only daughter.

The vexation of Jephthah. At the end of a 60-day mourning period, a heartbroken Jephthah kept his vow.

The vengeance of Jephthah. After all this, his troubles were not yet over, for he was provoked into battle by the jealous tribe of Ephraim. As a result of this tragic battle, 42,000 Ephraimite troops were killed. They were identified by their inability to pronounce a Hebrew word, *Shibboleth* (meaning, "stream").

Ninth judge: Ibzan

* Oppressing nation: unrecorded
* Length of oppression: unrecorded
* Years of peace: 7 years
* Accomplishments: unrecorded

Tenth judge: Elon

* Oppressing nation: unrecorded
* Length of oppression: unrecorded
* Years of peace: 10
* Accomplishments: unrecorded

Eleventh judge: Abdon

* Oppressing nation: unrecorded
* Length of oppression: unrecorded
* Years of peace: 8 years
* Accomplishments: unrecorded

God's Ordinary People

COMMENTS

The spiritual revival under Gideon's ministry was short-lived—the people returned to worshiping Baal (8:33). Gideon not only had the weakness of being fearful, he had a weakness for women. He had many wives by whom he had 70 sons. He also had at least one concubine by whom he had another son, Abimelech who slew 69 of his 70 half-brothers (9:5) and set himself up as king of the land (v. 6). Abimelech died by a brutality similar to that by which he had seized power (9:50-56).

After Abimelech, two minor judges arose, Tola and Jair, whose main function was to fill in the space between Abimelech and Jephthah (10:1-18). Jephthah was the son of Gilead and a harlot (11:1). He was put out of his home by Gilead's other sons. Jephthah fled to the land of Tob taking with him a group of worthless men (v. 3). Jephthah must have had a strong character and leadership abilities for the elders of Gilead came to him seeking his help in their plight (vv. 5-10). A deal was struck, and Jephthah became the leader of Israel's forces (vv. 9-11). Jephthah entered into negotiations with the king of Ammon, but no agreement was reached (vv. 12-28). The Spirit of the Lord came on Jephthah (v. 29) to equip him for the forthcoming conflict. Jephthah made a vow to the Lord that if He would grant him victory over Ammon, at his return he would offer as a burnt offering to Jehovah whatsoever came out of the door of his house first to meet him (v. 30). God gave Jephthah a mighty victory (v. 33). At his return, his only daughter came out to meet her father (v. 34). Jephthah realized the rashness of his vow (v. 35) but nonetheless kept his vow (vv. 36-40).

Was Jephthah right in making his vow? The Scripture does not say. It is certain that the vow did nothing to persuade God. Israel would have won the victory whether he had made the vow or not. Had he not made it, he would not have lost his only daughter at his own hands, nor would he have been without descendant, nor would his daughter have been deprived of life and its privileges. Jephthah, who had been born an illegitimate child, was sinned against before he was born. In making the rash vow, Jephthah sinned against his only child. Worse than making the vow, perhaps, was Jephthah's unwillingness to admit that he had erred in the vain attempt to guarantee something that God had determined.

The jealous Ephraimites, who had refused to help Jephthah earlier, threatened to do him evil (12:1). Jephthah gathered his troops together and took a strategic pass (through which the Ephraimites had to pass (12:5). In order to detect Ephraimites from other Israelites, Jephthah had them pronounce the word *"Shibboleth."* The "sh" sound was one which Ephraimites could not make. When a captive said *"Sibboleth,"* his identity as an Ephraimite was certain and Jephthah's men took him and slew him. Forty-two thousand Ephraimites failed the test that day and were slain (12:6). This is not the only time in the Bible or in history that a similar test was used to determine friend from foe. In the New Testament, Peter was detected by his speech to be a Galilean and a follower of Jesus as he warmed himself by the fire in Pilate's courtyard (Matt. 26:73). In the days of World War II, American troops in the Solomon Islands required the pronunciation of "lollapalooza" when they challenged a suspected infiltrator at night. The Japanese soldiers, incapable of pronouncing "l," substituted the sound of "r" and would say something like "roraparooza." Those failing the pronunciation tests were slain.

Jephthah's tenure as a judge was short—six years (12:7). God used him to unite Israel and purify the tribe of Ephraim. Three minor judges followed him, Ibzan, Elon, and Abdon, whose main function is to bridge the gap between the judgeships of Jephthah and Samson.

Preview

The Messiah's Military Men (Part Three)

JUDGES 13–16

He looked so peaceful, lying there asleep in her lap. A twinge of conscience suddenly swept through her. Perhaps it was wrong to do him in. But she wanted the money. Besides, maybe he was lying to her about his strength, as he had done three other times. Some Nazarite! Well, she would know soon enough.

"The Philistines be upon thee, Samson!" she screamed.

Instantly the Hebrew strong man sprang to his feet. But to his horror he realized his power was gone. His head had been shaved. He was helpless. Sensing this the Philistines, like hungry vultures, moved in. With gleeful revenge they gouged out his eyes, then tied him up as a wild animal. There he stood, before Delilah and the Philistines, bald, blinded, and bound. Could it be, they asked? Was this pitiful and powerless creature the same mighty warrior who had previously burned their fields, carried off their city gates, and slaughtered their army? It was indeed.

What in the world had happened? The answer was simple: God had once raised him up, but now sin had laid him low. Of course, they could not know at that moment that his hair and strength would come back, and they would die.

Overview

<table>
<tr><td>SCRIPTURE</td><td colspan="7">Judges 13–16</td></tr>
<tr><td>SUBJECT</td><td colspan="7">Ministry of Samson</td></tr>
<tr><td rowspan="6">SPECIFICS</td><td rowspan="2">His selection by God</td><td colspan="3">The occasion</td><td colspan="3">The office</td></tr>
<tr><td colspan="3">He was to deliver God's people</td><td colspan="3">He was to be a Nazarite</td></tr>
<tr><td rowspan="2">His strength from God</td><td colspan="2">Subduing animals</td><td colspan="2">Subduing soldiers</td><td colspan="2">Subduing objects</td></tr>
<tr><td colspan="2">A lion
300 foxes</td><td colspan="2">Killing 30 Philistines
Killing 1,000 Philistines</td><td colspan="2">Ripping up a gate
Tearing down a temple</td></tr>
<tr><td rowspan="2">His sins against God</td><td colspan="3">Action sins</td><td colspan="3">Attitude sins</td></tr>
<tr><td colspan="3">Immorality
Inebriation</td><td colspan="3">Impiety
Ingratitude</td></tr>
<tr><td>SAINTS AND SINNERS</td><td colspan="7">Manoah, Samson, Samson's wife, Delilah</td></tr>
<tr><td rowspan="2">SENTENCE SUMMARIES</td><td>O.T. Verses</td><td colspan="6">"My son, keep my words, and lay up my commandments with thee. . . . That they may keep thee from the strange woman, from the stranger which flattereth with her words. . . . For she hath cast down many wounded; yea, many strong men have been slain by her" (Prov. 7:1, 5, 26).</td></tr>
<tr><td>N.T. Verse</td><td colspan="6">"And what shall I more say? For the time would fail me to tell of Gideon, and of Barak, and of Samson, and of Jephthah, of David also, and Samuel, and of the prophets" (Heb. 11:32).</td></tr>
</table>

SRAEL'S STRONGMAN

Samson

* Oppressing nation: Philistia
* Length of oppression: 40 years
* Years of peace: 20 years
* Accomplishments: Set apart before birth as a Nazarite, fought against the Philistines; killed more Philistines at his death than in life.

His mission. Samson's mother was visited by the Angel of the Lord, who told her of his future birth.

"And there was a certain man of Zorah, of the family of the Danites, whose name was Manoah; and his wife was barren, and bare not. And the Angel of the Lord *appeared unto the woman, and said unto her, 'Behold now, thou art barren, and bearest not; but thou shalt conceive, and bear a son'" (Jud. 13:2-3).*

This heavenly messenger instructed the parents that their child was to be raised a Nazarite. According to Numbers 6:1-6, the Nazarite had three restrictions placed on him.

(1) He was not to touch wine.

(2) His hair was to remain untouched by a razor.

(3) He must not touch a dead body.

NOTE: Samson's mother was also commanded not to drink wine (Jud. 13:4, 7, 14).

On this occasion Samson's parents prayed a prayer all expectant Christian parents should pray.

"Then Manoah entreated the Lord, *and said, 'O my* Lord, *let the Man of God which thou didst send come again unto us, and teach us what we shall do unto the child that shall be born.' . . .*

"And Manoah said, 'Now let Thy words come to pass. How shall we order the child, and how shall we do unto him?' " (vv. 8, 12)

Samson was born and empowered by the Holy Spirit even as he grew up.

His marriage. To the dismay of his parents he determined to marry an unbelieving Philistine girl. Already Samson's carnal nature was coming to the surface. In spite of his sensuality, God used him for His glory.

"But his father and his mother knew not that it was of the Lord, *that he sought an occasion against the Philistines; for at that time the Philistines had dominion over Israel" (14:4).*

On route to Philistia he killed a lion. Later he discovered that a swarm of bees had chosen the carcass of the lion to make honey in it. At his wedding feast, Samson used this experience as a basis for a riddle.

"And he said unto them, 'Out of the eater came forth meat, and out of the strong came forth sweetness.' And they could not in three days expound the riddle" (v. 14).

The guests eventually would dishonestly solve this riddle, getting it from Samson's bride. Furious, Samson paid his debt to the wedding guests, but only at the expense of 30 Philistine victims. He then returned to his parents' home. He returned to his bride only to find that the girl's father had given her to Samson's best man. In an act of revenge, the Hebrew strongman did the following:

"And Samson went and caught 300 foxes, and took firebrands, and turned tail to tail, and put a firebrand in the midst between the tails. And when he had set the brands on fire, he let them go into the standing corn of the Philistines, and burnt up both the shocks, and also the standing corn, with the vineyards and olives" (15:4-5).

His miracles. Samson then killed many Philistines. After this, the Philistines threatened to destroy the tribe of Judah unless they delivered Samson bound to them. Samson meekly allowed himself to be tied up, but as the enemy came in view, he broke the ropes, grabbed the jawbone of an ass, and slaughtered 1,000 Philistines. He then prayed one of his only two recorded prayers. Both were totally carnal and self-centered (cf. v. 18 with 16:28).

"And he was sore athirst, and called on the Lord, *and said, 'Thou hast given this great deliverance into the hand of Thy servant; and now shall I die for thirst, and fall into the hand of the uncircumcised?'*

"But God clave a hollow place that was in the jaw, and there came water thereout; and when he had drunk, his spirit came again, and he revived; wherefore he called the name thereof Enhakkore, which is in Lehi unto this day" (15:18-19).

His misconduct. At Gaza (a Philistine city) Samson once again avoided capture, this time by ripping apart the iron gate of the city. His purpose in going to Gaza was to visit a harlot. Samson was finally done in by a Philistine woman named Delilah, who discovered the source of his great strength.

At this point, Samson had violated all three Nazarite vows.

(1) He had touched the carcass of a lion.

(2) He had drunk wine.

(3) He had allowed his hair to be cut.

His misery. Samson then learned the high cost of low living. *"But the Philistines took him, and put out his eyes, and brought him down to Gaza, and bound him with fetters of brass; and he did grind in the prison house" (16:21).*

In prison he regained his strength as his hair grew out again. He was then allowed by God to destroy thousands of Philistines who had gathered in their heathen temple for a drunken orgy. In the following destruction Samson himself perished.

"And Samson called unto the LORD, and said, 'O LORD God, remember me, I pray Thee, and strengthen me, I pray Thee, only this once, O God, that I may be at once avenged of the Philistines for my two eyes.'

"And Samson took hold of the two middle pillars upon which the house stood, and on which it was borne up, of the one with his right hand, and of the other with his left. And Samson said, 'Let me die with the Philistines.' And he bowed himself with all his might; and the house fell upon the lords, and upon all the people that were therein. So the dead which he slew at his death were more than they which he slew in his life" (vv. 28-30).

S amson: God's Mirror to Israel and Us

COMMENTS

Samson especially illustrates what the psalmist proclaimed; "Lo, children are a heritage of the LORD; and the fruit of the womb is His reward" (Ps. 127:3). To his parents came the Angel of the Lord (the preincarnate Christ) to announce that Samson was going to be born (Jud. 13:3) and that he was to be a Nazarite (one who is set aside for God's special purpose) whom God would use to deliver Israel out of the hand of the Philistines (v. 5). As a testimony of his Nazarite vow and life, his hair was not to be cut and he was to drink no wine or eat anything that was unclean. His mother was commanded to engage in special prenatal care which consisted of similar rules.

All of these things let Samson's parents, and later, Samson himself, and still later, the reader of the narrative, know that God had a special ministry for Samson to perform. Samson was born as promised (v. 24). His name, Samson ("distinguished" or "strong") was a testimony of his mission.

Samson was used of God to accomplish great feats of strength. It might be thought that he was a man with great bulging muscles. That this is not the case is evident from the following considerations. (1) The main point of the story of his life is that his strength was supernatural (v. 25; 14:6; 19; 15:14). (2) People were puzzled at the source of his strength and wondered what it was (16:5). (3) When he actually lost his strength he did not know it until he tried to use it (v. 20). (4) His strength completely left him when his vow was broken (13:5; 16:19-22). The true source of Samson's strength was in the ministry of the Spirit of God to him (13:25; 14:6; 15:14).

Samson is an illustration of what God can do with one totally surrendered and separated unto Him. To the degree that the believer is separated, to that degree he will have the strength of God operating in his life. Samson also shows what happens when one goes back on his separation from the world unto God. When Samson renounced his vow, he lost: (1) his power and strength (16:19); (2) his liberty, honor, and dignity; (3) his vision (v. 21); and (4) his testimony (v. 23).

Interesting parallels can be drawn between the life of Samson and the nation Israel. Samson was a mirror in which the nation could see itself: (1) both were called to be Nazarites to God; (2) the secret of strength in both was separation from the world and separation unto God; (3) God's strength was lost when the vow of separation was broken; (4) Samson was and Israel will be restored to a place of God's favor.

God used Samson as a negative example to purify Israel. His life stands as an object lesson to the virtues and blessings of being totally separated unto God and as a tragic warning of the dangers of illicit sex and sex appeal.

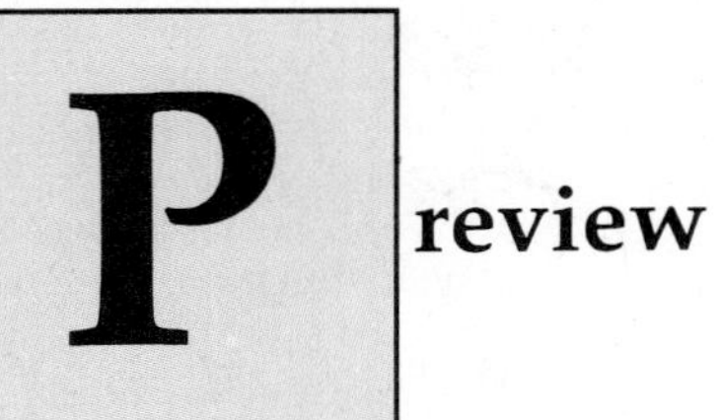

Studies in Sin: A Threefold Travesty

JUDGES 9; 17–21

Could any more depressing and depraved conditions possibly exist? Had the whole world suddenly gone mad? It was bad enough when Israel was plagued by its enemies from without. But now the land had been literally tormented by its own tribal inhabitants.

First there was the rise and fall of Abimelech, the mad-dog killer, a son of Gideon. Three cheers for that unknown woman who crushed the skull of this bloodthirsty bramble king. Then Micah the religious apostate had come along, and with him a money-grabbing minister. Their ungodly actions would seriously weaken the spiritual condition of the tribe of Dan. Finally, and by far the most horrible, was the city of Gibeah's problem. An especially vicious crime of rape and murder had initiated the crisis. Before it ended 40,000 Israelite troops lay dead, the result of a tragic intertribal war. Eleven tribes against one. When the battle smoke cleared, Benjamin, the one tribe, was reduced to 600 fighting men. Had it not been for some dancing damsels at Shiloh, Benjamin would have been no more.

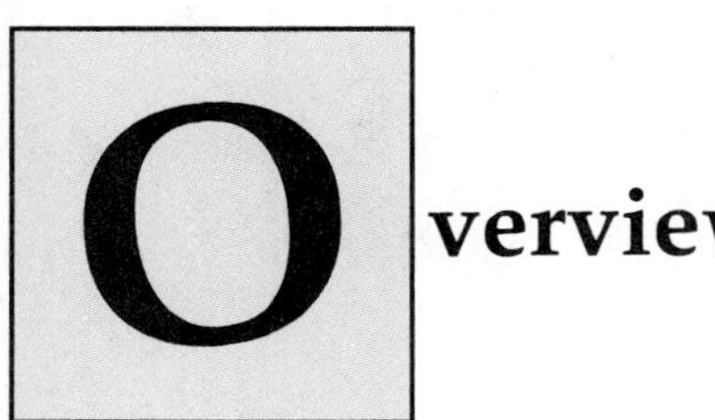

Overview

<table>
<tr><td>SCRIPTURE</td><td colspan="4">Judges 9; 17–21</td></tr>
<tr><td>SUBJECT</td><td colspan="4">Murder, idolatry, and intertribal war</td></tr>
<tr><td rowspan="3">SPECIFICS</td><td colspan="4">Three terrible tales</td></tr>
<tr><td></td><td>Number 1</td><td>Number 2</td><td>Number 3</td></tr>
<tr><td>The root</td><td>Insane lust for power</td><td>Indulgence
Apostasy
Greed</td><td>Rape
Murder</td></tr>
<tr><td></td><td>The fruit</td><td>The murder of 69 of Gideon's sons</td><td>Adding to the carnality of the tribe of Dan</td><td>The near-extinction of the tribe of Benjamin</td></tr>
<tr><td>SAINTS AND SINNERS</td><td colspan="4">Abimelech, Jotham, Micah, two Levites, an old man</td></tr>
<tr><td rowspan="2">SENTENCE SUMMARIES</td><td>O.T. Verses</td><td colspan="3">"Where there is no vision, the people perish; but he that keepeth the Law, happy is he" (Prov. 29:18).</td></tr>
<tr><td>N.T. Verses</td><td colspan="3">"Now the works of the flesh . . . are these: adultery, fornication, uncleanness, lasciviousness, idolatry, witchcraft, hatred, variance, emulations, wrath, strife, seditions, heresies, envyings, murders, drunkenness, revelings, and such like. Of the which I tell you before, as I have also told you in time past, that they which do such things shall not inherit the kingdom of God" (Gal. 5:19-21).</td></tr>
</table>

I SRAEL'S INTERNAL WAR

A BLOODY BUTCHER— ABIMELECH

Abimelech was the mad-dog son of Gideon by a concubine in Shechem. He arranged for the brutal murder of 69 of his 70 half-brothers and was crowned "king" of his mother's hometown.

Jotham, the half-brother who escaped, related one of the two fables in the Bible and directed it at Abimelech. (See Jud. 9:7-15; 2 Kings 14:9.)

"The trees went forth on a time to anoint a king over them; and they said unto the olive tree, 'Reign thou over us.'

"But the olive tree said unto them, 'Should I leave my fatness, wherewith by me they honor God and man, and go to be promoted over the trees?'

"And the trees said to the fig tree, 'Come thou, and reign over us.'

"But the fig tree said unto them, 'Should I forsake my sweetness, and my good fruit, and go to be promoted over the trees?'

"Then said the trees unto the vine, 'Come thou, and reign over us.'

"And the vine said unto them, 'Should I leave my wine, which cheereth God and man, and go to be promoted over the trees?'

"Then said all the trees unto the bramble, 'Come, thou, and reign over us' " (Jud. 9:8-14).

Three years later God (using an evil spirit) stirred up trouble between Abimelech and the citizens of Shechem. In the ensuing struggle, Abimelech was killed.

"And a certain woman cast a piece of a millstone upon Abimelech's head, and all to break his skull. Then he called hastily unto the young man his armor-bearer, and said unto him, 'Draw thy sword, and slay me, that men say not of me, "A woman slew him." ' And his young man thrust him through, and he died" (vv. 53-54).

AN IDOL-WORSHIPING SON— MICAH

Micah, a spoiled thief and idol-worshiper, was encouraged by his indulgent mother to "start his own religion." This he did by (among other things) hiring his own personal priest, a money-grabbing Levite from Bethlehem. This perverted "private pastor" was later enticed by the tribe of Dan to become their official priest.

At this time the tribe of Dan left their previously allotted land area located near the Philistines and migrated north. Afterward, the common expression "from Dan to Beersheba" was used to designate the extreme northern and southern boundaries of Israel. (See 20:1; 1 Sam. 3:20; 2 Sam. 3:10.)

A COWARDLY LEVITE

The wickedness in Benjamin. These chapters are among the most depressing in all the Bible. It all began when a Levite and his unfaithful concubine wife stopped overnight in Gibeah, a city located in the tribal territory of Benjamin. The couple stayed with an old man, whose house was surrounded that very night by a group of sex perverts who demanded the Levite come out and partake in their disgusting and degrading actions. The cowardly Levite saved himself by giving his concubine over to this miserable mob. By morning, the perverts had sexually murdered her. The Levite (who apparently was emotionally sick himself) thereupon cut up her dead body into 12 pieces, and sent a bloody chunk to each tribe in Israel along with the story of what happened.

The war against Benjamin. Israel was enraged at this sexual crime and gathered an army of over 400,000 troops to punish the guilty perverts of Gibeah. However, the citizens of Benjamin refused to surrender the criminals and a civil war broke out. After an especially bloody three-battle war in which Israel lost 40,000 men, Benjamin was defeated. Only 600 Benjamin soldiers were left alive.

The wives for Benjamin. A sobered and saddened Israel provided wives for these 600, lest the very name of Benjamin disappear from the face of the earth. They did this by giving them 400 Israelite girls from the city of Jabesh-gilead, and then allowing the remaining 200 soldiers to "kidnap" their wives during a festival held at Shiloh.

"Therefore they commanded the children of Benjamin, saying, 'Go and lie in wait in the vineyards; and see, and, behold, if the daughters of Shiloh come out to dance in dances, then come ye out of the vineyards, and catch you every man his wife of the daughters of Shiloh, and go to the land of Benjamin.' . . .

"And the children of Benjamin did so, and took them wives, according to their number, of them that danced, whom they caught; and they went and returned unto their inheritance, and repaired the cities, and dwelt in them" (Jud. 21:20-21, 23).

The End Result of Anarchy

COMMENTS

What would it be like if everyone could do anything he wanted to do any time he wanted to do it? To some that might sound like the ultimate of freedom and utopia itself. Consider these statements. "In those days there was no king in Israel, but every man did that which was right in his own eyes" (17:6). "In those days there was no king in Israel" (18:1); "There was no magistrate in the land, that might put them to shame in anything" (v. 7). "And there was no deliverer" (v. 28); "There was no king in Israel" (19:1). "In those days there was no king in Israel; every man did that which was right in his own eyes" (21:25). To the libertine it would seem as if his dreams had indeed come true. He could do whatever he wanted to do without fear of rebuke, condemnation, or chastisement. He would feel as if he were truly free.

We don't have to wonder what man would do in such a circumstance for that was exactly the situation at the end of the period of the Judges. What did freedom from restraint produce? Apart from the dreadful things encountered in the opening 16 chapters of the book for which God delivered the people into bondage at least seven times, we find in chapters 17–21 that anarchy produced: (1) Idolatry and rebellion against God—the private practice of one's god of his own creation with his own personal priest—all contrary to the worship of Jehovah (chap. 17). (2) Defection—the entire tribe of Dan stole Micah's worship and his private priest and worshiped Micah's graven image until they were taken away in the Assyrian captivity (chap. 18, esp. v. 30). (3) Immorality and cowardice of the priesthood—the immoral cowardly priest permitted the brutal sexual violation of his concubine rather than to protect her with his own life (chap. 19). (4) Homosexuality, rape, and murder—the depraved Benjamites who lived in Gibeah were practicing homosexuals, who desired to have sexual relations with the priest but settled for gang-raping his concubine which ultimately resulted in her death (vv. 21-28). (5) A grisly butchering—the Levite cut up the corpse of his concubine and sent a chunk of her body to each of the tribes of Israel together with a report of what had happened (vv. 29-30). (6) Shock—Israel was shocked at the depths of degradation to which it had sunk (v. 30). (7) Vengeance—Israel was galvanized into action to punish the men of Benjamin for what they had done (this is probably the only redeeming feature in the entire narrative) (20:1-12). (8) Civil war and mass death—instead of delivering up the guilty offenders, Benjamin decided to protect them. This resulted in a civil war in which Israel lost 40,000 men (10 percent of its total army) and Benjamin lost 25,100—only 600 men remained in all the tribe of Benjamin (chap. 20). (9) Rash vows—in anger the men of Israel made an oath not to permit any of their daughters to marry one of the men of Benjamin (21:1-6). (10) Murder and contrived marriages—so that the name of Benjamin would not vanish into extinction the men of Israel murdered every man and woman of Jabesh-gilead except for 400 young virgins whom they gave to 400 of the men of Benjamin and arranged for the 200 remaining to "kidnap" wives during the festival held at Shiloh (21:7-24).

These sordid pages in the Book of Judges and these sordid blots on Israel's history demonstrate what man does when there is "no king in Israel" and every man does that which is "right in his own eyes" (v. 25). The result is not happiness and freedom. The result is sorrow and bondage for all. Anarchy is not good for the individual or the nation. True freedom is found only in restraint. Only in looking into "the perfect law of liberty" and doing what God says to do is there true freedom and happiness.

Preview

David's Great Grandparents: Their Personal Story

THE BOOK OF RUTH

As she watched the simple ceremony through tear-filled eyes, her thoughts drifted back to her own wedding so many years ago, right here in Bethlehem. She also remembered two other weddings and three rapid funerals in another land. How bitter and broken she had become. After all, the death of one's own husband and two sons in quick succession was almost more than a human heart could stand. The truth was, she probably would have given up, had it not been for her faithful daughter-in-law. Was ever a mother-in-law so blessed?

The turn of events had been truly amazing. She could actually feel her resentment melting away as the service progressed. No longer would she demand that her neighbors call her Mara, meaning bitterness. She would return to her original name, Naomi, meaning pleasant one. How wonderful the ways of God!

Suddenly she was jarred to reality. The ceremony was over. Gentle Boaz had married gracious Ruth. Her widowed daughter-in-law was once more a wife. Probably they would have children, Naomi thought. They would indeed. In fact, in the marvelous providence of God, Ruth would later become the great-grandmother of King David, and wonder of wonders, occupy a place in the genealogy leading to Israel's Messiah Himself, the Lord Jesus Christ!

Overview

<table>
<tr><td>SCRIPTURE</td><td colspan="4">The Book of Ruth</td></tr>
<tr><td>SUBJECT</td><td colspan="4">The story of Boaz and Ruth</td></tr>
<tr><td rowspan="3">SPECIFICS</td><td>Ruth in Moab</td><td colspan="3">Ruth in Bethlehem</td></tr>
<tr><td>Her tears</td><td>Her ministry to Naomi</td><td colspan="2">In a barley field
By a threshing floor</td></tr>
<tr><td>Her testimony</td><td>Her marriage to Boaz</td><td colspan="2">The shoe
The son</td></tr>
<tr><td>SAINTS AND SINNERS</td><td colspan="4">Elimelech, Naomi, Mahlon, Chilion, Ruth, Orpah, Boaz, “such a one”</td></tr>
<tr><td rowspan="2">SENTENCE SUMMARIES</td><td>O.T. Verse</td><td colspan="3">“They that know Thy name will put their trust in Thee; for Thou, LORD, hast not forsaken them that seek Thee” (Ps. 9:10).</td></tr>
<tr><td>N.T. Verse</td><td colspan="3">“Nevertheless let every one of you in particular so love his wife even as himself; and the wife see that she reverence her husband” (Eph. 5:33).</td></tr>
</table>

A MOABITE GIRL —RUTH

RUTH RENOUNCING

The famine. During a famine, a Bethlehem citizen named Elimelech (which means, "God as King"), his wife Naomi ("pleasant one") and their two sons, Mahlon and Chilion ("sick" and "pining") left Palestine and went into Moab.

The funerals. The two boys married, but soon tragedy struck, for first the father died, and then both sons, leaving three saddened widows. Naomi decided to return to Palestine and was accompanied by her daughter-in-law, Ruth. Naomi attempted to persuade Ruth to go back to her own home. Ruth's answer must be counted as one of the most beautiful statements ever to come from the human throat.

The faith. "And Ruth said, 'Entreat me not to leave thee, or to return from following after thee; for whither thou goest, I will go; and where thou lodgest, I will lodge; thy people shall be my people, and thy God my God. Where thou diest, will I die, and there will I be buried. The LORD do so to me, and more also, if aught but death part thee and me' " (Ruth 1:16-17).

The frustration. Ruth and Naomi began their difficult trip, walking nearly 100 miles and crossing mountains a mile high. When they returned, a disillusioned Naomi informed her old neighbors to call her Mara, which means, "bitter," and not Naomi.

Ruth requesting. Ruth went out to glean wheat and, in the providence of God, picked a field belonging to Boaz, a near relative of Elimelech. Boaz was the son of the ex-harlot, Rahab. Boaz saw her, and apparently fell in love with her. He treated her ever so kindly and ordered his hired hands to do the same.

"And Boaz answered and said unto her, 'It hath fully been showed me, all that thou hast done unto thy mother-in-law since the death of thine husband; and how thou hast left thy father and thy mother, and the land of thy nativity, and art come unto a people which thou knewest not heretofore. The LORD recompense thy work, and a full reward be given thee of the LORD God of Israel, under whose wings thou art come to trust.' . . .

"And when she was risen up to glean, Boaz commanded his young men, saying, 'Let her glean even among the sheaves, and reproach her not, and let fall also some of the handfuls of purpose for her, and leave them, that she may glean them and rebuke her not' " (2:11-12, 15-16).

Ruth brought home some 30 pounds of barley and reported the kindness of Boaz to Naomi, who immediately began planning a wedding.

Ruth resting. Naomi sent Ruth to Boaz with instructions for her to assume a position at his feet. This has been looked on by some as an immoral act, but no one who knew the customs of Israel and the ancient oriental world would make such a claim. According to Hebrew law, Ruth was entitled to call on her nearest of kin to fulfill the various duties of a kinsman redeemer. By this course of action, Ruth was doing just this. Boaz understood fully her request to *"spread therefore thy skirt over thine handmaid; for thou art a near kinsman" (3:9).* From this point on, Boaz took the necessary steps to marry Ruth. Boaz then explained to Ruth why he had not proposed marriage to her before this time. He said, *"There is a kinsman nearer than I" (v. 12).*

Ruth returned home to Naomi with a full report. Naomi reassured her concerning Boaz.

"Then said she, 'Sit still, my daughter, until thou know how the matter will fall; for the man will not be in rest, until he have finished the thing this day' " (v. 18).

Ruth reaping. Boaz called a council meeting to determine whether the nearest kinsman (who may have been a brother to Elimelech) wanted to assume his obligations. Boaz's heart must have dropped to his kneecap when the man said, "I will redeem it." But Boaz continued the meeting, saying: *"What day thou buyest the field of the hand of Naomi, thou must buy it also of Ruth the Moabitess, the wife of the dead, to raise up the name of the dead upon his inheritance" (4:5).*

With a great sigh of relief and no doubt a silent prayer of thanksgiving to God, Boaz heard the nearest redeemer conclude: *"I cannot redeem it for myself, lest I mar mine own inheritance. Redeem thou my right to thyself; for I cannot redeem it" (v. 6).*

The issue was no longer in doubt. Boaz would now marry Ruth. To confirm this decision, the man plucked off his shoe. It was the custom at that time in Israel for a man transferring a right of purchase to pull off his sandal and hand it to the other party. This publicly validated the transaction.

The song. Ruth and Boaz were married. She gave birth to Obed, who later became the grandfather of King David himself.

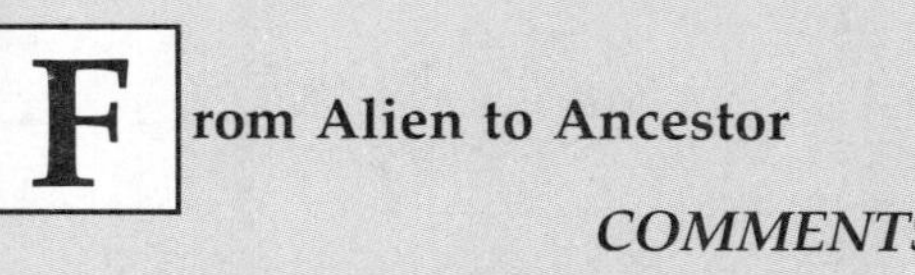

From Alien to Ancestor

COMMENTS

Against the dark backdrop of the unfaithfulness and apostasy of the period of the Judges stands the bright jewel of Ruth. A Gentile woman, Ruth, came to know the true and only God; left her homeland to go with her mother-in-law; supported her mother-in-law in her newly adopted country; and fell in love with and married the most eligible bachelor in Bethlehem, thus becoming an ancestor of Messiah. She was one of four women mentioned in Christ's genealogy and the only one who did not come from a sordid moral background.

In the Book of Ruth, the shoe covenant was the process by which Ruth was enabled to marry Boaz and thus be brought into the ancestral lineage of Messiah. It was enacted in connection with the right of the kinsman redeemer. Ruth was a widow. Her husband, Mahlon, Naomi's older son, was of the line of David (cf. 1:1; 4:17). He and Ruth had no children. This meant that at his death his nearest relative was to marry Ruth and have children by her so that the children would be able to care for their mother in her old age. Ruth had no thought of her own needs but set about to take care of the needs of her mother-in-law. She did this by going out into the fields and gathering that which the harvesters had failed to harvest. Boaz noticed Ruth (2:5) and made provision for her (vv. 8-9). He also learned all that he could about Ruth and of his own relationship to her. Ruth may have been entirely unfamiliar with the concept of the kinsman redeemer. When she returned home and gave Naomi the good news, she learned of her relationship to Boaz (v. 20).

The process by which Ruth went about to claim her right to Boaz as a kinsman redeemer must be seen in the light of the custom of the day. There were no sexual connotations at all. Boaz remained at the threshing floor to protect his crop. Ruth followed Naomi's instructions and went down to the threshing floor, uncovered his feet, and lay down at his feet. It was the way in which a woman claimed her right of marriage to her husband's next of kin. Boaz had already been thinking in these terms for he had done research and found that there was one closer to Ruth than he (3:12). However, he was willing and ready to do his part (v. 13).

To secure his right as the kinsman redeemer to marry Ruth, Boaz met with the man who was nearer to her than he. Boaz introduced the subject skillfully by telling "such a one" (4:1) about a parcel of land that was available. "Such a one" was eager to obtain the land (v. 4) until he learned that in order to get the land he must also marry Ruth (v. 5). At this point, he gave up his privilege (v. 6) and was willing to relinquish his right to marry Ruth to Boaz, who wanted it all along. To "seal the deal" Boaz and "such a one" entered into a shoe covenant. "Such a one" took off one of his shoes and Boaz took off one of his shoes. They exchanged shoes. The covenant was binding as long as each one possessed the other's shoe, or until something else happened to make the agreement irreversible.

The shoe covenant was the legal means whereby Ruth was brought into the line of Christ. She had a son, Obed, who had a son, Jesse, who had a son, David, who had a son . . . Jesus. Naomi's friends recognized Ruth's love for her and said that she was better to Naomi than if Naomi had had seven sons.

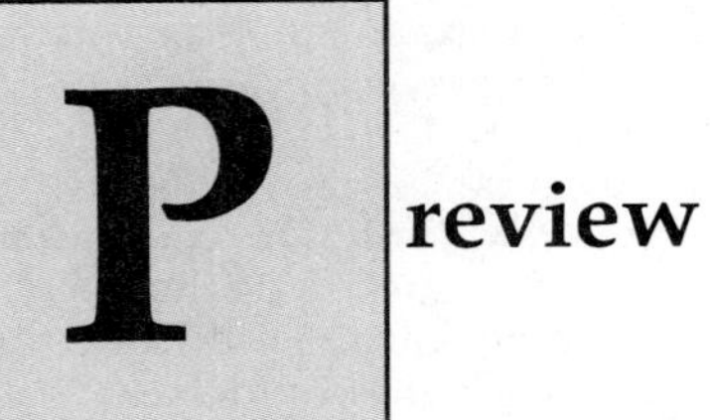

From Ichabod to Ebenezer

1 SAMUEL 1–7

Ichabod and Ebenezer! Strange words indeed. But in the fullest sense they summarize the latter part of the Judges Stage. One served as a reminder of Israel's failures, and the other of God's faithfulness. The first was whispered by a dying mother, while the second was proclaimed by a thankful prophet. Each word brought to mind a certain city. Ichabod, meaning "the glory of the LORD has departed" was connected to the destruction of the tabernacle by the Philistines at Shiloh. Ebenezer, meaning "Hitherto hath the LORD helped us," described the eventual victory over the Philistines at Mizpeh.

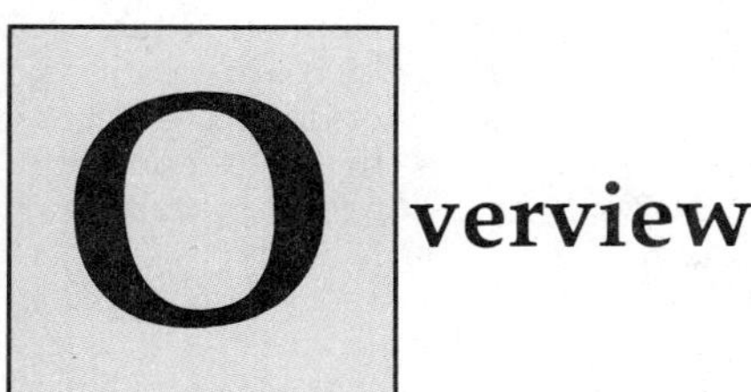

Overview

<table>
<tr><td>SCRIPTURE</td><td colspan="4">1 Samuel 1–7</td></tr>
<tr><td>SUBJECT</td><td colspan="4">Ministry of Eli and Samuel</td></tr>
<tr><td rowspan="4">SPECIFICS</td><td rowspan="4">Two births</td><td>Sorrowful</td><td rowspan="4">Two battles</td><td>Sorrowful</td></tr>
<tr><td>The birth of Ichabod</td><td>Israel defeated by the Philistines</td></tr>
<tr><td>Joyful</td><td>Joyful</td></tr>
<tr><td>The birth of Samuel</td><td>Israel victorious over the Philistines</td></tr>
<tr><td>SAINTS AND SINNERS</td><td colspan="4">Hannah, Eli, Samuel, wife of Phinehas</td></tr>
<tr><td rowspan="2">SENTENCE SUMMARIES</td><td>O.T. Verse</td><td colspan="3">"God is our refuge and strength, a very present help in trouble" (Ps. 46:1).</td></tr>
<tr><td>N.T. Verse</td><td colspan="3">"Strengthened with all might, according to His glorious power, unto all patience and long-suffering with joyfulness" (Col. 1:11).</td></tr>
</table>

DEDICATED MOTHER—HANNAH

HER PAIN

The account begins with a barren woman who stood weeping and praying at the altar in Shiloh. Her name was Hannah.

HER PRAYER

"And she vowed a vow, and said, 'O LORD of hosts, if Thou wilt indeed look on the affliction of Thine handmaid, and remember me, and not forget Thine handmaid, but wilt give unto Thine handmaid a man child, then I will give him unto the LORD all the days of his life, and there shall no razor come upon his head' " (1 Sam. 1:11).

We observe several factors in Hannah's request. Part of Hannah's sorrow was due to the constant ridicule from her husband's other wife, Peninnah.

Hannah vowed to raise a son, if given to her, as a Nazarite. Thus her boy, Samuel, would become one of the three Nazarites mentioned in the Bible. The other two were Samson (Jud. 13) and John the Baptist (Luke 1).

In her agony, Hannah moved her lips, but made no audible sound, which caused the old high priest Eli (who had been secretly watching her) to conclude that she was drunk. When rebuked for this supposed drunkenness, Hannah immediately denied the charge and then shared with Eli the true nature of her heartache. The old priest reassured her that God would indeed answer her prayer.

HER PRAISE

In the course of time God did "remember Hannah" with a son whom she called Samuel. When he was weaned (probably two-three years of age) Hannah brought him to Eli to dedicate him to God.

" 'For this child I prayed; and the LORD hath given me my petition which I asked of Him. Therefore, also, I have lent him to the LORD; as long as he liveth he shall be lent to the LORD.' And he worshiped the LORD there" (1 Sam. 1:27-28).

After the dedication, Hannah uttered a beautiful ode of praise which appears to be the basis of Mary's song found in Luke 1:46-55. (See 1 Sam. 2:1-10). In this remarkable prayer, Hannah mentioned a number of God's divine attributes.

(1) His holiness. *"There is none holy as the LORD" (v. 2).*

(2) His omniscience. *"The LORD is a God of knowledge" (v. 3).*

(3) His omnipotence. *"He bringeth low, and lifteth up" (v. 7).*

(4) His mercy. *"He raiseth up the poor . . . and . . . beggar . . . to set them among princes" (v. 8).*

(5) His faithfulness. *"He will keep the feet of His saints" (v. 9).*

(6) His justice. *"The LORD shall judge the ends of the earth" (v. 10).*

(7) His Messiah. *"He shall give strength unto His King, and exalt the horn of His anointed" (v. 10).*

N UNDISCIPLINED PRIEST

THE DEGENERATION OF ELI'S SONS

A sad note was now introduced concerning the two priestly sons of Eli.

According to the sacred account: (1) They were unsaved. (2) They regarded Belial as the true God. (3) They stole the offerings from God. (4) They bullied the people of God. (5) They committed adultery right in the tabernacle.

"Now Eli was very old, and heard all that his sons did unto all Israel; and how they lay with the women that assembled at the door of the tabernacle of the congregation" (v. 22).

(6) They caused God's people to transgress.

"Wherefore the sin of the young men was very great before the LORD; for men abhorred the offering of the LORD" (v. 17).

Eli attempted to correct this by a mild and weak "slap on the wrist," but his wicked sons remained unmoved and unrepentant.

"And he said unto them, 'Why do ye such things? For I hear of your evil dealings by all this people. Nay, my sons; for it is no good report that I hear; ye make the LORD's people to transgress. If one man sin against another, the judge shall judge him; but if a man sin against the LORD, who shall entreat for him?'

"Notwithstanding they hearkened not unto the voice of their father, because the LORD would slay them" (vv. 23-25).

THE RENUNCIATION OF ELI'S SONS

Eli was warned by an unnamed prophet of God concerning the following: (1) That his two wicked sons would both die on the same day. (2) That God would raise up a faithful priest.

God revealed Himself to Samuel one night as the boy lay in the tabernacle. This divine message contained the future judgment of Eli's household. The next morning a reluctant Samuel related all this to Eli.

"And ere the lamp of God went out in the temple of the LORD, where the ark of God was, and Samuel was laid down to sleep; that the LORD called Samuel; and he answered, 'Here am I.'

"And he ran unto Eli, and said, 'Here am I; for thou calledst me.'

"And he said, 'I called not; lie down again.' And he went and lay down.

"And the LORD called yet again, 'Samuel.' And Samuel arose and went to Eli, and said, 'Here am I' for thou didst call me.' And he answered, 'I called not, my son; lie down again.'

"Now Samuel did not yet know the LORD, neither was the word of the LORD revealed unto him.

"And the LORD called Samuel again the third time. And he arose and went to Eli, and said, 'Here am I; for thou didst call me.' And Eli perceived that the LORD had called the child.

"Therefore, Eli said unto Samuel, 'Go, lie down; and it shall be, if He call thee, that thou shalt say, "Speak, LORD, for Thy servant heareth." ' So Samuel went and lay down in his place.

"And the LORD came, and stood, and called as at other times, 'Samuel, Samuel.' Then Samuel answered, 'Speak, for Thy servant heareth' " (3:3-10).

Samuel was not elevated by God to the office of a prophet.

THE DESTRUCTION OF ELI'S SONS

After this, Israel was soundly defeated by the Philistines. During the battle, the ark of the covenant was captured, and Eli's two sons, Hophni and Phinehas, were killed. At this time, the tabernacle at Shiloh was also destroyed by the Philistines. (See Jer. 7:11-14.) The tragic news was brought back to Shiloh, resulting in the death of Eli and the total despair of his daughter-in-law, who with her dying breath, named her newborn son Ichabod, meaning, "the glory of the LORD has departed from Israel."

THE PHILISTINES AND THE ARK

The captured ark of the covenant proved a curse among the Philistines wherever it was taken. At Ashdod, it destroyed the statue of the idol god Dagon and smote the people with boils. At Gath it wrought great destruction and similar boils. At Ekron it brought great fear and more boils.

THE TRAVELS OF THE ARK

The ark was then placed by the Philistines on a wooden cart hitched to two cows. On this cart were also placed five golden mice. The ark was carried to an Israelite town called Beth-shemesh, where it was first received with great rejoicing, but later brought great sorrow, for some foolish men looked into the ark and caused a divine punishment from God.

From Beth-shemesh, the ark was taken to another Israelite town named Kirjath-jearim. Here it remained for 20 years.

A CIRCUIT-RIDING PREACHER—SAMUEL

"And Samuel grew, and the LORD was with him, and did let none of his words fall to the ground. And all Israel, from Dan even to Beer-sheba, knew that Samuel was established to be a prophet of the LORD. And the LORD appeared again in Shiloh . . . [and] revealed Himself to Samuel" (vv. 19-21).

THE REVIVAL

At this time, the great prophet and priest Samuel gathered all of Israel at Mizpeh (another town in Palestine) for a great revival.

"And Samuel spake unto all the house of Israel, saying, 'If ye do return unto the LORD with all your hearts, then put away the strange gods and Ashtaroth from among you, and prepare your hearts unto the LORD, and serve Him only; and He will deliver you out of the hand of the Philistines.'

"Then the Children of Israel did put away Baalim and Ashtaroth, and served the LORD only. And Samuel said, 'Gather all Israel to Mizpeh, and I will pray for you unto the LORD.'

"And they gathered together to Mizpeh, and drew water, and poured it out before the LORD, and fasted on that day, and said there, 'We have sinned against the LORD.' And Samuel judged the Children of Israel in Mizpeh" (7:3-6).

THE REMEMBRANCE

To celebrate this wonderful victory Samuel did a significant thing. *"Then Samuel took a stone, and . . . called the name of it Ebenezer, saying, 'Hitherto hath the Lord helped us' " (v. 12).*

"And Samuel judged Israel all the days of his life. And he went from year to year in circuit to Bethel, and Gilgal, and Mizpeh, and judged Israel in all those places. And his return was to Ramah; for there was his house, and there he judged Israel; and there he built an altar unto the Lord" (vv. 15-17).

other's Prayers

COMMENTS

The biblical view of children is far different than the way children are viewed today. In the Bible, childlessness was regarded as an indication of the curse of God. Women wanted to have children even though the women of the Bible knew nothing of the modern conveniences in raising children and knew nothing of the medical advantages that modern women have in childbearing. In today's society, children are sometimes regarded as an economic liability to be avoided if at all possible. Millions of children have perished in abortion chambers in America alone. How different the biblical view as expressed by the psalmist, who states: "Lo, children are a heritage of the Lord; and the fruit of the womb is His reward" (Ps. 127:3). Hannah knew that many years before the psalmist penned those words.

Hannah's burden was made heavier by the fact that her home life was unhappy. She was one of two wives in a polygamous union. She shared her husband, Elkanah, with Peninnah. God blessed Peninnah with sons and daughters, "but Hannah had no children" (1 Sam. 1:2). At least, Elkanah loved her. To Elkanah's credit, he did love God and annually took his wives and family to the house of God at Shiloh to worship and sacrifice unto Jehovah. His home life was a testimony to the moral depths to which Israel sank during the period of the Judges when "every man did that which was right in his own eyes" (cf. Jud. 21:25).

Because she did have children and was jealous of Elkanah's evident love for Hannah, Peninnah taunted Hannah for her barrenness (1 Sam. 1:6-7). Hannah's barrenness, however, was not due to her misconduct nor as a judgment of God on her. It was God's doing (cf. v. 5) because He had a greater purpose for Hannah than Hannah could possibly have understood or appreciated. He was going to use her to be the channel through whom the last of the judges and the first of the prophets, Samuel, would come into the world.

Hannah knew what to do with her burden—she took it to the Lord in prayer (v. 11). In addition, she made a vow to the Lord. She promised that if God would hear her prayer and grant her a man child that she would give him back to the Lord all the days of his life and that he would be a Nazarite (v. 11). She uttered this prayer in the house of God at Shiloh. Eli, the priest, thought that she was drunk—another indication of the depths to which Israel's women had sunk during the days of the Judges. God heard Hannah's prayer and gave her the son she desired (v. 20). She named her son Samuel, "asked of God." Hannah was true to her vow. When she had weaned her son, she took him back to the house of God, not for a visit, but to live there permanently to be raised for the priesthood by Eli the high priest. Israelite mothers nursed their children as a matter of course until their third year, thus, Samuel was probably a toddler of about three years of age at this time. Hannah readily recognized the fact that Samuel was not only asked of the Lord but that he had been given to her by the Lord. Therefore, she returned him to the Lord who had given him to be whatever God wanted him to be.

God took Hannah up on her vow. She came to the temple annually to visit Samuel and bring him a new coat (2:19). God rewarded Hannah by giving her three more sons and two daughters (v. 21). That little son which Hannah gave back to God, God called to Himself (3:1-14) and used him to pronounce God's judgment on Eli's house (vv. 12-14, 18). The hand of the Lord on Samuel was evident to all for "all Israel from Dan to Beer-sheba knew that Samuel was established to be a prophet of the Lord" (v. 20). Undoubtedly, Samuel knew of his mother's prayers for his birth and her dedicating him to be whatever God wanted him to be. Truly, his mother's prayers followed him.

The Consequences of Disobedience

COMMENTS

If a popular vote were taken, Eli would probably have been voted as being the outstanding success of his day. He was a judge and high priest of Israel for 40 years (4:18). What greater sign of success could one want?

In spite of all of his success and wonderful qualifications, there was one area in which Eli was deficient—he failed to discipline his sons. He was a disobedient parent. "So what?" one might say, "You can't succeed at everything." In the New Testament, Paul gives one of the qualifications for a bishop (pastor) as being "one that ruleth well his own house, having his children in subjection with all gravity." His reasoning is that "if a man know not how to rule his own house, how shall he take care of the church of God?" (1 Tim. 3:4-5) The New Testament teaching clearly is that if one is disqualified in the parsonage, he is disqualified from the pulpit! Though Eli was a qualified priest and judge he was not qualified as a parent and that failure had some far-reaching effects on his sons, himself, and on the nation Israel. Let us consider some of the consequences of Eli's disobedience.

Because they were not disciplined by their father, Hophni and Phinehas "knew not the LORD" (1 Sam. 2:12) and "abhorred the offering of the LORD" (v. 17). They were priests in profession only. There was no heart reality in their service. As a further indication of their spiritual insensitivity, they committed illicit sexual acts right in the house of God before the view of the people (v. 22). Because Eli's sons were not disciplined by their father, God sent a message of judgment against them (vv. 27-34) and the house of Eli was rejected from the priesthood (v. 35). The worship of Jehovah degenerated into empty formalism and superstition. When the Philistines came against Israel, the Israelites thought that if they had the ark of the covenant with them in the field of battle that it would change their fortune (4:3). So, they took the ark of the covenant out into the battlefield and in the ensuing battle 30,000 Israelites died, the ark of God was captured, and Eli's sons, Hophni and Phinehas, were killed (v. 11). When the news reached 98-year-old Eli he fell backward and died of a broken neck. Eli's daughter-in-law, Phinehas' wife, died in childbirth, but not before she had named her son "Ichabod" (lit. "where is the glory?"), because the glory of God had departed from Israel and the ark of God had been taken captive (vv. 21-22). The difficulties that the Philistines had with the ark of God are a direct outgrowth of Eli's failure to discipline his sons. Had he disciplined them properly, it may be that the Philistines would have come to know God in truth through the gracious message of redemption. Instead, they experienced the judgment of God as they tried to show that their god, Dagon, had been the source of their great victory. Finally, wearied of having the ark of God among them, they determined to return it to Israel with an offering that they deemed appropriate (6:3-5). What a sight it must have been as the two milk cows (indicating that they were fresh and, contrary to nature, were leaving behind new calves) made their way straight to Beth-shemesh (v. 12). The men of Beth-shemesh looked into the ark of the Lord and 50,070 of their countrymen died as an indirect result of Eli's failure to discipline his sons (v. 19). If only Eli had been a faithful father as well as a faithful priest. How different history might have been.

In stark contrast to Eli's sons is Samuel who was given to the Lord even before he was born. He led the people in repentance and confession of sin (7:5-6) and interceded to Jehovah for them (vv. 7-8). Through Samuel's obedience, God wrought a mighty victory (vv. 10-14).

United Kingdom

The Israelite crowds began gathering by tribes at Mizpeh, just north of Jerusalem. Unfortunately, they could not meet in Jerusalem, for the Holy City was still occupied by pagans. Finally the great Prophet Samuel appeared and made his announcement. So it was true after all—Israel was to have its very own king, like all other nations! But from what tribe would he come? The popular view was from Judah, largest of them all. Others felt, however, he might be from Ephraim, the most influential tribe in the North. Both guesses proved wrong. Audible gasps were heard when the official selection was announced. Israel's first king would be Saul, son of Kish, and a Benjamite, smallest of all the tribes!

The United Kingdom is the tale of three kings. Saul was the first, David the second, and Solomon the third. The latter two were not only rulers but writers also. Many of the psalms came from David's pen, while Solomon authored the Books of Proverbs, Ecclesiastes, and Song of Solomon. These books, written by Israel's first kings, predict the glorious future reign of her final King, the Lord Jesus Christ!

Preview

The Big Man with a Small Heart

1 SAMUEL 8–15

True, he had experienced some nagging doubts at the beginning. For one thing, it had all come about so suddenly and in such an unexpected manner. It seemed only hours ago that they had presented him with their demand: "Give us a king!" Now here they were, joyously shouting, "God save the king!"

Observing the new monarch, Samuel wondered just what the man was thinking. After all, one did not normally begin his day seeking for lost farm animals and finish it by obtaining the throne of Israel! Whatever else, the prophet had to admit he did indeed look impressive. If big was best, then no more qualified candidate could possibly have been chosen. There he stood, head and shoulders above the crowd. Who would have thought a tall farmer from tiny Benjamin would be afforded such honor! Maybe it would all work out, the old man concluded, bothered by the painful reminder that he had personally and miserably failed in raising his own sons for such a leadership position.

But enough for silent speculation. Israel now had a king. Saul was his name. It was time for Samuel to quiet the crowd and explain the nature of their kingdom.

Overview

SCRIPTURE	1 Samuel 8–15		
SUBJECT	The life of King Saul		
SPECIFICS	The stormy story of Saul		
	His attributes	His accomplishments	His apostasy
	From humble background Tall and impressive Appointed by God Appointed by Samuel	United the 12 tribes of Israel Defeated the vicious enemies of Israel	Disobedience Self-will Murder Suicide
SAINTS AND SINNERS	Samuel, Saul, Nahash, Jonathan, Agag		
SENTENCE SUMMARIES	O.T. Verses	"For the kingdom is the LORD's, and He is the governor among the nations" (Ps. 22:28).	
	N.T. Verses	"Afterward they desired a king; and God gave unto them Saul the son of Kish, a man of the tribe of Benjamin, by the space of 40 years" (Acts 13:21).	

SAUL, ISRAEL'S FIRST KING

THE SELECTION OF SAUL

The circumstances leading to his selection. Israel's elders had gathered at Ramah and demanded that Samuel give them a king.

"And said unto him, 'Behold, thou art old, and thy sons walk not in thy ways; now make us a king to judge us like all the nations' " (1 Sam. 8:5).

Samuel was displeased and listed the many disadvantages of having a king. God nevertheless informed Samuel that He would give Israel a king and that Samuel could expect the new leader at his doorstep in 24 hours. The next day Saul unknowingly fulfilled this prophecy by seeking Samuel's help in locating some lost animals.

The chronology of his selection. Saul was privately anointed by Samuel at Ramah. He was publicly acclaimed by Samuel at Mizpeh (10:24). At this stage Saul was a very humble man. He felt he was unworthy of being king and actually had to be brought out of hiding when Samuel officially proclaimed him king.

The confirmation of his selection. Following his inaugural service, Saul returned to his farm in Gibeah. He later raised an army of 330,000 to rescue a surrounded Israelite city called Jabesh-gilead from a cruel enemy and thus established his ability to lead the kingdom. Samuel then gathered Israel to Gilgal and there delivered his final recorded sermon to the people.

Samuel reminded them of his own personal integrity, not mentioning, however, his failure as a father. He reviewed God's faithfulness to Israel during the days of Moses and the various judges. He set before Israel the two ways. To obey God would result in blessing. To disobey God would mean disaster. He reminded them that they were God's special people. He promised to pray for them. He issued one final challenge and warning. God Himself sanctioned all this by sending a supernatural thunderstorm.

THE REJECTION OF SAUL

Saul caused this by offering the sacrifice of a priest. *"And Saul said, 'Bring hither a burnt offering to me, and peace offerings.' And he offered the burnt offering. . . . And Samuel said to Saul, 'Thou hast done foolishly. Thou hast not kept the commandment of the LORD thy God, which He commanded thee; for now would the LORD have established thy kingdom upon Israel forever. But now thy kingdom shall not continue. The LORD hath sought Him a man after His own heart, and the LORD hath commanded him to be captain over His people, because thou hast not kept that which the Lord commanded thee' " (13:9, 13-14).*

He also ordered the death of his own son. Israel was threatened by a Philistine attack. Not having yet discovered the secret of smelting iron, as had the enemy, Israel was at a terrible disadvantage. Jonathan and his bodyguard were led by God to conduct a surprise attack on a Philistine stronghold. The attack was so successful it resulted in the total route of the Philistines. NOTE: See evidence of Jonathan's faith in 14:6. Prior to the battle however, Saul had foolishly issued a command which prohibited his soldiers from eating until they defeated their enemies. This would later cause the famished troops to break the levitical Law of God. Unaware of this stupid order by his father, Jonathan had eaten. When Saul discovered this, he ordered his son be killed. However, he was saved from death by the grateful soldiers.

Saul then opposed the command of God to destroy a pagan named Amalek and his city. This event was significant because it marked the total rejection of Saul by God. It illustrated a great biblical principle.

"And Samuel said, 'Hath the LORD as great delight in burnt offerings and sacrifices, as in obeying the voice of the LORD? Behold, to obey is better than sacrifice, and to hearken than the fat of rams' " (15:22).

It was the last meeting between Saul and Samuel before Samuel died.

The Institution of Kingship in Israel

COMMENTS

The office of king was, of course, common in the ancient Near East long before Israel appeared on the scene. It appears that kingship first originated in Mesopotamia when one elder was given temporary charge over a city by the other elders. Though the purpose of this arrangement was initially intended only to provide leadership in case of an emergency, it soon became a permanent establishment. The hereditary aspect associated with kingship was also a later development derived from the notion that a king was established by divine election. Since the favor of the local deity was thus associated with the elect king, his line was assumed to be under divine blessing and worthy of continued rule. This idea was carried to great extremes in ancient cultures: in Assyria the king came to represent the god and in Egypt he was actually equated with the god. In Israel, however, the king was always under God's sovereignty.

Kingship in the Bible is mentioned quite early in the person of Nimrod whose kingdom included Babylon (Gen. 10:8-10). A number of peoples also had kings much earlier than Israel: the Canaanites (14:2), the Philistines (20:2), the Edomites (36:31), the Moabites (Num. 22:4), and the Midianites (31:8). Another important early king was Melchizedek, king of Salem (Jerusalem), who is taken by the writer of Hebrews as a type of Christ.

The earliest idea of centralized rule among the Hebrew people may be traced to the patriarchal control over the nomadic tribes as exercised by Abraham, Isaac, Jacob, and Joseph. During the Exodus from Egypt, Moses, a leader especially chosen by God, led the people. He was succeeded by Joshua who was chosen by God and recognized publicly. These men were not kings however; they exercised their leadership only under the rule of the Lord. Such a government with God Himself as the Head is called a theocracy.

With the death of Joshua there was no special representative of the Lord in Israel. The Israelites were therefore left under the direct rule of God. While they were able to determine the divine will by the casting of the lot by the high priest, there was no centralized leadership. Consequently, the Israelites lost their sense of religious unity, fell into idolatry, and became disunited militarily. The awful cycles of sin, servitude, supplication, and salvation in the Book of Judges attest to the chaos of this period. The temporary leaders sent by the Lord were called judges but were limited in authority and locale. As a result, their successes were short-lived.

In light of the failure of the institution of the Judges to lead Israel successfully, it is not surprising that the people came to Samuel to request a king. Such desires were not new since the Israelites had earlier pressured Gideon, though unsuccessfully, to serve as king (Jud. 8:23). This time, however, the people were more persistent. The motivation seems to have been for military leadership, and the request itself was regarded by God as a rejection of the theocracy. God had in fact intended to establish kingship in Israel. This is evident from the promise given to Abraham, "Kings shall come out of thee"; from Moses' provision for kingship and from the typology of Christ as King. That this occasion was not God's ideal time to crown a king over Israel, however, is apparent from the Lord's explicit rejection of the people's motives and from Saul's tragic reign and humiliating death. Nevertheless, just as He had fulfilled the Israelites' wanton desires in the wilderness, the Lord again let them have the king they wanted. The disastrous life and rule of Saul speaks for itself as to the wisdom of requesting a king.

The divinely ordained duties of the king included in a general sense responsibility for the welfare of all the people. More specifically, he was obligated to defend the people, recruit and maintain an army, lead the army during warfare, and act as a judge of final appeal. He himself was subject to the Law. In a religious sense, he was "the LORD'S anointed," was seated on the throne of the "kingdom of the LORD over Israel," and even bore the title "son" of the Lord as Israel had done earlier. The king was intended to be God's representative on earth, a calling sorely miscarried by Israel's first king, but well exemplified by her second.

Preview

David: The First Years

1 SAMUEL 16–31

Israel's first king was dead. The sword- and arrow-pierced body of Saul lay cold at the base of Mount Gilboa. What a spotted and stormy reign he had conducted! It had all begun so promisingly. Few if any of his surviving soldiers were even born at the time of that unforgettable day 40 years back, when before an adoring crowd he was acclaimed king by Samuel at Mizpeh. Self-confidence and courage had been Saul's mainstay then. But all too soon his self-confidence turned into self-will and his courage into envy.

Even Saul's closest acquaintances had difficulty understanding his illogical and insane hatred for David. After all, this young shepherd from Bethlehem had not only served as a loyal soldier in his army, but later, on two occasions, spared Saul's life when Saul was attempting to kill him! Who could justify Saul's cruelty in light of David's kindness? Then, there was Saul's midnight visit to a witch, a desperate attempt to conjure up the dead! Spooky stuff indeed!

But all this was history. What would happen now? Who would lead Israel? David, the heir apparent, was living in Philistia. Would he return from exile? Would he command the necessary popular support, to say nothing of the ability, to rule God's people? The answers to all these questions would soon be forthcoming.

Overview

SCRIPTURE	1 Samuel 16–31	
SUBJECT	Life of David: part 1	
SPECIFICS	The early years	The evil years
	A staff	Hated by Saul
	A harp	
	A sling	Hounded by Saul
SAINTS AND SINNERS	Samuel, Jesse, David, Saul, Jonathan, Goliath, Eliab, Abner, Michal, Ahimelech, Achish, Doeg, Nabal, Abigail, witch of Endor	
SENTENCE SUMMARIES	O.T. Verses	"He chose David also His servant, and took him from the sheepfolds; from following the ewes great with young He brought him to feed Jacob His people, and Israel His inheritance" (Ps. 78:70-71).
	N.T. Verses	"Afterward they desired a king; and God gave unto them Saul the son of Kish, a man of the tribe of Benjamin, by the space of 40 years. And when He had removed him, He raised up unto them David to be their king; to whom also He gave testimony, and said, 'I have found David the son of Jesse, a man after Mine own heart, which shall fulfill all My will' " (Acts 13:21-22).

DAVID, ISRAEL'S FINEST KING

DAVID, THE SHEPHERD

David was anointed by Samuel in Bethlehem, after his seven brothers had been rejected by God.

"And it came to pass, when they were come, that he looked on Eliab, and said, 'Surely the LORD's anointed is before Him.'

"But the LORD said unto Samuel, 'Look not on his countenance, or on the height of his stature; because I have refused him. For the LORD seeth not as man seeth; for man looketh on the outward appearance, but the LORD looketh on the heart.' . . .

"And he sent, and brought him in. Now he was ruddy, and withal of a beautiful countenance, and goodly to look to. And the LORD said, 'Arise, anoint him; for this is he.'

"Then Samuel took the horn of oil, and anointed him in the midst of his brethren; and the Spirit of the LORD came upon David from that day forward. So Samuel rose up, and went to Ramah" (1 Sam. 16:6-7, 12-13).

DAVID, THE SINGER

King Saul was from this point troubled by an evil spirit. Hearing of David's fame as a skilled harpist, the king invited him to the palace, where his beautiful music helped the troubled ruler.

DAVID, THE SOLDIER

With but a sling (and God's anointing) David defeated a mighty, 10-foot, Philistine giant named Goliath and won a battle for Israel.

DAVID, THE SOUGHT

The persecution by Saul. David began a long friendship with Jonathan. He incurred Saul's jealousy because during a parade to celebrate the victory some women sang the following song:

"Saul hath slain his thousands, and David his ten thousands" (18:7).

Saul then attempted to deal with the situation as follows:

*By demotion (cf. v. 5 with v. 13).

*By private attempts on his life (see v. 11; 19:10-17).

*By trickery: Saul promised the hand of Michal (his youngest daughter) in marriage if David would kill 100 Philistines. Saul hoped that David would die in battle. But David went out and killed 200 Philistines!

David now married the first of his many wives, Michal. She would later save his life. Saul's attempts at that time to curse and kill David were as unsuccessful as had been Balaam's efforts to blaspheme Israel four centuries back (cf. vv. 19-24 with Num. 23:5-12).

David learned from Jonathan that Saul had dropped all secret efforts to kill him and was now publicly gunning for him. Jonathan at first could not believe this about his own father. But his eyes were opened when Saul cursed him and actually attempted to kill him too.

The flight from Saul. *David at Nob: David went to Nob and (after lying about the nature of his visit) received bread and a sword from Ahimelech, the high priest.

*David at Gath: He then went to the Philistine city of Gath and faked insanity before King Achish.

*David at Adullam: He made the Cave of Adullam his headquarters and began gathering his "outlaw army." This army at first totaled 400 men. It then greatly expanded. During this period 3 of his mighty men slipped through enemy lines to bring David water from the well in Bethlehem he had so longed for. David was so impressed that he refused to drink it, but poured it out as an offering to God.

*David at Moab: David went to Moab, but was ordered back to Judah through the mouth of Gad, the prophet of the Lord. God had already gone to the trouble of bringing David's great grandmother from Moab into Judah. A vicious Edomite named Doeg betrayed Ahimelech to Saul, whereupon the insane king ordered the slaughter of 85 priests at Nob simply because Ahimelech had offered some bread to David.

*David at Keilah: David saved Keilah, a city in Judah, from the Philistines. In spite of this action, the men of this city planned to betray David into the hand of Saul, but being warned by God, he escaped. Jonathan visited David at this time, reassuring him of his loyalty and friendship.

*David at Ziklag: David backslid and moved to the Philistine city of Ziklag.

"And David said in his heart, 'I shall now perish one day by the hand of Saul. There is nothing better for me than that I should speedily escape into the land of the Philistines; and Saul shall despair of me, to seek me anymore in any coast of Israel. So shall I escape out of his hand' " (1 Sam. 27:1).

David now completed his army of mighty men. These men were known for both:

*Their strength: *"Men of might, and men of war fit for the battle, that could handle shield and buckler, whose faces were like the faces of lions, and who were as swift as roes upon the mountains" (1 Chron. 12:8).*

*Their spiritual perception: *"Then the spirit came upon Amasai, who was the chief of the captains, and he said, 'Thine are we, David, and on thy side. . . . Peace . . . be unto thee, and . . . to thine helpers; for thy God helpeth thee' " (v. 18).*

During this time, a period of 16 months, David carried out numerous plundering raids on various non-Israelite cities, but convinced the Philistine King Achish that the cities were actually Israelite ones.

The kindness to Saul. David spared Saul's life in a cave in the wilderness of En-gedi, by cutting off a piece of Saul's coat when he could have sliced off his head! We are told, however, that on this occasion David's heart smote him. Saul acknowledged both his stupidity and the fact that he knew God had chosen David to rule Israel. David married his second wife, Abigail. She was the widow of an arrogant and rich Judean sheepherder who had refused to help David in his time of need and was slain by the Lord for this 10 days later. Just prior to this time, Samuel died and was buried at Ramah. At this time Saul gave Michal, David's first wife, to another man.

David spared Saul's life the second time on a hillside in the wilderness of Ziph. To prove this to Saul, he took his spear and water canteen while the king lay sleeping (1 Sam. 26:7-12). NOTE: The wicked and frustrated king apparently, this time, kept his word.

The death of Saul. Saul visited the witch of En-dor in a desperate attempt to call up Samuel from the dead so that he might receive advice concerning a fearful Philistine military threat. Samuel appeared, apart, however, from any actions of the evil witch, and predicted Saul's defeat and death on the battlefield the following day. Saul was defeated by the Philistines and sorely wounded. He then fell on his sword to avoid torture at the hands of the enemy. His sons, including Jonathan, were also killed in battle. His death was a punishment from God because of his sin.

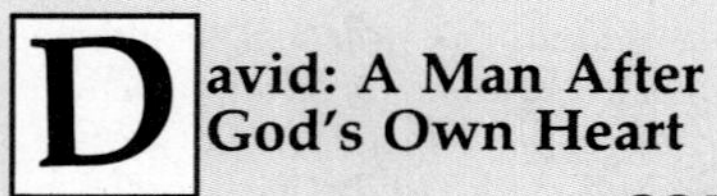

David: A Man After God's Own Heart

COMMENTS

Most Christians have often heard David referred to as "a man after God's own heart." However, it is not generally recognized that this characterization was made long before David became king. The occasion on which it was said was the repudiation of Saul's line from the monarchy. Saul had foolishly usurped the priest's office by offering a burnt offering when Samuel delayed coming to Gilgal. Consequently, Samuel announced to Saul that his line was rejected in favor of "a man after God's own heart," a reference to the king who would replace Saul. Since this statement was made of David before his coronation and rule, it is appropriate to consider the remark as God's evaluation of David's entire life. Of course the omniscient Lord knew of David's ultimate failures in the episode with Bathsheba and Uriah. Nevertheless, He evaluated David's life as a whole with gracious approval. It is appropriate then to inquire as to what traits made David "a man after God's own heart."

The first quality that is apparent about David in the biblical text is his courage. His storybook victory over Goliath has been a source of strength for "giant-killers" of all ages. It was no little matter for a youngster to stand up against a huge soldier, but David had so developed his daring for God that he was naive enough to believe that God would honor courage displayed for God's honor and glory. This great victory served only to further David's godly heroism.

A second attribute of David is his remarkable kindness. This reality is no more evident than in his dealings with Saul. When the insanely jealous king began to pursue the life of his young rival, David did not retaliate. In fact, on two occasions David could have easily taken Saul's life. The elimination of one's rivals to the throne was widely practiced in ancient times, but David refused to fall into this awful custom. In the wilderness of En-gedi he simply cut off the skirt of Saul's robe against the insistence of his men that he kill Saul (1 Sam. 24:1-15). Again, in the Wilderness of Ziph David resisted the suggestion of his aide to slay the sleeping king in favor of taking Saul's spear and water canteen. In addition to his kindness to Saul, David displayed his good nature on numerous other occasions. Time and again he treated his former enemies with grace and benevolence. Another of the notable examples of his kindness was his charitable treatment of Mephibosheth, the son of Jonathan, who could easily have been a challenger to the throne.

Another quality well exhibited by David was his loyalty. There is no better example of this fact than in his friendship with Jonathan. It is said that Jonathan loved David "as his own soul" (18:1) and that Jonathan's love for David was "wonderful, passing the love of women" (2 Sam. 1:26). David likewise loved Jonathan as "he loved his own soul" (1 Sam. 20:17). David's loyalty to his friend is clearly revealed in his lifelong covenant with Jonathan (18:3), in his woeful lament on the occasion of Jonathan's tragic death (2 Sam. 1:17-27), and in his kindness to Jonathan's son (chap. 9). David thus faithfully honored his commitments to others.

David's attitude of trust and reliance in God constitutes yet another example of his fine qualities. One need only read a few of the 73 psalms attributed to David to gain an indelible impression of the righteous spirit which David brought to God. Whether lamenting his present dire circumstances to his Lord, expressing his confidence in God, or speaking prophetically as a type of Christ, David was always a man of prayer and faith.

Psalm 3, written when he fled from Absalom, forms a fine example of David's trust in God. Though we know from 2 Samuel 15 that David had sent his friend Hushai back to Jerusalem to give deceptive counsel to Absalom—a plan that kept Absalom from getting the victory over David, there is no mention of Hushai's part in Psalm 3. Rather, David praised his God for deliverance for he knew that salvation is from the Lord alone. It is no wonder then that Paul, citing Old Testament examples of faith in Romans 4, sets David alongside Abraham as men who believed God and found His blessing.

Finally, much could be said about David's military successes. Though they could easily have engendered a spirit of pride and self-sufficiency, David never lost his sense of calling to further God's name and glory. His concern and joy in bringing the ark to Jerusalem is an outstanding example of this zeal (2 Sam. 6). Though God prohibited David from building the temple, he nevertheless set in motion much of its preparation and organization for his son Solomon to complete. Much of the credit for the erection of the temple can therefore be given to David.

Though David certainly had his failures, he is remembered by the New Testament writers (who mention him 58 times as the real founder of the kingdom of Israel, the ideal king, and the foreshadower of the Messiah, the Lord Jesus Christ). It is no accident then that one of the favorite titles of Jesus in the New Testament is "Son of David" (Rev. 22:16), a term openly claimed by Jesus Himself in the Bible's final chapter.

Samuel's Appearance to Saul at En-dor

COMMENTS

The strange scene which occurs in 1 Samuel 28 has provoked much discussion among Bible scholars. Did Samuel really appear to Saul? If so, what power do witches have to call up the dead? These and other important questions merit an examination of this unusual event. Several interpretations have been set forth. First, some have suggested that both the witch and Saul were under a hallucination. It seems unlikely, however, that both would hallucinate at the same time. Both did in fact talk to Samuel. Also, the woman was frightened when the vision of Samuel did appear. This fact seems to indicate that she really did see Samuel.

Other Bible scholars have suggested that the woman deceived Saul. In other words, she fooled Saul into thinking that she had called up Samuel from the dead. She was the deceiver, and Saul was the deceived. There is much that may be said against this view. It is unlikely that Saul, who knew Samuel well, could have been tricked by the woman's voice or another's voice. Also, the woman herself was terrified at what she saw. Finally, she would not have had the knowledge to predict such an accurate prophecy as that which is attributed to Samuel in the passage. The dire content of the prophecy itself militates against deception also, since the witch would most likely have delivered a more flattering prediction if she in fact had originated the oracle.

Still another view advocates that a demon impersonated Samuel. It is true that Satan and his demons can appear in deceptive ways (cf. 2 Cor. 11:14). Nevertheless, the content of the prophecy delivered by the apparition is in such accord with Samuel's earlier pronouncements to Saul that one can scarcely believe that a demon, if he could, would reproduce such a prophecy. Demons do not usually promulgate the truth, but deception. The prophecy involved here was proven to be true to the minutest detail.

Finally, the view of the majority of scholars is that Samuel actually appeared to Saul. This appearance occurred apart from any actions on the part of the witch, as her own fright indicates. Reasons cited for this view include the following: Saul believed that the apparition was really Samuel; the prophecy delivered was in accord with what Samuel had said to Saul when Samuel was still alive; the prophecy was fulfilled literally; the Septuagint translation of 1 Chronicles 10.13b reads "And Samuel the prophet answered him" (so also in the apocryphal Ecclesiasticus 46:20); this view was held by the early rabbis; and finally, it was held by church fathers Justin Martyr, Origen, and Augustine (though Tertullian and Jerome opted for the third view).

If Samuel really did appear to Saul, one question remains: Why would God allow such an ungodly woman to bring up a man of God and for what purpose? It has already been noted that the appearance occurred apart from any magic on the witch's part. God's purposes in the matter may have included the following: to make Saul's sin of witchcraft an occasion of his punishment; to demonstrate that God has control over all the spirit world; and to warn men of all time that they should stay away from spiritism. In any case, the prophecy given on this occasion was true, and Saul's ignominious death ensued on the following day.

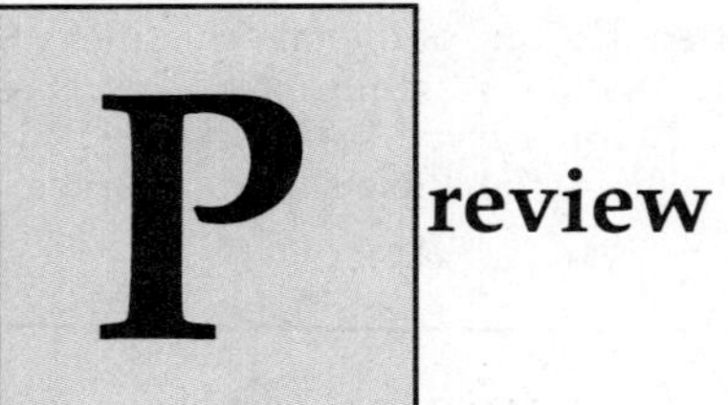

David: The Finest Years

2 SAMUEL 1–10; 1 CHRONICLES 11–20

His joy and sheer energy seemed boundless as he danced hour after hour to the praise and glory of God. In fact, his zeal superceded even that of the large levitical choir, whose sole assigned ministry was to continually worship and thank the Lord God of Israel. Small wonder, however, for did any man alive have more to praise God for than David? It seemed as if heaven itself had swooped down and utterly enveloped him during those past few weeks. First there was that fantastic three-day parade and celebration at Hebron to mark the beginning of his reign over all Israel. What memories flooded his mind as he viewed the 400,000 honor troops from all 12 tribes, briskly performing their maneuvers.

This was quite different from that quiet day in Bethlehem when Samuel had first anointed him as king, with only his father and brothers in attendance. That was 20 years back, when he was a mere lad of 17. So much had transpired since then. He had come from living off the land as a fugitive to ruling over the land as its king! But even more wonderful than this, his troops had just conquered Canaan's prize city. Jerusalem belonged to Israel. And wonder of wonders, that holiest of all objects, the ark of the covenant, had been recovered and now resided in his new capital of Jerusalem. All this was why the king danced with such genuine enthusiasm before the Lord during that unforgettable night. If only this jubilation could go on forever. But it would not. Sorrow, brought about by sin, would soon replace the singing.

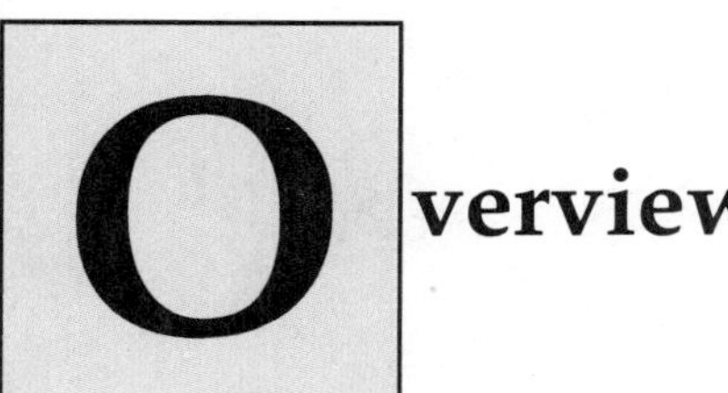

Overview

<table>
<tr><td>SCRIPTURE</td><td colspan="5">2 Samuel 1–10; 1 Chronicles 11–20</td></tr>
<tr><td>SUBJECT</td><td colspan="5">Life of David: part 2</td></tr>
<tr><td rowspan="8">SPECIFICS</td><td colspan="5">The three anointings of David</td></tr>
<tr><td rowspan="2">Place of anointing</td><td>Number 1</td><td>Number 2</td><td colspan="2">Number 3</td></tr>
<tr><td>Bethlehem</td><td>Hebron</td><td colspan="2">Hebron</td></tr>
<tr><td>Officiating over the anointing</td><td>Samuel</td><td>Two tribes</td><td colspan="2">Twelve tribes</td></tr>
<tr><td>Age when anointed</td><td>17</td><td>30</td><td colspan="2">37</td></tr>
<tr><td>Occupation when anointed</td><td>Shepherd</td><td>Soldier</td><td colspan="2">King</td></tr>
<tr><td rowspan="2">Events following anointing</td><td rowspan="2">Victory over Goliath</td><td rowspan="2">Death of Abner</td><td colspan="2">Capture of Jerusalem</td></tr>
<tr><td colspan="2">Possession of the ark</td></tr>
<tr><td>SAINTS AND SINNERS</td><td colspan="5">David, Abner, Ishbosheth, Joab, Asahel, Mephibosheth, Michal, Nathan, Ziba, Hanun</td></tr>
<tr><td rowspan="2">SENTENCE SUMMARIES</td><td>O.T. Verse</td><td colspan="4">"Thus saith the LORD: 'David shall never want a man to sit upon the throne of the house of Israel' " (Jer. 33:17).</td></tr>
<tr><td>N.T. Verse</td><td colspan="4">"Blessed are they which are persecuted for righteousness' sake; for theirs is the kingdom of heaven" (Matt. 5:10).</td></tr>
</table>

KING OF ALL ISRAEL

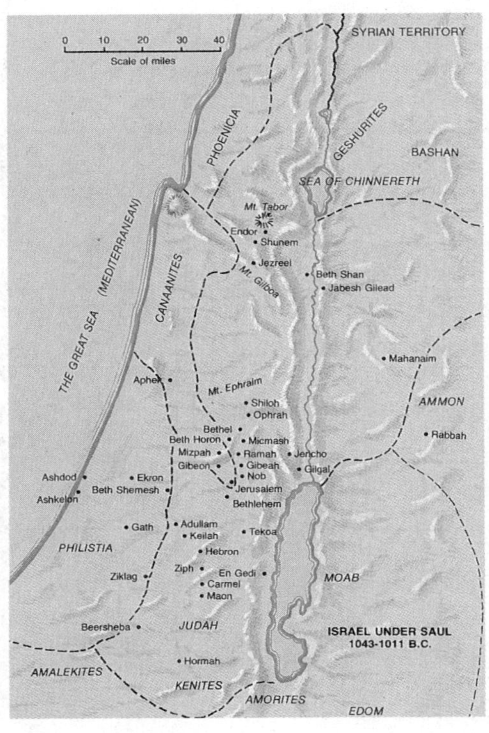

DAVID, THE SOVEREIGN

At Hebron, his first capital. *King over the two tribes: David heard the news of the death of Saul and Jonathan and grieved for them in Ziklag.

"Tell it not in Gath, publish it not in the streets of Askelon; lest the daughters of the Philistines rejoice, lest the daughters of the uncircumcised triumph. . . .

"Saul and Jonathan were lovely and pleasant in their lives, and in their death they were not divided. They were swifter than eagles, they were stronger than lions. . . .

"I am distressed for thee, my brother Jonathan. Very pleasant hast thou been unto me. Thy love to me was wonderful, passing the love of women" (2 Sam. 1:20, 23, 26).

At God's command, David returned to Palestine and was anointed at Hebron by the men of Judah as their king. This was his second anointing. David was now around 30, and he ruled over Judah for the next seven-and-one-half years. Abner, Saul's general, made Ish-bosheth, Saul's son, king over the 11 tribes.

Abner killed Asahel younger brother of Joab (David's general) in self-defense. Abner later attempted to join David's side, but was murdered by Joab for reasons of revenge and jealousy. David never forgave Joab for this act of treachery. At this time David got Michal, his first wife, back. He then married four more women, for a grand total of seven wives while in Hebron. It was here that four of his many children who would later bring sorrow to his life were born. They were: Amnon, who would rape his half-sister Tamar; Tamar; Absalom, who would murder Amnon for this crime and later lead a revolt against the king himself (13:28; 15:13-14); and Adonijah, who would later attempt to steal David's throne while the old king lay dying (1 Kings 1).

After a long war between Saul's house and David's house, Ish-bosheth was murdered by two of his own servants. This was the turning point, for now nothing could stop David from taking the entire kingdom of Israel.

King over the 12 tribes. David was anointed king over all Israel at Hebron. This marked his third anointing. It was a fantastic three-day celebration with nearly 400,000 honor troops taking part from the 12 tribes of Israel. Especially to be noted were 2 tribes: The men of Issachar *"which were men that had understanding of the times, to know what Israel ought to do" (1 Chron. 12:32);* and the men of Zebulun who were *"expert in war, with all instruments of war . . . [who] were not of double heart" (v. 33).*

At Jerusalem, his final capital. David then captured Jerusalem and made it his permanent capital. From this time on God declared Jerusalem to be His chosen city. David enlarged his kingdom, hired Hiram, the king of Tyre, to build him a palace, and married more wives and concubines (2 Sam. 5:6-16).

The ark of God. David brought the ark of

the covenant to Jerusalem. His method of carrying the ark (in a new cart) displeased God, resulting in the death of a man called Uzzah, and a three-month delay. David then recognized the scriptural way to transport the ark.

"Then David said, 'None ought to carry the ark of God but the Levites; for them hath the LORD chosen to carry the ark of God, and to minister unto Him forever.' . . .

"So the priests and the Levites sanctified themselves to bring up the ark of the LORD God of Israel. And the children of the Levites bare the ark of God upon their shoulders with the staves thereon, as Moses commanded according to the Word of the LORD" (1 Chron. 15:2, 14-15).

Finally, with much shouting, singing, and making of music, the ark entered the city. David then appointed some of the Levites to *"minister before the ark of the LORD, and to record, and to thank and praise the LORD God of Israel" (16:4).* This choir, numbering 288, was to do nothing but praise and thank the Lord.

David now delivered his first recorded psalms. (Cf. 16:7-22 with Ps. 105:1-15; and 1 Chron. 16:23-36 with Ps. 96.)

When David returned home, he was severely rebuked for all this "religious emotional nonsense" by his wife Michal.

The temple of God. David desired to build a temple for God, but this request was not allowed by God.

*The reason for this plan: *"Lo, I dwell in a house of cedars, but the ark of the covenant of the LORD remaineth under curtains" (1 Chron. 17:1).*

*The reaction to this plan: *"Then Nathan said unto David, 'Do all that is in thine heart; for God is with thee' " (v. 2).*

*The rejection of this plan: *"The same night . . . the word of God came to Nathan, saying, 'Go and tell David My servant, "Thus saith the LORD, 'Thou shalt not build Me a house to dwell in' " ' " (v. 4).*

The covenant of God. He was now given the Davidic Covenant from God (2 Sam. 7:8-17). This all-important covenant stated:

*David was to have a child, yet to be born, who would succeed him and establish his kingdom.

*This son (Solomon) would build the temple instead of David.

*The throne would not be taken away from him (Solomon) even though his sins might justify chastisement.

*David's house, throne, and kingdom would be established forever.

David responded to this by offering a beautiful prayer of thanksgiving.

"Wherefore Thou art great, O LORD God. For there is none like Thee, neither is there any God beside Thee, according to all that we have heard with our ears. . . . And let Thy name be magnified forever, saying, 'The LORD of hosts is the God over Israel: and let the house of Thy servant David be established before Thee' " (vv. 22, 26).

The blessings of God. David now consolidated his kingdom by defeating in rapid succession the Philistines, the Moabites, the Syrians, and the Edomites.

"Which also King David did dedicate unto the LORD, with the silver and gold that he had dedicated of all nations which he subdued. . . .

"And David reigned over all Israel, and David executed judgment and justice unto all his people" (8:11, 15).

He sought out and showed kindness to Mephibosheth, Jonathan's lame son (chap. 9).

"And David said unto him, 'Fear not. For I will surely show thee kindness for Jonathan thy father's sake, and will restore thee all the land of Saul thy father; and thou shalt eat bread at my table continually' " (v. 7).

David defeated the Ammonites after his offer of peace and friendship was ridiculed.

Jerusalem: the Holy City

COMMENTS

The capture of Jerusalem by David and its establishment as the Israelite capital were indicative of the glory that was to follow for this great city. This occasion was not the first reference to the city, however, since it already had a long history of occupation. In all likelihood it is referred to in Genesis twice: as Salem (14:18) and as the mountain in the "land of Moriah" (22:2). According to later Jewish tradition the temple was built on the latter site. Outside of the Bible, Jerusalem is known as early as around 1500 B.C., being mentioned frequently in letters written to and from an Egyptian Pharaoh.

When the Israelites began their southern campaign they faced a coalition of kings, including Adoni-zedek, the Jebusite king who reigned in Jerusalem. Though the Israelites were victorious under Joshua, they were not able to take the city itself since it forms a natural stronghold (Josh. 10). Part of the city was later captured by Judah and occupied by Benjamin, the latter tribe being able to live peaceably alongside the Jebusites (Jud. 1:8, 21). This situation prevailed until David, who, while reigning over Israel from Hebron, recognized the strategic value of capturing Jerusalem. This he was able to do by unexpected means. Though the proper translation of the word "gutter" in the expression "getteth up to the gutter" (2 Sam. 5:8) is uncertain—suggestions include "water shaft" and "scaling hook"—it may well be that a weakness in the water supply was exploited, allowing entry to the city. In any case, David made it his capital, fortified it, built his palace there, and later brought the ark there. The word "Zion" occurring in this passage (v. 7) probably refers to the hill on which the Jebusite fortress had stood. This word later became a synonym for Jerusalem, particularly in the psalms and among the prophets.

The achievement of Solomon in constructing the temple and fortifying the city gave it fame and glory during his reign. However, after his death the city began to decline, resulting in numerous occasions of plundering, looting, and destruction by foreign powers. Finally, the Babylonian monarch Nebuchadnezzar destroyed the city about 586 B.C. It was later rebuilt, along with the temple, and flourished again, only to be destroyed yet again by the Roman general Titus in A.D. 70.

The history of Jerusalem subsequent to biblical times is unfortunately one of constant warfare. Its history includes the following: captured from the Romans by the Jewish rebel Bar-Kochba (A.D. 32); recaptured by the Romans and made a pagan city dedicated to the god Jupiter (A.D. 135); declared a Christian city by the Roman Emperor Constantine (325); conquered by the Persians (614); recaptured by the Byzantine emperor (629); taken by the Moslem Caliph Omar (637); held alternately by the Crusaders (1099-1187; 1229-1244), Moslems (1187-1229) and Egyptians (in the main, 1244-1517); captured by the Ottoman Turks (1517); taken by the British general Allenby (1917); divided between Arabs and Jews (1948); and, finally, unified under Israeli rule in the famous Six-Day War (1967). There can be little doubt that Jerusalem is one of the greatest battlegrounds in the history of mankind.

The future of Jerusalem is well-outlined in Scripture in relation to two crucial periods: the Millennium and the eternal state. During the Millennium, Jerusalem will possess the following blessings: (1) It will be the home of the millennial King, the Lord Jesus Christ; (2) It will be the center of attention over the entire world; (3) It will be the center of the King's rule; (4) It will bring honor and glory to the Lord; (5) It will be greatly expanded in size; (6) It will be safe because of the King's power; (7) It will be an accessible source of worship for the entire earth; and (8) It will be blessed with an eternal existence.

In the eternal state Jerusalem will be recreated into "the New Jerusalem" (Rev. 21:2). Its beauty is compared to that of "a bride adorned for her husband" and its luxurious symmetry defies complete description by the Apostle John. One need only read Revelation 21 to realize that this city with its foundation, gates, walls, jewels, gold, power, and holiness will truly be a happy and suitable place for God's people. Most importantly, the Lord God Almighty and the Lamb, who is Jesus Christ, will be its chief residents and accessible to all (Rev. 21:22).

Importance of the Davidic Covenant

COMMENTS

The Davidic Covenant is the second great biblical covenant, occurring some 1,000 years after the first great covenant, the Abrahamic (Gen. 12:1-3). The importance of this covenant for biblical theology cannot be overstated. A proper interpretation of it is crucial to understanding the role of Jesus as Messiah and King.

The occasion of the covenant should first be explained. David had gained victory over his enemies for the time being and was at peace. He was at rest in his palace when the idea came to him that he should build a temple for the Lord. The ark of God was then in Jerusalem, having been recently moved there by David. David openly confessed his desire to build a temple to Nathan the prophet. At first, Nathan encouraged David to carry out his plans. This advice seems to have represented only Nathan's opinion, however, since the Lord spoke to Nathan that night and prohibited David from building the temple. Nevertheless, David's motives were pure, and the Lord took this occasion to give to David one of the greatest covenants recorded in Scripture.

It is important to take notice of the provisions of the covenant. First, the Lord promised to make David's name great. This aspect of the covenant is much like that which was promised to Abraham. Certainly David's name has become great. Throughout history, and even today, David is still looked on as the real founder of the Israelite monarchy, not Saul.

Second, God promised that He would plant His people securely in their land and that their enemies would oppress them no more. This aspect of the covenant awaits fulfillment.

Third, in the real heart of the covenant, the Lord promised that David would have a son in the future who would succeed him and establish his kingdom. Though David already had a number of wives and sons accumulated at Hebron, the son who would succeed him was yet to be born. That son was Solomon, of course, who was born to Bathsheba.

Fourth, David's successor would build the temple rather than David. Though not mentioned in 2 Samuel 7, it is revealed elsewhere that David was not permitted to build the temple because he was a man of war and bloodshed. This statement does not mean that war is morally wrong, but it does mean that David had been much too ruthless on occasion (see 8:2, for example).

Fifth, the successor would be established forever on his throne. The prophecy here is clearly predictive of the Messiah since no earthly line could truly exist forever.

Sixth, the successor's right to rule would not be revoked, even though his sins justified it. The sins of Solomon certainly merited his rejection by the Lord, but the Lord did not depose him because of this covenant. It is interesting to note that the Lord appeared to Solomon after Solomon dedicated the temple and reiterated the provisions of the Davidic Covenant to him, except that some of them were now conditional for Solomon and his successors.

Seventh, David's house, kingdom, and throne would be established forever. This promise did not mean that David's descendants would rule in an uninterrupted line forever. The line of rule was, of course, broken by the Babylonian Captivity and remains so today. The point of the promise seems to be that the right to rule would always belong to David's line. An important question must now be posed: Will this covenant be literally fulfilled? Will a descendant of David rule literally from the throne of David over God's people? The answer to this question must be found in the manner in which the New Testament treats this promise. It clearly reveals that the Davidic Covenant will be fulfilled ultimately by Jesus, who is a Son of David. Luke 1:31-33 is particularly instructive at this point: Gabriel set forth to Mary a series of seven promises, five of which have been fulfilled literally. The remaining two must also await a literal fulfillment: "The Lord God shall give unto Him the throne of His father David, and He shall reign over the house of Jacob forever; and of His kingdom there shall be no end" (vv. 32-33). At His second coming Jesus will assuredly assume this throne (Matt. 19:28; Acts 15:15-18).

Preview

David: The Frustrating Years

2 SAMUEL 11–20

The terrible truth was out, and frankly, David was relieved. Whatever the consequences, surely nothing could be worse than the crushing burden of guilt he had carried for over a year. In retrospect, it seemed so out of character for him. Few leaders of men had ever demonstrated the kindness and integrity that David had. Surely the one who had once shepherded sheep and spared his enemies could be fully trusted in matters of state. But not so. A more sordid situation could scarcely be imagined. First there had been adultery with the wife of one of his loyal soldiers. Then the shocking news—she was pregnant with David's child. Finally, in a desperate and despicable attempt to cover his crime, David ordered the murder of her husband so he could have the widowed spouse.

But thank God for faithful Nathan! Like a surgeon, that bold prophet exposed David's putrid and festering spiritual cancer. David would soon discover just how costly the cure would be. Reaping always involves more than sowing. But the king did the right thing. He agreed with Nathan's charge and confessed his sin. Let the punishment and the healing begin!

Overview

SCRIPTURE	2 Samuel 11–20				
SUBJECT	Life of David: part 3				
SPECIFICS	The transgressions and tears of David				
	His transgressions	The sin of adultery	His tears	Death of his infant son	
				Rape of his daughter	
		The sin of murder		Murder of one son	
				Rebellion by another son	
SAINTS AND SINNERS	David, Bathsheba, Uriah, Joab, Tamar, Amnon, Absalom, woman of Tekoa, Ittai, Zadok, Abiathar, Ahithophel, Hushai, Ziba, Shimei, Barzillai, Sheba, Amasa				
SENTENCE SUMMARIES	O.T. Verse	"Have mercy upon me, O God, according to Thy loving-kindness; according unto the multitude of Thy tender mercies blot out my transgressions" (Ps. 51:1).			
	N.T. Verses	"David also describeth the blessedness of the man unto whom God imputeth righteousness without works, saying, 'Blessed are they whose iniquities are forgiven, and whose sins are covered. Blessed is the man to whom the Lord will not impute sin' " (Rom. 4:6-8).			

D AVID'S DECLINE

DAVID, THE SINNER

His sin of adultery. The indulgent king lusted after and lay with Bathsheba, the wife of Uriah, one of his soldiers. Bathsheba became pregnant and reported this to David. Uriah was hurriedly called home from the battlefield under a pretext that he might visit his wife and thus later believe that the unborn child was his. Uriah refused to cooperate.

His sin of murder. In an act of desperation, David sent him back with a sealed letter to Joab to arrange for Uriah to be killed in battle. Uriah was killed, and David married Bathsheba.

DAVID, THE SORROWFUL

The confrontation by the prophet. After Bathsheba's child was born, Nathan the prophet related to David a story of how a rich farmer who owned thousands of sheep stole a little pet lamb from a poor farmer, his only one, then butchered and ate it (2 Sam. 12:1-4). David's anger knew no limit, and he vowed that the cruel rich man would pay back fourfold for his sin. Nathan then boldly pointed out to David that he, the king, was that man.

The confession of the king. David confessed his sin and repented. Two psalms directly relate to this terrible sin in David's life. Psalm 32 describes the terrible year following his sin and before his confession. Psalm 51 records his actual prayer of confession.

The chastisement from the Lord. God forgave David, but would require His servant to pay back fourfold, the same price the king would have made the rich man pay.

First sin payment. Seven days after David's confession, the first installment came due, for the child died. The king accepted this by faith, believing he would someday see him again.

Second sin payment. David's son, Amnon, lusted after and eventually raped his own half-sister, Tamar. The second installment on David's debt had come due.

Third sin payment. Absalom, the full brother of Tamar, began plotting the murder of Amnon and killed him two years later. This would be installment number three. Absalom then fled.

Fourth sin payment. *The rebellion: A woman sent by Joab tricked David into bringing Absalom back from exile. Absalom returned, but was refused an audience with his father for two years. Finally, after burning a barley field to get attention, Absalom began planning a revolt against his father. After four years, he was ready, and instigated the plot in Hebron.

"Absalom said moreover, 'Oh, that I were made judge in the land, that every man which hath any suit or cause might come unto me, and I would do him justice!'

"And it was so, that when any man came nigh to him to do him obeisance, he put forth his hand, and took him, and kissed him.

"And on this manner did Absalom to all Israel that came to the king for judgment. So Absalom stole the hearts of the men of Israel" (2 Sam. 15:4-6).

*The retreat: The rebellion gathered strength, and David was forced to leave Jerusalem. God had now exacted the fourth installment. Abiathar and Zadok also accompanied him. However, David ordered these joint high priests back to Jerusalem. They returned carrying God's ark with them.

"And the king said unto Zadok, 'Carry back the ark of God into the city. If I shall find favor in the eyes of the LORD, He will bring me again, and show me both it, and His habitation. But if He thus say, "I have no delight in thee"; behold, here am I, let Him do to me as seemeth good unto Him' " (vv. 25-26).

*The remorse: David walked up the road that led to the Mount of Olives and wept.

*The ruse: When David learned that his adviser Ahithophel had joined Absalom's rebellion, David ordered another loyal adviser Hushai to pretend to sell out to Absalom also, that he might frustrate and counter Ahithophel's advice (v. 34).

The plan worked. (See 16:15–17:14.)

Ahithophel gave this correct advice: *"Moreover Ahithophel said unto Absalom, 'Let me now choose out 12,000 men, and I will arise and pursue after David this night. And I will come upon him while he is weary and weakhanded, and will make him afraid. And all the people that are with him shall flee; and I will smite the king only' " (17:1-2).*

Hushai gave this crafty advice: *"Therefore I counsel that all Israel be generally gathered unto thee, from Dan even to Beer-sheba, as the sand that is by the sea for multitude; and that thou go to battle in thine own person" (v. 11).*

When his advice was refused, Ahithophel went home and hanged himself. Hushai then sent messengers warning David to cross the Jordan and mobilize his troops.

The reviling. David was cursed and had stones thrown at him by Shimei, a member of Saul's family. In spite of this, David refused to order his execution.

"Then said Abishai the son of Zeruiah unto the king, 'Why should this dead dog curse my lord the king? Let me go over, I pray thee, and take off his head.' . . .

"And David said to Abishai, and to all his servants, 'Behold, my son, which came forth of my bowels, seeketh my life. How much more now may this Benjamite do it? Let him alone, and let him curse; for the LORD *hath bidden him' " (16:9, 11).*

The route. Absalom's green soldiers were no match for David's seasoned troops and they quickly lost some 20,000 men and the entire battle. Note the great love in the hearts of David's followers for their king.

"But the people answered, 'Thou shalt not go forth. For if we flee away, they will not care for us; neither if half of us die, will they care for us; but now thou art worth 10,000 of us. Therefore now it is better that thou succor us out of the city' " (18:3).

Absalom attempted to escape, but was caught in some underbrush and killed by Joab. David learned of Absalom's death at Joab's hand and grieved over his dead son (v. 33; 19:1-4).

"And the king was much moved, and went up to the chamber over the gate, and wept. And as he went, thus he said, 'O my son Absalom, my son, my son Absalom! Would God I had died for thee, O Absalom, my son, my son!' " (18:33)

The return. David's trip back to Jerusalem was delayed by some intertribal friction (19:41-43) and by an attempted rebellion by a Benjamite named Sheba. David forgave a terrified Shimei, who begged for mercy. David then promised Amasa (former leader of Absalom's troops) that he would replace Joab with him, providing he could convince the fickle men of Judah to accept their king back. The king himself issued a personal plea.

"And King David sent to Zadok and to Abiathar the priests, saying, 'Speak unto the elders of Judah, saying, "Why are ye the last to bring the king to his house? Seeing the speech of all Israel is come to the king, even to his house. Ye are my brethren, ye are my bones and my flesh. Wherefore then are ye the last to bring back the king?" ' " (vv. 11-12)

Joab, however, murdered Amasa out of jealousy. A Benjamite named Sheba then led a 10-tribe revolt against David. Joab had Sheba killed.

David attempted to reward an 80-year-old Gileadite named Barzillai who had befriended him during Absalom's rebellion. David once again returned to Jerusalem, a sadder and wiser man. He would have more troubles later, but they would not include wars and rebellions. He could now burn the mortgage on his sin-debt with Bathsheba!

The Sin and Confession of David

COMMENTS

The tragic account of David's sin with Bathsheba is the subject of two psalms: Psalm 32 and Psalm 51. Each psalm emphasizes a particular aspect of sin that is true for every sinning Christian today: the awful consequences of unconfessed sin (Ps. 32) and the nature of true confession (Ps. 51). Both psalms also stress the blessedness of forgiveness. Key features of these psalms are worthy of special comment as they relate to David's sin.

Though Psalm 32 does not specifically state that it was written on the occasion of David's sin, the content of the psalm has forced many Bible scholars to that conclusion. The psalm begins with a twofold pronouncement of blessing upon the man who is forgiven (vv. 1-2). The word "blessed" may also be translated "happy" and thus points to the exuberant condition of having been cleansed from sin. Forgiveness itself is beautifully described as the lifting or removing of sin ("forgiven"); its concealment from sight ("covered"); and the subsequent imputation of righteousness to the sincere believer (v. 2).

In verses 3-4 David describes in excruciating language exactly how he felt when living with unconfessed sin. The figures of speech used are quite vivid: "my bones waxed old," "my roaring all the day long," "Day and night Thy hand was heavy upon me," and "My moisture is turned into the drought of summer." These figures seem to describe a state of physical debilitation but may well be more of an attempt to describe extreme psychological trauma. If these figures seem exaggerated, one needs only remember that David carried his unconfessed sin within him for the entire length of Bathsheba's pregnancy. Verse 5, however, provided a happy conclusion to the emotional distress by once again describing the blessedness of the forgiveness which God gave to David immediately at his confession.

The rest of the psalm provides instruction to the righteous to find in God a place of safety (vv. 6-7), to learn the lesson of submission to His will (vv. 8-9), and to rejoice in the Lord's abundant mercy (vv. 10-11).

We are not left to wonder if Psalm 51 is related to David's sin with Bathsheba since the superscription specifically assigns the composition of this psalm to that occasion. As such, it yields the deepest insight into David's self-knowledge and into the nature of true confession. The psalm opens with a straightforward appeal for mercy based on the Lord's "loving-kindness" (v. 1). Here is a practical illustration of how deliberate sin was dealt with in the Old Testament. Since there was no sacrifice for willful sin (as David's), the sinner was left to plead for the mercy of God. The plea continues with three imperatives for the removal of sin: "blot out," "wash me," and "cleanse me." The picture of washing is taken from the imagery of washing dirty laundry as though David were a filthy garment which needed to be sent to the cleaners.

The confession of David's sin is described quite soberly in verses 3-5. Worthy of special notice is the consciousness of offense to a holy God (v. 4) and of the ultimate source of sins in a deep-rooted sin nature (v. 5). David recognized that this one glaring sin sprang from a deep-seated corruption.

The joy of restoration is now sought on the heels of David's confession (vv. 6-13). The figures for cleansing from sin are again piled up conspicuously: purging with hyssop refers to ritual cleansing from defilement (v. 7; cf. Num. 19:16-19); the result of washing is said to be purity like snow (Ps. 51:7); and forgiveness is described as a hiding of God's face from sin and a blotting out of iniquity (v. 9). The result of this cleansing from sin is "a clean heart" (v. 10), "a right spirit" (v. 10), the continued presence of the Holy Spirit (v. 11), the joy of salvation (v. 12), and a renewal of David's ministry to others (v. 13). There seems to be a sense of eagerness in this plea for restoration and, at the same time, a humble assumption that it is being granted.

Finally, the psalm closes with a renewed worshiper freely expressing to God his heartfelt concerns. These include: grateful worship, unencumbered with sin (vv. 14-15); maintenance of "a broken and contrite heart" (v. 17); and a petition for the spiritual rebuilding of Jerusalem (vv. 18-19).

It is crucial then that the reader of 2 Samuel 11–12, with its candid picture of the blackness of David's heart, also read Psalms 32 and 51 with their heartfelt confession of sin. Though God did not take away all of the consequences of David's sin, He did restore his fellowship with Him and placed David back into service.

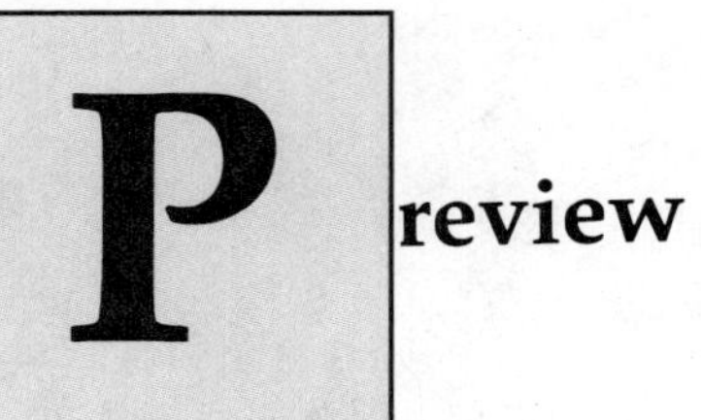

David: The Final Years

2 SAMUEL 21–24; 1 CHRONICLES 21–29

How disappointed David had been that day over 20 years back, when God had announced through Nathan that the king would not be allowed to build the temple. That responsibility would fall to his son, Solomon. The truth was, as David soon learned, that God had something far better in mind for him—a promise that someday the Messiah Himself would come from David's line. Who would not be awed with that? But in regard to the temple, David would be permitted to prepare for its construction. And prepare he did. How good God is. He began by providing the future king with the actual blueprints. Given that blessed supernatural encouragement, David directed his full energies to raising the money, gathering the materials, recruiting the workers, and assigning the musicians. He even found the time to build a temple army of sorts. Finally, the vast preparations were completed. All David could do, he had done. With great satisfaction he viewed the results. What did it matter that he would not live to see the actual construction? In his mind it was already up. But even more comforting, he would soon leave the pain and problems of earth to dwell eternally in God's heavenly temple. What more could a former shepherd lad possibly ask for?

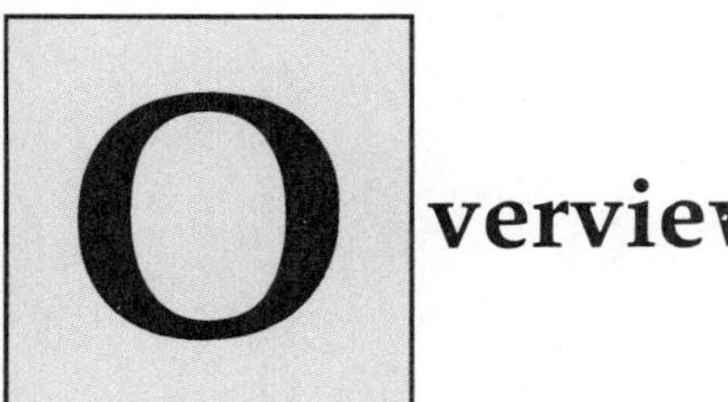

verview

<table>
<tr><td>SCRIPTURE</td><td colspan="7">2 Samuel 21–24; 1 Chronicles 21–29</td></tr>
<tr><td>SUBJECT</td><td colspan="7">Life of David: part 4</td></tr>
<tr><td rowspan="8">SPECIFICS</td><td colspan="7">The latter years of David's reign</td></tr>
<tr><td colspan="2">Punishment</td><td colspan="2">Preparation</td><td colspan="3">Praise</td></tr>
<tr><td rowspan="6">His plagues from God</td><td rowspan="3">A three-year famine, caused by Saul</td><td rowspan="6">His place for God</td><td rowspan="3">The first temple—conceived by David</td><td rowspan="6">His psalms to God</td><td>David the soldier</td><td>3 psalms written</td></tr>
<tr><td>The outlaw</td><td>15 psalms</td></tr>
<tr><td>The king</td><td>9 psalms</td></tr>
<tr><td rowspan="3">A three-day plague, caused by David</td><td rowspan="3">The first temple—completed by Solomon</td><td>The sinner</td><td>2 psalms</td></tr>
<tr><td>The sufferer</td><td>5 psalms</td></tr>
<tr><td>The intercessor</td><td>1 psalm</td></tr>
<tr><td>SAINTS AND SINNERS</td><td colspan="7">David, Rizpah, Gad, Joab, Ornan</td></tr>
<tr><td rowspan="2">SENTENCE SUMMARIES</td><td colspan="2">O.T. Verses</td><td colspan="5">"Bless the LORD, O my soul; and all that is within me, bless His holy name. . . . The LORD hath prepared His throne in the heavens; and His kingdom ruleth over all" (Ps. 103:1, 19).</td></tr>
<tr><td colspan="2">N.T. Verse</td><td colspan="5">"David, after he had served his own generation by the will of God, fell on sleep, and was laid unto his fathers, and saw corruption" (Acts 13:36).</td></tr>
</table>

S TATESMAN, CENSUS-TAKER, SCRIBE

DAVID, THE STATESMAN

A three-year famine from God had come on Israel. David was told it was because of the bloody house of Saul, who in the past, had slain the Gibeonites. In Joshua 9, Israel had made a covenant with these Gibeonites that they would not be harmed. This sin was now being punished.

David negotiated with the Gibeonite leaders, and they determined that justice could only be done by allowing them to execute seven of Saul's sons, all of whom doubtless participated in the former Gibeon massacre. This was done and the plague was stayed. The life of Mephibosheth, however, was spared.

DAVID, THE CENSUS-TAKER

David succumbed to the temptation of Satan and numbered Israel. He later repented of this and was offered by God one of three kinds of punishment: (1) A period of famine; (2) To flee 90 days before his enemies; (3) A three-day pestilence. He chose the last. As a result, 70,000 men died.

The plague was stopped by David at a threshing floor as he pleaded with God. David later bought this floor. Fire fell from heaven as David offered a burnt sacrifice to God.

It was upon this spot that the first temple would later be built.

DAVID, THE SPONSOR

David was now nearly 70 years old. When he was but 37, he determined to build a temple for God, but had been forbidden by the Lord to do so.

The old king was, however, allowed to lead in the preparations for the temple which Solomon would construct.

"And David said, 'Solomon my son is young and tender, and the house that is to be builded for the LORD must be exceeding magnifical, of fame and of glory throughout all countries. I will therefore now make preparation for it.' So David prepared abundantly before his death" (1 Chron. 22:5).

David may have written Psalm 18 at this time (cf. 2 Sam. 22).

Note the details of this preparation.

The reason for the temple. It was to provide a home for the ark of God and the other vessels from a temporary tabernacle which was located at Gibeon. The original tabernacle of Moses had been set up at Shiloh, but was destroyed along with the city of Shiloh by the Philistines.

The cost of the temple. *One hundred thousand talents of gold (120 million ounces).

*One million talents of silver (1.2 billion ounces). At today's prices this would equal 75 billion dollars.

David himself gave nearly 2 billion dollars. The total cost of the temple may have exceeded 100 billion dollars.

The assigned workers in the temple. David appointed 38,000 Levites to prepare for construction. Twenty-four thousand were to oversee the work. Six thousand were to function as officers and judges. Four thousand were gatekeepers. Four thousand were singers and musicians. At this time David divided the priesthood in 24 divisions.

The music in the temple. We have already noted the 4,000 regular musicians. To this number David then appointed 288 musical instructors.

The army of the temple. David had an army of 288,000 men, consisting of 12 divisions of 24,000 warriors (1 Chron. 27:1-15).

The blueprints for the temple. David gave Solomon the temple building plans which God had given him.

The challenge to the temple builders, the Israelite leaders. "David also commanded all the princes of Israel to help Solomon his son, saying, 'Is not the LORD your God with you? And hath He not given you rest on every side? For He hath given the inhabitants of the land into mine hand; and the land is subdued before the LORD, and before His people. Now set your heart and your soul to seek the LORD your God; arise therefore, and build ye the sanctuary of the LORD God, to bring the ark of the covenant of the LORD, and the holy vessels of God, into the house that is to be built to the name of the LORD' " (22:17-19).

The Use of Numbers in the Old Testament

COMMENTS

The obvious discrepancies between certain parallel passages in the Books of Samuel and Chronicles highlight the problem of numbers in the Old Testament. These disagreements are actually part of a greater problem which encompasses the transmission and accuracy of all numbers in the Old Testament.

The problems involved fall into one of two categories: first, exceptionally large numbers which seem to the modern reader too fantastic to be true and, second, places in the historical books where parallel passages disagree. As regards the first problem, excessively large numbers are restricted primarily to the earliest ages in the Bible, though they are also present in the historical books. The lengthy lifespans assigned to the pre-Flood inhabitants are well known and need not be recounted here. Suffice it to say that the problem seems certainly to be of a textual nature since the number of years between Creation and the Flood are totalled differently by our three major witnesses to the Old Testament text: the Hebrew gives 1,656 years; the Septuagint 2,262 years, and the Samaritan Pentateuch 1,307. It is clear then that numbers were not transmitted with as much accuracy as other parts of the Old Testament. This fact may explain some of the seemingly excessive numbers in the historical books. For example, most Hebrew manuscripts and the Septuagint record that 50,070 men were killed at Beth-shemesh for looking into the ark. A few Hebrew manuscripts, however, record the much more reasonable number of 70. It is unreasonable to believe that so many thousands would continue to look into the ark when their fellow Israelites were falling dead because of that same sin. The number of fighting men listed under Jehoshaphat's rule is set at 1,161,000, which also seems quite high, though no parallel passage exists by which to compare it, and all manuscripts agree on this point. It also seems quite fantastic that one city wall could fall on and kill 27,000 Aramean soldiers! Other numbers which seem quite immense include the following: (1) Solomon's daily provisions: 30 measures of fine flour (about 185 bushels); (2) Solomon's yearly receipts: 666 talents of gold (25 tons); (3) The Ammonites' hire of mercenaries: 1,000 talents of silver paid (37 tons); 32,000 chariots hired; (4) Solomon's sacrifices at the dedication of the temple—all in one day—22,000 head of cattle and 120,000 sheep and goats; (5) Solomon's importing of gold from Ophir: 450 talents of gold (17 tons).

At least two suggestions may be made to account for these large numbers. First, in the case of the precious metals mentioned, the tonnage involved may actually refer to ore and not to purely refined metals. This is a reasonable assumption. In the case of large numbers of soldiers or cattle, another suggestion may prove helpful. A number of scholars have observed that the Hebrew word for "thousand" may also in some instances be translated "family" or "clan." For example, Gideon says in Judges 6:15: "My family is poor." Thus the word may represent one family or, in the case of the animals mentioned above, a unit much smaller than a thousand. Others have pointed out that by a slight revocalization of the Hebrew the word for thousand may also be translated "captain." The observation, if applied to military contexts, would reduce significantly the numbers of troops involved.

Other problems with numbers may be solved by comparing parallel texts which exhibit more reasonable readings. For example, the 40,000 stalls for Solomon's horses, mentioned in 1 Kings 4:26, may be reduced to 4,000 stalls, in accord with 2 Chronicles 9:25 and the Septuagint. The height of the temple portico is set at 120 cubits (180 feet) according to the Hebrew text in 2 Chronicles 3:4, but this figure may be reduced to 20 cubits (30 feet) according to some Septuagint and Syriac manuscripts.

These suggestions obviously do not solve all of the problems, but at least they do demonstrate that there are reasonable explanations for the supposed contradictions. In the final analysis, we must wait in faith for additional information to be found to help solve these problems. Our present difficulty is due, not to the presence of errors in the Bible, but to our lack of knowledge.

The response of the temple builders. "Then the chief of the fathers and princes of the tribes of Israel, and the captains of thousands and of hundreds, with the rulers of the king's work, offered willingly. And gave for the service of the house of God of gold 5,000 talents and 10,000 drams, and of silver 10,000 talents, and of brass 18,000 talents, and 100,000 talents of iron. And they with whom precious stones were found gave them to the treasure of the house of the LORD, by the hand of Jehiel the Gershonite. Then the people rejoiced, for that they offered willingly, because with perfect heart they offered willingly to the LORD; and David the king also rejoiced with great joy" (29:6-9).

The advice to the temple builder—Solomon. "Now, my son, the LORD be with thee; and prosper thou, and build the house of the LORD thy God, as He hath said of thee. Only the LORD give thee wisdom and understanding, and give thee charge concerning Israel, that thou mayest keep the Law of the LORD thy God. Then shalt thou prosper, if thou takest heed to fulfill the statutes and judgments which the LORD charged Moses with concerning Israel. Be strong, and of good courage; dread not, nor be dismayed" (22:11-13).

" 'And thou, Solomon my son, know thou the God of thy father, and serve Him with a perfect heart and with a willing mind. For the LORD searcheth all hearts, and understandeth all the imaginations of the thoughts. If thou seek Him, He will be found of thee; but if thou forsake Him, He will cast thee off forever. Take heed now; for the LORD hath chosen thee to build an house for the sanctuary; be strong, and do it.' . . .

"And David said to Solomon his son, 'Be strong and of good courage, and do it. Fear not, nor be dismayed: for the LORD God, even my God, will be with thee; He will not fail thee, nor forsake thee, until thou hast finished all the work for the service of the house of the LORD' " (28:9-10, 20).

The prayer to the God of the temple. "Wherefore David blessed the LORD before all the congregation. And David said, 'Blessed be Thou, LORD God of Israel our Father, forever and ever. Thine, O LORD, is the greatness, and the power, and the glory, and the victory, and the majesty. For all that is in the heaven and in the earth is Thine; Thine is the kingdom, O LORD, and Thou art exalted as Head above all.

" 'Both riches and honor come of Thee, and Thou reignest over all; and in Thine hand is power and might; and in Thine hand it is to make great, and to give strength unto all. Now therefore, our God, we thank Thee, and praise Thy glorious name.

" 'But who am I, and what is my people, that we should be able to offer so willingly after this sort? For all things come of Thee, and of Thine own have we given Thee. For we are strangers before Thee, and sojourners, as were all our fathers. Our days on the earth are as a shadow, and there is none abiding.

" 'O LORD our God, all this store that we have prepared to build Thee a house for Thine holy name cometh of Thine hand, and is all Thine own.

" 'I know also, my God, that Thou triest the heart, and hast pleasure in uprightness. As for me, in the uprightness of mine heart I have willingly offered all these things. And now have I seen with joy Thy people, which are present here, to offer willingly unto Thee.

" 'O LORD God of Abraham, Isaac, and of Israel, our fathers, keep this forever in the imagination of the thoughts of the heart of thy people, and prepare their heart unto Thee. And give unto Solomon my son a perfect heart, to keep Thy commandments, Thy testimonies, and Thy statutes, and to do all these things, and to build the palace, for the which I have made provision' " (29:10-19).

DAVID, THE SCRIBE

Of the 150 psalms, David wrote 73 of them. The historical background for some of the Davidic psalms are as follows: His victory over Goliath; while he was still living in Saul's court; when Michal helped save him; when fleeing from Saul; when fleeing from Saul to King Achish; the slaughter of Doeg at Nob; while living in the cave of Adullam; the theology by the citizens of Ziph; after Saul had given up trying to kill him; to celebrate the capture of Jerusalem; when the ark was brought into Jerusalem; after receiving the Davidic Covenant; Joab's victory over the Edomites; after his kingdom was established; after his sin of adultery and murder but before his confession; after he was convicted of these terrible sins by Nathan the prophet; fleeing from Absalom; at the end of a divine plague caused by his forbidden census; and his prayer for Solomon his son.

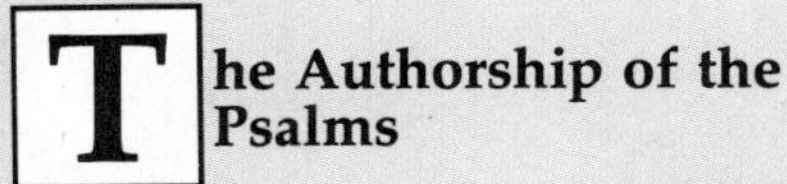

The Authorship of the Psalms

COMMENTS

Since David wrote roughly half of the psalms, he will be considered first. Critical scholars have long questioned the biblical statements that David wrote these psalms. The reason cited for this denial is the simple observation that the psalmist bears little resemblance to David the warrior in Samuel and Kings. A number of reasons may be cited to support the biblical indications that David actually authored the psalms so attributed to him.

First, the historical books clearly picture David, not just as a warrior, but as a poet: "David took a harp, and played with his hand" (1 Sam. 16:23); "David played [the harp] with his hand" (19:9); and David is called "the sweet psalmist of Israel" (2 Sam. 23:1). Besides these passages there are explicit statements that David authored specific poetic compositions. These include a lament over the deaths of Saul and Jonathan, the song of 2 Samuel 22 (same as Ps. 18), and the psalm of 1 Chronicles 16 (same as Ps. 105).

Second, later testimony in the Old Testament also supports the Davidic authorship of the psalms. In Amos 6:5 David is cited as a proverbial example of a musician some three centuries after his death.

Third, the New Testament writers assume, in quoting Davidic psalms, that David actually wrote them. Jesus assigned Psalm 110 to David (Matt. 22:43-45), Peter stated that Psalm 2 was authored by David (Acts 4:25), Paul quoted Psalm 32 as a Davidic hymn (Rom. 4:6-8), and the author of Hebrews refers to Psalm 95 as coming from the hand of David (Heb. 4:7). All of these citations point to the fact that Christ and the early Christians accepted without hesitation the Davidic authorship of those psalms which claimed it (and also a few which did not).

Fourth, in the Hebrew text of the psalms which are ascribed to David, the particular form which the superscription takes is the simple *lamedh* preposition (corresponding to English "of") plus the personal name David. While it is true that this preposition can often mean "to" or "for" David, as the heading of a literary work it is best taken as indicating authorship: "of David," i.e., written by David. In sum, there is excellent evidence for following the superscriptions, the historical evidence, and the New Testament church in assigning the Davidic psalms to David himself.

Twelve psalms are ascribed to the sons of Korah. These were Levites who were descended from the rebel leader by the same name. Their ancestor, along with Dathan, Abiram, On, and 250 Israelites, rebelled against Moses in the wilderness. As a result of their rebellion, the rebels and their followers were destroyed by the earth opening up to consume them and by fire. Korah's line, however, was spared. One part of his descendants became the temple doorkeepers; another part became the singers and musicians who composed the temple choir.

Another 12 psalms were authored by Asaph. He was a descendant of Gershom, son of Levi. He was a leading singer of the Levites who preceded the ark when it was brought to Jerusalem. Later, David appointed him leader of the choral worship. His descendants were known as "the sons of Asaph," and they constituted the chief family of musicians until the restoration period.

One psalm each is ascribed to Heman (88) and Ethan (89) the Ezrahites (Ethan is probably another name for Jeduthun). Both men founded choirs and were also known for their wisdom. There is some confusion as to whether Psalm 88 should be ascribed to Heman or to the sons of Korah since both are mentioned in the superscription. It is possible that Heman was the author and the sons of Korah the performers; otherwise, it is a case of dual authorship.

Among the other psalms only two authors were named: Moses (90) and Solomon (72; 127). Since Psalm 90 is by Moses, that makes it the oldest psalm in the Psalter. The rest of the psalms are anonymous, though the background and authorship of certain of them are implied.

Preview

Solomon: His Wisdom and Works

1 KINGS 1–8; 2 CHRONICLES 1–6

"The King is dead! Long live the King!" Solomon would never forget that cry, even though 11 years had elapsed since he heard it. It seemed at first a hollow cry, in light of that frightening rebellion instigated by his own half brother. But the merciful and mighty God preserved him from all enemies, as He had done for David. However, that day in November, 11 years later, a more fitting chorus would be, "The temple is up! Long endure the temple!"

If only his father could be here to see it! For that matter, if only Moses and Samuel could be present. Moses had built the tabernacle at Sinai, and Samuel saw its destruction at Shiloh, four centuries later. That had occurred before Saul's time, nearly a century ago. In many ways this new edifice was vastly superior to the old tent structure of Moses. It was certainly larger, more permanent, and elaborate. It featured, for example, 10 golden lampstands and tables of showbread as opposed to 1 each in the tabernacle.

But, Solomon may have wondered on dedication day, would the most important feature of the tabernacle be found here also, without which its size and splendor would prove utterly worthless? Whatever doubts he may have entertained would quickly vanish however, for after the prayer and benediction were over, the Shekinah glory cloud of God filled the temple. As in Moses' day, heaven had approved. The priests were in business again!

Overview

<table>
<tr><td>SCRIPTURE</td><td colspan="3">1 Kings 1–8; 2 Chronicles 1–6</td></tr>
<tr><td>SUBJECT</td><td colspan="3">Life of Solomon: part 1</td></tr>
<tr><td rowspan="7">SPECIFICS</td><td colspan="3">His provisions from God</td></tr>
<tr><td colspan="2">The absence of war</td><td>The abundance of wisdom</td></tr>
<tr><td colspan="3">His project for God</td></tr>
<tr><td rowspan="4">Construction of the first temple</td><td colspan="2">The materials involved</td></tr>
<tr><td colspan="2">The music involved</td></tr>
<tr><td colspan="2">The miracle involved</td></tr>
<tr><td colspan="2">The message involved</td></tr>
<tr><td>SAINTS AND SINNERS</td><td colspan="3">David, Solomon, Abishag, Adonijah, Joab, Abiathar, Zadok, Nathan, Bathsheba, Shimei, two mothers, Hiram the artisan, Hiram the king</td></tr>
<tr><td rowspan="2">SENTENCE SUMMARIES</td><td>O.T. Verses</td><td colspan="2">“Blessed are they that dwell in Thy house; they will still be praising Thee. Selah. . . . For a day in Thy courts is better than a thousand. I had rather be a doorkeeper in the house of my God than to dwell in the tents of wickedness” (Ps. 84:4, 10).</td></tr>
<tr><td>N.T. Verses</td><td colspan="2">“But Solomon built Him an house. Howbeit the Most High dwelleth not in temples made with hands, as saith the prophet” (Acts 7:47-48).</td></tr>
</table>

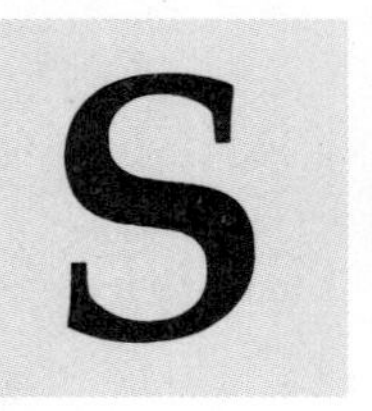

SOLOMON, ISRAEL'S FABULOUS KING

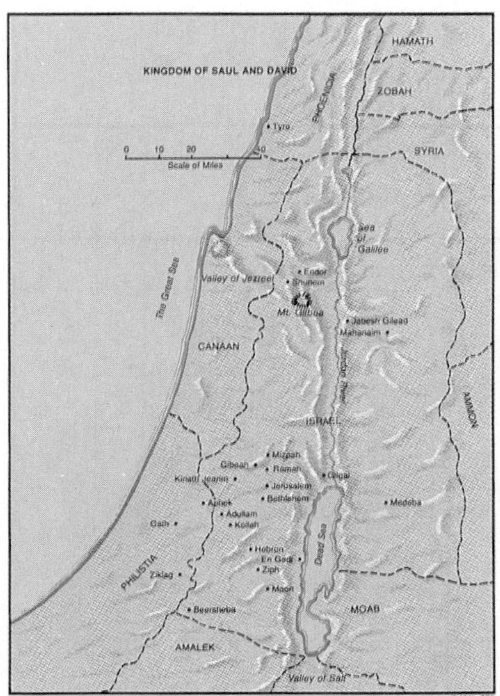

HIS TRIUMPH OVER HIS ENEMIES

Over Adonijah. When David was on his deathbed, his oldest living son, Adonijah, attempted to steal the throne from his half brother, Solomon.

Bathsheba visited her dying husband, and arranged for Solomon to be anointed by Zadok. Adonijah was placed on probation, but later executed.

Over Abiathar. He was a loyal priest in David's time but joined in with Adonijah's revolt. Because of his faithfulness to David, Abiathar was allowed to live but was banished from the priesthood.

Over Joab. This bloody general under David was finally executed, not only because he too supported Adonijah, but for past crimes, including the murder of Abner (Saul's general who wanted to surrender to David), and Absalom (David's son).

Over Shimei. Shimei, like Adonijah, was for a time placed on parole, but he broke this trust and suffered the death penalty for it.

HIS TALENT FROM GOD

Solomon was visited by the Lord in a dream when he went to Gibeon to the tabernacle to sacrifice. God told him he could have anything he desired and the new king asked for wisdom. This answer pleased God who then promised Solomon riches, power, and fame besides. Solomon then offered 1,000 animals on the bronze altar built by the grandson of Hur.

When he returned to Jerusalem, he was immediately confronted with a situation which tested his newly acquired wisdom. Two harlot mothers approached him concerning two babies, one dead and the other living. Both mothers claimed the living one as theirs. Solomon suggested he divide the living child with a sword and give half to each woman. The real mother, of course, was horrified at this, and thus her true identity was revealed.

His total and tranquil reign over all Israel (1 Kings 4). Solomon's reign at this time is a beautiful foreshadow of Christ's perfect millennial reign. Thus we see: Solomon had 12 cabinet members to aid in his reign; Jesus will confer this on His 12 disciples; Solomon ruled "over all kingdoms" in the Holy Land area, while Christ will rule over all kingdoms everywhere; Solomon's subjects served him as we will serve Christ; Solomon brought in local peace (v. 24), as Christ will usher in universal peace; Judah and Israel dwelt safely, *"every man under his vine" (v. 25).* So will it be during Christ's reign.

HIS TEMPLE OF WORSHIP

The preparation. It was begun in May during Solomon's fourth year and completed in November of his eleventh year, thus making a total of seven years.

It was exactly twice the size of Moses' tabernacle, 90 feet long, 30 feet wide, 45 feet high. (Cf. Ex. 26:16, 18.)

It was built by the partial slave labor project instituted by Solomon which consisted of 100,000 Israelites, 80,000 stonecutters, and 3,300 foremen.

The floors and the walls were made of stone covered with cedar and overlaid with gold (6:16, 21-22).

It was built without the sound of hammer, axe, or any other tool (v. 7).

It had 10 lampstands and 10 tables of showbread as opposed to 1 each in Moses' tabernacle.

Solomon paid King Hiram of Tyre nearly a million bushels of wheat and some 850 gallons of pure olive oil for the timber alone from the forest of Lebanon to construct the temple shell.

There were two golden cherubim in the holy of holies.

The dedication. Solomon briefly reviewed the historical circumstances which led up to this glad day.

The supplication. Solomon prayed that the influence of this beautiful temple would extend itself in a threefold manner: over the individual; over the nation; over the heathen.

The benediction. "Blessed be the LORD, *that hath given rest unto His people Israel, according to all that He promised. There hath not failed one word of all His good promise, which He promised by the hand of Moses His servant. . . .*

"Let your heart therefore be perfect with the LORD *our God, to walk in His statutes, and to keep His commandments, as at this day" (8:56, 61)*

He then placed the ark of the covenant into the holy of holies. One hundred and twenty Levite trumpeters sounded forth.

"Also the Levites which were the singers, all of them of Asaph, of Heman, of Jeduthun, with their sons and their brethren, being arrayed in white linen, having cymbals and psalteries and harps, stood at the east end of the altar, and with them 120 priests sounding with trumpets. It came even to pass, as the trumpeters and singers were as one, to make one sound to be heard in praising and thanking the LORD; *and when they lifted up their voice with the trumpets and cymbals and instruments of music, and praised the* LORD, *saying, 'For He is good; for His mercy endureth forever'; that then the house was filled with a cloud, even the house of the* LORD; *so that the priests could not stand to minister by reason of the cloud. For the glory of the* LORD *had filled the house of God" (2 Chron. 5:12-14).*

The manifestation. "Now when Solomon had made an end of praying, the fire came down from heaven and consumed the burnt offering and the sacrifices; and the glory of the LORD *filled the house. And the priests could not enter into the house of the* LORD, *because the glory of the* LORD *had filled the* LORD*'s house" (7:1-2).*

The presentation. This offering, consisting of 120,000 sheep and 22,000 oxen was the largest in the Bible, and perhaps of all time.

The Beginning of the Wisdom Movement in Israel

COMMENTS

The flourishing of wisdom pursuits in the age of Solomon must be seen against a backdrop of the development of wisdom literature throughout the ancient Near East. The roots of wisdom literature began no doubt with oral wisdom consisting of short, pithy sayings about life. Beginning around 2500 B.C. in Egypt, oral wisdom began to be supplemented with literary wisdom. At some point an entire class of wise men developed, whose task was the creation, collection, revision, and preservation of wise sayings (cf. Ecc. 12:9). During the reign of Solomon this movement came to prominence in Israel under his direction: "And there came of all people to hear the wisdom of Solomon, from all kings of the earth, which had heard of his wisdom" (1 Kings 4:34). Hezekiah, a later king, also shared an interest in the promotion of wisdom.

The position of the wise man within the Israelite society is not completely clear. It is known that David employed wise men on his staff, the most famous of which were Ahithophel and Hushai. These men were obviously attached to the royal court, and their wisdom was utilized for political and military purposes. Another class of wise men were writers and speakers, and their wisdom was utilized for the public moral good: "The words of the wise are as goads, and as nails fastened by the masters of assemblies, which are given from one shepherd" (Ecc. 12:11). At least two collections of sayings within the Book of Proverbs are collected from various wise men. By the time of Jeremiah (seventh century B.C.) the wise man was considered a social fixture as prominent as the prophet and priest: "For the law shall not perish from the priest, nor counsel from the wise, nor the word from the prophet" (Jer. 18:18). Besides highlighting the unique duties of the wise man in comparison to the priest and prophet, this verse shows clearly that there was a class of wise men within Israel.

Wisdom literature developed within Israel (as in the entire ancient Near East) along two broad lines: instructive literature and reflective literature. Of the first type, the Book of Proverbs is the best example. It is composed of 10 homilies in which the father instructs his son to choose the way of wisdom and to reject the way of folly (chaps. 1–9). The rest of the book is composed of individual proverbs, or short, pithy statements which expose a fundamental reality about life. Each of these in some way contains the antithesis of the way of wisdom versus the way of folly.

Regarding the reflective type of wisdom literature, Job and Ecclesiastes may be cited as examples. These writings seek to delve into the problems of existence and the basic questions faced by mankind: Why do the righteous suffer? How does man find value in life? How can man confront God? The form of reflective literature may be the monologue (Ecc.) or the dialogue (Job). It is important to note however that the reflective literature is not theoretical. Its content is couched in terms of concrete human examples: Job and the Preacher.

The literary devices employed by the wise men are numerous. Foremost is poetic parallelism (treated elsewhere in this volume). Special forms of this phenomenon are the acrostic and the numerical sequence. The latter device is used as a way of maintaining parallelism when numbers are used: "There are three things that are never satisfied, yea, four things say not, It is enough" (Prov. 30:15). Since there are no synonyms for numbers, the poets devised this creative way of maintaining the parallel structure. Other types of wisdom literary methods include riddles (Jud. 14:12-18; Prov. 1:6), fables (Jud. 9:7-15; Ezek. 17:3-24; 19), argument or plea (Job 29:1), sermon (Prov. 5), and parables (2 Sam. 12:1-4; Isa. 28:4; Prov. 24:30-34).

The wise men obviously influenced the historical and prophetic writings, as the preceding verses demonstrate. Some psalms show wisdom influence as well. Amos also seems to have utilized several wisdom motifs such as numerical patterns (Amos 1:3–2:6), cause and effect questions and the impossible question.

There can be no question that, as an intellectual, social, and political force, the wisdom movement contributed greatly to the history of Israel. Its successes must be traced, however, to Solomon who first set its gears in motion by virtue of his personal example and his promotion of wisdom.

onstruction and History of Solomon's Temple

COMMENTS

It may seem strange to the modern reader to find out that close to 50 chapters in the Old Testament deal with the construction of the tabernacle or temple. It should be remembered, however, that the tabernacle and the temple symbolized the presence of God's concern that His dwelling place be built as He would have it. Some idea of the purpose and importance of the temple may be gleaned by simply observing the numerous titles assigned to Solomon's temple: "temple of the LORD" (2 Kings 11:10), "palace" (1 Chron. 29:1), "house of my God" (v. 2), "holy house" (v. 3), "house of sacrifice" (2 Chron. 7:12), "sanctuary" (20:8), "house of the LORD" (23:5), "tabernacle of witness" (24:6), "house of their sanctuary" (36:17), "holy temple" (Ps. 79:1), "house of the God of Jacob" (Isa. 2:3), "holy mount" (27:13), "house of prayer" (56:7), "house of My glory" (60:2), "holy and beautiful house" (64:11). Most of these titles signify the fact that the temple was God's visible dwelling place on earth. It represented a great act of condescension on God's part to inhabit an earthly building.

Solomon's temple was built with the help of Hiram of Tyre, a Phoenician, whose people were known for their expertise in building. The temple, unlike the tabernacle before it, contained more than the three key parts and was a much more elaborate structure with the following main contents: (1) the holy of holies, also called the "most holy house" and "the inner house" (1 Kings 6:27; 2 Chron. 3:8), contained the ark of the covenant. (2) The holy place, also called "the greater house" (v. 5), contained the table of showbread (1 Kings 7:48), other tables of gold and silver (1 Chron. 28:16), candlesticks and their utensils (1 Kings 7:49-50), and the altar of incense with its furniture (6:22). (3) The porch, also called "the porch of the LORD" (2 Chron. 15:8), extended past the width of the temple about 30 feet and projected about 15 feet from the front of the temple (1 Kings 6:3). It was overlaid with gold and adorned with two magnificent pillars called Jachin and Boaz (2 Chron. 3:15-17). (4) The chambers of the temple, used for storage, extended around both the sides and the rear of the building (1 Kings 6:5-10). Their height was about 7 ½ feet and their width 7 ½ feet to 10 ½ feet. (5) The courts of the temple, which were surrounded by rows of stones and cedar beams, contained the altar of burnt offering, the brazen sea, and 10 lavers. (6) The gates included the higher gate, the new gate, the beautiful gate, and the eastern gate.

A summary listing of the uses of the temple throughout its history reveals that its utilization varied from the spiritual to the most earthly and mundane; a dwelling place of the Lord, the foremost reason for its erection; to contain the ark of the covenant; for the offering of sweet incense; for the continual placing of showbread and offering of burnt offerings; for prayer and worship; as a focal point for prayer; as an armory for weapons; and for refuge.

Solomon's lengthy prayer of dedication for the temple is unmatched for its beauty and theology (8:23-53). It contains, for example, a classic statement of the omnipresence of God: "But will God indeed dwell on the earth? Behold, the heaven and heaven of heavens cannot contain Thee; how much less this house that I have builded?" (v. 27) The student of the Bible, however, can never read this glorious prayer without tracing the history of the temple to its tragic end. It was pillaged by Shishak of Egypt and by Jehoash of Israel; it had to be repaired by Jehoash of Judah and by Josiah and purified by Hezekiah; it was converted into an idolatrous shrine by Manasseh; its treasures were plundered by Judah's own kings who tried to purchase peace with their enemies (Asa from Ben-hadad; Jehoash of Judah from Hazael, and Hezekiah, from Sennacherib); and, finally, it was destroyed by the Babylonian king Nebuchadnezzar who carried its remaining treasures to the temple of his god.

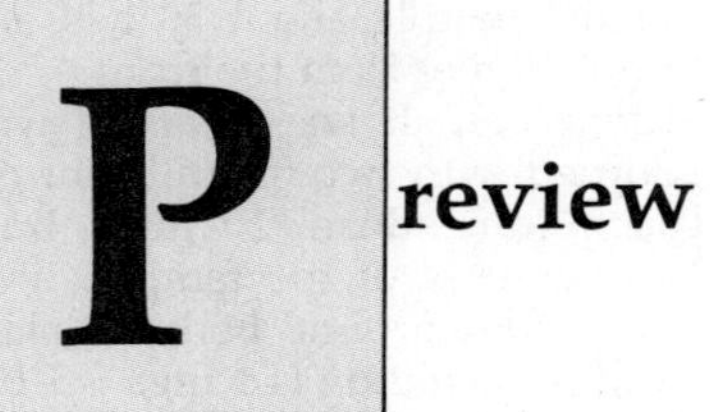

Solomon: His Fame and Shame

1 KINGS 9–11; 2 CHRONICLES 7–9

What had gone wrong? It was, at first glance, so unexpected. How could the king who began his reign by rejoicing in God, end it by rebelling against God? For one thing, it was not an overnight affair. Early in his reign Solomon had displayed certain inward flaws. His marriage to an Egyptian for political reasons was probably the first visible sign. Then fame and fortune, those treacherous twins, moved down on him, enhancing his reputation, but eating away at his character. Finally, lust replaced love, and gold was substituted for God. The end could not be far off. In retrospect it can be argued that, outwardly at least, Solomon's failures did not approach those of his father. But external conclusions are often wrong. The true test always centers in attitude, not appearance. The tragic truth was, that despite his vast wealth and wisdom, Solomon lacked that greatest of all qualities, so unmistakably possessed by David—a burning desire after God's own heart!

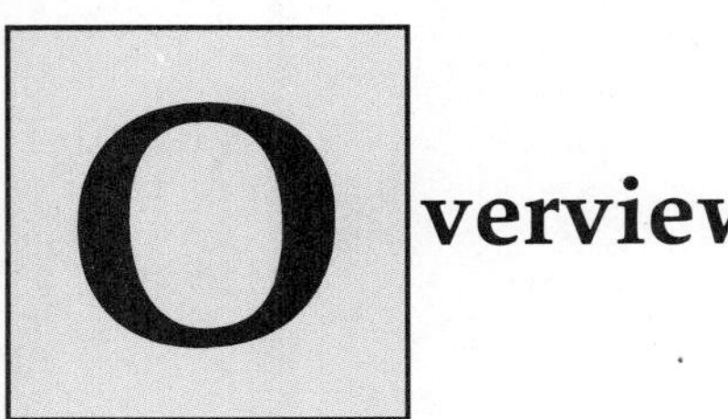

verview

<table>
<tr><td>SCRIPTURE</td><td colspan="6">1 Kings 9–11; 2 Chronicles 7–9</td></tr>
<tr><td>SUBJECT</td><td colspan="6">Life of Solomon: part 2</td></tr>
<tr><td rowspan="3">SPECIFICS</td><td colspan="6">The King of Israel</td></tr>
<tr><td>1 Kings 10:1-9</td><td>His reputation for God</td><td>1 Kings 10:14-27</td><td>His riches from God</td><td>1 Kings 11:1-13</td><td>His reprimand by God</td></tr>
<tr><td colspan="6">The King of kings</td></tr>
<tr><td>SAINTS AND SINNERS</td><td colspan="6">Solomon, Hiram the king, the queen of Sheba, Hadad, Rezon, Jeroboam, Ahijah</td></tr>
<tr><td rowspan="2">SENTENCE SUMMARIES</td><td>O.T. Verse</td><td colspan="5">“Did not Solomon king of Israel sin by these things? Yet among many nations was there no king like him, who was beloved of his God, and God made him king over all Israel; nevertheless even him did outlandish women cause to sin” (Neh. 13:26).</td></tr>
<tr><td>N.T. Verse</td><td colspan="5">“The queen of the South shall rise up in the judgment with this generation, and shall condemn it. For she came from the uttermost parts of the earth to hear the wisdom of Solomon; and, behold, a greater than Solomon is here” (Matt. 12:42).</td></tr>
</table>

RICHES, TESTIMONY, SIN

HIS TREASURY OF RICHES

He had 700 wives and 300 concubines.

He had fantastic quantities of gold. His personal income was 666 talents of gold yearly (799,000 ounces)–roughly one half billion dollars.

"And the king made silver and gold at Jerusalem as plenteous as stones, and cedar trees . . . as the sycamore trees" (2 Chron. 1:15).

His drinking vessels were made of gold.

"And King Solomon passed all the kings of the earth in riches and wisdom" (9:22).

He owned 40,000 horses.

He owned 1,400 chariots, each costing 400 dollars.

He commanded 12,000 cavalrymen.

He owned an extensive fleet of ships. These ships brought him more gold and silver, along with ivory, apes, and peacocks.

He built a huge ivory throne and overlaid it with pure gold. It had six steps and a rounded back with armrests. It was surrounded by 12 lions, 2 resting on each step.

He constructed an iron-smelting industry at Ezion-Geber.

HIS TESTIMONY THROUGHOUT THE LAND

The ruler of Arabia came to see for herself the riches of Solomon and also to test his universally known wisdom. She entered Jerusalem a skeptic, but left a believer.

"And she said to the king, 'It was a true report that I heard in mine own land of thy acts and of thy wisdom. Howbeit I believed not the words, until I came, and mine eyes had seen it. And, behold, the half was not told me; thy wisdom and prosperity exceedeth the fame which I heard' " (1 Kings 10:6-7).

Solomon's wisdom was testified to universally in matters of jurisprudence, administration, poetry, natural science, architecture and engineering, commercial enterprise, philosophy, and horticulture.

"And God gave Solomon wisdom and understanding exceeding much, and largeness of heart, even as the sand that is on the seashore. And Solomon's wisdom excelled the wisdom of all the children of the east country, and all the wisdom of Egypt" (4:29-30).

"And he spake 3,000 proverbs; and his songs were 1,005" (v. 32).

"And he spake of trees, from the cedar tree that is in Lebanon even unto the hyssop that springeth out of the wall. He spake also of beasts, and of fowl, and of creeping things, and of fishes" (v. 33).

HIS TRANSGRESSIONS AGAINST GOD

The warnings to Solomon against transgressing. Solomon received two warnings from David.

He received three warnings from God.

"But if ye shall at all turn from following Me, ye or your children, and will not keep My commandments and My statutes which I have set before you, but go and serve other gods, and worship them; then will I cut off Israel out of the land which I have given them; and this house, which I have hallowed for My name, will I cast out of My sight; and Israel shall be a proverb and a byword among all people" (9:6-7).

"Wherefore the LORD said unto Solomon, 'Forasmuch as this is done of thee, and thou hast not kept My covenant and My statutes, which I have commanded thee, I will surely rend the kingdom from thee, and will give it to thy servant' " (11:11).

The nature of Solomon's transgressions. Some four and one half centuries before Solomon, God had written the following qualification concerning all future kings of Israel:

"But he shall not multiply horses to himself, nor cause the people to return to Egypt, to the end that he should multiply horses. Forasmuch as the LORD hath said unto you, 'Ye shall henceforth return no more that way.' Neither shall he multiply wives to himself, that his heart turn not away: neither shall he greatly multiply to himself silver and gold" (Deut. 17:16-17).

But Solomon had disobeyed in all three areas. He had much gold and silver; he owned thousands of horses; he gathered

Polygamy in the Bible

COMMENTS

The remarkable fact that Solomon had 700 wives and 300 concubines raises the issue of polygamy in the Bible. Though Solomon is remembered as the greatest polygamist in the Bible, this evil practice was observed much earlier than he. The list of polygamists in the Bible reads like a "Who's Who" of biblical characters. It was begun by Lamech and continued by Abraham, Esau, Jacob, Gideon, Elkanah, David, Solomon, Rehoboam, Abijah, Jehoram, Joash, Ahab, Jehoiachin, and Belshazzar.

In light of God's intended monogamous pattern, some explanation should be offered to explain the toleration of such sin in the Bible. First, in the earliest ages of biblical history God did not clearly prohibit man from multiple marriages. Though God's monogamous intention should have been clear from the fact that He created one woman for one man, God apparently decided that man should learn from experience that His plan was best. It is obvious that either man could not deduce the divine pattern from Creation or else he chose not to obey.

Second, God did reveal in due time, that polygamy represented a gross violation of the institution of marriage. Deuteronomy 17:17 seems to be the first stated prohibition against polygamy, though it is addressed solely to kings. Leviticus 18:18 likewise contains a limited application of the prohibition: a man must not marry his wife's sister. Jesus of course taught, on the basis of Creation alone, that monogamy was God's ordination and that polygamy and divorce were both violations of the divine will. It is true that Exodus 21:10-11 seems to imply that polygamy was acceptable to God. However, this law must be understood as the regulation of an existing practice and not the condoning of it. The fact is that people did commit polygamy; therefore, laws were written to minimize the cruelty inherent in that practice.

Third, whenever polygamy is mentioned in the Bible, its woeful results are clearly expressed. These problems include favoritism toward a certain wife (by Jacob), rivalry (between Sarah and Hagar; between Rachel and Leah, between Hannah and Peninnah), and idolatry (by Solomon, by the repatriated Jews in Ezra and Nehemiah's day). In the case of Solomon the historian's evaluation is quite succinct but pointed: "His wives turned away his heart after other gods" (1 Kings 11:4).

Fourth, in many cases of polygamy in the Bible the guilty parties suffer specific judgments, either as the natural consequences of their sin, or by direct intervention of God. Abraham, Esau, Jacob, and Elkanah, for example, all suffered as a result of their sin. It was left to them to mediate between quarreling wives or, in the case of Esau, between his mother and his wives. On the other hand, in the divine commentary on Solomon's sin we are specifically instructed that the Lord was angry with Solomon and told him that He would take the kingdom away from Solomon because his heart was turned away from the Lord.

Fifth, it seems that the man was always held accountable by God for the sin involved. This fact is due to the reality that polygamy was a problem whereas polyandry (multiple husbands) was not.

Sixth, even in the case of the polygamous Solomon, the Bible has preserved for all time a beautiful story of married love that was conducted according to God's design: the Song of Solomon. This little book, which is the only one in the Bible completely devoted to love and marriage, evidently should be placed chronologically near the beginning of Solomon's reign, before his many wives turned his heart away. In any case, it does serve to rescue at least one beautiful love story from the life of the man who had 1,000 wives and concubines.

hundreds of wives and concubines (1 Kings 11:3). This transgression was by far the most serious, for these pagan women influenced Solomon to actually worship Ashtoreth, Milcom, and Chemosh, devilish idols of the Sidonians, Ammonites, and Moabites.

The results of Solomon's transgressions. Solomon would, for the first time in his reign, be plagued with troublemakers and minor revolts. Two of these troublemakers are named: Hadad, an Edomite, and Rezon, a bandit.

After his death, God would take the kingdom from Solomon's son and give a large portion of it to another (vv. 9-13, 26-40). This person was an Ephraimite named Jeroboam.

Jeroboam was told by the Prophet Ahijah that when Solomon died he would rule over 10 of the 12 tribes.

After a reign of 40 years, Solomon died.

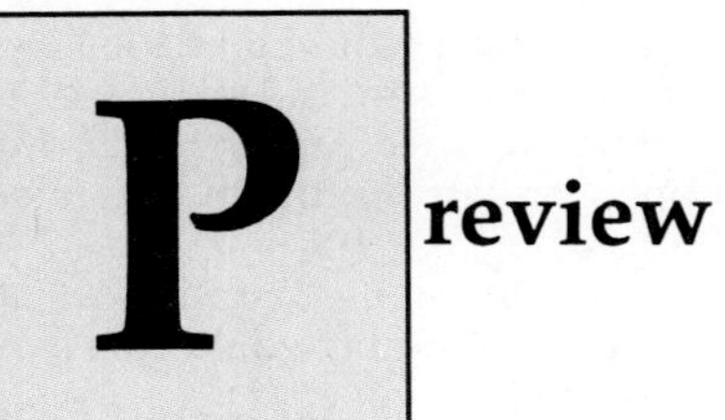

Previewing the Psalms

THE BOOK OF PSALMS

Heaven's handbook on prayer and praise! These are the Psalms, 150 in number, written by at least eight authors over a period of some seven centuries. In no other biblical book is the soul of man so totally and vividly exposed. We hear choruses of devotion coming from the highest mountains, and cries of despair proceeding from the deepest valleys. Its pages are filled with singing, sobbing, shouting, and sorrowing. God's face, eyes, voice, arms, hands, fingers, and feet are referred to. He is seen as a Fortress, Rock, Shield, Shepherd, Soldier, Creator, Ruler, Judge, Redeemer, Sustainer, and Avenger. He possesses love, hate, anger, and compassion. He is all-present, all-knowing, and almighty. The works, will, ways, and words of the Lord are stressed. As for believers, they are called sheep, the apple of His eye, saints, the upright, and the righteous. God has rescued them from the miry pit, placed their feet on the rock, established their journey, created new songs in their hearts, satisfied their longings, provided for their every need, forgiven their sins, and prepared an eternal home for them.

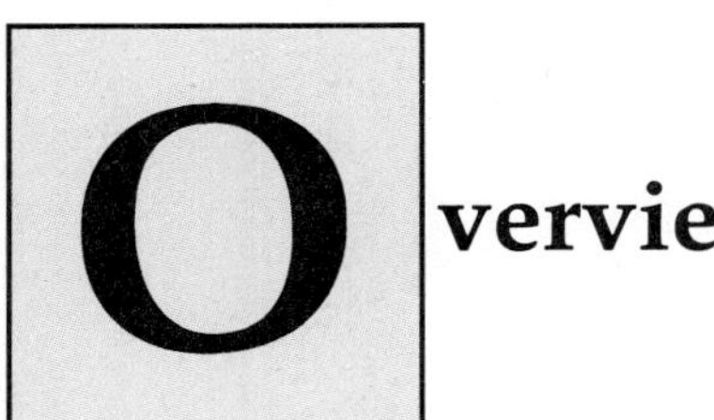

verview

SCRIPTURE	The Book of Psalms				
SUBJECT	Book division and authorship of the Psalms				
SPECIFICS	Sections in the Psalms			Scribes of the Psalms	
	Psalm divisions	Key phrase	Corresponding Pentateuch book	The name	The number
	1–41	Man	Genesis	David	At least 73
	42–72	Deliverance	Exodus	Sons of Korah	12
				Asaph	12
	73–89	Sanctuary	Leviticus	Heman	1
				Ethan	1
	90–106	Wandering	Numbers	Solomon	2
				Moses	1
	107–150	Word of God	Deuteronomy	Hezekiah	10
SAINTS AND SINNERS					
SENTENCE SUMMARIES	O.T. Verse	"Hezekiah commanded to offer the burnt offering upon the altar. And when the burnt offering began, the song of the LORD began also with the trumpets, and with the instruments ordained by David king of Israel" (2 Chron. 29:27).			
	N.T. Verse	"They sing the song of Moses the servant of God, and the song of the Lamb, saying, 'Great and marvelous are Thy works, Lord God Almighty; just, and true are Thy ways, Thou King of saints' " (Rev. 15:3).			

BOOKS OF THE BIBLE WRITTEN DURING THE UNITED KINGDOM PERIOD

JESSE
(Father)

DAVID

ZERUIAH
(Sister)

ASAHEL
(Nephew)

ABISHAI
(Nephew)

JOAB
(Nephew)

WIVES

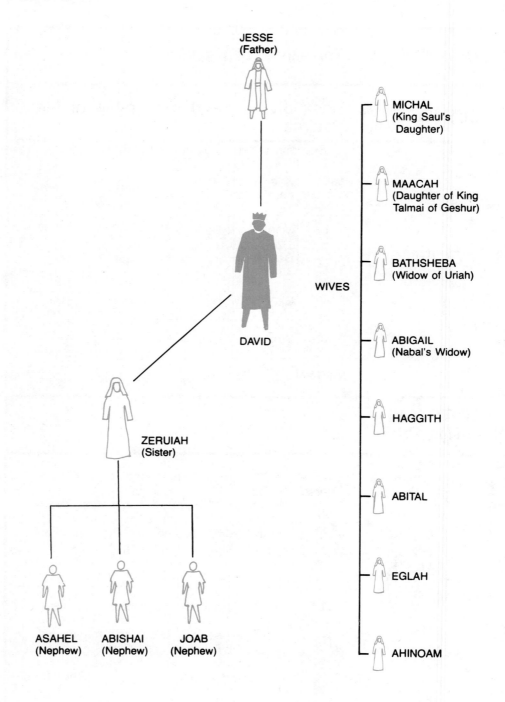

MICHAL
(King Saul's Daughter)

MAACAH
(Daughter of King Talmai of Geshur)

BATHSHEBA
(Widow of Uriah)

ABIGAIL
(Nabal's Widow)

HAGGITH

ABITAL

EGLAH

AHINOAM

Four Old Testament poetical books were written (for the most part) during the United Kingdom stage. These are: Psalms, Proverbs, Ecclesiastes, and Song of Solomon.

THE PSALMS

There are at least five ways one may study the Psalms.

By book division (each division ends with a doxology). "Blessed be the LORD *God of Israel from everlasting, and to everlasting. Amen, and Amen" (Ps. 41:13).*

"Blessed be the LORD *God . . . of Israel, who only doeth wondrous things. And blessed be His glorious name forever. And let the whole earth be filled with His glory. Amen, and Amen" (72:18-19).*

"Blessed be the LORD *forevermore. Amen, and Amen" (89:52).*

"Blessed be the LORD *God of Israel from everlasting to everlasting. And let all the people say, Amen. Praise ye the* LORD*" (106:48).*

"Let everything that hath breath praise the LORD*. Praise ye the* LORD*" (150:6).*

Some believe these five divisions reflect the main thought expressed in the Pentateuch (first 5 books in the Bible). Note some examples: *Psalms 1–41 (correspond to Gen.): Key word is *man*. *"Blessed is the man that walketh not in the counsel of the ungodly" (Ps. 1:1).*

"What is man, that Thou art mindful of him?" (8:4)

"What man is he that feareth the Lord?" (25:12)

"Verily, every man at his best state is altogether vanity" (39:5).

*Psalms 42–72 correspond to Exodus: The key word is *deliverance*. *"Thou art my King, O God; command deliverances for Jacob" (Ps. 44:4).*

"For He hath delivered me out of all trouble" (54:7).

"For Thou has delivered my soul from death" (56:13).

"Deliver me from mine enemies, O my God" (59:1).

"For He shall deliver the needy when He crieth" (72:12).

*Psalms 73–89 correspond to Leviticus: The key word is *sanctuary*. *"For I was envious . . . when I saw the prosperity of the wicked. . . . Until I went into the sanctuary of God; then understood I their end" (Ps. 73:3, 17).*

"Thy way, O God, is in the sanctuary" (77:13).

"And He built His sanctuary . . . which He hath established forever" (78:69).

*Psalms 90–106 correspond to Numbers: the key words are *unrest* and *wandering*. Especially to be noted under this section are two entire psalms which are given over to Israel's failures as recorded in the Book of Numbers. These psalms are 90 and 106.

*Psalms 107–150 correspond to Deuteronomy: The key phrase is *Word of God.*

"He sent His Word and healed them" (Ps. 107:20).

"I wait for the LORD *. . . and in His Word do I hope" (130:5).*

"Thou hast magnified Thy Word" (138:2).

In addition to these verses this final section contains Psalm 119, Scripture's longest chapter. It is totally given over to the Word of God. It is mentioned in 171 of the 176 verses in the chapter. The author gives the Bible eight titles in this psalm and ascribes some 12 ministries to it.

The titles. His Law (v. 1), His testimonies (v. 2), His ways (v. 3), His precepts (v. 4), His statutes (v. 5), His commandments (v. 6), His righteous judgments (v. 7), His Word (v. 9), and His ordinances (v. 91).

The ministries. It cleanses (v. 9), it quickens (v. 25), it strengthens (v. 28), it establishes (v. 38), it defends (v. 42), it comforts (v. 50), it instructs (vv. 98-99), it enlightens (v. 105), it assures (v. 114), it upholds (v. 116), it brings peace (v. 165), and it delivers (v. 170).

Note but a few statements about the Word in Psalm 119.

"Wherewithal shall a young man cleanse his way? By taking heed thereto according to Thy Word" (v. 9).

"Thy Word have I hid in mine heart, that I might not sin against Thee" (v. 11).

"Forever, O LORD*, Thy Word is settled in heaven" (v. 89).*

"Thy Word is a lamp unto my feet, and a light unto my path" (v. 105).

"Thy Word is very pure; therefore, Thy servant loveth it" (v. 140).

By authorship. *David—73 psalms. These can be divided into four categories: The shepherd psalms (Examples—23, 100); the sinner psalms (Examples—32, 38, 51); the suffering psalms (Examples—22, 55, 69); the satisfied psalms (Examples—37, 103, 139).

*By the sons of Korah: 12. Psalms 42–49, 84–85, 87–88.

*By Asaph: 12. Psalms 50, 73–83.

*By Heman: 1. Psalm 88.

*By Ethan: 1. Psalm 89.

*By Solomon: 2. Psalms 72, 127.

*By Moses: 1. Psalm 90.

*By Hezekiah: 10. Psalms 120–121, 123, 125–126, 128–130, 132, 134.

*Anonymous: 38.

The Nature of Hebrew Poetry

COMMENTS

It is important to preface any study of the Old Testament poetical books with a few remarks about Hebrew poetry. Poetry in the Old Testament does not rhyme the last words of lines as is common in English poetry. Rather, Hebrew poetry rhymes ideas. This phenomenon is commonly called parallelism. There are at least six types of parallelism evident in Old Testament poetry.

Synonymous. Two consecutive lines are very similar. "O LORD, rebuke me not in Thine anger, neither chasten me in Thy hot displeasure" (Ps. 6:1).

It should be noted that the verses are not always precisely synonymous. "Keep me as the apple of the eye, hide me under the shadow of Thy wings" (17:8).

Antithetic. The second line is contrasted with the first. "The thoughts of the righteous are right, but the counsels of the wicked are deceit" (Prov. 12:5).

Synthetic. The second line further develops a thought from the first line. "For the LORD is a great God, and a great King above all gods" (Ps. 95:3).

Emblematic. One line conveys the main point; the other line illuminates it with an image or illustration. "As the hart panteth after the water brooks, so panteth my soul after Thee, O God" (42:1).

Climactic. The second line repeats the first line with the exception of the last term. "O sing unto the LORD a new song: sing unto the LORD, all the earth" (96:1).

Formal. Two lines are joined together with none of the obvious logical relationships outlined above. "Yet have I set My King upon My holy hill of Zion" (2:6).

While it is true that five of the Old Testament books are called "poetical books" (Job through Song of Solomon), this title is really a misnomer since most of the prophetic books are also written in poetical form. Many modern editions of the Bible set the poetical sections in verse so that the reader can readily identify them.

Meter, or systematically measured rhythm, is not found in Hebrew poetry. The only measurable rhythm is that of accent or grammatical stress. The reader should not look for stanzas in Hebrew poetry either. The enigmatic word *selah* is clearly not used to indicate stanzas.

Songs form a special type of Hebrew poetry. Evidently the Jews loved music and became famous for their songs (cf. Ps. 137:3). Examples of songs composed for various occasions abound in the Old Testament: the song of the well, taunt or mocking songs, a love song (Song), laments, songs of victory, and benedictions.

Songs were most often accompanied by music. Numerous musical instruments are mentioned in Scripture. These include stringed instruments (harp, psaltery), wind instruments (pipe, flute, organ, horn, trumpet), and percussion (bells, cymbals, timbrel).

There can be little doubt that music played an extremely important role in the worship of ancient Israel. First Chronicles 16:4 contains an excellent summary of the basic purposes of the psalms: "And he [David] appointed certain of the Levites to minister before the ark of the LORD, and to record, and to thank and praise the LORD God of Israel." The word "record" could be better translated "petition" and refers to requests made to God through psalms. "To thank" means to offer thanksgiving to God for what He does for man, and "to praise" refers to the exaltation of God for who He is.

The importance of Hebrew poetry is clear, not only from the fact that the largest book in the Old Testament is the hymnbook (Pss.), but from the simple fact that almost all of the communication between God and man in the Old Testament is in poetry. God loves beauty and is pleased with man's creative expression of his needs, thanks, and praise to God.

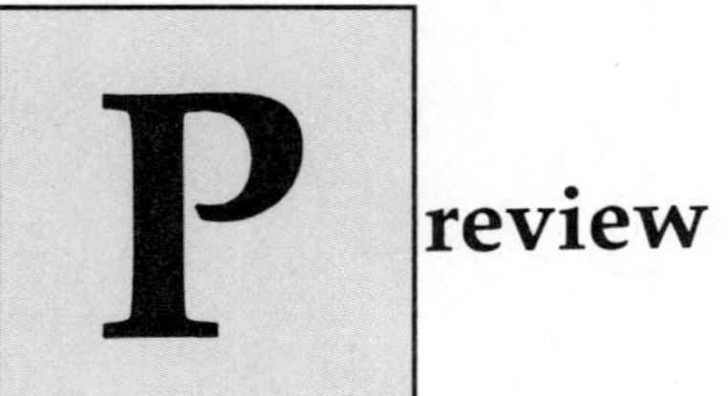

Preview

Six Suggested Study Plans

PSALMS 6; 32; 35; 38; 51; 69; 102; 109; 130; 137; 143

As a believer, how does my sin affect both myself and God? Should I ever pray for God to judge His enemies? When and how did the Old Testament saints use the Psalms? Where can I find the best survey of the Old Testament in the Old Testament? What learning device did the Holy Spirit once use to help believers memorize entire sections of Scripture? These and other questions are answered as one studies the penitential, imprecatory, degree, hallelujah, historical, and acrostic psalms. These six subjects can be classified under three divisions: those psalms dealing with sin, celebrations, and surveys.

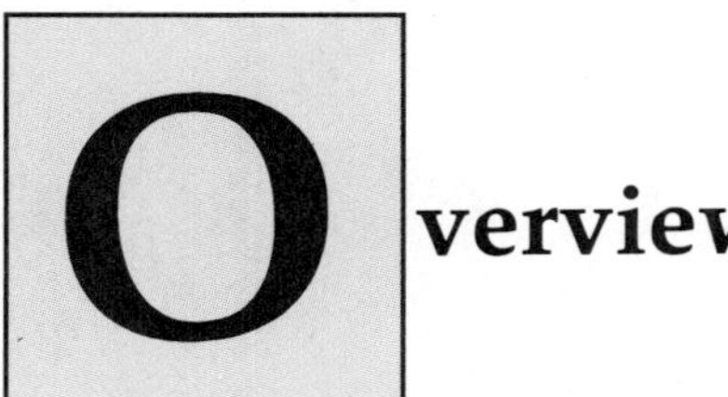

verview

<table>
<tr><td>SCRIPTURE</td><td colspan="6">Psalms 6; 32; 35; 38; 51; 69; 102; 109; 130; 137; 143</td></tr>
<tr><td>SUBJECT</td><td colspan="6">Topical approach to the Psalms</td></tr>
<tr><td rowspan="3">SPECIFICS</td><td colspan="2">Sin psalms</td><td colspan="2">Special occasion psalms</td><td colspan="2">Schoolbook psalms</td></tr>
<tr><td>Penitential</td><td>Asking God to cleanse His own</td><td>Ascent</td><td>Psalms sung in the temple</td><td>Historical</td><td>Psalms to be studied as history</td></tr>
<tr><td>Imprecatory</td><td>Asking God to condemn His enemies</td><td>Hallelujah</td><td>Psalms sung during the Passover</td><td>Acrostic</td><td>Psalms to be committed to memory</td></tr>
<tr><td>SAINTS AND SINNERS</td><td colspan="6"></td></tr>
<tr><td rowspan="2">SENTENCE SUMMARIES</td><td colspan="2">O.T. Verse</td><td colspan="4">“From the uttermost part of the earth have we heard songs, even glory to the righteous. But I said, ‘My leanness, my leanness, woe unto me! The treacherous dealers have dealt treacherously; yea, the treacherous dealers have dealt very treacherously’ ” (Isa. 24:16).</td></tr>
<tr><td colspan="2">N.T. Verse</td><td colspan="4">“And when they had sung a hymn, they went out into the Mount of Olives” (Matt. 26:30).</td></tr>
</table>

SALMS BY TOPICS

By subject matter. *The penitential psalms (6, 32, 38, 51, 102, 130, 143): These are psalms where the author confesses his sins to God.

"When I kept silence, my bones waxed old through my roaring all the day long. For day and night Thy hand was heavy upon me; my moisture is turned into the drought of summer. I acknowledged my sin unto Thee, and mine iniquity have I not hid. I said, 'I will confess my transgressions unto the LORD; and Thou forgavest the iniquity of my sin' " (32:3-5).

"For my iniquities are gone over mine head. As a heavy burden they are too heavy for me. . . . For I will declare mine iniquity; I will be sorry for my sin" (38:4, 18).

"Have mercy upon me, O God, according to Thy loving-kindness; according unto the multitude of Thy tender mercies blot out my transgressions. Wash me thoroughly from mine iniquity, and cleanse me from my sin. For I acknowledge my transgressions; and my sin is ever before me. Against Thee, Thee only, have I sinned, and done this evil in Thy sight; that Thou mightest be justified when Thou speakest, and be clear when Thou judgest. . . .

"Purge me with hyssop, and I shall be clean; wash me, and I shall be whiter than snow. . . .

"Hide Thy face from my sins, and blot out all mine iniquities. Create in me a clean heart, O God; and renew a right spirit within me. Cast me not away from Thy presence; and take not Thy Holy Spirit from me. Restore unto me the joy of Thy salvation; and uphold me with Thy free Spirit" (51:1-4, 7, 9-12).

"If Thou, LORD, shouldest mark iniquities, O LORD, who shall stand? But there is forgiveness with Thee, that Thou mayest be feared" (130:3-4).

*The imprecatory psalms: To imprecate is to call down judgment on God's enemies.

"Let them be confounded and put to shame that seek after my soul. Let them be turned back and brought to confusion that devise my hurt. Let them be as chaff before the wind; and let the Angel of the LORD chase them. Let their way be dark and slippery; and let the Angel of the LORD persecute them. . . .

"Let destruction come upon him at unawares; and let his net that he hath hid catch himself; into that very destruction let him fall" (35:4-6, 8).

"Let their table become a snare before them, and that which should have been for their welfare, let it become a trap. Let their eyes be darkened, that they see not, and make their loins continually to shake. Pour out Thine indignation upon them, and let Thy wrathful anger take hold of them" (69:22-24).

"Set Thou a wicked man over him, and let Satan stand at his right hand. When he shall be judged, let him be condemned. And let his prayer become sin. Let his days be few, and let another take his office. Let his children be fatherless, and his wife a widow. Let his children be continually vagabonds, and beg; let them seek their bread also out of their desolate places.

"Let the extortioner catch all that he hath; and let the strangers spoil his labor. Let there be none to extend mercy unto him. Neither let there be any to favor his fatherless children. Let his posterity be cut off; and in the generation following let their name be blotted out. Let the iniquity of his fathers be remembered with the LORD; and let not the sin of his mother be blotted out. Let them be before the LORD continually, that He may cut off the memory of them from the earth" (109:6-15).

*The degree or ascent psalms: There are several theories to explain the meaning of the name for these psalms:

1. Hezekiah (who authored 10 of them) introduced this title as a reminder of his supernatural healing, during which time the sun retreated 10 degrees on its dial.
2. They were sung as the Levite choir ascended the 15 stairs in the temple court.
3. They were sung by Jewish pilgrims in route to the temple during various annual feast days.

Psalm 137: An Imprecatory Psalm

COMMENTS

Psalm 137 is an appropriate psalm to consider since it raises the issue of imprecatory prayers in the psalms. This term refers to occasions in which the psalmist prays for God's justice, or an imprecation, to fall on his enemies. This issue will be examined here as the psalm is considered as a whole.

The background of this psalm is clearly revealed from its contents. It expresses the woeful situation of the Israelite exiles in Babylon. One need only read Jeremiah 52 to gain some sense of what the Israelites must have felt after they were carried away captive into Babylon. Their nation had been destroyed; their temple had been ransacked; and their king had been blinded by the Babylonians. Then they were forced to march hundreds of miles to a distant, pagan land where most of them died. This psalm reflects their mourning for their homeland as they wasted away in Babylon.

The psalm may be divided into three parts. First, there is a *cry in captivity* (vv. 1-4). The mention of the "rivers of Babylon" provides some local color to the psalm since it is widely known that Babylon had a system of many canals (cf. Ezekiel's visions by the river in Ezek. 1:1; 3:15). It was in this foreign land that the captives remembered their homeland with mourning. Evidently the Israelites were well known in the ancient Near East for their musical ability because the Babylonians requested that they sing for them. By this time most of the psalms had been written, and these Israelites would have had a large selection from which to choose in their performances. However, they felt that they could not sing the Lord's song in a strange land (v. 4). That would have been a compromise of God's truth.

The second part of the psalm may be appropriately titled *a vow of remembrance* (vv. 5-6). The mention of Zion causes the psalmist to vow never to forget his homeland. Since singing had been requested, the psalmist vowed that his hand, which played the instrument, and his tongue, which sang the song, might both be annulled if he forgot Jerusalem. Jerusalem represents the place of blessing and promise for the Israelite, and therefore its importance is preeminent.

The third part of the psalm may be described as *a prayer for judgment* (vv. 7-9). It is this passage that is most troublesome to the modern reader. Here the psalmist prays for the destruction of both the Edomites and Babylonians. The Edomites had given moral support to the Babylonians while the latter destroyed Jerusalem and took its people captive. The prayer for vengeance is quite vivid. The psalmist requested that the Babylonians' infants might be dashed against the rocks and slain. On the face of it, this request seems quite cruel and unduly vengeful. However, there are several reasons by which such imprecatory psalms and prayers may be justified. First, it must be remembered that the Israelites were building a political kingdom of God. The psalmist realized that as long as the wicked prospered, God's glory was tarnished and His kingdom on earth, which was Israel, was thwarted in its attempt to establish God's ethical rule over men. Actually, this prayer is in the same spirit as the disciples' petition, "Thy kingdom come," since the coming of Christ's kingdom includes the destruction of the wicked.

Second, the petition is consistent with God's revealed will. If this prayer be a problem, then God's order for the Israelites to completely destroy the Canaanites must present a greater difficulty. In God's economy it was important that both of these wicked societies be completely obliterated or else their ungodly traits would be passed on to another generation. Certainly the Babylonians passed their lust for power and international dominion from one generation to the next. The only thing that could break this cycle was for them to be destroyed.

Third, at least the psalmist did pray and put the matter into God's hands. His spirit of animosity is poured out to God in prayer which is the best place to take one's feelings in heartfelt confession.

A final question may be raised: Is it legitimate or permissible for Christians to pray such prayers today? While there may be occasions on which a Christian might pray such a prayer, as Paul did for Alexander (2 Tim. 4:14), or as the Tribulation saints will do against their enemies (Rev. 6:10), the pattern of prayer for the New Testament Christian must be conducted in light of the new display of God's grace in Christ. We should pray prayers that are consistent with our calling, which is not to establish a political kingdom, but to get the Gospel to every creature (cf. Paul's prayer in Rom. 10:1).

*The hallel or hallelujah psalms: These psalms were sung on the night of the Passover. Our Lord and His disciples doubtless sung them during the close of the Passover in the Upper Room.

"And when they had sung a hymn, they went out into the Mount of Olives" (Matt. 26:30).

What must have gone through the Saviour's mind on that emotion-filled night as He sang the following (among the many) hallelujah verses, knowing full well of His impending death at Calvary.

"But our God is in the heavens; He hath done whatsoever He hath pleased" (Ps. 115:3; cf. Isa. 53:10).

"The sorrows of death compassed me, and the pains of hell got hold upon me; I found trouble and sorrow. Then called I upon the name of the LORD. . . . I will take the cup of salvation, and call upon the name of the LORD" (Ps. 116:3-4, 13; cf. Mark 14:34, 36).

"The stone which the builders refused is become the head stone of the corner. This is the LORD's doing; it is marvelous in our eyes. This is the day which the LORD hath made; we will rejoice and be glad in it" (Ps. 118:22-24; cf. Matt. 21:42).

*The historical psalms: These three psalms, which depict the history of Israel, may be summarized as follows: Israel refused to walk in His Law; forgot His works; spoke against Him; did not trust His salvation; lied to Him; grieved Him; limited Him; worshiped graven images; envied His leader Moses; despised the Promised Land; murmured in their tents; ate the sacrifices of the dead; mingled among the heathen; sacrificed their sons and daughters to devils; and shed innocent blood.

The grace of God. God remembered His covenant when they cried unto Him. He divided the sea; He led them with a cloud by day; He led them with a fire by night; He provided water for them out of rocks; He rained down manna for them; He was full of compassion and forgave their iniquity; He wrought signs for them in Egypt; He brought them to the border of the Promised Land; He cast out the heathen before them; He chose David to lead them; He allowed no man to hurt them; He fed them; He reproved kings for their sake; He elevated them through Joseph; He gave them the riches of Egypt; He kept them all strong; He continually forgave them; and He continually heard their cry.

*The acrostic psalms: The nine psalms are also called the alphabetical psalms. This is so because each line of these psalms begins with a successive letter of the 22 letters in the Hebrew alphabet.

Psalm 119 is, of course, the most famous of the acrostic psalms. It has 22 stanzas. Each stanza has eight verses, for a total of 176. Each of these stanzas begins with 1 of the 22 Hebrew letters. Not all of these psalms are complete in this arrangement. That is, some are missing a letter or more. Thus we find:

—Psalms 9–10, 25 are missing several letters.

—Psalms 34, 145 have all but one letter.

—Psalms 37, 111–112, 119 have all the letters.

It is reasonable to suppose that the acrostic device was designed to assist the memory.

Psalm 117: A Short Psalm with a Big Message

COMMENTS

Psalm 117 is one of the hallel psalms, but it is better known for being the shortest psalm in the Psalter. With only two verses, it also constitutes the shortest chapter in the Bible. In spite of its brevity, however, it strikes a note which no other psalm in the book emphasizes quite so forcefully. It might well be compared to the one-note musician in an orchestra. His only duty is to strike one note during the entire concert, yet his one note cannot be removed without doing damage to the composition. Such is the case with Psalm 117. That one note is worth investigating.

The psalm itself may be divided into three distinct parts. First, there is the *call to praise* (v. 1). The most important point to make about this verse is the fact that the writer addresses "all ye nations" and "all ye people." The first expression refers to all nations without distinction, that is, rich and poor, black and white, etc.; the second refers to all nations without exception. In other words, this psalm is clearly addressed to Gentiles. That makes it the only psalm in the Psalter which is written in its entirety to the Gentile nations. It thus contains an evangelistic tone. The second word translated "praise" also adds a Gentile flavor since it is an Aramaic word borrowed into Hebrew. Aramaic was the language of the Gentiles and would have evoked warm feelings in their response. It would be equivalent to calling a Spanish friend "amigo" in an attempt to encourage him.

A second point to be noticed in verse 1 is the One to whom these Gentile nations are encouraged to offer their praise: to the God of Israel. The psalmist calls on the nations to worship Israel's God alone as the one true God. Some might charge the psalmist with overzealous nationalism, but as Christians we know that the God of Israel is the Lord Jesus Christ of the New Testament, who alone is truth. The godly Israelite knew that Israel was destined to rule the entire world, and thus he calls on the nations to submit now while there is hope for them.

The second part of the psalm may be entitled the *cause for praise* (v. 2a-b). The verse begins with the word "for" and therefore cites the reasons why the Gentiles should believe in and praise the God of Israel. Two specific reasons are cited: first, "His merciful kindness is great toward us." The particular attribute singled out here is God's "merciful kindness," which could be translated "loyal love." It refers to God's loyalty to His covenantal commitment to Israel. God had entered into covenant with Abraham, had reaffirmed that covenant to his descendants many times, and had never forgotten it. God loved to be loyal to His commitment. All of these ideas are bound up in the word. It is strange, however, that the psalmist states that the Gentiles should praise God because of His love "toward *us*," that is, toward Israel. The psalmist is not overstepping the bounds, however, if it be remembered that God had promised Abraham: "In thee shall all families of the earth be blessed" (Gen. 12:3). If God is not loyal to His promises to Israel, then all Gentiles are without hope also. Therefore, the Gentiles should rejoice that God continues to honor His promises to Abraham's seed.

The second reason cited in the cause for praise is the fact that "the truth of the LORD endureth forever." The word "truth" in the Old Testament contains the ideas of dependability, faithfulness, and firmness. It is a way of saying that God never forgets His promises and His Word. They are firm and reliable.

Finally, the third part of the psalm is the *conclusion* (v. 2c). It consists simply of the words, "Praise ye the LORD." These words actually translate one Hebrew word, "Hallelujah." It is a closing call to the readers to praise the God of Israel. It almost has the idea of bragging on the Lord. It means to tell how good He is; how great His loyal love is; how dependable His truth is, etc.

In sum, the brevity of the psalm must not be allowed to obscure its message. As the only psalm addressed in its entirety to the Gentile world, its message was still too big for some Jews in the first century who did not think Gentiles could be saved. When Paul wanted to quote proof from the Old Testament to show that God was interested in the salvation of the Gentiles, he chose four passages. This psalm is among them (Rom. 15:11). With its brief but unique note in the Psalter, it stands as a rebuke to anyone who would seek to restrict salvation or the love of God.

Tell Me the Story of Jesus

PSALMS 2; 8; 16; 22; 24; 40–41; 45; 68–69; 72; 89; 102; 110; 118

Reduced to its purest and most precise form, the Bible is a Book about Jesus. He alone is its subject, Saviour, and song. The following outline aptly brings this into focus.

> The Old Testament gives us the preparation for Jesus.
> The Gospel accounts give us the manifestation of Jesus.
> The Book of Acts gives us the propagation of Jesus.
> The Epistles give us the explanation for Jesus.
> The Book of Revelation gives us the coronation of Jesus.

The messianic psalms (predictions about Jesus) help us, as do few other Old Testament passages, to prepare for the Saviour. In them we read of His future submission, sufferings, and sovereign rule over all the earth!

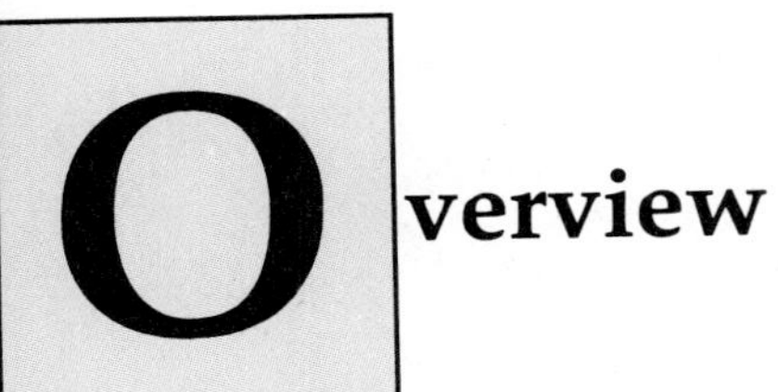

Overview

<table>
<tr><td>SCRIPTURE</td><td colspan="5">Psalms 2; 8; 16; 22; 24; 31; 34; 40–41; 45; 55; 68–69; 72; 89; 102; 109–110; 118; 129</td></tr>
<tr><td>SUBJECT</td><td colspan="5">Messianic psalms</td></tr>
<tr><td rowspan="10">SPECIFICS</td><td colspan="4">The role</td><td>The record</td></tr>
<tr><td rowspan="2">The servant</td><td colspan="3">Obedience to the Father</td><td rowspan="2">Psalms 40; 69</td></tr>
<tr><td colspan="3">Zeal for the father</td></tr>
<tr><td rowspan="2">The sufferer</td><td colspan="3">Forsaken by man</td><td rowspan="2">Psalms 22; 31; 34; 41; 55; 69; 109; 118; 129</td></tr>
<tr><td colspan="3">Forsaken by God</td></tr>
<tr><td>The soldier</td><td>Resur-rection</td><td>Ascen-sion</td><td>Triumphal Entry</td><td>Psalms 16; 24; 68</td></tr>
<tr><td>The sanctifier</td><td colspan="3">His high priestly word</td><td>Psalm 110</td></tr>
<tr><td>The sovereign</td><td>His wedding</td><td>His warfare</td><td>His reign</td><td>Psalms 2; 8; 45; 72; 89; 102; 110</td></tr>
<tr><td>SAINTS AND SINNERS</td><td colspan="5"></td></tr>
<tr><td rowspan="2">SENTENCE SUMMARIES</td><td>O.T. Verses</td><td colspan="4">"Give thanks unto the LORD, call upon His name, make known His deeds among the people. Sing unto Him; sing psalms unto Him; talk ye of all His wondrous works" (2 Chron. 16:8-9).</td></tr>
<tr><td>N.T. Verse</td><td colspan="4">"He said unto them, 'These are the words which I spake unto you, while I was yet with you, that all things must be fulfilled, which were written in the Law of Moses, and in the Prophets, and in the Psalms, concerning Me' " (Luke 24:44).</td></tr>
</table>

BY MESSIANIC CONTENT

His obedience. "Sacrifice and offering Thou didst not desire; mine ears hast Thou opened. Burnt offering and sin offering hast Thou not required.

"Then said I, 'Lo, I come: in the volume of the book it is written of Me, I delight to do Thy will, O My God. Yea, Thy Law is within My heart.'

"I have preached righteousness in the great congregation; lo, I have not refrained My lips. O LORD, Thou knowest. I have not hid Thy righteousness within My heart; I have declared Thy faithfulness and Thy salvation. I have not concealed Thy loving-kindness and Thy truth from the great congregation" (Ps. 40:6-10).

His zeal. "For the zeal of Thine house hath eaten Me up; and the reproaches of them that reproached Thee are fallen upon Me" (69:9).

His rejection. "The stone which the builders refused is become the head stone of the corner" (118:22).

His betrayal. "Yea, Mine own familiar friend, in whom I trusted, which did eat of My bread, hath lifted up his heel against Me" (41:9).

"For it was not an enemy that reproached me; then I could have borne it. Neither was it he that hated me that did magnify himself against me; then I would have hid myself from him. But it was thou, a man mine equal, my guide, and mine acquaintance. We took sweet counsel together, and walked unto the house of God in company" (55:12-14).

His suffering. "My God, My God, why hast Thou forsaken Me? Why art Thou so far from helping Me, and from the words of My roaring?" (22:1)

"But I am a worm, and no man; a reproach of men, and despised of the people. All they that see Me laugh Me to scorn. They shoot out the lip, they shake the head, saying, 'He trusted on the LORD that He would deliver Him. Let Him deliver Him, seeing He delighted in Him' " (22:6-8).

"The plowers plowed upon My back; they made long their furrows" (129:3).

"For dogs have compassed Me; the assembly of the wicked have enclosed Me; they pierced My hands and My feet. I may tell all My bones; they look and stare upon Me" (22:16-17).

"They gave Me also gall for My meat; and in My thirst they gave Me vinegar to drink" (69:21).

"They part My garments among them, and cast lots upon My vesture" (22:18). (See Matt. 27:34, 48; Luke 23:34; John 19:33-36.)

"For Thou wilt not leave My soul in hell; neither wilt Thou suffer Thine Holy One to see corruption" (Ps. 16:10).

His victories. "Thou hast ascended on high, Thou hast led captivity captive. Thou hast received gifts for men; yea, for the rebellious also, that the LORD God might dwell among them" (68:18).

"Lift up your heads, O ye gates; and be ye lifted up, ye everlasting doors; and the King of glory shall come in. Who is this King of glory? The LORD strong and mighty, the LORD mighty in battle" (24:7-8).

"The LORD said unto my Lord, 'Sit Thou at My right hand, until I make Thine enemies Thy footstool.' . . .

"He shall judge among the heathen, He shall fill the places with the dead bodies; He shall wound the heads over many countries" (110:1, 6).

"Also I will make Him My firstborn, higher than the kings of the earth" (89:27).

"When the LORD shall build up Zion, He shall appear in His glory" (102:16).

"His name shall endure forever: His name shall be continued as long as the sun: and men shall be blessed in Him. All nations shall call Him blessed" (72:17).

Types of Messianic Psalms

COMMENTS

It is quite obvious from the way the New Testament writers apply the psalms to Christ that the psalms contain many pictures of Christ. Thus they are referred to as messianic psalms because they in some way prefigure the Messiah, or Christ. The content of these passages is quite explicit as the material in this lesson shows. One way to study these psalms is to list the specific statements about Christ within them. Another way to study them is to divide them into different types of messianic psalms. All of the messianic psalms can be placed into one of five categories. These provide a helpful and organized manner of studying these psalms.

First, many psalms are *typically messianic.* This means that some subject in these psalms is in some way a type of Christ. Psalm 34:20, for example, reads: "He keepeth all His bones; not one of them is broken." In the context of the psalm this statement is made of any righteous person. It is a description of how God protects the righteous man—any righteous man. In John 19:36 however, the verse is quoted and applied to Christ. Christ as the righteous Man, the only God-Man, can easily be the recipient of passages in the Psalms which speak of the ideal righteous man.

Second, some psalms are both *typical and prophetic.* These are psalms in which the author, in describing his own outward and inward experiences, transcends his present condition and expresses statements that become historically true only in Christ. Therefore, not only is his life and situation typical, but his words are prophetic and have become true of Christ's life and situation. Psalm 22 is the best example of this type. The psalm describes the awful persecution which David was enduring from his enemies. In verse 1 David cries out: "My God, my God, why hast Thou forsaken me?" At that moment David did literally express this thought to God in prayer. He probably had no idea that his experience was to be used by God to be prophetic of the experience of one of his own descendants, the Lord Jesus Christ, who repeated the same cry on the cross (Matt. 27:46). Other elements in the psalms are similarly used of Christ's experiences by the New Testament writers: David's ridicule (Ps. 22:6-8; Matt. 27:43); David's pierced feet (Ps. 22:16; John 20:20-25, though this may not have literally happened to David); and David's garments divided (Ps. 22:18; Matt. 27:35, though David's enemies may have only intended to do this).

A third type of messianic psalm may be called *indirectly messianic.* These psalms refer to a literal king, either David or one in his line, but, ultimately, they find their fulfillment in Christ. Psalm 2 is an example of this type. In verse 7 the Lord says of the earthly king (probably David): "Thou art My son; this day have I begotten thee." This statement is in keeping with the Davidic Covenant in which the Lord promised David that every one of his descendants would be adopted as God's son (2 Sam. 7:14). Thus, every Davidic king was adopted as a son of the Lord and was a potential Messiah. We know, however, that the intention of this adoption is ultimately fulfilled only in Jesus Christ, who is God's beloved Son (Heb. 1:5). Psalms 45 and 72 may also be included in this category.

A fourth type of messianic psalm is *purely prophetic.* Only Psalm 110 may be placed in this category. In this psalm there is no reference to any earthly king or individual. The reference is solely to Christ and is thus purely prophetic. This seems to have been one of the points Jesus was trying to make with the Pharisees when he quoted this psalm: "How then doth David in spirit call Him [i.e., Christ] Lord, saying, 'The LORD said unto my Lord, "Sit Thou on My right hand, till I make Thine enemies Thy footstool" '?" The LORD (Jehovah) said to David's Lord, or Master, "Sit at My right hand." David's Lord must be the Messiah. Jesus was thus trying to prove that, while Christ is a Son of David, He is also the Son of God.

A final type of messianic psalm speaks of the *reign of the Lord.* These psalms speak of the Lord coming to reign on earth in His kingdom. These will only be fulfilled when Christ establishes His kingdom on earth during the Millennium. These psalms are distinguished by the expression "The LORD reigns" and include Psalms 47, 93, 96–97, 99.

One can readily see that, while the Psalms are filled with beautiful and priceless devotion to God, their prophetic content is also rich with significance. The New Testament writers recognized this aspect and so should we.

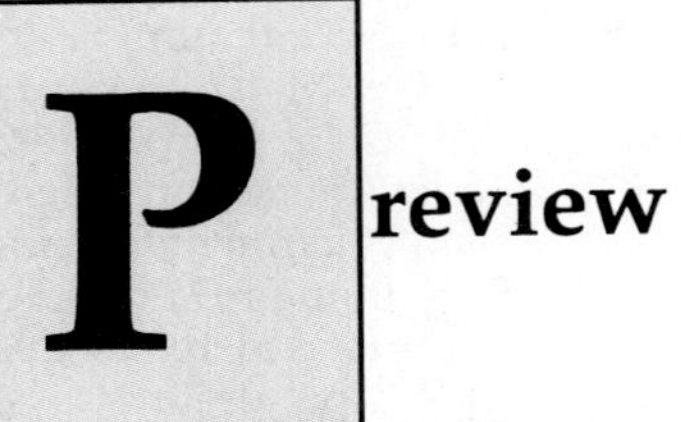

Preview

The Glory of God (Part One)

PSALMS 8; 33; 37; 48; 71; 87; 114; 121–122; 126–128; 137; 139; 147

Origin, abortion, traditional family unit, old age, and the nation Israel. Few issues in our day are more discussed and debated than are these. What about origin? Am I an accidental product of a muddy glob, or am I a deliberate creation of a mighty God? What about abortion? Does God actually see me as a person even while in my mother's womb? What about traditional family units? Should they be dissolved in favor of alternate life-styles, such as homosexuality, free love, and live-in arrangements? What about old age? Should it be legal to kill our infirmed, as society now permits doing to its unborn? Finally, what about the nation Israel? Has God cast off His people? What are His thoughts concerning Jerusalem? Clear and concise answers to these questions are given in this section of the Psalms.

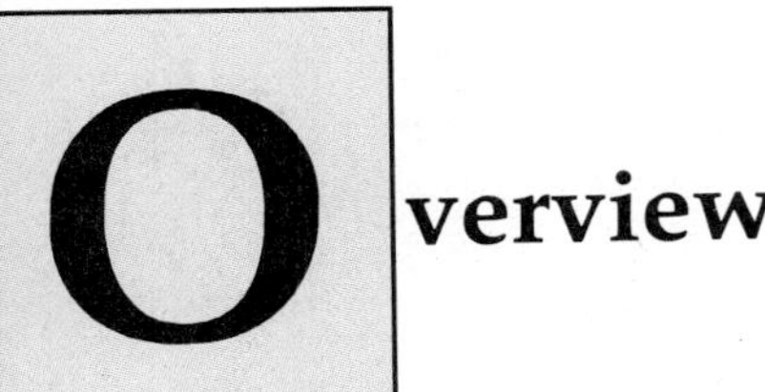

Overview

SCRIPTURE	Psalms 8; 33; 37; 48; 71; 87; 114; 121–122; 126–128; 137; 139; 147
SUBJECT	Suggested chapter titles—part 1

SPECIFICS

The characteristics of God		The commands of God		The city of God		The chosen of God	
Psalms 8; 33; 139; 147	His omnipresence	Psalm 37	Trust	Psalms 48; 87; 122	The splendor of Jerusalem	Psalms 71; 114; 121; 126–128; 137	Israel
	His omniscience		Delight		The sanctity of Jerusalem		Elderly believers
	His omnipotence		Commit		The security of Jerusalem		Family members
			Rest				Travelers

SAINTS AND SINNERS		
SENTENCE SUMMARIES	O.T. Verse	"Sing, O heavens; and be joyful, O earth; and break forth into singing, O mountains; for the LORD hath comforted His people, and will have mercy upon His afflicted" (Isa. 49:13).
	N.T. Verse	"Speaking to yourselves in psalms and hymns and spiritual songs, singing and making melody in your heart to the Lord" (Eph. 5:19).

B Y SUBJECT MATTER

The "omni" psalms. These psalms describe the omniscience, omnipresence, and omnipotence of God.

"O LORD, *Thou hast searched me, and known me. Thou knowest my downsitting and mine uprising; Thou understandest my thought afar off. Thou compassest my path and my lying down, and art acquainted with all my ways. For there is not a word in my tongue, but, lo, O* LORD, *Thou knowest it altogether.*

"Thou hast beset me behind and before, and laid Thine hand upon me. Such knowledge is too wonderful for me; it is high, I cannot attain unto it.

"Whither shall I go from Thy spirit? Or whither shall I flee from Thy presence? If I ascend up into heaven, Thou art there; if I make my bed in hell, behold, Thou art there.

"If I take the wings of the morning, and dwell in the uttermost parts of the sea; Even there shall Thy hand lead me, and Thy right hand shall hold me.

"If I say, 'Surely the darkness shall cover me; even the night shall be light about me.'

"Yea, the darkness hideth not from thee; but the night shineth as the day. The darkness and the light are both alike to Thee. For Thou hast possessed my reins. Thou hast covered me in my mother's womb. I will praise Thee; for I am fearfully and wonderfully made; marvelous are Thy works; and that my soul knoweth right well.

"My substance was not hid from Thee, when I was made in secret, and curiously wrought in the lowest parts of the earth. Thine eyes did see my substance, yet being unperfect; and in Thy book all my members were written, which in continuance were fashioned, when as yet there was none of them.

"How precious also are Thy thoughts unto me, O God! How great is the sum of them! . . .

"Search me, O God, and know my heart; try me, and know my thoughts; and see if there be any wicked way in me, and lead me in the way everlasting" (139:1-17, 23-24).

"He healeth the broken in heart, and bindeth up their wounds. He telleth the number of the

stars; He calleth them all by their names. Great is our Lord, and of great power; His understanding is infinite" (147:3-5).

Psalms of Creation. "When I consider Thy heavens, the work of Thy fingers, the moon and the stars, which Thou hast ordained; what is man, that Thou art mindful of him? And the son of man, that Thou visitest him? For Thou hast made him a little lower than the angels, and hast crowned him with glory and honor.

"Thou madest him to have dominion over the works of Thy hands; Thou hast put all things under his feet" (8:3-6).

"By the word of the LORD were the heavens made; and all the host of them by the breath of His mouth. He gathereth the waters of the sea together as a heap. He layeth up the depth in storehouses. Let all the earth fear the LORD. Let all the inhabitants of the world stand in awe of Him. For He spake, and it was done; He commanded, and it stood fast" (33:6-9).

The psalm of the Exodus. "When Israel went out of Egypt, the house of Jacob from a people of strange language; Judah was His sanctuary, and Israel His dominion. The sea saw it, and fled; Jordan was driven back. . . .

"Tremble, thou earth, at the presence of the Lord, at the presence of the God of Jacob; which turned the rock into a standing water, the flint into a fountain of waters" (114:1-3, 7-8).

The ladder of faith psalm. "Trust in the LORD, and do good; so shalt thou dwell in the land, and verily thou shalt be fed.

"Delight thyself also in the LORD; and He shall give thee the desires of thine heart. Commit thy way unto the LORD; trust also in Him; and He shall bring it to pass. . . .

"Rest in the LORD, and wait patiently for Him. Fret not thyself because of him who prospereth in his way, because of the man who bringeth wicked devices to pass. . . .

"The steps of a good man are ordered by the LORD; and He delighteth in his way. Though he fall, he shall not be utterly cast down; for the LORD upholdeth him with His hand.

"I have been young, and now am old; yet have I not seen the righteous forsaken, nor His seed begging bread" (37:3-5, 7, 23-25).

Psalms of Jerusalem. "Great is the LORD, and greatly to be praised in the city of our God, in the mountain of His holiness. Beautiful for situation, the joy of the whole earth, is Mount Zion, on the sides of the north, the city of the great King. God is known in her palaces for a refuge. . . .

"Walk about Zion, and go round about her; tell the towers thereof. Mark ye well her bulwarks, consider her palaces; that ye may tell it to the generation following" (48:1-3, 12-13).

"His foundation is in the holy mountains. The LORD loveth the gates of Zion more than all the dwellings of Jacob. Glorious things are spoken of Thee, O city of God" (87:1-3).

"Our feet shall stand within thy gates, O Jerusalem. Jerusalem is builded as a city that is compact together. . . .

"Pray for the peace of Jerusalem; they shall prosper that love thee. Peace be within thy walls, and prosperity within thy palaces" (122:2-3, 6-7).

Psalm of the Babylonian Captivity. "By the rivers of Babylon, there we sat down, yea, we wept, when we remembered Zion. We hanged our harps upon the willows in the midst thereof. For there they that carried us away captive required of us a song; and they that wasted us required of us mirth, saying, 'Sing us one of the songs of Zion.'

" 'How shall we sing the LORD's song in a strange land?'

"If I forget thee, O Jerusalem, let my right hand forget her cunning. If I do not remember thee, let my tongue cleave to the roof of my mouth; if I prefer not Jerusalem above my chief joy" (137:1-6).

Psalm of the return to Jerusalem. "When the LORD turned again the captivity of Zion, we were like them that dream. Then was our mouth filled with laughter, and our tongue with singing. Then said they among the heathen, 'The LORD hath done great things for them.'

"The LORD hath done great things for us; whereof we are glad. . . .

"They that sow in tears shall reap in joy. He that goeth forth and weepeth, bearing precious seed, shall doubtless come again with rejoicing, bringing his sheaves with him" (126:1-3, 5-6).

The spiritual senior saints' psalm. "For Thou art my hope, O Lord GOD. Thou art my trust from my youth. By Thee have I been holden up from the womb; Thou art He that took me out of my mother's bowels. My praise shall be continually of Thee. . . .

"Cast me not off in the time of old age; forsake me not when my strength faileth. . . .

"O God, Thou hast taught me from my youth; and hitherto have I declared Thy wondrous works. Now also when I am old and greyheaded, O God, forsake me not; until I have showed Thy strength unto this generation, and Thy power to everyone that is to come" (71:5-6, 9, 17-18).

Family psalms. "Lo, children are a heritage of the LORD; and the fruit of the womb is His reward. As arrows are in the hand of a mighty man; so are children of the youth. Happy is the man that hath his quiver full of them. They shall not be ashamed, but shall speak with the enemies in the gate" (127:3-5).

"Blessed is every one that feareth the LORD; that walketh in His ways. . . .

"Thy wife shall be as a fruitful vine by the sides of thine house. Thy children like olive plants round about thy table. . . .

"Yea, thou shalt see thy children's children, and peace upon Israel" (128:1, 3, 6).

The traveler's psalm. "I will lift up mine eyes

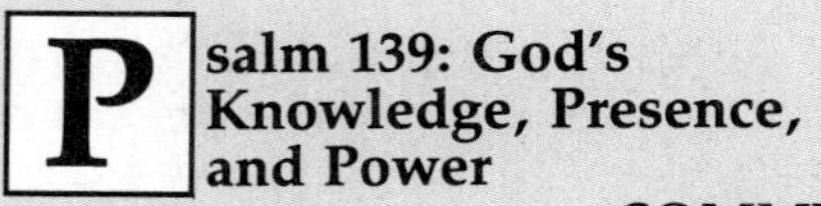

Psalm 139: God's Knowledge, Presence, and Power

COMMENTS

Whenever we study a psalm, we need to determine, if possible, the historical situation in which the psalm was written. Unfortunately, only a few psalms contain a historical superscription which states the occasion of the psalm. Psalm 139 does not have such a superscription. The next place we can look, however, is in the psalm itself to see if there is some hint at its background. In Psalm 139 there is such a statement. In verses 19-22 the reader finds out that David was experiencing opposition as he wrote this psalm. Wicked men were opposing God's program and were opposing David. The truths expounded in the rest of the psalm were those which encouraged David in the midst of his persecution. The psalm is then extremely important to Christians today who may be suffering for God's cause.

Psalm 139 naturally falls into four parts of six verses each. The first six verses might be titled appropriately "Lord, You know me." In these verses David expressed very beautifully the omniscience of God or the fact that God knows all things, both actual and possible. In verse 1 David writes, "Thou hast searched me." This means that God had dug through to David's basic being as one might dig deep into a mine for precious ore. The extent of God's knowledge is further explained in verse 2: it covers "my downsitting and mine uprising." This means that God knew David all the time. In verse 3 he adds that, "Thou . . . art acquainted with all my ways." The "ways" were David's characteristics, including his idiosyncrasies. God knew them all. There was nothing about David that God did not know. He even knew the words that David would speak before he said them (v. 4) and is said to have completely surrounded David. Such knowledge on God's part staggers the human mind and is incomprehensible to it.

The next section might well be summarized, "Lord, You are with me" (vv. 7-12). Here David expresses the truth of God's omnipresence, the fact that God is everywhere at the same time with His full being. This attribute means that God is everywhere on the vertical plane—from heaven above to hell below (v. 8), and is everywhere on the horizontal plane—from the present location to the distant island (vv. 9-10). David then anticipated what a reader might ask: "What about when it becomes dark—will God be with me then?" The answer is of course affirmative: God sees as well in the dark as in the day. To God, the night is as bright as the day (vv. 11-12).

One might well ask: How did David know that God was omniscient and omnipresent? The next section (vv. 13-18) gives the answer. Verse 13 begins with the word "for" which indicates that David will explain the source of his information. Briefly put, it may be summarized in this statement: "Lord, You created me." David knew from the fact that God created him, that God must know him and be with him. God's creative act is described here as beautifully as anywhere in Scripture. "Thou hast covered me in my mother's womb" might better be translated "You knit me together in my mother's womb." It means that God was like a fine craftsman who knit together David with all his sinews, bones, and parts. David's embryo was known to God while he was being formed in the womb (vv. 15-16). The words "curiously wrought" are particularly vivid because the expression means to weave with colors. This means that God wove David together with all his colors: his blue eyes, black hair, olive skin, etc. Furthermore, God did all of this work in the darkness of the womb where no light could enter! Verse 16 seems to refer to David's body but would be better taken to refer to his days. God knew all of David's days before any one of them ever came to pass. Certainly God's thoughts about David were innumerable as the sand (vv. 17-18).

Finally, David returned in the fourth section (vv. 19-24) to the present reality: he was being persecuted by his enemies. This section could well be summarized as "Lord, Your cause is my cause." It is here that David expresses his identification with God's cause. At first glance, Christians today recoil at the expression of hatred in verses 21-22. However, we must remember that David lived in the old dispensation of warfare when God's people were trying to establish God's political kingdom on the earth. Anyone who opposed that kingdom opposed God. In light of David's knowledge of God's knowledge of him, he closed the psalm with six imperatives (vv. 23-24) which expressed his desire for openness before God. It was essentially a petition that God would search through him; remove any wicked thought; and lead him into the way that counted for eternity. After all, nothing can be hidden from God.

unto the hills, from whence cometh my help. My help cometh from the Lord, *which made heaven and earth. He will not suffer thy foot to be moved; He that keepeth thee will not slumber. Behold, He that keepeth Israel shall neither slumber nor sleep.*

"The Lord *is thy keeper; the* Lord *is thy shade upon thy right hand. The sun shall not smite thee by day, nor the moon by night.*

"The Lord *shall preserve thee from all evil; He shall preserve thy soul.*

"The Lord *shall preserve thy going out and thy coming in from this time forth, and even forevermore" (121:1-8).*

The Glory of God (Part Two)

PSALMS 18–19; 27; 29; 42; 50; 63; 89; 104; 107; 115; 119; 135–136

"Who is the LORD, that I should obey His voice to let Israel go?"

"Who is that God that shall deliver you out of my hands?"

Two arrogant questions, asked by two arrogant monarchs, both of whom were soon humbled by the very God they sought to ridicule. The first question was directed to Moses by the Egyptian Pharaoh, and the second from Nebuchadnezzar to three Hebrew young men.

Who is the Lord? Whoever He is, He certainly takes care of His own, as these two rulers would learn, for God's people could not be drowned or burned! Who is the Lord? It would almost seem that the authors of the following psalms wrote their words with these two questions in mind. In glowing terms they speak of His house, wealth, word, care, mercy, voice, goodness, and uniqueness! Who is the Lord? He is the Creator, Redeemer, Sustainer, Ruler, and Judge of all things.

Overview

SCRIPTURE	Psalms 18–19; 27; 29; 42; 50; 63; 84; 104; 107; 115; 119; 135–136
SUBJECT	Suggested chapter titles—part 2

<table>
<tr><td rowspan="7">SPECIFICS</td><td colspan="2">The greatness of God</td><td colspan="2">The gentleness of God</td></tr>
<tr><td>Psalm</td><td>Attribute</td><td>Psalm</td><td>Attribute</td></tr>
<tr><td>50</td><td>His wealth</td><td rowspan="2">136</td><td rowspan="2">His mercy</td></tr>
<tr><td rowspan="2">19; 29; 119</td><td rowspan="2">His Word</td></tr>
<tr><td rowspan="2">107</td><td rowspan="2">His goodness</td></tr>
<tr><td>18</td><td>His witness</td></tr>
<tr><td>84
27; 42; 63; 115; 135</td><td>His workmanship
His worthiness</td><td>104</td><td>His care
for vegetation
for animals
for humans</td></tr>
<tr><td>SAINTS AND SINNERS</td><td colspan="4"></td></tr>
<tr><td rowspan="2">SENTENCE SUMMARIES</td><td>O.T. Verse</td><td colspan="3">"Sing unto the LORD a new song, and His praise from the end of the earth, ye that go down to the sea, and all that is therein; the isles, and the inhabitants thereof" (Isa. 42:10).</td></tr>
<tr><td>N.T. Verse</td><td colspan="3">"At midnight Paul and Silas prayed, and sang praises unto God; and the prisoners heard them" (Acts 16:25).</td></tr>
</table>

GOD'S GOODNESS

The house of God psalm. "How amiable are Thy tabernacles, O LORD of hosts! My soul longeth, yea, even fainteth for the courts of the LORD. My heart and my flesh crieth out for the living God.

"Yea, the sparrow hath found a house, and the swallow a nest for herself, where she may lay her young, even Thine altars, O LORD of hosts, my King, and my God.

"Blessed are they that dwell in Thy house; they will be still praising thee. Selah. . . . For a day in Thy courts is better than a thousand. I had rather be a doorkeeper in the house of my God, than to dwell in the tents of wickedness" (84:1-4, 10).

The wealth of God psalm. "For every beast of the forest is Mine, and the cattle upon a thousand hills. I know all the fowls of the mountains; and the wild beasts of the field are Mine. If I were hungry, I would not tell thee; for the world is Mine, and the fullness thereof" (50:10-12).

The Word of God psalms. "The Law of the LORD is perfect, converting the soul; the testimony of the LORD is sure, making wise the simple. The statutes of the LORD are right, rejoicing the heart; the commandment of the LORD is pure, enlightening the eyes. The fear of the LORD is clean, enduring forever; the judgments of the LORD are true and righteous altogether.

"More to be desired are they than gold, yea, than much fine gold; sweeter also than honey and the honeycomb. Moreover by them is Thy servant warned; and in keeping of them there is great reward" (19:7-11).

"Wherewithal shall a young man cleanse his way? By taking heed thereto according to Thy Word. . . .

"Forever, O LORD, Thy Word is settled in heaven. . . .

"Thy Word is a lamp unto my feet, and a light unto my path. . . .

"The entrance of Thy words giveth light; it giveth understanding unto the simple. . . .

"Thy Word is very pure: therefore Thy servant loveth it. . . . Great peace have they which love

Thy Law; and nothing shall offend them" (119:9, 89, 105, 130, 140, 165).

The providential care of God psalm. "He sendeth the springs into the valleys, which run among the hills. They give drink to every beast of the field; the wild asses quench their thirst. By them shall the fowls of the heaven have their habitation, which sing among the branches. . . .

"He causeth the grass to grow for the cattle, and herb for the service of man, that he may bring forth food out of the earth; and wine that maketh glad the heart of man, and oil to make his face to shine, and bread which strengtheneth man's heart.

"The trees of the LORD are full of sap; the cedars of Lebanon, which He hath planted. Where the birds make their nests; as for the stork, the fir trees are her house. The high hills are a refuge for the wild goats; and the rocks for the conies. He appointed the moon for seasons; the sun knoweth his going down.

"Thou makest darkness, and it is night; wherein all the beasts of the forest do creep forth. The young lions roar after their prey, and seek their meat from God. The sun ariseth, they gather themselves together, and lay them down in their dens.

"Man goeth forth unto his work and to his labor until the evening.

"O LORD, how manifold are Thy works! In wisdom hast Thou made them all. The earth is full of Thy riches" (104:10-12, 14-24).

The pursuit of God psalms. "One thing have I desired of the LORD, that will I seek after; that I may dwell in the house of the LORD all the days of my life, to behold the beauty of the LORD, and to inquire in His temple. . . .

"When Thou saidst, 'Seek ye My face'; my heart said unto Thee, 'Thy face, LORD, will I seek.' . . .

"When my father and my mother forsake me, then the LORD will take me up" (27:4, 8, 10).

"As the hart panteth after the water brooks, so panteth my soul after Thee, O God. My soul thirsteth for God, for the living God; when shall I come and appear before God? . . .

"Why art thou cast down, O my soul? And why art thou disquieted within me? Hope thou in God; for I shall yet praise Him, who is the health of my countenance, and my God" (42:1-2, 11).

"O God, Thou art my God; early will I seek Thee. My soul thirsteth for Thee, my flesh longeth for Thee in a dry and thirsty land, where no water is. . . .

"My soul followeth hard after Thee; Thy right hand upholdeth me" (63:1, 8).

The mercy of God psalm. "O give thanks unto the LORD; for He is good; for His mercy endureth forever" (136:1).

The voice of God psalm. "The voice of the LORD is upon the waters; the God of glory thundereth; the LORD is upon many waters. The voice of the LORD is powerful; the voice of the LORD is full of majesty.

"The voice of the LORD breaketh the cedars of Lebanon. . . . He maketh them also to skip like a calf; Lebanon and Sirion like a young unicorn.

"The voice of the LORD divideth the flames of fire. The voice of the LORD shaketh the wilderness; the LORD shaketh the wilderness of Kadesh. The voice of the LORD maketh the hinds to calve, and discovereth the forests; and in His temple doth everyone speak of His glory" (29:3-9).

The goodness of God psalms. "O give thanks unto the LORD, for He is good: for His mercy endureth forever. Let the redeemed of the LORD say so, whom He hath redeemed from the hand of the enemy. . . .

"Oh, that men would praise the LORD for His goodness, and for His wonderful works to the children of men! For He satisfieth the longing soul, and filleth the hungry soul with goodness" (107:1-2, 8-9).

The manifestation of God psalm. "In my distress I called upon the LORD, and cried unto my God. He heard my voice out of His temple, and my cry came before Him, even into His ears.

"Then the earth shook and trembled; the foundations also of the hills moved and were shaken, because He was wroth. There went up a smoke out of His nostrils, and fire out of His mouth devoured. Coals were kindled by it.

"He bowed the heavens also, and came down; and darkness was under His feet. And He rode upon a cherub, and did fly; yea, He did fly upon the wings of the wind. He made darkness His secret place; His pavilion round about Him were dark waters and thick clouds of the skies. At the brightness that was before Him His thick clouds passed, hailstones and coals of fire.

"The LORD also thundered in the heavens, and the Highest gave His voice; hailstones and coals of fire. Yea, He sent out His arrows, and scattered them; and He shot out lightnings, and discomfited them. Then the channels of waters were seen, and the foundations of the world were discovered at Thy rebuke, O LORD, at the blast of the breath of Thy nostrils" (18:6-15).

Psalms of the only true God. "But our God is in the heavens; He hath done whatsoever He hath pleased.

"Their idols are silver and gold, the work of men's hands. They have mouths, but they speak not; eyes have they, but they see not. They have ears, but they hear not; noses have they, but they smell not. They have hands, but they handle not; feet have they, but they walk not. Neither speak they through their throat" (115:3-7).

"For I know that the LORD is great, and that our Lord is above all gods. . . . The idols of the heathen are silver and gold, the work of men's hands. . . . They that make them are like unto them; so is everyone that trusteth in them" (135:5, 15, 18).

Psalm 19: The Revelation of God Exalted

COMMENTS

The word "revelation," when used theologically, refers to God's disclosure of Himself to man. It means that God has revealed something about Himself that man would not know otherwise. Psalm 19 is a perfect psalm to use in explaining God's revelation because it includes both types of revelation: natural and special. Natural revelation means simply that God has revealed Himself in nature; special revelation refers to the revelation of God in special ways, such as the Scriptures, miracles, Christ, prophecy, etc. Because of its clear inclusion of both of these themes, Psalm 19 is certainly the plainest exposition of these truths in the Old Testament.

The psalm may be outlined under three headings. The first section might be entitled the *revelation of God in Creation* (vv. 1-6). It is God's answer to the hypothesis of evolution. The evolutionists say that the ultimate factors which make evolution feasible are time and chance. They state that if evolution were only given enough time, all known life forms would be produced by random process from nonliving material.

Psalm 19, however, clearly indicates that the very existence of the heaven and earth point to the objective fact of God's existence. They are a permanent testimony to the fact that a creative, intelligent Being made the entire universe. Verse 1 is a summary statement for the section. It affirms two truths that are evident from the existence of the heavens: God is glorious and God is Creator. This revelation is then further described in four ways in verses 2-6. First, it is a continual declaration (v. 2). Day and night the heavenly bodies proclaim the existence of God. It is as though they are God's "preachers in the sky," and they preach 24 hours a day. Second, it is a communication without words (v. 3). In other words, they do not speak a certain language, but men of all languages can understand their message. Third, it is a universal declaration (v. 4). Just as one would survey and mark off a tract of land, the heavens have lined off the whole earth as the place where they will declare their message. Fourth, it is a declaration that is illustrated by the sun (vv. 5-6). The sun is the best example of a heavenly body. It is here compared to a bridegroom. This speaks of the sun's vigor and power. Furthermore, the sun is like a runner. The morning is the starting gate, and the evening is the finishing line, and the sun never tires of running this race. Surely there can be no question for the thinking person that the existence of the universe points to the existence of the Creator.

As important as Creation is, it cannot bring a man to Christ. Therefore, special revelation is needed. The second section of the psalm now takes up this aspect: the *revelation of God in the Scriptures* (vv. 7-11). Verses 7-9 contain six parallel statements which exalt the Word of God. In each statement there is a synonym for the Word, an adjective describing the Word, and a participle telling what the Word can do. Thus, the Word is called the Law, the testimony, the statutes, the commandment, the fear of the LORD, and the judgments. The Word is described as perfect, sure, right, pure, clean, and true. Its work and character include converting the soul, making wise the simple, rejoicing the heart, enlightening the eyes, enduring forever, and being true and righteous. To add the capstone to this description, David adds that the Word is more desirable than wealth (v. 10a), more satisfying than sensual pleasures (v. 10b), and contains both warning and reward (v. 11).

Finally, as is always the case, man must respond to God's revelation. Thus verses 12-14 form an appropriate conclusion to the psalm and may be labeled *response of the man of faith*. In light of what God has created and what God has revealed in His Word, David prays for three things: first, for deliverance from errors and hidden sins (v. 12); second, for preservation from presumptuous or willful sins (v. 13); and third, for acceptable words and thoughts (v. 14). David's prayer thus encompasses the entire range of one's standing before God. Negatively, he wants to be delivered from sin, whether unintentional or intentional; positively, he wants everything he says and thinks to be pleasing to God. No wonder that David is called "a man after God's own heart." David can only pray such prayers however because he has made the Lord his "Strength and Redeemer" (v. 14). These last three verses then form the only appropriate response to God's revelation.

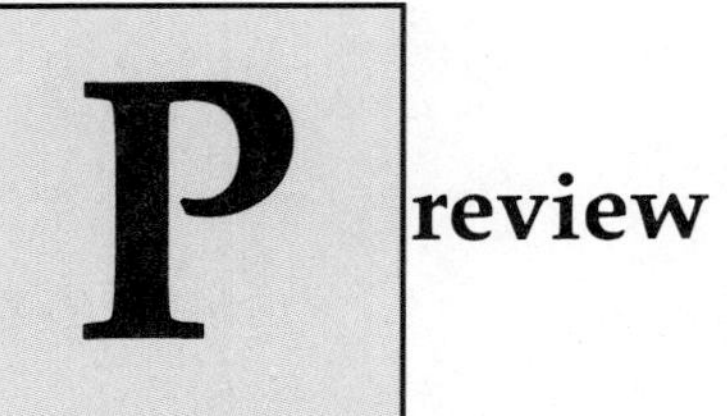

Saints and Sinners in the Psalms

PSALMS 4–5; 9–10; 13–14; 31; 49; 58; 73; 88; 116; 121

Approach number one: Why worry when you can pray? Approach number two: Why pray when you can worry? In times of trial and trouble, a believer can apply either of these approaches to his problem. Unfortunately, and unnecessarily, the second method is all too often selected over the first. The following psalms strongly suggest the first approach. In short, Christians are commanded to pray. These psalms suggest the when (morning and evening), the why (for assurance and answers), and the how (by praise and persistence) concerning our prayer life. In fact, the actions of the wicked are simply the results of their attitudes—they don't pray. "God is not in all his thoughts" (Ps. 10:4).

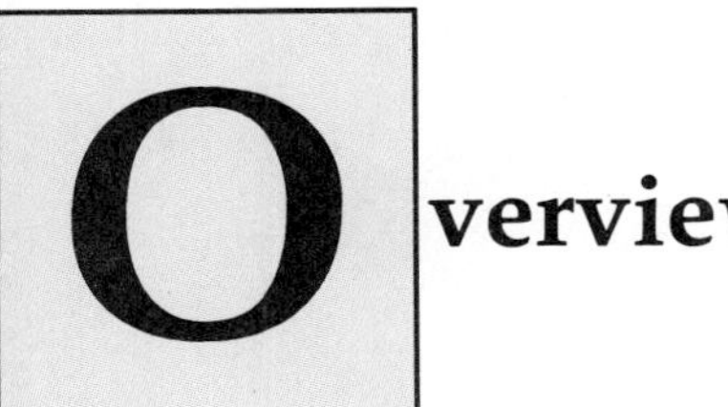

Overview

SCRIPTURE	Psalms 4–5; 9–10; 13–14; 31; 49; 58; 73; 88; 116; 121			
SUBJECT	Suggested chapter titles—part 3			
SPECIFICS	Psalms describing the godly		Psalms describing the godless	
	4–5; 31; 116; 121	God will hear them	9–10; 14; 58	Their works condemn them wicked conscience wicked conversation
	13; 73; 88	God will help them answering their questions alleviating their fears	49	Their wealth condemns them it cannot satisfy them it cannot save them
SAINTS AND SINNERS				
SENTENCE SUMMARIES	O.T. Verse	"Sing unto the LORD; for He hath done excellent things; this is known in all the earth" (Isa. 12:5).		
	N.T. Verse	"They sang a new song, saying, 'Thou art worthy to take the book, and to open the seals thereof; for Thou wast slain, and hast redeemed us to God by Thy blood out of every kindred and tongue and people and nation" (Rev. 5:9).		

HE GODLY AND THE GODLESS

The evening psalm. "Stand in awe, and sin not. Commune with your own heart upon your bed, and be still. Offer the sacrifices of righteousness, and put your trust in the LORD. . . . I will both lay me down in peace, and sleep: for Thou, LORD, only makest me dwell in safety" (4:4-5, 8).

The morning psalm. "Give ear to my words, O LORD, consider my meditation. Hearken unto the voice of my cry, my King and my God; for unto Thee will I pray. My voice shalt Thou hear in the morning, O LORD; in the morning will I direct my prayer unto Thee, and will look up" (5:1-3).

The security psalm. "I will lift up mine eyes unto the hills, from whence cometh my help. My help cometh from the LORD, which made heaven and earth. He will not suffer thy foot to be removed. . . . He shall preserve thy soul. The LORD shall preserve thy going out and thy coming in from this time forth" (121:1-3, 7-8).

Psalms of deliverance. "Into Thine hand I commit my spirit. Thou hast redeemed me, O LORD God of truth. . . .

"My times are in Thy hand. Deliver me from the hand of mine enemies, and from them that persecute me. . . .

"Oh, how great is Thy goodness, which Thou hast laid up for them that fear Thee; which Thou hast wrought for them that trust in Thee before the sons of men! Thou shalt hide them in the secret of Thy presence from the pride of man; Thou shalt keep them secretly in a pavilion from the strife of tongues" (31:5, 15, 19-20).

"The sorrows of death compassed me, and the pains of hell got hold upon me; I found trouble and sorrow. Then called I upon the name of the LORD; 'O LORD, I beseech Thee, deliver my soul.' Gracious is the LORD, and righteous; yea, our God is merciful. The LORD preserveth the simple. I was brought low, and He helped me. Return unto thy rest, O my soul; for the LORD hath dealt bountifully with thee" (116:3-8).

The "if-only" psalm. "I am the LORD thy God, which brought thee out of the land of Egypt; open thy mouth wide, and I will fill it. But My people would not hearken to My voice; and Israel would none of Me. So I gave them up unto their own hearts' lust; and they walked in their own counsels. Oh, that My people had hearkened unto Me, and Israel had walked in My ways! I should soon have subdued their enemies, and turned My hand against their adversaries" (81:10-14).

The "how-long" psalm. "How long wilt Thou forget me, O LORD? Forever? How long wilt Thou hide Thy face from me? How long shall I take counsel in my soul, having sorrow in my heart daily? How long shall mine enemy be exalted over me?

"Consider and hear me, O LORD my God; lighten mine eyes, lest I sleep the sleep of death; lest mine enemy say, 'I have prevailed against him'; and those that trouble me rejoice when I am moved.

"But I have trusted in Thy mercy; my heart shall rejoice in Thy salvation. I will sing unto the LORD, because He hath dealt bountifully with me" (13:1-6).

The judgment of nations psalm. "Thou hast rebuked the heathen, Thou hast destroyed the wicked, Thou hast put out their name forever and ever. . . .

"The heathen are sunk down in the pit that they made; in the net which they hid is their own foot taken. . . .

"The wicked shall be turned into hell, and all the nations that forget God. . . .

"Arise, O LORD; let not man prevail; let the heathen be judged in Thy sight. Put them in fear, O LORD; that the nations may know themselves to be but men" (9:5, 15, 17, 19-20).

Psalms of the wicked. "The wicked in his pride doth persecute the poor; let them be taken in the devices that they have imagined. For the wicked boasteth of his heart's desire, and blesseth the covetous, whom the LORD abhorreth. The wicked, through the pride of his countenance, will not seek after God; God is not in all his thoughts.

"His ways are always grievous; Thy judgments are far above out of his sight. As for all his enemies, he puffeth at them. He hath said in his heart, 'I shall not be moved: for I shall never be in adversity.'

"His mouth is full of cursing and deceit and fraud; under his tongue is mischief and vanity. He sitteth in the lurking places of the villages; in the secret places doth he murder the innocent: his eyes are privily set against the poor. He lieth in wait secretly as a lion in his den; he lieth in wait to catch the poor. He doth catch the poor, when he draweth him into his net. . . .

"He hath said in his heart, 'God hath forgotten; He hideth His face; He will never see it' " (10:2-9, 11).

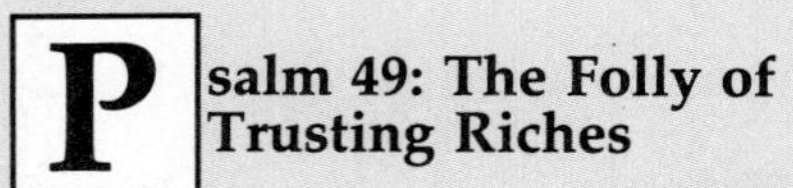

Psalm 49: The Folly of Trusting Riches

COMMENTS

Because of the wealth in society today, Christians stand in grave danger of allowing wealth and the pursuit of it to become the preoccupation of their time and energy. The problem is not new, however. The author of Psalm 49 lived in a society which was inordinately concerned with money. This psalm might well be characterized as the Old Testament counterpart to 1 Timothy 6:17: "Charge them that are rich in this world, that they be not high-minded, nor trust in uncertain riches, but in the Living God, who giveth us richly all things to enjoy." The psalm therefore has tremendous application to Christians today.

The psalm may be divided into three parts. First, there is an *invitation to listen* (Ps. 49:1-4). The psalmist calls on "all people" and "all inhabitants." His message concerns all humanity and has universal application, not just to Israel. Verse 2 is even more specific: "low and high, rich and poor." This means that both common men and men of means are addressed. The middle class is not omitted either, since the psalmist's real point is that all men should take heed to his message. In verses 3-4 he uses four key words to describe his message: "wisdom," or skill in living; "understanding," or insight into life; "parable," or, better, "proverb," which is a miniature illustration about life; and, finally, "dark saying," or a perplexing problem that requires much thought to understand.

The second part begins the actual message of the psalm to its readers and may be entitled the *insufficiency of wealth* (vv. 5-12). The section begins with a question which, in essence, asks: Why should I fear because wealthy men boast? (vv. 5-6) The psalmist then answers his own question in verse 7 by plainly stating the inadequacy of wealth; riches cannot answer man's basic need, which is redemption. No man, regardless of the mass of his wealth, can redeem his brother by a monetary payment (v. 7). The redemption of a soul is too costly for any amount to buy it (v. 8). The proof of this thesis is obvious: both wise and stupid alike die. No man is smart enough or brilliant enough to avoid death. Therefore, both wise and stupid alike leave their wealth to others. No matter how much education one has, no matter how sophisticated one may be, he must die alongside the common man (v. 10). In spite of this obvious common destiny of all men, rich men still try to obtain immortality: "Their inward thought is, that their houses shall continue forever" (v. 11). This statement means that the rich even have pretensions that their wealth will persist and abide. Furthermore, "They call their lands after their own names," i.e., they try to obtain a measure of immortality by having lands named after them. Nevertheless, the psalmist brings man back to the cold, hard facts: in the final analysis, he is like a beast because he perishes in death like a beast (v. 12).

The final section of the psalm drives home the difference between the wealthy wicked and the righteous psalmist. It may be entitled a *difference in destinations* (vv. 13-20). The psalmist evaluates the foolishness of trusting in riches with some of the most vivid metaphors in the Old Testament. After stating forthrightly the folly of trusting riches (v. 13), he describes, with gruesome imagery, death as a shepherd ruling over the wicked dead (v. 14). The fate of the righteous, on the other hand, is a glorious resurrection from the dead (v. 15). What the wealth of man could not do (v. 7), the power of God accomplishes. Then in verse 16 the psalmist records only the second command in the psalm (the other is in verse 1). In essence he says here, "Do not be afraid of the wealthy because, when he dies, he will take none of it with him" (vv. 16-17). Though men may praise the wealthy in this life (v. 18), they all must die, and then this praise is meaningless (v. 19). Finally, the same refrain that closed the second section is repeated, just in case the reader missed it: men are like the beasts that perish (v. 20). This is the final thought which the psalmist wants to leave with the reader: in spite of all the wealth a man may accumulate, he still must die like a beast. How great the need for redemption appears in the light of this sobering message. Only God can redeem. Riches, when viewed in the light of eternity, can, in no wise, possess the significance that is attached to them in our society.

"The fool hath said in his heart, 'There is no God.' They are corrupt, they have done abominable works, there is none that doeth good. The LORD *looked down from heaven upon the children of men, to see if there were any that did understand, and seek God. They are all gone aside, they are all together become filthy. There is none that doeth good, no, not one"* (14:1-3).

"The wicked are estranged from the womb; they go astray as soon as they be born, speaking lies. Their poison is like the poison of a serpent; they are like the deaf adder that stoppeth her ear" (58:3-4).

The folly of riches psalm. "They that trust in their wealth, and boast themselves in the multitude of their riches; none of them can by any means redeem his brother, nor give to God a ransom for him (For the redemption of their soul is precious, and it ceaseth forever), that he should still live forever, and not see corruption.

"For he seeth that wise men die, likewise the fool and the brutish person perish, and leave their wealth to others. . . .

"For when he dieth he shall carry nothing away; his glory shall not descend after him" (49:6-10, 17).

The psalm of the question why. "For I was envious at the foolish, when I saw the prosperity of the wicked. . . . They are not in trouble as other men; neither are they plagued like other men. . . . Their eyes stand out with fatness: they have more than heart could wish. . . .

"And they say, 'How doth God know?' And, 'Is there knowledge in the Most High?'

"Behold, these are the ungodly, who prosper in the world; they increase in riches. Verily I have cleansed my heart in vain, and washed my hands in innocency. For all the day long have I been plagued, and chastened every morning. . . .

"When I thought to know this, it was too painful for me; until I went into the sanctuary of God; then understood I their end. Surely Thou didst set them in slippery places; Thou castedst them down into destruction. How are they brought into desolation, as in a moment! They are utterly consumed with terrors" (73:3, 5, 7, 11-14, 16-19).

The psalm of deepest distress. "O LORD *God of my salvation, I have cried day and night before Thee. . . . For my soul is full of troubles; and my life draweth nigh unto the grave. . . .*

"Mine eye mourneth by reason of affliction. LORD, *I have called daily upon Thee, I have stretched out my hands unto Thee. . . .* LORD, *why castest Thou off my soul? Why hidest Thou Thy face from me?"* (88:1, 3, 9, 14)

The Redeemer and His Redeemed

PSALMS 1–2; 22–24; 90–91; 100; 103; 110; 133

"For they drank of that spiritual rock that followed them; and that Rock was Christ" (1 Cor. 10:4). Thus wrote Paul, describing Christ's relationship to Israel in the Old Testament. And what a relationship that was, as spoken of by these psalms. In essence, He was the bountiful Shepherd of His flock, giving them abundant and eternal life, and the beloved Son of His Father. That glorious relationship thus assured obedient believers of both fruitfulness and fellowship.

Overview

SCRIPTURE	Psalms 1–2; 22–24; 90–91; 100; 103; 110; 133
SUBJECT	Suggested chapter titles—part 4
SPECIFICS	**Fellowship** — Psalm 133: Defined; Described **Stewardship** — Psalms 1; 90: Be faithful; Be fruitful **Guardianship** — Psalm 91: Protection; Provision **Relationship** — Psalms 2; 22–24; 110: Relationship of Christ to the faithful: The Good Shepherd; The Great Shepherd; The Chief Shepherd. Relationship of Christ to the Father: He is a Priest; He is a King **Lordship** — Psalms 100; 103: He is Lord of Creation; He is Lord of redemption
SAINTS AND SINNERS	
SENTENCE SUMMARIES	O.T. Verse: "Sing, O ye heavens; for the LORD hath done it; shout, ye lower parts of the earth; break forth into singing, ye mountains, O forest, and every tree therein; for the LORD hath redeemed Jacob, and glorified Himself in Israel" (Isa. 44:23) N.T. Verse: "Let the word of Christ dwell in you richly in all wisdom; teaching and admonishing one another in psalms and hymns and spiritual songs, singing with grace in your hearts to the Lord" (Col. 3:16).

RELATIONSHIP TO GOD

Psalm of the Good Shepherd. This corresponds to John 10:11 and describes the sacrifice of Christ.

"My God, My God, why hast Thou forsaken Me? Why art Thou so far from helping Me, and from the words of My roaring? . . . All they that see Me laugh Me to scorn; they shoot out the lip, they shake the head, saying, 'He trusted on the LORD, *that He would deliver Him; let Him deliver Him, seeing He delighted in Him.' . . .*

"For dogs have compassed Me; the assembly of the wicked have enclosed Me; they pierced My hands and My feet. I may tell all My bones; they look and stare upon Me. They part My garments among them, and cast lots upon My vesture" (22:1, 7-8, 16-18).

Psalm of the Great Shepherd. This corresponds to Hebrews 13:20-21 and describes the sufficiency of Christ.

"The LORD *is my Shepherd; I shall not want. He maketh me to lie down in green pastures; He leadeth me beside the still waters. He restoreth my soul. He leadeth me in the paths of righteousness for His name's sake.*

"Yea, though I walk through the valley of the shadow of death, I will fear no evil; for Thou art with me; Thy rod and Thy staff they comfort me. Thou preparest a table before me in the presence of mine enemies. Thou anointest my head with oil; my cup runneth over. Surely goodness and mercy shall follow me all the days of my life; and I will dwell in the house of the LORD *forever" (23:1-6).*

Psalm of the Chief Shepherd. This corresponds to 1 Peter 5:4 and describes the sovereignty of Christ.

"Lift up your heads, O ye gates; and be ye lifted up, ye everlasting doors; and the King of glory shall come in. Who is this King of glory? The LORD *strong and mighty, the* LORD *mighty in battle.*

"Lift up your heads, O ye gates; even lift them up, ye everlasting doors; and the King of glory shall come in. Who is this King of glory? The LORD *of hosts, He is the King of glory" (24:7-10).*

Psalms of supreme praise. "Make a joyful

noise unto the LORD, *all ye lands. Serve the* LORD *with gladness; come before His presence with singing. Know ye that the* LORD *He is God. It is He that hath made us, and not we ourselves. We are His people, and the sheep of His pasture.*

"Enter into His gates with thanksgiving, and into His courts with praise. Be thankful unto Him, and bless His name. For the LORD *is good; His mercy is everlasting; and His truth endureth to all generations" (100:1-5).*

"Bless the LORD, *O my soul; and all that is within me, bless His holy name. Bless the* LORD, *O my soul, and forget not all His benefits. Who forgiveth all thine iniquities; who healeth all thy diseases. Who redeemeth thy life from destruction; who crowneth thee with loving-kindness and tender mercies. Who satisfieth thy mouth with good things; so that thy youth is renewed like the eagle's.*

"The LORD *executeth righteousness and judgment for all that are oppressed. He made known His ways unto Moses, His acts unto the Children of Israel. The* LORD *is merciful and gracious, slow to anger, and plenteous in mercy. He will not always chide; neither will He keep His anger forever. He hath not dealt with us after our sins; nor rewarded us according to our iniquities.*

"For as the heaven is high above the earth, so great is His mercy toward them that fear Him. As far as the east is from the west, so far hath He removed our transgressions from us.

"Like as a father pitieth his children, so the LORD *pitieth them that fear Him. For He knoweth our frame; He remembereth that we are dust. As for man, his days are as grass; as a flower of the field, so he flourisheth. For the wind passeth over it, and it is gone; and the place thereof shall know it no more.*

"But the mercy of the LORD *is from everlasting to everlasting upon them that fear Him, and His righteousness unto children's children. To such as keep His covenant, and to those that remember His commandments to do them.*

"The LORD *hath prepared His throne in the heavens; and His kingdom ruleth over all.*

"Bless the LORD, *ye His angels, that excel in strength, that do His commandments, hearkening unto the voice of His word.*

"Bless ye the LORD, *all ye His hosts; ye ministers of His, that do His pleasure.*

"Bless the LORD, *all His works in all places of His dominion. Bless the* LORD, *O my soul" (103:1-22).*

Psalm of the godly man. "Blessed is the man that walketh not in the counsel of the ungodly, nor standeth in the way of sinners, nor sitteth in the seat of the scornful. But his delight is in the Law of the LORD; *and in His Law doth he meditate day and night.*

"And he shall be like a tree planted by the rivers of water, that bringeth forth his fruit in his season; his leaf also shall not wither; and whatsoever he doeth shall prosper.

"The ungodly are not so; but are like the chaff which the wind driveth away. Therefore the ungodly shall not stand in the judgment, nor sinners in the congregation of the righteous. For the LORD *knoweth the way of the righteous, but the way of the ungodly shall perish" (1:1-6).*

The Father and Son psalms. "Why do the heathen rage, and the people imagine a vain thing? The kings of the earth set themselves, and the rulers take counsel together, against the LORD, *and against His Anointed, saying, 'Let us break Their bands asunder, and cast away Their cords from us.'*

"He that sitteth in the heavens shall laugh; the LORD *shall have them in derision. Then shall He speak unto them in His wrath, and vex them in His sore displeasure. 'Yet have I set My King upon My holy hill of Zion.'*

"I will declare the decree: 'The LORD *hath said unto me, "Thou art My Son; this day have I begotten Thee." '*

"Ask of Me, and I shall give Thee the heathen for Thine inheritance, and the uttermost parts of the earth for Thy possession. Thou shalt break them with a rod of iron; Thou shalt dash them in pieces like a potter's vessel.

"Be wise now therefore, O ye kings; be instructed, ye judges of the earth. Serve the LORD *with fear, and rejoice with trembling. Kiss the Son, lest He be angry, and ye perish from the way, when His wrath is kindled but a little. Blessed are all they that put their trust in Him" (2:1-12).*

"The LORD *said unto my Lord, 'Sit Thou at My right hand, until I make Thine enemies Thy footstool.'*

"The LORD *shall send the rod of Thy strength out of Zion; rule Thou in the midst of thine enemies. . . . The* LORD *hath sworn, and will not repent, 'Thou art a Priest forever after the order of Melchizedek' " (110:1-2, 4).*

*The psalm of death. "*LORD, *Thou hast been our dwelling place in all generations. Before the mountains were brought forth, or ever Thou hadst formed the earth and the world, even from everlasting to everlasting, Thou art God.*

"Thou turnest man to destruction; and sayest, 'Return, ye children of men.'

"For a thousand years in Thy sight are but as yesterday when it is past, and as a watch in the night. Thou carriest them away as with a flood; they are as asleep. In the morning they are like grass which groweth up. In the morning it flourisheth, and groweth up; in the evening it is cut down, and withereth. . . .

"The days of our years are threescore years and ten; and if by reason of strength they be fourscore years, yet is their strength labor and sorrow; for it is soon cut off, and we fly away. . . . So teach us to number our days, that we may apply our hearts unto wisdom" (90:1-6, 10, 12).

Psalm 1: How to Be Happy

COMMENTS

One of the greatest lies of Satan is that one cannot be a Christian and be happy at the same time. Nothing could be farther from the truth. God is love, and He wants His children to be happy and fulfilled. Psalm 1 presents a simple formula for happiness that cannot be improved. The first word in the psalm, "Blessed," may be translated "happy." Thus the psalm becomes a pronouncement about the happy man.

The psalmist first describes the happy man (vv. 1-3). The happy man is said to avoid evil influences, deeds, and attitudes (v. 1). It is important to note how the psalmist begins with a negative at the outset—things the happy man does not do. These negatives serve as forceful means to communicate the holiness of God (much like the Ten Commandments where negatives also dominate).

The first thing the happy man does not do is "walk in the counsel of the ungodly." This means simply that he does not listen to the advice of the wicked. The happy man does not obtain his values from the wicked. The word "ungodly" used here refers to the criminal element in the Old Testament community, the ones who broke God's Law. The happy man is aware of the fact that everyone has a worldview, and he refuses to allow his values to come from the people around him.

The second thing the happy man does not do is "stand in the way of sinners." This means that he does not take part in their activities. He does not do the same things; he does not go to the same places; and he does not keep the same company. This statement is, of course, an advancement over the first since involving oneself in the activities of the wicked is worse than simply listening to their advice.

The third thing the happy man does not do is "sit in the seat of the scornful." This statement means that the happy man does not adopt the attitude of the wicked. This activity reflects the deepest involvement of the three statements since the "scornful" are the group which are farthest from repentance. These are they who openly mock moral and spiritual values and are antagonistic toward God and His people. The happy man does not take part in these godless attitudes.

As important as these negatives are, they are not sufficient to provide man with the spiritual fuel he needs to be godly. Therefore the psalmist moves quickly to the positive side of the happy man's life (v. 2). The happy man delights in God's Word. The "Law of the LORD" in this verse answers to the "counsel of the ungodly" in verse 1. The source of the happy man's values is the Word of God. It is said to be his "delight" and to be a source of meditation day and night for him. The Word of God is for the happy man a constant source of help throughout the day and the night. The mind is assumed here to be the key to the whole man. The happy man realizes this and fills his mind with God's Word.

Because the happy man avoids the wicked and because he meditates on God's Word, he is rewarded with God's blessing (v. 3). Here the happy man is compared to a tree. Three comparisons are drawn. First, the tree is said to be planted by streams. This speaks of the happy man's continual rejuvenation by God. Second, the tree is fruitbearing. Therefore, the happy man is productive in his character and influence on others. Third, the leaf of the tree does not wither. This means that the happy man has vitality and energy to serve God. The psalmist then summarizes what God does for the happy man: "Whatever he doeth shall prosper."

The psalmist anticipated the obvious question: What is the alternative to being a happy man? One might think the answer would be an unhappy man, but it is not. The alternative is to be a wicked man, and this is what the psalmist now describes (vv. 4-5). The worth of the wicked man is revealed in a comparison to chaff. Nothing is more worthless than chaff. When a farmer winnowed his grain, he would toss the threshed grain into the air for the husks and bits of straw to be blown away, leaving behind only the grain. The wicked man is like that chaff. Further, his destiny is certain doom (v. 5). He will be expelled from the assembly of the righteous without recourse.

Finally, the psalmist relates the Lord's evaluation of the two men: God knows the righteous and takes care of him, but He rejects the ungodly and judges him (v. 6). The pleasures of the wicked are short-lived. Their prosperity is short-term. They will be judged. In the final analysis, there is an inseparable link between happiness and holiness and between judgment and ungodliness.

The psalm of life. "He that dwelleth in the secret place of the Most High shall abide under the shadow of the Almighty. I will say of the LORD, 'He is my refuge and my fortress, my God; in Him will I trust.'

"Surely He shall deliver thee from the snare of the fowler, and from the noisome pestilence. He shall cover thee with His feathers, and under His wings shalt thou trust. His truth shall be thy shield and buckler. Thou shalt not be afraid for the terror by night; nor for the arrow that flieth by day; nor for the pestilence that walketh in darkness; nor for the destruction that wasteth at noonday.

"A thousand shall fall at thy side, and ten thousand at thy right hand; but it shall not come nigh thee. . . .

"There shall no evil befall thee, neither shall any plague come nigh thy dwelling. For He shall give His angels charge over thee, to keep thee in all thy ways. They shall bear thee up in their hands, lest thou dash thy foot against a stone. Thou shalt tread upon the lion and adder; the young lion and the dragon shalt thou trample under feet" (91:1-7, 10-13).

The unity psalm. "Behold, how good and how pleasant it is for brethren to dwell together in unity! It is like the precious ointment upon the head, that ran down upon the beard, even Aaron's beard; that went down to the skirts of his garments. As the dew of Hermon, and as the dew that descended upon the mountains of Zion; for there the LORD commanded the blessing, even life forevermore" (133:1-3).

Preview

Advice from the Manufacturer (Part One)

PROVERBS 5; 7; 10; 22–23; 27; 30-31

An old Arab proverb goes as follows:

> He that knows not and knows not that he knows not—that man is a fool: Avoid him!
>
> He that knows not and knows that he knows not—that man is teachable: Teach him!
>
> He that knows and knows not that he knows—that man is asleep: Wake him!
>
> He that knows and knows that he knows—that man is wise: Follow him!

If one reads and heeds the words of the Old Testament Book of Proverbs, he will be like that man who knows and knows that he knows.

Overview

<table>
<tr><td>SCRIPTURE</td><td colspan="3">Proverbs 5; 7; 10; 22–23; 27; 30–31</td></tr>
<tr><td>SUBJECT</td><td colspan="3">Proverbs dealing with a good name, youth, business matters, marriage, immorality</td></tr>
<tr><td rowspan="3">SPECIFICS</td><td colspan="2">Cottage advice</td><td>Community advice</td></tr>
<tr><td colspan="2">Parents and children
Children should be counseled
Children should be chastened</td><td>Concerning one's reputation</td></tr>
<tr><td colspan="2">Husbands and wives
The wisdom of sexual purity
The wickedness of sexual promiscuity</td><td>Concerning one's riches</td></tr>
<tr><td>SAINTS AND SINNERS</td><td colspan="3"></td></tr>
<tr><td rowspan="2">SENTENCE SUMMARIES</td><td>O.T. Verse</td><td colspan="2">"He spake 3,000 proverbs, and his songs were 1,005" (1 Kings 4:32).</td></tr>
<tr><td>N.T. Verse</td><td colspan="2">"The Queen of the South shall rise up in the judgment with this generation, and shall condemn it; for she came from the uttermost parts of the earth to hear the wisdom of Solomon; and, behold a greater than Solomon is here" (Matt. 12:42).</td></tr>
</table>

AMILIES, REPUTATION, AND MONEY

PROVERBS

It is impossible to construct a chronological outline of this book. At least 11 main subjects are discussed. These are:

A good name. "The memory of the just is blessed; but the name of the wicked shall rot" (10:7).

"A good name is rather to be chosen than great riches, and loving favor rather than silver and gold" (22:1).

Youth and discipline. A man with a levelheaded son is happy, but a rebel's mother is sad (see 10:1; 17:21, 25; 19:13).

A wise youth will listen to his father but a younger mocker won't (see 13:1).

"He that spareth his rod hateth his son; but he that loveth him chasteneth him betimes" (v. 24).

"Chasten thy son while there is hope, and let not thy soul spare for his crying" (19:18).

"Train up a child in the way he should go, and when he is old, he will not depart from it" (22:6).

"Foolishness is bound in the heart of a child: but the rod of correction shall drive it far from him" (22:15; see 29:15, 17).

"Withhold not correction from the child; for if thou beatest him with the rod, he shall not die. Thou shalt beat him with the rod, and shalt deliver his soul from hell" (23:13-14).

Business matters. God hates a dishonest scale and delights in honesty (see 11:1; 16:11; 20:10, 23).

Don't sign a note for someone you barely know (see 6:1-5; 11:15; 17:18).

Don't withhold repayment of your debts (see 3:27).

God will not let a good man starve to death (see 10:3).

Lazy men are soon poor; hard workers have an abundant supply (see v. 4; 22:29).

A lazy fellow is a pain to his employer—like smoke in his eyes or vinegar that sets the teeth on edge (see 11:26).

He that trusteth in his riches shall fall (see v. 28).

Develop your business first before building your house (see 24:27).

Riches can disappear quickly. And the king's crown doesn't stay in his family forever—so watch your business interests closely. Know the state of your flocks and your herds; then there will be lamb's wool enough for clothing, and goat's milk enough for food for all your household after the hay is harvested, and the new crop appears, and the mountain grasses are gathered in (see 27:23-27).

Marriage. "Drink waters out of thine own cistern" (5:15).

"Rejoice with the wife of thy youth" (v. 18).

A beautiful woman lacking discretion and modesty is like a fine gold ring in a pig's snout (see 11:22).

"He that troubleth his own house shall inherit the wind" (v. 29).

"A virtuous woman is a crown to her husband; but she that maketh ashamed is as rottenness in his bones" (12:4).

"Every wise woman buildeth her house: but the foolish plucketh it down with her hands" (14:1).

"Whoso findeth a wife findeth a good thing, and obtaineth favor of the LORD" (18:22).

"It is better to dwell in a corner of the housetop, than with a brawling woman in a wide house" (21:9; 25:24).

"It is better to dwell in the wilderness, than with a contentious and angry woman" (21:19).

"Who can find a virtuous woman?" (31:10)

Immorality. It means to flout the law of God (see 2:17).

It leads along the road to death and hell (see v. 18; 7:27; 9:18).

It causes one to groan in anguish and shame when disease consumes the body (see 5:11).

It leads to bitter remorse (see vv. 12-13).

It will be judged by God (see v. 21).

It will bring a man to poverty (see 6:26).

It will burn the soul as surely as fire burns the skin (see vv. 27, 32).

It can be compared to an ox going to the butcher, a trapped stag awaiting the death arrow, or a bird flying into a snare (see 7:22-23).

The Structure and Argument of the Book of Proverbs

COMMENTS

Bible students have long questioned whether the Book of Proverbs has an organized structure or outline. A careful reading of the book will reveal however that there is a clear, logical structure embedded in the text. The following expressions serve as guides to introduce new sections in the outline: "the proverbs of Solomon" (1:1); "my son" (v. 8; 2:1; 3:1; 4:10, 20; 5:1; 6:1, 20; 7:1); "ye children" (4:1); "the proverbs of Solomon" (10:1); "the words of the wise" (22:17); "these things also belong to the wise" (24:23); "these are also proverbs of Solomon" (25:1); "the words of Agur" (30:1); "the words of King Lemuel" (31:1); "who can find a virtuous woman?" (31:10) The argument of the book may then be outlined as follows:

- I. Introduction (1:1-7)
  - A. Title (1:1))
  - B. Purpose (1:2-6)
  - C. Motto (1:7)
- II. Exhortations to be wise (1:8–9:18)
  - A. Rejection of sinners and acceptance of wisdom (1:8-33)
  - B. Benefits of wisdom (2:1-22)
  - C. Right relationships and wisdom (3:1-35)
  - D. Supremacy of wisdom (4:1-9)
  - E. Righteousness versus wickedness (4:10-19)
  - F. Wisdom of self-discipline (4:20-27)
  - G. Admonition against adultery (5:1-23)
  - H. Freedom from folly (6:1-19)
  - I. Admonition against adultery (6:20-35)
  - J. Invitations from two women (7:1–8:36)
  - K. Epilogue: Wisdom versus Folly (9:1-18)
- III. Proverbs of Solomon (second collection) (10:1–22:16)
- IV. Words of the wise, part 1 (22:17–24:22)
- V. Words of the wise, part 2 (24:23-34)
- VI. Proverbs of Solomon (third collection, or Hezekiah's collection) (25:1–29:27)
- VII. Words of Agur (30:1-33)
- VIII. Words of King Lemuel (31:1-9)
- IX. The Perfect Wife from *A* to *Z* (31:10-31)

The argument of the book may now be traced. The introduction states the title, purpose, and motto. The purpose of the book is to give the reader wisdom, or skill in living. The motto of the book is, "The fear of the LORD is the beginning of knowledge." The controlling principle of wisdom and knowledge is the fear of the Lord. The fear of the Lord is the common expression for faith in God in the Old Testament and means submission to Him and His will. The Book of Proverbs states that true wisdom is more than intellectual: it has a crucial spiritual dimension.

There are 10 consecutive exhortations, each beginning with the words "my son" or "ye children." This shows that the book is essentially the words of a father to his son. The word "son" should not be taken here as referring to a disciple because the original setting of the book was the home. The frequent references to the mother prove this point. The purpose of these exhortations is to set before the son the theology of the two ways: reject folly and pursue wisdom. The son is constantly admonished to heed his father's counsel while he is young and thus instill in his life the principle of wisdom which will carry him through his life. There are five passages which warn against sexual sin (2:16-19; 5:1-23; 6:20-35; 7:1-27; 9:1-18). Young people then faced many of the same temptations as today.

This book contains 375 proverbs of Solomon. Each verse is a single proverb which expresses a complete thought. Each proverb represents in miniature the choice between wisdom and folly. These proverbs are then followed by two collections of the words of wise men. It is known that Solomon's reign was a time when an international wisdom movement flourished and that Solomon himself collected the sayings of others (1 Kings 10:24). The sixth section is Hezekiah's collection of Solomon's proverbs. This reference shows that the Book of Proverbs itself was compiled over a period of many years, since Hezekiah lived over 200 years after Solomon. The next two collections are evidently the words of foreign wise men, Agur and King Lemuel.

Finally, the last 22 verses are set off from the words of King Lemuel because they are in the form of an acrostic, a poem in which each verse begins with a consecutive letter of the Hebrew alphabet. It has been suggested that the reason the passage on the excellent wife occurs at the end is because she, of all persons, will have the greatest impact in communicating right values in the home. In conclusion, the question of the structure of Proverbs can no longer be raised since a logical structure can be easily demonstrated from the book itself.

Marriage and Family in the Book of Proverbs

COMMENTS

One of the best ways to study the Book of Proverbs (especially 10:1–31:9) is by topics. One key subject of the book is the family. Numerous important principles of family living emerge when the book is carefully studied. First, marriage is to be monogamous. This fact is assumed throughout the book. Marriage occurs when one man marries one woman for one lifetime. In spite of Solomon's own sin of polygamy, his book of wise living is to be followed since it records inspired words for he who would be wise.

Second, the home is to be the place where moral and spiritual values are passed on to the children. This principle is commanded in Deuteronomy 6:6-7: "And these words, which I command thee this day, shall be in thine heart. And thou shalt teach them diligently unto thy children, and shalt talk of them when thou sittest in thine house, and when thou walkest by the way, and when thou liest down, and when thou risest up." The Book of Proverbs may be regarded as a practical application of these verses. In it the reader sees a father (and mother) trying to communicate their values to their children. It should also be noted that both father and mother are involved in this teaching process (Prov. 1:8; 6:20).

Third, children are to be submissive to their parents. Over and over again the father commands the son to listen to his father and his mother (1:8; 2:1-4; 3:1; 4:1-2, etc.). Children are naive and need to learn from those who are older and wiser. Young people must realize that they are malleable in their moral and spiritual outlook and that the only place for this shaping of values to occur is under the parents' tutelage. Proverbs is a reflection of Ephesians 6:1 in this regard.

Fourth, parents are responsible for the discipline of their children. Not only are they to teach them with words, they also must discipline them with physical punishment (13:24; 22:15; 23:13; 29:15). The "rod" referred to in these verses is used for wise, corporal punishment, done in love (13:24), not for abuse. The Bible recognizes that "foolishness is bound in the heart of a child." Judicious physical discipline is a means of teaching.

Fifth, sexual immorality destroys the family. In the first nine chapters of Proverbs there occur at least five passages in which the father admonishes his son to refrain from sexual sin. This fact shows the importance of the subject and how necessary it is for every parent to teach his children about sex. Chapters 5 and 7 are classic passages on this subject and are worthy of specific treatment here. In chapter 5 the father instructs his son that the father's words, if applied, will protect him against the harlot (vv. 1-2) whose words are enticing (v. 3) though they lead to a cruel death (vv. 4-6). The word "death" here does not refer to a literal death but to the absence of a full life. In other words, the adulterer misses out on the real meaning of life. The father admonishes the son to stay away from the occasion of temptation (vv. 7-8). He explains that the price of unchastity is immense: he will lose health and wealth (vv. 9-11); he will regret it and may be rejected by the community (vv. 12-14), and he will suffer the Lord's punishment (vv. 21-23). Sandwiched between these foreboding commands, however, is a ray of hope: the son should find real satisfaction and sexual pleasure in his wife (vv. 15-23).

In chapter 7 the father describes a specific occasion on which a young man fell. The harlot's tactics are especially evident in this chapter: she kissed the young man (v. 13); she told him that it was the ideal occasion (vv. 14-15), and that she had the ideal place (vv. 16-17). Furthermore, there was nothing to fear (vv. 19-20). With such strong temptations the youth yielded as an ox going to the slaughter. His first fault was simply that he did not avoid her paths (vv. 8-9). As a result of his foolishness he will miss out on legitimate sexual relations as intended by God. Only a fool would satisfy his lust at such a price. Two important principles emerge out of these passages: first, it is the duty of parents to teach their children about sex and, second, sexual immorality destroys real life, especially that of the family.

The family in Proverbs is seen as a training ground for the children in which both parents actively teach their children the values that will guide them through life (cf. 22:6).

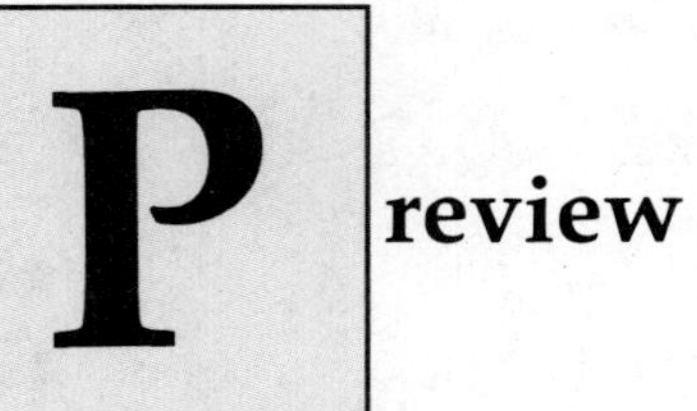

Advice from the Manufacturer (Part Two)

PROVERBS 1; 3; 15; 17–18; 23; 25; 27

"Let your speech be always with grace, seasoned with salt, that ye may know how ye ought to answer every man" (Col. 4:6).

"Sound speech, that cannot be condemned" (Titus 2:8).

The thrust of the following Proverbs deal with a believer's wise usage of his tongue. Two poems (authors unknown) aptly summarize this section.

ON WHEN TO SPEAK

A wise old owl sat in an oak;
The more he saw, the less he spoke;
The less he spoke, the more he heard;
Oh, to be like that wise old bird!

ON WHAT TO SPEAK

A careless word may kindle strife.
A cruel word may wreck a life.
A gracious word may smooth the way.
A joyous word may light the day.
A timely word may lessen stress.
A loving word may heal and bless!

Overview

<table>
<tr><td>SCRIPTURE</td><td colspan="4">Proverbs 1; 3; 15; 17–18; 23; 25; 27</td></tr>
<tr><td>SUBJECT</td><td colspan="4">Proverbs dealing with evil companions, wisdom, self-control, strong drink, friendship, the tongue</td></tr>
<tr><td rowspan="4">SPECIFICS</td><td rowspan="4">Virtues to acquire</td><td>Wisdom</td><td rowspan="4">Vices to avoid</td><td rowspan="2">Evil companions</td></tr>
<tr><td>Self-control</td></tr>
<tr><td>Friendship</td><td rowspan="2">Strong drink</td></tr>
<tr><td>Sound speech</td></tr>
<tr><td>SAINTS AND SINNERS</td><td colspan="4"></td></tr>
<tr><td rowspan="2">SENTENCE SUMMARIES</td><td>O.T. Verse</td><td colspan="3">"Who hath put wisdom in the inward parts? Or who hath given understanding to the heart?" (Job 38:36)</td></tr>
<tr><td>N.T. Verse</td><td colspan="3">"Walk in wisdom toward them that are without, redeeming the time" (Col. 4:5).</td></tr>
</table>

VIRTUES AND VICES

Evil companions. Refuse them, for in attempting to trap others they only trap themselves (see 1:10-19).

Refuse them, *"for they eat the bread of wickedness and drink the wine of violence" (4:17).*

Refuse them, for their kindness is a trick; they want to use you as their pawn (see 23:6-8).

Refuse them, for a man's true character is reflected by the friends he chooses (see 27:19).

Wisdom. The fear of God is its root (see 1:7; 9:10).

It will gain one many honors (see 1:9).

It will keep one from immorality (see 2:16).

It will direct all one's paths (see 3:6).

It will give one renewal, health, and vitality (see v. 8).

It will (as one wisely tithes) fill one's barns with wheat and barley and overflow the wine vats with the finest wines (see vv. 9-10).

It is better than silver, gold, and precious rubies (see v. 14; 8:11, 19).

It gives a long life, riches, honor, pleasure, and peace (see 3:16-17; 9:11).

It was God's method in Creation (see 3:19-20).

It is the principal thing (see 4:7).

It should be loved like a sweetheart (see 7:4).

It brings the favor of God (see 8:35).

Self-control. It is better to have self-control than to capture a mighty city (see 16:32).

An uncontrolled man often begins something he can't finish (see 25:8).

A man without self-control is as defenseless as a city with broken-down walls (see v. 28).

Strong drink. It gives false courage and leads to brawls (see 20:1).

It fills the heart with anguish and sorrow (see 23:29).

It causes bloodshot eyes and many wounds (see v. 29).

It bites like a poisonous serpent and stings like an adder (see v. 32).

It leads to hallucinations and delirium tremens (see v. 33).

It makes one say silly and stupid things (see v. 33).

It causes one to stagger like a sailor at sea (see v. 34).

It allows one to be beat up without even being aware of it (see v. 35).

It causes leaders to forget their duties and thus pervert justice (see 31:5).

Friendship. A true friend is always loyal and is born to help in time of need (see 17:17).

Wounds from a friend are better than kisses from an enemy (see 27:6).

Never abandon a friend—either yours or your father's (see v. 10).

Friendly suggestions are as pleasant as perfume (see v. 9).

A friendly discussion is as stimulating as the sparks that fly when iron strikes iron (see v. 17).

A man who would have friends must himself be friendly (see 18:24).

True is a friend *"that sticketh closer than a brother" (v. 24).*

The Meaning and Acquisition of Wisdom

COMMENTS

The key word in the Book of Proverbs is of course the word *wisdom*. It is important, therefore, to delve into its precise meaning. Fortunately, the word is used often in the Old Testament, and its meaning can be readily determined. The Hebrew word for wisdom is used frequently in the Old Testament to refer to a physical skill: tailoring (Ex. 28:3), metalworking and woodworking (31:3, 6; 35:31), spinning (v. 26), engraving, designing and embroidering (v. 35), and warfare (Isa. 10:13). In Exodus 28, for example, the tailors who were chosen to make Aaron's beautiful high priestly garments were said to have "wisdom." This means simply that they had a physical skill. They could take flax, work it into thread, dye that thread, and then weave it into a beautiful garment. It takes skill to do that. So it is in life, according to the Book of Proverbs: one needs skill in living. It takes a great deal of skill to live life successfully and to produce something beautiful with your life. The Book of Proverbs promises that skill or wisdom to the one who lives by its truths.

Other key words are introduced in the purpose statement of the book (Prov. 1:3-6). These words further amplify the meaning of wisdom. "Instruction" (v. 2) refers to moral discipline. It has a note of sternness to it. One must take life seriously. "Understanding" (v. 2) means the capability of distinguishing between the true and false, the good and bad, what matters most in life, and what does not matter at all. "Wisdom" (v. 3), a different Hebrew word than in verse 2, encompasses the ideas of wise dealing, good sense, and practical wisdom. "Justice" (v. 3) might better be translated "righteousness" since it refers to conformity to God's character. "Judgment" (v. 3) is used of a judge's verdict. It means to meet the demands of God's Law. "Equity" (v. 3) is a way of thought and conduct that is right and true. These are the character qualities that one can build into his life by living by the Book of Proverbs.

Some word should be said about the recipients of wisdom in the Book of Proverbs. While it is true that the book promises that even wise men can learn from it (v. 5), most of the book is addressed to the most needy recipients of wisdom. These are, listed in order of increasing need, as follows: (1) The "young man" (v. 4). The youth is open-minded and immature. (2) The "simple" (v. 4). This is the untutored young person whose mind is open to any influence though he seems to be inclined toward evil. (3) The "fool" (v. 7). There are actually several words for fool in the Book of Proverbs but each emphasizes not mental deficiency but moral deficiency, or a lack of moral principle. (4) The "sluggard" (6:6). This word refers to the habitually lazy person who has many unfulfilled desires (13:4), refuses to plow in season (20:4), and even begins to believe his own preposterous excuses for not working, such as: "There is a lion in the way!" (26:13) (5) The "sinner" (1:10). The word refers to those to whom sin has become a character trait, a way of life. (6) The "scorner" (v. 22). The scorner or scoffer is the farthest from repentance. This word refers to the one who mocks things that are spiritual and moral. The Book of Proverbs thus promises its wisdom, not only to those who are already wise and to the young who need its counsel, but also to those who have drifted by one degree or another from its teaching.

Finally, one question remains: what are the requirements for wisdom? These are simple but require much diligence: (1) Its controlling principle is the fear of the Lord (v. 7), (2) It can only be gained by hard work in seeking understanding and insight (2:4-5), (3) It takes time to be achieved and cannot be acquired overnight or only in a time of need (1:28-29), (4) Its goal is the knowledge of God (2:5), (5) Its method is the inculcation of received teaching (vv. 1-4), (6) It is personalized in Jesus Christ (Col. 2:3, 10). For the New Testament Christian then, all that Proverbs says about wisdom is available in one's relationship to Christ as one grows in Him.

The Importance of Words

COMMENTS

Few topics appear more often in the Book of Proverbs than the subject of words. Though a number of words are used to introduce the subject, such as "tongue," "speech," "words," etc., the point remains clear: words are extremely important in the course of human relations. The first thing to note about words is their power. Proverbs 18:21 expresses it quite clearly: "Death and life are in the power of the tongue." As is often the case in Proverbs, the words "death" and "life" refer to a quality of life. In other words, the tongue has the power to bring life and death to someone, to revitalize their spirits and bring a deeper quality of life, or to discourage them and take away the enjoyment of life. The following truths regarding the power of words may be gleaned from the book: (1) Bad words can pierce like a sword (12:18a). (2) A timely good word can boost one's spirit and revitalize one's energy (v. 18b). (3) Good words can cure anxiety or add to it (v. 25). (4) Pleasant words can make a person feel good and do for one's soul what good health does for the body (16:24). (5) Gossip, on the other hand, does for one's soul what wounds do to the body. One's attitude toward others may be deeply affected by a mere whisper (26:22). (6) Flattery or unjust praise does not help one's neighbor but actually hinders him and may help destroy him (29:5). (7) One righteous man can, by using good words, make his words a spring of life to others; on the other hand, a wicked man's words can spread like violence (10:11). (8) Words are like seeds planted that bear fruit for good or for evil, in accord with the spirit in which they were planted. (9) A wholesome tongue is like a tree of life spreading good health to the souls of all who listen (15:4). (10) On the other hand, the words of an ungodly man are like a fire. They do not burn literally of course, but they burn a fire inside the listener (16:22b).

In spite of the power of words, their awesome ability to revitalize or to destroy, they are, at the same time, quite weak.This truth is expressed in several key verses: (1) Mere talk with no action brings one to poverty (14:23). As powerful as words are, they cannot substitute for action. (2) Words, no matter how deceitful they may be, cannot really change the way things are. Just as glaze over pottery cannot change its earthen interior, so burning lips cannot change the underlying wicked heart (26:23). A hateful man may try to disguise his evil intentions with words, but he cannot thereby change his evil heart (26:24-26). (3) Words cannot make people respond. This fact is especially evident in the unrequited appeals of wisdom (1:20-23), but is expressed as well specifically in the proverb "A servant will not be corrected by words" (29:19).

If words are both powerful and weak, how may one concentrate on making the best words? The Book of Proverbs also tells the reader how to do this. Good words will be true (16:13), few (13:3; 17:28), calm and irenic (15:1; 17:27), appropriate (15:23; 25:11), and thought through (15:28). Ultimately, however, good words spring from a good heart (4:23). A man must have the right character to make the right words. What a man says ultimately will reveal what he is. It is as Jesus said: "Out of the abundance of the heart the mouth speaketh" (Matt. 12:34). The only way to say good words is to have good character. As one's character improves, so do his words.

Words and the tongue. *"The tongue of the just is as choice silver"* (10:20).

"He that refraineth his lips is wise" (*v.* 19; see 11:12).

"The lips of the righteous feed many" (10:21).

"A hypocrite with his mouth destroyeth his neighbor" (11:9).

"A talebearer revealeth secrets; but he that is of a faithful spirit concealeth the matter" (*v.* 13).

"There is that speaketh like the piercings of a sword, but the tongue of the wise is health" (12:18).

"He that keepeth his mouth keepeth his life; but he that openeth wide his lips shall have destruction" (13:3).

"A true witness delivereth souls" (14:25).

"A soft answer turneth away wrath; but grievous words stir up anger" (15:1).

"A wholesome tongue is a tree of life; but perverseness therein is a breach in the spirit" (*v.* 4).

"A word spoken in due season, how good is it!" (*v.* 23)

"The heart of the righteous studieth to answer" (*v.* 28).

"Pleasant words are as a honeycomb, sweet to the soul, and health to the bones" (16:24).

"A froward man soweth strife, and a whisperer separateth chief friends" (*v.* 28; see 17:9).

"The beginning of strife is as when one letteth out water; therefore leave off contention, before it be meddled with" (*v.* 14).

"He that hath knowledge spareth his words" (17:27).

"The words of a talebearer are as wounds" (18:8).

"He that answereth a matter before he heareth it, it is folly and shame unto him" (*v.* 13).

"Death and life are in the power of the tongue" (*v.* 21).

"He that speaketh lies shall not escape" (19:5).

"A word fitly spoken is like apples of gold in pictures of silver" (25:11).

"By long forbearing is a prince persuaded, and a soft tongue breaketh the [hard] bone" (*v.* 15).

"He that passeth by and meddleth with strife belonging not to him, is like one that taketh a dog by the ears" (26:17).

"Where no wood is, there the fire goeth out; so where there is no talebearer, the strife ceaseth" (*v.* 20).

"Let another man praise thee, and not thine own mouth" (27:2).

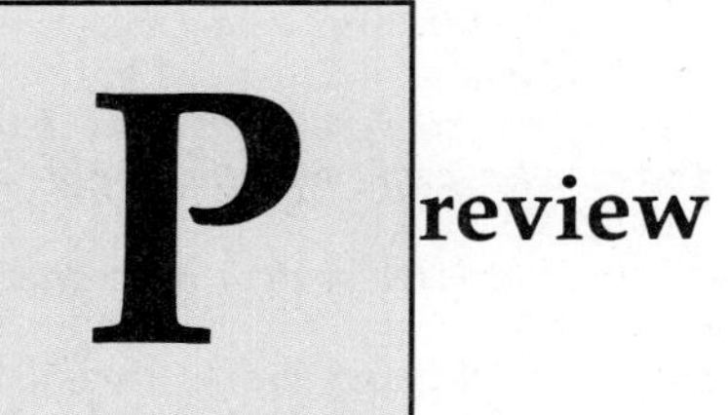

Advice from the Manufacturer (Part Three)

PROVERBS 1; 3; 6; 8; 24–25; 30–31

The warning from God. The woman of God. The Book of Proverbs begins and ends with these two subjects. The warning from God: the ultimate in insanity is to refuse the clear call of God.

The woman of God: At least three types of women are described in the Proverbs. There is the filthy woman (Prov. 7), the foolish woman (chap. 9), and the faithful woman (chap. 31). The latter is the woman of God!

Overview

SCRIPTURE	Proverbs 1; 3; 6; 8; 24–25; 30–31			
SUBJECT	Classical passages in the Proverbs			
SPECIFICS	Graphic guidelines		General groupings	
	Concerning . . .	The rejection of God	Concerning . . .	7 things God hates
		The blessings of God		4 unsatisfied things
		The Son of God		4 wonderful things
		The ways of God		4 unbearable things
		The Word of God		4 small and wise things
		The woman of God		4 stately monarchs
SAINTS AND SINNERS				
SENTENCE SUMMARIES	O.T. Verse	"And the Spirit of the LORD shall rest upon him, the Spirit of wisdom and understanding, the Spirit of counsel and might, the Spirit of knowledge and of the fear of the LORD" (Isa. 11:2).		
	N.T. Verse	"O the depth of the riches both of the wisdom and knowledge of God! How unsearchable are His judgments, and His ways past finding out" (Rom. 11:33).		

LASSICAL PASSAGES

Classical passages in the Book of Proverbs. "Because I have called, and ye refused; I have stretched out My hand, and no man regarded; but ye have set at nought all My counsel, and would none of My reproof. I also will laugh at your calamity; I will mock when your fear cometh; when your fear cometh as desolation, and your destruction cometh as a whirlwind; when distress and anguish cometh upon you. Then shall they call upon Me, but I will not answer; they shall seek Me early, but they shall not find Me" (1:24-28).

"Trust in the LORD with all thine heart; and lean not unto thine own understanding. In all thy ways acknowledge Him, and He shall direct thy paths. . . .

"Honor the Lord with thy substance, and with the firstfruits of all thine increase; so shall thy barns be filled with plenty, and thy presses shall burst out with new wine. My son, despise not the chastening of the LORD; neither be weary of His correction; for whom the LORD loveth He correcteth; even as a father the son in whom he delighteth. . . .

"The LORD by wisdom hath founded the earth; by understanding hath He established the heavens. By His knowledge the depths are broken up, and the clouds drop down the dew. My son, let not them depart from thine eyes; keep sound wisdom and discretion. So shall they be life unto thy soul, and grace to thy neck. Then shalt thou walk in thy way safely, and thy foot shall not stumble. When thou liest down, thou shalt not be afraid; yea, thou shalt lie down, and thy sleep shall be sweet. Be not afraid of sudden fear, neither of the desolation of the wicked, when it cometh. For the LORD shall be thy confidence, and shall keep thy foot from being taken" (3:5-6, 9-12, 19-26).

Christ in eternity past. "The LORD possessed me in the beginning of His way, before His works of old. I was set up from everlasting, from the beginning, or ever the earth was. . . . Then I was by Him, as one brought up with Him, and I was daily His delight, rejoicing always before Him" (8:22-23, 30).

"The fruit of the righteous is a tree of life; and he that winneth souls is wise" (11:30).

"There is a way which seemeth right unto a man; but the end thereof are the ways of death. . . . Righteousness exalteth a nation; but sin is a reproach to any people" (14:12, 34).

"Commit thy works unto the LORD, and thy thoughts shall be established. . . . When a man's ways please the LORD, He maketh even his enemies to be at peace with him. . . .

"Pride goeth before destruction, and a haughty spirit before a fall" (16:3, 7, 18).

"The name of the LORD is a strong tower; the righteous runneth into it, and is safe" (18:10).

How to treat one's enemy. "Rejoice not when thine enemy falleth, and let not thine heart be glad when he stumbleth" (24:17).

"If thine enemy be hungry, give him bread to eat; and if he be thirsty, give him water to drink. For thou shalt heap coals of fire upon his head, and the LORD shall reward thee" (25:21-22).

"Boast not thyself of tomorrow; for thou knowest not what a day may bring" (27:1).

"He that covereth his sins shall not prosper; but whoso confesseth and forsaketh them shall have mercy" (28:13).

"He, that being often reproved hardeneth his neck, shall suddenly be destroyed, and that without remedy. . . . Where there is no vision, the people perish; but he that keepeth the Law, happy is he" (29:1, 18).

God's holiness revealed. "Who hath ascended up into heaven, or descended? Who hath gathered the wind in his fists? Who hath bound the waters in a garment? Who hath established all the ends of the earth? What is His name, and what is His Son's name, if thou canst tell?

"Every word of God is pure. He is a shield unto them that put their trust in Him. Add thou not unto His words, lest He reprove thee, and thou be found a liar. . . . There is a generation that curseth their father, and doth not bless their mother" (30:4-6, 11).

A virtuous woman. * Her worth: "Who can find a virtuous woman? For her price is far above rubies" (31:10).

* Her works: "She looketh well to the ways of her household, and eateth not the bread of idleness" (v. 27).

"She considereth a field, and buyeth it. With the fruit of her hands she planteth a vineyard" (v. 16).

"She stretcheth out her hand to the poor; yea, she reacheth forth her hands to the needy" (v. 20).

The Perfect Wife from A to Z

COMMENTS

The final 22 verses of the Book of Proverbs contain the most beautiful description of the virtuous wife found in Scripture. It is therefore worthy of a verse-by-verse examination. One must first observe that the passage is written in the form of an acrostic, a literary device used to list various statements with each verse beginning with a consecutive letter of the alphabet. Since there are 22 letters in the Hebrew alphabet, the verses number the same. The author is thus describing the perfect wife from *A* to *Z*. There does not seem to be a specific structure in mind in the passage, but each verse emphasizes one key trait of the excellent wife. These will now be examined.

(1) Rare and valuable (v. 10). An excellent wife is difficult to find so her worth cannot be measured by economic standards.

(2) Trustworthy or dependable (v. 11). She has proven to her husband that she is equal to her tasks. Therefore, he has confidence in her.

(3) Constant love (v. 12). Her love for her husband is not dependent on circumstances but on her own steadfast moral commitment to him. Therefore, it is a constant love that builds up and does not destroy.

(4) Enjoys work (v. 13). She uses elbow grease. She directs her mind intentionally and purposefully.

(5) Seeks the most advantageous bargains (v. 14). Exotic foods are not in view here but simply the necessary foods. She goes beyond the immediate supply of food and could be called a "bargain hunter."

(6) Self-starter (v. 15). She cares more for her household than for her own comfort. She prepares the food early in the day. She is there to set the work of the household in motion at the beginning of each working day. She has a well-coordinated plan.

(7) Enterprising (v. 16). She invests her money rather than squandering it.

(8) Willing to do hard labor (v. 17). It will take strength to work the vineyard. She does not shirk physical labor.

(9) Does not rest on her successes (v. 18). While she senses that her enterprises have brought good results, she still burns the midnight oil.

(10) Willing to do monotonous work (v. 19). This quality may explain why she is burning the midnight oil (v. 18). Spinning is tedious and monotonous work, but she does it willingly.

(11) Compassionate (v. 20). She gives to the needy in accordance with the requirements of the Law (cf. Deut. 15:11).

(12) Prepared for predictable circumstances (Prov. 31:21). She prepares for winter well ahead of it. The "scarlet" here is wool for warmth. It is red for beauty.

(13) Maintains personal appearance (v. 22). Though she has fine clothing, she is not a spendthrift. Much of it she made herself.

(14) Enhances her husband's reputation (v. 23). Her character lends respect to her husband. Such a well-ordered household and wife is a benefit to his reputation in the community.

(15) Uses spare time wisely (v. 24). She uses her spare time to contribute to the family income.

(16) Not swayed by circumstances (v. 25). She does not worry about the future because her household is secure. She is not swayed by temporal circumstances.

(17) Wise and kind (v. 26). Wisdom means that she has skill in living. Kindness means that she is loyal to her obligations within the family and community.

(18) Looks for opportunities to serve (v. 27). She keeps a close oversight of her household so that she can serve it with diligence. As new opportunities arise, she is industrious in meeting the need rather than being idle.

(19) Her excellence is apparent (v. 28). Those who know her best are so impressed by her devotion and ability that they spontaneously bless and praise her.

(20) Not satisfied with the mediocre (v. 29). It is not that she is in competition with others but simply that her striving for excellence has marked her out above others.

(21) A woman of God (v. 30). The fear of the Lord is the fundamental expression for faith in God in the Old Testament. She is a believer in the one true God.

(22) Praiseworthy (v. 31). Her best praise is her works. This verse is actually a closing command that the family of the excellent wife should reward her virtue with praise, even before others. She deserves a good reputation and high standing in the community.

* Her wisdom: *"She openeth her mouth with wisdom; and in her tongue is the law of kindness" (v. 26).*

* Her witnesses: *"The heart of her husband doth safely trust in her, so that he shall have no need of spoil" (v. 11).*

"Her children arise up, and call her blessed; her husband also, and he praiseth her" (v. 28).

* Her worship: *"Favor is deceitful, and beauty is vain; but a woman that feareth the LORD, she shall be praised" (v. 30).*

Seven things that God hates. The seven things God hates are: a proud look, a lying tongue, hands that shed innocent blood, a wicked plotting heart, eagerness to do wrong, a false witness, and sowing discord among brothers.

Four things which are never satisfied. These are: the grave, the barren womb, a barren desert, and a fire.

Four wonderful and mysterious things. The four are: how an eagle glides through the sky, how a serpent crawls upon a rock; how a ship finds its way across the heaving ocean, and the growth of love between a man and a woman.

Four things which the earth finds unbearable. These are: a slave who becomes a king, a rebel who prospers, a bitter woman when she finally marries, and a servant girl who marries her mistress' husband.

Four small but wise things. The four are: ants, who are not strong, but store up food for the winter. Cliff badgers, who are delicate little animals that protect themselves by living among the rocks. Locusts, though they have no leader, stay together in swarms. Lizards, which are easy to catch and kill, yet are found even in kings' palaces.

Four stately monarchs. These are: the lion, king of animals. He will not turn aside for anyone. The peacock, the he-goat, and a king as he leads his army.

Two things Agur requested of God. Agur asked God to remove from him vanity and lies, and to give him neither poverty nor riches—but feed him with food convenient for him: *"Lest I be full, and deny Thee, and say, 'Who is the LORD?' "* or, *"Lest I be poor, and steal, and take the name of my God in vain."*

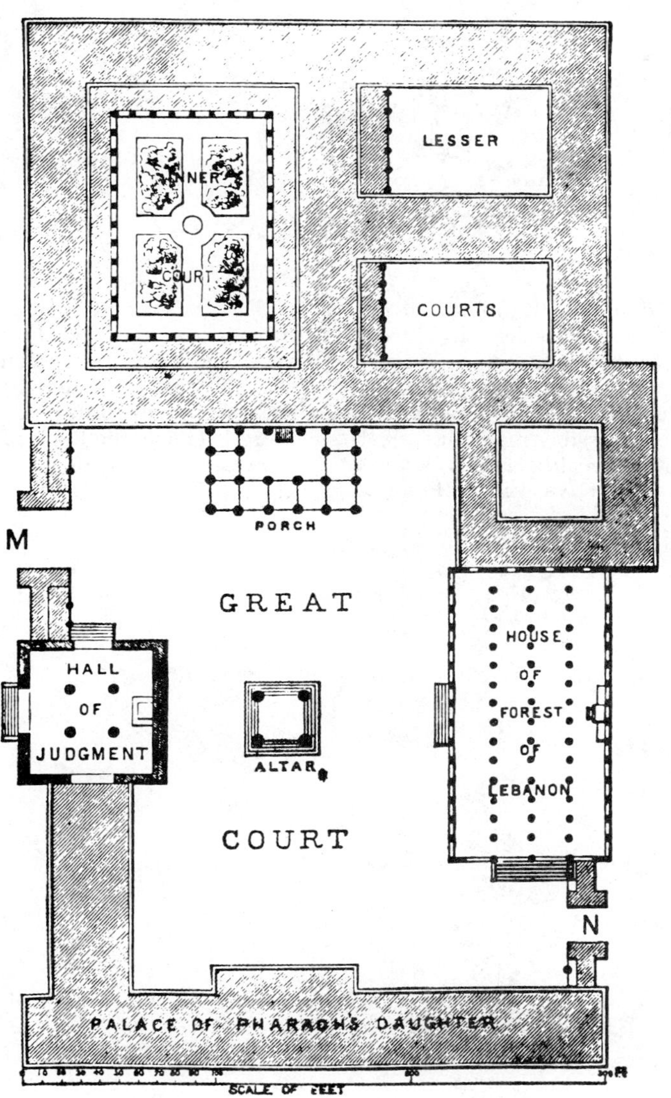
INNER COURT
LESSER
COURTS
PORCH
M
GREAT
HALL OF JUDGMENT
ALTAR
COURT
HOUSE OF FOREST OF LEBANON
N
PALACE OF PHARAOH'S DAUGHTER
SCALE OF FEET

The Mystery of Life

ECCLESIASTES 1–2

There was little doubt in the minds of his court officials. If the universally sought treasure really existed, their leader would surely find it. Certainly no other man in history was as highly qualified as he to attempt the search. Who could possibly match his great power, popularity, wealth, and wisdom? The man in this account was King Solomon, and the sought-after treasure was purposeful meaning to the mystery of life. From the very beginning it was determined that the search would be systematic and specific. No rock would be unturned or corner unexplored. This is the Book of Ecclesiastes, the saga of a search for peace and purpose.

Overview

<table>
<tr><td>SCRIPTURE</td><td colspan="3">Ecclesiastes 1–2</td></tr>
<tr><td>SUBJECT</td><td colspan="3">In search of peace and purpose</td></tr>
<tr><td rowspan="9">SPECIFICS</td><td colspan="3">13 dead-end streets</td></tr>
<tr><td>Lust of the flesh</td><td>Lust of the eyes</td><td>Pride of life</td></tr>
<tr><td rowspan="2">Pleasure</td><td rowspan="3">Beautiful gardens</td><td>Human wisdom</td></tr>
<tr><td>Massive wealth</td></tr>
<tr><td>Alcohol</td><td>Reputation</td></tr>
<tr><td rowspan="2">Personal indulgences</td><td rowspan="4">Great building projects</td><td>Literature</td></tr>
<tr><td>Natural science</td></tr>
<tr><td rowspan="2">Sex</td><td>Military power</td></tr>
<tr><td>Music</td></tr>
<tr><td>SAINTS AND SINNERS</td><td colspan="3"></td></tr>
<tr><td rowspan="2">SENTENCE SUMMARIES</td><td>O.T. Verse</td><td colspan="2">"There is a way that seemeth right unto a man, but the end thereof are the ways of death" (Prov. 16:25).</td></tr>
<tr><td>N.T. Verse</td><td colspan="2">"For what is a man profited, if he shall gain the whole world, and lose his own soul? Or what shall a man give in exchange for his soul?" (Matt. 16:26)</td></tr>
</table>

PEACE AND PURPOSE

ECCLESIASTES

This book is the inspired record of Solomon's search for peace and purpose in this world apart from the person of God.

"I the preacher was king over Israel in Jerusalem. And I gave my heart to seek and search out by wisdom concerning all things that are done under heaven. This sore travail hath God given to the sons of man to be exercised therewith" (1:12-13).

The quest—man's problems stated. Even before he started the search, Solomon had doubts. In his opinion: everything seemed so futile; generations come and go, but it seems to make no difference; the sun rises and sets, the wind twists back and forth, but neither seems to get any place or accomplish any purpose; the river runs into the sea, but the sea is never full. The water returns again to the rivers and flows again to the sea; everything appears so unutterably weary and tiresome; no man seems satisfied, regardless of what he has seen or heard; history merely repeats itself—absolutely nothing new ever occurs under the sun; 100 years from now everything will have been forgotten, regardless of what occurs today.

Was life truly this way everywhere? Could a wise and wealthy man, by searching the length and breadth of the land, find peace and purpose? Solomon would try! This he diligently did by drinking deeply at many wells.

*Human wisdom: *"I communed with mine own heart, saying, 'Lo, I am come to great estate, and have gotten more wisdom than all they that have been before me in Jerusalem.' Yea, my heart had great experience of wisdom and knowledge. And I gave my heart to know wisdom, and to know madness and folly; I perceived that this also is vexation of spirit. For in much wisdom is much grief; and he that increaseth knowledge increaseth sorrow" (1:16-18).*

*Pleasure: *"I said in mine heart, 'Go to now, I will prove thee with mirth, therefore enjoy pleasure.' And, behold, this also is vanity. I said of laughter, 'It is mad'; and of mirth, 'What doeth it?' " (2:1-2)*

*Alcohol: *"I sought in mine heart to give myself unto wine" (v. 3).*

*Great building projects: *"I made me great works; I builded me houses" (v. 4).*

*Beautiful gardens and parks: *"I planted me vineyards; I made me gardens and orchards, and I planted trees in them of all kinds of fruits; I made me pools of water, to water therewith the wood that bringeth forth trees" (vv. 4-6).*

*Personal indulgences: *"I got me servants and maidens, and had servants born in my house" (v. 7).*

*Sex: *"And he had 700 wives, princesses, and 300 concubines" (1 Kings 11:3).*

*Massive wealth: *"I had great possessions of great and small cattle above all that were in Jerusalem before me. I gathered me also silver and gold, and the peculiar treasure of kings and of the provinces" (Ecc. 2:7-8).*

*International reputation: *"And she [the Queen of Sheba] said to the king, 'It was a true report that I heard in mine own land of thy acts and of thy wisdom. Howbeit, I believed not the words, until I came, and mine eyes had seen it; and behold, the half was not told me. Thy wisdom and prosperity exceedeth the fame which I heard' " (1 Kings 10:6-7).*

*Literature: *"And he spoke 3,000 proverbs, and his songs were 1,005" (4:32).*

*Natural science: *"And he spake of trees, from the cedar tree that is in Lebanon even unto the hyssop that springeth out of the wall; he spake also of beasts, and of fowl, and of creeping things, and of fish" (v. 33).*

*Military power: *"And Solomon had 40,000 stalls of horses for his chariots, and 12,000 horsemen" (v. 26).*

"And King Solomon made a navy of ships . . . on the shore of the Red Sea" (9:26).

*Music: *"I got me men singers and women singers, and the delights of the sons of men, as musical instruments, and that of all sorts" (Ecc. 2:8).*

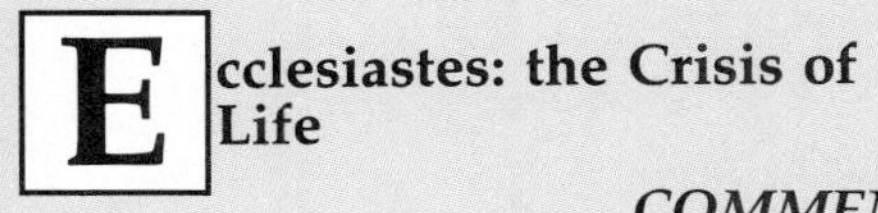

Ecclesiastes: the Crisis of Life

COMMENTS

The Book of Ecclesiastes has been interpreted primarily in one of two ways. Some have suggested that the book represents the musings of a weary, cynical old man who has drifted away from God. The author is described as skeptical and pessimistic. On the other hand, others suggest just the opposite, that the author is a man of faith who simply tells his readers that man cannot find lasting profit and value in this life apart from the only ultimate values in God's Word. It is this latter view that is here defended.

Organizing the thought of Ecclesiastes is difficult because the argument of the book is repetitive, contains different literary types, and seems to alternate between negative and positive ideas. However, as one reads through the book he quickly becomes aware that the author of the book is concerned primarily with a problem or crisis. This crisis revolves around two main ideas. The first idea expressing the crisis of life is found in passages which emphasize that man cannot observe lasting value and significance in life. This idea is expressed in a number of different ways. Foremost among these is the recurring refrain, "All is vanity." This expression is the theme of the book and the most apparent method of expressing the problem faced by the author. The interpretation of the key word "vanity" then becomes very important. The Hebrew word for "vanity" occurs 38 times in Ecclesiastes (out of 73 in the entire Old Testament). Since it is difficult to translate in Ecclesiastes, many suggestions have been offered: "vanity," "emptiness," "meaningless," "breath," "absurd," and "nothingness." The key idea of the word however is clearly revealed in 1:3 where the initial refrain, "All is vanity," is followed by this explanatory question: "What profit hath a man of all his labor which he taketh under the sun?" Thus the primary idea of "vanity" is a lack of profit and value in life. It must quickly be added that the author does not say that value is not present. He simply emphasizes that value cannot be *observed*. He uses such expressions as "I saw"; "I have seen"; "I perceived," etc. Also, the thesis statement is limited to that which one sees "under the sun" (29 times), "under heaven" (3 times), or "on the earth" (4 times). In sum, the author's judgment on life is that man cannot visibly see its profitability or value. He cannot determine purpose and value in life by observation. Life is therefore futile to the observer, and this is the crisis man faces.

Closely related to the thesis that "all is vanity" is the related theme that man is limited. This idea is expressed in a number of passages: man's power is limited (1:3-11); man cannot change things (v. 15); man cannot alter God's actions (3:14); man's power declines in old age (12:1-7); man's knowledge is limited (3:11); man cannot know the future (8:7); man cannot comprehend God's work (v. 17), etc. Thus, man's limitations complicate the crisis of life. Man not only cannot observe profit in life, but he has neither the power nor the knowledge to deal adequately with the crisis. This leaves only God Himself as the source of help to deal with man's crisis.

The second idea which expresses the crisis of life is centered in God. The first idea emphasizes man's crisis and his woefully inadequate limitations in dealing with it. The second idea emphasizes the fact that God does not resolve man's crisis but remains hidden in His person, work, and justice. More specifically, God's person is present, but He remains hidden (5:1-7); God's work is hidden (3:9-14; 7:13-14; 8:17; etc.); and God's justice is hidden (3:16-17; 8:11-13; 9:1-2; 11:9; 12:14). One should especially note 3:9-14. This passage shows not only that God has an active part in earthly activity but that God's work is a unit ("work" not "works"), includes all events, is eternal, is immutable, and cannot be comprehended by man.

In sum, the Book of Ecclesiastes pictures man in a crisis. Man is like the person who is trying to put a puzzle together without all of the pieces. He cannot see its value or profit. On the other hand, God, who alone can provide the missing pieces, has chosen not to reveal them. Man is left to rely solely on what God has revealed.

Preview

The Meaning of Life

ECCLESIASTES 3–12

Lord Byron, the famed English poet, wrote:

"Count o'er the joys thine hours have seen,
Count o'er the days from anguish free,
And know, whatever thou hast been,
'Tis something better not to be!"

These words represent possibly the most direct and depressing summary of life from a nonbeliever's perspective ever penned. Byron, like Solomon of old, had apparently once conducted his own search for peace and purpose. And his conclusion? Simply this: Even if your life had consisted only of those revered joyful and fruitful days, it would still have been better if you had never been born! An epitaph on a tombstone once read:

I was not
I became
I am not
I care not

How different the conclusion of King Solomon. Here his wisdom shines in its most brilliant light—"Find God early and fear God always!"

Overview

<table>
<tr><td>SCRIPTURE</td><td colspan="4">Ecclesiastes 3–12</td></tr>
<tr><td>SUBJECT</td><td colspan="4">Discoveries and decisions</td></tr>
<tr><td rowspan="5">SPECIFICS</td><td rowspan="5">What Solomon discovered about life</td><td>It is hopeless</td><td rowspan="5">What Solomon decided about life</td><td rowspan="5">"Let us hear the conclusion of the whole matter: Fear God, and keep His commandments; for this is the whole duty of man" (Ecc. 12:13).</td></tr>
<tr><td>It is merciless</td></tr>
<tr><td>It is comfortless</td></tr>
<tr><td>It is powerless</td></tr>
<tr><td>It is rudderless</td></tr>
<tr><td>SAINTS AND SINNERS</td><td colspan="4"></td></tr>
<tr><td rowspan="2">SENTENCE SUMMARIES</td><td>O.T. Verse</td><td colspan="3">"Seek ye the LORD while He may be found; call ye upon Him while He is near" (Isa. 55:6).</td></tr>
<tr><td>N.T. Verse</td><td colspan="3">"Having therefore these promises, dearly beloved, let us cleanse ourselves from all filthiness of the flesh and spirit, perfecting holiness in the fear of God" (2 Cor. 7:1).</td></tr>
</table>

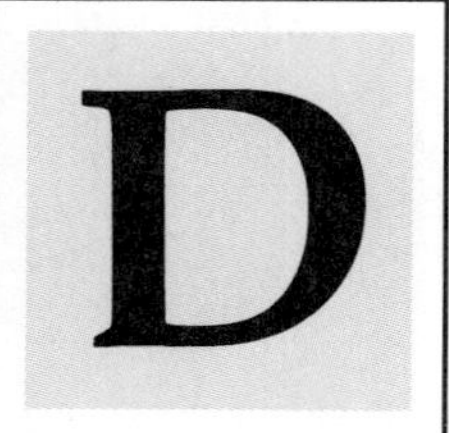

ISCOVERIES AND DECISIONS

The digest—man's problems studied. After completing an exhaustive (and doubtless exhausting) journey, Solomon returned home and contemplated his travels. He concluded the following about life apart from God.

*It is utterly futile: *"Then I looked on all the works that my hands had wrought, and on the labor that I had labored to do; and, behold, all was vanity and vexation of spirit, and there was no profit under the sun" (Ecc. 2:11).*

*It is permeated with sorrow: *"So I returned, and considered all the oppressions that are done under the sun. And behold the tears of such as were oppressed, and they had no comforter; and on the side of the oppressors there was power; but they had no comforter" (4:1).*

*It is grievous and frustrating: *"Therefore I hated life; because the work that is wrought under the sun is grievous unto me: for all is vanity and vexation of spirit" (2:17).*

*It is uncertain: *"I returned, and saw under the sun, that the race is not to the swift, nor the battle to the strong, neither yet bread to the wise, nor yet riches to men of understanding, nor yet favor to men of skill; but time and chance happeneth to them all. For man also knoweth not his time; as the fishes that are taken in an evil net, and as the birds that are caught in the snare; so are the sons of men snared in an evil time, when it falleth suddenly upon them" (9:11-12).*

*It is without purpose: *"Wherefore I praised the dead which are already dead more than the living which are yet alive. Yea, better is he than both they, which hath not yet been, who hath not seen the evil work that is done under the sun" (4:2-3).*

"Then I commended mirth, because a man hath no better thing under the sun, than to eat, and to drink, and to be merry; for that shall abide with him of his labor the days of his life, which God giveth him under the sun" (8:15).

*It is incurable: *"That which is crooked cannot be made straight; and that which is wanting cannot be numbered" (1:15).*

*It is unjust: *"All things have I seen in the days of my vanity: there is a just man that perisheth in his righteousness, and there is a wicked man that prolongeth his life in his wickedness" (7:15).*

"Folly is set in great dignity, and the rich sit in low place. I have seen servants upon horses, and the princes walking as servants upon the earth" (10:6-7).

*It is on the level of animal existence: *"For that which befalleth the sons of men befalleth beasts; even one thing befalleth them; as the one dieth, so dieth the other; yea, they have all one breath; so that a man hath no preeminence above a beast. For all is vanity" (3:19).*

The best—man's problems solved. Solomon concluded that even with God, life is a mystery, but apart from Him it becomes a horrible nightmare. Therefore, it was best if man could do the following things.

*Find God early in his life: *"Rejoice, O young man, in thy youth; and let thy heart cheer thee in the days of thy youth, and walk in the ways of thine heart, and in the sight of thine eyes. But know thou, that for all these things God will bring thee into judgment. Therefore remove sorrow from thy heart, and put away evil from thy flesh: for childhood and youth are vanity" (11:9-10).*

"Remember now thy Creator in the days of thy youth, while the evil days come not, nor the years draw nigh, when thou shalt say, 'I have no pleasure in them.' While the sun, or the light, or the moon, or the stars, be not darkened, nor the clouds return after the rain" (12:1-2).

*Fear God throughout life: *"Let us hear the conclusion of the whole matter: Fear God, and keep His commandments. For this is the whole duty of man. For God shall bring every work into judgment, with every secret thing, whether it be good, or whether it be evil" (vv. 13-14).*

Some of the most striking sentences ever written concerning a human being growing old are found here in this final chapter. Especially note verses 3-7.

"In the day when the keepers of the house [legs] shall tremble, and the strong men shall bow themselves [shoulders], and the grinders [teeth] cease because they are few, and those that look out of the windows [eyes] be darkened. And the doors [ears] shall be shut in the streets; when the sound [voice] of the grinding is low, and he shall rise up at the voice of the bird [old people rise early], and all the daughters of music shall be brought low [inability to sing]. Also when they shall be afraid of that which is high, and fears shall be in the way [fear of traveling] and the almond tree [gray hair, or no hair] shall flourish, and the grasshopper

shall be a burden [frayed nerves], and desire [romance] shall fail; because man goeth to his long home, and the mourners go about the streets. Or ever the silver cord [spinal column] is loosed, or the golden bowl [brain] be broken, or the pitcher [lungs] be broken at the fountain, or the wheel [heart] broken at the cistern."

Ecclesiastes: The Crisis of Life Resolved

COMMENTS

It has been argued that there are two "negative" aspects of Ecclesiastes' thought: first, man is faced with a crisis of value in life (and is too limited to deal with it) and second, God, who alone can solve the crisis, remains hidden in His person, work, and justice. One might therefore conclude that no positive drives remain for man and that the author of the book might encourage men to join with sinners in their wickedness. Such is not the case. At least three key ideas from the book are quite positive and give to man an adequate, though not complete, solution to his problem.

The first clear resolution to man's crisis of value is found in the commands to fear God. There are at least six commands in the book which compel man to fear God (3:14; 5:7; 7:15-18; 8:12-13; 12:1, 13-14). The most important of these is the last one which puts the capstone to the book: "Fear God and keep His commandments." The single-most important response to man's crisis is to submit himself to God. The primary meaning of the expression "to fear God" means to submit oneself to God. When you fear something, you either run from it or submit to it. This latter idea is obviously what is involved here. The commandments referred to here represent God's laws which must be obeyed. Certainly therefore, the conclusion of the book shows that the author is not a cynic, pessimist, skeptic, or the like, but rather a man of God who counsels his readers to obey God. The epilogue of the book itself places Ecclesiastes among the wise (v. 11) and states that his words were acceptable, upright, and true (v. 10).

A second resolution to the crisis of man is found in the exhortations to enjoy one's life and work. At least seven passages in the book contain such exhortations: 2:24-25; 3:12-13, 22; 5:18-20; 8:15; 9:7-10; 11:7-10. The expression "to eat and drink" occurs in five out of these seven passages. Some have interpreted the expression in a negative sense, as though the writer were a hedonist who encouraged his readers to live it up with no thought of God. This view cannot be true, however, since the author wrote a number of times that man should fear God. Rather, these exhortations must be taken in a positive sense because God desires man to enjoy life. These passages could be summarized as follows: (1) To enjoy the good things God has given man is to do His will. (2) In light of our inability to deal with life's crisis, we must be content with our lot in life and enjoy it. (3) Labor, which is one of the main problems in the crisis of life, can actually become a source of enjoyment when one realizes its proper place in God's plan. Therefore, Ecclesiastes is far from a negative book. The author encourages his readers to enjoy life but within God's revealed will. Not to enjoy life is to fall short of God's intention.

Finally, there is a third resolution to the crisis of value in life: the proper use of wisdom. It is true that Ecclesiastes often records explicit statements of wisdom's limitations (2:15; 6:8; 7:16; 8:17), but these are designed only to show that wisdom cannot solve man's basic problem. Ecclesiastes does not contradict the Book of Proverbs. The latter book is concerned with wisdom's benefit, but Ecclesiastes with wisdom's limitations. Both emphases have their proper place. On the other hand, Ecclesiastes contains explicit statements which show that wisdom is essential to life (7:11-12, 19; 9:17-18). Also, in many places the author quotes the sayings of the wise, as examples of appropriate conduct to follow (7:1-14; 9:17–10:20).

To sum up Ecclesiastes' ideas, one may say that Solomon pictures man under a crisis of value. Man cannot put life together and his own limitations in power and wisdom fail him. Then too God Himself does not relieve the crisis. Man is therefore left to live by that which God has revealed: submission to God and His commands, enjoyment of one's life and work, and the proper use of wisdom. The Book of Ecclesiastes in this particular understanding then becomes a very positive book which helps man cope with a puzzling life in a fallen world.

Preview

How a Shepherd and His Sweetheart Became a King and a Queen

SONG OF SOLOMON

How could he best depict the love Christ has for His church? Perhaps it could be compared to that affection a father has for his only son, or the devotion felt by a daughter for her mother. These human comparisons would certainly have been readily understood. But no, the Apostle Paul would be directed by God's Spirit to employ the most intimate and immeasurable love of all in describing the Saviour's love for His church: "Husbands, love your wives, even as Christ also loved the church, and gave Himself for it" (Eph. 5:25).

The Song of Solomon in a very real sense serves both as a review and preview.

The review: That love which should exist between a man and his wife. That love which God had for Israel.

The preview: That love Christ showed when He died for His bride, the church.

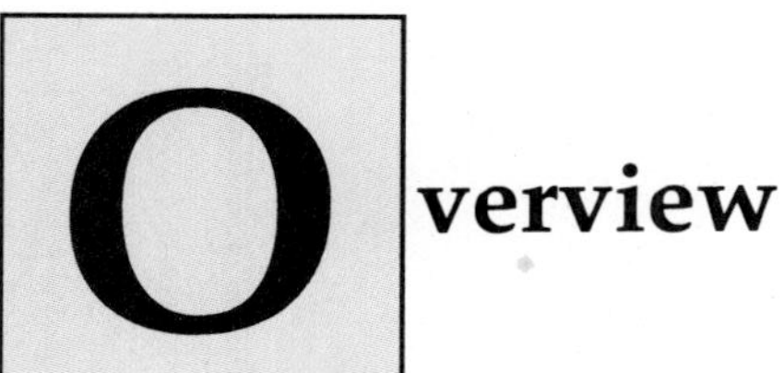

Overview

<table>
<tr><td>SCRIPTURE</td><td colspan="2">Song of Solomon</td></tr>
<tr><td>SUBJECT</td><td colspan="2">Solomon and his bride</td></tr>
<tr><td rowspan="4">SPECIFICS</td><td>The Shulamite Cinderella</td><td>The mighty monarch</td></tr>
<tr><td>Her drudgery</td><td rowspan="2">Choosing his bride as a shepherd</td></tr>
<tr><td>Her dreams</td></tr>
<tr><td>Her discovery</td><td>Claiming his bride as a sovereign</td></tr>
<tr><td>SAINTS AND SINNERS</td><td colspan="2"></td></tr>
<tr><td rowspan="2">SENTENCE SUMMARIES</td><td>O.T. Verses</td><td>"She shall be brought unto the king in raiment of needlework; the virgins her companions that follow her shall be brought unto thee. With gladness and rejoicing shall they be brought; they shall enter into the king's palace" (Ps. 45:14-15).</td></tr>
<tr><td>N.T. Verses</td><td>"Let us be glad and rejoice, and give honor to Him; for the marriage of the Lamb is come, and His wife hath made herself ready" (Rev. 19:7).</td></tr>
</table>

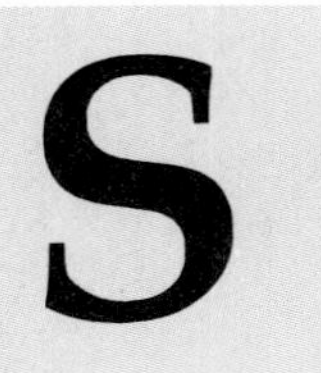

SOLOMON AND HIS BRIDE

Act one—the Shulamite Cinderella. Solomon had a vineyard in the hill country of Ephraim, just outside the little town of Shunam, about 50 miles north of Jerusalem. This vineyard was rented out to a family of sharecroppers consisting of a mother, two sons, and two daughters. The oldest of these girls was the Shulamite. The Shulamite was the Cinderella of the family, having great natural beauty, but unnoticed by the world. Her brothers made her work very hard tending the vineyards, so that she had little opportunity to care for her personal appearance. She pruned the vines, set traps for the little foxes, and kept the flocks. Being out in the open so often, she became sunburned.

Act two—the shepherd stranger. One day a mysterious handsome stranger came to the vineyard and soon won the heart of the Shulamite girl. Unknown to her, he was Solomon, disguised as a lowly shepherd. She asked about his flocks. He answered evasively, but was very definite concerning his love for her. He left her, but promised he would someday return to her.

During his absence she dreamed of him twice. In the first dream they were already married and one night she awakened to find him missing from her bed. She quickly dressed and went out looking for him.

In the second dream her beloved returned and besought her to open the door and let him in. But she refused for she was unwilling to reclothe herself and soil her feet going to the door. Soon, however, her heart smote her for this shabby action and she leaped for the door. But he had already gone. The bride then began her frantic search for the lover she had so carelessly ignored. During her search the guards of the city mistreated her, and the watchman on the wall tore off her veil. She then pleaded with the women of Jerusalem to aid her in finding her lover and informing him of her love for him. Suddenly and joyfully she discovered his whereabouts.

"My beloved is gone down into his garden, to the beds of spices, to feed in the gardens, and to gather lilies. I am my beloved's and my beloved is mine. He feedeth among the lilies" (6:2-3).

These then, are the two dreams concerning the mysterious shepherd lover of the Shulamite girl. But why did he leave her? Where did he go? Would he ever return?

Act three—the mighty monarch. One day the little town of Shunam received some electrifying news. King Solomon himself was approaching their city. But the lovesick and lonely maiden was not interested, and took no further notice until word was brought to her that the powerful potentate himself desired to see her.

She was puzzled until she was brought into his presence where she recognized him as her beloved shepherd. He then gently explained to her that she would be his choice bride and true love. He invited her to come with him and promised to care for her little sister.

The bride was then placed into the king's chariot, made from the wood of Lebanon, with silver posts, a golden canopy, and purple seating. Together they rode off to the royal palace in Jerusalem, accompanied by 60 mighty swordsmen and experienced bodyguards.

Note the language of love used by the bride and bridegroom as they describe each other. She was the most beautiful girl in the world (1:8); she was like a bouquet of flowers in a garden (v. 14); her eyes were as soft as doves (v. 15); she was as a lily among the thorns (2:2); her hair fell across her face like flocks of goats which frisked across the slopes of Gilead (4:1); her teeth were as white as sheep's wool (v. 2); her lips were like a thread of scarlet (v. 3) and made of honey (v. 11); her neck was as stately as the Tower of David (v. 4); her bosom was as twin fawns of a gazelle, feeding among the lilies (v. 5); she was like a lovely orchard, bearing precious fruit (v. 13); she was as a garden fountain, a well of living water, refreshing as the streams from the Lebanon mountains (v. 15); her thighs were like jewels, the work of the most skilled craftsmen (7:1); her navel was as lovely as a goblet filled with wine (v. 2); her waist was like a heap of wheat set about with lilies (v. 2); her nose was shapely like the Tower of Lebanon overlooking Damascus (v. 4); and he was completely overcome by a single glance of her beautiful eyes (4:9).

He was as swift as a young gazelle leaping and bounding over the hills (2:9); he was tanned and handsome, the fairest of 10,000 (5:10); his head was as purest gold, covered by wavy, raven hair (v. 11); his eyes were as doves beside the water brooks, deep and quiet (v. 12); his cheeks were like sweetly scented beds of spice (v. 13); his lips were as perfumed lilies and his breath like myrrh (v. 13); his arms were as round bars of gold set with beryl (v. 14); and his eyes were pillars of marble set in sockets of finest gold, like cedars of Lebanon (v. 15).

The Interpretation of the Song of Solomon

COMMENTS

Interpretations of the Song of Solomon down through the ages are much too numerous for any one man to compass. By about 1700, for example, there were already over 500 commentaries on this unusual book. The reasons for such varied interpretations are obvious: spiritual themes seem to be lacking; the plot, if any, is vague; and its erotic descriptions seem to many to be out of place in God's Word, if taken literally. In light of these problems several key views have been defended by Bible scholars and are worthy of examination.

One early interpretation, which is no longer held, may be labeled as *allegorical.* This view provided an easy escape for those offended by the explicit descriptions in the book. The literal contents of the book were ignored and every item was said to represent some deeper truth. The entire Song, for example, was said to represent God's love and dealings with Israel. More specifically, the maiden's breasts were said to represent the Old and New Testaments! This view fell into disrepute since interpreters found themselves constantly vying for the most ingenious new suggestion.

Another popular interpretation, which is still advocated by many today, is the *typical* interpretation. Unlike the allegorical view, the typical view does accept the literal nature of the love described in the book but, at the same time, it minimizes its application. The Song is said to be a type of Christ's love for the church. It is true that marriage is used to illustrate Christ's relationship to the church (Eph. 5:22-33) and that types of Christ in the Old Testament certainly do exist as, for example, the serpent in the wilderness (Num. 21:4-9; John 3:14). However, there seems little indication in the text that an extended story such as the Song is to be taken in its entirety as typical.

In light of the subjectivity of the preceding interpretations, there has been a return in recent times to the *literal* view. This interpretation may be subdivided into two views. The three character view (or "shepherd hypothesis") interprets the book as an example of the proverbial "lover's triangle." Solomon is depicted as the wealthy king who tries to win the Shulamite maiden from her shepherd lover. In this view Solomon becomes the villain and the local shepherd boy the hero. This view is said to account for the fact that the lover is called a shepherd (1:7-8), but there is no reason why Solomon could not be pictured in the story as both king and shepherd since he had many flocks and herds (Ecc. 2:7). It is this literal two-character view that fits best with a literal interpretation of the book, the same method of interpretation which we try to use elsewhere.

Other interpretations include the following: a collection of marriage songs used in a week-long marriage feast; a liturgy for the fertility rites of the Tammuz cult, and a collection of love songs unrelated to any specific occasion. All of these views are fraught with difficulties, however, and force us back to a literal view.

If the book is to be taken literally, how then can it adequately picture married love, since Solomon had 1,000 wives and concubines? (1 Kings 11:3) The probable answer to this question is found in the suggestion that this romance and marriage occurred early in Solomon's reign before his apostasy and polygamy later distorted his moral and spiritual values.

The value of the book for today lies in its main theme which is best expressed in Song 8:7: "Many waters cannot quench love." It is a tribute to the power and vitality of love and marriage. As the only book of the Bible completely devoted to married love, it serves as a testimony to the joy, satisfaction, and fulfillment available to those who follow God's pattern for marriage.

Chaotic Kingdom

"Daddy, what did you do during the war?" All those fathers living from 931 B.C. onward probably had to answer this penetrating question. During that fateful year a nasty—and needless—civil war broke out among Israel's 12 tribes, resulting in two separate kingdoms. The 10 Northern tribes left the 2 Southern ones to form their own nation.

Perhaps Jesus had this very event in mind centuries later when He uttered the following: *"Every kingdom divided against itself is brought to desolation; and every city or house divided against itself shall not stand"* (Matt. 12:25).

The Chaotic Kingdom stage is best characterized through the actions of two official groups—potentates and prophets. More of each appear at this time than at any other period in biblical history.

No less than 39 rulers sat on two thrones, 20 in the South and 19 in the North. Thirty-eight were men, and 1 was a woman. The longest reign was 55 years, and the shortest a mere 7 days.

Ministering to, and more often than not, preaching against these 39 monarchs came the prophets.

Who were they? For the most part, they were God's 11 admonishing authors! Each man appeared and fell like a heavenly hammer on sin and sinners. Their names? Obadiah, Jonah, Nahum, Amos, Hosea, Joel, Isaiah, Micah, Zephaniah, Habakkuk, and Jeremiah.

To whom did they write? One directed his writings to Edom, two to Nineveh, six to the Southern Kingdom, and two to the Northern Kingdom. In fact, an additional two—Elijah and Elisha—were so busy pronouncing judgment and performing miracles that they didn't even take time to write down anything.

What did they write? In a nutshell, shape up spiritually, or be shipped out physically! Or, stated another way, seek God's pardon, or suffer God's punishment. Revival or ruin—which would it be?

How did they fare? Some were ridiculed, others murdered, and the rest totally ignored. And the results? Satan's twin wolves were permitted to prey on God's 12 tribes. Assyria would devour the Northern 10, while Babylon would destroy the Southern 2. The sad words of heartbroken Hosea would become a terrible reality: *"My people are destroyed for lack of knowledge. Because thou hast rejected knowledge, I will also reject thee, that thou shalt be no priest to Me; seeing thou hast forgotten the Law of thy God, I will also forget thy children"* (Hosea 4:6).

Preview

Rulers in the North
(Part One)

1 KINGS 11–16; 2 CHRONICLES 9–16

A sensible request followed by a senseless reply! These eight pointed and pathetic words sadly summarize Israel's tragic Civil War. The year was 931 B.C. The place was Shechem. The occasion was the anointing of Rehoboam, son of Solomon, as Israel's fourth king. But it was not to be. The planned coronation would give way to an unplanned separation.

Here was the sensible request:

"The congregation of Israel . . . spake unto Rehoboam, saying, 'Thy father made our yoke grievous; now, therefore, make thou . . . his heavy yoke which he put upon us, lighter, and we will serve thee' " (1 Kings 12:3-4).

Here was the senseless reply:

"My father made your yoke heavy, and I will add to your yoke: my father also chastised you with whips, but I will chastise you with scorpions" (v. 14).

Well, that did it! Solomon's love for women, wealth, pomp, and power had already seriously weakened the fragile unity among the 12 tribes. But his son's arrogant and abrasive answer was absolutely the last straw, triggering a tragic split. At this time in history, two opposing Hebrew Kingdoms came into being, one in the South and one in the North. Jeroboam, a former cabinet member during Solomon's reign, returned from Egyptian exile and led the 10 Northern tribes' revolt against Judah and Benjamin. Jewish harmony was over. Jewish hostilities would begin.

Overview

SCRIPTURE	1 Kings 11–16; 2 Chronicles 9–16
SUBJECT	Introduction; reigns of Jeroboam, Nadab, Baasha, Elah, Zimri, Omri

SPECIFICS

Two kingdoms		
History	Northern Kingdom	Southern Kingdom
Duration	931–722 B.C.	931–586 B.C.
First ruler	Jeroboam	Rehoboam
Final ruler	Hoshea	Zedekiah
Number of rulers	19	20
Number of tribes	10	2
Capital	Samaria	Jerusalem
Captured by	Assyria	Babylon
Return	No return	3 returns

Six kings	
Jeroboam	His perversion His punishment
Nadab	Assassinated by Baasha
Baasha	Built a wall against Jerusalem
Elah	Assassinated by Zimri
Zimri	Reigned only 7 days
Omri	Founder of Samaria Father of Ahab

SAINTS AND SINNERS	Jeroboam, Nadab, Baasha, Elah, Zimri, Omri, unnamed man of God, false prophet, wife of Jeroboam

SENTENCE SUMMARIES

O.T. Verse	"When the righteous are in authority, the people rejoice; but when the wicked beareth rule, the people mourn" (Prov. 29:2).
N.T. Verse	"Jesus knew their thoughts, and said unto them, 'Every kingdom divided against itself is brought to desolation; and every city or house divided against itself shall not stand' " (Matt. 12:25).

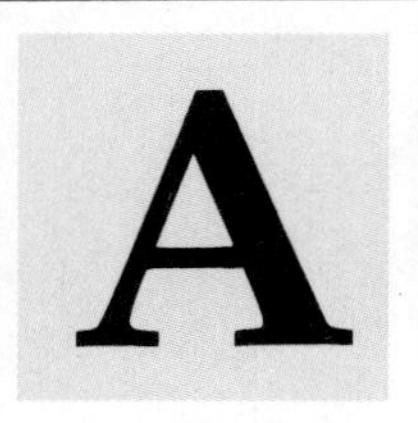

N INTRODUCTION TO THE CHAOTIC KINGDOM STAGE

After the death of Solomon, a tragic civil war split Israel into two opposing Kingdoms, the North and the South.

THE NORTHERN KINGDOM

- It began in 931 B.C. and lasted 209 years.
- The first ruler was Jeroboam.
- The last ruler was Hoshea.
- The total number of kings was 19. Not 1 was godly.
- It consisted of 10 tribes.
- Its capital later became Samaria.
- It was captured by the Assyrians in 722 B.C.
- There was no return from captivity.

THE SOUTHERN KINGDOM

- It began in 931 B.C. and lasted 345 years.
- The first ruler was Rehoboam.
- The last ruler was Zedekiah.
- The total number of rulers was 20, 19 kings and 1 queen. Eight of the 20 were godly.
- It consisted of two tribes (Judah and Benjamin).
- Its capital remained Jerusalem.
- It was captured by the Babylonians in 586 B.C.
- There were three separate returns from Captivity.

NOTE: The Chaotic Kingdom Stage may thus be divided into two time periods:

(1) The Divided Kingdom (both North and South). From 931-722 B.C.

(2) The Single Kingdom (only the South). From 722-586 B.C.

THE RULERS OF THE CHAOTIC KINGDOM STAGE

JEROBOAM—FIRST KING

He reigned for 22 years. Jeroboam was an ex-cabinet member under Solomon. He introduced a false religious system to keep his people from returning to the Jerusalem temple during the three yearly visits required by Moses.

"Whereupon the king took counsel, and made two calves of gold, and said unto them, 'It is too much for you to go up to Jerusalem. Behold thy gods, O Israel, which brought thee up out of the land of Egypt.' And he set the one in Bethel, and the other put he in Dan" (1 Kings 12:28-29).

He degraded the levitical priesthood. "He . . . made priests of the lowest of the people, which were not of the sons of Levi" (v. 31).

He heard an amazing prophecy from a nameless prophet. It was that a Judean king named Josiah would someday destroy Jeroboam's false religion and would burn the bones of the dead priests on the very altar where Jeroboam stood sacrificing (cf. v. 2 with 2 Kings 23:15-16).

He fought against Rehoboam constantly. He was defeated by Abijah (Rehoboam's son) despite outnumbering him two to one. Jeroboam lost one-half million troops in that battle (2 Chron. 13:2-17). It is said of him 21 times that he caused Israel to sin. God continued to speak of his sin even during the days of King Josiah, some 285 years after Jeroboam's death!

His plagues. He died as a result of a plague sent from God.

NADAB—SECOND KING

His reign. He reigned for two years.

His death. He was assassinated by a rebel named Baasha.

BAASHA—THIRD KING

His reign. He reigned for 24 years (909-886).

His works. He killed Nadab and thus fulfilled Ahijah the prophet's prediction. Compare 1 Kings 14:4-16 with 15:29. He fought with Asa (third king of the South) and built a wall to cut off trade to Jerusalem.

His judgment. His seed was predicted to suffer the same judgment as that of Jeroboam.

ELAH—FOURTH KING

His reign. Elah, the son of Baasha, reigned for two years. He was assassinated by a rebel.

ZIMRI—FIFTH KING

His reign and death. He reigned for seven days (885). He fulfilled a prophecy by slaughtering Baasha's seed. He was trapped by rebel soldiers in his own palace, resulting in a fiery suicidal death.

OMRI—SIXTH KING

His reign. He reigned for 12 years (885-873).

His capital. Omri made the city of Samaria the new Northern capital.

His distinction. He was the most wicked king of the North up to that time.

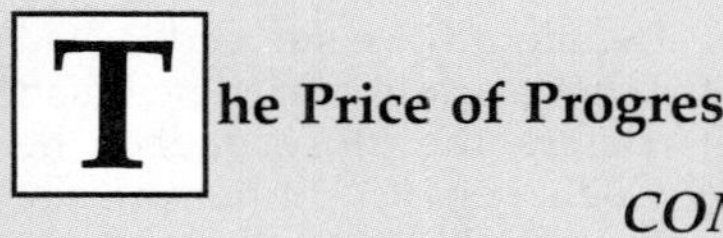

The Price of Progress

COMMENTS

One of the cries growing out of John F. Kennedy's campaign for the presidency of the United States was, "We've got to get this country moving." The country had, indeed, gone through a time of economic recession and Kennedy's youth and vigor caught the imagination of the nation. He was swept into office by a large popular vote, the youngest man ever to be elected to the presidency. His charming young wife and their two beautiful small children also caught the nation's heart. Kennedy appointed the youngest men in history to hold cabinet positions as well as important offices at all levels of government. The entire government had the look of youth and vitality. A new day had come to government.

The idea of "if it's old, it's no good and must be replaced" is not new. Rehoboam, who succeeded his father, Solomon, fell victim to that myth. Before Rehoboam came to power, Saul, David, and Solomon had each ruled Israel for 40 years—120 years and only three kings. Rehoboam thought that the nation had become stagnant and needed a fresh start with bright young men in positions of responsibility in the government. A fresh idea. To implement it, Rehoboam replaced the "old men" who had constituted the administration of Solomon's government with young men of his own appointment. He adopted a policy which said, in effect, "We've got to get this country moving." The government, of course, moves on its resources. There is the problem. The government has no resources except the resources given it from its citizens in the form of taxation. Rehoboam's people were already reeling under the tax burden placed on them by Solomon. Jeroboam I was sent as the representative of the Northern tribes to ask Rehoboam to give the people tax relief (1 Kings 12:3-4). The old men counseled Rehoboam against his new proposals (vv. 6-7) but the young men urged him on (vv. 8-11). Rehoboam rejected the counsel of the old men saying, "My little finger shall be thicker than my father's loins" (v. 10). The new program went into effect. But what was the price of progress? The 10 Northern tribes withdrew to form their own nation. Only Judah and Benjamin were left in the South. Under the leadership of Jeroboam I, the Northern Kingdom went into idolatry. He made two golden calves and set up one in Bethel and the other one in Dan. He instituted a whole worship system of these false gods. "And this thing became a sin" (v. 30) from which they never recovered. They were ultimately carried into captivity by Assyria and never returned.

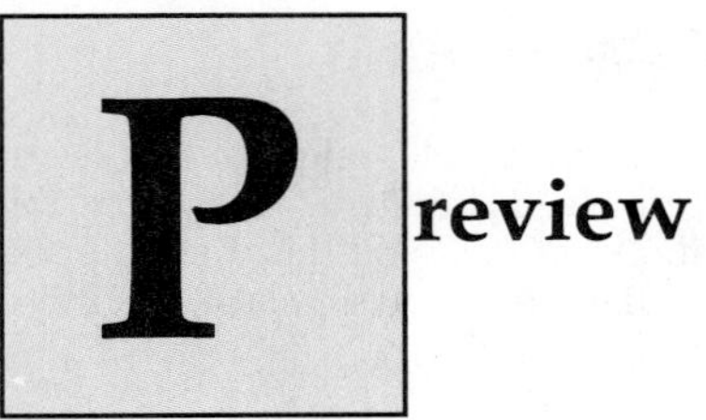

Rulers in the North
(Part Two)

1 KINGS 16–2 KINGS 17; 2 CHRONICLES 18; 20; 22; 28

What a terrible time it was in the North. Six heartless and godless kings in less than 60 years. Jeroboam, Nadab, Baasha, Elah, Zimri, and Omri. Would the ruthless reigns ever end? But now Omri was dead. Perhaps his son, soon to become the seventh ruler of the 10 tribes, would be different. If those hopes were entertained by citizens of the Northern Kingdom, they soon would be cruelly and completely dashed to the ground.

Far from being better, Ahab, the new monarch, proved to be more bloody and blasphemous than the first six combined. His marriage to Jezebel, a beautiful Phoenician princess whose cruelty far surpassed her charm, only intensified Ahab's terrible reign. The queen was a fanatical believer in the devil god Baal. No sooner was Ahab in power than she feverishly began to replace Israel's true God with her fake one. Humanly speaking, she might have succeeded had it not been for that fearless crusader, Elijah the prophet. Before the story ended, he would revive God's people, kill her priests, and predict doom for both Ahab and Jezebel. Mangy dogs, according to the prophecy, would be connected with each death. Those wild creatures would lick up Ahab's spilled blood, and eat Jezebel's crushed flesh.

Ahab died in 852 B.C. During the next 131 years 12 more kings would sit on the Northern throne, none of whom sought God. Finally, during the reign of Hoshea, Israel's last monarch, the brutal Assyrians invaded the land, carrying its citizens off into captivity. Thus, the once-free people of God became slaves of Satan. Such is the terrible cost of sin.

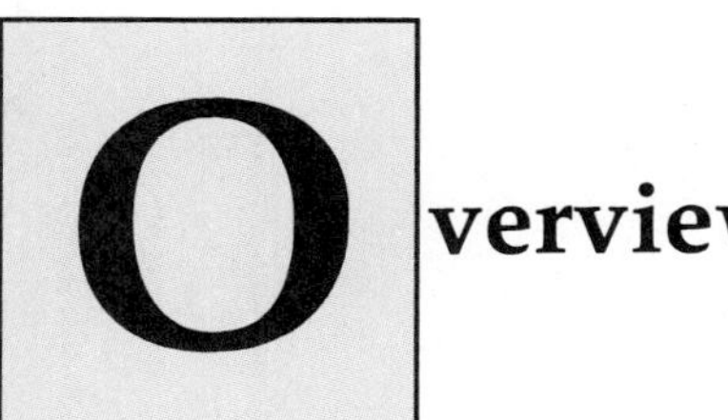

verview

SCRIPTURE	1 Kings 16–2 Kings 17; 2 Chronicles 18; 20; 22; 28			
SUBJECT	Reigns of Ahab, Ahaziah, Jehoram, Jehu, Jehoahaz, Jehoash, Jeroboam II, Zechariah, Shallum, Menahem, Pekahiah, Pekah, Hoshea			
SPECIFICS	Ahab	His debauchery in Samaria His death in Syria	Jehoahaz	His sin led to a temporary Syrian occupation
			Jehoash	Visited Elisha on his deathbed
	Ahaziah	Attempted to arrest Elijah	Jeroboam II	Most powerful Northern ruler
	Jehoram	The king and a Syrian leper The king and 4 Israelite lepers	Zechariah	Murdered by Shallum
			Shallum	Murdered by Menahem
			Menahem	Most brutal Northern ruler
			Pekahiah	Murdered by Pekah
	Jehu	The chariot driver The blood-letter	Pekah	Beginning of Assyrian invasions
			Hoshea	Completion of Assyrian captivity
SAINTS AND SINNERS	Ahab, Ahaziah, Jehoram, Jehu, Jehoahaz, Jehoash, Jeroboam II, Zechariah, Shallum, Menahem, Pekahiah, Pekah, Hoshea, Micaiah, Jezebel, Elijah, Elisha, Zedekiah, 2 resurrected sons, Obadiah, priests of Baal, Naboth			
SENTENCE SUMMARIES	O.T. Verse	"Whoso loveth wisdom rejoiceth his father; but he that keepeth company with harlots spendeth his substance" (Prov. 29:3).		
	N.T. Verse	"Let them alone. They be blind leaders of the blind. And if the blind lead the blind, both shall fall into the ditch" (Matt. 15:14).		

HIRTEEN EVIL KINGS

1 Kings 12-22
2 Kings
2 Chronicles 10-36
Obadiah
Joel
Jonah
Amos
Hosea
Isaiah
Micah
Nahum
Zephaniah
Jeremiah
Habakkuk

THE SOUTHERN KINGDOM

REHOBOAM	JOTHAM
ABIJAM	AHAZ
ASA	HEZEKIAH
JEHOSHAPHAT	MANASSEH
JEHORAM	AMON
AHAZIAH	JOSIAH
ATHALIAH	JEHOAHAZ
JOASH	JEHOIAKIM
AMAZIAH	JEHOIACHIN
UZZIAH	ZEDEKIAH

THE NORTHERN KINGDOM

JEROBOAM	JEHOAHAZ
NADAB	JEHOASH
BAASHA	JEROBOAM II
ELAH	ZECHARIAH
ZIMRI	SHALLUM
OMRI	MENAHEM
AHAB	PEKAHIAH
AHAZIAH	PEKAH
JEHORAM	HOSHEA
JEHU	

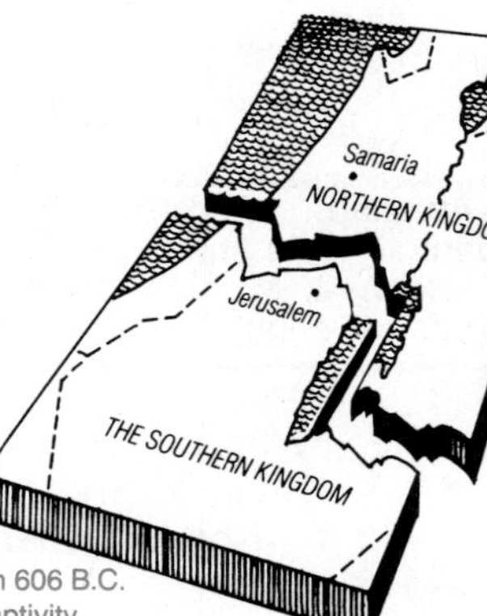

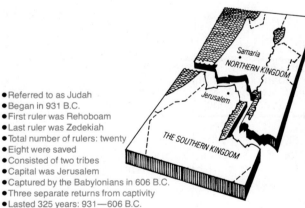

- Referred to as Judah
- Began in 931 B.C.
- First ruler was Rehoboam
- Last ruler was Zedekiah
- Total number of rulers: twenty
- Eight were saved
- Consisted of two tribes
- Capital was Jerusalem
- Captured by the Babylonians in 606 B.C.
- Three separate returns from captivity
- Lasted 325 years: 931—606 B.C.

- Referred to as Israel and Ephraim
- Began in 931 B.C.
- First ruler was Jeroboam
- Last ruler was Hoshea
- Total number of rulers: nineteen
- Not one was saved
- Consisted of ten tribes
- Capital was Samaria
- Captured by the Assyrians in 721 B.C.
- No return from captivity
- Lasted 210 years: 931—721 B.C.

AHAB—SEVENTH KING

Ahab and Jezebel. Ahab married Jezebel and built a temple to Baal in Samaria. He was more wicked than his father Omri. *"And Ahab the son of Omri did evil in the sight of the* L*ORD above all that were before him. And it came to pass, as if it had been a light thing for him to walk in the sins of Jeroboam the son of Nebat, that he took to wife Jezebel the daughter of Ethbaal king of the Zidonians, and went and served Baal, and worshiped him. And he reared up an altar for Baal in the house of Baal, which he had built in Samaria" (1 Kings 16:30-32).*

At the beginning of his reign a 500-year-old prophecy was fulfilled concerning the rebuilding of Jericho (v. 34; compare with Josh. 6:26). After destroying the city, Joshua predicted that the man who would presume to rebuild Jericho would lose his firstborn son at the foundational laying, and his youngest son at the setting up of the gates. During the reign of Ahab a man from Bethel named Hiel rebuilt Jericho. His firstborn son, Abiram, died at its completion.

Ahab and Elijah. He was confronted by Elijah and warned that due to his sin and Israel's wickedness, a three-and-one-half-year famine would occur. Ahab saw his Baalite priests defeated and destroyed by Elijah on Mount Carmel. This included all 850 priests supported by Jezebel.

Ahab and God. He was allowed by God to defeat the arrogant Syrians on two occasions to prove a point, the point being that Jehovah is Lord over all. After their first defeat the Syrians concluded their problem was of a geographical nature. *"And the servants of the king of Syria said unto him, 'Their gods are gods of the hills; therefore, they were stronger than we. But let us fight against them in the plain, and surely we shall be stronger than they' " (20:23).*

However, the real difficulty was theological.

"And there came a man of God, and spoke unto the king of Israel, and said, 'Thus saith the LORD, "Because the Syrians have said, 'The LORD is God of the hills, but He is not God of the valleys,' therefore, will I deliver all this great multitude into thine hand, and ye shall know that I am the LORD" ' " (v. 28).

As a result of divine intervention, the Syrians lost 127,000 troops.

After the final battle, Ahab disobeyed God and treated the Syrian king, his former enemy, as a long-lost brother. Because of this, Ahab's death was predicted by an unnamed prophet.

"And he said unto him, 'Thus saith the LORD, "Because thou hast let go out of thy hand a man whom I appointed to utter destruction, therefore thy life shall go for his life, and thy people for his people" ' " (v. 42).

Ahab and Naboth. Ahab attempted unsuccessfully to buy a vineyard from Naboth. He then permitted Jezebel to plot the murder of Naboth. Elijah met him in the vineyard and issued a threefold prediction: (a) the dogs would lick Ahab's blood where they had licked Naboth's blood; (b) Ahab's dynasty would be destroyed; and (c) the dogs would eat Jezebel. As a result, Ahab experienced a brief (but temporary) remorse.

Ahab and Micaiah. During a war meeting against Syria between Ahab and Jehoshaphat, his death was once again predicted by a godly prophet named Micaiah.

"And he said, 'I saw all Israel scattered upon the hills, as sheep that have not a shepherd: and the LORD said, "These have no master; let them return every man to his house in peace" ' " (22:17).

Ahab was killed in battle during his third Syrian campaign as God had predicted. To win a bet, a Syrian soldier shot a random arrow in the sky. God guided it to plunge into a small area in Ahab's chest which was not protected by his armor.

"So the king died, and was brought to Samaria; and they buried the king in Samaria. And one washed the chariot in the pool of Samaria; and the dogs licked up his blood; and they washed his armor; according unto the word of the LORD which He spake" (vv. 37-38).

AHAZIAH—EIGHTH KING

Ahaziah reigned for two years (853-852). He was the oldest son of Ahab and Jezebel.

He persuaded Jehoshaphat to enter into a shipbuilding enterprise with him at Ezion-Geber.

He suffered a severe fall (which proved fatal) in his palace in Samaria. When he turned to the pagan god Baal-Zebub for healing, he was rebuked by Elijah, whom he unsuccessfully attempted to arrest.

JEHORAM—NINTH KING

He reigned for 12 years (852-841).

He was the youngest son of Ahab and Jezebel.

He persuaded Jehoshaphat to ally with him against Syria. Elisha the prophet performed a miracle (for Jehoshaphat's sake) which won the battle. Elisha later helped Jehoram by warning him of several planned Syrian ambushes. Elisha would, however, prevent him from slaughtering some supernaturally blinded Syrian troops.

He was on the throne when Naaman came to be healed of leprosy and when God used four lepers to save Samaria from starvation.

He was finally murdered by Jehu in the Valley of Jezreel.

The Gods of the Hills

COMMENTS

"I will lift up mine eyes unto the hills, from whence cometh my help. My help cometh from the LORD, which made heaven and earth" (Ps. 121:1-2). These frequently quoted verses are usually misunderstood by those who quote them. The problem is in the way they are rendered in the common English versions. The "from whence cometh my help" clause appears to be adverbial telling the source of the psalmist's strength, i.e., in the hills. To understand the psalmist's thought properly, the words should be translated: "I will lift up mine eyes unto the hills. From whence cometh my help? My help cometh from the LORD which made heaven and earth." The thought is clear. He is distinguishing the Lord (Jehovah) from the gods worshiped by the heathen. This psalm was one of the songs of "degrees" or "ascents" sung as the pilgrims approached Jerusalem which was built on the highest mountain in Israel. The psalmist is saying that he will lift up his eyes to the hills on which Jerusalem is situated. He clearly recognizes that Jehovah does not dwell in the mountains like the tribal mountain deities. His help comes from the Jehovah who not only made the mountains in which the heathen think their deities dwell, but also the heavens and the earth.

From early days mankind, being ignorant of Jehovah, has mistakenly thought that their gods dwelt in the hilltops. The Greeks thought that the gods of their pantheon dwelt on Mount Olympus. Ben-hadad, king of the Syrians, and the 32 kings with him, made the mistake of thinking that the God of Israel was a simple god of the hills. They thought this because though they had successfully warred against Samaria and had besieged it and demanded "unconditional surrender" (1 Kings 20:1-3) to which Ahab, king of Israel, agreed (v. 4), the God of Israel intervened (v. 13) and put Ben-hadad to rout (vv. 20-21). The people with Ben-hadad had a ready explanation for the defeat. The battle had taken place in the mountains in which Samaria was situated. They reasoned that the God of Israel was a god of the hills (v. 23). Since the battle had taken place in the hills, Israel's superiority must be attributable to their gods. The gods of the Syrians, by contrast, were gods of the plain. Their theology governed their military strategy. They reasoned that if they could lure Israel to fight in the plain they would have superiority over them. A year later, Ben-hadad returned to Aphek on the coastal plain southwest of Samaria (v. 26). Jehovah sent His prophet to the king of Israel to assure him of victory "Because the Syrians have said, 'The LORD is God of the hills, but He is not God of the valleys' " (v. 28). In the ensuing battle Israel slew 100,000 infantrymen. The 27,000 who escaped the slaughter, retreated to Aphek only to be slain by a wall which fell on them (vv. 29-30). Ben-hadad threw himself on the mercy of the king of Israel and successfully negotiated a covenant of surrender which displeased the Lord because Ben-hadad's life was spared (vv. 31-36).

While Israel benefited from Jehovah's deliverance, the victory was not primarily given for that purpose. Jehovah wanted Israel to know that He definitely was not a god of the hills nor a god of the valleys. He wanted Israel to know that He was "the LORD" (v. 28), the eternal Jehovah whom the psalmist proclaimed to be the Creator of the heavens and the earth. He not only is the Maker of the hills and valleys, He is also the Creator of the heavens and heavenly bodies above. Jehovah is infinite and infinitely superior to the heathen deities which exist only as products of their own creation. He is not to be confused with the gods of man's imagination. Before Him, they and all mankind are helpless. The victory, then, was a call for Israel to change its mind about Him. Israel, however, failed to learn this all-important message.

JEHU—TENTH KING

The anointed. Jehu reigned for 28 years (841-814).

Elijah had been commanded to anoint Jehu as king, but for some reason had not done so. Therefore, Elisha anointed him, using the services of a young preacher boy.

The assassin. Jehu became notorious for his chariot-riding and bloodletting. He would execute Judean King Ahaziah, grandson of Jehoshaphat, Northern King Jehoram, who was ruler of Israel at the time, and Jezebel.

"And when Jehu was come to Jezreel, Jezebel heard of it; and she painted her face, and tired her head, and looked out at a window.

"And as Jehu entered in at the gate, she said, 'Had Zimri peace, who slew his master?'

"And he lifted up his face to the window, and said, 'Who is on my side? Who?' And there looked out to him two or three eunuchs.

"And he said, 'Throw her down.' So they threw her down; and some of her blood was sprinkled on the wall, and on the horses, and he trode her underfoot.

"And when he was come in, he did eat and drink, and said, 'Go, see now this cursed woman, and bury her; for she is a king's daughter.'

"And they went to bury her; but they found no more of her than the skull, and the feet, and the palms of her hands. Wherefore they came again, and told him. And he said, 'This is the word of the LORD, which He spake by His servant Elijah the Tishbite, saying, "In the portion of Jezreel shall dogs eat the flesh of Jezebel. And the carcass of Jezebel shall be as dung upon the face of the field in the portion of Jezreel; so that they shall not say, 'This is Jezebel' " ' " (2 Kings 9:30-37).

Jehu also killed Ahab's 70 sons, 42 royal princes of Judah, and the Baalite worshipers.

The apostate. In spite of his Baalite reforms, Jehu continued worshiping the golden calves set up by Jeroboam.

JEHOAHAZ—ELEVENTH KING

He reigned for 17 years (814-798). He was the son of Jehu. He saw his army almost wiped out by the Syrians.

"And the anger of the LORD was kindled against Israel, and He delivered them into the hand of Hazael king of Syria, and into the hand of Ben-hadad the son of Hazael, all their days. And Jehoahaz besought the LORD, and the LORD hearkened unto him; for He saw the oppression of Israel, because the king of Syria oppressed them. (And the LORD gave Israel a savior, so that they went out from under the hand of the Syrians, and the Children of Israel dwelt in their tents, as beforetime)" (13:3-5).

He experienced a brief period of remorse over his sins but apparently not genuine repentance.

JEHOASH—TWELFTH KING

He reigned for 16 years (798-782), 11 of those years in a coregency with Jeroboam II.

He visited Elisha on his deathbed and defeated Amaziah (sixth king of Judah) on the battlefield. He related one of the two Old Testament fables to ridicule the arrogant claims of Amaziah.

"And Jehoash the king of Israel sent to Amaziah king of Judah, saying, 'The thistle that was in Lebanon sent to the cedar that was in Lebanon, saying, "Give thy daughter to my son to wife": and there passed by a wild beast that was in Lebanon, and trode down the thistle' " (14:9). He plundered Jerusalem, taking many hostages and much wealth.

JEROBOAM II—THIRTEENTH KING

He reigned 41 years (793-753); part of his reign was a coregency with Jehoash. Jeroboam was the most powerful of all the Northern kings. He restored much of Israel's land which had been previously taken by the Syrians.

"For the LORD saw the affliction of Israel, that it was very bitter: for there was not any shut up, nor any left, nor any helper for Israel" (v. 26).

This was prophesied by Jonah, who lived during the reign of Jeroboam II.

ZECHARIAH—FOURTEENTH KING

He reigned for six months (753-752). He was the great-great-grandson of Jehu and fourth ruler in his dynasty. He was murdered by a rebel named Shallum, thus fulfilling God's prophecy against Jehu (10:30; 14:29; 15:8-12).

SHALLUM—FIFTEENTH KING

He reigned for one month (752) and was murdered by a cruel soldier named Menahem.

MENAHEM—SIXTEENTH KING

He reigned for 10 years (752-742) and was one of Israel's most brutal dictators. His reign overlapped that of Pekah.

"Then Menahem smote Tiphsah, and all that were therein, and the coasts thereof from Tirzah, because they opened not to him, therefore he smote it; and all the women therein that were with child he ripped up" (2 Kings 15:16).

He bought off Assyrian king Tiglath-Pileser, with a 2-million-dollar bribe.

PEKAHIAH—SEVENTEENTH KING

He reigned for two years (742-740) at the same time as Pekah. He was the son of Menahem. He was killed by his army commander, Pekah.

PEKAH—EIGHTEENTH KING

He reigned for 20 years (752-732). It should be noted that only 8 years are actually in view here (740-732). It is thought that the first 12 years (752-740) were shared by a coregency arrangement between Pekahiah and Menahem.

The various Assyrian attacks against Isaiah began during his reign.

HOSHEA—NINETEENTH KING

He reigned for nine years (732-722). He was Israel's last king.

After becoming a vassal to Assyrian king Shalmaneser, Hoshea joined with Egypt in rebelling against that empire. For this he was imprisoned by Shalmaneser. It was at this time that Samaria fell and the citizens of the Northern Kingdom were carried away into Assyrian captivity.

The reasons for this carrying away. 1. Israel had turned their hearts over to Canaanite gods.

"For so it was, that the Children of Israel had sinned against the LORD their God, which had brought them up out of the land of Egypt, from under the hand of Pharaoh king of Egypt, and had feared other gods, and walked in the statutes of the heathen, whom the LORD cast out from before the Children of Israel, and of the kings of Israel, which they had made.

"And the Children of Israel did secretly those things that were not right against the LORD their God, and they built them high places in all their cities, from the tower of the watchmen to the fenced city. And they set them up images and groves in every high hill, and under every green tree; and there they burnt incense in all the high places, as did the heathen whom the LORD carried away before them; and wrought wicked things to provoke the LORD to anger, for they served idols, whereof the LORD had said unto them, 'Ye shall not do this thing' " (17:7-12).

2. They then turned their children over to be sacrificed to these devil deities.

"And they caused their sons and their daughters to pass through the fire, and used divination and enchantments, and sold themselves to do evil in the sight of the LORD, and to provoke Him to anger" (v. 17).

3. They refused to hear God's prophets.

4. They rejected God's Word.

"Therefore the LORD was very angry with Israel, and removed them out of His sight. There was none left but the tribe of Judah only. . . .

"For the Children of Israel walked in all the sins of Jeroboam which he did; they departed not from them; until the LORD removed Israel out of His sight, as He had said by all His servants the prophets. So was Israel carried away out of their own land to Assyria unto this day" (vv. 18, 22-23).

The results of this carrying away. The land of Israel was now settled by pagan homesteaders. The remnant of Israel (the few who were left) intermarried with these Gentiles, thus creating the Samaritan race.

House Divided

COMMENTS

When Jesus was accused by the Pharisees of casting out demons by the power of Beelzebub the prince of demons, He responded, "Every kingdom divided against itself is brought to desolation" (Matt. 12:25). Those words, spoken many years after the nation Israel divided into two parts, summarize its history and explain why ultimately both kingdoms passed out of existence. The two kingdoms can be contrasted in at least eight ways, and in each contrast God's working to preserve the Davidic line for the coming of Messiah can be seen.

(1) *In duration.* The period of the Divided Kingdom lasted for approximately 209 years with the Northern Kingdom taken captive by Assyria in 722 B.C. and the Southern Kingdom taken captive by Babylon in 586 B.C. God used the longer duration of Judah to strengthen the godly remnant for the coming Captivity. Of the 20 nations taken captive by Nebuchadnezzar, Judah was the only 1 that maintained its own identity and returned to its own homeland.

(2) *In the numbers of tribes.* Israel consisted of 10 tribes while Judah was comprised of only Judah and Benjamin plus the godly remnant from the 10 tribes and the priests who sought asylum in Judah. In relation to tillable land available, Judah had three times more people than Israel depending on its soil for sustenance. One would expect Israel to outlast Judah and yet Judah outlasted Israel because the Messiah was to come from them and God was preparing them for the coming Captivity.

(3) *In numbers of dynasties.* Israel had nine dynasties while Judah had only one, the Davidic dynasty, in partial fulfillment of 2 Samuel 7:12-16. While the South had some of the assassination that characterized the North, never was the only heir to the throne assassinated. The Davidic line was kept intact till the coming of Christ.

(4) *In internal conditions.* Israel was characterized by continual warfare while Judah was relatively peaceful. It was only 25 miles from Jerusalem to Israel's southern border. God brought just enough wars into Judah's history to keep it humbled before Him. God caused the division so as to be able to preserve Judah in times of relative peace.

(5) *In numbers of kings.* During its 209 years of history, Israel had 19 kings. During the 345 years of its history, Judah had 19 kings (plus Athaliah, the usurping queen). The Northern kings averaged an 11-year reign while the Southern kings averaged a 17-year reign. The longer reigns and the single dynasty of the Southern kings had a great unifying effect on the kingdom of Judah. They never forgot their Davidic lineage.

(6) *In numbers of revivals.* Israel had no sweeping revival but Judah had four great revivals under: (a) Asa and Jehoshaphat, (b) Joash, (c) Hezekiah, and (d) Josiah. These revivals worked to provide a depth of spiritual consciousness not present in Israel.

(7) *In the number of good kings.* All of Israel's 19 kings were evil. Of Judah's 19 kings, 4 were good (Asa, Uzziah, Hezekiah, Josiah), 4 were relatively good (Jehoshaphat, Joash, Amaziah, Jotham), while 11 were bad. God balanced the events in Judah's history so that the good and relatively good kings reigned for twice as many years as the bad kings reigned. Though the bad kings outnumbered the good kings, their combined reigns were significantly shorter. The effect of the good kings was felt throughout Judah's history.

(8) *In the policies of capturing nations.* Assyria sent colonists to occupy the land vacated by Israel. These people intermarried with the people of Israel left behind resulting in the Samaritans. Babylon did not send colonists. Judah's land was left vacant so that they could return and the Messiah could be born in precisely the place indicated by the prophets.

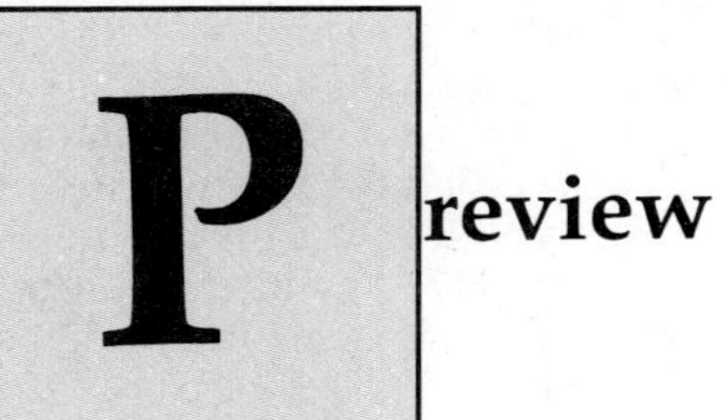

Preview

Rulers in the South (Part One)

1 KINGS 12–22; 2 CHRONICLES 9–20

The older men shook their heads sadly, their hearts filled with a mixture of both dismay and disgust. Just look at him, barely out of his teens, yet strutting around as if he had subdued empires. Totally immature, inexperienced, and insensitive. These words best described him. Part of his problem, of course, was his equally untested and unbending young companions whose heartless and senseless advice merely confirmed his own inflated self-importance. Well, at least his grandfather wasn't around to witness such a sordid sight. True, Grandfather had once been guilty of both adultery and murder, but after being chastened by God, David walked in a hushed and humble way before the Lord the remaining days of his life. But apparently none of David's spirit had rubbed off on Rehoboam, his arrogant grandson.

These were the thoughts of the older men as they awaited Rehoboam's coronation in the city of Shechem. Mercifully at that moment they could not know the extent of that arrogance, or what would happen on the very day scheduled for Rehoboam's anointing, turning it into a spiritual blizzard of anarchy and rebellion. Nor were the older men remotely aware that before the skies would clear again, Israel would suffer invasion and imprisonment at the hands of both Assyrians and Babylonians. Sometimes we are blessed by our ignorance.

Overview

<table>
<tr><td>SCRIPTURE</td><td colspan="4">1 Kings 12–22; 2 Chronicles 9–20</td></tr>
<tr><td>SUBJECT</td><td colspan="4">Reigns of Rehoboam, Abijam, Asa, Jehoshaphat</td></tr>
<tr><td rowspan="5">SPECIFICS</td><td>Rehoboam</td><td>Asa</td><td colspan="2">Jehoshaphat</td></tr>
<tr><td>His tactlessness
The arrogant reply
The awful results</td><td>The first years: Asa, the godly
His concern for the Lord
His cry to the Lord</td><td>The glory</td><td>Teaching the Word
Testing the Word</td></tr>
<tr><td>His godlessness
Forsaking God's Word
Feeling God's wrath</td><td>The final years: Asa, the godless
Opposing the precepts of God
Oppressing the people of God</td><td>The grief</td><td>Caused by an unwise mission
Caused by an unwise marriage</td></tr>
<tr><td colspan="4">Abijam</td></tr>
<tr><td colspan="4">He defeated, by supernatural intervention, Northern King Jeroboam on the battlefield</td></tr>
<tr><td>SAINTS AND SINNERS</td><td colspan="4">Rehoboam, Abijam, Asa, Jehoshaphat, Ahab, Micaiah, Zedekiah, Azariah, Hanani, Jahaziel</td></tr>
<tr><td rowspan="2">SENTENCE SUMMARIES</td><td>O.T. Verse</td><td colspan="3">"Be wise now therefore, O ye kings; be instructed, ye judges of the earth" (Ps. 2:10).</td></tr>
<tr><td>N.T. Verse</td><td colspan="3">"What I tell you in darkness, that speak ye in light; and what ye hear in the ear, that preach ye upon the housetops" (Matt. 20:27).</td></tr>
</table>

OUR SOUTHERN RULERS

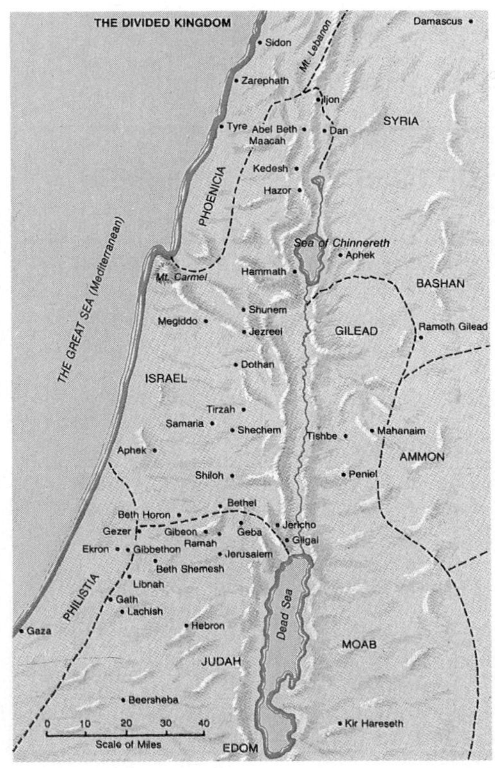

REHOBOAM—FIRST KING

His arrogance. He reigned 17 years. His cruel and tactless answer to the demands of some of Israel's leaders helped trigger the tragic civil war.

"And the king answered the people roughly, and forsook the old men's counsel that they gave him; and spake to them after the counsel of the young men, saying, 'My father made your yoke heavy, and I will add to your yoke; my father also chastised you with whips, but I will chastise you with scorpions.' . . .

"So when all Israel saw that the king hearkened not unto them, the people answered the king, saying, 'What portion have we in David? Neither have we inheritance in the son of Jesse. To your tents, O Israel; now see to thine own house, David.'

"So Israel departed unto their tents" (1 Kings 12:13-14, 16).

He was unknowingly helped by Jeroboam who had driven the faithful Levite priests from the north to Jerusalem. These godly men were responsible in the main for Judah's continuation a century after Assyria had captured the Northern Kingdom (2 Chron. 11:13-17).

His adultery. Like his father Solomon, Rehoboam committed the sin of polygamy. His favorite wife (out of 18 wives and 60 concubines) was Maachah, the ungodly daughter of Absalom.

His affliction. Due to his wickedness, God allowed Jerusalem to be invaded by a foreign power for the first time in nearly 100 years.

"And it came to pass, when Rehoboam had established the kingdom, and had strengthened himself, he forsook the Law of the LORD, and all Israel with him. And it came to pass, that in the fifth year of King Rehoboam, Shishak king of Egypt came up against Jerusalem, because they had transgressed against the LORD. With 1,200 chariots, and threescore thousand horsemen; and the people were without number that came with him out of Egypt; the Lubims, the Sukkiims, and the Ethiopians. And he took the fenced cities which pertained to Judah, and came to Jerusalem" (2 Chron. 12:1-4).

The city was saved, however, by the repentance of both Rehoboam and the people. In spite of this the king soon returned to his evil ways.

ABIJAM—SECOND KING

He reigned for three years (913-911).

He defeated (by supernatural intervention) the Northern king Jeroboam on the battlefield.

In spite of God's help, he degenerated into a wicked king.

ASA—THIRD KING

Asa, the godly. He ruled for 41 years (911-870), part of which was a coregency with Jehoshaphat. Asa was the first godly king. During the first 10 years of his reign, the land was at peace. Asa used the time wisely. He led the people in a great revival.

"And Asa did that which was good and right in the eyes of the LORD his God. For he took away the altars of the strange gods, and the high places, and brake down the images, and cut down the groves; and commanded Judah to seek the LORD God of their fathers, and to do the Law and the commandment" (14:2-4).

He built up and fenced in the cities of Judah. This peace was suddenly shattered, however, when he was threatened with invasion by a million Ethiopian troops. Hopelessly outnumbered, Asa cried out to God:

"LORD, it is nothing with Thee to help, whether with many, or with them who have no power. Help us, O LORD our God; for we rest on Thee, and in Thy name we go against this multitude. O LORD, Thou art our God; let not man prevail against Thee" (v. 11).

God graciously answered this prayer and personally smote the Ethiopians. A thankful Asa returned home and continued his reforms.

"And they entered into a covenant to seek the LORD God of their fathers with all their heart and with all their soul" (15:12).

He even deposed his own grandmother Maachah because of her idolatry.

Asa, the godless. Some 25 years later, however, when again threatened by invasion, Asa sought help from a pagan Syrian king instead of the Lord. A godly prophet named Hanani severely rebuked him for this, saying: *"For the eyes of the LORD run to and fro throughout the whole earth, to show Himself strong in the behalf of them whose heart is perfect toward Him. Herein thou hast done foolishly; therefore, from henceforth thou shalt have wars" (16:9).*

An angry Asa had Hanani thrown in prison for this. He then ended the good reign he began by oppressing the people. Two years prior to his death he became seriously diseased in his feet, *"yet in his disease he sought not to the LORD, but the physicians" (v. 12).*

JEHOSHAPHAT—FOURTH KING

Communications in the Word of God.

He reigned 25 years (873-848). Part of his reign was a coregency with both Asa and Joram.

He began by continuing the moral reforms and building projects his father Asa had started.

"And the LORD was with Jehoshaphat, because he walked in the first ways of his father David, and sought not unto Baalim. . . . And his heart was lifted up in the ways of the LORD; moreover he took away the high places and groves out of Judah" (17:3, 6).

During his third year in power he instituted a nationwide religious education program, sending out Bible teachers to all important Judean cities who lectured to the people from the Law of Moses.

"And they taught in Judah, and had the Book of the Law of the LORD with them, and went about throughout all the cities of Judah, and taught the people" (v. 9).

He grew in power and accepted tribute from the Philistines.

Compromising the Word of God. In the latter years of his reign, however, he marred his testimony by compromising with three ungodly Northern kings—Ahab, and his two sons, Ahaziah and Jehoram.

*His matrimonial alliance with Ahab: He foolishly allowed his son Jehoram to marry Athaliah, the wicked daughter of Ahab and Jezebel. She would later become queen of Judah and shed much innocent blood, all as a result of this compromise of Jehoshaphat.

*His military alliance with Ahab against Syria: This interesting account records the conversation of two kings, two prophets, and a devious demon.

The kings. Ahab, the apostate, persuaded Jehoshaphat to join forces against the Syrians.

Jehoshaphat, the appeaser, had some doubts, despite the reassurances of 400 false court preachers. His question: *"Is there not here a prophet of the LORD besides, that we might inquire of him?" (18:6)*

*Ahab's answer: *"There is yet one man, by whom we may inquire of the LORD, but I hate him; for he never prophesied good unto me, but always evil" (v. 7).*

The Lamp of God—Part I

COMMENTS

"And unto his son [i.e., Rehoboam] will I give one tribe, that David My servant may have a light [lit., a lamp] alway before Me in Jerusalem" (1 Kings 11:36; cf. 15:4; 2 Kings 8:19). In this promise, God guaranteed that the Davidic line would remain intact through the stormy days ahead until the time when the Messiah ultimately would be born. The "lamp of God" would not be put out.

Satan's first attempt to put out the "lamp of God" came in the days of Rehoboam and Abijam, Judah's first two kings. During the reigns of these kings Satan's attempt to *destroy* the Davidic line is seen by: (1) Rehoboam's determination to attack Israel with an army of 180,000 men (1 Kings 12:21-24; 2 Chron. 11:1-4). God sent Shemaiah, His prophet, to show Rehoboam that the division of the kingdom was in His will and for Rehoboam to reunite the kingdom was not. (2) The king of Egypt's (Shishak) invasion of Judah with 1,200 chariots and 60,000 horsemen (1 Kings 14:25-28; 2 Chron. 12:1-12). God worked so as to change Shishak's mind so that he took the spoil but left the people totally untouched. (3) Jeroboam I, king of Israel, continually fought with Rehoboam, king of Judah, and in the reign of Abijam came against Judah with an army of 800,000. Abijam's army only numbered 400,000 (1 Kings 15:7-8; 2 Chron. 13:1-20). Even though Abijam was fighting 2-1 odds, God gave him the victory and enabled his army to slay 500,000 Israelites—more than they had in their own army.

Failing to destroy the Davidic line in this period, Satan tried to *corrupt* it by: (1) Jeroboam I's introduction of idolatry thus making "Israel to sin" (1 Kings 12:26-33). God counteracted this danger by special miracles of judgment (13:1-32), a remarkable prophecy concerning Josiah (vv. 1-2), the Prophet Ahijah's prophecy about the death of Jeroboam's child (14:1-6), and the end of Jeroboam's dynasty (v. 10; 15:25-30). (2) Judah's idolatry and sodomy (14:22-28). God counteracted this by Shishak's invasion of Judah and by the wars between Jeroboam and Rehoboam—these caused the people of Judah to repent. (3) Abijah's wickedness and his polygamous unions (15:3; 2 Chron. 13:21). God counteracted these through causing Abijah to have to fight Jeroboam against overwhelming odds and by sending revival to the land (chaps. 14–20).

In the period of the good kings Asa and Jehoshaphat, Judah's third and fourth kings, Satan's attacks were intensified. God sent one of the greatest revivals in the history of His people. Satan attempted to *destroy* the Davidic line by: (1) Zerah, the Ethiopian's, invasion of Judah (chap. 14). Judah fought against 2-1 odds and God gave them a mighty victory. (2) The battle Jehoshaphat fought in league with Ahab, king of Israel, against Ben-hadad, king of Syria (1 Kings 22:29-40; 2 Chron. 18:28-34). Jehoshaphat was nearly killed in a case of mistaken identity. Ahab was killed by a "chance" arrow. (3) The invasion of Judah by the Moabites and Ammonites (20:1-30). Jehoshaphat met the threat by having national prayer meetings. They met all of God's conditions. God gave them the victory.

Failing to destroy the Davidic line in this period, Satan tried to *corrupt* the Davidic line in the following ways: (1) By King Asa's league with Ben-hadad, king of Syria (1 Kings 15:16-24; 2 Chron. 16:1-4). God counteracted Asa's sin by taking his life. (2) Jehoshaphat's league with Ahab and Ahaziah, kings of Israel (1 Kings 22:1-50; 2 Chron. 18:1-34; 20:35-37). God counteracted this through the death of Ahab and the ministries of Elijah and Elisha.

The events of this period clearly show that God is fully capable of keeping His word and that no one was able to put out "the lamp of God."

Rulers in the South (Part Two)

2 KINGS 8–17; 2 CHRONICLES 21–28; ISAIAH 7

The news quickly traveled through Jerusalem, then rapidly spread out to nearby cities. It was received with mixed feelings. Some felt the whole idea was preposterous. A few voiced great optimism. But the vast majority seemed to adopt an uneasy wait-and-see attitude. All agreed, however, that the new situation would require some real getting used to.

And the nature of this news? For the first time in Judah's history the little southern country was about to be ruled by a woman! Following the death of her son, Athaliah quickly assumed his throne. But the priesthood, to a man, opposed her ascension, pointing out (doubtless in private circles) she was utterly disqualified, not being a direct descendant of King David, as had been the previous six monarchs who sat on the Judean throne following Solomon's death. To make matters worse, if her cruelty and idolatry even remotely approached that of her mother and father, Judah could be in for real trouble. In a nutshell, Athaliah's brief but bloody reign would actually surpass that of her parents, Jezebel and Ahab. After a ruthless rule of six years this evil queen was herself executed. It is ironic that she was killed by a spear once belonging to King David. Thus Athaliah, who had attempted to steal his throne, would die by his sword.

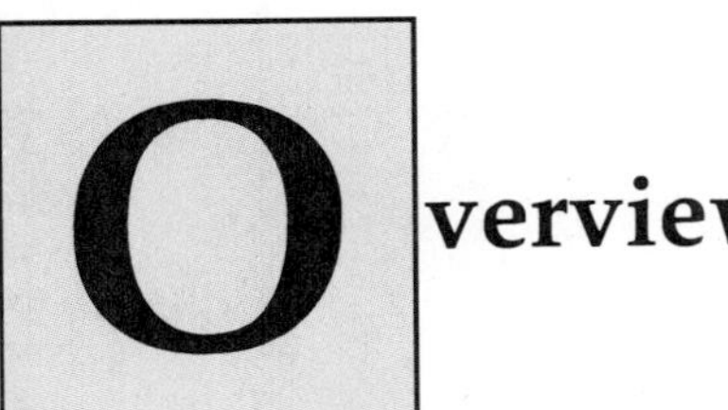

Overview

<table>
<tr><td>SCRIPTURE</td><td colspan="4">2 Kings 8–17; 2 Chronicles 21–28; Isaiah 7</td></tr>
<tr><td>SUBJECT</td><td colspan="4">Reigns of Joram, Ahaziah, Athaliah, Joash, Amaziah, Uzziah, Jotham, Ahaz</td></tr>
<tr><td rowspan="4">SPECIFICS</td><td>Joram</td><td>Ahaziah</td><td>Athaliah</td><td>Joash</td></tr>
<tr><td>His wicked wife
His wicked ways</td><td>Killed by Jehu</td><td>The executions
The retribution</td><td>The reformation
The degeneration</td></tr>
<tr><td>Amaziah</td><td>Uzziah</td><td>Jotham</td><td>Ahaz</td></tr>
<tr><td>The instruction for a battle
The idolatry following a battle</td><td>His proficiency
His pride</td><td>He built the upper gate of the temple</td><td>The Virgin Birth revealed
The Virgin Birth rejected</td></tr>
<tr><td>SAINTS AND SINNERS</td><td colspan="4">Joram, Ahaziah, Athaliah, Joash, Amaziah, Uzziah, Jotham, Ahaz, Zechariah, Azariah, Isaiah</td></tr>
<tr><td rowspan="2">SENTENCE SUMMARIES</td><td>O.T. Verse</td><td colspan="3">"It is an abomination to kings to commit wickedness; for the throne is established by righteousness" (Prov. 16:12).</td></tr>
<tr><td>N.T. Verse</td><td colspan="3">"Submit yourself to every ordinance of man for the Lord's sake; whether it be to the king, as supreme" (1 Peter 2:13).</td></tr>
</table>

IGHT SOUTHERN RULERS

JORAM—FIFTH KING

He reigned 12 years (853-841). Part of his reign was a coregency with Jehoshaphat. He began his reign by murdering his six brothers.

He received a posthumous message from Elijah predicting judgment on him because of his wicked and murderous reign.

He was attacked and defeated by the Philistines and Arabians.

He died of a horrible disease and was unmourned at the funeral.

"And after all this the LORD smote him in his bowels with an incurable disease. And it came to pass, that in process of time, after the end of two years, his bowels fell out by reason of his sickness; so he died of sore diseases. And his people made no burning for him like the burning of his fathers" (2 Chron. 21:18-19).

AHAZIAH—SIXTH KING

He reigned one year (841). He was the son of Joram and Athaliah. He was killed by Jehu (tenth Northern king).

ATHALIAH—SEVENTH RULER

The purge. She reigned for six years (841-835). It has already been noted that Athaliah (Jezebel's daughter) had married Joram (Jehoshaphat's son). They had one son and named him Ahaziah. When he was killed by Jehu, Athaliah mounted the throne. This murderous hag then ordered the slaughter of all of the royal seed of the house of Judah.

But Athaliah's own daughter, Jehosheba (along with her husband Jehoiada, who was high priest at that time) hid one sole survivor of the blood bath, a little lad named Joash.

The purge. After six years of secret preparation, a coup was brought about which dethroned and saw the execution of Athaliah.

JOASH—EIGHTH KING

The better years of his reign. He reigned 39 years (835-796). The greater part of Joash's rule was good. He cooperated with Jehoiada the high priest in some much-needed religious reforms. He then ordered Jehoiada to repair the temple of Solomon. To finance the work, Jehoiada constructed a special offering box.

The bitter years of his reign. As long as the high priest lived, Joash walked the spiritual line but at Jehoiada's death things quickly degenerated.

"Now after the death of Jehoiada came the princes of Judah, and made obeisance to the king. Then the king hearkened unto them. And they left the house of the LORD God of their fathers, and served groves and idols; and wrath came upon Judah and Jerusalem for this their trespass" (24:17-18).

The spirit of God then came on Zechariah (Jehoiada's son) and he severely rebuked both people and king for idolatry and immorality.

"Thus saith God, 'Why transgress ye the commandments of the LORD, that ye cannot prosper? Because ye have forsaken the LORD, He hath also forsaken you' " (v. 20).

Finally, at Joash's order, Judah murdered their own high priest by stoning. This was probably the high-water mark of sin by Abraham's seed in the Old Testament. See Jesus' words in Matthew 23:35.

Shortly after this, God allowed the Syrian army to briefly capture Jerusalem. Joash was severely wounded and the chief leaders executed. After a reign of 39 years, Joash was murdered by his own palace officials.

AMAZIAH—NINTH KING

He reigned for 29 years (796-767).

He was a good king for a while, executing the killers of his father, Joash.

He was rebuked by a prophet for hiring some mercenary Israelite soldiers to help him fight against Edom.

He reluctantly dismissed these paid soldiers and with God's help, defeated Edom with his own soldiers.

He foolishly brought back some of the Edomite gods for worshiping purposes.

The reckless king then declared war on Northern Israel and was soundly defeated.

UZZIAH—TENTH KING

The leader reigned for 50 years (790-740). Part of his reign was a coregency with both Amaziah and Jotham. Uzziah did more to strengthen Judah both from a military and economic standpoint than any other king. He defeated most of Judah's enemies. He organized his army into peak fighting strength. He built towers and water reservoirs. He laid out farms and vineyards and he raised great herds of cattle.

The lawless. But in the midst of his strength, he was cut down by pride. We are told: *"But when he was strong, his heart was*

The Lamp of God—Part II

COMMENTS

God pledged Himself to preserve the Davidic line, "the lamp of God," until Messiah should be born (2 Sam. 21:17; 1 Kings 11:36; 15:4; 2 Kings 8:19). In Part I we saw two times when Satan attempted to put out the lamp of God and failed.

Satan's third attempt to put out the lamp of God came in the person of the usurping Queen Athaliah, who tried to kill every member of the Davidic line (11:1-3; 2 Chron. 24:7). She prohibited people from going to the temple for six years. The temple thus became the ideal place for Jehosheba to hide the infant Joash whom she secreted away. Joash was enthroned at age seven and Athaliah was deposed. Later he was assassinated, but by then there were other members of the Davidic line.

Satan's fourth attempt to put out the lamp of God came under the four relatively good kings, Joash, Amaziah, Uzziah, and Jotham (2 Kings 12–15; 2 Chron. 24:17-27). Joash killed the son of Jehoiada who was the priest and spiritual leader. God counteracted by causing Joash to be assassinated. Amaziah succeeded Joash and was also assassinated, but not while he was the only link in the Davidic line. Uzziah offered incense on the altar. God counteracted by causing Uzziah to be stricken with leprosy.

Satan's fifth attempt to put out the lamp of God came in the person of King Ahaz, Judah's most wicked king, who reigned for 20 years (2 Kings 16–17; 2 Chron. 28). God counteracted in three ways: (1) through good King Hezekiah's reign; he tore down all the idols his father had built, (2) through causing the Northern Kingdom to go into captivity, and (3) through the Prophets Isaiah and Micah and the revival resulting from their ministries.

Satan's sixth attempt to put out the lamp of God came during the reign of good King Hezekiah (2 Kings 18–20; 2 Chron. 29–32). Satan attacked the Davidic line through the invasion of Sennacherib which God counteracted in two ways: (1) by sending the Angel of Jehovah to slay 185,000 Assyrians during the night and (2) by the death of Sennacherib when he returned to Assyria.

Satan's seventh attempt to put out the lamp of God came during the reigns of Manasseh and Amon (2 Kings 21; 2 Chron. 33). Manasseh would have been Judah's most wicked king except for the fact that he repented late in life. Manasseh introduced human sacrifice, Baal worship, and spiritism into Judah. He had sodomites in the temple. Amon succeeded Manasseh and was assassinated at the age of 24 after a two-year reign. God counteracted the evil Manasseh with Josiah who, at 8, became king just two years after Manasseh's death. Josiah was a good king who read the Law and introduced reforms to undo the evil of Manasseh (2 Kings 22–23).

Satan's eighth attempt to put out the lamp of God came during the reign of good King Josiah (22:1–23:30; 2 Chron. 34–35). Josiah went out against the will of God to fight Pharaoh as he was on his way to invade Assyria. God counteracted Josiah's sin by having him killed and causing the people to mourn for him. In the process they recalled the wonderful deeds that he had done.

Satan's ninth attempt to put out the lamp of God came during the reigns of Josiah's sons, Jehoahaz, Jehoiakim, Jehoiachin, and Zedekiah (2 Kings 23:31–25:30; 2 Chron. 36)—all of them were evil. God counteracted their evil ways through giving them short reigns, bringing terrible judgments against them, and ultimately by allowing Judah to be taken captive into Babylon.

All of Satan's attempts to extinguish or to corrupt the lamp of God met with failure. "But when the fullness of the time was come, God sent forth His Son, made of a woman, made under the Law, to redeem them that were under the Law, that we might receive the adoption of sons" (Gal. 4:4-5).

lifted up to his destruction" (26:16).

His sin was intrusion into the office of the priesthood by the burning of incense on the golden altar. Caught in this act, he was severely rebuked by the high priest Azariah and 80 other godly priests.

"And they withstood Uzziah the king, and said unto him, 'It appertaineth not unto thee, Uzziah, to burn incense unto the LORD, but to the priests the sons of Aaron, that are consecrated to burn incense. Go out of the sanctuary; for thou hast trespassed; neither shall it be for thine honor from the LORD God" (v. 18).

The leper. Uzziah was furious and refused to repent, causing God to punish him with leprosy. *"And Uzziah, the king, was a leper unto the day of his death, and dwelt in a several house . . . for he was cut off from the house of the LORD" (v. 21).*

JOTHAM—ELEVENTH KING

He reigned for 19 years (750-731). He had a coregency with both Uzziah and Ahaz.

He was a good king.

He built the upper gate of the temple and erected fortresses and towns.

He defeated his enemies and received huge annual tribute from them.

AHAZ—TWELFTH KING

The glorious revelation. He reigned 20 years (735-715), 4 years in a coregency with Jotham. Ahaz was the first person to hear the prophecy from Isaiah about the Virgin Birth of Christ. This amazing account began when Jerusalem was threatened with invasion by an alliance of the Northern Kingdom and Syria. God then informed the terrified Ahaz through Isaiah that the invasion would fail, and as proof, Ahaz was invited to: *"Ask thee a sign of the LORD, thy God; ask it either in the depth, or in the height above" (Isa. 7:11).*

But the wicked young monarch refused to trust the Lord. As a result, God then promised a special sign to demonstrate His eventual plan to save Jerusalem forever from all her enemies. *"Therefore the LORD Himself shall give you [the whole house of Israel] a sign; Behold, the virgin shall conceive, and bear a son, and shall call His name Immanuel" (v. 14).*

The grievous rejection. The young king not only rejected this prophecy, but completely turned his back on God and actually sacrificed his own children to the evil gods in the valley of Hinnom outside Jerusalem. As a result of all this, *"the LORD brought Judah low because of Ahaz . . . for he made Judah naked, and transgressed sore against the LORD" (2 Chron. 28:19).*

Ahaz's wickedness seemed to know no limits. He humbled himself before the Assyrian king, seeking his help against his enemies, bribing him with silver and gold taken from the temple. He then rebuilt the brazen altar so that it resembled the one found in a heathen Assyrian temple. Because of this, God allowed his enemies to inflict much grief on him.

"For he sacrificed unto the gods of Damascus . . . and he said . . . 'I will sacrifice to them, that they may help me.' But they were the ruin of him, and of all Israel" (v. 23).

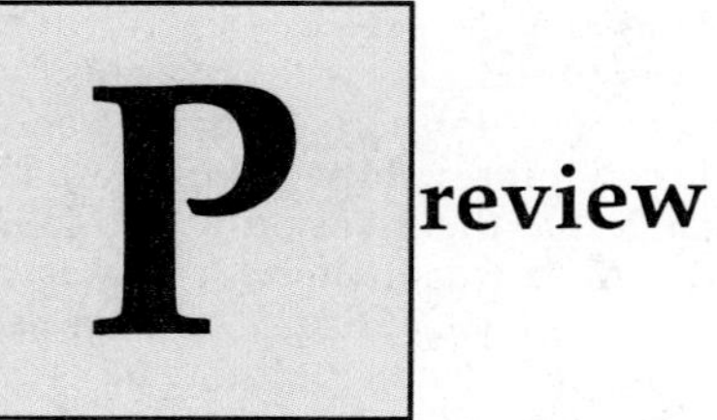

Rulers in the South (Part Three)

2 KINGS 18–21; 2 CHRONICLES 29–33; ISAIAH 36–39

A famous evangelist once began a sermon: "Tonight I'm going to speak on the meanest man who ever lived!" After pausing for a moment, he continued; "Now I saw several of you ladies looking at your husbands, but I'm not going to talk about any of them." He then said, "Some of you husbands might think I plan to preach on Adolf Hitler, or Judas Iscariot, or the bloodthirsty Nero. But you're wrong. Tonight I'm going to speak about a man even more terrible than all these." With that, the evangelist preached on Manasseh, Judah's fourteenth king. One would almost think this evil monarch rose at sunrise so he could get an early start on the scheduled blasphemy and bloodletting for that day. But, miracle of miracles, in the plan and grace of God, this vicious vehicle of Satan was temporarily imprisoned by his enemies. There, in that dark dungeon of despair and death, he cried out to the God he had once hated. After his release he returned to Jerusalem and immediately began tearing down what he had once built up (the worship of many false gods) and building up what he had once torn down (the worship of the true God). Centuries later, the Apostle Paul may well have had Manasseh in mind when he wrote: *"But where sin abounded, grace did much more abound" (Rom. 5:20).* So it did then. So it does now.

Overview

SCRIPTURE	2 Kings 18–21; 2 Chronicles 29–33; Isaiah 36–39			
SUBJECT	Reigns of Hezekiah and Manasseh			
SPECIFICS	Hezekiah, the father	A demonstration of God's might The miracle of Jerusalem's redemption The miracle of Hezekiah's restoration	Manasseh, the son	A demonstration of God's mercy The perversions The prison The prayer The pardon
SAINTS AND SINNERS	Hezekiah, Manasseh, Isaiah, Rabshakeh, Sennacherib			
SENTENCE SUMMARIES	O.T. Verse	"The king's heart is in the hand of the LORD, as the rivers of water; He turneth it whithersoever He will" (Prov. 21:1).		
	N.T. Verses	"I exhort, therefore, that first of all supplications, prayers, intercessions, and giving of thanks, be made for all men: for kings, and for all that are in authority, that we may lead a quiet and peaceable life in all godliness and honesty" (1 Tim. 2:1-2).		

TWO SOUTHERN RULERS

HEZEKIAH—THIRTEENTH KING

The heart of Hezekiah. He reigned for 29 years (715-686). He was the godliest king since David.

"He trusted in the LORD God of Israel; so that after him was none like him among all the kings of Judah, nor any that were before him. For he clave to the LORD, and departed not from following Him, but kept His commandments, which the LORD commanded Moses" (2 Kings 18:5-6).

The hands of Hezekiah. He revived the people of God. He led his people in a great revival by reopening and repairing the temple and by cleansing the land of idols. Even Moses' serpent of brass was destroyed, for the people had been burning incense to it.

He reinstituted the Passover of God. Hezekiah planned for and carried out the greatest Passover service since Solomon. A special invitation was even sent out to the Northern Kingdom tribes to attend.

*Some ridiculed: *"So the posts passed from city to city through the country of Ephraim and Manasseh even unto Zebulun; but they laughed them to scorn, and mocked them" (2 Chron. 30:10).*

*Some responded: *"Nevertheless divers of Asher and Manasseh and of Zebulun humbled themselves, and came to Jerusalem" (v. 11).* The sacrifices during this Passover numbered 2,000 bulls and 17,000 sheep. This all resulted in the receiving of a tremendous freewill offering.

"Then Hezekiah questioned with the priests and the Levites concerning the heaps. And Azariah the chief priest of the house of Zadok answered him, and said, 'Since the people began to bring the offerings into the house of the LORD, we have had enough to eat, and have left plenty; for the LORD hath blessed His people; and that which is left is this great store' " (31:9-10).

He reorganized the priests of God. He organized the priests and Levites into service corps, appointing some to offer animal sacrifices to God, and others simply to thank and praise Him.

Under Ahaz, Hezekiah's father, Judah had paid tribute, but Hezekiah successfully stood up to the Assyrians and refused to do this.

The health of Hezekiah. He was stricken with a fatal boil-like disease, possibly due to his pride.

*His sickness: *"In those days was Hezekiah sick unto death. And the Prophet Isaiah the son of Amoz came to him, and said unto him, 'Thus saith the LORD, "Set thine house in order; for thou shalt die, and not live" ' " (2 Kings 20:1).*

*His supplication: *"Then he turned his face to the wall, and prayed unto the LORD, saying, 'I beseech Thee, O LORD, remember now how I have walked before Thee in truth and with a perfect heart, and have done that which is good in Thy sight.' And Hezekiah wept sore" (vv. 2-3).*

*His sign: *"And Hezekiah said unto Isaiah, 'What shall be the sign that the LORD will heal me, and that I shall go up into the house of the LORD the third day?'*

"And Isaiah said, 'This sign shalt thou have of the LORD, that the LORD will do the thing that He hath spoken. Shall the shadow go forward 10 degrees, or go back 10 degrees?'

"And Hezekiah answered, 'It is a light thing for the shadow to go down 10 degrees. Nay, but let the shadow return backward 10 degrees.' And Isaiah the prophet cried unto the LORD: and He brought the shadow 10 degrees backward, by which it had gone down in the dial of Ahaz" (vv. 8-11).

Hezekiah's prayer for recovery was answered by God and the king was granted an additional 15 years. God then effected a supernatural sign to assure Hezekiah that his life would really be spared. At the king's own request, the shadow on the royal sundial was moved back 10 degrees. Isaiah 38:9-20 recorded Hezekiah's personal account of those days.

His despondency prior to the promised healing. "I said, 'I shall not see the LORD, even the LORD, in the land of the living: I shall behold man no more with the inhabitants of the world. Mine age is departed, and is removed from me as a shepherd's tent; I have cut off like a weaver my life. He will cut me off with pining sickness; from day even to night will Thou make an end of me.' . . . Like a crane or a swallow, so did I chatter: I did mourn as a dove. Mine eyes fail with looking upward. 'O LORD, I am oppressed; undertake for me' " (vv. 11-12, 14).

His delight following the promised healing.

"Behold, for peace I had great bitterness; but Thou hast in love to my soul delivered it from the pit of corruption. For Thou hast cast all my sins behind Thy back. . . . The LORD *was ready to save me; therefore we will sing my songs to the stringed instruments all the days of our life in the house of the* LORD*" (vv. 17, 20).*

The hastiness of Hezekiah. He received an envoy from the rising Babylonian Empire who came both to congratulate him on his recovery and also to secretly determine how much loot Babylon could take from Jerusalem after coming into power. Isaiah rebuked the king for showing these spies the riches of the temple.

The helplessness of Hezekiah. Hezekiah found himself surrounded by the Assyrians. Hezekiah's initial (and correct) response was that of confidence in the Lord.

"Be strong and courageous, be not afraid nor dismayed for the king of Assyria, nor for all the multitude that is with him; for there be more with us than with him. With him is an arm of flesh; but with us is the LORD *our God to help us, and to fight our battles. And the people rested themselves upon the words of Hezekiah king of Judah" (2 Chron. 32:7-8).*

This confidence, however, turned to fear as the Assyrian threats and troops increased. *"And . . . Hezekiah . . . rent his clothes, and covered himself with sackcloth, and went into the house of the* LORD. *. . . And . . . said . . . 'This . . . is a day of trouble' " (Isa. 37:1, 3).*

He then offered a cry to God for deliverance in the temple. *"O* LORD *of hosts, God of Israel, that dwellest between the cherubim, Thou art the God, even Thou alone, of all the kingdoms of the earth. Thou hast made heaven and earth. . . .*

"Now therefore, O LORD *our God, save us from his hand, that all the kingdoms of the earth may know that Thou art the* LORD, *even Thou only" (vv. 16, 20).*

The help of Hezekiah. In answer to Hezekiah's desperate prayer, God (through Isaiah) predicted that not only would the Assyrians fail to take the city of Jerusalem, but that not even an enemy arrow would land inside the walls. That very night God's death angel slew 185,000 enemy troops and Jerusalem was saved. See 2 Kings 19:14-19, 35-37; 2 Chronicles 32:21-22; Isaiah 37:14-20, 33-38.

MANASSEH—FOURTEENTH KING

The unique king. He reigned for 55 years (695-642). Part of his reign was a coregency with Hezekiah. The fourteenth ruler of Judah was, without doubt, the most unique king ever to sit on either the Northern or Southern throne. Note the following: he was king longer than any other of either kingdom, ruling 55 years; he had the godliest father up to that time of all Judean kings (Hezekiah); his grandson Josiah was finest of all; he was the only wicked king to genuinely repent prior to his death; and he was the most wicked of all kings prior to his salvation.

The ungodly king. The preconversion reign (as recorded in 2 Kings 21:1-18; 2 Chron. 33:1-20) of Manasseh would probably have surpassed that of Stalin and Hitler in terms of sheer wickedness. Consider the following blasphemous and bloody actions: he rebuilt all pagan Baalite altars his father had destroyed; he set up a zodiac center for the heathen worship of the sun, moon, and stars in every house of God; he sacrificed his own children to satanic gods in the Valley of Hinnom as his grandfather Ahaz had done; he consulted spirit-mediums and fortune-tellers; tradition says he murdered Isaiah by having him sawn asunder; God said he was more wicked than heathen nations which had once occupied Palestine; he shed innocent blood from one end of Jerusalem to the other; he totally ignored repeated warnings of God in all this; and was imprisoned temporarily by the king of Assyria.

The upright king. He repented while in prison and was forgiven by God. He was later allowed to return as king of Judah.

*The record of his conversion: *"And when he was in affliction, he besought the* LORD *his God, and humbled himself greatly before the God of his fathers, and prayed unto Him. And He was entreated of him, and heard his supplication, and brought him again to Jerusalem into his kingdom. Then Manasseh knew that the* LORD *He was God" (33:12-13).*

*The results of his conversion: *"And he took away the strange gods, and the idol out of the house of the* LORD, *and all the altars that he had built in the mount of the house of the* LORD, *and in Jerusalem, and cast them out of the city. And he repaired the altar of the* LORD *and sacrificed thereon peace offerings and thank offerings, and commanded Judah to serve the* LORD *God of Israel" (vv. 15-16).*

The Peril of Answered Prayer

COMMENTS

Believers are conditioned to the idea that they should pray and expect their prayers to be answered. To many believers prayer is simply a matter of persuading God so that they can get from God the things that they want. Prayer thus becomes a tool of persuasion to convince God to do something that otherwise He might not wish to do. It is thought that the worst thing that could happen would be for the believer's prayers not to be answered at all or to be answered with a no. While prayer never causes God to diverge from His purpose, Hezekiah's life affords a striking example of a time when seemingly his prayer did cause God to change His mind. When one looks at the outworkings of that answer he cannot but wonder if it would not have been better if God had not answered that prayer at all or simply said, no.

It must be remembered that Hezekiah was a good king. He was the godliest king to come to the throne since David. Under his reign some wonderful things were accomplished: (1) he led his people in a great revival, (2) he reinstituted the observance of the Passover, (3) he reorganized the priesthood, and (4) he refused to pay tribute to Assyria. He reigned for 14 years and then became deathly ill with a boil-like disease. God sent the Prophet Isaiah to him with some of the strongest language in the Old Testament. He literally said, "Set your house in order for in dying you shall certainly die!" Similar words had been spoken to Adam (cf. Gen. 2:17). Hezekiah's future was set—he would certainly die.

Hezekiah reacted to the prophet's pronouncement predictably and humanly—he prayed and wept (2 Kings 20:2-3). He reminded God of the good life that he had lived and cried as he prayed. Seemingly he was successful in causing God to change His mind for before Isaiah got out of the king's courtyard the Word of the Lord came to him telling him to return to Hezekiah and tell him that not only would he be healed but 15 years would be added to his life. Hezekiah asked for a sign to guarantee that it was true. In compliance, God caused the shadow on the sundial to go backward 10 degrees.

It would seem that Hezekiah had successfully "prayed through" and had convinced God to change His mind. He had engaged in prevailing prayer. But consider the things that happened following the answering of this prayer: (1) Shortly after he was healed, he received an envoy from the Babylonian empire and he showed them all the wealth of his country. God sent Isaiah to deliver the word of judgment telling Hezekiah that all that wealth would be carried away into Babylon (v. 17). (2) Three years after Hezekiah was healed, Manasseh was born. Manasseh was the longest-reigning and most wicked king to reign over Judah. The only redeeming feature of his life was the fact that at the end of his life he repented of the evil he had done (2 Chron. 33:19).

What could be worse than not having one's prayers answered? In Hezekiah's case it was to have his prayers answered. Why then did God answer Hezekiah's prayer when, seemingly, it was not in Judah's best interest? The answer is found in 2 Kings 20:6. God did not answer Hezekiah's prayer for Hezekiah's sake. He did it for His own sake and for His servant David's sake. Apparently, Hezekiah had forgotten the promise given to David that the line of David would not ever pass out of existence. At the time of his illness, Hezekiah had no offspring. He should have realized that he could not die at least until an heir was born to him, but he didn't. The reason, then, that God answered Hezekiah's prayer was so that the Davidic line would continue, even if through one who was a wicked king, just as He had done through Ahaz, Manasseh's grandfather. Truly, God is sovereign when it comes to answering prayer and never is persuaded against His will.

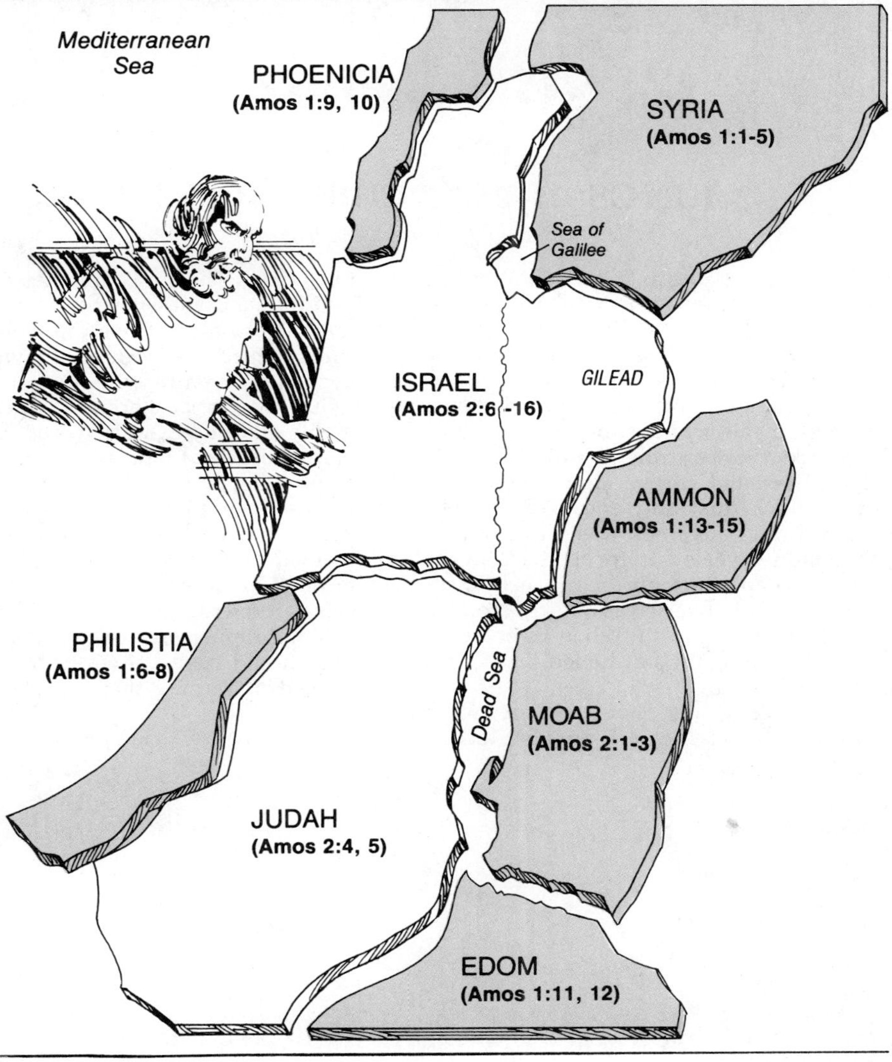

Mediterranean Sea

PHOENICIA
(Amos 1:9, 10)

SYRIA
(Amos 1:1-5)

Sea of Galilee

ISRAEL
(Amos 2:6-16)

GILEAD

AMMON
(Amos 1:13-15)

PHILISTIA
(Amos 1:6-8)

Dead Sea

MOAB
(Amos 2:1-3)

JUDAH
(Amos 2:4, 5)

EDOM
(Amos 1:11, 12)

Preview

Rulers in the South
(Part Four)

2 KINGS 21–25; 2 CHRONICLES 33–36

Question: Is it possible to lose God's Word in God's house? *Answer:* It is indeed tragically possible. The last godly king of Judah was Josiah. After ascending the throne, this monarch began an extensive project to repair the temple of Solomon which had suffered great neglect under the reigns of previous wicked Judean rulers. Suddenly, in a dark and isolated corner, doubtlessly covered by thick dust and encircled by cobwebs, a mysterious Book was found. Close examination revealed it to be the Law of Moses, perhaps the only one in existence. This precious discovery was quickly brought to Josiah and read to him. When he heard its words of warning on sin, he led his people in a great revival.

Think of it: God's Word lost in God's house. Is this sad situation possible today? It is indeed. There are churches that display beautiful and massive Bibles on Communion tables only to have the Bible's blessed truths denied by apostate clergymen standing behind nearby pulpits.

Question: What happens when one attempts to destroy God's Word? *Answer:* In a word, disaster. Jehoiakim, Judah's eighteenth king, could give a pointed and painful response to this. The section he destroyed was that portion written by Jeremiah the prophet. The method was by burning. The results were swift and terrible. Jeremiah rewrote the book and added to it a chilling prophecy relating to Jehoiakim. The king should have known better. It is wiser to heed a warning than to kill the watchman.

Overview

SCRIPTURE	2 Kings 21–25; 2 Chronicles 33–36		
SUBJECT	Reigns of Amon, Josiah, Jehoahaz, Jehoiakim, Jehoiachin, Zedekiah		
SPECIFICS	Amon	Executed by his own household servants	
	Josiah	Doing God's work	Discovering God's Word
	Jehoahaz	Carried off into Egyptian captivity	
	Jehoiakim	His cruelty to the sheep of God	His contempt for the Scriptures of God
	Jehoiachin	Incurred a curse from God	
	Zedekiah	Blinded to the facts	Blinded by his foes
SAINTS AND SINNERS	Amon, Josiah, Jehoahaz, Jehoiakim, Jehoiachin, Zedekiah, Hilkiah, Huldah, Jeremiah, Nebuchadnezzar		
SENTENCE SUMMARIES	O.T. Verse	"The king that faithfully judgeth the poor, his throne shall be established forever" (Prov. 29:14).	
	N.T. Verse	"Honor all men. Love the brotherhood. Fear God. Honor the king" (1 Peter 2:17).	

AST YEARS OF THE SOUTHERN KINGDOM

AMON—FIFTEENTH KING

He reigned for two years (642-640).

He was wicked like his father Manasseh, but did not repent as did his father.

He was executed by his own household servants.

JOSIAH—SIXTEENTH KING

Doing the works of God. He reigned for 31 years (640-609). Josiah was the finest king since Solomon. *"And like unto him was there no king before him, who turned to the LORD with all his heart, and with all his soul, and with all his might, according to all the Law of Moses; neither after him arose there any like him" (2 Kings 23:25).*

He was also the last godly king of Judah. He began seeking God as a youth. He destroyed all the altars of Baal including the one at Bethel, thus fulfilling a 300-year-old prophecy. Compare 1 Kings 13:1-3 with 2 Chronicles 34:3-5.

Discovering the Word of God. At age 26 he began to repair the temple. When the Law of Moses (which had doubtless been lost during Manasseh's reign) was discovered in the temple, Josiah led his nation in a great revival.

Josiah's reaction to the Word of God. "And it came to pass, when the king had heard the words of the Law, that he rent his clothes. . . . 'Go, inquire of the LORD for me, and for them that are left in Israel and in Judah, concerning the words of the Book that is found. For great is the wrath of the LORD that is poured out upon us, because our fathers have not kept the Word of the LORD, to do after all that is written in this Book' " (vv. 19, 21).

Huldah's reassurance from the God of the Word. This prophetess predicted future judgment on Judah for their sins, but not during the reign of Josiah because of his godliness. He then planned for and presided over the greatest Passover service ever held in Judah. Thirty thousand sheep, 3,000 bulls, 7,600 cows, and 800 oxen were offered. At this time, Josiah ordered the ark of the covenant to be put back in the holy of holies. For some unexplained reason it had apparently been removed. This is the last mention of the ark in the Bible. Its fate is not known.

Josiah was tragically killed in battle while attempting to keep the Egyptians from crossing his land to do battle with the Assyrians.

"And Jeremiah lamented for Josiah; and all the singing men and the singing women spake of Josiah in their lamentations to this day, and made them an ordinance in Israel: and, behold, they are written in the lamentations" (35:25).

JEHOAHAZ—SEVENTEENTH KING

He was the middle son of Josiah, and reigned for three months (609). He was deposed after only 90 days by the Pharaoh who had killed his father and he was eventually carried into Egyptian captivity where he died.

JEHOIAKIM—EIGHTEENTH KING

The butchery. He reigned for 9 years (609-597). With the exception of Manasseh (his great-great grandfather), Jehoiakim may be regarded as Judah's most evil king. Note this sordid record: he built a plush palace, having huge rooms, many windows, paneled throughout with a fragrant cedar, and painted a beautiful red. This he accomplished with forced slave labor while his own people were suffering; he was full of selfish greed and dishonesty; he murdered the innocent, oppressed the poor, and reigned with ruthlessness; he butchered with a sword a godly and fearless prophet named Uriah, having him first tracked down in Egypt and brought back to Jerusalem; and he often attempted to silence the Prophet Jeremiah.

The burning. He, on one occasion, burned a scroll which contained the inspired writings and prophecies of Jeremiah. But this backfired, as the prophet rewrote all the

The Measure of Indispensability

COMMENTS

The story is told of an executive in a large corporation who kept a five-gallon bucket of water by his office door. He called it his "Indispensability Meter." Whenever an employee came into the executive's office seeking a raise in pay, the executive would promise to give him a raise in keeping with his indispensability to the company. "Stick your arm into the bucket so that your hand rests flat on the bottom of it," he would tell the hopeful employee. When the employee had complied, the executive would direct, "Now pull your hand out of the bucket as fast as you can!" The employee would comply eagerly. The executive would then ask, "How large a hole is left?" The employee had to say, "None." The executive then said, "You are as indispensable to the company as the hole that your arm left behind in the bucket. That's how much of a raise you can expect!"

God does not use such an indispensability meter in His rating of individuals. There is, however, an interesting way in which the indispensability of an individual to God's program can be measured. It is not by what the individual accomplished or by how long he lived or served. It is by how much space is accorded to him in the Bible. Consider how this works out with reference to some of the outstanding kings of Judah as their reigns are recorded in the Book of 2 Kings. Ahaz was Judah's most wicked king. He reigned over Judah for 16 years. To him was given the amazing prophecy of Isaiah 7:14. A scant 46 verses are given to his reign (2 Kings 16:2-20; 2 Chron. 28). If Manasseh had not repented at the end of his life, he would have been Judah's most wicked king. He ruled Judah for 55 years, the longest reign of any king of Judah. A scant 38 verses are dedicated to his long and wicked reign (2 Kings 21:1-18; 2 Chron. 33:1-20). By contrast, Hezekiah, who followed Ahaz's wicked reign, reigned over Judah for 29 years. He was a good king who sought to please Jehovah in his kingdom. Two hundred and twelve verses are devoted to the reign of Hezekiah (2 Kings 18–20; 2 Chron. 29–32). Manasseh was succeeded by his son Amon who reigned only two years. Thirteen verses are given to his reign (2 Kings 21:19-26; 2 Chron. 33:21-24). Josiah, Amon's son, succeeded him in the kingdom and reigned for 31 years. One hundred and ten verses are given to his reign (2 Kings 22:1–23:30; 2 Chron. 34–35). The last four kings of Judah reigned a total of 22 years and six months. All of them did evil in the sight of the Lord. To their combined reigns is given the total of 70 verses (2 Kings 23:31–25:30; 2 Chron. 36:1-13). This averages out to a little over 17 verses for each king. The evil kings were obviously a part of God's ultimate program or they would never have come to power. Their contribution was twofold: (1) they kept the Davidic line intact and (2) the corruption of the nation leading to its setting aside and bringing in the times of the Gentiles was realized. Their contribution to the nation was negative. God's indispensable heroes were the good kings. They not only preserved the Davidic line, but in their reigns the nation experienced great revivals. Through their reforms much of the harm done by the evil kings was undone. Though the nation rebounded from evil under the good kings, yet, like a bouncing tennis ball, each time it rebounded it did not achieve the heights of the previous good king. Ultimately the nation was delivered over to the 70-year Babylonian Captivity.

God's heroes are those men and women who determined to do what God wanted them to do and did it when God put them in the place where they could exercise that determination for the welfare of the nation. Their indispensability can be seen by the amount of space that God devoted to them in His revelation. If God were in the process of giving His revelation to man today, how much space would He devote to you?

king had burned and added a chilling prophecy against Jehoiakim.

Jehoiakim was made a vassal by Nebuchadnezzar after the Babylonians had defeated the Assyrians and Egyptians at the battle of Carchemish. During the last part of his reign, Nebuchadnezzar captured Jerusalem and took some of the sacred temple vessels to Babylon. He also bound Jehoiakim, intending to carry him along, but apparently for some reason, restored him to the Judean throne as his puppet king. He did, however, carry into Captivity some royal Jewish youths, one of which was Daniel.

After three years of this, Jehoiakim was deluded by the Egyptian party in his court to rebel against Nebuchadnezzar.

Though Nebuchadnezzar apparently could not rise up immediately at that time to crush this rebellion, God punished the wicked Judean king by allowing the land to be invaded by the Syrians, Moabites, and Ammonites.

The burial. Jehoiakim died, and as prophesied by Jeremiah, received the burial of a wild animal. He was dragged out of Jerusalem and thrown on the garbage dump beyond the gate, unmourned by even his immediate family. He was succeeded by his son, Jehoiachin.

JEHOIACHIN—NINETEENTH KING

He reigned for three months (597).

He incurred a curse from God stating that his sons would not sit on Judah's throne. Both Ezekiel and Jeremiah predicted he would be carried off into Babylonian Captivity. This happened during Nebuchadnezzar's second "visit" (597) to Jerusalem. Ezekiel was also carried away at this time. Jehoiachin eventually died in Babylon.

ZEDEKIAH—TWENTIETH KING

The coming of the Babylonians. He reigned for 11 years (597-586). Zedekiah was the youngest son of Josiah. He often persecuted Jeremiah. Zedekiah foolishly refused the counsel of Jeremiah and rebelled against Nebuchadnezzar, even though he had taken an oath of loyalty. Rising to this revolt, Nebuchadnezzar came against him. For some 30 months, Jerusalem held out, but on July 18, 586 B.C. it totally collapsed. During the final night, Zedekiah attempted to escape, but was captured near Jericho and brought back to Nebuchadnezzar for punishment. He was forced to witness the execution of his own sons and then his eyes were gouged out. He was finally taken in chains to Babylon where he died.

NOTE: Jeremiah had warned Zedekiah that he would look into the very eyes of Nebuchadnezzar, but Ezekiel prophesied that he would not see Babylon with his eyes. These horrible prophecies came true.

The conquering of the Babylonians. During the latter part of July 586, Nebuchadnezzar's captain of the guard, Nebuzaradan, burned the temple, along with most private and public buildings. The walls of the city were torn down. Nebuchadnezzar then ordered the execution of Seraiah the high priest along with 73 other important officials. Judah's exile was now complete. From this date on, until May 14, A.D. 1948, Israel would cease to be a nation.

The reasons for the Babylonian onslaught. Israel had polluted the temple of God; they had despised the Word of God. *"And the LORD God of their fathers sent to them by His messengers, rising up betimes, and sending; because He had compassion on His people, and on His dwelling place. But they mocked the messengers of God, and despised His words, and misused His prophets, until the wrath of the LORD arose against His people, till there was no remedy" (2 Chron. 36:15-16).*

They had abused the land of God. *"To fulfill the word of the LORD by the mouth of Jeremiah, until the land had enjoyed her Sabbaths. For as long as she lay desolate she kept Sabbath, to fulfill threescore and ten years" (v. 21).*

The results of the Babylonian onslaught. And the Chaldeans burned the king's house, and the houses of the people, and broke down the walls of Jerusalem. *"And they burnt the house of God and brake down the wall of Jerusalem, and burnt all the palaces thereof with fire, and destroyed all the goodly vessels thereof" (v. 19).*

This marked the beginning of that tragic period referred to by Jesus: *"And Jerusalem shall be trodden down of the Gentiles, until the times of the Gentiles be fulfilled" (Luke 21:24).*

This period will not end until the second coming of Christ.

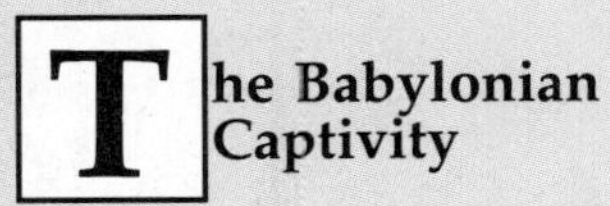

The Babylonian Captivity

COMMENTS

Up to this point in Israel's history, the events comprising it can be summarized as follows: God began with a single individual, Abraham, and promised to make of him a great nation (Gen. 12:1-3). From that point through 2 Samuel God brought that nation into existence in four steps: (1) He gave them the people to comprise the nation during the 430-year Egyptian bondage, (2) He gave them a culture (the Mosaic Law) at Mount Sinai, (3) He gave them the land under Joshua, and (4) He gave them a strong central government under their first king, Saul. In three masterful strokes, God disassembled the nation that He had brought into existence: (1) the division of the kingdom under Rehoboam, (2) the delivery of the Northern Kingdom to Assyrian captivity (from which they never returned), and (3) the delivery of the Southern Kingdom to the Babylonian Captivity.

The Babylonian Captivity was a momentous event in Israel's history. It was a "watershed," for from this point in God's economy God set Israel aside and began the times of the Gentiles so graphically portrayed in Daniel's visions and prophecies. It was also at this time that God began specifically to prepare the world for the coming of His Son, the Messiah, to take away the sins of the world. It might be said that from Creation to Abraham, God's focus was universal, dealing with all mankind. From Abraham to the Babylonian Captivity, God's focus was national, dealing primarily with the nation Israel. With the Babylonian Captivity God's focus is national/universal. National in the sense of bringing to Israel its prophesied Messiah but universal in the sense of bringing to the world its Saviour.

Jeremiah had prophesied that the Babylonian Captivity would last for 70 years (Jer. 25:11-12; 29:10-14). The very fact that he had prophesied a specific length of the Captivity was an encouragement to the faithful of Israel who believed the Word of God. Daniel, for example, studied Jeremiah's prophecy and used it as the basis for his prayer to God to bring to realization the deliverance of His people from that Captivity (Dan. 9:2-19).

The reason why the Babylonian Captivity lasted for exactly 70 years was that God had commanded Israel to let the land rest a full year every seventh year. The people disobeyed God and thus God forced them to give the land a Sabbath of Sabbath rests (Lev. 26:33-35, 43-45; 2 Chron. 36:20-21).

The chief reason for the Babylonian Captivity was to purify the nation from its idolatry. They had forsaken the ways of Jehovah and given themselves wholly to idol worship. God cured them by the saturation method. He took them to the fountainhead of idolatry so that they would become so sick of it that they would forsake it forever.

God used at least three instruments to purify Israel from its idolatry: (1) miracles of deliverance, (2) miracles of judgment, and (3) the deep humiliation that Israel experienced at the hands of the Babylonians (Lam. 2:20-21; 5:9-13). With miracles of deliverance God delivered the Hebrew children from the fiery furnace while the idolatrous soldiers who threw them in were slain. God delivered Daniel from the lions' den while the 120 men with their wives and children were devoured before they reached the bottom of the den. With miracles of judgment God humbled the great Nebuchadnezzar by causing him to eat grass like an animal for seven years and delivered Belshazzar's kingdom to Darius the Mede in one night. Through these miracles God demonstrated His greatness and the impotence of the heathen idols. So effective was the Babylonian Captivity in accomplishing its purpose that even today, Israel is militantly monotheistic to the point of denying the Trinity!

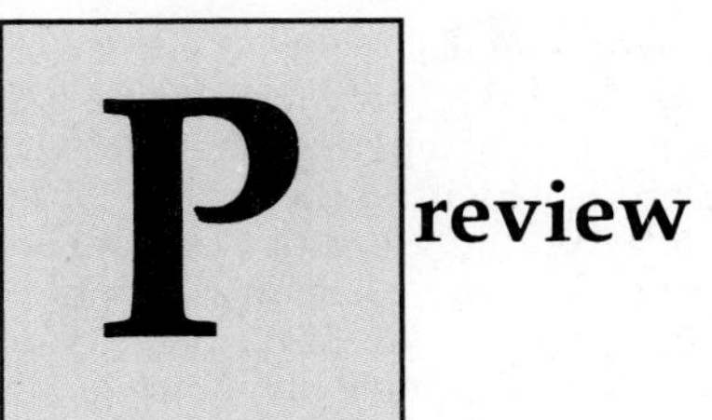

Messengers of God with a Message from God

VARIOUS SCRIPTURE PASSAGES

In spite of the fierce desert heat, the woman shivered as she stood there, watching Him sitting so composed on the platform rim of the well. How could He have possibly known? Until a few minutes ago, they had never even met. Yet, He was fully aware of her five previous marriages, and even more devastating, the fact that she was at that moment living with a sixth man who was not her husband. Attempting to disguise her shock, she weakly responded:

"Sir, I perceive that Thou art a Prophet" (John 4:19). Thus did a Samaritan woman speak to Jesus at Jacob's well. She addressed Him as a Prophet. This lesson is about prophecy and prophets. Over 30 prophets in the Old Testament are mentioned by name, not counting the 18 writing prophets such as Amos, Joel, and Daniel. In this list of 30 are the names of 4 women: Miriam, Deborah, Isaiah's wife, and Huldah. A prophet both forthtold and foretold. He told it like it was and like it would be. Are there prophets today? Yes, but only in the forthtelling sense of the word.

Overview

SCRIPTURE	Various Scripture passages
SUBJECT	Introduction to the Old Testament prophets

SPECIFICS

Description				Duties	Delineation
One who exercised divine	Hindsight	Concerning	The past	To represent	The oral prophets
	Insight		The present	To reveal	
	Foresight		The future	To rebuke	The writing prophets
				To reassure	

Divisions			Destinations			
Six main themes	First coming of Christ	Regathering of Israel	Concerning cities	Jericho	Concerning nations	Assyria
	Second coming of Christ	The Great Tribulation		Jerusalem		Babylon
	Dispersion of Israel	The Millennium		Nineveh		Egypt
				Samaria		Greece
				Tyre		Israel
						Persia
						Rome
						Russia

SAINTS AND SINNERS	Various Old Testament prophets

SENTENCE SUMMARIES

O.T. Verse	"Since the day that your fathers came forth out of the land of Egypt unto this day I have even sent unto you all my servants the prophets, daily rising up early and sending them" (Jer. 7:25).
N.T. Verses	"Knowing this first, that no prophecy of the Scripture is of any private interpretation. For the prophecy came not in old time by the will of man; but holy men of God spake as they were moved by the Holy Ghost" (2 Peter 1:20-21).

THE PROPHETS OF THE CHAOTIC KINGDOM STAGE

The nature of the prophets. The Hebrew word for prophet is *nabhi,* meaning "to boil." The Greek words are: *pro,* meaning, "in place of," and *phemi,* meaning "to speak." Thus, a prophet was God's ambassador and one who spoke His message fervently.

He was different from a priest. A priest represented men to God, while a prophet represented God to men. Furthermore, a prophet did not inherit his office as many Old Testament priests and kings did. He exercised hindsight, insight, and foresight. He reviewed the past and previewed the future. A prophet both forthtold and foretold.

Samuel is generally acknowledged as the first man to hold the office of a prophet. However, a number of men prior to him on occasion did function as prophets. Some of the more well known are Enoch, Jacob, and Moses. Samuel also organized schools for the prophets. Agabus is the last recorded prophet in the Bible. The prophets were fierce revivalists and intense patriots. They were for the most part unpopular.

The predictive messages of the Old Testament prophets covered six main themes: the first advent of Christ, the second advent of Christ, the dispersion of Israel, the regathering of Israel, the coming Great Tribulation, and the coming glorious Millennium.

The Old Testament prophets were not told about the Church Age. *"Which in other ages was not made known unto the sons of men, as it is now revealed unto His holy apostles and prophets by the Spirit. That the Gentiles should be fellow heirs, and of the same body, and partakers of His promise in Christ by the Gospel" (Eph. 3:5-6).*

Because of this, they did not always fully understand everything they wrote about. *"Of which salvation the prophets have inquired and searched diligently, who prophesied of the grace that should come unto you, searching what, or what manner of time the Spirit of Christ which was in them did signify, when it testified beforehand the sufferings of Christ, and the glory that should follow" (1 Peter 1:10-11).*

"Then He said unto them, 'O fools, and slow of heart to believe all that the prophets have spoken. Ought not Christ to have suffered these things, and to enter into His glory?' And beginning at Moses and all the prophets, He expounded unto them in all the Scriptures the things concerning Himself" (Luke 24:25-27).

Prophets were, in Old Testament times, often described as watchmen on a wall. Both the Assyrian and Babylonian captivities were caused (in part) by the lying ministries of false prophets.

There were a number of tests laid down in the Bible whereby a false prophet might be distinguished from a true one. Did they ever predict things that did not come to pass? If so, they were false prophets. Did they turn people away from the true God to other gods? If so, they were false prophets. Did they use instruments of divination (crystal balls, tea leaves, etc.)? If so, they were false prophets.

The names of the prophets. The true prophets were Abel, Enoch, Noah, Abraham, Isaac, Jacob, Deborah, Unknown prophet, Man of God in days of Eli, Samuel, Bands of prophets, Moses, Miriam, Aaron, 70 elders, Gad, Nathan, David, Ahijah, Shemaiah, Man of God from Judah, Iddo, Azariah, Hanani, Jehu, Elijah, Unknown prophet, A son of the prophets, Micaiah, Jahaziel, Eliezer, Elisha, Sons of the prophets, Zechariah, Man of God, Unknown prophet, Zechariah, Obed, Isaiah's wife, and Huldah.

NOTE: This list does not include the writing prophets, like Isaiah, Amos, etc., and John the Baptist, Anna, Agabus, Judas, Silas, Philip's four daughters, and the two tribulational prophets.

NOTE: While He was on earth, our Lord was also recognized as a Prophet.

The false prophets were the prophets of Baal, the Prophet Balaam, Saul, an old prophet from Bethel, Zedekiah, Hananiah, the Prophetess Noadiah, Elymas, the Prophetess Jezebel, and the false prophet (helper to the Antichrist) during the Great Tribulation.

Prophet or Parrot?

COMMENTS

Throughout the course of history many have undertaken the task of speaking for God. Some of them have been divinely appointed and were God's prophets. Others have either been self-appointed or hired by others and dutifully parroted the message they were given. What is the difference between a prophet and a parrot? It is not the claim or desire of the messenger but rather the true source of the message.

The acid test for telling a prophet from a parrot is found in Deuteronomy 18:20-22. Two factors are involved: (1) he was to speak in the name of the Lord (*Yahweh*) and (2) the prophesied event must happen. If the prophet did not speak in the name of the Lord or if the prophesied event did not transpire it was proof that he was a parrot and not a prophet. To be a parrot was a capital offense—the false prophet was to die.

In the Old Testament there are three primary names for God: (1) *Elohim,* usually represented in the English text by "God," (2) *Adonai,* usually represented in the English text by "Lord," and (3) *Yahweh,* usually represented in the English text by "LORD." In delivering his message, the true prophet was to say, "Thus saith the LORD" or, "Thus saith Jehovah." If he used any other name it was an admission that he was not a prophet but was a parrot.

An incident in the life of Jehoshaphat, king of Judah, graphically brings out the difference. Jehoshaphat agreed to ally his army with Ahab, king of Israel, to deliver Ramoth-gilead out of Syrian control (1 Kings 22). Jehoshaphat had some reservations about the whole arrangement for he said to Ahab, "Inquire, I pray thee, at the word of the LORD [*Yahweh*] today" (v. 5). In response, Ahab gathered together about 400 prophets and asked them whether he should undertake the mission to rescue Ramoth-gilead. The prophets simply answered, "Go up, for the Lord [*Adonai*] shall deliver it into the hand of the king" (v. 6). Note that Ahab's prophets did not say, "thus saith the LORD [*Yahweh*]." Jehoshaphat instantly recognized that they were parrots, not prophets, as he said, "Is there not here a prophet of the LORD [*Yahweh*] besides, that we might inquire of him?" (v. 7) Ahab responded, "There is yet one man, Micaiah . . . by whom we may inquire of the LORD. But I hate him; for he doth not prophesy good concerning me, but evil" (v. 8). Jehoshaphat's ears were keenly tuned to the note of authenticity ("Thus saith the LORD") and failing to hear it, was duly alarmed. To satisfy Jehoshaphat, Ahab dispatched a messenger to summon Micaiah (v. 9). While they waited, Jehoshaphat and Ahab sat down garbed in their official robes to hear the messages delivered by the various prophets (v. 10). Zedekiah was particularly brash as he claimed, "Thus saith the LORD, 'With these [horns] shalt thou push the Syrians, until thou have consumed them' " (v. 11). All the other false prophets, encouraged by his daring, agreed, and said, "Go up to Ramoth-gilead, and prosper; for the LORD shall deliver it into the king's hand" (v. 12). They were much bolder than they were earlier (cf. v. 6). When Micaiah arrived on the scene, he amazingly gave the same message (cf. vv. 14-15). Even Ahab detected a note of insincerity (cf. v. 16). Micaiah then explained that it was God's will for Ahab to go up against Ramoth-gilead not to deliver it, but to be slain (cf. vv. 17-23) and then explained the message sent not only by him, but by the false prophets as well. The Lord [*Yahweh*] had sent a lying spirit into the mouths of Ahab's prophets to cause Ahab's death. Ensuing events confirmed that Micaiah was the prophet and Ahab's prophets were parrots, for in spite of Ahab's attempt to frustrate the plan of God (vv. 29-33) "a certain man drew a bow at a venture, and smote the king of Israel. . . . So the king died" (vv. 34, 37) as Micaiah had prophesied.

The Sensational Prophet

1 KINGS 17–2 KINGS 2

The amazing account of earth's second astronaut! The only other human in history to leave this planet without dying. The first to do it was Enoch, and the second, Elijah. Before departing, however, Elijah would select an equally famous successor, Elisha. Elijah and Elisha. What a tremendous team they were. This dynamic duet literally tore up the Middle East countryside during the middle of the eighth century B.C. Rivers were rolled back, kings were rebuked, and corpses were raised. Even as they departed this life, the excitement continued. One left without dying, and the other raised a corpse long after he himself had died. In fact, to these men went the honor of restoring to life the first three of eight dead bodies in the Word of God.

This first mighty messenger, Elijah, began his ministry by rebuking a greedy king, and ended it by sparing a frightened soldier. He then rolled back a river, mounted a fiery chariot, and was gone. Small wonder he wrote no recorded Scripture. He was too busy to pick up a pen.

Overview

SCRIPTURE	1 Kings 17–2 Kings 2			
SUBJECT	Elijah the prophet			
SPECIFICS	God ministering through Elijah		God ministering to Elijah	
	Condemning	Chastising	West of the Jordan	Beside a brook Under a tree In a cave
	Ahab The Baalite priests Ahaziah	Obadiah Israel		
	Comforting	Commissioning	East of the Jordan	The chariot of fire
	The widow of Zarephath	Elisha		
SAINTS AND SINNERS	Elijah, Ahab, Widow of Zarephath, Obadiah, priests of Baal, Jezebel, Naboth, Ahaziah, Elisha			
SENTENCE SUMMARIES	O.T. Verse	"Behold, I will send you Elijah the prophet before the coming of the great and dreadful Day of the LORD" (Mal. 4:5).		
	N.T. Verse	"Elijah was a man subject to like passions as we are, and he prayed earnestly that it might not rain; and it rained not on the earth by the space of three years and six months" (James 5:17).		

ELIJAH

Elijah and King Ahab. Elijah announced a three and-one-half year drought to Ahab. *"And Elijah the Tishbite, who was of the inhabitants of Gilead, said unto Ahab, 'As the LORD God of Israel liveth, before whom I stand, there shall not be dew nor rain these years, but according to my word' " (1 Kings 17:1).*

After three and one half years, Elijah challenged Ahab to a contest on Mount Carmel. *"And it came to pass, when Ahab saw Elijah, that Ahab said unto him, 'Art thou he that troubleth Israel?'*

"And he answered, 'I have not troubled Israel; but thou, and thy father's house, in that ye have forsaken the commandments of the LORD, and thou hast followed Baalim. Now therefore, send, and gather to me all Israel unto Mount Carmel, and the prophets of Baal 450, and the prophets of the groves 400, which eat at Jezebel's table' " (18:17-19).

Elijah predicted the end of the drought. *"And Elijah said unto Ahab, 'Get thee up, eat and drink; for there is a sound of abundance of rain.'*

"So Ahab went up to eat and to drink. And Elijah went up to the top of Carmel; and he cast himself down upon the earth, and put his face between his knees, and said to his servant, 'Go up now, look toward the sea.' And he went up, and looked, and said, 'There is nothing.' And he said, 'Go again seven times.'

"And it came to pass at the seventh time, that he said, 'Behold, there ariseth a little cloud out of the sea, like a man's hand.' And he said, 'Go up, say unto Ahab, "Prepare thy chariot, and get thee down, that the rain stop thee not." ' And it came to pass in the meanwhile, that the heaven was black with clouds and wind, and there was a great rain. And Ahab rode, and went to Jezreel" (vv. 41-45).

Elijah pronounced the death sentence on Ahab and his wife.

Elijah and the ravens at the Brook Cherith. "And the ravens brought him bread and flesh in the morning, and bread and flesh in the evening; and he drank of the brook" (17:6).

Elijah and the widow at Zarephath. Elijah supernaturally fed her family. *"For thus saith the LORD God of Israel, 'The barrel of meal shall not waste, neither shall the cruse of oil fail, until the day that the LORD sendeth rain upon the earth' " (v. 14).*

He supernaturally raised her son. *"And he stretched himself upon the child three times, and cried unto the LORD, and said, 'O LORD my God, I pray Thee, let this child's soul come into him again.'*

"And the LORD heard the voice of Elijah; and the soul of the child came into him again, and he revived" (vv. 21-22).

Elijah and Obadiah. Obadiah was the superintendent of Ahab's household. He had hidden and cared for 100 prophets of God, thus saving them from Jezebel's wrath, but he was afraid to take a public stand for Jehovah God.

Elijah and the people of Israel. "And Elijah came unto all the people, and said, 'How long halt ye between two opinions? If the LORD be God, follow Him; but if Baal, then follow him.' And the people answered him not a word" (18:21).

Elijah and the priests of Baal. *The proposal: Elijah said that two bullocks should be offered, one to Baal, the other to God, with the true Deity to respond by sending down fire to consume His bullock.

*The problem: *"And they took the bullock which was given them, and they dressed it, and called on the name of Baal from morning even until noon, saying, 'O Baal, hear us.' But there was no voice, nor any that answered. And they leaped upon the altar which was made. . . . And they cried aloud, and cut themselves after their manner with knives and lancets, till the blood gushed out upon them.*

"And it came to pass, when midday was past, and they prophesied until the time of the offering of the evening sacrifice, that there was neither voice, nor any to answer, nor any that regarded" (vv. 26, 28-29).

*The preparation: Elijah then placed his bullock on a 12-stone altar and filled the trench surrounding it with 12 barrels of water.

*The prayer: *"Hear me, O LORD, hear me, that this people may know that Thou art the LORD God, and that Thou hast turned their heart back again" (v. 37).*

*The purification: *"Then the fire of the LORD fell, and consumed the burnt sacrifice, and the wood, and the stones, and the dust, and licked up*

Elijah: God's Baal-buster

COMMENTS

The worship of Baal was a long-standing cancer going back in human history to at least 1700 B.C. The word Baal in its primary sense means "master," "owner," or "lord." Baal was commonly thought to be the sun-god, the male counterpart of Asteroth (plural), the moon goddess. In reality, Baal was more of a god of nature supposedly owning and controlling the land and being responsible for the increase of fruits, crops, and cattle. The worship of Baal was accompanied by cruelty, even human sacrifice, and sexual immorality. The Israelites first came into contact with Baal worship during their wilderness wanderings when Balaam led them into the worship of Baal-peor (Num. 22:41). It was the religion of Canaan when Israel under Joshua invaded it. The Phoenician cities of Tyre and Sidon were the chief cities of Baal worship. Because the Phoenicians were sailors, the worship of Baal was widespread. The north African city of Carthage was a colony of Phoenicia. Their most famous general was Hannibal, whose name meant "the grace of Baal." The Babylonians were also involved in Baal worship. Their chief god was Bel, whose name was merely a Babylonian form of Baal.

When Joshua conquered Jericho he issued a prophecy (Josh. 6:26) which stood unchallenged until the days of Ahab, the most wicked king of Israel's history (1 Kings 16:33). In defiance of Jehovah he instituted the worship of Baal throughout the land of Judah. So deeply did Ahab's rebellion take root in Judah that Hiel decided to rebuild ancient Jericho. He did so in spite of the deaths of his firstborn and youngest sons (v. 34) in fulfillment of Joshua's prophecy.

Into such a spiritually rebellious and apostate climate God sent His man—Elijah. God used Elijah in the battle against Baal in at least nine ways: (1) through his first public act in announcing that there would be no dew or rain except at his word (17:1-7)—Baal was supposed to be the god of nature and live in heaven yet Elijah closed up heaven and imprisoned Baal; (2) through his ministry to the widow of Zarephath (vv. 8-14)—she lived in Phoenicia, Baal's stronghold; Elijah worked miracles of mercy showing that the true God is able to invade Baal's stronghold and use His power for acts of mercy, not cruelty; (3) through the contest with the priests of Baal on Mount Carmel (18:19-40)—one prophet of Jehovah opened the heavens in July, the dry season, and put to rout 450 prophets of Baal and 400 prophets of Ashteroth, having them put to death; (4) through his marathon race from Mount Carmel to Jezreel before Ahab's chariot (vv. 44-46)—Ahab was trying to outrun the coming rain yet God worked in Elijah's body enabling him to outrun the horses; (5) through anointing Elisha to be his successor (19:15-16)—God used Elisha to continue the battle against Baal; (6) through his prophecy of judgment against Ahab and Jezebel (21:17-24) and against the house of Ahab (22:37-38; 2 Kings 9:30-37; 10:1-17)—though the prophecy wasn't fulfilled for 20 years it showed the people the results of Baal worship; (7) through his last public act, his prophecy of Ahaziah's death (chap. 1)—Elijah's victory over Baal is shown as Baal's representative is on his knees before Elijah begging for mercy; (8) through his final visit to Gilgal, Bethel, and Jericho and dividing the waters of the Jordan (2:1-10; cf. 1 Sam. 7:16)—he was training those who would carry on the battle against Baal; and (9) through his translation to heaven (2 Kings 2:11)—he was caught up in a whirlwind and went through the atmosphere over which Baal was supposed to have dominion; Baal could not stop God's Baal-buster. The work begun by Elijah was continued by Elisha.

the water that was in the trench" (v. 38).

*The praise: *"And when all the people saw it, they fell on their faces, and they said, 'The LORD, He is the God; the LORD, He is the God' " (v. 39).*

*The purge: *"And Elijah said unto them, 'Take the prophets of Baal; let not one of them escape.' And they took them, and Elijah brought them down to the Brook Kishon, and slew them there" (v. 40).*

Elijah and God. Fleeing from Jezebel, he rested under a juniper tree, where he was reassured and fed by God Himself.

"And as he lay and slept under a juniper tree, behold, then an angel touched him, and said unto him, 'Arise and eat.' And he looked, and behold, there was a cake baken on the coals, and a cruse of water at his head. And he did eat and drink, and laid him down again.

"And the Angel of the LORD came again the second time, and touched him, and said, 'Arise and eat; because the journey is too great for thee' " (19:5-7).

God spoke to him in a still, small voice while he was hiding in a cave. *"And He said, 'Go forth, and stand upon the mount before the LORD.' And, behold, the LORD passed by, and a great and strong wind rent the mountains, and brake in pieces the rocks before the LORD; but the LORD was not in the wind. And after the wind an earthquake; but the LORD was not in the earthquake. And after the earthquake a fire; but the LORD was not in the fire. And after the fire a still small voice" (vv. 11-12).*

Elijah and King Ahaziah. Ahaziah, the wicked king, son of Ahab, commanded three bands of 50 soldiers each to seek out and kill Elijah for condemning his idolatry and predicting the ruler's death. The first two groups were consumed by fire called down from heaven by Elijah. The captain of the third group begged for mercy and was spared. As Elijah had predicted, Ahaziah soon died.

Elijah and Elisha. "So he [Elijah] departed thence, and found Elisha the son of Shaphat, who was plowing with 12 yoke of oxen before him, and he with the twelfth: and Elijah passed by him, and cast his mantle upon him" (v. 19).

Elisha refused to allow Elijah to abandon him or a band of fickle student prophets to discourage him. Note Elisha's request: *"And it came to pass, when they were gone over, that Elijah said unto Elisha, 'Ask what I shall do for thee, before I be taken away from thee.' And Elisha said, 'I pray thee, let a double portion of thy spirit be upon me' " (2 Kings 2:9).*

Elijah and the chariot of fire. "And it came to pass, as they still went on, and talked, that, behold, there appeared a chariot of fire, and horses of fire, and parted them both asunder; and Elijah went up by a whirlwind into heaven" (v. 11).

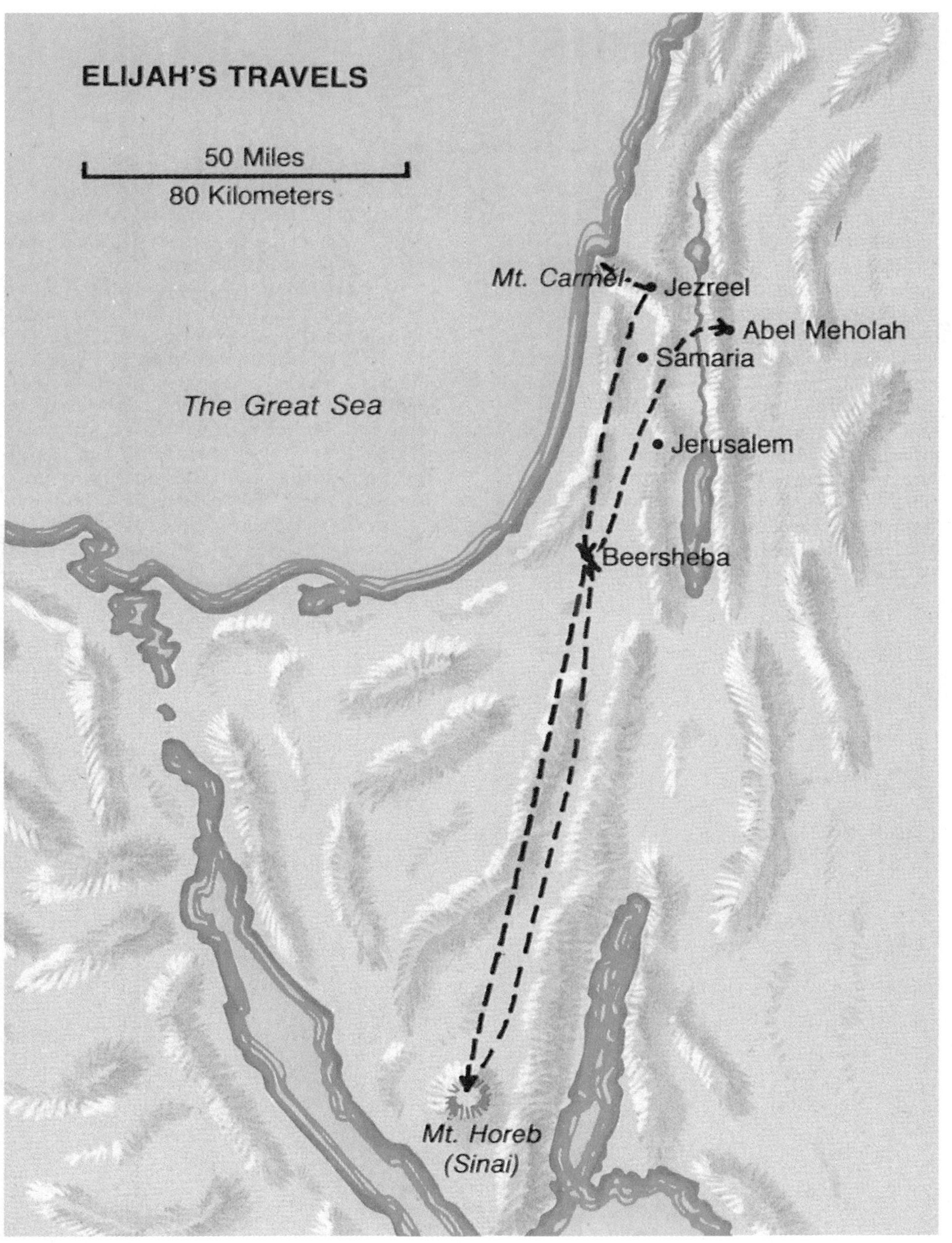
ELIJAH'S TRAVELS
50 Miles
80 Kilometers
Mt. Carmel
Jezreel
Abel Meholah
Samaria
The Great Sea
Jerusalem
Beersheba
Mt. Horeb
(Sinai)

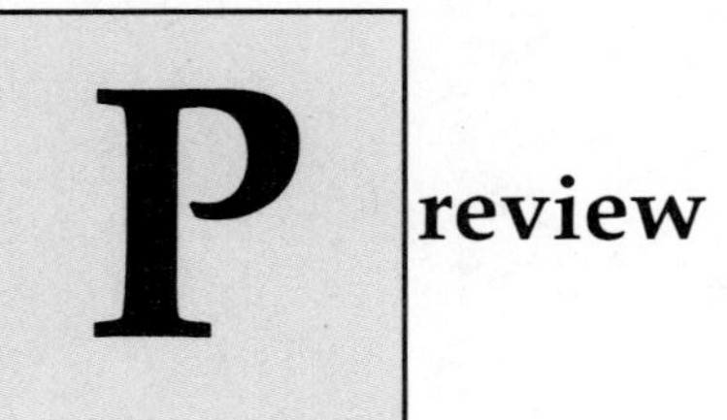

The Sensitive Prophet

2 KINGS 2–13

The blinding light and deafening sound at last subsided. All was now deathly quiet. Nothing around him had changed, and yet everything was different. He had both seen and heard sights and sounds never experienced by mortal man. Whatever happened, he would never be the same. Elisha stood on the Eastern Bank of the Jordan immediately after the stupendous homegoing of Elijah. What a moment! But now Elisha was emotionally drained. He needed answers and reassurance. Had a double portion of Elijah's divine power been given to him as requested? He would soon see. Taking Elijah's mantle, Elisha smote the river in front of him and cried out, *"Where is the* LORD *God of Elijah?"* In a flash, the Jordan waters parted. This all happened some 28 centuries ago. God answered his question.

But today a more piercing question is, "Where are the Elijahs of the Lord God?" Where indeed? Like the Marines, God is still looking for a few good men and women.

Elijah and Elisha. What were they really like? In a sense they can be considered the Peter and Paul of the Old Testament. Elijah was like Peter, vocal, dynamic, bold, impulsive, high-strung, with the capacity to move from elation to depression in a few moments. But what about Elisha? Like Paul, he was low-keyed, organized, productive, and absolutely tireless.

Overview

<table>
<tr><td>SCRIPTURE</td><td colspan="5">2 Kings 2–13</td></tr>
<tr><td>SUBJECT</td><td colspan="5">Elisha the prophet</td></tr>
<tr><td rowspan="8">SPECIFICS</td><td colspan="5">The Miracle-worker</td></tr>
<tr><td rowspan="4">Personal miracles</td><td colspan="4">For his students</td></tr>
<tr><td colspan="2">Purifying some water
Purifying a stew
Creating oil</td><td colspan="2">Feeding 100
Recovering an axhead</td></tr>
<tr><td>For himself</td><td>For a supporter</td><td>For a servant</td><td>For a soldier</td></tr>
<tr><td>Parting the Jordan
Judging some trouble-makers</td><td>Raising her son</td><td>Showing him God's angels</td><td>Healing his leprosy</td></tr>
<tr><td>Patriotic miracles</td><td>Deceiving the enemy</td><td colspan="2">Revealing the war plans of the enemy</td><td>Blinding the enemy</td></tr>
<tr><td>Predictive miracles</td><td colspan="4">7 prophecies that were fulfilled</td></tr>
<tr><td>Posthumous miracle</td><td colspan="4">Raising a man from the dead</td></tr>
<tr><td>SAINTS AND SINNERS</td><td colspan="5">Elisha, Elijah, some student prophets, Jehoram, a widow, Gehazi, a Shunammite woman, Naaman, 4 lepers, Joash</td></tr>
<tr><td rowspan="2">SENTENCE SUMMARIES</td><td>O.T. Verse</td><td colspan="4">"The Angel of the LORD encampeth round about them that fear Him, and delivereth them" (Ps. 34:7).</td></tr>
<tr><td>N.T. Verse</td><td colspan="4">"Many lepers were in Israel in the time of Elisha the prophet; and none of them was cleansed, saving Naaman the Syrian" (Luke 4:27).</td></tr>
</table>

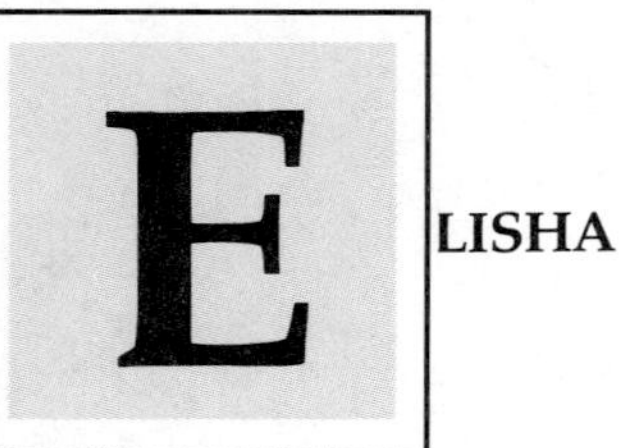

ELISHA

Parting the waters at Jordan. "And he took the mantle of Elijah that fell from him, and smote the waters, and said, 'Where is the LORD God of Elijah?' And when he also had smitten the waters, they parted hither and thither; and Elisha went over" (2 Kings 2:14).

Judging some hoodlums at Bethel. "And he went up from thence unto Bethel. And as he was going up by the way, there came forth little children out of the city, and mocked him, and said unto him, 'Go up, thou bald head; go up, thou bald head.'

"And he turned back, and looked on them, and cursed them in the name of the LORD. And there came forth two she bears out of the wood, and tare forty and two children of them" (vv. 23-24).

Causing some empty ditches to fill with water. Jehoshaphat had foolishly joined forces with King Jehoram (Ahab's second son) against the Moabites. For Jehoshaphat's sake Elisha supernaturally caused some empty ditches to fill with water. This water served to slacken the thirst of the allies, and was mistaken by the Moabites for blood, who assumed it was evidence of fighting between the allies. Because of this supernatural deception, the Moabites were defeated.

Creating oil in empty vessels. This allowed a prophet's poverty-stricken widow to pay her creditors.

Raising a dead boy at Shunem. This boy's mother had provided Elisha with a guest room. After the boy's death his mother refused to tell Gehazi (Elisha's carnal servant) about her terrible need. When she finally told Elisha, he took immediate action. "And he went up, and lay upon the child, and put his mouth upon his mouth, and his eyes upon his eyes, and his hands upon his hands. And he stretched himself upon the child; and the flesh of the child waxed warm. Then he returned, and walked in the house to and fro; and went up, and stretched himself upon him: and the child sneezed seven times, and the child opened his eyes" (4:34-35).

Feeding 100 men by supernaturally increasing 20 loaves of bread and a sack of corn.

Healing of Naaman. Naaman, the Syrian soldier, had leprosy, but because of the testimony of a faithful Israelite slave girl, left Syria to find healing in Samaria.

"And she said unto her mistress, 'Would God my lord were with the prophet that is in Samaria. For he would recover him of his leprosy' " (5:3).

Naaman, the seeking soldier. Jehoram, wicked king of Israel, was unable to help Naaman. Elisha, godly prophet in Israel, was fully able to help him.

"And it was so, when Elisha the man of God had heard that the king of Israel had rent his clothes, that he sent to the king, saying, 'Wherefore hast thou rent thy clothes? Let him come now to me, and he shall know that there is a prophet in Israel' " (v. 8).

Naaman, the sulking soldier. Elisha commanded Naaman to wash himself seven times in the Jordan River. Furious, but desperate, Naaman obeyed.

"Then he went down, and dipped himself seven times in Jordan, according to the saying of the man of God, and his flesh came again like unto the flesh of a little child, and he was clean" (v. 14).

Naaman, the singing soldier. "And he returned to the man of God, he and all his company, and came, and stood before him. And he said, 'Behold, now I know that there is no God in all the earth, but in Israel. Now therefore, I pray thee, take a blessing of thy servant' " (v. 15).

Recovering a lost axhead. A student prophet lost a borrowed axhead in the Jordan River. Elisha caused it to float and be recovered.

Revealing the secret war plans of Syria. On several occasions Elisha had revealed to King Jehoram the location of his enemies, the Syrians, thus preventing an ambush.

Praying that his servant could see an invisible angelic army. The Syrian king sent troops to arrest Elisha for revealing the location of his armies. Elisha prayed that Gehazi, his frightened servant, might see what the old prophet knew existed.

"And Elisha prayed, and said, 'LORD, I pray Thee, open his eyes, that he may see.' And the LORD opened the eyes of the young man; and he saw. And, behold, the mountain was full of horses and chariots of fire round about Elisha" (6:17).

Blinding some Syrian soldiers. These soldiers, sent to arrest Elisha, were then led blinded to Samaria where they received their sight, were fed, and were allowed to return home, having experienced the

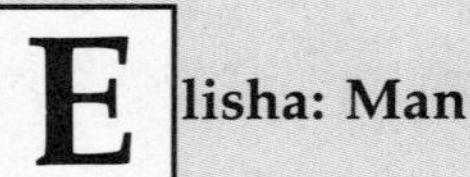

Elisha: Man of Miracles

COMMENTS

God used Elijah to undermine the foundations of Baal worship and He used Elisha to restrain Baal worship after Elijah passed from the scene. The ministries of both men were located in the Northern Kingdom of Israel and were characterized by miracles. Most of Elijah's miracles were worked during the reign of Ahab and were primarily miracles of judgment. Most of Elisha's 16 recorded miracles were worked during the reign of Jehoram, Ahab's son, and were primarily miracles of mercy showing that Jehovah is a God of mercy. Elisha's recorded miracles are as follows:

(1) Dividing the River Jordan by smiting it with Elijah's mantle (2 Kings 2:13-15). This miracle showed Elisha that he had indeed received a double portion of Elijah's spirit as he had requested. The power that Elijah had had was with him. It also showed the sons of the prophets that Elisha was the God-appointed successor to Elijah.

(2) The healing of the poisonous waters at Jericho by casting salt into them from a new cruse (vv. 18-22; cf. Josh. 6:26; 1 Kings 16:34). This miracle was directed as a call to repentance to the rebellious inhabitants of rebuilt Jericho. It was also directed to the sons of the prophets who resided at Jericho (cf. 2 Kings 2:5) to show them that God would purify Israel by casting some of the prophets who were "salt" from a new cruse among impure Israel.

(3) The destruction at Bethel of the 42 disrespectful young men by two she bears (vv. 23-25). Jeroboam I instituted calf worship at Bethel (cf. 1 Kings 12:28-29) where some of the sons of the prophets also lived (cf. 2 Kings 2:3). The term "bald head" was actually a curse against Elisha. In their attitude toward God's prophet the lads were expressing their attitude toward God. They wanted to be rid of Elisha and his God. The miracle shows that the young men, probably about 20 years of age, were responsible for their actions before God. The miracle showed the sons of the prophets at Bethel that God would supernaturally protect them.

(4) The victory over King Mesha and the Moabites, won by the kings of Israel (Jehoram), Judah (Jehoshaphat), and Edom by miraculously filling trenches with water which resembled blood (3:4-27). This miracle was directed toward Judah and Jehoshaphat (who really should not have been there in league with the kings of Israel and Edom who did not believe in Jehovah). Through the miracle God preserved Jehoshaphat and the Davidic line. The miracle also exerted a restraining influence on Jehoram who, during the 12 years of his reign, forsook the Baal worship of his parents (vv. 2-3). The minstrel's playing is indicative of the value of music to prepare one's heart to be receptive to the message of God.

(5) The miraculous supply of oil for the widow of one of the sons of the prophets (4:1-7). This miracle was directed primarily to the wives of the sons of the prophets. The wives of God's ministers needed to see the power of God and realize that God would supply their needs too even though they were very poor.

(6) The supernatural birth of the Shunammites' son and his resurrection from the dead (vv. 8-37). This miracle was worked in response to a woman of great faith. When her son died, she made no provisions for his burial. She didn't even tell her husband that their son had died. She traveled about four hours to reach Elisha and when asked, "Is it well with thee . . . with thy husband . . . with the child?" she answered simply, "It is well." In response to faith God's prophet raised the son to life. The fact that the son sneezed seven times showed that he was very much alive—it takes a great deal of energy to sneeze.

(7) Counteracting the poisoned food of the sons of the prophets at Gilgal by casting meal into the pot (vv. 38-41). This miracle was twofold for it not only counteracted the uneaten food in the pot but also the food that had already been eaten. It showed the sons of the prophets that God would care for and protect them. It also showed them that God was going to use them to counteract the poison of sin in Israel by casting them into the "pot."

(8) The miraculous feeding of 100 men during the famine at Gilgal with 20 barley loaves and fresh ears of grain brought by a man from Baal-shalisha (vv. 42-44). This miracle showed the sons of the prophets that God could care for them even in the worst of circumstances. Baal-shalisha had been a center of Baal worship in the days of Ahab and Jezebel. When this incident was related there it would be an additional influence to restrain Israel from returning to Baal worship.

(9) Healing Naaman the Syrian of leprosy (5:1-19). Naaman was a Syrian national hero. His leprosy was white leprosy, the worst kind. Naaman's flesh was made purer than it had been before. The miracle was

absolutely free. All Syria would hear of Naaman's healing and would be called to repentance. God demonstrated His principle of showing mercy to one's enemies.

(10) The judgment of leprosy on Gehazi (vv. 20-27). This miracle warned against the sin of covetousness. Even Elisha's servant was not exempt from punishment when he sinned. God's curse was passed from Naaman, the Gentile who obeyed, to Gehazi, the Jew who disobeyed. God's servants must not mistake God's favor for favoritism.

(11) Making the axhead swim (6:1-7). This miracle showed the sons of the prophets that God cared about their personal obligations ("it was borrowed") incurred to accomplish His work.

(12) Israel's victory over Syria through supernatural blindness inflicted on the Syrians (vv. 8-23). Elisha led the entire Syrian army captive to Samaria where they were treated kindly and released. It was a call to repentance to Syria to forsake the cruel ways of Baal worship and seek Jehovah, the God of mercy.

(13) Israel's supernatural deliverance from famine through God's host (v. 24–7:20). Through this miracle God prolonged Israel's life and called them to repentance. In about 24 hours prices went from the highest to the lowest in Israel's history. It was a tangible illustration of 2 Peter 3:8.

(14) Elisha's prediction of the seven-year famine (2 Kings 8:1-6). God used this prediction not only to preserve the woman's life but also to vindicate Elisha as the prophet of Jehovah.

(15) Elisha's prediction of Hazael's victories (vv. 7-15, cf. 10:32-33; 12:17; 13:3, 7). This prediction was used to vindicate God's prophet before the Syrians. Not even Hazael expected to do these things which were accomplished over a period of many years.

(16) Raising a dead man to life whose corpse touched Elisha's (vv. 20-21). This was God's climactic seal of approval on Elisha's ministry against Baal. It showed that though Elisha was gone, the God of Elisha is still living and able to work miracles.

In summary, it can be observed that God had four purposes in making Elisha His man of miracles: (1) to restrain Israel from returning to Baal worship during the reign of Jehoram, Ahab's son, (2) to call the Syrians from their national religion, Baal worship, to the worship of Jehovah, the true and only God, (3) to call Israel from the calf worship instituted by Jeroboam I, and (4) to train young men of God and their wives in the miracle-working power of God.

mighty power and grace of God!

Predicting Gehazi's leprosy. Gehazi was smitten by leprosy for attempting to secure money from Naaman for the healing experienced at the hand of Elisha.

Predicting the salvation of Samaria from starvation. Samaria was surrounded by the Syrians. Horrible conditions soon prevailed, including starvation and cannibalism. In spite of all this: *"Elisha said, 'Hear ye the word of the LORD; Thus saith the LORD, "Tomorrow about this time shall a measure of fine flour be sold for a shekel, and two measures of barley for a shekel, in the gate of Samaria" ' " (7:1).*

The king's assistant denounced Elisha. "Behold, if the LORD would make windows in heaven, might this thing be?" (v. 2) He was in turn denounced by Elisha. *"Behold, thou shalt see it with thine eyes, but shall not eat of it" (v. 2).*

"And there were four leprous men at the entering in of the gate, and they said one to another, 'Why sit we here until we die? If we say, "We will enter into the city," then the famine is in the city, and we shall die there; and if we sit still here, we die also. Now therefore come, and let us fall unto the host of the Syrians. If they save us alive, we shall live; and if they kill us, we shall but die' " (vv. 3-4).

"And they rose up in the twilight, to go unto the camp of the Syrians; and when they were come to the uttermost part of the camp of Syria, behold, there was no man there. For the Lord had made the host of the Syrians to hear a noise of chariots, and a noise of horses, even the noise of a great host. And they said one to another, 'Lo, the king of Israel hath hired against us the kings of the Hittites, and the kings of the Egyptians, to come upon us' " (vv. 5-6).

After helping themselves to the spoils of war, they suddenly remembered those starving people within the city. *"Then they said one to another, 'We do not well. This day is a day of good tidings, and we hold our peace. If we tarry till the morning light, some mischief will come upon us. Now therefore come, that we may go and tell the king's household' " (v. 9).*

"And the king appointed the lord on whose hand he leaned to have the charge of the gate; and the people trode upon him in the gate, and he died, as the man of God had said, who spake when the king came down to him" (v. 17).

The reign of Hazael over Syria. Elisha not only predicted Hazael's reign, but foretold the terrible cruelties he would bring on Israel.

Raising a man years after the prophet himself had died. This happened when the corpse of a man being buried came in contact with Elisha's bones. *"And Elisha died, and they buried him. And the bands of the Moabites invaded the land at the coming in of the year. And it came to pass, as they were burying a man, that, behold, they spied a band of men; and they cast the man into the sepulchre of Elisha. And when the man was let down, and touched the bones of Elisha, he revived, and stood up on his feet" (13:20-21).*

Preview

Obadiah and Jonah: Prophets to the Pagans

BOOKS OF OBADIAH AND JONAH

Who were they? Well, for the most part they were God's 11 angry authors. Here are their names: Obadiah, Jonah, Nahum, Amos, Hosea, Joel, Isaiah, Micah, Zephaniah, Habakkuk, and Jeremiah.

To *whom* did they write? One wrote about the nation Edom, two concerning Nineveh, two to the Northern Kingdom, and six to the Southern Kingdom.

What did they write? In a nutshell, shape up or be shipped out! Revival or ruin, which would it be?

First, a word about Obadiah: Imagine that your city is surrounded by a brutal enemy. However, one dark night you manage to escape and find yourself, for the moment at least, out of danger. But suddenly out of the darkness you are pounced on by an unknown enemy and roughly dragged back to the city to be sold by your original captors into slavery. Only then, in the morning light, are you aware that the heartless bounty hunter is your own cousin! This is the story of Obadiah. The enemy was Assyria, the victims, the Israelites, and the bounty hunters, the Edomites. Both Edom and Israel were related, being descendants of Isaac.

Now, a word about Jonah. Think of him this way—his book contains the biggest fish story of all time, but it has nothing to do with the sea monster that swallowed him in chapter 1 or spewed him out in chapter 2. No, in reality it is found in chapter 3 where we read of perhaps the greatest revival in history. In other words Jonah caught more human fish with his Gospel net of repentance than any other spiritual "fisherman" either before or after his time.

Overview

<table>
<tr><td>SCRIPTURE</td><td colspan="5">Books of Obadiah and Jonah</td></tr>
<tr><td>SUBJECT</td><td colspan="5">General introduction to Chaotic Kingdom stage books; ministries of Obadiah and Jonah</td></tr>
<tr><td rowspan="7">SPECIFICS</td><td colspan="2">General introduction</td><td colspan="2">Obadiah</td><td>Jonah</td></tr>
<tr><td>Writer</td><td>Recipient</td><td colspan="2" rowspan="4">Edom's contempt for God</td><td rowspan="2">The refusal</td></tr>
<tr><td>Obadiah</td><td>Edom</td></tr>
<tr><td>Jonah
Nahum</td><td>Nineveh</td><td rowspan="2">The resolution</td></tr>
<tr><td>Amos
Hosea</td><td>Northern Kingdom</td></tr>
<tr><td rowspan="2">Joel
Isaiah
Micah
Zephaniah
Habakkuk
Jeremiah
Lamentations</td><td rowspan="2">Southern Kingdom</td><td colspan="2" rowspan="2">Edom's condem-nation by God</td><td>The revival</td></tr>
<tr><td>The resentment</td></tr>
<tr><td>SAINTS AND SINNERS</td><td colspan="5">Obadiah, Jonah, some sailors, king of Nineveh</td></tr>
<tr><td rowspan="2">SENTENCE SUMMARIES</td><td>O.T. Verses</td><td colspan="4">"Save me, O God; for the waters are come in unto my soul. I sink in deep mire, where there is no standing; I am come into deep waters, where the floods overflow me" (Ps. 69:1-2).</td></tr>
<tr><td>N.T. Verse</td><td colspan="4">"For as Jonah was three days and three nights in the whale's belly, so shall the Son of man be three days and three nights in the heart of the earth" (Matt. 12:40).</td></tr>
</table>

THE OLD TESTAMENT BOOKS WRITTEN DURING THE CHAOTIC KINGDOM STAGE

OBADIAH (DESTINATION EDOM)

Because of their thankless hearts. The Edomites had become proud and arrogant. They lived in high, inaccessible mountainous cliffs which surrounded their capital, the city of Petra. Because of this, they thought they were invincible.

"The pride of thine heart hath deceived thee, thou that dwellest in the clefts of the rock, whose habitation is high; that saith in his heart, 'Who shall bring me down to the ground?'

" 'Though thou exalt thyself as the eagle, and though thou set thy nest among the stars, thence will I bring thee down,' saith the LORD*" (Obad. 3-4).*

Every nook and cranny of Petra would be searched and robbed, and every treasure found and taken. Edom's allies would turn against them. Their wise men would be filled with stupidity. The mightiest soldiers of Teman (another Edomite city) would be confused and helpless to prevent this awful slaughter.

Because of their treacherous hand. They had deserted their blood brothers (Judah) in time of great need, standing aloof, refusing to lift even one finger to help. They had actually rejoiced over Judah's agony, mocking them, and occupying their lands after the Captivity. They stood at the crossroads killing some of those trying to escape and selling others into slavery as prisoners of war.

THE HOUSE OF JACOB TO BE REVIVED BY GOD

In spite of their terrible persecutions and punishments, some deserved and others undeserved, Judah will someday be fully restored to Palestine. The Israelites will then control tremendous land areas never before occupied, including the land of Edom. Judges will rule over Edom and Petra from Jerusalem during the Millennium.

"And saviors shall come up on Mount Zion to judge the mount of Esau; and the kingdom shall be the LORD*'s" (v. 21).*

JONAH (DESTINATION NINEVEH)

The prophet's order. God ordered Jonah to proceed to Nineveh and preach out against their wickedness.

The prophet's objection. Jonah refused and bought a ticket on a ship heading for Tarshish (Spain). God suddenly flung a terrific wind over the sea, causing a great storm. The frightened sailors prayed to their various pagan gods and frantically threw the cargo they were carrying overboard to lighten the ship. During this time, Jonah was sound asleep in the ship's hold. When the captain heard this, he awakened Jonah and ordered that he too make prayer to his God for salvation.

The prophet's ordeal. In desperation, the sailors cast lots to determine who among them had brought the storm by offending his god. The lot fell to Jonah. Jonah admitted to them his nationality and sin of disobeying God. He then advised them to throw him overboard.

After further useless strugglings, the sailors cried out a prayer for forgiveness for what they had to do with Jonah and quickly threw him overboard into the boiling sea. Immediately, the raging waters became calm as the storm ceased. The amazed sailors gave thanks to Jehovah God.

"Wherefore they cried unto the LORD*, and said, 'We beseech Thee, let us not perish for this man's life, and lay not upon us innocent blood; for Thou, O* LORD*, hast done as it pleased Thee.' So they took up Jonah, and cast him forth into the sea; and the sea ceased from her raging.*

"Then the men feared the LORD *exceedingly, and offered a sacrifice unto the* LORD*, and made vows" (Jonah 1:14-16).*

According to God's plan, Jonah was swallowed by a huge fish.

The petition. Jonah immediately began an earnest and all-out one-man prayer meeting. His altar was perhaps the strangest ever used, the slippery slopes of a fish's stomach.

"For Thou hadst cast me into the deep, in the midst of the seas; and the floods compassed me about; all Thy billows and Thy waves passed over

me. Then I said, 'I am cast out of Thy sight; yet I will look again toward Thy holy temple.' The waters compassed me about, even to the soul; the depth closed me round about, the weeds were wrapped about my head" (2:3-5).

Some advocate that Jonah's language seemed to indicate he actually died and was later resurrected by God. Note his phrases:

"I went down to the bottoms of the mountains; the earth with her bars was about me forever. Yet hast Thou brought up my life from corruption, O LORD my God. When my soul fainted within me I remembered the LORD; and my prayer came in unto Thee, into Thine holy temple" (vv. 6-7).

Jonah renounced his sin, remembered his vow of service, and reconsecrated his life to God.

"They that observe lying vanities forsake their own mercy. But I will sacrifice unto Thee with the voice of thanksgiving; I will pay that I have vowed. Salvation is of the LORD" (vv. 8-9).

The pardon. He ended his prayer with a five-word summary of the entire Bible and indeed, the very plan and purpose of God: *"Salvation is of the LORD"* (v. 9).

He was then vomited up on dry land by the fish.

The warning. "Yet 40 days, and Nineveh shall be overthrown" (3:4).

The transforming. "So the people of Nineveh believed God, and proclaimed a fast, and put on sackcloth, from the greatest of them even to the least of them. For word came unto the king of Nineveh, and he arose from his throne, and he laid his robe from him, and covered him with sackcloth, and sat in ashes. . . .

"And God saw their works, that they turned from their evil way; and God repented of the evil that He had said that He would do unto them; and He did it not" (3:5-6, 10).

NOTE: The greatest revival in the history of the world may have taken place at this time.

Two phrases in this verse deserve a brief comment: *"God repented"*—that is, God changed His previously intended course of action. See also Genesis 6:6; Exodus 32:14; 2 Samuel 24:16.

"Of the evil"—While it is true the Hebrew word *ra* (here translated "evil") is usually connected with sin, it can also be (and often is) translated by such words as affliction, calamity, distress, grief, harm, trouble, and sorrow. The context would show that the latter meaning is meant here in Jonah 3:10. See also 1:7-8 and Isaiah 45:7 for similar examples.

Lamenting over a city. This chapter, along with Genesis 9, 12, 2 Samuel 11, 1 Kings 19 and others demonstrate beyond any reasonable doubt that the Bible is not a book man would write if he could. Jonah, God's chosen minister, is presented as a petty and pouting prophet, sitting on a hill outside Nineveh and hoping the city would refuse his previous message and be destroyed.

He reluctantly acknowledged the grace, mercy, and goodness of God and then in brazen desperation and disappointment dared to pray: *"Therefore now, O LORD, take, I beseech Thee, my life from me; for it is better for me to die than to live"* (Jonah 4:3).

Learning under a gourd. Jonah made a leafy lean-to shelter and continued to sit sulking on the hillside. When the sun had withered the leafy shelter, to Jonah's surprise and relief, God arranged for a vine to grow quickly and shade him. But God also prepared a worm, which soon ate through the vine's stem and killed it.

Finally the Lord subjected His prophet to a scorching east wind, until he once again cried out for God to kill him. Jonah was asked then if he regretted the destruction of the vine. The prophet loudly assured God he did indeed, and the divine trap was sprung. God's final recorded words to Jonah must have softened his stubborn and carnal heart.

"Then said the LORD, 'Thou hast had pity on the gourd, for the which thou hast not labored, neither madest it grow; which came up in a night, and perished in a night. And should not I spare Nineveh, that great city, wherein are more than sixscore thousand persons that cannot discern between their right hand and their left hand; and also much cattle?" (vv. 10-11)

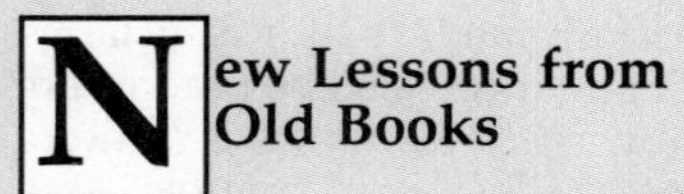

COMMENTS

Though they were written thousands of years ago, the books of the minor prophets are always up to date. Each of them answers a question that is as relevant today as in the days of the prophets. The prophecy of Obadiah answers the question, "What happens when brotherly love turns sour?" The prophecy of Jonah answers the question, "How do you neutralize an enemy world power that threatens you with obliteration?"

In the case of Obadiah the brothers were twin brothers—Jacob and Esau. God had chosen Jacob and his descendants to be His chosen people and the channel through whom the Messiah would come into the world. Though Jacob was the one through whom God always had intended to work, he got the blessing through subterfuge in cooperation with his mother. The enmity between him and his twin brother (Gen. 27) was passed on to their descendants. The descendants of Jacob were called Israelites. They lived in the land of Israel which God gave to them in the days of Joshua. The descendants of Esau were called Edomites. They lived to the south and east of Israel in the impregnable area of Petra. They were proud of their heritage and of their location (Obad. 3). They violated the bond between Judah and themselves, aroused God's displeasure (vv. 10-14), and ultimately passed out of existence.

The tragic history of Judah and Edom could have been avoided if Jacob had been content to wait for God to give him the promised blessing. It could have been avoided if Jacob and Esau had truly asked forgiveness and forgiven each other before their descendants multiplied. What happens when brotherly love sours? It gets worse and worse until the descendants reap the judgment of God; Judah by going into the Babylonian Captivity and Edom by passing out of existence.

The prophecy of Obadiah is the shortest book in the Old Testament and is the only book in the Old Testament to have but one chapter. Nothing is known about Obadiah except his name, which means "servant," or "worshiper of Jehovah."

The only thing known of Jonah is what is learned of him through his prophecy and a brief statement made about him in 2 Kings 14:25. The entire prophecy is written in the third person. The prophecy begins with the prophet running away from God and ends with the prophet in dejection and discouragement—hardly fit demeanor for a prophet of God. The use of the third person, however, lets the reader know that the prophet wrote after his mission to Assyria was completed and that he responded favorably to God's rebuke. His prophecy contains the record of God's dealing with himself as an individual; with the heathen Gentile sailors as a group; and with the heathen Gentile world power Assyria as a nation.

While Jonah's prophecy makes no specific mention of the nation Israel, it is itself a clear testimony to the workings of God on behalf of His disobedient prophet, whose life He preserved and whose desires He modified; to the heathen sailors to whom He gave abundant testimony of Himself; to the heathen Assyrians, whom He brought to national repentance; and to the nation Israel whose security He guaranteed and whose captivity He delayed for 130 years. Jonah answers the question, "How do you neutralize an enemy world power?" The answer: Evangelize that nation with the truth of God.

The Books of Obadiah and Jonah have two pertinent lessons for us to learn today: (1) brotherly differences must be resolved before they get out of control; and (2) national enemies can be neutralized and turned into friends by evangelism.

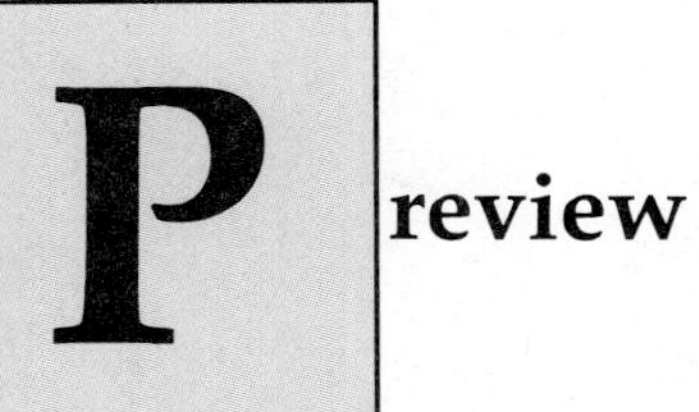

Bugs, Beetles, and Blessings

BOOK OF JOEL

Joel had never seen anything like it. The old men had never seen anything like it. The land of Judah had never seen anything like it. Uncounted millions of fast-moving locusts with ferocious appetites stripping the land till scarcely a green blade of anything was left. At the prophet's command, a public meeting was called to allow the Israel of God to cry out to the God of Israel. Perhaps heaven would respond, if not by salvation, at least by explanation. Why was this happening to them?

The divine explanation was immediate. The terrible locust plague occurred to accomplish a twofold purpose. First to serve as a punishment, and second as a prophecy. Judah's sin demanded Jehovah's punishment. But what about the prophecy? God used the locust plague as an illustration to preview that coming calamity when future enemy troops would invade Judah, much as the locusts had done. The earth would quake, stars would fall, blood would flow, and men would die. But after the grievous night, the glorious light would come. God's Spirit would descend on the chosen and God's Son would rule over them.

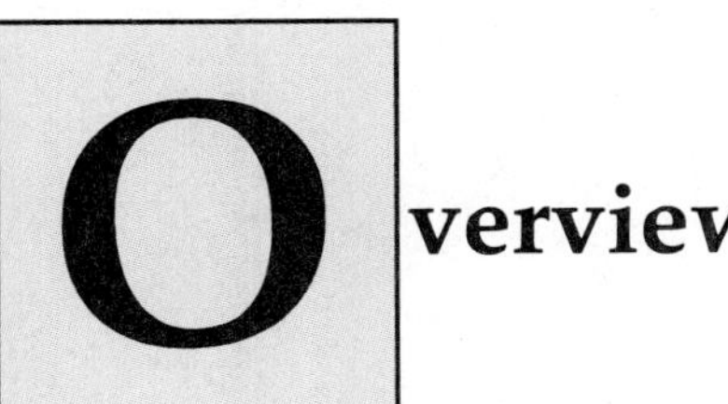

Overview

SCRIPTURE	Book of Joel			
SUBJECT	Ministry of Joel			
SPECIFICS	Prophecies about Pentecost, Armageddon, and Millennium			
	The illustration	The information		
	A terrible locust plague	Pentecost	Armageddon	Millennium
		Foretold in Joel 2	The heavens to be darkened	God's Spirit will guide all flesh
		Fulfilled (in part) in Acts 2	The heathen to be destroyed	God's Son will govern all flesh
SAINTS AND SINNERS	Joel			
SENTENCE SUMMARIES	O.T. Verse	"Behold, the Lord maketh the earth empty, and maketh it waste, and turneth it upside down, and scattereth abroad the inhabitants thereof" (Isa. 24:1).		
	N.T. Verse	"The heaven departed as a scroll when it is rolled together; and every mountain and island were moved out of their places" (Rev. 6:14).		

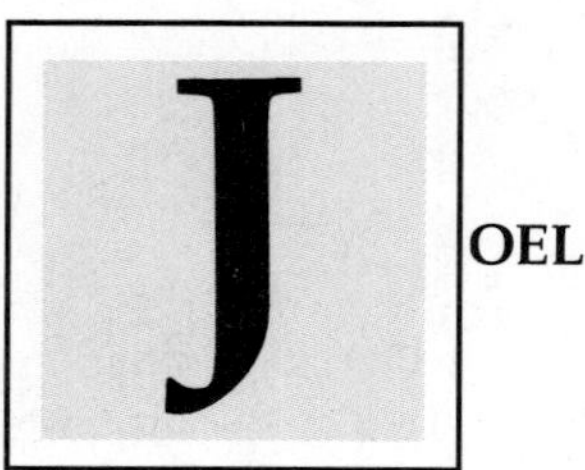

OEL

Kings of Israel and Judah

About 800-700

Judah	Israel
Amaziah (29) 796-767	Joash (16) 798-782
mostly Uzziah (52) 791-740	Jeroboam II (41) 793-753
Jotham (16) 750-735	Zechariah (6 mos.) 753-752
Ahaz (20) 736-716	Shallum (1 mo.) 752
Hezekiah (29) 716-687	Menahem (10) 752-742
	Pekahiah (2) 742-740
	Pekah (9) 740-732
	Hoshea (11) 732-722

Two Centuries—Amaziah to Zedekiah

Good King *Bad King* *796-767 Approximate time of reign (years B.C.)*
Overlapping Dates–Two Kings Reigning Together

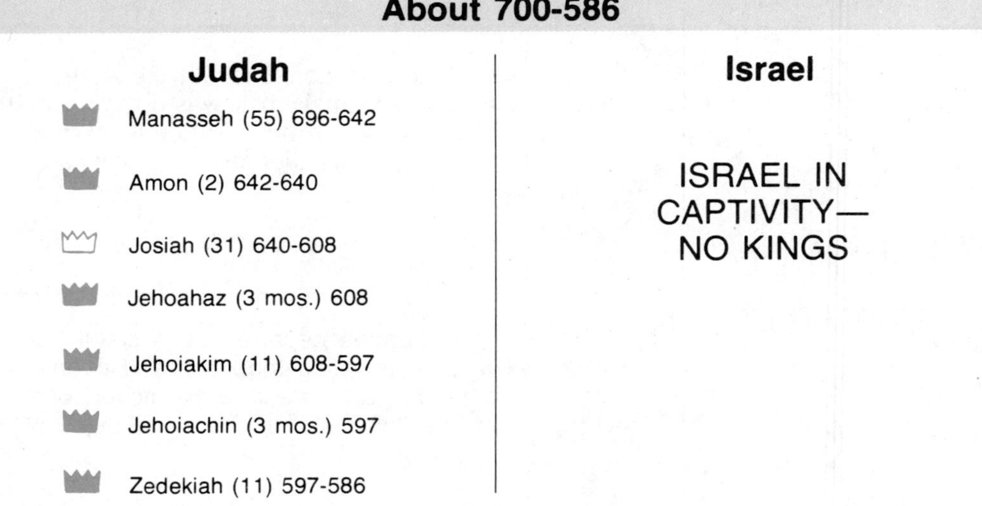

About 700-586

Judah	Israel
Manasseh (55) 696-642	ISRAEL IN CAPTIVITY—NO KINGS
Amon (2) 642-640	
Josiah (31) 640-608	
Jehoahaz (3 mos.) 608	
Jehoiakim (11) 608-597	
Jehoiachin (3 mos.) 597	
Zedekiah (11) 597-586	

ISRAEL AND GOD'S JUDGMENT: A REVIEW OF THE PAST

The severity of the locust judgment. "That which the palmerworm hath left hath the locust eaten; and that which the locust hath left hath the cankerworm eaten; and that which the cankerworm hath left hath the caterpiller eaten" (Joel 1:4).

The name for the locust judgment. "Alas for the day! For the Day of the LORD *is at hand, and as a destruction from the Almighty shall it come" (v. 15).*

ISRAEL AND GOD'S JUDGMENT: A PREVIEW OF THE FUTURE

"Blow ye the trumpet in Zion, and sound an alarm in My holy mountain. Let all the inhabitants of the land tremble; for the Day of the LORD *cometh, for it is night at hand; a day of darkness and of gloominess, a day of clouds and of thick darkness, as the morning spread upon the mountains. A great people and a strong; there hath not been ever the like, neither shall be any more after it, even to the years of many generations. . . . The earth shall quake before them; the heavens shall tremble. The sun and the moon shall be dark, and the stars shall withdraw their shining" (2:1-2, 10).*

"I will also gather all nations, and will bring them down into the Valley of Jehoshaphat, and will plead with them there for My people and for My heritage Israel, whom they have scattered among the nations, and parted My land. . . . Proclaim ye this among the Gentiles: Prepare war, wake up the mighty men, let them come up. Beat your plowshares into swords, and your pruning hooks into spears. Let the weak say, 'I am strong.' Assemble yourselves, and come, all ye heathen, and gather yourselves together round about; thither cause thy mighty ones to come down, O LORD.

" 'Let the heathen be wakened, and come up to the Valley of Jehoshaphat: for there will I sit to judge all the heathen round about. Put ye in the sickle, for the harvest is ripe: come, get you down; for the press is full, the vats overflow; for their wickedness is great.'

"Multitudes, multitudes in the valley of decision. For the Day of the LORD *is near in the valley of decision. The sun and the moon shall be darkened, and the stars shall withdraw their shining" (3:2, 9-15).*

THE IDENTITY OF THIS INVASION

What nation or enemy was Joel speaking of here in chapters 2 and 3? He might have been referring to several in general, giving special emphasis to the last in particular.

The Assyrian invasion in 701 B.C., led by Sennacherib and crushed at the very gates of Jerusalem by God's death angel; the Babylonian invasion in 586 B.C., led by Nebuchadnezzar; the Russian invasion, during the middle of the Tribulation, to be led by Gog; and the final invasion, at the end of the Tribulation, to be led by the Antichrist at the Battle of Armageddon.

THE GATHERING PLACE OF THIS INVASION

"I will also gather all nations, and will bring them down into the Valley of Jehoshaphat; and will plead with them there" (v. 2).

THE TWOFOLD PURPOSE FOR THIS INVASION GATHERING

The purpose of the Antichrist. To destroy Israel and her God. See Psalm 2.

The purpose of God. To destroy Antichrist and his allies.

THE OUTCOME OF THIS INVASION

"The LORD *also shall roar out of Zion, and utter His voice from Jerusalem; and the heavens and the earth shall shake. But the* LORD *will be the hope of His people, and the strength of the Children of Israel" (v. 16).*

THE BLESSINGS AFTER THIS INVASION HAS BEEN CRUSHED

God's Spirit will be poured out on all flesh. "And it shall come to pass afterward, that I will pour out My Spirit upon all flesh; and your sons and your daughters shall prophesy, your old men shall dream dreams, your young men shall see visions. And also upon the servants and upon the handmaids in those days will I pour out My Spirit. And I will show wonders in the heavens and in the earth, blood, and fire, and pillars of smoke. The sun shall be turned into darkness, and the moon into blood, before the great and the terrible Day of the LORD *come.*

"And it shall come to pass, that whosoever shall call on the name of the LORD *shall be deliv-*

The Pentecostal Prophet

COMMENTS

The main theme of the prophecy of Joel is the Day of the Lord which he views from two perspectives: (1) the near view—the locust plague (1:4–2:27) and (2) the far view—the Day of the Lord (2:28–3:17). In bringing judgment on His people, God does not need to use some great force such as an earthquake or flood. He uses the lowliest weapon in His arsenal, the locust, with which the land is laid bare with such devastation that the only thing worse is the Day of the Lord itself which will precede the establishment of the millennial kingdom.

That the locust plague and the Day of the Lord are not the same is seen by the words, "And it shall come to pass afterward" (2:28). The chronology of Joel's prophecy calls for: (1) the coming of a locust plague which is preceded by nothing, (2) the outpouring of the Spirit which is preceded by the locust plague, and (3) the coming of the Day of the Lord which is preceded by the universal outpouring of the Spirit accompanied by signs and wonders in nature. In true prophetic fashion, Joel compresses together events separated by thousands of years. The crucial events are: (1) the locust plague of his day (ca. 836 B.C.), (2) the Day of Pentecost on which the Holy Spirit was universally poured out (ca. A.D. 33), (3) the Day of the Lord, the Tribulation period which is separated from Pentecost by more than 1,900 years, and (4) the establishment of the earthly Davidic millennial kingdom following the Day of the Lord.

In his famous Pentecostal sermon (Acts 2:17-21), Peter introduced his quotation of Joel 2:28-32 with: "But this is that which was spoken by the Prophet Joel" (Acts 2:16). His purpose was to explain the phenomenon of speaking in tongues which those observing were attributing to drunkenness. Peter's words can be understood in three ways: (1) this is *like* that; i.e., this is a manifestation of something like that prophesied by Joel; (2) this is a *partial fulfillment* of that; i.e., what you are witnessing is a partial fulfillment of what Joel prophesied, the complete fulfillment will come when the kingdom is established; or (3) this *is* that; i.e., this is the fulfillment of what Joel prophesied would take place.

The first view is untenable for Peter spoke in a metaphor, not a simile. The second view would of necessity involve the understanding of the church in Joel's prophecy for part of his prophecy would be understood to initiate the church while the remainder instituted the kingdom. The third view, then is to be preferred. Two things are necessary for the establishment of Israel's kingdom: (1) the death of the Messiah and (2) the coming of the Holy Spirit. At the time of Peter's preaching, the death of Christ was a historical fact. The Spirit, however, had not made His advent into the world. Peter identified the phenomenon of speaking in tongues as the outward manifestation of the outpouring of the Spirit prophesied by Joel. With the death of the Messiah and the coming of the Spirit God provided all that is necessary for the establishment of Israel's earthly, Davidic, millennial kingdom. The only thing that prohibits the establishment of the kingdom is the nation's unbelief and rejection of its Messiah. The time is coming, however, when the King will return to set up His earthly kingdom. At that time He will not have to die again nor will He have to make the Holy Spirit available—these things have been accomplished. Zechariah 13 shows that the day is coming when Israel will avail herself of the death of the Messiah ("the fountain that cleanses"). The prophecy of Joel, the Pentecostal Prophet, shows that at that same time Israel will avail herself of the person and work of the Holy Spirit. Then the provision made by the fulfillment of Joel's prophecy as recorded in Acts 2:16 will be realized as well as the provisions made by the fulfillment of the death of the Messiah.

ered. For in Mount Zion and in Jerusalem shall be deliverance, as the LORD *hath said, and in the remnant whom the* LORD *shall call'' (2:28-32).*

It should be noted that this event marked the fulfillment of Moses' desire. (See Num. 11:29.)

Peter later quoted this passage in Joel on the Day of Pentecost. (See Acts 2:16-21.) This he did, not so much to indicate that Pentecost was the fulfillment of Joel's prophecy, but rather as an example of it.

All human needs will be provided for. ''And ye shall eat in plenty, and be satisfied, and praise the name of the LORD *your God, that hath dealt wondrously with you; and My people shall never be ashamed. And ye shall know that I am in the midst of Israel, and that I am the* LORD *your God, and none else. And My people shall never be ashamed'' (Joel 2:26-27).*

Nature itself will be transformed. ''And it shall come to pass in that day, that the mountains shall drop down new wine, and the hills shall flow with milk, and all the rivers of Judah shall flow with waters, and a fountain shall come forth of the house of the LORD*, and shall water the Valley of Shittim'' (3:18).*

Christ Himself will reign in Zion.

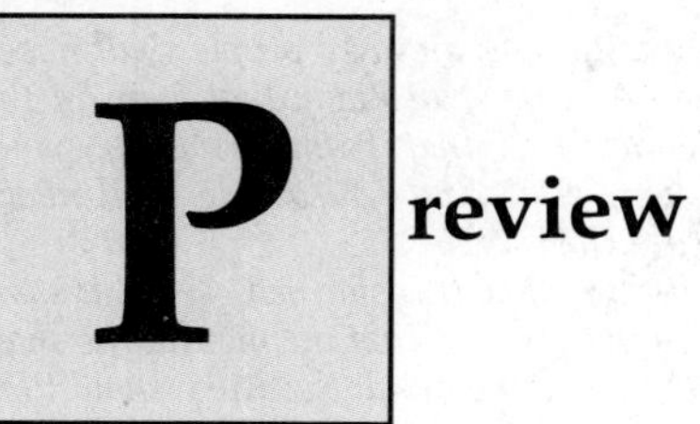

The Old Testament Billy Sunday

BOOK OF AMOS

"No, I'm not a prophet! No, I'm not the son of a prophet! It's true, I'm just a fruit-picker and flock-tender. But I'll tell you something else. Even though I'm a lowly layman, I'm far more qualified to speak for God than are you, a professional priest!"

This little confrontation took place around 760 B.C. in the Northern Kingdom city of Bethel. The speaker was Amos, and his angry listener, Amaziah, a faithless priest of Bethel. Amaziah had started the whole thing by his efforts to muzzle Amos. It was like attempting to silence an electrical storm! No other single writing prophet so thundered away at sin, righteousness, and judgment as did Amos. Before he finished Jews, Gentiles, laymen, and leaders alike were boldly denounced. Justice had been spurned. Judgment would fall. Four terrible visions spoke of this. But wait—there would be one more! After the fury of the storm had abated, the glory of the Lord would appear. Israel would be redeemed, regathered, and restored to the land. Thus did the fruit-picker and flock-tender speak. No professional prophet, or son of a prophet, could have done better.

Overview

<table>
<tr><td>SCRIPTURE</td><td colspan="6">Book of Amos</td></tr>
<tr><td>SUBJECT</td><td colspan="6">Ministry of Amos</td></tr>
<tr><td rowspan="10">SPECIFICS</td><td colspan="4">The sinful countries</td><td colspan="2">The sovereign Creator</td></tr>
<tr><td>Identity</td><td colspan="3">Iniquities</td><td rowspan="9">As revealed through five visions</td><td rowspan="2">The locust plague</td></tr>
<tr><td>Syria</td><td rowspan="4">Cruelty & murder</td><td rowspan="4">Blasphemy</td><td rowspan="4">Drunkenness</td></tr>
<tr><td>Philistia</td><td rowspan="2">The great fire</td></tr>
<tr><td>Phoenicia</td></tr>
<tr><td>Edom</td><td rowspan="2">The plumb line</td></tr>
<tr><td>Ammon</td><td rowspan="4">Slave-running</td><td rowspan="4">Immorality & idolatry</td><td rowspan="4">Materialism</td></tr>
<tr><td>Moab</td><td rowspan="2">The basket of fruit</td></tr>
<tr><td>S. Kingdom</td></tr>
<tr><td>N. Kingdom</td><td>The Lord at the altar</td></tr>
<tr><td>SAINTS AND SINNERS</td><td colspan="6">Amos, Amaziah</td></tr>
<tr><td rowspan="2">SENTENCE SUMMARIES</td><td>O.T. Verse</td><td colspan="5">"I have also spoken by the prophets, and I have multiplied visions, and used similitudes, by the ministry of the prophets" (Hosea 12:10).</td></tr>
<tr><td>N.T. Verses</td><td colspan="5">"To this agree the words of the prophets, as it is written: 'After this I will return, and will build again the tabernacle of David, which is fallen down; and I will build again the ruins thereof, and I will set it up' " (Acts 15:15-16).</td></tr>
</table>

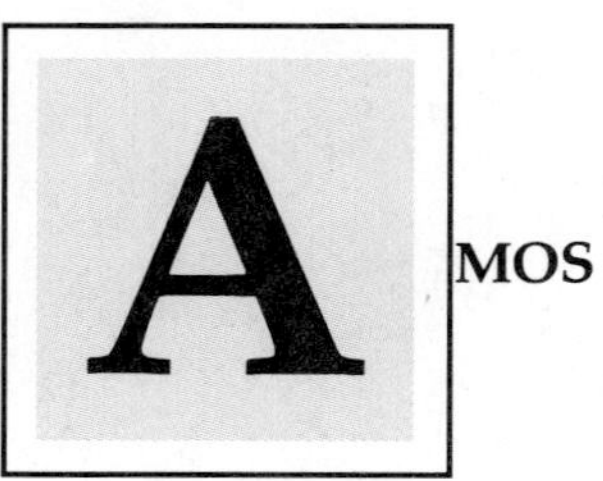

MOS

EIGHT NATIONS DENOUNCED

Syria (capital city, Damascus). They would be punished for their cruelty to those Israelites living on the Eastern Bank of Jordan.

Philistia (capital city, Gaza). Their crime was selling Israelites into slavery to Edom.

Phoenicia (capital city, Tyre). They had broken the treaty made with Israel during David's time, attacking Israel and selling its citizens as slaves to Edom.

Edom (capital cities, Teman and Bozrah).

Ammon (capital city, Rahbah). "They have ripped up the women with child of Gilead, that they might enlarge their border" (Amos 1:13).

Moab (capital city, Kerioth). This nation had committed blasphemous acts.

Judah (capital city, Jerusalem). Judah had rejected the Word of God and disobeyed the God of the Word.

Israel (capital city, Samaria). They had become immoral, unthankful, and totally materialistic. They had even caused the Nazarites to sin by tempting them to drink wine.

But all this was only the introduction. Now Amos singled out the whole house of Jacob (both North and South) and called down the fire of heaven. He summarized all this in fearful language.

Jacob's punishment must equal her past privileges. "Hear this word that the LORD hath spoken against you, O children of Israel, against the whole family which I brought up from the land of Egypt, saying, 'You only have I known of all the families of the earth. Therefore I will punish you for all your iniquities.' Can two walk together, except they be agreed?" (3:1-3)

God was issuing them one final warning through His prophets. "Surely the Lord God will do nothing, but He revealeth His secret unto His servants the prophets" (v. 7).

Jacob's enemies are called on to attest to her wickedness. Her women had become cruel and demanding. Her formal and empty religious ceremonies had become an insult to divine holiness. *"Come to Beth-el, and transgress; at Gilgal multiply transgression; and bring your sacrifices every morning, and your tithes after three years" (4:4).*

"I hate, I despise your feast days, and I will not smell in your solemn assemblies. Though ye offer Me burnt offerings and your meat offerings, I will not accept them. Neither will I regard the peace offerings of your fat beasts. Take thou away from Me the noise of thy songs; for I will not hear the melody of thy viols. But let judgment run down as waters, and righteousness as a mighty stream" (5:21-24).

They had surrounded themselves with gross luxury, with ivory beds to lie on, and the choicest food to eat. They thought more of worldly music than their own Messiah. They had drunk wine by the bucketful, perfumed themselves with sweet ointments, and totally neglected the poor and needy.

God had tried everything to bring His people to their senses. He had tried famine, drought, crop plagues, and human plagues. What He then did: *" 'I have overthrown some of you, as God overthrew Sodom and Gomorrah, and ye were as a firebrand plucked out of the burning. Yet have ye not returned unto Me,' saith the LORD. 'Therefore thus will I do unto thee, O Israel; and because I will do this unto thee, prepare to meet thy God, O Israel' " (4:11-12).*

One final invitation was extended by God. "For thus saith the LORD unto the house of Israel, 'Seek ye Me, and ye shall live.' . . .

"Seek good, and not evil, that ye may live; and so the LORD, the God of hosts, shall be with you, as ye have spoken. Hate the evil, and love the good, and establish judgment in the gate. It may be that the LORD God of hosts will be gracious unto the remnant of Joseph" (5:4, 14-15).

This invitation was rejected and judgment fell. Jacob was consumed as a lion devours a sheep. There was crying in the streets and on every road. In that day they were like a man who escaped from a lion, only to meet a bear. They were as one who leans against a wall in a dark room and puts his hand on a snake. Ninety percent of their soldiers fell in battle.

FIVE VISIONS ANNOUNCED

The locust plague. In a vision God revealed to Amos His intention to destroy all the main crops that sprang up after the first mowing. Amos interceded for Israel and a merciful God changed His course of action.

The vision of the great fire. Amos saw a destructive fire, the heat from which was so fierce that it consumed the very waters of Palestine. This was to fall on the land to punish sin. Again the prophet pled for mercy and again God set aside this deserved judgment.

The vision of the plumb line. Amos viewed the Lord as He stood beside a wall built with a plumb line to see if it was straight. God informed Amos that He would continue testing Israel with the plumb line of heavenly justice and that He would no longer turn away from punishing.

At this point in his preaching ministry, Amos was viciously opposed by a false religious leader named Amaziah. Amos responded by pronouncing judgment both on him and his ungodly family.

"Therefore, thus saith the LORD; 'Thy wife shall be a harlot in the city, and thy sons and thy daughters shall fall by the sword, and thy land shall be divided by line; and thou shalt die in a polluted land; and Israel shall surely go into captivity forth of his land' " (7:17).

The vision of the basket of summer fruit. God showed Amos a basket filled with ripe fruit, explaining that it symbolized Israel, which was now ripe for judgment. The riotous sound of singing in the temple would be turned to weeping, dead bodies would be scattered everywhere, fearful heavenly signs would occur.

" 'And it shall come to pass in that day,' saith the LORD God, 'that I will cause the sun to go down at noon, and I will darken the earth in the clear day' " (8:9).

This frightening punishment will have its ultimate fulfillment during the coming Great Tribulation. There would be no comforting words from God.

" 'Behold, the days come,' saith the LORD God, 'that I will send a famine in the land, not a famine of bread, nor a thirst for water, but of hearing the words of the LORD. . . . They shall run to and fro to seek the Word of the LORD, and shall not find it' " (vv. 11-12).

The vision of the Lord at the altar. The condemnation of Israel's transgressors. *"Though they dig into hell, thence shall Mine hand take them; though they climb up to heaven, thence will I bring them down. And though they hide themselves in the top of Carmel, I will search and take them out thence; and though they be hid from My sight in the bottom of the sea, thence will I command the serpent, and he shall bite them" (9:2-3).*

The restoration of David's tabernacle. The Davidic monarchy was in a degraded condition with 10 out of the 12 tribes refusing to give homage to it. But during the glorious Millennium all this will change. The blessings of this restored monarchy (under Christ, the rightful Seed of David) will be manifold.

" 'For, lo, I will command, and I will sift the house of Israel among all nations, like as corn is sifted in a sieve, yet shall not the least grain fall upon the earth. . . .

" 'In that day will I raise up the tabernacle of David that is fallen, and close up the breaches thereof; and I will raise up his ruins, and I will build it as in the days of old. . . .

" 'Behold, the days come,' saith the LORD, 'that the plowman shall overtake the reaper, and the treader of grapes him that soweth seed; and the mountains shall drop sweet wine, and all the hills shall melt. And I will bring again the captivity of My people Israel, and they shall build the waste cities, and inhabit them; and they shall plant vineyards, and drink the wine thereof; they shall also make gardens, and eat the fruit of them. And I will plant them upon their land, and they shall no more be pulled up out of their land which I have given them,' saith the LORD thy God" (vv. 9, 11, 13-15).

Amos: The Hillbilly Diplomat

COMMENTS

Tucked away in the middle of his prophecy is a little autobiographical insert in which Amos lets his readers know that he has no misgivings concerning his origin, his mission, or his message (7:14-15). He definitely was not a legend in his own mind.

In this brief autobiographical statement, Amos tells us that he was not a member of the student body nor a graduate of the school of the prophets which had been in operation since the days of Elijah. Nor was he introduced to the prophetical office by his father, for his father was not a prophet either. In other words, Amos did not *choose* to be a prophet and had no formal training to prepare him for the office. Amos was the most unlikely candidate for the office of prophet. He was a simple shepherd and gatherer of sycamore fruit—both considered to be lowly occupations. Amos was from Tekoa (cf. 1:1) situated on a 2,700-foot hill in one of the bleakest areas of Judah. By the standards of today, Amos would be considered to be nothing but an uneducated, low-class, economically deprived hillbilly. Amos probably would not contest the classification. He was a southern country boy preaching in Bethel, the affluent religious capital of the Northern Kingdom.

Hillbilly though he may have been, Amos had one great ability—availability! He had sense enough to obey God when God reached down and "took" him and made him His instrument to deliver His message of judgment against the Northern Kingdom, Israel. Amos may not have had any formal education, but when it came to delivering his message he did so with great boldness and great tact that would make any skilled rhetorician envious.

It must be remembered that Amos delivered his message orally to a hostile audience before he wrote it down. He had no rank, glamour, or special charisma to gain their empathy. One of the principal laws of rhetoric is that the speaker must gain the attention and interest of his audience. Note how skillfully Amos went about his communication task.

Amos' first message of judgment was to the northeast against Damascus, the capital of Syria, Israel's perennial enemy (vv. 3-5). The crowd must have roared its approval. His second message of judgment was to the southwest against Philistia, another long-standing enemy (vv. 6-8)—again to the crowd's delight. The third message of judgment was directed to the northwest against Phoenicia (vv. 9-10)—with the audience's continued approval. These first three messages of judgment were delivered against peoples who were raw heathens. The fourth message of judgment was directed to the southeast against Edom (vv. 11-12). The fifth message of judgment was directed to the east against Ammon (vv. 13-15). The sixth message of judgment was directed to the east but a little bit south against Moab (2:1-3). This second group of three messages were directed against nations who, while heathen, were blood-relatives to Israel. The seventh message of judgment was delivered directly to the south against Israel's brother and archenemy, Judah (vv. 4-5). The crowd must have given Amos a standing ovation on that one. At this point, Amos must have been the favorite orator of the day. He not only gained his audience's attention, but also had their enthusiastic approval of his message. With the skill of an expert artilleryman he had bracketed his target in every direction and then delivered the eighth and final message of judgment directed against Israel itself (vv. 6-16). The remainder of the prophecy is concentrated on Israel concerning whom he delivers four messages of condemnation (3:1–6:14) and five symbolic visions of judgment (7:1–9:10). From man's vantage point Amos was a simple hillbilly, but from God's he was an amazing diplomat.

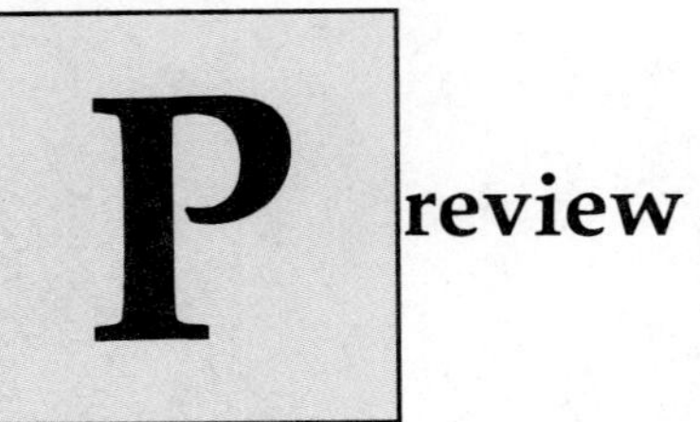

Two Sinful Spouses

BOOK OF HOSEA

Some were sympathetic, others displayed indifference, but many were openly critical. After all, he had asked for it. What could have possibly possessed any sensible man, especially a man of God as he was, to knowingly marry a harlot. The whole matter was simply incredible and inexcusable! None, of course, knew that God Himself had ordered him to marry her. So, in quiet obedience, Hosea, the man of God, took Gomer, the harlot, as his wife. But before the birth of their third child the marriage had deteriorated. Gomer, a harlot before marriage, soon became an adulteress after marriage. But why would the sovereign God require His prophet to suffer such an ordeal? Slowly the truth dawned on the heartbroken husband. God desired that Hosea understand in some small measure the agony He Himself was enduring over the unfaithfulness of Israel, His chosen wife. And what of their three children? Their very names would serve as a prophetic summary of the total relationship between Jehovah and Judah. What terrible names they bore—"scattered," "unpitied," and "not My people."

Question: Did Hosea and Gomer eventually reconcile? God's goodness might suggest they did.

Question: Will God and Israel eventually reconcile? Israel will indeed be cleansed and restored. "Scattered" will become "gathered," "unpitied," "full of pity," and "not My people," "My beloved people."

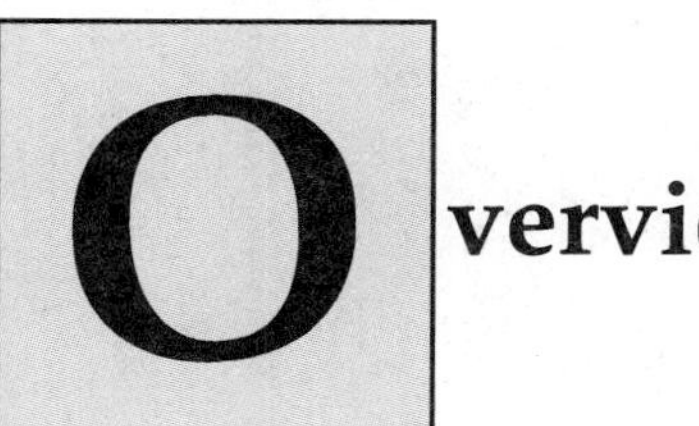

Overview

<table>
<tr><td>SCRIPTURE</td><td colspan="7">Book of Hosea</td></tr>
<tr><td>SUBJECT</td><td colspan="7">Ministry of Hosea</td></tr>
<tr><td rowspan="6">SPECIFICS</td><td colspan="7">Adultery: two case studies</td></tr>
<tr><td rowspan="5">Case study no. 1</td><td rowspan="2">Individuals</td><td>Injured spouse</td><td>Immoral spouse</td><td rowspan="5">Case study no. 2</td><td rowspan="2">Individuals</td><td>Injured spouse</td><td>Immoral spouse</td></tr>
<tr><td>Hosea</td><td>Gomer</td><td>God</td><td>Israel</td></tr>
<tr><td rowspan="2">Evaluation</td><td colspan="2">The children from the marriage</td><td rowspan="2">Evaluation</td><td colspan="2">The wife is corrupted</td></tr>
<tr><td colspan="2">The concern for the marriage</td><td colspan="2">The wife is chastened</td></tr>
<tr><td>Ending</td><td colspan="2">Not told</td><td>Ending</td><td>The wife will be resur-rected</td><td>The wife will be restored</td></tr>
<tr><td>SAINTS AND SINNERS</td><td colspan="7">Hosea, Gomer, Jezreel, Lo-ruhamah, Lo-ammi</td></tr>
<tr><td rowspan="2">SENTENCE SUMMARIES</td><td>O.T. Verse</td><td colspan="6">"For thy Maker is thy husband; the LORD of Hosts is His name; and thy Redeemer the Holy One of Israel; the God of the whole earth shall He be called" (Isa. 54:5).</td></tr>
<tr><td>N.T. Verse</td><td colspan="6">"As He saith also in Hosea, 'I will call them My people, which were not My people; and her beloved, which was not beloved' " (Rom. 9:25).</td></tr>
</table>

OSEA (DESTINATION NORTHERN KINGDOM)

GRIEVING HUSBAND AND HIS GRIEVOUS WIFE

Hosea's wife, ill-famed. His wife Gomer was apparently a harlot before marriage and an adulteress after marriage. Hosea attempted in vain to save this marriage by barring her from the markets of the world.

"Therefore, behold, I will hedge up thy way with thorns, and make a wall, that she shall not find her paths" (Hosea 2:6).

Hosea thought he could force her to remain home in this manner.

He even sought the help of his first son, Jezreel, asking him to reason with his mother concerning the folly of her ways.

"Plead with your mother, plead: for she is not my wife, neither am I her husband, let her therefore put away her whoredoms out of her sight, and her adulteries from between her breasts" (v. 2).

But all this was to no avail. Gomer apparently ran off at the first opportunity.

Hosea attempted to buy her out of the markets of the world. It was not long before Gomer had been used, abused, and abandoned by her lustful lovers, and found herself in a slave market. God ordered Hosea to find and redeem her from this market.

"So I bought her for myself for 15 pieces of silver, and for a homer of barley and a half homer of barley" (3:2).

Hosea's children, ill-named. The prophet fathered three children through Gomer. Each child (at God's command) was given a name which carried with it prophetical meaning. The first child, a boy, was named Jezreel, meaning "to be scattered." His name predicted two future events: (1) the setting aside of the dynasty of a Northern king named Jehu; (2) the Assyrian invasion, at which time the entire Northern Kingdom would be scattered.

The second child, a girl, was named Loruhamah. This name literally meant, "no more mercy," indicating that God's judgment was just around the corner. Along with this baby, however, came the promise that God would spare Judah, the Southern Kingdom, of this coming Assyrian invasion.

"But I will have mercy upon the house of Judah, and will save them by the LORD their God, and will not save them by bow, nor by sword, nor by battle, by horses, nor by horsemen" (1:7). This, of course, happened as recorded in 2 Kings 19:35.

The third child, a boy, was named Loammi. Here the name means "not My people."

A GRIEVING HUSBAND AND HIS GRIEVOUS WIFE

Ephraim denounced. Because of her ignorance. *"My people are destroyed for lack of knowledge. Because thou hast rejected knowledge, I will also reject thee, that thou shalt be no priest to Me, seeing thou hast forgotten the law of thy God, I will also forget thy children" (Hosea 4:6).*

*Because of her idolatry: Ephraim had prayed to idols. She had sacrificed her sons to idols. She had totally joined herself to idols.

Ephraim desired. In spite of her wickedness, God still loved her. *"O Ephraim, what shall I do unto thee? O Judah, what shall I do unto thee? For your goodness is like a morning cloud, and as the early dew it goeth away" (6:4).*

Ephraim described. She was aflame with lust like a baker's hot oven. God said the hearts of the people smoldered with evil plots during the night, and burst into flaming fire the next morning. They mingled with the heathen and had become as useless as a half-baked cake. They were as a silly dove, calling to Egypt, and flying to Assyria for help. They were as a crooked bow, always missing the target, which was God's glory. They lay among the nations as a broken pot. They were as a wandering and lonely wild ass. They were as a dried-up root. They were as an empty vine. They were as a backsliding heifer.

Ephraim disciplined. God declared, *"For they have sown the wind, and they shall reap the whirlwind" (8:7).* (See also 10:13.)

God would, therefore (for a while) withhold His mercy from them. They would be many days without the following: *A king: In 722 B.C. Hoshea, Israel's last king, was dethroned, and in 586 B.C., Zedekiah, Judah's final king, was deposed. Some six centuries later Israel's only true King was rejected. Thus, this tragic situation will continue until He comes again (Rev. 19:11-16).

*A prince: The next recorded prince in Israel's future will not minister until the Millennium. (See Ezek. 44:3.)

*A sacrifice: In A.D. 70 Titus destroyed the temple and all animal sacrifices ceased. During the Tribulation they will once again be instituted, only to be stopped by the Antichrist (Dan. 9:27).

*An image: This literally means, "the pillars," and may refer to the temple. A temple will be rebuilt during the Tribulation (Rev. 13), destroyed (Zech. 14:2), and again raised during the Millennium (Ezek. 40:48).

*An ephod: A reference to Israel's high priesthood. The ephod was a garment he wore. The last high priest personally planned the murder of the nation's own Messiah (Matt. 26:57-68; John 11:49-51).

*Teraphim: These were normally figurines, or images in human form. (See Gen. 31:34.) It is not known what Hosea had in mind here.

They would go off as slaves into Assyria. "[They] shall be also carried unto Assyria" (Hosea 10:6).

They would be (for a while) swallowed up among the nations. "Israel is swallowed up; now shall they be among the Gentiles as a vessel wherein is no pleasure" (8:8).

"My God will cast them away, because they did not hearken unto Him. And they shall be wanderers among the nations" (9:17).

Ephraim delivered. Someday this glorious event will indeed take place. Note the following passages: *"And I will betroth thee unto Me forever; yea, I will betroth thee unto Me in righteousness, and in judgment, and in lovingkindness, and in mercies. . . . And I will sow her unto Me in the earth; and I will have mercy upon her that had not obtained mercy; and I will say to them which were not My people, 'Thou art My people'; and they shall say, 'Thou art my God' " (2:19, 23).*

"Afterward shall the Children of Israel return, and seek the LORD their God, and David their king; and shall fear the LORD and His goodness in the latter days" (3:5).

"Come, and let us return unto the LORD. For He hath torn, and He will heal us; He hath smitten, and He will bind us up. After two days will He revive us; in the third day He will raise us up, and we shall live in His sight. Then shall we know, if we follow on to know the LORD. His going forth is prepared as the morning; and He shall come unto us as the rain, as the latter and former rain unto the earth" (6:1-3).

"When Israel was a child, then I loved him, and called My son out of Egypt. . . .I drew them with cords of a man, with bands of love; and I was to them as they that take off the yoke on their jaws, and I laid meat unto them. . . . How shall I give thee up, Ephraim? How shall I deliver thee, Israel? How shall I make thee as Admah? How shall I set thee as Zeboim? Mine heart is turned within Me; My repentings are kindled together. I will not execute the fierceness of Mine anger, I will not return to destroy Ephraim; for I am God, and not man; the Holy One in the midst of thee; and I will not enter into the city" (11:1, 4, 8-9).

"I will be thy King. Where is any other that may save thee in all thy cities, and thy judges of whom thou saidst, 'Give me a king and princes'? . . . I will ransom them from the power of the grave; I will redeem them from death. O death, I will be thy plagues; O grave, I will be thy destruction; repentance shall be hid from Mine eyes" (13:10, 14).

"I will heal their backsliding, I will love them freely; for Mine anger is turned away from him. I will be as the dew unto Israel; he shall grow as the lily, and cast forth his roots as Lebanon. His branches shall spread, and his beauty shall be as the olive tree, and his smell as Lebanon. They that dwell under his shadow shall return; they shall revive as the corn, and grow as the vine; the scent thereof shall be as the wine of Lebanon" (14:4-7).

Hosea: The Guide for Today's Marital Problems

COMMENTS

In obedience to God Hosea married "a wife of whoredoms" (1:2a). As distasteful as the events between him and his wife (1:2–3:5) might have been to the prophet, they were divinely intended by God to portray the relationship between Him and idolatrous Israel (4:1–14:8).

If ever anyone had "grounds for divorce," Hosea did. He could easily have divorced Gomer within the provisions given by Moses in Deuteronomy 24:1. In spite of the darkness of the picture and the hopelessness of the sinful Gomer, Jehovah did not command Hosea to divorce Gomer, but commanded him to go and reclaim her (Hosea 3:1). This command of God to Hosea ought to lay to rest any speculation concerning the permanency of marriage and the husband's responsibility in the matter. If adultery were sufficient grounds to break the marital union, Gomer's adulteries would have obliterated the union between Hosea and her. Though the union certainly was damaged by her infidelity, it was not broken. Nothing breaks the marital tie but the death of one of the partners (cf. Rom. 7:3; 1 Cor. 7:39). In obedience to God, Hosea went and found Gomer and redeemed her to himself "for 15 pieces of silver . . . a homer of barley, and a half homer of barley." The price paid is indicative of the depths to which Gomer had sunk. Barley was a coarse grain eaten only by the poorest of people and animals. The price commonly paid for a slave in good health was 30 pieces of silver (cf. Ex. 21:32). So deep had been the inroads of sin on Gomer that Hosea bought her for only half the price commonly paid for a slave plus about 10 bushels of animal food.

Hosea's serious words to Gomer, "Thou shalt abide for me many days; thou shalt not play the harlot, and thou shalt not be for another man; so will I also be for thee" (Hosea 3:3), can be understood either as spoken sternly or in great love. While Hosea had every right to speak them to Gomer sternly, it fits the context better to view them as having been spoken in great love and assurance.

Hosea illustrates several truths concerning marriage: (1) the responsibility for marriage is on the husband's shoulders—the command to consummate the marriage was given to Hosea; (2) the husband is responsible for keeping the marital union together—God commanded Hosea to go and reclaim his wife; (3) sexual infidelity does not break the marital union—while it may damage and strain the relationship, only death breaks the marital bond; and (4) divorce is not the solution for marital problems—Hosea could have divorced Gomer on "biblical grounds" but it would not have solved either his problem or hers. Divorce has never solved marital problems; it only compounds them. It should be observed that in commenting on Deuteronomy 24:1, Jesus said that Moses made this provision because of "the hardness of your hearts" (Matt. 19:8). Thus whether it was in Moses' day, Hosea's day, Jesus' day, or today, there is no such thing as a "spiritual divorce." Whenever anyone gets a divorce it is testimony to the hardness and spiritual insensitivity of his heart. Those who are seeking guidance in how to deal with marital problems would do well to consider spiritual Hosea and follow his example of seeking his wayward wife, forgiving her, restoring her to himself, and loving her with a never-failing love. There is no marital problem that Hosea's method would not cure.

Preview

The Peerless Prophet

ISAIAH 7; 13–23

It was early spring in 1947. The place was a desert region just west of a world famous body of water. Ahmed Mohammed, a Bedouin shepherd, was somewhat upset. Another goat had strayed away from his flock. Where was that frustrating creature hiding? Perhaps he was in a cave, located in the wall of a large cliff which rose up from the desert floor. Well, he would soon see. Tossing a rock into the cave brought an immediate response, but not the cry of a goat Ahmed had expected. Instead, it resembled a crushing sound, as if something had been broken. Hurriedly entering the cave, the shepherd found eight large jars. From one of these he drew out three leather scrolls.

Standing there in the cave, pondering the strange figures on those ancient parchments, the humble goat-tender was utterly oblivious to the fact that he was an integral part of a momentous historical event. As it turned out, that famous body of water near the cave would later give Ahmed's amazing discovery its official name—the Dead Sea Scrolls. Those scrolls were probably hidden there sometime during the second century B.C. by a Jewish group called the Essenes. They included fragments of every Old Testament book in the Hebrew Bible, except the Book of Esther. Especially exciting was a complete scroll of the Book of Isaiah. During the next five lessons we will discover just why the Essenes so carefully preserved it, and why both Jews and Christians revere the Book of Isaiah so highly today.

Overview

<table>
<tr><td>SCRIPTURE</td><td colspan="6">Isaiah 7; 13–23</td></tr>
<tr><td>SUBJECT</td><td colspan="6">Introduction to the prophecies of Isaiah</td></tr>
<tr><td rowspan="7">SPECIFICS</td><td colspan="2">The classification</td><td>The countries</td><td colspan="2">The certainty</td></tr>
<tr><td rowspan="2">1–35</td><td>God's chosen</td><td rowspan="7">Babylon
Assyria
Philistia
Moab
Damascus
Ethiopia
Egypt
Edom
Arabia
Tyre
The entire world</td><td rowspan="4">Fulfilled prophecies</td><td>During Isaiah's life</td></tr>
<tr><td>The failures of Israel
The future of Israel</td><td>Ten prophecies</td></tr>
<tr><td rowspan="2">36–39</td><td>God's city</td><td>Following Isaiah's life</td></tr>
<tr><td>Jerusalem surrounded by her foes
Jerusalem saved from her foes</td><td>Ten prophecies</td></tr>
<tr><td rowspan="2">40–66</td><td>God's Christ</td><td rowspan="2">Future prophecies</td><td rowspan="2">The Great Tribulation
The glorious Millennium</td></tr>
<tr><td>His mission
His majesty</td></tr>
<tr><td>SAINTS AND SINNERS</td><td colspan="6">Isaiah</td></tr>
<tr><td rowspan="2">SENTENCE SUMMARIES</td><td>O.T. Verse</td><td colspan="5">"Surely the Lord God will do nothing, but He revealeth His secret unto His servants the prophets" (Amos 3:7).</td></tr>
<tr><td>N.T. Verse</td><td colspan="5">"God, who at sundry times and in divers manners spake in time past unto the fathers by the prophets" (Heb. 1:1).</td></tr>
</table>

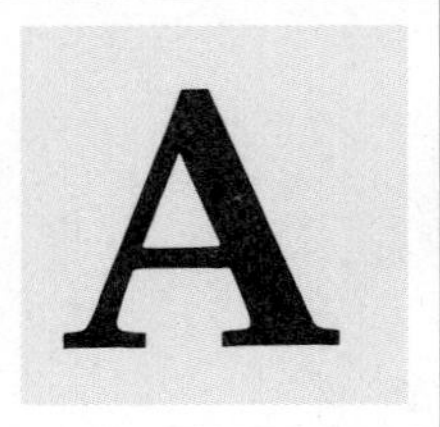

GENERAL OUTLINE OF ISAIAH

ISRAEL, GOD'S FAITHLESS SERVANT (AND HER VARIOUS ENEMIES)

Her sins listed.
Her future predicted.
Her great prophet's vision.
Her wicked king's unbelief.
Her enemies judged. Babylon, Assyria, Philistia, Moab, Damascus, Ethiopia, Egypt, Edom, Arabia, Tyre, the entire world.

HEZEKIAH, GOD'S FRIGHTENED SERVANT

Hezekiah and the king of Assyria.
Hezekiah and the King of heaven.
Hezekiah and the king of Babylon.

CHRIST, GOD'S FAITHFUL SERVANT (ISA. 40–66)

THE DELIVERANCE—THE COMFORT OF JEHOVAH

God and the idols (chaps. 40–46).
God and the nations (chaps. 47–48).

THE DELIVERER—THE SALVATION OF JEHOVAH

THE DELIVERED—THE GLORY OF JEHOVAH

A SUMMARY OF ISAIAH'S PROPHECIES

PROPHECIES FULFILLED DURING HIS OWN LIFETIME

- Judah would be saved from the threatened Syrian and Israelite invasion.
- Syria and Israel would later be destroyed by Assyria.
- Assyria would invade Judah.
- Jerusalem would be saved during this invasion.
- Moab would be judged by the Assyrians within three years.
- Egypt and Ethiopia would be conquered by the Assyrians.
- Arabia would be destroyed.
- Tyre would be destroyed.
- Hezekiah's life would be extended by 15 years.
- Assyria would be judged by God.

PROPHECIES FULFILLED AFTER HIS LIFETIME

- The Babylonian Captivity.
- Babylon overthrown by Cyrus.
- The conquests of a Persian named Cyrus.
- The return to Jerusalem decree of Cyrus.
- The joy of the returning remnant.
- The restoration of Tyre.
- The perpetual desolation of Edom.
- The birth, earthly life, sufferings, death, resurrection, ascension, and exaltation of Jesus Christ.
- The ministry of John the Baptist.

PROPHECIES YET TO BE FULFILLED

- The Tribulation.
- The Battle of Armageddon.
- The Millennium.

THE GENTILE NATIONS IN ISAIAH

BABYLON

Babylon was to be destroyed by the Medes: *"And Babylon, the glory of kingdoms, the beauty of the Chaldees' excellency, shall be as when God overthrew Sodom and Gomorrah" (Isa. 13:19).*

Their armies would be chased back to their own land as a wild dog would pursue a frightened deer. Their soldiers would be butchered, their children murdered, and their wives raped. The Prophet Isaiah was horrified and became physically ill at God's description of Babylon's punishment.

"Therefore are my loins filled with pain, pangs have taken hold upon me, as the pangs of a woman that travaileth, I was bowed down at the hearing of it; I was dismayed at the seeing of it. . . . My heart panted, fearfulness affrighted me; the night of my pleasure hath He turned into fear unto me" (21:3-4).

Isaiah also vividly described the watchman as he brought the word to the king that the city had fallen (vv. 6-10). Babylon was to become a desolate land of porcupines and swamps; the wild animals would make it their home, and demons would come there to dance.

Babylon was never to be rebuilt on that site.

ASSYRIA

God had determined to crush the Assyrian army on the mountains of Israel. This would be done to remove the awful Assyrian yoke from His people.

PHILISTIA

Philistia was warned not to rejoice over the death of the Judean king Ahaz, who had smote them. His son (Hezekiah) would be even more demanding. Finally, Philistia suffered total doom under the cruel attack of Sargon, the Assyrian king.

MOAB

Moab was to be punished by God, with its chief cities destroyed in one night. The whole land would be filled with weeping from one end to another. Lions would hunt down the survivors. Moab's refugees were invited by God to avail themselves of His mercies. They were enjoined to pay tribute to Israel according to their past arrangement. However, pride kept Moab from doing this. Isaiah wept because of God's judgment on this stubborn pride. Judgment was officially set to fall within three years. The Assyrians at that time invaded Moab.

DAMASCUS

Ephraim (another title for the Israelite Northern Kingdom) and Damascus had allied together against Judah, thus linking that kingdom with the divine judgment. Partners in crime meant partners in punishment. Both allies were later besieged by Tiglath-Pileser and were finally deported by Shalmaneser.

ETHIOPIA

This nation marched against Israel (historically or prophetically?) but was cut off by God Himself. Their army will be left dead on the field for the birds and animals to eat. After this (the Tribulation?) Ethiopia will bring gifts to the Lord of hosts in Jerusalem.

EGYPT

Egypt was to be severely punished because of her idolatry. Her people were originally monotheistic but gradually lapsed into the basest idolatry. They worshiped the bull, the frog, the fish, and various birds. Egypt was to be given over to a cruel ruler. Egyptian would fight against Egyptian. The channels along the Nile River were filled and fouled with rotting reeds. The paper reeds by the brooks withered away. Egypt's fishing industry disappeared. Her linen industry disappeared. Egypt staggered along in world history as a *"drunken man staggereth in his vomit" (19:14).* Judah was a terror to Egypt.

But all this would someday gloriously change. God would smite Egypt in the Tribulation, but would then graciously heal her. Egypt and Iraq will be connected by a highway, thus allowing both nations to freely travel to Jerusalem to worship God.

"In that day shall Israel be the third with Egypt and with Assyria, even a blessing in the midst of the land, whom the LORD of hosts shall bless, saying, 'Blessed be Egypt My people, and Assyria the work of My hands, and Israel Mine inheritance' " (vv. 24-25).

saiah: Miniature Bible and Dilemma Deluxe

COMMENTS

The Book of Isaiah in its present form claims to be the work of Isaiah the son of Amoz (1:1). This prophecy has long posed a deluxe dilemma to many who have poured over it. Scholars have long recognized a decided shift in style, historical background, and theological thought between chapters 1–39 and 40–66. Some scholars have come to the conclusion that chapters 1–39 were written by Isaiah as they claim but that a "second Isaiah" wrote chapters 40–66. This view is called the "deutero-Isaiah" view of the authorship of the prophecy. Other scholars have noted that within chapters 40–66 there is a decided shift between chapters 40–55 and chapters 56–66, the former being more theological and poetical, the latter being more prophetical. This view is called the "trito-Isaiah view." According to it there are at least three Isaiahs: Isaiah the son of Amoz who wrote chapters 1–39; Second Isaiah who wrote chapters 40–55; and Third Isaiah who wrote chapters 56–66. Modern scholars would posit many more Isaiahs noting there are many logical contradictions, especially throughout Third Isaiah. They would assign the sections not to particular individuals but to categories of writings each being more or less homogeneous in its content.

Two insurmountable objections can be raised against any partition theory of Isaiah. Isaiah was one of Jesus' favorite books and He quotes from all three sections of it, in each instance saying, "As Isaiah says" (cf. John 12:38-40 quoting Isa. 53:1 and 6:9). Jesus only recognized one Isaiah as being the author of the prophecy bearing his name. The most important manuscript find of the text of Isaiah was among the Dead Sea Scrolls. This manuscript consists of 17 parchment sheets sewn together and measures 24 feet in length and has the complete text of Isaiah. The manuscript evidence to support a textual division of Isaiah simply does not exist.

Those who observe a decided shift between chapters 1–39 and chapters 40–66 observe correctly. Chapters 1–39 deal with the Assyrian crisis while chapters 40–66 deal with the Babylonian crisis. In this way, the Book of Isaiah is like a Bible in miniature. The Bible is divided into two testaments consisting of 39 books in the Old Testament and 27 books in the New Testament.

If one looks at format of writing, the 66 chapters of Isaiah should be divided into three sections: chapters 1–35 being poetical in form, chapters 36–39 being historical, and chapters 40–66 being poetical. There is a practical reason for the shift in form. Content-wise chapters 1–35 deal with the Assyrian crisis while chapters 40–66 deal with the Babylonian crisis. Chapters 36–39 constitute a historical bridge with chapters 36–37 drawing the curtain on the Assyrian crisis while chapters 38–39 raise the curtain on the Babylonian crisis. Using a musical figure, chapters 1–35 are written in the key of A while chapters 40–66 are written in the key of B. Chapters 36–39 are a modulation from the key of A to the key of B.

Two main arguments are raised which are thought to make it impossible for both sections of the prophecy of Isaiah to be written by the same person: (1) the events of the Babylonian crisis are 135 years after the Assyrian crisis and the same prophet could not have ministered to both crises and (2) Cyrus is mentioned in 44:28 and 45:1 as if he were already on the scene when in actuality he did not come on the scene until some 60 years after the Children of Israel were taken captive. It is thought that it would be impossible for one prophet's ministry to cover not only the Assyrian crisis, but the Babylonian crisis 135 years later, and the rise of Cyrus 60 years later. What to man is a dilemma deluxe is child's play to God. Such is the genius of predictive prophecy!

EDOM

This passage includes a question and an answer:

The question—"Watchman, what of the night?"

The answer—"The morning cometh, and also the night."

Both morning and night are coming. What would be glory for some (the Medes, who will overrun Edom), would be shame for others (the Edomites).

ARABIA

Arabia was the land of the Ishmaelites, the Bedouin tribes of the desert. They would be so severely judged that only a few of their stalwart archers would survive.

TYRE

Tyre was to be destroyed by the Babylonians and carried into captivity for 70 years. This was to be done because of their pride and utter materialism. Nebuchadnezzar would lay siege to the coastland city, raze its palaces, and make it a heap of ruins. Egypt, its ally, would sorrow over its swift destruction, along with its sailors, who would not even be able to return home. After 70 years, Tyre would be rebuilt (as was Jerusalem) but would soon degenerate into the same gross materialism and pride of former days. In the Millennium Tyre will be rebuilt and be blessed by God.

Preview

The Elect and the Enemy

ISAIAH 1; 3; 5; 14

The enemy of God and the elect of God! The story of how both rebelled, and how one was restored. Perhaps heaven's holy angels shook their heads, indicating shock and sadness. They had witnessed this kind of sordid thing before. On neither occasion did they understand it. How could any finite creature possibly revolt against the holy and glorious Creator? But it had happened in time past and was right then happening again.

The first instance involved one of their own, Lucifer by name. Disregarding God's person, and defying His power, this ambitious and apostate angel unsuccessfully attempted a celestial coup, only to become the devil.

Now it was happening again. This time, however, humans, not angels, were involved. The sad truth was that the Israel of God had turned against the God of Israel. This then was the reason for the angelic surprise and sadness.

But before the story ended, another emotion would be experienced by these heavenly creatures, that of praise to God. The reason? Unlike Lucifer, whose sin was unforgivable, Israel would be forgiven, redeemed, and restored.

Overview

<table>
<tr><td>SCRIPTURE</td><td colspan="7">Isaiah 1; 3; 5; 14</td></tr>
<tr><td>SUBJECT</td><td colspan="7">Facts about Israel and Satan</td></tr>
<tr><td rowspan="7">SPECIFICS</td><td colspan="4">Israel: the elect of God</td><td colspan="3">Satan: the enemy of God</td></tr>
<tr><td colspan="2">Her rebellion</td><td colspan="2">Her rebuke</td><td rowspan="6">The wicked "I wills" of the devil</td><td rowspan="6">"I will assume"</td><td>God's possessions</td></tr>
<tr><td>Vertical sins</td><td>Ignorance
Idolatry
Impunity
Insincerity</td><td>Northern Kingdom</td><td>To be captured by the Babylonians</td><td>God's preeminence</td></tr>
<tr><td>Horizontal sins</td><td>Godlessness
Their leaders
Their women
Covetousness
Drunkenness
Bloodiness</td><td>Southern Kingdom</td><td>To be captured by the Assyrians</td><td>God's program</td></tr>
<tr><td colspan="2">Her repentance</td><td>Her rebirth</td><td>Her restoration</td><td rowspan="2">God's person</td></tr>
<tr><td colspan="2">Confessing her sin</td><td>The travail involved</td><td>By the Lord</td></tr>
<tr><td colspan="2">Forsaking her sin</td><td>The time involved</td><td>To the land</td><td>God's power</td></tr>
<tr><td>SAINTS AND SINNERS</td><td colspan="7">Isaiah</td></tr>
<tr><td rowspan="2">SENTENCE SUMMARIES</td><td colspan="2">O.T. Verse</td><td colspan="5">"O Ephraim, what shall I do unto thee? O Judah, what shall I do unto thee? For your goodness is as a morning cloud, and as the early dew it goeth away" (Hosea 6:4).</td></tr>
<tr><td colspan="2">N.T. Verse</td><td colspan="5">"Well hath Isaiah prophesied of you hypocrites, as it is written, 'This people honoreth Me with their lips, but their heart is far from Me' " (Mark 7:6).</td></tr>
</table>

THE NATION ISRAEL IN ISAIAH

HER SIN

Willful ignorance. "The ox knoweth his owner, and the ass his master's crib; but Israel doth not know; My people doth not consider" (Isa. 1:3).

"Therefore My people are gone into captivity, because they have no knowledge. And their honorable men are famished, and their multitude dried up with thirst" (5:13).

Hypocrisy in their burnt offerings. "Your new moons and your appointed feasts My soul hateth; they are a trouble unto Me; I am weary to bear them. And when ye spread forth your hands, I will hide Mine eyes from you. Yea, when ye make many prayers, I will not hear; your hands are full of blood" (1:14-15).

Corrupt leadership. "Thy princes are rebellious, and companions of thieves. Everyone loveth gifts, and followeth after rewards; they judge not the fatherless, neither doth the cause of the widow come unto them" (v. 23).

"For the leaders of this people cause them to err; and they that are led of them are destroyed" (9:16).

Idolatry. "Their land also is full of idols; they worship the work of their own hands, that which their own fingers have made" (2:8).

Gross materialism. "Their land also is full of silver and gold, neither is there any end of their treasures; their land is also full of horses, neither is there any end of their chariots" (v. 7).

Godless women. Before God judged them they were haughty with their noses in the air. They had wanton eyes. They wore ornaments about their feet and chains around their ankles. They had necklaces and bracelets. They had veils of shimmering gauze. They wore headbands. They wore nose jewels and earrings. They sported party clothes, negligees, and capes. They wore ornate combs and carried purses. How far removed was all this from Peter's description of real beauty and adornment? See 1 Peter 3:1-4.

After God judged them. Instead of sweet fragrance, there would be rottenness; instead of a girdle (sash), a rope; instead of well-set hair, baldness; instead of beauty, shame, disgrace, and widowhood.

Fruitlessness. The Parable of the Lord's Vineyard. This parable employed one of the two figures taken from the botanical world to represent the nation Israel. The other figure was a fig tree. See Matthew 21:33-46.

God planted His vineyard on a very fertile hill with the choicest vine. He plowed it and took out all the rocks. He built a watchtower and cut a winepress in the rocks. He waited patiently for the harvest.

God received nothing from His vineyard but wild and sour grapes.

He would tear down the fences and let the vineyard go to pasture, to be trampled by cattle and sheep. He would not prune nor hoe it, but let it be overgrown with briars and thorns. He would even command the clouds not to rain on it anymore.

Drunkenness. "Woe unto them that rise up early in the morning, that they may follow strong drink; that continue until night, till wine inflame them!" (Isa. 5:11)

"But they also have erred through wine, and through strong drink are out of the way; the priest and the prophet have erred through strong drink, they are swallowed up of wine, they are out of the way through strong drink; they err in vision, they stumble in judgment" (28:7).

Amorality. "Woe unto them that call evil good, and good evil; that put darkness for light, and light for darkness; that put bitter for sweet, and sweet for bitter" (5:20).

Humanism. "Woe unto them that are wise in their own eyes, and prudent in their own sight" (v. 21).

Unscriptural alliances. "Woe to them that go down to Egypt for help; and stay on horses, and trust in chariots, because they are many; and in horsemen, because they are very strong; but they look not unto the Holy One of Israel, neither seek the LORD!" (31:1)

Rebellion. "That this is a rebellious people, lying children, children that will not hear the Law of the LORD" (30:9-11).

"I have spread out My hands all the day unto a rebellious people, which walketh in a way that was not good, after their own thoughts" (65:2).

Infant sacrificing. "Enflaming yourselves with idols under every green tree, slaying the children in the valleys under the clefts of the rocks?" (57:5)

Overall condition. "From the sole of the foot even unto the head there is no soundness in it; but wounds, and bruises, and putrefying sores.

421

The Life of Christ According to Isaiah

COMMENTS

Messiah is one of Isaiah's most prominent themes because He is the ultimate hope for the nation. From Isaiah's prophecy one can construct a rather complete life of Christ from before the time He was born in Bethlehem's manger to the time He will be invested with His messianic crown. Consider the following:

(1) *His ancestry (Isa. 11:1).* Messiah is the Branch who will descend from Jesse the father of David and reign on David's throne.

(2) *His forerunner (Isa. 40:3-5).* The ministry of John the Baptist is only prophesied here and in Malachi 3:1. John the Baptist used Isaiah's words in his ministry (cf. Matt. 3:2-3).

(3) *His Virgin Birth (Isa. 7:14).* While this prophecy immediately was fulfilled in the birth of Isaiah's son, Mahershalalhashbaz (cf. 8:1-4), Matthew applied it specifically to Jesus' birth (Matt. 1:22-23).

(4) *His anointing by the Holy Spirit (Isa. 11:2).* This aspect of the Holy Spirit's ministry began when He descended on Jesus at His baptism (Matt. 3:16).

(5) *His character and qualifications for universal kingship (Isa. 11:2-5; 42:1-4).* Jesus will reign with righteousness and will establish righteousness throughout all the world. He will direct the "rod of His mouth" against the wicked and punish them.

(6) *His work as Prophet (Isa. 61:1-3).* Jesus quoted these words of Isaiah's prophecy and applied them to Himself when He preached at His hometown synagogue in Nazareth (cf. Luke 4:16-21) and pronounced them "fulfilled." It should be noted that He stopped midway in His reading of Isaiah 61:2 (following the word Lord) separating His first and second comings to earth.

(7) *His work as Teacher (Isa. 50:4).* Most of the Gospel records are made up of the teachings of Jesus. Truly, "No man ever spake as this Man."

(8) *His work as Jehovah's true slave (Isa. 50:5).* Only one Person in all history was truly Jehovah's slave in every aspect—Jesus, who came to do the Father's will (Heb. 10:7).

(9) *His miracles of healing sicknesses (Isa. 53:4).* Matthew specifically applied these words to Jesus in His ministry of casting out demons and healing the sick (Matt. 8:17).

(10) *His rejection and sufferings (Isa. 50:6; 53:1-4).* More amazing than the fact that Messiah would come was the fact that when He came He would suffer and be rejected.

(11) *His vicarious sufferings (Isa. 53:5-6).* The description of Christ's sufferings comes in the middle of a section in Isaiah's prophecy that describes the glory of the Messiah. While He is intrinsically glorious, in a real sense His sufferings are His glory.

(12) *His death (Isa. 53:8-9).* The great mystery of the prophecies of the Messiah is the fact that He would die. They thought He was coming to reign. This caused the prophets great consternation and caused them to study their own prophecies (1 Peter 1:10-12).

(13) *His burial in a rich man's tomb (Isa. 53:9).* People who were crucified were usually buried in unmarked common graves. Jesus was buried in a tomb belonging to a rich man (Matt. 27:57-60).

(14) *His work of judgment and second coming (Isa. 63:1-6).* Jesus will come and execute vengeance on all of God's enemies and will establish His earthly Davidic millennial kingdom.

(15) *His millennial reign (Isa. 9:6-7; 11:1-10; 32; 42; 49; 52:13-15; 60; 65:17).* No theme is so recurrent in Isaiah's prophecy as that expressed by the hymn writer, "Jesus shall reign where'er the sun does his successive journeys run; His kingdom spread from shore to shore, till moons shall wax and wane no more."

They have not been closed, neither bound up, neither mollified with ointment" (1:6).

"Behold, the LORD*'s hand is not shortened, that it cannot save; neither His ear heavy, that it cannot hear. But your iniquities have separated between you and your God, and your sins have hid His face from you, that He will not hear. For your hands are defiled with blood, and your fingers with iniquity; your lips have spoken lies, your tongue hath muttered perverseness. . . .*

"Their feet run to evil, and they make haste to shed innocent blood. Their thoughts are thoughts of iniquity; wasting and destruction are in their paths. The way of peace they know not; and there is no judgment in their goings. They have made them crooked paths; whosoever goeth therein shall not know peace" (59:1-3, 7-8).

"But we are all as an unclean thing, and all our righteousnesses are as filthy rags; and we all do fade as a leaf; and our iniquities, like the wind, have taken us away" (64:6).

Preview

The Majesty of Our Maker

ISAIAH 6; 40–41; 43; 55; 63

The same basic defiant question had been asked on two occasions. First it was heard by the River Nile in Egypt. Pharaoh demanded of Moses: *"Who is the LORD, that I should obey His voice to let Israel go?" (Ex. 5:2)*

Centuries later it was repeated by the River Euphrates in Babylon. Nebuchadnezzar hurled it at three young Hebrew men: *"Who is that God that shall deliver you out of my hands?" (Dan. 3:15)*

Both monarchs got their answers soon enough. Who is this God? Well, for starters He could and would protect His own. Pharaoh found he couldn't drown them and Nebuchadnezzar discovered he couldn't burn them. In this portion of his book, Isaiah expands on the question posed by these two pagans. Who indeed is the God of Israel? In glowing terms the prophet speaks of His salvation, righteousness, grace, glory, holiness, mercy, compassion, wrath, power, eternality, long-suffering, triunity, uniqueness, faithfulness, and love! What more need be said? In fact, what more could be said?

Overview

<table>
<tr><td>SCRIPTURE</td><td colspan="5">Isaiah 6; 40–41; 43; 55; 63</td></tr>
<tr><td>SUBJECT</td><td colspan="5">The greatness of God</td></tr>
<tr><td rowspan="8">SPECIFICS</td><td colspan="5">Fifteen sovereign attributes</td></tr>
<tr><td rowspan="7">His intrinsic attributes</td><td rowspan="2">His righteousness</td><td rowspan="2">His omnipotence</td><td rowspan="7">His imparted attributes</td><td>His grace</td></tr>
<tr><td>His mercy</td></tr>
<tr><td rowspan="2">His glory</td><td rowspan="2">His eternality</td><td>His compassion</td></tr>
<tr><td>His wrath</td></tr>
<tr><td rowspan="2">His holiness</td><td rowspan="2">His triunity</td><td>His long-suffering</td></tr>
<tr><td>His faithfulness</td></tr>
<tr><td>His omniscience</td><td>His uniqueness</td><td>His love</td></tr>
<tr><td>SAINTS AND SINNERS</td><td colspan="5">Isaiah</td></tr>
<tr><td rowspan="2">SENTENCE SUMMARIES</td><td>O.T. Verse</td><td colspan="4">"Thine, O LORD, is the greatness, and the power, and the glory, and the victory, and the majesty; for all that is in the heavens and in the earth is Thine; Thine is the kingdom, O LORD, and Thou art exalted as head above all" (1 Chron. 29:11).</td></tr>
<tr><td>N.T. Verse</td><td colspan="4">"These things said Isaiah, when he saw His glory, and spake of Him" (John 12:41).</td></tr>
</table>

THE GREATNESS OF GOD IN ISAIAH

HIS SALVATION

"Behold, God is my salvation; I will trust, and not be afraid. For the LORD JEHOVAH is my strength and my song; He also is become my salvation. Therefore with joy shall ye draw water out of the wells of salvation. And in that day shall ye say, 'Praise the LORD, call upon His name, declare His doings among the people, make mention that His name is exalted. Sing unto the LORD; for He hath done excellent things; this is known in all the earth' " (Isa. 12:2-5).

"He will swallow up death in victory; and the Lord GOD will wipe away tears from off all faces; and the rebuke of His people shall He take away from off all the earth. For the LORD hath spoken it. And it shall be said in that day, 'Lo, this is our God; we have waited for Him, and He will save us. This is the LORD; we have waited for Him, we will be glad and rejoice in His salvation' " (Isa. 25:8-9).

"I, even I, am the LORD; and beside Me there is no savior" (43:11).

"Ho, everyone that thirsteth, come ye to the waters, and he that hath no money; come ye, buy, and eat; yea, come, buy wine and milk without money and without price. Wherefore do ye spend money for that which is not bread? And your labor for that which satisfieth not? Hearken diligently unto Me, and eat ye that which is good, and let your soul delight itself in fatness. . . .

"Seek ye the LORD while He may be found, call ye upon Him while He is near. Let the wicked forsake his way, and the unrighteous man his thoughts; and let him return unto the LORD, and He will have mercy upon him; and to our God, for He will abundantly pardon" (55:1-2, 6-7).

"I will greatly rejoice in the LORD, my soul shall be joyful in my God; for He hath clothed me with the garments of salvation, He hath covered me with the robe of righteousness, as a bridegroom decketh himself with ornaments, and as a bride adorneth herself with her jewels" (61:10).

HIS RIGHTEOUSNESS

"For He put on righteousness as a breastplate, and a helmet of salvation upon his head; and He put on the garments of vengeance for clothing, and was clad with zeal as a cloak" (59:17).

HIS GRACE

"For the people shall dwell in Zion at Jerusalem. Thou shalt weep no more; He will be very gracious unto thee at the voice of thy cry; when He shall hear it, He will answer thee" (30:19).

HIS GLORY

"I am the LORD; that is My name: and My glory will I not give to another, neither My praise to graven images" (42:8).

"So shall they fear the name of the LORD from the west, and His glory from the rising of the sun. When the enemy shall come in like a flood, the spirit of the LORD shall lift up a standard against him" (59:19).

HIS HOLINESS

"In the year that King Uzziah died I saw also the Lord sitting upon a throne, high and lifted up, and His train filled the temple. Above it stood the seraphim; each one had six wings; with twain he covered his face, and with twain he covered his feet, and with twain he did fly. And one cried unto another, and said, 'Holy, holy, holy, is the LORD of hosts; the whole earth is full of His glory' " (6:1-3).

"For thus saith the high and lofty One that inhabiteth eternity, whose name is Holy; 'I dwell in the high and holy place, with him also that is of a contrite and humble spirit, to revive the spirit of the humble, and to revive the heart of the contrite ones' " (57:15).

HIS MERCY

"For the LORD will have mercy on Jacob, and will yet choose Israel, and set them in their own land; and the strangers shall be joined with them, and they shall cleave to the house of Jacob" (14:1).

"For Thou hast been a strength to the poor, a strength to the needy in his distress, a refuge from the storm, a shadow from the heat, when the blast of the terrible ones is as a storm against the wall" (25:4).

HIS COMPASSION

"I will mention the loving-kindness of the LORD, and the praises of the LORD, according to all that the LORD hath bestowed on us, and the great goodness toward the house of Israel, which He hath bestowed on them according to His mercies, and according to the multitude of His loving-kindnesses.

"For He said, 'Surely they are My people, children that will not lie'; so He was their Saviour.

"In all their affliction He was afflicted, and the angel of His presence saved them. In His love and in His pity He redeemed them; and He bare them, and carried them all the days of old" (63:7-9).

HIS WRATH

"Behold, the name of the LORD cometh from far, burning with His anger, and the burden thereof is heavy. His lips are full of indignation, and His tongue as a devouring fire" (30:27).

HIS WISDOM

"Who hath directed the spirit of the LORD, or being His counselor hath taught Him? With whom took He counsel, and who instructed Him, and taught Him in the path of judgment, and taught Him knowledge, and showed to Him the way of understanding?" (40:13-14)

"Behold, the former things are come to pass, and new things do I declare; before they spring forth I tell you of them" (42:9).

HIS POWER

"Who hath measured the waters in the hollow of His hand, and meted out heaven with the span, and comprehended the dust of the earth in a measure, and weighed the mountains in scales, and the hills in a balance? . . .

"Behold, the nations are as a drop of a bucket, and are counted as the small dust of the balance. Behold, He taketh up the isles as a very little thing. And Lebanon is not sufficient to burn, nor the beasts thereof sufficient for a burnt offering. All nations before Him are as nothing; and they are counted to Him less than nothing, and vanity. . . .

"Have ye not known? Have ye not heard? Hath it not been told you from the beginning? Have ye not understood from the foundations of the earth? It is He that sitteth upon the circle of the earth, and the inhabitants thereof are as grasshoppers; that stretcheth out the heavens as a curtain, and spreadeth them out as a tent to dwell in. . . .

" 'To whom then will ye liken Me, or shall I be equal?' saith the Holy One. Lift up your eyes on high, and behold who hath created these things, that bringeth out their host by number; He calleth them all by names by the greatness of His might, for that He is strong in power; not one faileth. . . .

"Hast thou not known? Hast thou not heard, that the everlasting God, the LORD, the Creator of the ends of the earth, fainteth not, neither is weary? There is no searching of His understanding. He giveth power to the faint; and to them that have no might He increaseth strength. Even the youths shall faint and be weary, and the young men shall utterly fall. But they that wait upon the LORD shall renew their strength; they shall mount up with wings as eagles; they shall run, and not be weary; and they shall walk, and not faint" (40:12, 15-17, 21-22, 25-26, 28-31).

"Thus saith God the LORD, He that created the heavens, and stretched them out; He that spread forth the earth, and that which cometh out of it; He that giveth breath unto the people upon it, and spirit to them that walk therein" (42:5).

"Thus saith the LORD, thy Redeemer, and He that formed thee from the womb, 'I am the LORD that maketh all things; that stretcheth forth the heavens alone; that spreadeth abroad the earth by Myself' " (44:24).

" 'I form the light, and create darkness. I make peace, and create evil. I the LORD do all these things. . . . I have made the earth, and created man upon it. I, even My hands, have stretched out the heavens, and all their host have I commanded.' . . .

"For thus saith the LORD that created the heavens; God Himself that formed the earth and made it; He hath established it, He created it not in vain, He formed it to be inhabited: 'I am the LORD; and there is none else' " (45:7, 12, 18).

"Declaring the end from the beginning, and from ancient times the things that are not yet done, saying, 'My counsel shall stand, and I will do all My pleasure' " (46:10).

"Mine hand also hath laid the foundation of the earth, and My right hand hath spanned the heavens; when I call unto them, they stand up together" (48:13).

"For, behold, I create new heavens and a new

Pictures of Christ in Isaiah

COMMENTS

In the science of the interpretation of Scripture (hermeneutics), a type is an Old Testament person, place, thing, or event which is divinely intended to portray spiritual truth which is fully revealed in the New Testament. In the strictest sense of the word, a type must be expressly so-declared in the New Testament (cf. 1 Cor. 10:6, 11—the word translated "examples" and "ensamples" is the Greek word *tupos*, "type"). In a less-strict sense, there are many people, places, things, or events which provide some interesting illustrations of New Testament spiritual truths. In the prophecy of Isaiah there are at least five persons or things that provide interesting illustrations or pictures of the person and work of Christ.

(1) *The Prophet Isaiah.* The names Jesus and Isaiah are similar. Jesus means "Jehovah saves" and Isaiah means "salvation of Jehovah." Isaiah was a faithful prophet of Jehovah and as such is a foreshadowing of God's perfect Prophet, Jesus. Isaiah says of himself, "Behold I and the children whom Jehovah hath given me are for signs" (Isa. 8:18). The writer of Hebrews applies this very statement to Jesus and His spiritual children (Heb. 2:13).

(2) *The nation Israel.* Israel provides a picture of Christ by contrast. Isaiah shows Israel to be a false vine (Isa. 5:1-7). Jesus, by contrast, calls Himself the "true Vine" (John 15:1). Because of the work of the true Vine, Israel will one day be purged of its sins and will be a true vine bringing forth fruit for Jehovah (Isa. 27:2-6).

(3) *The sacrifices.* One of the reasons why God was angry with Israel was because they were not observing the required sacrifices properly (1:11-13). Their attitude toward the sacrifices was indicative of their attitude toward God. In their disgust for the sacrifices, the Children of Israel were showing their disgust for what the sacrifices pictured, the person and work of Christ.

(4) *Eliakim, the son of Hilkiah.* Eliakim's name means "God doth establish." He was a true child of God whom King Hezekiah placed over his household (cf. Isa. 36:3, 11, 22; 37:2; 2 Kings 18:18, 26, 37; 19:2). He was the official spokesman for the king of Judah in his dealings with the representatives of the evil king of Assyria. In a much greater way Jesus was on a mission for His Father to represent Him against all the forces of evil in this world. Just as victory is predicted for Eliakim (cf. Isa. 22:20-25) so Jesus will be victorious over all of the forces of evil and will reign forever.

(5) *Cyrus, the king of Persia.* While many things in the character of Cyrus are pictures of Christ by contrast, there is one notable way in which he is a positive picture of Christ. The king of Assyria had practiced the policy of colonization. Under that policy the population of Israel was taken to Assyria and never returned. The king of Assyria sent colonists to occupy the land vacated by the Israelites. They became a half-Jew and half-Gentile race called Samaritans who were hated by the Jews.

Nebuchadnezzar did not follow the foreign policy of Assyria but simply took prisoners from Judah and left the land vacant. Cyrus conquered Babylon in one night and instituted the policy of colonization again. Under him the people of Judah were restored to their land. Jehovah said of him, " 'He is My shepherd, and shall perform all My pleasure.' . . . Thus saith the LORD to His anointed, to Cyrus" (44:28; 45:1). Cyrus, then, is Jehovah's messiah under whom Israel experienced a partial and temporary restoration. Jesus is Jehovah's Messiah under whom Israel will experience a complete and permanent restoration.

earth; and the former shall not be remembered, nor come into mind" (65:17).

HIS ETERNALITY

" 'Ye are My witnesses,' saith the LORD, 'and My servant whom I have chosen, that ye may know and believe Me, and understand that I am He. Before Me there was no God formed, neither shall there be after Me' " (43:10).

"Thus saith the LORD the King of Israel, and His Redeemer the LORD of hosts, 'I am the first, and I am the last; and beside Me there is no God' " (44:6).

"Hearken unto Me, O Jacob and Israel, My called; I am He; I am the first. I also am the last" (48:12).

"For thus saith the high and lofty One that inhabiteth eternity, whose name is holy; 'I dwell in the high and holy place, with him also that is of a contrite and humble spirit, to revive the spirit of the humble, and to revive the heart of the contrite ones' " (57:15).

HIS LONG-SUFFERING

" 'Come now, and let us reason together,' saith the LORD. 'Though your sins be as scarlet, they shall be as white as snow; though they be red like crimson, they shall be as wool' " (1:18).

"Therefore is the anger of the LORD kindled against His people . . . and the hills did tremble, and their carcasses were torn in the midst of the streets. For all this His anger is not turned away, but His hand is stretched out still" (5:25).

HIS TRIUNITY

"Come ye near unto me, hear ye this; I have not spoken in secret from the beginning; from the time that it was, there am I: and now the Lord GOD, and His Spirit, hath sent me" (48:16).

HIS UNIQUENESS

"I am the LORD, and there is none else, there is no God beside Me. I girded thee, though thou hast not known Me, that they may know from the rising of the sun, and from the west, that there is none beside Me. I am the LORD, and there is none else" (45:5-6).

"Remember the former things of old, for I am God, and there is none else; I am God, and there is none like Me" (46:9).

HIS FAITHFULNESS

"O LORD, Thou art my God; I will exalt Thee, I will praise Thy name; for Thou hast done wonderful things; Thy counsels of old are faithfulness and truth" (25:1).

HIS LOVE

For Israel. "But thou, Israel, art My servant, Jacob whom I have chosen, the seed of Abraham My friend. Thou whom I have taken from the ends of the earth, and called thee from the chief men thereof, and said unto thee, 'Thou art My servant; I have chosen thee, and not cast thee away. Fear thou not; for I am with thee: be not dismayed; for I am thy God: I will strengthen thee; yea, I will help thee; yea, I will uphold thee with the right hand of My righteousness' " (41:8-10).

"But now thus saith the LORD that created thee, O Jacob, and He that formed thee, O Israel, 'Fear not, for I have redeemed thee, I have called thee by thy name; thou art Mine. When thou passest through the waters, I will be with thee; and through the rivers, they shall not overflow thee: when thou walkest through the fire, thou shalt not be burned; neither shall the flame kindle upon thee. . . . Since thou wast precious in My sight, thou hast been honorable, and I have loved thee. Therefore will I give men for thee, and people for thy life' " (43:1-2, 4).

"Behold, I have refined thee, but not with silver; I have chosen thee in the furnace of affliction" (48:10).

"But Zion said, 'The LORD hath forsaken me, and my Lord hath forgotten me.' Can a woman forget her sucking child, that she should not have compassion on the son of her womb? Yea, they may forget, yet will I not forget thee. Behold, I have graven thee upon the palms of My hands; thy walls are continually before Me" (49:14-16).

" 'For a small moment have I forsaken thee; but with great mercies will I gather thee. In a little wrath I hid My face from thee for a moment; but with everlasting kindness will I have mercy on thee,' saith the LORD thy Redeemer. . . .

" 'No weapon that is formed against thee shall prosper; and every tongue that shall rise against thee in judgment thou shalt condemn. This is the heritage of the servants of the LORD, and their righteousness is of Me,' saith the LORD" (54:7-8, 17).

"And the LORD shall guide thee continually, and satisfy thy soul in drought, and make fat thy bones, and thou shalt be like a watered garden, and like a spring of water, whose waters fail not" (58:11).

For the world. "Look unto Me, and be ye saved, all the ends of the earth; for I am God, and there is none else" (45:22).

The Place of Christ in Isaiah

COMMENTS

Though Isaiah was written more than 600 years before Christ's birth, He is the main character of the prophecy. Consider the prominent place given Him in Isaiah's prophecy.

He is Jehovah. The name Jehovah is properly used in three ways in the Old Testament. It is usually used to refer to the Triune God (cf. Deut. 6:4). It is also used to refer to each of the Persons of the Trinity. This is as would be expected, for where one Person of the Godhead is, the other members are also present. What is true of One is true of each of the others. There are four classic examples in the prophecy of Isaiah where the name Jehovah is used of Christ. (1) In Isaiah 2:3 we read: "Come ye, and let us go up to the mountain of the LORD [Jehovah]. . . and He will teach us of His ways, and we will walk in His paths." The One who will do the teaching in those millennial days will be Christ. (2) Concerning his majestic vision, Isaiah said (6:5), "Woe is me! . . . For mine eyes have seen the King, the LORD [Jehovah] of hosts." John tells us that the "Holy One of Israel" whom Isaiah saw was none other than Christ Himself because "he saw His glory; and spake of Him" (John 12:41). (3) Isaiah 40:3, 5, and 10 describe the ministry and message of John the Baptist. "Prepare ye the way of the LORD [Jehovah] . . . .And the glory of the LORD [Jehovah] shall be revealed. . . . Behold the Lord GOD [Jehovah] will come." The One of whom Isaiah spoke and the One for whom John the Baptist prepared the way was Jesus Christ (Messiah) who did come and did reveal the glory of God. (4) Isaiah 45:18, 21-22 are particularly significant in showing that Jesus is Jehovah: "I am the LORD [Jehovah]; and there is none else. . . . There is no God else beside Me. . . . Look unto Me, and be ye saved, all the ends of the earth." The One who will accomplish this is none other than Jesus.

He is the subject of many direct prophecies. Isaiah provides a good illustration of Revelation 19:10b: "For the testimony of Jesus is the spirit of prophecy." From the extensive prophecies of Christ in the Book of Isaiah one can easily construct a "Life of Christ." Many of Isaiah's darkest prophecies also include beautiful promises concerning our Lord Jesus. Jesus Himself read Isaiah 61:1-2 and applied it to Himself, accurately separating His first coming to earth from His second coming (cf. Luke 4:16-19). In addition to the many direct prophecies of Christ in Isaiah, many names and titles for Jesus are found, a few of which are: "the God of Jacob" (Isa. 2:3), "The King, the LORD of hosts" (6:5), "Immanuel" (7:14), "Child . . . Son . . . Wonderful, Counselor, Mighty God, Everlasting Father, Prince of Peace" (9:6), "a rod out of the stem of Jesse . . . a branch shall grow out of his roots" (11:1), "The Root of Jesse" (11:10), "a foundation, a stone, a tried stone, a precious cornerstone" (28:16), "Judge . . . Lawgiver . . . King" (33:22), "My Servant" (42:1; 52:13; 53:11), "My Elect" (42:1), "Shepherd" (40:11), "a light of the Gentiles" (42:6; 49:6), "a Man of Sorrows" (53:3), "Arm of the Lord" (v. 1), "tender plant . . . root out of a dry ground" (v. 2), "David" (55:3), "Witness . . . Leader . . . Commander" (v. 4), "Lamb . . . Sheep" (53:7), and "a Redeemer" (59:20).

He is the Angel of the LORD. The Angel of the LORD is mentioned twice in Isaiah (37:36; 63:9). The Angel of the LORD is the name given to Jesus in His preincarnate Old Testament appearances.

He is the One for whom the nation was preserved. In His providence, God used the prophecy of Isaiah to preserve the nation Israel for the coming of the Messiah. Jesus is the Messiah who came to be born and die and will yet come to reign. Apart from the Messiah, Isaiah's preaching ministry and message are meaningless.

His Word. "The voice said, 'Cry.' And he said, 'What shall I cry?' 'All flesh is grass, and all the goodliness thereof is as the flower of the field. The grass withereth, the flower fadeth: because the spirit of the Lord *bloweth upon it. Surely the people is grass. The grass withereth, the flower fadeth, but the Word of our God shall stand forever' " (40:6-8).*

"I have sworn by Myself, the word is gone out of My mouth in righteousness, and shall not return, that unto Me every knee shall bow, every tongue shall swear" (45:23).

"For as the rain cometh down, and the snow from heaven, and returneth not thither, but watereth the earth, and maketh it bring forth and bud, that it may give seed to the sower, and bread to the eater; so shall My Word be that goeth forth out of My mouth: it shall not return unto Me void, but it shall accomplish that which I please, and it shall prosper in the thing whereto I sent it" (55:10-11).

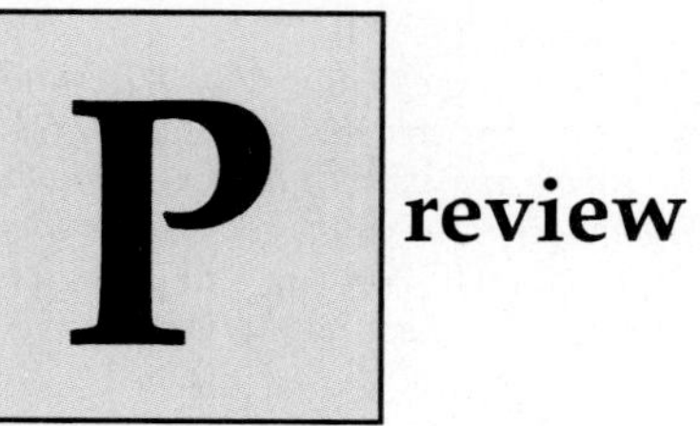

review

From the Cradle to the Cross to the Crown

ISAIAH 7; 9; 11; 49; 52–53

"Tell me the story of Jesus, write on my heart every word. Tell me the story most precious, sweetest that ever was heard."

Here it is, the wonderful story of Jesus, as told by Isaiah the prophet some seven centuries before it actually happened. A glorious story about a glorious Saviour. Isaiah has been called the author of the fifth Gospel because of his detailed and accurate account of Christ's earthly ministry. Beginning with the Virgin Birth, he reverently and relevantly traces Jesus' route from the cradle, to the cross, and finally to the crown. Along the way we are told of His lowliness and youth in Nazareth, His special relationship with the Father, and His ministry to both Jews and Gentiles. In fact, Isaiah predicts His miracles and actually writes one of His sermons. What a privileged task. But the prophet must have wiped the tears from his eyes as he spoke of the Saviour's agony in chapter 53. Soon, however, Isaiah's sobbing turns to singing, for he is allowed to preview his Messiah's glorious resurrection, ascension, exaltation, and future millennial reign.

verview

SCRIPTURE	Isaiah 7; 9; 11; 49; 52–53
SUBJECT	Christ in Isaiah
SPECIFICS	(see below)

SPECIFICS	The Lamb of God				The Lion of Judah	
	Incarnation	His humanity "A child is born" His deity "A Son is given"	Preparation	The Branch of Nazareth The Beloved of God	His current glory	The Resurrection The Ascension The Exaltation
	Demonstration	His meekness His miracles His message	Humiliation	Condemned Crucified	His coming glory	A universal rule An external reign

SAINTS AND SINNERS	Isaiah	
SENTENCE SUMMARIES	O.T. Verse	"But thou, Bethlehem Ephratah, though thou be little among the thousands of Judah, yet out of thee shall He come forth unto Me that is to be ruler in Israel; whose goings forth have been from of old, from everlasting" (Micah 5:2).
	N.T. Verses	"When the even was come, they brought unto Him many that were possessed with devils; and He cast out the spirits with His word, and healed all that were sick. That it might be fulfilled which was spoken by Isaiah the prophet, saying, 'Himself took our infirmities, and bare our sicknesses'" (Matt. 8:16-17).

THE SON OF GOD IN ISAIAH

HIS INCARNATION

Isaiah 7:14. "Therefore the Lord Himself shall give you a sign; Behold, a virgin shall conceive, and bear a son, and shall call His name Immanuel."

Isaiah 9:6. "For unto us a Child is born, unto us a Son is given. And the government shall be upon His shoulder; and His name shall be called Wonderful, Counselor, the Mighty God, the Everlasting Father, the Prince of Peace."

HIS LOWLINESS AND YOUTH IN NAZARETH

Isaiah 11:1-2. "And there shall come forth a rod out of the stem of Jesse, and a Branch shall grow out of his roots; And the Spirit of the LORD shall rest upon Him, the spirit of wisdom and understanding, the spirit of counsel and might, the spirit of knowledge and the fear of the LORD."

The Hebrew word for "branch" is *netser*, and was probably what Matthew referred to when he stated that Christ, *"Came and dwelt in a city called Nazareth; that it might be fulfilled which was spoken by the prophets, 'He shall be called a Nazarene' " (Matt. 2:23).*

Isaiah 53:2. "For He shall grow up before Him as a tender plant, and as a root out of a dry ground; He hath no form nor comeliness; and when we shall see Him, there is no beauty that we should behold Him."

(This verse is only quoted here. It will be dealt with under the aspect of His suffering in connection with Isa. 53.)

Isaiah 7:15. "Butter and honey shall He eat, that He may know to refuse the evil, and choose the good." This refers to the relative poverty of the Saviour's family. Thickened milk and honey were the food of desert wanderers. They were, of course, not the only articles of food, but provided the staples.

HIS RELATIONSHIP TO THE FATHER

Beloved by the Father. "Behold My Servant, whom I uphold; Mine Elect in whom My soul delighteth; I have put My Spirit upon Him; He shall bring forth justice to the nations" (42:1).

This was quoted in Matthew 12:18 and demonstrated in 3:17 and 17:5.

Obedience to the Father. "The Lord GOD hath given Me the tongue of the learned, that I should know how to speak a word in season to him that is weary; He wakeneth morning by morning; He waketh Mine ear to hear like the learned. The Lord God hath opened Mine ear, and I was not rebellious, neither turned away back" (Isa. 50:4-5).

HIS SPECIFIC MINISTRY TO THE GENTILES

"The people that walked in darkness have seen a great light; they that dwell in the land of the shadow of death, upon them hath the light shined" (9:2).

HIS GRACIOUS MINISTRY TO ALL

"He shall not cry, nor lift up, nor cause His voice to be heard in the street. A bruised reed shall He not break, and the smoking flax shall He not quench; He shall bring forth justice in truth" (42:2-3).

HIS MIRACLES

"Then the eyes of the blind shall be opened, and the ears of the deaf shall be unstopped. Then shall the lame man leap as a hart, and the tongue of the dumb sing" (35:5-6).

HIS MESSAGE

"The Spirit of the Lord God is upon Me, because the LORD hath anointed Me to preach good tidings unto the meek; He hath sent Me to bind up the brokenhearted, to proclaim liberty to the captives, and the opening of the prison to those who are bound; to proclaim the acceptable year of the LORD, and day of vengeance of our God; to comfort all that mourn" (61:1-2).

Isaiah 7:14 in the Light of a True Prophet

COMMENTS

According to Deuteronomy 18:20-22, two criteria must be met for a prophet to be regarded as a true prophet: (1) he must speak in the name of the Lord (Yahweh/Jehovah) and (2) whatever he prophesied must come true. If either of these criteria were wanting, the prophet was considered to be a false prophet and was to be put to death.

Many well-intentioned preachers in dealing with Isaiah 7:14 fail to recognize its partial fulfillment in Isaiah's day. They feel that to do so is to compromise Isaiah's intention in using the word "virgin" (Heb., *almah*) to describe the young woman who was to conceive and bear the child. They fail to realize that in order for Isaiah to be a true prophet of Jehovah what he prophesied *must* come to pass. If Isaiah were not a true prophet then not only is his prophecy invalid for Ahaz, it is also invalid for Matthew and us. There *must* be a fulfillment in Isaiah's day, and there was. This realization does not in any way violate the meaning of *almah* nor do violence to the Virgin Birth of Christ. It does show that the word *almah* is more elastic than some have thought, for whatever an *almah* is, the term is broad enough to include both Isaiah's wife (who was not a virgin in the technical sense for she had already given birth to Shearjashub) and Mary the mother of Jesus (who *was* a virgin in the technical sense, Matt. 1:20, 23). Some translations translate Isaiah 7:14, "Behold a young woman shall conceive." That is an accurate translation, for both Mary and Isaiah's wife were truly young women, though Mary was the only one of the two who was a virgin in the technical sense. Some would point out that "the Greeks had a word for it" and when they translated Isaiah's word *almah*, they used the Greek word for virgin, *parthenos.* Even the Greek word had much more elasticity than many have recognized. In the city of Athens at the top of the acropolis stand the remains of a historical building, the Parthenon. The Greek words *parthenon* and *parthenos* are the same word; the former is neuter (agreeing with the neuter noun *to heiron,* temple, which is what the Parthenon was) and the latter is feminine. In the Parthenon were young priestesses (called *parthenai,* feminine, nominative, plural of *parthenos*). These "virgins" were hardly virgins in the technical sense after their initial religious observance. Yet they were called *parthenai* or "virgins" as long as they were at the Parthenon. The proof of the Virgin Birth of Christ does not rest on the meaning of either the Hebrew word *almah* or the Greek word *parthenos* nor is it hurt by translating both of those words as "young woman." For Isaiah to be a true prophet, a baby had to be born in his day, and he was (8:1-4). For Jesus to be the Saviour of the world He had to be born of a woman who was a virgin in the technical sense of the word, and He was. This is shown conclusively by the statement made by Gabriel to Joseph, "That which is conceived in her is of the Holy Ghost" (Matt. 1:20) and demonstrated conclusively in a comparison of the genealogies of Matthew (1:1-17, esp. v. 11, cf. Jer. 22:24-30) and Luke (3:23-38) which shows that Jesus got His legal rights to David's throne through Joseph but His blood rights to David's throne through Mary. Both the fulfillments of Isaiah 7:14 in Isaiah's day and in the birth of Jesus are partial fulfillments. Viewed together, the prophecy of Isaiah 7:14 is completely fulfilled. There is one note of particular interest. Neither child was specifically called "Immanuel" though both were Immanuel—Mahershalalhashbaz in the sense that in his day God was with Judah in delivering them from the threat of Israel and Syria (8:8-10); Jesus in the sense of being God in human form. In this way Isaiah's prophecy is not violated. Rather, it is demonstrated to be accurate and true.

HIS SUFFERINGS AND DEATH

In three key passages Isaiah described in accurate and awesome detail the crucifixion of Christ some 700 years before it historically took place.

Isaiah 50:6. "I gave My back to the smiters, and My cheeks to them that plucked off the hair; I hid My face from shame and spitting."

Isaiah 52:14. "As many were astounded at Thee; His visage was so marred more than any man, and His form more than the sons of men."

Isaiah 53:1-10a. Verses 1-3 may be the voices of the believing Israelite remnant of all ages as they discussed His death. The first verse is literally, "Who believed what we heard?" Verses 2 and 3 tell the life story of the Saviour from the cradle to the cross.

He was despised (counted as nothing) because of His lowly background (v. 2). See also John 1:46. He was rejected because of His message (Isa. 53:3). See also Luke 4:16-30. He was a man of sorrows and acquainted with grief because of His earthly mission (Isa. 53:3). See also Luke 19:10.

His humble beginning seemed so unimportant. Who really noticed Him as a Lad in Nazareth? He could be likened as an insignificant "shoot," a bit of vegetation that is scarcely noticed.

The last part of Isaiah 53:4 informs us that the nation Israel in general looked on the cross as a righteous sentence imposed by God Himself on a blasphemer named Jesus. See Matthew 27:38-44.

Verse 5 tells us He was wounded (translated "tormented" by *Lang's Commentary*) and bruised ("crushed") for our iniquities. These two words, "wounded" and "bruised," are the strongest terms to describe a violent and agonizing death.

Verse 6 is the "all" verse, as it begins and ends with this word. *"All we like sheep have gone astray . . . the LORD hath laid on Him the iniquity of us all."*

Some might ask how we can know that Isaiah was really referring to Christ in chapter 53, since the Saviour was not mentioned by name. But His identity was clearly brought out in the two New Testament passages which linked Him directly to Isaiah 53. The Apostle John quoted Isaiah 53:1 (John 12:37-38). Isaiah 53:7-8 was quoted by Philip (Acts 8:32-33).

We are told that though He was oppressed (treated unsparingly), yet He opened not His mouth. Verse 8 might be rendered:

"By oppression and an unjust sentence He was taken away; and as to His fate, who gave it any thought?"

Verse 9 tells us the religious officials planned to dump Him into a potter's field along with the two thieves. Of course, God stepped in and He was placed in a new tomb owned by a rich man (Matt. 27:57-60).

Who really killed Christ? Many, of course, played a part in His death. This would include Judas, Caiaphas, Annas, the wicked Jewish religious leaders, Pilate, Herod, the Roman soldiers, the devil, and the sins of all sinners. But who actually masterminded the original plan? Here we are told it was God Himself.

HIS RESURRECTION, ASCENSION, AND EXALTATION

Isaiah 52:13. "Behold, My Servant shall deal prudently; He shall be exalted and extolled, and be very high."

Isaiah 53:10b-12 and Isaiah 52:15. "When Thou shalt make His soul an offering for sin, He shall see His seed, He shall prolong His days, and the pleasure of the LORD shall prosper in His hand. He shall see of the travail of His soul, and shall be satisfied; by His knowledge shall My righteous Servant justify many; for He shall bear their iniquities. Therefore will I divide Him a portion with the great, and He shall divide the spoil with the strong, because He hath poured out His soul unto death; and He was numbered with the transgressors; and He bore the sin of many, and made intercession for the transgressors" (53:10b-12).

"So shall He sprinkle many nations; the kings shall shut their mouths at Him; for that which had not been told them shall they see, and that which they had not heard shall they consider" (52:15).

HIS MILLENNIAL REIGN

Isaiah 9:7. "Of the increase of His government and peace there shall be no end. Upon the throne of David, and upon His kingdom, to order it, and to establish it with judgment and with justice from henceforth even forever. The zeal of the LORD of hosts will perform this."

Isaiah 42:4-7. "I the LORD have called thee in righteousness, and will hold thine hand, and will keep thee, and give thee for a covenant of the people, for a light of the Gentiles" (v. 6).

Isaiah 59:16-21. "For He put on righteousness as a breastplate, and a helmet of salvation upon His head; and He put on the garments of vengeance for clothing, and was clad with zeal as a cloak. . . . 'And the Redeemer shall come to Zion, and unto them that turn from transgression in Jacob,' saith the LORD" (vv. 17, 20).

Isaiah 11:3-5. "And shall make Him of quick understanding in the fear of the LORD; and He shall not judge after the sight of His eyes, neither reprove after the hearing of His ears. But with righteousness shall He judge the poor, and reprove with equity for the meek of the earth; and He shall smite the earth with the rod of His mouth, and with the breath of His lips shall He slay the wicked. And righteousness shall be the girdle of His loins, and faithfulness the girdle of His reins."

Isaiah 49:1-12. "Thus saith the LORD, *the Redeemer of Israel, and His Holy One, to Him whom man despiseth, to Him whom the nation abhorreth, to a servant of rulers, 'Kings shall see and arise, princes also shall worship, because of the* LORD *that is faithful, and the Holy One of Israel, and He shall choose Thee.'*

"Thus saith the LORD, *'In an acceptable time have I heard Thee, and in a day of salvation have I helped Thee: and I will preserve Thee, and give Thee for a covenant of the people, to establish the earth, to cause to inherit the desolate heritages; that Thou mayest say to the prisoners, "Go forth"; to them that are in darkness, "Show yourselves." They shall feed in the ways, and their pastures shall be in all high places. They shall not hunger nor thirst; neither shall the heat nor sun smite them; for He that hath mercy on them shall lead them, even by the springs of water shall He guide them. And I will make all My mountains a way, and My highways shall be exalted' " (vv. 7-11).*

Isaiah 32:1. "Behold, a king shall reign in righteousness, and princes shall rule in judgment."

Isaiah 33:22. "For the LORD *is our Judge, the* LORD *is our Lawgiver, the* LORD *is our King; He will save us."*

Two Views of Isaiah 53

COMMENTS

The story is told of two women who were arguing from the back porches of their homes separated by a narrow alley. Neither could see the other's point of view because they were arguing from different premises. Such is the case when both Jew and Christian come to such a majestic passage in the Old Testament as Isaiah 53. Each looks at it from his own perspective and neither can see the other's point of view. Both Jew and Christian recognize that Isaiah's thought begins at 52:13 describing the Servant of Jehovah and the sufferings that befall Him.

We must recognize at the outset that the Jewish interpretation of Isaiah 53 has not always been the same. In the earliest days Jews understood Isaiah to be talking of the Messiah who was to come and bear the sins of the world. This is clearly shown in the case of the Ethiopian eunuch (Acts 8:26-39), a Jewish proselyte who was returning from Jerusalem where he had gone to worship Jehovah. As he was going along the way he was reading Isaiah 53 (cf. Acts 8:28, 32-33). He was captivated by Isaiah's words and asked Philip, "I pray thee, of whom speaketh the prophet this? Of himself, or of some other man?" (v. 34) Philip gave him the earliest Jewish interpretation of Isaiah 53 as he "opened his mouth, and began at the same Scripture and preached unto him Jesus" (Acts 8:35). That day the Ethiopian eunuch came to know the Messiah of Isaiah 53 as his own personal Saviour from sin and was baptized (Acts 8:36-38).

In the dark days of the Medieval Age, rabbinical Judaism was threatened by the traditional Jewish interpretation of Isaiah 53. The most outstanding eleventh-century medieval Jewish commentator, Rabbi Solomon Yitzchaki (called "Rashi" for short) wrote: "Since Christians interpret Isaiah 53 as being a prophecy concerning Jesus, we maintain that this is a prophecy concerning the people of Israel." In spite of the clear meaning of Isaiah's prophecy, modern Jews, especially Reformed Jews and even some Orthodox Jews, prefer to understand Isaiah to be talking about Israel, the Servant of God, who redeems the nations of the world by taking the griefs of the world on itself. Isaiah 53 is carefully avoided in the modern synagogue so as not to invite embarrassing questions. The idea of a suffering Messiah is repulsive and distasteful to modern Jews, for it implies that man is a sinner in need of a Saviour. They prefer to dream of a golden Messianic Age brought about by man's genius; but without a personal Messiah. The fact that Israel has suffered so much at the hand of man does not deter their persistence in their unbelief. Most Orthodox Jews hope for a Messiah who will be a wise and powerful glorified national king, but not a Messiah who is the Saviour of mankind from their sins. Their Messiah is far from the Messiah pictured by Isaiah.

The Christian view of Isaiah 53 is as different from the Jewish as light is from darkness or, more realistically, life from death. To Christians, with Isaiah 53 all Old Testament prophecy stands or falls. Even more, with the Person of Isaiah 53, the Servant of Jehovah, all of the promises of God must stand or fall. Without His willing sacrifice for sins no matter how much God loved us, salvation would not be possible. Isaiah 53 is to the Old Testament what John 3:16 is to the New Testament. Isaiah 53 is the Gospel of the Old Testament telling of the Messiah who was first promised in Genesis 3:15 and came into the world to suffer, die, and redeem mankind to Himself. God's plan of salvation is neatly summarized in Isaiah 53:6: "All we like sheep have gone astray; we have turned everyone to his own way; and the LORD hath laid on Him the iniquity of us all." Someone has observed that the way to be saved is to come to Isaiah 53:6, enter in at the first "all" and come out at the last "all."

Preview

Seven Years of Hell, Ten Centuries of Heaven

ISAIAH 24; 35

Question: Is this the worst or best of all possible worlds to live in?

Biblical answer: Yes. Earthly philosophers have throughout the centuries pondered this question.

Isaiah responds as follows:

Is this the worst possible world to live in? In the future, for a period of seven years, yes. This coming evil time is known as the Great Tribulation. According to the prophet, the skies will darken, the stars will fall, the earth will shake, and sinners will die. At the end of this frightful era, Armageddon, the biggest, bloodiest, and most blasphemous battle in all history, will be fought. Heaven's mighty Conqueror will appear, and earth's miserable creatures will be crushed like overripe grapes.

Is this the best possible world to live in? In the future, for a period of 1,000 years, yes. After describing the agony of Armageddon, Isaiah depicts in breathtaking terms the blessed Millennium. Wars will cease. Gentiles will worship God in Jerusalem. Israel will be redeemed and regathered. The curse on Creation imposed by the first Adam will be removed by the second Adam. The infirmed will be healed. The valleys will be exalted and the mountains abased. The earth itself will glow with the glory of God.

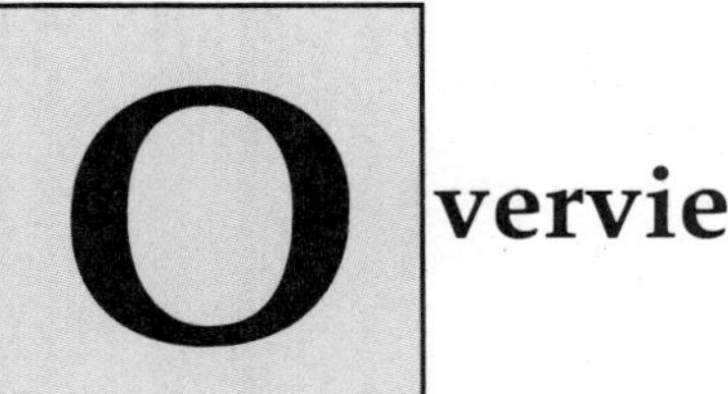

Overview

SCRIPTURE	Isaiah 24; 35
SUBJECT	The Tribulation and Millennium
SPECIFICS	(see below)
SAINTS AND SINNERS	Isaiah

SPECIFICS

The coming grief		
The final woes	Fierce plagues to fall	Upon the soil Upon the sea Upon the sky Upon sinners
The final war	The agony of Armageddon	The vengeance of the Lord The victory of the Lord

The coming glory					
The bestowal of God's salvation	Upon the nations	The Jews	Their citizens to be purified Their capital to be magnified	The Gentiles	Wars to cease Worship to commence
	Upon the needy	The blind will see The deaf will hear The lame will walk			
	Upon all nature	Countryside	Valleys to rise Mountains to sink Deserts to bloom	Creatures — Perfect harmony	Between lion & lamb Between child and cockatrice

SENTENCE SUMMARIES

O.T. Verse	"At that time shall Michael stand up, the great prince which standeth for the children of thy people; and there shall be a time of trouble, such as never was since there was a nation even to that same time; and at that time thy people shall be delivered, every one that shall be found written in the book" (Dan. 12:1).
N.T. Verses	"Then shall be Great Tribulation. . . . And then shall appear the sign of the Son of man in heaven; and then shall all the tribes of the earth mourn, and they shall see the Son of man coming in the clouds of heaven with power and great glory" (Matt. 24:21, 30).

HE TRIBULATION IN ISAIAH

THE MAIN PASSAGES

Isaiah 2:10-22.
Isaiah 13:6-13.
Isaiah 24:1-23.
Isaiah 26:20-21.
Isaiah 34:1-10.
Isaiah 42:13-14.
Isaiah 51:6.
Isaiah 63:1-6.
Isaiah 66:15-16, 24.

THE MAIN ACTION

The earth's disturbance. During this period the earth will be terribly shaken, moved out of its place, made waste and turned upside down, burned with fire, broken down and dissolved, reel to and fro like a drunkard, and be unable to cover its dead.

The heavens. The stars, sun, and moon will be darkened. The hosts of heaven will be dissolved and rolled up as a scroll. The stars shall fall as figs from a tree when shaken.

Sinful mankind. Men and women will hide in the caves and holes of the earth, faint with fear and their hearts will melt, suffer the agonies of childbirth, experience no joy whatsoever, cover the mountains with their blood and overpower the valleys with the stench of their dead, and be utterly trampled by a wrathful God like overripe grapes.

The Battle of Armageddon. "Come, my people, enter thou into thy chambers, and shut thy doors about thee. Hide thyself as it were for a little moment, until the indignation be overpast. For, behold, the LORD cometh out of His place to punish the inhabitants of the earth for their iniquity. The earth also shall disclose her blood, and shall no more cover her slain" (26:20-21).

"Come near, ye nations, to hear; and hearken, ye people. Let the earth hear, and all that is therein; the world, and all things that come forth of it. For the indignation of the LORD is upon all nations, and His fury upon all their armies; He hath utterly destroyed them, He hath delivered them to the slaughter. Their slain also shall be cast out, and their stink shall come up out of their carcasses, and tne mountains shall be melted with their blood" (34:1-4).

"Who is this that cometh from Edom, with dyed garments from Bozrah? This that is glorious in His apparel, traveling in the greatness of His strength? I that speak in righteousness, mighty to save. Wherefore art Thou red in Thine apparel, and Thy garments like him that treadeth in the winevat? I have trodden the winepress alone; and of the people there was none with Me: for I will tread them in Mine anger, and trample them in My fury; and their blood shall be sprinkled upon My garments, and I will stain all My raiment.

"For the day of vengeance is in Mine heart, and the year of My redeemed is come. And I looked, and there was none to help; and I wondered that there was none to uphold. Therefore Mine own arm brought salvation unto Me; and My fury, it upheld Me. And I will tread down the people in Mine anger, and make them drunk in My fury, and I will bring down their strength to the earth" (63:1-6).

"For behold, the LORD will come with fire, and with His chariots like a whirlwind, to render His anger with fury, and His rebuke with flames of fire. For by fire and by His sword will the LORD plead with all flesh; and the slain of the LORD shall be many. . . . And they shall go forth, and look upon the carcasses of the men that have transgressed against Me; for their worm shall not die, neither shall their fire be quenched; and they shall be an abhorring unto all flesh" (66:15-16, 24).

The Storm before the Calm

COMMENTS

The Tribulation period will begin after the church is removed from the scene. It's official beginning is marked by the signing of a defense pact or peace treaty between the king of the west and the nation Israel. It is at that time that God's timepiece for Israel, which has been stopped for nearly 2,000 years, will start and begin to mark off Daniel's 70th week. For Israel, it will be a time of unparalleled judgment. It will be the storm before the calm.

At the time the church is removed from the earth, no believers will be left on the face of the earth. Shortly after the beginning of the Tribulation period, 144,000 Jews living in all the countries of the earth will have an experience similar to that the Apostle Paul had on the Damascus Road—they will be sovereignly saved. The identity of the tribes is lost to man, but not to God. At that time the identity of the tribes will be known and 144,000 (12,000 from each tribe) will become the true witnesses of Jehovah. To protect them from the wrath of the Antichrist, God will sovereignly seal them so they cannot be killed. They will be wonderfully successful in their witness. John tells us that he saw a great multitude whom no man could number coming out of the Great Tribulation having washed their robes white in the blood of the Lamb. It will be a wonderful time of evangelism, the most successful that the world will ever see. During this time more and more Jews will immigrate to Israel from all over the world. There will be some great global catastrophes but the overall tenor of things will be "business as usual." During this time the Jews will rebuild the temple and will institute worship in it. In the middle of the Tribulation period, the king of the north will say to the king of the south, "You go into the land from the south and I will come into the land from the north. Together we'll put a great pincer movement on the land and crush Israel out of existence." Because of the defense pact that he has signed with Israel, the king of the west will have to come into the land to protect Israel. He will be successful in his effort and will defeat the king of the north and the king of the south. International Communism will be wiped out. The king of the west will be impressed with his own power and will become convinced that he must be God. He will take over the temple of the Jews and will install himself in it showing himself off to be God. One will arise out of Israel (the false prophet) and will convince the Jews that truly the king of the west is the Messiah for he has guaranteed to them all the things promised to Abraham, Moses, David, and Jeremiah. The fact that he is a Gentile won't matter (perhaps he will be of Jewish descent); they will worship him gladly. The king of the west, Antichrist, will vent his wrath on every other religion and it will be outlawed. He will particularly turn his wrath on the converts of the 144,000 and the nation Israel and will kill myriads of them. At the end of the Tribulation period the king of the east, who has been jealously watching the success of the king of the west, will come into the land to do battle with the king of the west. They will gather their armies together on the plain of Esdralon stretching from Mount Carmel eastward to the Jordan Valley and southward past Jerusalem to Petra in the land of Edom. Before they can do battle, some sign is given them in the heavens letting them know that Jesus Christ is about to return to the earth to set up His kingdom. They will become confederates in the attempt to keep Jesus from returning to the earth to set up His kingdom. Their league is futile, for Jesus will return with His church to set up His kingdom and will slay every unbeliever with the breath of His mouth. This is the Battle of Armageddon.

THE MILLENNIUM IN ISAIAH

THE SALVATION OF GENTILE NATIONS

Isaiah 2:2-4. "And it shall come to pass in the last days, that the mountain of the LORD's house shall be established in the top of the mountains, and shall be exalted above the hills; and all nations shall flow into it. And many people shall go and say, 'Come ye, and let us go up to the mountain of the LORD, to the house of the God of Jacob; and He will teach us of His ways, and we will walk in His paths.' For out of Zion shall go forth the law, and the word of the LORD from Jerusalem. And He shall judge among the nations, and shall rebuke many people. And they shall beat their swords into plowshares, and their spears into pruning hooks. Nation shall not lift up sword against nation, neither shall they learn war any more."

Isaiah 11:10. "And in that day there shall be a root of Jesse, which shall stand for an ensign of the people; to it shall the Gentiles seek; and His rest shall be glorious."

Isaiah 19:18-25. Israel suffered perhaps more under the brutal reigns of Assyria and Egypt than any other two nations. But during the Millennium God will supernaturally unite these three into a beautiful trio of fellowship. The Egyptians will speak the Hebrew language. They will build an altar and monument to the Lord. God will answer their prayers and heal them. Both Egypt and Assyria (Iraq) will be connected by a highway. Both shall worship Jehovah and receive His rich blessings.

Isaiah 52:10. "The LORD hath made bare His holy arm in the eyes of all the nations; and all the ends of the earth shall see the salvation of our God."

Isaiah 56:6-8.

Isaiah 66:23. " 'And it shall come to pass, that from one new moon to another, and from one Sabbath to another, shall all flesh come up to worship before Me,' saith the LORD."

THE SALVATION OF ISRAEL AND JERUSALEM

Isaiah 4:2-6. They will be washed and rinsed of all their moral filth. They will once again be blessed by the fiery and cloudy pillar.

Isaiah 11:12. "And He shall set up an ensign for the nations, and shall assemble the outcasts of Israel, and gather together the dispersed of Judah from the four corners of the earth."

Isaiah 14:3. "And it shall come to pass in the day that the LORD shall give thee rest from thy sorrow, and from thy fear, and from the hard bondage wherein thou wast made to serve."

Isaiah 25:8-9. "He will swallow up death in victory; and the Lord God will wipe away tears from off all faces; and the rebuke of His people shall He take away from off all the earth; for the LORD hath spoken it. And it shall be said in that day, 'Lo, this is our God; we have waited for Him, and He will save us; this is the LORD; we have waited for Him, we will be glad and rejoice in His salvation."

Isaiah 26:1-4. "In that day shall this song be sung in the land of Judah; 'We have a strong city; salvation will God appoint for walls and bulwarks. Open ye the gates, that the righteous nation which keepeth the truth may enter in. Thou wilt keep him in perfect peace, whose mind is stayed on Thee, because he trusteth in Thee. Trust ye in the LORD forever; for in the LORD Jehovah is everlasting strength.' "

Isaiah 30:19. "For the people shall dwell in Zion at Jerusalem; thou shalt weep no more. He will be very gracious unto thee at the voice of thy cry; when He shall hear it, He will answer thee."

Isaiah 32:18. "And My people shall dwell in a peaceable habitation, and in sure dwellings, and in quiet resting places."

Isaiah 33:17. "Thine eyes shall see the King in His beauty; they shall behold the land that is very far off."

Isaiah 40:4-5. "Every valley shall be exalted, and every mountain and hill shall be made low, and the crooked shall be made straight, and the rough places plain. And the glory of the LORD shall be revealed, and all flesh shall see it together, for the mouth of the LORD hath spoken it."

Isaiah 44:23. "Sing, O ye heavens; for the LORD hath done it. Shout, ye lower parts of the earth. Break forth into singing, ye mountains, O forest, and every tree therein. For the LORD hath redeemed Jacob, and glorified Himself in Israel."

Isaiah 49:1-13. "They shall not hunger nor

thirst; neither shall the heat nor sun smite them; for He that hath mercy on them shall lead them, even by the springs of water shall He guide them" (v. 10).

Isaiah 51:3, 11. "For the Lord *shall comfort Zion; He will comfort all her waste places; and He will make her wilderness like Eden, and her desert like the garden of the* Lord*; joy and gladness shall be found therein, thanksgiving, and the voice of melody. . . . Therefore the redeemed of the* Lord *shall return, and come with singing unto Zion; and everlasting joy shall be upon their head. They shall obtain gladness and joy; and sorrow and mourning shall flee away."*

Isaiah 52:1, 7-9. "Awake, awake; put on thy strength, O Zion; put on thy beautiful garments, O Jerusalem, the Holy City; for henceforth there shall no more come into thee the uncircumcised and the unclean. . . . How beautiful upon the mountains are the feet of him that bringeth good tidings, that publisheth peace; that bringeth good tidings of good, that publisheth salvation; that saith unto Zion, 'Thy God reigneth!' "

Isaiah 59:20-21. " 'And the Redeemer shall come to Zion, and unto them that turn from transgression in Jacob,' saith the Lord*. 'As for Me, this is My covenant with them,' saith the* Lord*; 'My spirit that is upon thee, and My words which I have put in thy mouth, shall not depart out of thy mouth, nor out of the mouth of thy seed, nor out of the mouth of thy seed's seed,' saith the* Lord*, 'from henceforth and forever.' "*

Isaiah 60:1-3, 11, 19-22. "Arise, shine; for thy light is come, and the glory of the Lord *is risen upon thee. For, behold, the darkness shall cover the earth, and gross darkness the people: but the* Lord *shall arise upon thee, and His glory shall be seen upon thee. And the Gentiles shall come to thy light, and kings to the brightness of thy rising. . . .*

"Therefore thy gates shall be open continually; they shall not be shut day nor night; that men may bring unto thee the forces of the Gentiles, and that their kings may be brought. . . . The sun shall be no more thy light by day; neither for brightness shall the moon give light unto thee; but the Lord *shall be unto thee an everlasting light, and thy God thy glory. Thy sun shall no more go down; neither shall thy moon withdraw itself; for the* Lord *shall be thine everlasting light, and the days of thy mourning shall be ended."*

Isaiah 62:1-4. "For Zion's sake will I not hold My peace, and for Jerusalem's sake I will not rest, until the righteousness thereof go forth as brightness, and the salvation thereof as a lamp that burneth. And the Gentiles shall see thy righteousness, and all kings thy glory: and thou shalt be called by a new name, which the mouth of the Lord *shall name. Thou shalt also be a crown of glory in the hand of the* Lord*, and a royal diadem in the hand of thy God. Thou shalt no more be termed Forsaken; neither shall thy land any more be termed Desolate; but thou shalt be called Hephzibah, and thy land Beulah, for the* Lord *delighteth in thee, and thy land shall be married."*

Isaiah 65:19-20, 24. "And I will rejoice in Jerusalem, and joy in My people; and the voice of weeping shall be no more heard in her, nor the voice of crying. There shall be no more thence an infant of days, nor an old man that hath not filled his days; for the child shall die a hundred years old; but the sinner being a hundred years old shall be accursed. . . . And it shall come to pass, that before they call, I will answer; and while they are yet speaking, I will hear."

Isaiah 66:10, 12. " 'Rejoice ye with Jerusalem, and be glad with her, all ye that love her; rejoice for joy with her, all ye that mourn for her.' . . . For thus saith the Lord*, 'Behold, I will extend peace to her like a river, and the glory of the Gentiles like a flowing stream; then shall ye suck, ye shall be borne upon her sides, and be dandled upon her knees.' "*

THE SALVATION OF THE AFFLICTED

Isaiah 29:18. "And in that day shall the deaf hear the words of the Book, and the eyes of the blind shall see out of obscurity, and out of darkness."

Isaiah 35:5-6. "Then the eyes of the blind shall be opened, and the ears of the deaf shall be unstopped. Then shall the lame leap as a hart, and the tongue of the dumb sing; for in the wilderness shall waters break out, and streams in the desert."

Isaiah 42:16. "And I will bring the blind by a way that they knew not; I will lead them in paths that they have not known; I will make darkness light before them, and crooked things straight. These things will I do unto them, and not forsake them."

THE SALVATION OF ALL NATURE

Isaiah 11:6-9. "The wolf also shall dwell with the lamb, and the leopard shall lie down with the kid; and the calf and the young lion and the fatling together; and a little child shall lead them. And the cow and the bear shall feed; their young ones shall lie down together; and the lion shall eat straw like the ox.

"And the sucking child shall play on the hole of the asp, and the weaned child shall put his hand on the cockatrice's den. They shall not hurt nor destroy in all My holy mountain; for the earth shall be full of the knowledge of the Lord*, as the waters cover the sea."*

Isaiah 14:7-8. "The whole earth is at rest, and

is quiet; they break forth into singing. Yea, the fir trees rejoice at Thee, and the cedars of Lebanon, saying, 'Since Thou art laid down, no feller is come up against us.' "

Isaiah 30:23-26. "Moreover the light of the moon shall be as the light of the sun, and the light of the sun shall be sevenfold, as the light of seven days, in the day that the Lord *bindeth up the breach of His people, and healeth the stroke of their wound" (v. 26).*

Isaiah 35:1-2, 7-10. "The wilderness and the solitary place shall be glad for them; and the desert shall rejoice, and blossom as the rose. It shall blossom abundantly, and rejoice even with joy and singing; the glory of Lebanon shall be given unto it, the excellency of Carmel and Sharon, they shall see the glory of the Lord, *and the excellency of our God. . . .*

"And the parched ground shall become a pool, and thirsty land springs of water; in the habitation of dragons, where each lay, shall be grass with reeds and rushes. And a highway shall be there, and a way, and it shall be called 'the way of holiness'; the unclean shall not pass over it; but it shall be for those; the wayfaring men, though fools, shall not err therein. No lion shall be there, nor any ravenous beast shall go up thereon, it shall not be found there; but the redeemed shall walk there. And the ransomed of the Lord *shall return, and come to Zion with songs and everlasting joy upon their heads; they shall obtain joy and gladness, and sorrow and sighing shall flee away."*

Isaiah 40:4-5. "Every valley shall be exalted, and every mountain and hill shall be made low; and the crooked shall be made straight, and the rough places plain. And the glory of the Lord *shall be revealed, and all flesh shall see it together; for the mouth of the* Lord *hath spoken it."*

The Calm Following the Storm

COMMENTS

When Jesus returns to the earth with His church, His feet will land on the Mount of Olives. Jesus will call for His people, Israel, and they will come from all corners of the earth, look on Him whom they have pierced, and receive a new heart. Then all Israel shall be saved. The whole world will experience the calm following the storm. What a day that will be.

The members of the church, the body of Christ who return with Him, will take up residence in "satellite city"—the heavenly city New Jerusalem, 1,000 miles square—suspended in permanent orbit over the earthly city Jerusalem. They will have access to the earth which will be restored to Edenic conditions. The lion will lie down with the lamb, a little child will be able to play at a cockatrice's (which is an adder or viper) den and will not be harmed. Jesus Christ will be visibly present ruling on the throne of David and will speak peace to the nations. There will be no warfare and no violence for Jesus will rule with a rod of iron and any insurrection will be put down before it can be started. To add to the bliss, Satan will be chained in the bottomless pit and will not be able to bother the earth or its inhabitants for 1,000 years. At the time of Jesus' return to the earth and the establishment of His kingdom, all of the believing dead from Adam down to the establishment of the church, together with the dead Tribulation saints, will be raised from the dead. Abraham will personally witness the realization of all the things promised to him. Moses will realize the promises made to him. David will realize the promises made to him and will be the vice-regent reigning with his greater Son, Jesus.

Think how wonderful it will be! A believing human being will be able to look up into the heavens and see the huge satellite filled with glorified human beings. Further, he will be able to see them and interview them on one of their frequent trips to the millennial earth. He will also be able to talk to Abraham, to David, to any one of the resurrected, glorified, Old Testament saints and learn from him firsthand all the wonderful things God promised and kept. He will be able to see Jesus Christ visibly present and reigning on David's throne in Jerusalem. Conceivably he will be able to get an audience with Him and will be able to see for himself the wounds on His hands and side, for those wounds are His glory. They not only guaranteed the realization of Israel's New Covenant but also paid the penalty to redeem the residents of "satellite city" and those who paid for their faith by being put to death during the Tribulation. In fact, it will be possible to be a living Tribulation saint and be able to talk with glorified saints who were put to death during the Tribulation and now are raised again. Unglorified Tribulation saints will be the ones who will populate the millennial earth at first. Their children will still have Adamic sin natures and will have to become regenerate by believing on Jesus as their Saviour. Surely in all of these wonderful millennial conditions with all the glorified Old and New Testament and Tribulation saints present they will all believe in Him. In all the beauty and wonder of the millennial picture there is one flaw—man's sin nature. At the end of the Millennium, Satan will briefly be released from the bottomless pit to come to the millennial earth. When he arrives, he will find a great number of people who have only overtly bowed to the lordship of Christ. He will gather them for one final rebellion which will be met summarily. Satan will be cast immediately into hell. The rebellious ones will join the resurrected unsaved dead to stand before the Great White Throne judgment and be cast into the lake of fire forever. The present heaven and earth will be destroyed by fire. God will create a New Heaven and Earth in which righteousness will dwell forever. Amen.

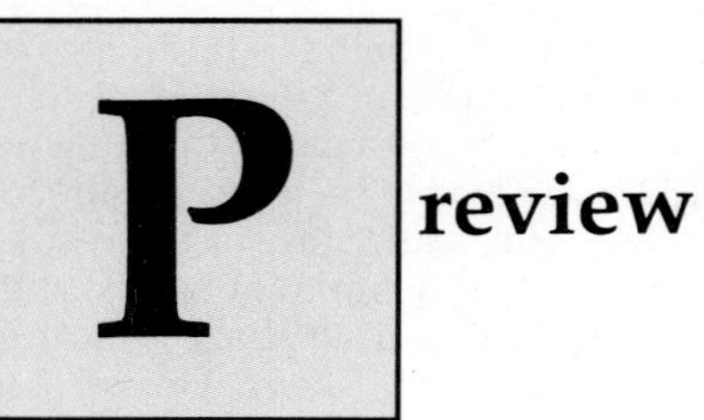

When God Chastens His Chosen

BOOKS OF ZEPHANIAH & HABAKKUK

"I'm so sorry, but I must be absolutely honest with you. Your illness is terminal. You will soon die." These are undoubtedly the most difficult words a physician must say to a patient.

In the Old Testament account three spiritual doctors were commanded by God to make this announcement, not to a patient, but to an entire nation. These "medical messengers" were Zephaniah, Habakkuk, and Jeremiah. The patient was Judah and the fatal disease, sin. This by itself was sad enough. But the real tragedy was even more heartbreaking, if not downright frustrating! Judah's condition was not incurable! There *was* a balm in Gilead. A cure did exist. Genuine repentance would immediately arrest the disease and heal both body and soul. But the dying patient was utterly unwilling to cooperate, apparently preferring death to deliverance. Did those three prophets of God know each other? They doubtless did, for all lived at the same time and in the same city, Jerusalem.

Here is the story of the first two, Zephaniah and Habakkuk. Each reacted differently to his unpleasant mission and message. Zephaniah remained somewhat detached, but Habakkuk experienced great doubt. Both, however, agreed on three basic conclusions: Judah would indeed be destroyed for its sin; God would be perfectly just in causing this; the story would eventually have a happy ending. Judah would someday be made whole.

Overview

<table>
<tr><td>SCRIPTURE</td><td colspan="4">Books of Zephaniah and Habakkuk</td></tr>
<tr><td>SUBJECT</td><td colspan="4">Ministry of Zephaniah and Habakkuk</td></tr>
<tr><td rowspan="10">SPECIFICS</td><td rowspan="10">Judgment on Judah</td><td>Spokesmen</td><td>Zephaniah</td><td>Habakkuk</td></tr>
<tr><td>Recipients</td><td>Judah
Five other nations</td><td>Judah</td></tr>
<tr><td>Reason for</td><td>Idolatry
Corrupt leaders</td><td>Ignoring the Law
Perverting justice</td></tr>
<tr><td>Source of</td><td>Babylon</td><td>Chaldeans</td></tr>
<tr><td>Title for</td><td>The Day of the Lord
Past-Babylonian Captivity
Future-Great Tribulation</td><td></td></tr>
<tr><td>Problem of</td><td></td><td>Why the usage of Babylon?</td></tr>
<tr><td>Answer</td><td></td><td>The just shall live by his faith</td></tr>
<tr><td>Aftermath</td><td>Judah and her enemies to be united</td><td>Babylon to be judged
Christ to appear</td></tr>
<tr><td>Effect on the prophet</td><td></td><td>Tremendous effect on his head, heart, and hands</td></tr>
<tr><td></td><td></td><td></td></tr>
<tr><td>SAINTS AND SINNERS</td><td colspan="4">Zephaniah, Habakkuk</td></tr>
<tr><td rowspan="2">SENTENCE SUMMARIES</td><td>O.T. Verse</td><td colspan="3">"Why art thou cast down, O my soul? And why art thou disquieted within me? Hope thou in God; for I shall yet praise Him, who is the health of my countenance, and my God" (Ps. 42:11).</td></tr>
<tr><td>N.T. Verse</td><td colspan="3">"I am crucified with Christ; nevertheless I live; yet not I, but Christ liveth in me; and the life which I now live in the flesh I live by the faith of the Son of God, who loved me, and gave Himself for me" (Gal. 2:20).</td></tr>
</table>

Z EPHANIAH (DESTINATION: SOUTHERN KINGDOM)

A BAD DAY—THE PROPHET PRONOUNCES JUDGMENT

The fact of this judgment. God would sweep away everything in the land and destroy it to the ground. This would include man, birds, and even fish.

The reason for this judgment. Judah had worshiped Baal (the great god of the Canaanite pantheon), and Milcom (chief Ammonite deity), thus ignoring the only true God. The city's leaders were like roaring lions and ravenous wolves, devouring any and all victims.

The name of this judgment. The prophet calls it "the Day of the LORD." This term is used no less than seven times. (See Zeph. 1:7-8, 14, 18; 2:2-3.) The immediate, historical meaning of this term referred to the Babylonian Captivity under Nebuchadnezzar. The ultimate, prophetical meaning of this term refers to the Battle of Armageddon under the Antichrist.

The results of this judgment. "The great Day of the LORD is near, it is near, and hasteth greatly, even the voice of the Day of the LORD; the mighty man shall cry there bitterly. That day is a day of wrath, a day of trouble and distress, a day of wasteness and desolation, a day of darkness and gloominess, a day of clouds and thick darkness, a day of the trumpet and alarm against the fenced cities, and against the high towers. And I will bring distress upon men, that they shall walk like blind men, because they have sinned against the LORD; and their blood shall be poured out as dust, and their flesh as the dung. Neither their silver nor their gold shall be able to deliver them in the day of the LORD's wrath; but the whole land shall be devoured by the fire of His jealousy; for He shall make even a speedy riddance of all them that dwell in the land" (1:14-18).

On the enemies of God. There would be judgment on the Philistine cities, Moab and Ammon, Ethiopia, Assyria and its capital Nineveh. This would include the enemies of Judah in all directions.

On the city of God. A cry of alarm would begin at the northern fish gate in Jerusalem. It would be heard from gate to gate until it reached the highest part of the city. God planned to search with lanterns in Jerusalem's darkest corners to find and destroy all sinners. He urged the godly remnant to hide themselves.

"Seek ye the LORD, all ye meek of the earth, which have wrought His judgment; seek righteousness, seek meekness. It may be ye shall be hid in the day of the LORD's anger" (2:3).

A GLAD DAY—THE PROPHET ANNOUNCED JUSTICE

On thee (once) enemies of God. "For then will I turn to the people a pure language, that they may all call upon the name of the LORD, to serve Him with one consent. From beyond the rivers of Ethiopia My suppliants, even the daughters of My dispersed, shall bring Mine offering" (3:9-10).

On the land of God. "The remnant of Israel shall not do iniquity, nor speak lies; neither shall a deceitful tongue be found in their mouth; for they shall feed and lie down, and none shall make them afraid" (v. 13).

On the city of God. Jerusalem will once again be filled with singing, for the theme of their songs, the King of Israel, will be there. God, Himself, will lead this happy song.

ABAKKUK (DESTINATION: SOUTHERN KINGDOM)

THE DOUBTS

His question. "Will You punish our nation?" The prophet was grieved over the wickedness of Judah. The Law was ignored, justice was perverted, and righteousness was surrounded by wickedness.

God's answer. "I will, through Judah's foes." This would be done during Habakkuk's lifetime. He was raising a new force on the world scene, the Chaldeans.

"For, lo, I raise up the Chaldeans, that bitter and hasty nation, which shall march through the breadth of the land, to possess the dwelling places that are not theirs" (Hab. 1:6).

They were a law unto themselves. Their horses were swifter than leopards and more fierce than wolves. Their riders were like hungry eagles circling their prey. They collected captives like sand. They mocked at kings.

His question. "Will You punish these Chaldeans also?" Habakkuk could not comprehend why God would let this pagan nation punish His own people, even though they were admittedly guilty of gross sin.

"Thou art of purer eyes than to behold evil, and canst not look on iniquity: wherefore lookest Thou upon them that deal treacherously, and holdest Thy tongue when the wicked devoureth the man that is more righteous than he?" (v. 13)

Habakkuk knew the Chaldeans would snare and treat their Hebrew captives like fish.

God's answer. "I will, through My woes!" Habakkuk climbed upon his watchtower to await God's answer. Soon it comes.

" 'I will stand upon my watch, and set me upon the tower, and will watch to see what He will say unto me, and what I shall answer when I am reproved.' And the LORD answered me, and said, 'Write the vision, and make it plain upon tables, that he may run that readeth it' " (2:1-2).

God told him the Chaldeans would indeed be punished, but only at His appointed time. Babylon was judged for their many sins of slavery, robbery, bloodshedding, drunkenness, and idolatry. Until then, Habakkuk was to live by faith. God was still in control over all the earth.

"But the LORD is in His holy temple; let all the earth keep silence before Him" (v. 20).

God will someday rule over all the earth. *"For the earth shall be filled with the knowledge of the glory of the LORD, as the waters cover the sea" (v. 14).*

Habakkuk's final testimony revealed that he apparently learned to live by faith. *"When I heard, my belly trembled; my lips quivered at the voice: rottenness entered into my bones, and I trembled in myself, that I might rest in the day of trouble. When He cometh up unto the people, He will invade them with His troops" (3:16).*

THE SHOUTS

THE SOUL OF THE PROPHET IS REVIVED

"O LORD, I have heard Thy speech, and was afraid. O LORD, revive Thy work in the midst of the years, in the midst of the years make known; in wrath remember mercy" (3:2).

THE EYES OF THE PROPHET ARE REASSURED

Habakkuk 3:3-16 records Habakkuk's awesome manifestation of God's majestic glory. Hebrew scholar Charles L. Feinberg believed all the verbs found in 3:3-15 should be regarded as describing future events. If this be true, Habakkuk actually gave us the future coming of the returning Christ.

His schedule. "God came from Teman, and the Holy One from Mount Paran. Selah. His glory covered the heavens, and the earth was full of His praise" (v. 3).

He will touch down on the Mount of Olives. He will then go to Teman (an ancient settlement in Edom), perhaps to rescue the Jews hiding out in Petra. (See Isa. 63:1; Rev. 12:13-17.)

His appearance. "And His brightness was as the light; He had horns coming out of His hand: and there was the hiding of His power" (Hab. 3:4).

His actions. "Before Him went the pestilence, and burning coals went forth at His feet. He stood, and measured the earth; He beheld, and drove asunder the nations; and the everlasting mountains were scattered, the perpetual hills did bow. His ways are everlasting. . . .

"Thou didst march through the land in indignation, Thou didst thresh the heathen in anger" (Hab. 3:5-6, 12).

His purpose. "Thou wentest forth for the salvation of Thy people, even for salvation with Thine anointed; Thou woundest the head out of the house of the wicked, by discovering the foundation unto the neck. Selah" (v. 13).

THE HEART OF THE PROPHET IS REJOICED

"Yet I will rejoice in the Lord, I will joy in the God of my salvation" (v. 18).

THE FEET OF THE PROPHET ARE RENEWED

"The LORD God is my strength, and He will make my feet like hinds' feet, and He will make me to walk upon mine high places" (v. 19).

The Prophetical Trio

COMMENTS

God sent three prophets to Judah as its kingdom was coming to an end: Zephaniah the preaching prophet, Jeremiah the weeping prophet, and Habakkuk the praying prophet. All three began their ministries in a five-year period in the days of good King Josiah. Zephaniah was first on the scene (ca. 625 B.C.), followed by Jeremiah (ca. 622 B.C.), and then Habakkuk (ca. 620 B.C.). Zephaniah was a bold and outspoken prophet. Of the three, he is the only one who gives his lineage in great detail. He was the great-great-grandson of good King Hezekiah (cf. 1:1). His royal pedigree would give him access to the king's court and he may have delivered his stinging message of judgment from there. If so, his rebuke of the princes and nobles (cf. vv. 8, 13, 18) is all the more significant.

Zephaniah's oratorical style pervades his written prophecy. He was a prophet of contrasts. No other prophet painted so black a picture of God's judgment on Judah and no other prophet painted so bright a picture of Judah's future glory. In greater detail than any other minor prophet, Zephaniah showed what the Day of the Lord would mean for ungodly Judah and her enemies (1:2–3:7) and what it would mean for the godly remnant of Judah (3:8-20). On the immediate scene, God used Zephaniah's preaching to prepare the nation for the revival and reforms under King Josiah.

Concerning Habakkuk personally, nothing is known except what may be gleaned from his prophecy. In response to Judah's sin he prayed to God asking God to punish His people and purify them of their sin of idolatry. He had prayed for some time and felt that God would never hear him (1:2-4). He was appalled when God answered his prayer and told him that He was going to punish His people using the Chaldeans (Babylonians) (v. 6). Habakkuk was perplexed for he could not understand how God could use Chaldea to punish Judah. Judah was bad, but not nearly as bad as Chaldea. Habakkuk then assumed the role of advocate for Judah and opponent of God as he sought to dissuade God (vv. 12-17). God was gracious and long-suffering not only with Judah but with His prophet. He responded to the prophet's suit with a gracious explanation summarized by contrasting Chaldea with Judah (2:4). God was not fooled by either of them. The Chaldeans were proud and haughty. They would be the victors in the coming conflict, but their very arrogance and independence from God would cause God to destroy them. In contrast, the righteous of Judah would appear to be defeated but in reality they would be the victors because of faith in Jehovah—"the just shall live by his faith." Chaldea would be victorious temporarily but would be lost eternally. The faithful of Judah would suffer loss temporarily but would be saved eternally. This encouragement from Jehovah has been popular with God's people of all ages. It is quoted three times in the New Testament (cf. Rom. 1:17; Gal. 3:11; Heb. 10:38) and was the battle cry of the Protestant Reformation under Martin Luther. The last chapter of Habakkuk is unique among the prophecies for it is a psalm complete with instructions to the musicians for its proper rendering. In the first two chapters of his prophecy Habakkuk contended with Jehovah. In the last chapter, he submitted to Jehovah.

Jeremiah was the only prophet of the three to survive and to see the words of judgment delivered, not only by himself, but also by Zephaniah and Habakkuk come to pass. His words of lament over the Chaldean destruction of Jerusalem comprise the Book of Lamentations.

In summary, this prophetic trio represents the responses that the man of God should have to sin. With Jeremiah he should weep about it, with Habakkuk he should pray about it, and with Zephaniah he should preach against it.

Preview

A Background of the Brokenhearted

BOOK OF JEREMIAH

Among the thousands of mourners who attended King Josiah's state funeral in Jerusalem, probably no one was more unnoticed, unhappy, or unsettled than a young unmarried son of a priest from the city of Anathoth. He was unnoticed because of his youth, unhappy because of Josiah's death, and unsettled because God had previously called him to assume the office of a prophet. Never had there been a more unwilling candidate. His timid protests, however, were of no avail whatsoever. God had, even from the womb, closely observed and sanctified this young man for special service.

Such was the condition of Jeremiah in the year 610 B.C. After a long, hard, and hectic ministry, Jeremiah was forced against his will by his own countrymen into Egypt. In addition to the Books of Jeremiah and Lamentations, the weeping prophet could have written an autobiography entitled, *Head Honchos Who Have Heard Me,* for he prophesied under Judah's final four kings, plus Nebuchadnezzar the Babylonian monarch, and finally Gedaliah and Johanan, Judah's two post-Captivity governors.

Overview

<table>
<tr><td>SCRIPTURE</td><td colspan="5">Book of Jeremiah</td></tr>
<tr><td>SUBJECT</td><td colspan="5">Biographical background of Jeremiah</td></tr>
<tr><td rowspan="8">SPECIFICS</td><td colspan="2">Jeremiah: the man</td><td colspan="3">Jeremiah: the mission</td></tr>
<tr><td>The selection</td><td>The symbols</td><td rowspan="7">God's spokesman to the following</td><td>Josiah</td><td>Judah's last saved king</td></tr>
<tr><td rowspan="2">Jeremiah's reservations
Jeremiah's reassurance</td><td rowspan="2">An almond tree
A pot of boiling water
A basket of fruit</td><td>Jehoiakim</td><td>Burned Jeremiah's scroll</td></tr>
<tr><td>Jehoiachin</td><td>Received a curse from God</td></tr>
<tr><td>The search</td><td>The sale</td><td>Zedekiah</td><td>Judah's final king</td></tr>
<tr><td rowspan="3">His efforts to find an honest man</td><td rowspan="3">What he bought—a field
When he bought it—while in prison
Why he bought it</td><td>Nebuchadnezzar</td><td>Babylonian monarch</td></tr>
<tr><td>Gedaliah</td><td>Appointed governor in post-war Jerusalem</td></tr>
<tr><td>Johanan</td><td>Jewish leader who carried Jeremiah to Egypt</td></tr>
<tr><td>SAINTS AND SINNERS</td><td colspan="5">Jeremiah, Hanameel, Josiah, Jehoiakim, Jehoiachin, Zedekiah, Nebuchadnezzar, Gedaliah, Johanan</td></tr>
<tr><td rowspan="2">SENTENCE SUMMARIES</td><td>O.T. Verses</td><td colspan="4">"Blessed is the man that walketh not in the counsel of the ungodly, nor standeth in the way of sinners, nor sitteth in the seat of the scornful. But his delight is in the Law of the LORD; and in His Law doth he meditate day and night" (Ps. 1:1-2).</td></tr>
<tr><td>N.T. Verse</td><td colspan="4">"Ye have not chosen Me, but I have chosen you, and ordained you, that ye should go and bring forth fruit, and that your fruit should remain; that whatsoever ye shall ask of the Father in My name, He may give it you" (John 15:16).</td></tr>
</table>

PERSONAL HISTORY OF JEREMIAH

Jeremiah was the son of Hilkiah, a priest living in Anathoth, some three miles northeast of Jerusalem in the land of Benjamin. He received his call to full-time service during the thirteenth year of godly King Josiah.

Jeremiah at first protested this call (as Moses once did, Ex. 3–4), pleading his youth as an excuse.

"Then the word of the LORD came unto me, saying, 'Before I formed thee in the belly, I knew thee; and before thou camest forth out of the womb I sanctified thee, and I ordained thee a prophet unto the nations.'

"Then said I, 'Ah, Lord God! Behold, I cannot speak, for I am a child' " (Jer. 1:4-6).

He was quickly reassured by God. *"But the LORD said unto me, 'Say not, "I am a child": for thou shalt go to all that I shall send thee, and whatsoever I command thee thou shalt speak. Be not afraid of their faces, for I am with thee to deliver thee,' saith the LORD.*

"Then the LORD put forth His hand, and touched my mouth. And the LORD said unto me, 'Behold, I have put My words in thy mouth. See, I have this day set thee over the nations and over the kingdoms, to root out, and to pull down, and to destroy, and to throw down, to build, and to plant' " (vv. 7-10).

As Jeremiah began his ministry, God showed him three things which underlined the nature and importance of his call.

He was shown an almond tree rod. Because it flowered earlier than the other trees, the almond signified the near fulfillment of God's proposed judgment.

He saw a pot of boiling water, tipping southward from the north. This symbolized the Babylonian invasion.

He then saw two baskets of figs in the temple. One basket had fresh, well-ripened figs, but the other contained rotten ones. God explained that the fresh figs represented the Jewish exiles in Babylon (men such as Daniel and Ezekiel), while the rotten fruit depicted Zedekiah and his corrupt officials.

Jeremiah was ordered to make a yoke and fasten it on his neck with leather thongs. He was then to send messages to the kings of Edom, Moab, Ammon, Tyre, and Sidon, through their ambassadors in Jerusalem, warning them that God had given their nations over to Babylon. Those who submitted and wore the yoke of punishment with true repentance would be spared, but those who refused would be destroyed. After God had used Nebuchadnezzar to punish Judah and neighboring nations, He would chastise Babylon itself. Judah was reassured that after the Babylonian Captivity she would be gathered back to Jerusalem.

He was commanded (like the Greek Diogenes who once ran through the streets of Athens with a lantern trying to find an honest man) by God to *"run . . . to and fro through the streets of Jerusalem, and see now, and know, and seek in the broad places thereof if ye can find a man, if there be any that executeth judgment, that seeketh the truth, and I will pardon it"* (5:1). God had once made a similar arrangement with Abraham concerning Sodom (see Gen. 18:23-33).

Jeremiah admitted this dreadful condition existed among the poor and ignorant, but felt he could find honest men within the ranks of Judah's educated and rich rulers. But they too had utterly rejected God.

After a fruitful 31-year reign, Josiah died. A weeping prophet attended his funeral. Judah's last good king had gone, and it would be downhill spiritually from that point on.

Jeremiah visited the settlement where the Rechabite families lived. These individuals belonged to a religious order and were founded by Jonadab, son of Rechab, during the reign of Jehu (841-814 B.C.). They assisted in the eradication of Baalism from Israel. Avoiding city life, they lived as shepherds, drinking no wine.

He was commanded to test them by offering them wine. They immediately refused, saying: *"We will drink no wine; for Jonadab, the son of Rechab, our father, commanded us, saying, 'Ye shall drink no wine, neither ye, nor your sons forever' "* (Jer. 35:6).

Jeremiah then related this sterling example to Judah and contrasted the obedience of the Rechabites to the disobedience of Jerusalem. While in prison, Jeremiah was ordered by God to buy a field from his cousin Hanameel. This was to illustrate that in spite of the advancing Babylonian armies,

Jeremiah—Setting and Life

COMMENTS

The political setting. In order to understand the Book of Jeremiah, one must comprehend the political situation of Judah in the sixth and seventh centuries B.C. Israel had always been a small nation wedged between the superpowers of the day. Egypt to the south, Assyria and Babylon to the north and east. The Assyrian Empire reached its zenith when Sargon III took the Northern Kingdom capital, Samaria, in 722 B.C. Jerusalem and the Southern Kingdom of Judah were spared by a divine miracle (2 Kings 18:13–19:37; Isa. 36–37).

During the last quarter of the seventh century B.C. the Assyrian Empire declined. Egypt then asserted herself in Judah, the Southern Kingdom. Finally in 607 B.C. Nineveh, capital of the tottering Assyrian Empire, fell to the Babylonians. Conflict between Babylon and Egypt was inevitable.

In the fourth year of Jehoiakim's reign (605 B.C.) Pharaoh Neco of Egypt was defeated at Carchemish by Nebuchadnezzar, the crown prince of Babylon (as predicted in Jer. 46:1-12). Nebuchadnezzar pursued Neco through Judah to Egypt and was stopped only by the death of his father. This first invasion of Jerusalem marks the beginning of Jeremiah's prophecy of the 70-year Babylonian Captivity (25:11). Jeremiah, therefore, lived and ministered throughout this long political struggle between Egypt and Babylon.

The life of Jeremiah. The weeping prophet was born to Hilkiah, priest of Anathoth, in the land of Benjamin, during the reign of the wicked tyrant, Manasseh (1:1). He was about 20 years old when God called him to the prophetic ministry in the thirteenth year (626 B.C.) of the reign of Josiah (v. 2). Jeremiah's call was not some whim or fanciful dream, for God "knew" him (the word means approval or selection—Gen. 18:19; Ps. 1:6; Amos 3:2) before he was born. Samson (Jud. 13:3-5), John the Baptist (Luke 1:15), Paul (Gal. 1:15-16) and others were also chosen and set apart for service while still in their mothers' wombs.

Jeremiah was told that his message would not only be to Judah but also the nations (Jer. 1:10). His prophetic coin would have two sides—one negative (root out, pull down, destroy—God's judgment) and one positive (build and plant—God's mercy). When the effects of Josiah's revival wore off, Judah plunged into idolatry and unbelief. Jeremiah was called to warn the people of impending judgment—the great theme of his book. Jeremiah saw Babylon as the instrument of God's judgment. Judah would be conquered. Since their sin was indelible, divine judgment was inevitable. The only course of action, therefore, was to surrender to Babylon. For this Jeremiah was considered a traitor and persecuted by his friends (11:21), the priests and prophets (26:8-9), the civil leaders (36:19, 26; 38:4) and even his family (12:6).

Both the message and the messenger were rejected by the people. Jeremiah had preached repentance, but the people refused to repent. He counseled the kings to submit to Babylon, but they refused. He advised the remnant to remain in Judah, but they fled to Egypt. Even in Egypt Jeremiah continued to minister to his rebellious flock. Now between 70 and 80 years old he delivered his last prophecies in Tahpanhes (Daphne) in Lower Egypt (43:8–44:30). The Bible does not record the weeping prophet's death. Jerome and Tertullian believed he was stoned by the Jews at Tahpanhes. An Alexandrian tradition holds that Alexander the Great brought his bones to the city of Alexandria. A Jewish tradition held that he escaped to Babylon. He probably just died in Egypt, broken by men but loved and honored by God.

"Houses and fields and vineyards shall be possessed again in this land" (32:15).

The background of all this was interesting. God told Jeremiah that his cousin Hanameel was soon to visit him, attempting to sell the prophet a farm he owned in Anathoth. Jeremiah was to buy it for 17 shekels of silver. Baruch was then to place the sealed deed in a pottery jar and bury it. All this was to demonstrate that someday people would once again own property in Judah and buy and sell. Jeremiah was comforted at this time in prison by God's gracious promise: *"Call unto Me, and I will answer thee, and show thee great and mighty things, which thou knowest not" (33:3).*

These tremendous and thrilling "things" were listed in chapters 30–31, and 33. They included the following: In spite of the impending Babylonian Captivity, the time was coming when God would heal Jerusalem's hurt and give her prosperity and peace; He still loved Israel with an everlasting love; and Israel would be gathered into Palestine from the earth's farthest ends.

"They shall come with weeping, and with supplications will I lead them; I will cause them to walk by the rivers of waters in a straight way, wherein they shall not stumble; for I am a Father to Israel" (31:9).

"Therefore they shall come and sing in the height of Zion . . . a watered garden, and they shall not sorrow any more at all" (v. 12).

THE RULERS THAT JEREMIAH MINISTERED UNDER

JOSIAH

Jeremiah was called by God during the reign of Josiah, Judah's last good king.

JEHOAHAZ

JEHOIAKIM

This wicked king burned Jeremiah's original written prophecy scroll.

JEHOIACHIN

This 90-day wonder was soundly condemned by Jeremiah.

ZEDEKIAH

The prophet suffered much under the reign of Zedekiah, Judah's final king. Zedekiah sent to Jeremiah asking for his prayers after Nebuchadnezzar had declared war on Judah. Jeremiah sent word back to the wicked king stating prayers were useless on this subject, for God would use the Babylonians to punish Jerusalem, and Zedekiah himself was to be given over to Nebuchadnezzar. Jeremiah told Zedekiah that Jerusalem would be burned, and he would be captured and carried into Babylon.

Jeremiah rebuked those rich Jewish homeowners who had violated the Mosaic Law which demanded all Hebrew servants to be set free after serving six years.

Pharaoh Hophra's Egyptian armies had arrived to aid Judah in fighting Nebuchadnezzar. Jeremiah warned Zedekiah that their political alliance would fail, for Nebuchadnezzar would defeat the Egyptians.

NEBUCHADNEZZAR

Jeremiah was treated with respect by the great Babylonian conqueror.

Zedekiah attempted to escape the doomed city, but was captured near Jericho and brought back to Jerusalem. Here he was forced to witness the execution of his own sons, and then submit to the agony of his eyes being gouged out.

Nebuchadnezzar instructed his chief-of-staff, Nebuzaradan, to treat Jeremiah with kindness.

Jeremiah was released from prison and taken by Nebuzaradan to Ramah. Here he was offered his choice of going on to Babylon or returning to Jerusalem. Jeremiah chose to return and was placed under the protection of the new Jewish governor of Jerusalem, a man named Gedaliah.

GEDALIAH

He was appointed by Nebuchadnezzar to govern the fallen city of Jerusalem. Gedaliah attempted to institute a moderate postwar administration over the devastated city of Jerusalem. This soon aroused the fury of a Jewish rebel leader named Ishmael who plotted to assassinate Gedaliah. The governor was warned of this plot by a man named Johanan, but refused to take it seriously. Ishmael murdered Gedaliah along with many other Jewish officials, pilgrims, and some Babylonian soldiers. Some of their bodies were hurled down an empty cistern. Johanan arrived on the scene of the massacre and soon restored order.

JOHANAN

He took over after the tragic assassination of

Gedaliah and later forced Jeremiah to accompany a Jewish remnant to Egypt. After a 10-day prayer session with God, Jeremiah was told that the Lord desired the remnant to remain in Jerusalem and not go to Egypt, as some were already planning to do. When Johanan and other leaders heard this unwelcome report, they accused Jeremiah of lying. They then disobeyed the clearly revealed Word of God by going to Egypt. Jeremiah was forced to accompany them.

In Egypt, many of the Jews returned to their old habits of idolatry. They began burning incense to the Queen of Heaven. This pagan goddess was another name for Ishtar, the Mesopotamian goddess of love and war.

Jeremiah pronounced the divine death penalty on all who refused to repent and return to Jerusalem. To dramatize this bitter truth, he buried some large rocks between the pavement stones at the entrance of Pharaoh's palace. This signified that Nebuchadnezzar would occupy Egypt and set his throne on those stones. Jeremiah predicted Nebuchadnezzar would then kill many of the Jewish remnant who refused to return. The others would die of various plagues or be enslaved.

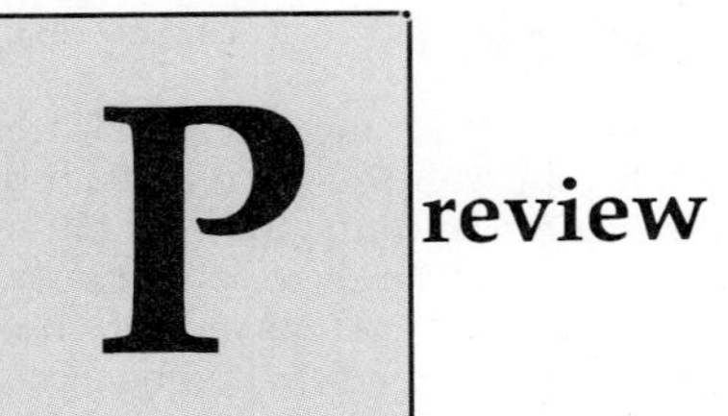

review

Becoming All Things to All Men

BOOK OF JEREMIAH

After being sworn in as President at the unexpected death of FDR, Harry Truman remarked he felt as if the sun, moon, and stars had suddenly fallen on him. Jeremiah the prophet doubtless felt the same way just prior to the destruction of both Jerusalem and its temple. He could see the terrible storm of judgment coming and actually feel its awful blast. But Judah would not hear him nor heed his words of warning. Crusading, comforting, and condemning. That's how he spent his long days. His crusade was directed toward Jerusalem, his comfort toward the remnant already in Captivity, and his condemning toward the nine pagan Gentile nations which surrounded Judah. The wickedness of man and the wrath of God. That was his message. Wrath and wickedness. But along with these terrible terms came his weeping. No other biblical prophet ever said more stern things against Judah or shed more bitter tears over its people than did Jeremiah.

Overview

<table>
<tr><td>SCRIPTURE</td><td colspan="5">Book of Jeremiah</td></tr>
<tr><td>SUBJECT</td><td colspan="5">Threefold ministry of Jeremiah</td></tr>
<tr><td rowspan="5">SPECIFICS</td><td colspan="2">Cautioning the majority</td><td colspan="2">Comforting the minority</td><td>Condemning the multitudes</td></tr>
<tr><td>Protesting</td><td>The rebellion of Israel</td><td rowspan="2">Some don'ts</td><td rowspan="2">Don't get discouraged
Don't believe the lies of false prophets</td><td rowspan="3">Egypt
Philistia
Moab
Ammon
Edom
Damascus
Kedar and Hazor
Elam
Babylon</td></tr>
<tr><td>Pleading</td><td>The repentance of Israel</td></tr>
<tr><td>Predicting</td><td>The retribution on Israel</td><td>Some do's</td><td>Settle down
Pray
Trust God to lead your children back</td></tr>
<tr><td colspan="2">The Jews still living in Judah</td><td colspan="2">The Jews in the Babylonian Captivity</td><td>Nine Gentile nations</td></tr>
<tr><td>SAINTS AND SINNERS</td><td colspan="5">Jeremiah</td></tr>
<tr><td rowspan="2">SENTENCE SUMMARIES</td><td>O.T. Verse</td><td colspan="4">"Should ye not hear the words which the LORD hath cried by the former prophets, when Jerusalem was inhabited and in prosperity, and the cities thereof round about her, when men inhabited the south and the plain?" (Zech. 7:7)</td></tr>
<tr><td>N.T. Verse</td><td colspan="4">"Therefore endure hardness, as a good soldier of Jesus Christ" (2 Tim. 2:3).</td></tr>
</table>

THE THREEFOLD MINISTRY OF JEREMIAH

CAUTIONING THE MAJORITY

Jeremiah warned the majority still in Judah about the coming Babylonian Captivity. He pleaded with Judah to return to God.

"Go and proclaim these words toward the north, and say, 'Return, thou backsliding Israel,' saith the LORD; 'and I will not cause Mine anger to fall upon you. For I am merciful,' saith the LORD, 'and I will not keep anger forever. Only acknowledge thine iniquity, that thou hast transgressed against the LORD thy God, and hast scattered thy ways to the strangers under every green tree, and ye have not obeyed My voice,' saith the LORD.

" 'Turn, O backsliding children,' saith the LORD; 'for I am married unto you . . . and I will bring you to Zion.' . . . Thus saith the LORD, 'Stand in the court of the LORD's house, and speak unto all the cities of Judah, which come to worship in the LORD's house, all the words that I command thee to speak unto them; diminish not a word. If so be they will hearken, and turn every man from his evil way, that I may repent Me of the evil, which I purpose to do unto them because of the evil of their doings. And thou shalt say unto them, "Thus saith the LORD; 'If ye will not hearken to Me, to walk in My Law, which I have set before you, to hearken to the words of My servants the prophets, whom I sent unto you, both rising up early, and sending them, but ye have not hearkened; then will I make this house like Shiloh, and will make this city a curse to all the nations of the earth.' " '

"So the priests and the prophets and all the people heard Jeremiah speaking these words in the house of the LORD" (Jer. 3:12-14; 26:2-7).

God would repeatedly invite Israel back to Him. He would receive Israel even after her immorality with other lovers. Jeremiah pleaded with them to plow up the hardness of their hearts, lest all be choked by thorns.

"For thus saith the LORD to the men of Judah and Jerusalem, 'Break up your fallow ground, and sow not among thorns. Circumcise yourselves to the LORD, and take away the foreskins of your heart, ye men of Judah and inhabitants of Jerusalem; lest My fury come forth like fire, and burn that none can quench it, because of the evil of your doings' " (4:3-4).

They could still escape judgment by cleansing their hearts and purifying their thoughts. To repent meant they could remain in the land. To refuse meant to be covered by thick darkness.

He fearlessly pronounced coming judgment at the hands of the Babylonians. He then listed Judah's sins.

Judah had forsaken the fountain of divine water and built broken cisterns which could not hold water.

The nation had become a race of evil men and no amount of soap or lye could make them clean.

The rulers had stained their clothes with the blood of the innocent and poor and were as an unashamed prostitute. They worshiped false gods on every hill and under every shade tree. They had killed their prophets as a lion would slaughter his prey. They were as insolent as brass, and hard and cruel as iron. They had set up idols right in the temple and worshiped the pagan Queen of Heaven goddess.

"The children gather wood, and the fathers kindle the fire, and the women knead their dough, to make cakes to the Queen of Heaven, and to pour out drink offerings unto other gods, that they may provoke Me to anger" (7:18).

They had actually sacrificed their little children as burnt offerings to devil gods. He finally warned them concerning the terrible results of their disobedience. Great armies marched on Jerusalem. Neither Assyria nor Egypt could help Judah against Babylon. People fled from Judah's cities as one runs from a hungry lion. Jerusalem was surrounded as hunters would move in on a wild and wounded animal. They cried out as a woman in delivery. Jerusalem's own trees were cut down and used against her walls as battering rams. The temple was destroyed.

" 'And now, because ye have done all these works,' saith the LORD, 'and I spake unto you, rising up early and speaking, but ye heard not; and I called you, but ye answered not; therefore will I do unto this house, which is called by My name, wherein ye trust, and unto the place which I gave to you and to your fathers, as I have done to Shiloh' " (vv. 13-14).

Enemy troops then moved among the

people like poisonous snakes. Many died by sword, disease, and starvation. Some were scattered as chaff by the fierce desert winds. Unburied corpses littered the valleys outside Jerusalem, and became food for wild animals and birds. Judah's enemies broke open the sacred graves of her kings, priests, and prophets, and spread out their bones on the ground before the sun, moon, and stars. Thousands were carried away into Babylon for a period of 70 years.

"And this whole land shall be a desolation, and an astonishment; and these nations shall serve the king of Babylon 70 years. . . . For thus saith the LORD, *'That after 70 years be accomplished at Babylon I will visit you, and perform My good word toward you, in causing you to return to this place' " (25:11; 29:10).*

The severity of Judah's punishment would astonish the onlooking pagan Gentile nations. When the people ridiculed and rejected his message, the warning prophet became the weeping prophet.

"Oh, that my head were waters, and mine eyes a fountain of tears, that I might weep day and night for the slain of the daughter of my people!" (9:1)

COMFORTING THE MINORITY

He comforted the minority already captive in Babylon. Jeremiah wrote a letter of encouragement to the Jewish exiles in Babylon. He told them to settle down for a 70-year stay and to pray for the peace and prosperity of Babylon, that their own lives might be peaceful. They were also to ignore the lies of those false prophets and mediums there in Babylon, lest they be punished along with them.

Jeremiah pronounced God's death sentence on two of these prophets named Ahab and Zedekiah for their lying messages and their sin of adultery. He also warned the exiles concerning a man named Shemaiah, who was sending poison-pen letters from Babylon to the influential leaders in Jerusalem against Jeremiah.

God still loved them and would someday bring them back to Jerusalem.

" 'For I know the thoughts that I think toward you,' saith the LORD, *'thoughts of peace, and not of evil, to give you an expected end. Then shall ye call upon Me, and ye shall go and pray unto Me, and I will hearken unto you. And ye shall seek Me, and find Me, when ye shall search for Me with all your heart. And I will be found of you,' saith the* LORD; *'and I will turn away your captivity, and I will gather you from all the nations, and from all the places whither I have driven you,' saith the* LORD; *'and I will bring you again into the place whence I caused you to be carried away captive' " (29:11-14).*

CONDEMNING THE MULTITUDES

He pronounced judgment on nine Gentile nations. These nations were: Egypt, Philistia, Moab, Ammon, Edom, Damascus, Kedar and Hazor, Elam, and Babylon.

After listing these nations, Jeremiah dealt with each one in a specific way.

Egypt. Egypt would be defeated by Nebuchadnezzar at the battle of Carchemish. Their armies would flee in terror and fill the Euphrates with corpses. Their sin wound (like that of Judah) was incurable. Pharaoh Hophra, the Egyptian leader, was ridiculed as a man of plenty of noise, but no power. Egypt would be occupied by Nebuchadnezzar.

Philistia. It was to be overrun by the Egyptians. This occurred in 606 B.C., the year King Josiah died. Strong Philistine men would scream and fathers would flee, leaving behind their helpless children. Philistia's allies, Tyre and Sidon, would also be destroyed at the same time. The two chief Philistine cities of Gaza and Ashkelon would be totally destroyed.

Moab. Nebuchadnezzar's armies would overrun Moab. Their god Chemosh was to be carried away with priests and princes. Prior to this time, Moab had been relatively undisturbed from various invasions. In the end, Moab will be as ashamed of her national idol-god Chemosh as Israel was of her calf-god at Bethel. The ancestor of the Moabites (Moab) was born in a cave. During the fearful Babylonian invasion, the Moabites will once again flee into caves.

Ammon. This nation would be punished for occupying the cities of Israel after the Captivity and worshiping the false god Milcom. Milcom, along with the Ammonite princes and priests, would be carried away. Ammon will be reestablished during the Millennium.

Edom. Edom's cities would become as silent as Sodom and Gomorrah. Their cry will be heard as far away as the Red Sea. God would, however, be merciful to her widows and orphans.

Damascus. Her entire army would be destroyed in one single day. A fire would start at the edge of the city and eventually burn up the palaces of Ben-hadad.

Kedar and Hazor. Kedar was the name of an Arab tribe living in the desert east of Palestine which was to be destroyed by Nebuchadnezzar. God Himself ordered

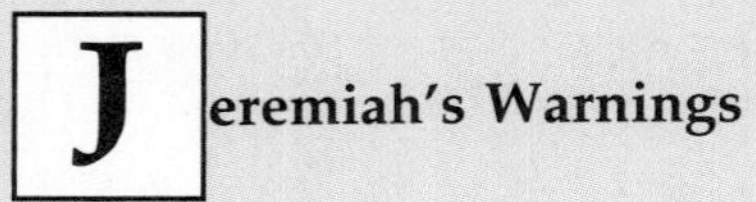

Jeremiah's Warnings

COMMENTS

The first 45 chapters of Jeremiah are a series of sermons, interspersed with historical narrative, warning Judah of the consequences of their sin and disobedience to God. The first sermon (2:1–3:5) developed the theme of national apostasy. God is faithful, but His people were unfaithful. The consequences could only be divine judgment.

The people had committed two evils. They had forsaken God—the Fountain of Living Waters. Both Isaiah and Jesus used this same imagery (Isa. 44:3; John 4:10-15; 7:37-39). Judah's second sin was idolatry described as broken cisterns (Jer. 2:13). Since Israel is an arid land (it rarely rains during the summer), this imagery was a powerful object lesson.

In Jeremiah's second sermon (3:6–6:30), he used Israel, the Northern Kingdom, as an example and warning to Judah, the Southern Kingdom. Judah's sin was greater than Israel's. Israel had openly revolted against God, but Judah was lukewarm, wanting both God and Baal. God called on Judah to return (Heb., *shub*), which may mean "return from exile"; but Jeremiah also meant to return to Jehovah (15:19; cf. 3:1, 12-14, 22; 8:4-7; 15:5-9; 23:14). The command to "circumcise yourselves to the Lord" was a challenge to true heart religion and not mere ceremony. All Jewish boys were circumcised at eight days old as a sign of covenant relationship to God (Gen. 17:1-14). The external sign, however, cannot make one a child of God without the accompanying circumcision of the heart (cf. Rom. 2:28-29).

Jeremiah's third sermon (Jer. 7:1–10:25) warned the people of God of the consequences of their sin. Delivered at the gate of the temple, this sermon first rebuked the people's superstitious faith and trust in a building, the temple, rather than Jehovah. The temple had become a fetish and even the phrase "the temple of the Lord" had become a religious chant (7:4). They reasoned that no foreign power could destroy the house of God. Therefore, Jerusalem could not be destroyed no matter how they lived.

The people had forgotten, however, that in the days of Eli, after the battle of Ebenezer (1 Sam. 4; Ps. 78:60) that Shiloh (the location of the tabernacle, Jer. 7:12) was destroyed by the Philistines and the ark taken. The temple in Jerusalem was no guarantee that God would not punish sin.

The other sermons of Jeremiah continue the theme of judgment resulting from sin. Since Judah's sin was indelible, judgment was inevitable.

In 597 B.C. Nebuchadnezzar deported King Jehoiachin and the best people to Babylon. Two years later word reached Jeremiah that false prophets exiled in Babylon were predicting its speedy demise and the immediate return of the Jewish exiles.

Jeremiah responded by penning a letter of comfort to this Jewish minority (chap. 29). In the letter Jeremiah advised the captives to settle in the land and become law-abiding exiles because their Captivity would be long (vv. 10-19).

Elasah and Gemariah (v. 3) were the two ambassadors sent by King Zedekiah to Babylon, who also carried Jeremiah's letter. Gemariah was a popular name of that time as evidenced by Shaphan's son (36:10) and its mention in the Lachish letters.

The exiles were not slaves but deportees. They were permitted to live in their own settlements (29:4-7). Tel Abib on the Grand Canal (the Chebar River) was perhaps the largest settlement. It was from here that Ezekiel carried out his prophetic ministry.

Ahab, Zedekiah (v. 21), and Shemaiah (v. 24) were the false exile prophets. Ahab and Zedekiah were "roasted in the fire" (v. 22) by Nebuchadnezzar. This atrocity definitely dates this passage during the reign of Nebuchadnezzar, since under the Persians (who regarded fire as sacred), ingestion by lions was the form of capital punishment employed (cf. Dan. 6:16).

God had ordained Jeremiah as "a prophet unto the nations" (Jer. 1:5; cf. v. 10), as well as to Israel. Chapters 46 through 51 are Jeremiah's prophetic condemnation on the Gentile nations surrounding Israel. Since Jeremiah's purpose was to describe God's judgment rather than particular sins, we find little reference to actual national sins in these chapters.

From Egypt to Babylon the pagan Gentile nations would not escape the wrath of God. Though Nebuchadnezzar was God's servant of judgment on Judah, yet Babylon would be punished for their sins of pride and greed. In 539 B.C. Cyrus, the Persian, conquered Babylon without a fight. Even the Babylonians almost welcomed him as a liberator from the misrule of Nebuchadnezzar's successors. With Cyrus' decree of returning the exiles, many Jews were repatriated and rebuilt Jerusalem.

Nebuchadnezzar to destroy these wealthy, materialistic, and arrogant Bedouin tribes. Hazor, another Arabian tribe located nearby, was to be leveled also.

Elam. Elam, east of the Tigris-Euphrates country, with its capital at Susa, was overrun by Nebuchadnezzar in the winter of 596 B.C. Zedekiah, Judah's last king, began ruling in Jerusalem at that time. Elam is to be reestablished during the Millennium.

Babylon. Two Babylons seemed to be referred to in these verses. One was the historical Babylon, captured by Darius the Persian in October of 539 B.C. (see Dan. 5) and the other is the future Babylon which will be destroyed by God Himself (see Rev. 17:18). After the destruction of both Babylons, Israel would seek their God. This happened historically (Ezra 1) and it will occur in the future (Zech. 13:9). After the final destruction of Babylon (Rev. 18), the city will never be inhabited again. The ungodly nations would weep over the destruction of both Babylons (v. 10, Jer. 50:46). The Israelites were to flee from both Babylons (Rev. 18:4; Jer. 51:6). Both cities are depicted as golden cups filled with iniquities from which the nations have drunk and become mad. All heaven rejoices over the destruction of both.

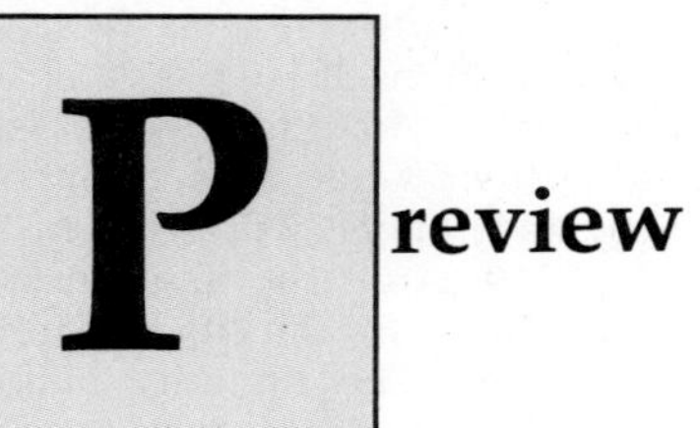

Preview

Future Facts

BOOK OF JEREMIAH

In ancient history a rich king once inquired of his seer whether or not he should declare war on another king. After a session of pretended crystal ball-gazing, the seer replied: "O King, if you attack, a great empire will be destroyed." Satisfied, the monarch moved his troops, only to be decidedly defeated!

In defending his prophecy the seer exclaimed: "You note I only predicted your attack would destroy a great kingdom. I did not specify which kingdom it would be."

One can immediately see the worthlessness of this kind of prophecy, which is in reality no prophecy at all. What a contrast is seen as one considers Jeremiah's predictions. Instead of being vague and worthless, his are pointed, precise, and if heeded, profitable to all involved. In matters of preciseness, his prophecy concerning the Babylonian Captivity is one of Scripture's most amazing. Not only did he foretell the Captivity itself, but specified the time element in the Captivity (70 years), and the Jewish return from the Captivity. Perhaps the most exciting of all, however, was his New Covenant prophecy, which promised that redeemed Israel will someday, yet in the future, live on God's soil, indwelled by God's Spirit, and ruled over by God's Son. This is prophecy at its very best.

Overview

<table>
<tr><td>SCRIPTURE</td><td colspan="6">Book of Jeremiah</td></tr>
<tr><td>SUBJECT</td><td colspan="6">Jeremiah's prophecies</td></tr>
<tr><td rowspan="6">SPECIFICS</td><td colspan="4">The group prophecies</td><td colspan="2">The great prophecy</td></tr>
<tr><td colspan="2">Judah's people</td><td colspan="2">Judah's potentates</td><td rowspan="5">God's new covenant</td><td rowspan="2">Its nature</td></tr>
<tr><td colspan="2" rowspan="2">Fall of Jerusalem
Fall of the temple
70-year Captivity
Kindly treatment in Captivity
Restoration
Future rule of Christ</td><td rowspan="2">Bad news concerning</td><td rowspan="2">Jehoahaz
Jehoiakim
Jehoiachin
Zedekiah</td></tr>
<tr><td>Its time element</td></tr>
<tr><td colspan="2">Judah's prophets</td><td colspan="2">Judah's persecutors</td><td>Its superiority</td></tr>
<tr><td>Death of 3 false prophets</td><td>Zedekiah
Ahab
Hananiah</td><td colspan="2">Defeat of Egypt by Babylon
Occupying of Egypt by Babylon
Defeat of Babylon</td><td>Its mediator</td></tr>
<tr><td>SAINTS AND SINNERS</td><td colspan="6">Jeremiah, Zedekiah, Ahab, Hananiah, Seraiah</td></tr>
<tr><td rowspan="2">SENTENCE SUMMARIES</td><td>O.T. Verse</td><td colspan="5">"In the first year of his reign I Daniel understood by books the number of the years, whereof the word of the LORD came to Jeremiah the prophet, that he would accomplish seventy years in the desolations of Jerusalem" (Dan. 9:2).</td></tr>
<tr><td>N.T. Verses</td><td colspan="5">"Then was fulfilled that which was spoken by Jeremiah the prophet, saying, 'In Ramah was there a voice heard, lamentation, and weeping, and great mourning, Rachel weeping for her children, and would not be comforted, because they are not' " (Matt. 2:17-18).</td></tr>
</table>

HE PROPHECIES OF JEREMIAH

THE FALL OF JERUSALEM

THE DESTRUCTION OF THE TEMPLE

THE DEATH OF THE DEPOSED JUDEAN KING JEHOAHAZ IN EGYPT

THE IGNOBLE AND UNLAMENTED DEATH OF KING JEHOIAKIM

Jeremiah soundly condemned Jehoiakim for his wicked reign. He was constructing an extravagant palace with forced labor. He had murdered the innocent and oppressed the poor. He was filled with selfish greed and dishonesty.

About this time one of Jeremiah's fellow prophets, Uriah, was murdered by Jehoiakim for his fearless preaching. Therefore, Jeremiah predicted that the king would die unlamented and be buried like a dead donkey, dragged out of Jerusalem and thrown on the garbage dump beyond the gate.

THE CUTTING OFF FROM THE ROYAL LINE OF KING JEHOIACHIN

This young son of Jehoiakim ruled only three months, but so aroused the divine wrath of heaven that, Jeremiah was told, had he been the signet ring of God's right hand, he would still have been cast off and given to the Babylonians.

Jeremiah predicted that this 90-day wonder would be given over to Nebuchadnezzar, be cast out of the land along with his mother, die in a foreign land, be regarded as a discarded and broken dish, and be considered childless (even though he had offspring) as far as the throne of David was concerned.

THE DEATH OF TWO FALSE PROPHETS AND THE PUNISHMENT OF ANOTHER

THE DEATH OF A FALSE JERUSALEM PROPHET NAMED HANANIAH

THE CAPTIVITY OF SERAIAH

Jeremiah warned a man named Seraiah that he would be taken captive by Nebuchadnezzar at a later date. This literally happened some six years later. Seraiah was then given a scroll containing Jeremiah's prophecies against Babylon. When he arrived there, the prophet commanded him to publicly read it and then to tie a rock to the scroll and throw it into the Euphrates River. This symbolized that Babylon would sink, never to rise again.

THE FAILURE OF THE EGYPTIAN-JUDEAN MILITARY ALLIANCE AGAINST BABYLON

THE DEFEAT OF EGYPT BY BABYLON

Jeremiah described in vivid detail the world-famous battle at Carchemish at the very moment when it was being fought. Egypt suffered a resounding defeat at the hands of Nebuchadnezzar.

THE EVENTUAL OCCUPYING OF EGYPT BY BABYLON

THE SEVENTY-YEAR CAPTIVITY OF JUDAH IN BABYLON

NOTE: In Jeremiah 31:15-16, Jeremiah predicted that the loud wails and bitter weeping of Rachel for her children in Ramah will disappear. Ramah was an ancient reference to the area in and around Bethlehem. It was here that Nebuchadnezzar killed many sick and feeble exile captives who would not be able to endure the long trip to Babylon. Rachel, the wife of Jacob, was, of course, symbolic of all weeping Israelite mothers. In Matthew 2:18 this sad verse was linked to that occasion when Herod murdered the babies of Bethlehem in an attempt to kill Christ.

THE RESTORATION TO JERUSALEM AFTER THE SEVENTY YEARS

Jeremiah promised ultimate restoration. Israel would be gathered back from all over the world.

"Behold, I will bring them from the north country, and gather them from the coasts of the earth, and with them the blind and the lame, the woman with child and her that travaileth with child together; a great company shall return thither. They shall come with weeping, and with supplications will I lead them; I will cause them to walk by the rivers of waters in a straight way, wherein they shall not stumble; for I am a Father to Israel, and Ephraim is My firstborn" (Jer. 31:8-9).

"Behold, I will gather them out of all countries, whither I have driven them in Mine anger, and in My fury, and in great wrath; and I will bring them again unto this place, and I will cause them to dwell safely. And they shall be My people, and I will be their God. And I will give them one heart, and one way, that they may fear Me forever, for the good of them and of their children after them" (32:37-39).

God would appoint leaders after His own heart. Palestine would once again be filled with the glory of God, and the people of God. This would be a far greater and grander event than that of the original Exodus, when He brought them out of Egypt.

A righteous Branch (the Saviour) will occupy King David's throne, ruling with wisdom and justice.

" 'Behold, the days come,' saith the LORD, 'that I will raise unto David a righteous Branch, and a King shall reign and prosper, and shall execute judgment and justice in the earth. In His days Judah shall be saved, and Israel shall dwell safely; and this is His name whereby he shall be called, THE LORD OUR RIGHTEOUSNESS' " (23:5-6).

Jerusalem will be rebuilt and filled with joy and great thanksgiving. During the Millennium Israel will understand the necessity for and the purpose of all their sufferings. The cities of Israel will be rebuilt, and Jerusalem will become the praise and power center of all the earth.

THE DEFEAT OF BABYLON AFTER THE SEVENTY YEARS

NOTE: The punishment Babylon would receive from God as found in Jeremiah 50–52 evidently referred not only to the historical judgment (see Dan. 5), but also that future judgment (see Rev. 18).

THE CAPTURE OF ZEDEKIAH

THE KINDLY TREATMENT OF THE GODLY EXILES IN BABYLON

The Prophecies of Jeremiah—Judgment

COMMENTS

Jeremiah was called to the prophetic office at the darkest hour of Israel's history. From both a political and moral standpoint the nation was in trouble. The people had rejected God's earlier prophets (7:25; 44:4). The revival under Josiah was short-lived. The judgment of God was inevitable. The great theme of Jeremiah's prophecies, therefore, is judgment. The judgment of God can be seen in two specific prophecies: the fall of Jerusalem and the cutting off of the line of Jehoiachin.

The fall of Jerusalem: The prophecy concerning the fall of Jerusalem first appears in the second confirming sign of Jeremiah's call (1:13-16). Jeremiah saw a large seething pot from the north boiling over. This seething pot (Heb., *sīr*) was a large caldron in which vegetables or meat for a large group could be cooked (2 Kings 4:38-41; Ezek. 24:3-7). As the pot boiled over, so too would disaster from the north fall on the land of Judah.

Jeremiah mentioned the foe from the north (Jer. 4:5-9; 5:15-17) and then gave his first description of the attack on Jerusalem in chapter 6 (vv. 1-6). Since the enemy would come from the north, the people would have to flee to the south toward Tekoa, the home of the prophet Amos, 12 miles south of Jerusalem. The invaders would be like shepherds whose flocks strip away the covering of the land (v. 3). So fierce would be the fighting that the invaders would not break at "noon," which was the normal practice due to the extreme heat, but would continue the attack through the night.

The greatest horror of the downfall of Jerusalem would be the destruction of the temple (7:11-15; 26:6-9). The people had placed their faith and trust in a building, the temple, rather than the Lord. Since Isaiah had taught the presence of God in Jerusalem (Isa. 8:18; 28:16) and this was confirmed by the Assyrian defeat in 701 B.C. (2 Kings 19:35), the people reasoned that no foreign power could destroy the house of God. They made the temple a fetish chiming a religious chant "the temple of the LORD" (Jer. 7:4).

Due to the indelible nature of Judah's sin even the temple would be destroyed. Jeremiah reminded them that as God destroyed Shiloh so too would He destroy Jerusalem (v. 12). Eighteen miles north of Jerusalem, Shiloh was the location of the tabernacle during the early days of the nation. After the battle of Ebenezer in 1050 B.C. (1 Sam. 4; Ps. 78:60) the city was destroyed and the ark taken by the Philistines. Jeremiah 37 through 39 describes historically the awful events of the siege and fall of Jerusalem. The Book of Lamentations is a funeral dirge written about this darkest day in Judah's history.

Royal roots—the cutting off of Jehoiachin: One of Jeremiah's most fascinating prophecies of judgment is the cutting off of the royal line of Jehoiachin. Jeremiah predicted that King Jehoiachin would be "childless" (Jer. 22:30). This did not mean that he would have no children, because he had seven sons (1 Chron. 3:17-18) and he is also mentioned in Matthew's genealogy (Matt. 1:12). Rather, due to divine judgment, Jehoiachin would have no physical descendant sit on the throne of David. Christ's dynastic right to the throne of David came through His foster father, Joseph, who was of the line of Jehoiachin (also called Coniah, Jer. 22:24; and Jeconiah, 24:1; 27:20; cf. 2 Kings 24:8-16; 25:27-30). Jesus' physical descent came through Mary, whose genealogy is traced through Nathan rather than Solomon to David (cf. Luke 3:31; Matt. 1:17). Had Joseph been the physical father of Jesus, the Lord would not be able to occupy the throne of David, and Luke 1:32-33 would contradict Jeremiah 22:24-30. This prophecy is then an indirect prediction of the Virgin Birth.

HE NEW COVENANT OF JEREMIAH

THE NATURE OF THE NEW COVENANT

It would embrace the entire house of Israel and be totally unlike the old Mosaic Covenant.

God would inscribe His laws on their hearts. Israel had always suffered with self-inflicted spiritual heart trouble. Note the divine diagnosis: *"The sin of Judah is written with a pen of iron and with the point of a diamond; it is engraved upon the table of their heart" (Jer. 17:1).*

But under the New Covenant the heavenly Physician would offer them perfect and guaranteed successful heart transplants. This nation with the new hearts would then once again become God's people, and He their God.

THE TIME OF THE NEW COVENANT

It will go into effect "after those days" and following the "time of Jacob's trouble." Both these terms refer to the coming Great Tribulation. Thus, the New Covenant will begin to function after the time of Jacob's trouble, at the start of the glorious Millennium.

THE SUPERIORITY OF THE NEW COVENANT

It will be immutable, unconditional, and eternal, as opposed to the Mosaic Covenant. M.F. Unger writes: "The Old Covenant was the Law covenant grounded in legal observance. The New Covenant (Heb. 8:8-12) will be entirely on the basis of grace and the sacrificial blood of Christ, which will be the foundation of Israel's future inward regeneration and restoration to God's favor. Israel's entering into the blessings of the New Covenant (Rom. 11:1-26) will insure her being an everlasting nation" (*Unger's Bible Dictionary* [Moody Press], p. 352).

God Himself assured Israel of the duration of this New Covenant when He declared: *"If heaven above can be measured, and the foundations of the earth searched out beneath, I will also cast off all the seed of Israel" (31:37).* See also 33:2-26.

THE MEDIATOR OF THE NEW COVENANT: THE SON OF DAVID HIMSELF

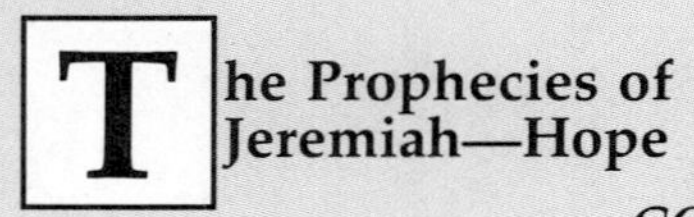

The Prophecies of Jeremiah—Hope

COMMENTS

Against the dark backdrop of judgment there is also a message of hope. Some of the greatest messianic prophecies of the Old Testament appear in Jeremiah. Like Isaiah a century earlier, Jeremiah's message of hope was in the coming of the Messiah. Two significant prophecies of hope in Jeremiah are the Righteous Branch and the New Covenant.

The Righteous Branch: In chapter 23 Jeremiah compares the wicked kings and leaders of Judah with the coming righteous King, the Messiah. The prophets, priests, and kings in the Old Testament were types of the messianic offices. Yet the prophets, priests, and kings of Judah did not live up to their names. Only the Righteous Branch, King David's greater Son, the King of kings and Lord of lords will be the hope of Judah.

Jeremiah uses the term "pastors" to signify leaders or rulers in general. The "pastors" (literally "shepherds" or "leaders") were not religious but civil leaders (3:15). Under the Old Testament theocracy their task was to lead the people in the way of the Lord. Yet these leaders were the greatest transgressors. They had "driven them [the people] away," just the opposite of the oriental shepherd's duty of leading the flock to the fold or pasture (Isa. 40:11; John 10:3-4).

The Righteous Branch is a messianic metaphor (cf. Isa. 4:2-4; Jer. 33:15; Zech. 3:8; 6:12). The branch was not a branch or twig of a tree, but a sprout directly from the root or from a fallen tree forming a second tree (cf. Ps. 65:10; Isa. 61:11; Ezek. 16:7; 17:9-10). From the fallen nations, therefore, would come the individual Messiah who would be the hope of Israel and the world.

This prophecy, like many Old Testament prophecies, has a double fulfillment. The first fulfillment came with the first advent of the Messiah. The second fulfillment awaits the millennial reign of the Messiah. That this prophecy has not yet been fulfilled is seen by the statements: "Judgment and justice" (Jer. 23:5), and "They shall no more say . . . out of the north country" (vv. 7-8).

The New Covenant: Chapters 30 to 33 counterbalance the message of impending disaster with a message of comfort and hope. Called by many the "Book of Consolation," this section points beyond the return from exile to the fulfillment of God's promise to Israel in the Millennium.

The promise of a literal return of both Israel and Judah (30:3) has been spiritualized by some commentators transferring it to the church. This does injustice to the natural meaning of the text. Jeremiah says that Israel and Judah will possess the land (v. 3). In the days after the Captivity, however, the land was not possessed. There were only a few Jews from the Northern tribes who returned with the remnant of Judah. Since Revelation 7 speaks of 12,000 from each tribe, the return from Babylonian Captivity cannot be the complete fulfillment of this prophecy.

Jeremiah predicts that "Jacob shall return, and shall be in rest" (Jer. 30:10). From the return under Zerubbabel to the destruction of Jerusalem in A.D. 70 (even unto this day), Israel has seen nothing but conflict, warfare, and unrest. The fulfillment of these prophecies awaits the future millennial kingdom.

The Old Testament frequently speaks of God's covenant with Israel (Ex. 19:3-8; 24:3-8; Deut. 29:1-29). Since Israel, however, had broken that covenant (Jer. 7:21-26; 11:1-13), God must one day make a New Covenant with His people. The New Covenant would be made in the last days (31:31-33); the parties of the covenant would be both Israel and Judah (v. 31); the terms of the covenant would be a knowledge of God and forgiveness of sins (v. 34); the people of the covenant would be preserved (vv. 35-37); and the guarantee of the covenant would be the rebuilding of Jerusalem (vv. 38-40). The Lord Jesus Christ instituted the New Covenant by His vicarious atonement (Heb. 7:22; 8:7-13; 10:15-22). Though some features of this covenant have been fulfilled in the church, Jeremiah 31:31 states that the ultimate fulfillment of the New Covenant will be with Israel and Judah.

Preview

The Prophet and His Pain

BOOK OF JEREMIAH

"From henceforth let no man trouble me, for I bear in my body the marks of the Lord Jesus." Thus did the Apostle Paul once write (Gal. 6:17).

In matters of pain and persecution, Jeremiah the prophet may be considered the Paul of the Old Testament. Perhaps no other pre-Calvary prophet suffered as much for God as did Jeremiah. The truth is, in many ways his sufferings foreshadowed the sufferings of the Saviour. Consider: both Jeremiah and Jesus were mistreated by their own families (Jer. 12:6; John 7:3-5); both were hated by the religious world (Jer. 26:7-8; John 11:47-53); both were plotted against by the citizens of their own hometowns (Jer. 11:21; Luke 4:28-30); both were denounced by the synagogue leaders of their day (Jer. 20:1-2; John 18:13, 24); both wept over the city of Jerusalem (Jer. 9:1; Luke 19:41); both were accused falsely and beaten (Jer. 37:12-15; Matt. 26:61; 27:26).

Were Jeremiah's sufferings because of his stand for God worth it? They were indeed. Surely his conclusion would have been that of Paul's along this line: *"For I reckon that the sufferings of this present time are not worthy to be compared with the glory which shall be revealed in us" (Rom. 8:18).*

Overview

<table>
<tr><td>SCRIPTURE</td><td colspan="6">Book of Jeremiah</td></tr>
<tr><td>SUBJECT</td><td colspan="6">The sufferings of Jeremiah</td></tr>
<tr><td rowspan="9">SPECIFICS</td><td rowspan="9">The source of his suffering</td><td rowspan="4">His family</td><td rowspan="4">His home-town</td><td rowspan="9">The nature of his suffering</td><td>Reviled and ridiculed</td></tr>
<tr><td>Rejected</td></tr>
<tr><td>Threatened</td></tr>
<tr><td>Plotted against</td></tr>
<tr><td rowspan="5">The religious world</td><td rowspan="5">The political world</td><td>Falsely accused</td></tr>
<tr><td>Flogged</td></tr>
<tr><td>Put in stocks</td></tr>
<tr><td>Thrown down empty cistern</td></tr>
<tr><td>Had his scroll burned</td></tr>
<tr><td>SAINTS AND SINNERS</td><td colspan="6">Jeremiah, Hananiah, Irijah, Pashur</td></tr>
<tr><td rowspan="2">SENTENCE SUMMARIES</td><td>O.T. Verse</td><td colspan="5">"I am the man that hath seen affliction by the rod of His wrath" (Lam. 3:1).</td></tr>
<tr><td>N.T. Verse</td><td colspan="5">"Blessed are they which are persecuted for righteousness' sake; for theirs is the kingdom of heaven" (Matt. 5:10).</td></tr>
</table>

HE SUFFERINGS OF JEREMIAH

HE WAS PERSECUTED BY HIS OWN FAMILY

HE WAS PLOTTED AGAINST BY THE PEOPLE OF HIS HOMETOWN

HE WAS REJECTED AND REVILED BY HIS PEERS IN THE RELIGIOUS WORLD

Pashhur, the chief temple priest, had him whipped and put in stocks.

He was almost murdered by a wild mob of priests and prophets after one of his messages. He preached a sermon at the temple gate and was nearly killed by an angry mob for predicting the temple would be destroyed. He was defended by some of Judah's wise old men who reminded the angry mob that Jeremiah's message was like that of the Prophet Micah. See Jeremiah 26:1-19.

Jeremiah was accused of lying by a false prophet named Hananiah who had predicted the Babylonian Captivity would only last for two years and that those already in exile (such as King Jehoiachin, Daniel, Ezekiel, etc.) would be returned along with all the temple treasury which had been taken. To dramatize his accusation, Hananiah broke the yoke worn by Jeremiah. Jeremiah predicted Hananiah's death in the near future by God's hand for his lying ministry. Within two years, he was dead.

HE WAS THREATENED BY KING JEHOIAKIM

HE WAS ARRESTED, FLOGGED, AND ACCUSED OF TREASON

Jeremiah attempted to visit the land of Benjamin on one occasion to inspect some property he had bought. However, a guard named Irijah arrested him at the city gate and accused him of defecting to the Babylonians. Jeremiah denied this, but was flogged and thrown into prison. He was soon secretly sent for by Zedekiah the king. Zedekiah placed him in the prison palace instead of returning him to the dungeon he was formerly in.

HE WAS CAST DOWN INTO AN EMPTY BUT FILTHY CISTERN

In the palace, however, pressure from the religious officials who despised Jeremiah eventually forced Zedekiah to return the prophet to a more crude confinement. This time he was lowered by ropes into an empty cistern in the prison yard where he soon sank down into a thick layer of mire at the bottom. Eventually, an Ethiopian friend, Ebed-melech, persuaded Zedekiah to remove him from this filthy place. It took 30 men to haul him from the cistern. He was returned to the prison palace. Jeremiah again predicted the fall of Jerusalem. He remained in prison until the city was taken.

HE SAW HIS ORIGINAL MANUSCRIPT BURNED BY WICKED KING JEHOIAKIM

He was ordered to have his scribe, Baruch, write down all those oral messages he had been given for the past 23 years. Baruch did this and read them to the people in the temple. He then was invited to read them to the religious officials. When he finished, they were badly frightened and decided King Jehoiakim should also hear them.

An official named Jehudi read them to Jehoiakim as the sullen king sat in front of his fireplace. As Jehudi finished reading three or four columns, Jehoiakim would take his knife, slit off the section of the roll, and throw it into the fire. Finally, the entire scroll was destroyed. Jeremiah was then commanded to rewrite the burned sections plus a good deal of additional material, including these fearful words about Jehoiakim.

"Therefore thus saith the LORD of Jehoiakim king of Judah: 'He shall have none to sit upon the throne of David, and his dead body shall be cast out in the day to the heat, and in the night to the frost. And I will punish him and his seed and his servants for their iniquity; and I will bring upon them, and upon the inhabitants of Jerusalem, and upon the men of Judah, all the evil that I pronounced against them; but they hearkened not.'

"Then took Jeremiah another roll, and gave it to Baruch the scribe, the son of Neriah; who wrote therein from the mouth of Jeremiah all the words of the book which Jehoiakim king of Judah had burned in the fire: and there were added besides unto them many like words" (36:30-32).

After Jehoiakim had burned the scroll, Baruch became despondent. It had probably taken him a year to write the material. God then both warned and encouraged him through Jeremiah.

HE EXPERIENCED FRUSTRATION AND DEPRESSION

Jeremiah had become frustrated over his inability to call Judah: *"Then I said, 'I will not make mention of Him, nor speak any more in His name.' But His Word was in mine heart as a burning fire shut up in my bones, and I was weary with forbearing, and I could not stay" (20:9).* (See also 1 Kings 19:3-4; Jonah 1:1-3; 1 Cor. 9:16.)

At this time he uttered one of the most despondent prayers in all the Bible: *"Cursed be the day wherein I was born. Let not the day wherein my mother bare me be blessed. Cursed be the man who brought tidings to my father saying, 'A man child is born unto thee'; making him very glad. And let that man be as the cities which the LORD overthrew, and repented not; and let him hear the cry in the morning, and the shouting at noontide. Because He slew me not from the womb; or that my mother might have been my grave, and her womb to be always great with me. Wherefore came I forth out of the womb to see labor and sorrow, that my days should be consumed with shame?" (Jer. 20:14-18)*

CLASSIC PASSAGES IN JEREMIAH

1. *"They have healed also the hurt of the daughter of My people slightly, saying, 'Peace, peace'; when there is no peace"* (6:14).

2. *" 'Is this house, which is called by My name, become a den of robbers in your eyes? Behold, even I have seen it,' saith the LORD"* (7:11).

3. *"The harvest is past, the summer is ended, and we are not saved. . . . Is there no balm in Gilead; is there no physician there? Why then is not the health of the daughter of My people recovered?"* (8:20, 22)

4. *" 'Who would not fear Thee, O King of nations? For to Thee doth it appertain; forasmuch as among all the wise men of the nations, and in all their kingdoms, there is none like unto Thee.' . . . He hath made the earth by His power, He hath established the world by His wisdom, and hath stretched out the heavens by His discretion"* (10:7, 12).

5. *"But I was like a lamb or an ox that is brought to the slaughter; and I knew not that they had devised devices against me, saying, 'Let us destroy the tree with the fruit thereof, and let us cut him off from the land of the living, that his name may be no more remembered' "* (11:19).

6. *"Can the Ethiopian change his skin, or the leopard his spots? Then may ye also do good, that are accustomed to do evil"* (13:23).

7. *"Then said the LORD unto me, 'Though Moses and Samuel stood before Me, yet My mind could not be toward this people. Cast them out of My sight, and let them go forth.' . . . Thy Words were found, and I did eat them; and Thy Word was unto me the joy and rejoicing of mine heart: for I am called by Thy name, O LORD God of hosts"* (15:1, 16).

8. *" 'Therefore, behold, the days come,' saith the LORD, 'that it shall no more be said, "The LORD liveth, that brought up the Children of Israel out of the land of Egypt"; but, "The LORD liveth, that brought up the Children of Israel from the land of the north, and from all the lands whither He had driven them"; and I will bring them again into their land that I gave unto their fathers' "* (16:14-15).

9. *"Thus saith the LORD: 'Cursed be the man that trusteth in man, and maketh flesh his arm, and whose heart departeth from the LORD. For he shall be like the heath in the desert, and shall not see when good cometh; but shall inhabit the parched places in the wilderness, in a salt land and not inhabited.*

" 'Blessed is the man that trusteth in the LORD, and whose hope the LORD is. For he shall be as a tree planted by the waters, and that spreadeth out her roots by the river, and shall not see when heat cometh, but her leaf shall be green; and shall not be careful in the year of drought, neither shall cease from yielding fruit. The heart is deceitful above all things, and desperately wicked, who can know it? I the LORD search the heart, I try the reins, even to give every man according to his ways, and according to the fruit of his doings' " (17:5-10).

10. *"The word which came to Jeremiah from the LORD saying, 'Arise and go down to the potter's house, and there I will cause thee to hear My words.' Then I went down to the potter's house, and, behold, he wrought a work on the wheels. And the vessel that he made of clay was marred in the hand of the potter, so he made it again another vessel, as seemed good to the potter to make it.*

"Then the word of the LORD came to me saying, 'O house of Israel, cannot I do with you as this potter?' saith the LORD. 'Behold, as the clay is in the potter's hand, so are ye in Mine hand, O house of Israel' " (18:1-6).

11. *"O LORD, Thou hast deceived me, and I was deceived. Thou art stronger than I, and hast prevailed. I am in derision daily, everyone mocketh me. For since I spake, I cried out, I cried violence and spoil; because the Word of the LORD was made a reproach unto me, and a derision daily. Then I said, 'I will not make mention of Him, nor speak anymore in His name.' But His Word was in mine heart as a burning fire shut up in my bones, and I was weary with forbearing, and I could not stay"* (20:7-9).

12. *"Sing unto the LORD, praise ye the LORD, for He hath delivered the soul of the poor from the hand of evildoers. Cursed be the day wherein I was born; let not the day wherein my mother bare me be blessed. Cursed be the man who brought tidings to my father, saying, 'A man child is born unto thee'; making him very glad"* (vv. 13-15).

13. *"And unto this people thou shalt say, 'Thus saith the LORD; "Behold, I set before you the way of life, and the way of death" ' "* (21:8).

14. *" 'Is not My word like as a fire?' saith the LORD; 'and like a hammer that breaketh the rock*

in pieces?' " (23:29)

15. *" 'For I know the thoughts that I think toward you,' saith the LORD, 'thoughts of peace, and not of evil, to give you an expected end. Then shall ye call upon Me, and ye shall go and pray unto Me, and I will hearken unto you. And ye shall seek Me, and find Me, when ye shall search for Me with all your heart. And I will be found of you,' saith the LORD, 'and I will turn away your captivity, and I will gather you from all the nations, and from all the places whither I have driven you,' saith the LORD; 'and I will bring you again into the place whence I caused you to be carried away captive' " (29:11-14).*

16. *"Alas! For that day is great, so that none is like it; it is even the time of Jacob's trouble; but he shall be saved out of it" (30:7).*

17. *"The LORD hath appeared of old unto me, saying, 'Yea, I have loved thee with an everlasting love; therefore with loving-kindness have I drawn thee. . . . Behold, I will bring them from the north country, and gather them from the coasts of the earth, and with them the blind and the lame, the woman with child and her that travaileth with child together; a great company shall return thither. They shall come with weeping, and with supplications will I lead them; I will cause them to walk by the rivers of waters in a straight way, wherein they shall not stumble; for I am a father to Israel, and Ephraim is My firstborn.' . . .*

"Thus saith the LORD: 'A voice was heard in Ramah, lamentation, and bitter weeping; Rachel weeping for her children refused to be comforted for her children, because they were not.' . . .

" 'How long wilt thou go about, O thou backsliding daughter? For the LORD hath created a new thing in the earth, a woman shall compass a man' " (31:3, 8-9, 15, 22).

18. *"Ah Lord God! Behold, Thou hast made the heaven and the earth by Thy great power and stretched out arm, and there is nothing too hard for Thee. . . . Behold, I am the LORD, the God of all flesh, is there anything too hard for Me?" (32:17, 27)*

19. *"Call unto Me, and I will answer thee, and show thee great and mighty things, which thou knowest not. . . . As the host of heaven cannot be numbered, neither the sand of the sea measured, so will I multiply the seed of David My servant, and the Levites that minister unto Me" (33:3, 22).*

20. *"But fear not thou, O My servant Jacob, and be not dismayed, O Israel. For, behold, I will save thee from afar off, and thy seed from the land of their captivity; and Jacob shall return, and be in rest and at ease, and none shall make him afraid" (46:27).*

21. *"O thou sword of the Lord, how long will it be ere thou be quiet? Put up thyself into thy scabbard, rest, and be still" (47:6).*

22. *" 'In those days, and in that time,' saith the LORD, 'the Children of Israel shall come, they and the Children of Judah together, going and weeping; they shall go, and seek the LORD their God. They shall ask the way to Zion with their faces thitherward, saying, "Come, and let us join ourselves to the LORD in a perpetual covenant that shall not be forgotten." My people hath been lost sheep; their shepherds have caused them to go astray, they have turned them away on the mountains; they have gone from mountain to hill, they have forgotten their resting place' " (50:4-6).*

The Weeping Prophet

COMMENTS

Jeremiah was called by God to the prophetic office during the darkest days of Old Testament history. Since his primary message was that of judgment, he was rejected by the many and received by the few. Because of his immense sorrows over the sinful people of God, he has been called "the weeping prophet."

Like many great men, Jeremiah was despised in life, but applauded in death. He was rejected by family (12:6), friends (11:21), and rulers (20:1-3; 26:7-9; 37:11-16; 38). He suffered more than perhaps any other prophet in the Old Testament.

Pashur, the chief of the temple police, arrested Jeremiah after his message on the "Sign of the Potter" (19:14–20:18). Harassment now turned to physical abuse. Jeremiah was beaten with 40 stripes. In Paul's day, the number of stripes was reduced for fear of exceeding the legal limits of the law (Deut. 25:3; cf. 2 Cor. 11:24). Jeremiah was then placed in the "stocks," a scaffold affair which held the prisoner's hands and legs in a contorted position causing great pain (cf. Jer. 29:26; Acts 16:24). The "chief governor" (Jer. 20:1) was the chief officer of the temple in charge of security.

The reaction to Jeremiah's temple sermon was so great that he was nearly killed by a wild mob of priests and false prophets (26:1-24). Arrested and falsely accused, Jeremiah was finally acquitted by the testimony of Ahikam and some of the other wise court officials. The king's wrath was not yet appeased. He, therefore, vented his anger against a lesser adversary, the Prophet Urijah, who had fled to Egypt for protection. Urijah was arrested by Elnathan, returned to Jerusalem, and executed by King Jehoiakim.

When Babylon lifted the siege of Jerusalem for a short time, Jeremiah took advantage of the reprieve to visit Anathoth, his hometown. He was falsely accused of treason by Irijah, one of the sentinels, and placed in prison (37:11–38:13).

While in prison King Zedekiah secretly (for fear of the princes) inquired of Jeremiah if there was any further word from the Lord. Again, the reply was one of inevitable judgment. Jeremiah, however, was moved from the dungeon (37:15) prison to the more accommodating palace prison. Not long afterward, however, Jeremiah was thrown into the dungeon of Malchiah (38:6). This was one of the cisterns so common in the ancient Near East, where water was collected during the rainy season to be used during the long dry summer (cf. 2 Kings 18:31; Prov. 5:15). There was no water in this cistern, however, and Jeremiah would have suffocated in the mud except for the intervention of an Ethiopian, Ebed-melech.

Jeremiah's persecution was not only physical but also mental. Both message and messenger had been rejected and persecuted. The most poignant example of the rejection of Jeremiah's message came during the fourth year of King Jehoiakim's reign (Jer. 36:1-32). God had commanded Jeremiah to write down his prophecies. Once completed, Baruch, Jeremiah's secretary, read the scroll to the people at the temple. The princes then read the scroll to the king, who violently reacted to the prophecy by cutting each column and burning it in the fire. The "winterhouse" (v. 22) was the winterized portion of the palace. In the typical two-story Palestinian house, the ground floor was used during the winter, while the second floor with its superior ventilation was used during the long hot summers. The "penknife" (v. 23) was the typical knife scribes used for sharpening reed pens and trimming the scrolls. Jeremiah's prophecy had been rejected, but God told him to compile a new scroll with additional prophecies.

The sufferings of Jeremiah brought on depression. The Word of God, however, was his comfort and strength. He could not remain silent. He had to declare the Word of the Lord (20:7-9).

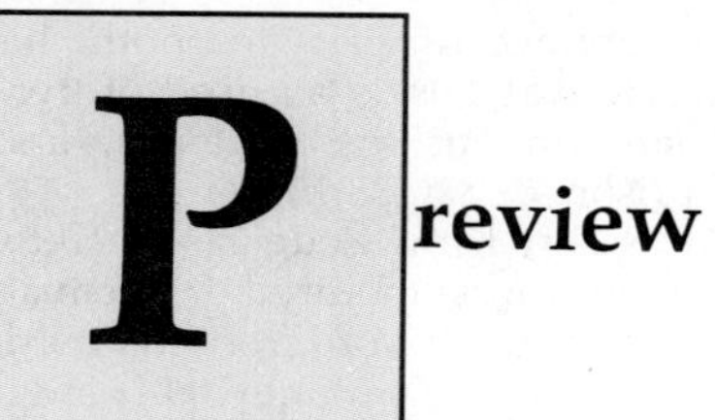

O Little Town of Bethlehem

BOOK OF MICAH

What on earth did the king want? It had to be important for all the city's religious community had hurriedly gathered at his command. Did it have anything to do with that visiting delegation assembled right outside the royal throne room? They could not say. Whatever the reason, those called immediately dropped everything and rushed over. One simply did not keep this particular ruler waiting. Soon the powerful and cruel monarch made his appearance. Ignoring all introductory formalities, he thundered out: "Where is this particular Baby to be born?"

The religious leaders sat there for a moment, utterly stunned. This was absolutely the last thing they had expected. Quickly recovering, however, they weakly responded: "In Bethlehem of Judea; for thus it is written by the prophet."

Who today is not familiar with this famous historical event, recorded in Matthew 2? The city was Jerusalem, the time 4 B.C., the religious community, the Jewish priests; the visitors, the magi; the king, Herod the Great; and the Babe, the Lord Jesus Christ! But which prophet did the priests and scribes quote to Herod on that historic day some 20 centuries back? His name was Micah and the words quoted to the king are found in chapter 5, verse 2 of his book. Isaiah had predicted both *how* and *why* the Messiah would be born (Isa. 7; 9). Daniel had hinted concerning *when* He would be born (Dan. 9). But it was left to Micah to tell us just *where* He would be born.

Overview

<table>
<tr><td>SCRIPTURE</td><td colspan="7">Book of Micah</td></tr>
<tr><td>SUBJECT</td><td colspan="7">Ministry of Micah</td></tr>
<tr><td rowspan="5">SPECIFICS</td><td colspan="3">Micah and Israel</td><td colspan="2">Micah and himself</td><td colspan="2">Micah and God</td></tr>
<tr><td rowspan="3">Sermons on sin</td><td>Pleading</td><td>For the repentance of Israel</td><td rowspan="3">A personal analogy</td><td rowspan="3">In attempting to find righteousness, he was like a frustrated fruit-picker in a barren land</td><td rowspan="3">Deciding and Describing</td><td>The prophet's decision for God</td></tr>
<tr><td>Pronouncing</td><td>The retribution on Israel</td><td rowspan="2">The prophet's description of God</td></tr>
<tr><td>Predicting</td><td>The restoration of Israel</td></tr>
<tr><td colspan="3">The outward look</td><td colspan="2">The inward look</td><td colspan="2">The upward look</td></tr>
<tr><td>SAINTS AND SINNERS</td><td colspan="7">Micah</td></tr>
<tr><td rowspan="2">SENTENCE SUMMARIES</td><td colspan="3">O.T. Verse</td><td colspan="4">"Unto us a Child is born, unto us a Son is given; and the government shall be upon His shoulder; and His name shall be called Wonderful, Counselor, the Mighty God, the Everlasting Father, the Prince of Peace" (Isa. 9:6).</td></tr>
<tr><td colspan="3">N.T. Verses</td><td colspan="4">"When Herod the king had heard these things, he was troubled, and all Jerusalem with him. And when he had gathered all the chief priests and scribes of the people together, he demanded of them where Christ should be born" (Matt. 2:3-4).</td></tr>
</table>

ICAH

THE OUTWARD LOOK: MICAH'S PUBLIC SERMONS

Three sermons proclaiming retribution on Israel (Micah 1–3). *First sermon: God Himself would soon respond in judgment because of the sins found in Samaria and Jerusalem. Samaria would be utterly destroyed. The sin of the city was terminal. The very foundations of its buildings would be exposed. The idols of Samaria would be thrown into the surrounding valleys. The enemy would come up to the very gates of Jerusalem.

*Second sermon: God condemned those who lie awake at night, plotting wickedness, and rise at dawn to perform them. Their punishment will only end when the Messiah (the Breaker and King of 2:13) leads them out of exile through the gates of their cities of captivity, back to their own land. God will then regather Israel.

"I will surely assemble, O Jacob, all of thee; I will surely gather the remnant of Israel; I will put them together as the sheep of Bozrah, as the flock in the midst of their fold. They shall make great noise by reason of the multitude of men" (v. 12).

*Third sermon: Israel's leaders were especially rebuked by God. They were supposed to know right from wrong, but were themselves the vilest sinners of all.

The shepherds had become the butchers of God's flock. The prophets had become treacherous liars. The Lord, therefore, would hide His face from both leaders and people.

Micah alone of the prophets, at that time, was *"full of power by the Spirit of the Lord, and of judgment, and of might, to declare unto Jacob his transgression, and to Israel his sin" (3:8).*

Because of those false money-loving prophets, Jerusalem would later be plowed as a field and become a heap of rubble. The very spot on Mount Moriah where the temple stood would be overgrown with brush (v. 12).

Prophesying the restoration of Israel. In spite of her terrible sins, God would someday, after her punishment had been consummated, restore her to Palestine.

The chronology leading to this restoration. Judah must first suffer the 70-year Babylonian Captivity.

"Be in pain and labor to bring forth, O daughter of Zion, like a woman in travail; for now shalt thou go forth out of the city, and thou shalt dwell in the field, and thou shalt go even to Babylon; there shalt thou be delivered; there the Lord shall redeem thee from the hand of thine enemies" (4:10).

This was a remarkable passage indeed, for at the time Micah wrote, Babylon was anything but a world power. Assyria was the strong nation then.

Judah's Messiah would be born in Bethlehem.

"But thou, Bethlehem Ephratah, though thou be little among the thousands of Judah, yet out of thee shall He come forth unto Me that is to be ruler in Israel; whose goings forth have been from of old, from everlasting" (5:2).

God would set them aside as a nation until their spiritual rebirth during the Tribulation.

"Therefore will He give them up, until the time that she which travaileth hath brought forth; then the remnant of his brethren shall return unto the Children of Israel" (v. 3).

The nations would gather together against Israel at Armageddon.

"Now also many nations are gathered against thee, that say, 'Let her be defiled, and let our eye look upon Zion' " (4:11).

These nations would be utterly destroyed.

"And I will execute vengeance in anger and fury upon the heathen, such as they have not heard" (5:15).

The final results of this restoration. "But in the last days it shall come to pass, that the mountain of the house of the Lord shall be established in the top of the mountains, and it shall be exalted above the hills; and people shall flow unto it. And many nations shall come, and say, 'Come, and let us go up to the mountain of the Lord, and to the house of the God of Jacob; and He will teach us of His ways, and we will walk in His paths'; For the Law shall go forth of Zion, and the Word of the Lord from Jerusalem.

"And He shall judge among many people, and rebuke strong nations afar off; and they shall beat their swords into plowshares, and their spears

into pruning hooks. Nation shall not lift up a sword against nation, neither shall they learn war anymore. But they shall sit every man under his vine and under his fig tree; and none shall make them afraid; for the mouth of the LORD of hosts hath spoken it" (4:1-4).

PLEADING FOR THE REPENTANCE OF ISRAEL

What God had done for Israel. He brought them out of Egypt; He showed them the right way. *"He hath showed thee, O man, what is good; and what doth the LORD require of thee, but to do justly, and to love mercy, and to walk humbly with thy God?" (Micah 6:8)*

What Israel was doing against God. They were walking in the evil ways of Ahab.

What God would do to Israel. "Thou shalt eat, but not be satisfied. . . . Thou shalt sow, but thou shalt not reap" (vv. 14-15).

THE INWARD LOOK: MICAH'S PERSONAL CONTEMPLATIONS

"Woe is me! For I am as when they have gathered the summer fruits, as the grape gleanings of the vintage; there is no cluster to eat, my soul desired the first ripe fruit" (7:1).

THE COLLAPSE OF THE JUDICIAL SYSTEM

THE COLLAPSE OF FRIENDSHIP

"Trust ye not in a friend, put ye not confidence in a guide" (v. 5).

THE COLLAPSE OF THE FAMILY UNIT

"Keep the doors of thy mouth from her that lieth in thy bosom" (v. 5).

"For the son dishonoreth the father, the daughter riseth up against her mother, the daughter-in-law against her mother-in-law; a man's enemies are the men of his own house" (v. 6).

THE UPWARD LOOK: MICAH'S PRAYERFUL PETITIONS

HIS DECISION FOR GOD

He would wait for the future salvation of the Lord. "Therefore I will look unto the LORD; I will wait for the God of my salvation: my God will hear me" (v. 7).

He would endure the present indignation from the Lord. "I will bear the indignation of the LORD, because I have sinned against Him, until He plead my cause, and execute judgment for me. He will bring me forth to the light, and I shall behold His righteousness" (v. 9).

HIS DESCRIPTION OF GOD

"Who is a God like unto Thee, that pardoneth iniquity, and passeth by the transgression of the remnant of His heritage? He retaineth not His anger forever, because He delighteth in mercy. He will turn again, He will have compassion upon us; He will subdue our iniquities; and thou wilt cast all their sins into the depths of the sea. Thou wilt perform the truth to Jacob, and the mercy to Abraham, which Thou hast sworn unto our fathers from the days of old" (vv. 18-20).

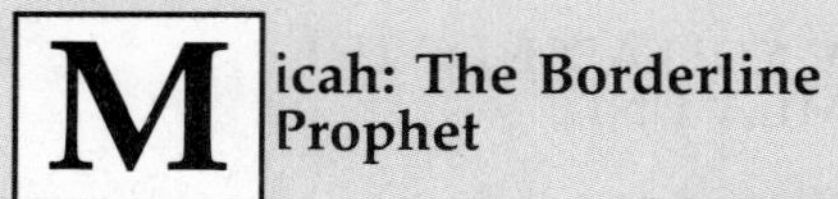

Micah: The Borderline Prophet

COMMENTS

Micah called himself "Micah the Morasthite" (1:1) because he was a native of Moresheth-gath in northern Judah. He was a borderline preacher because he ministered for nearly 50 years to the towns on the border between southern Israel and northern Judah. His name means "Who is like Jehovah?" He played on the meaning of his name in 7:18 as he asked, "Who is a God like unto Thee, that pardoneth iniquity, and passeth by the transgression?"

Along with Hosea and Amos, Micah was a contemporary of Isaiah, the prince of prophets, who had been prophesying some 17 or 18 years before Micah began his ministry. Though Amos had passed off the scene, Micah and Hosea, together with Isaiah, lived to see the immediate fulfillment of Isaiah 7:14 as Syria was obliterated and replaced by Assyria and Israel was taken captive by Assyria.

It is to be expected that prophets who ministered together would have some things in common, but Micah and Isaiah are noted more for their contrasts than their likenesses. Micah was virtually an obscure prophet while Isaiah was the most prominent. Micah was a country preacher, while Isaiah was a prophet of the city and the court. Micah ministered mostly to poor people and always ministered in their behalf. Isaiah ministered mainly to the leaders of the people. Micah ministered on the border area of southern Israel and northern Judah. Isaiah ministered mainly in Jerusalem. Micah is more like Isaiah when it comes to his writing ministry. Micah probably wrote his prophecy from Jerusalem. While his prophecy is severe in much of its tone, it does contain much of Isaiah's poetic beauty. Some have called it "Isaiah in shorthand."

The outstanding single prophecy of Micah concerns the birth of the Messiah in Bethlehem (5:2). This amazing prophecy not only foretold Messiah's birth but also His millennial reign over the nation in which He will (1) establish peace (v. 5); (2) deliver the nation from its enemies (v. 6); (3) empower His people to be victorious over their enemies (vv. 7-9); (4) destroy the weapons of warfare so that there will be no more warfare (v. 10); (5) destroy all military fortifications (v. 11); (6) destroy all witchcraft and idolatry (vv. 12-14); and (7) destroy all the sinful nations (v. 15). This prophecy, together with all the other millennial prophecies of Micah, provide proof of the correctness of the premillennial approach to the Scripture, for the things prophesied in Israel's restoration were not realized in the days following the Babylonian Captivity. This leaves the Bible student with two options. Either God will not specifically keep His promises or else there must yet be a time coming in which everything that He has promised and prophesied will be fulfilled exactly as He promised it. If the prophecies of Micah (and all the other prophets) are not dependable then the promises of everlasting life in the New Testament are not reliable either. The premillennial approach to prophecy provides the only acceptable answer and the proper framework for understanding Micah's (and all the other prophets') glorious promises concerning Israel's future restoration and the millennial reign of Messiah over His redeemed people.

God used Micah's ministry to face His people with their sins and to prepare them for His judgment which must fall. In delivering his message of judgment, Micah made use of a technique that every minister of God would do well to emulate. He completed each of his discourses with a word about their ultimate restoration. He never left his people without hope for the future. Though His people have sinned, God is in control and will sovereignly restore His people and will send His Messiah to reign over them. The future for Israel and Judah is as bright as the promises of God given through Micah, His borderline prophet.

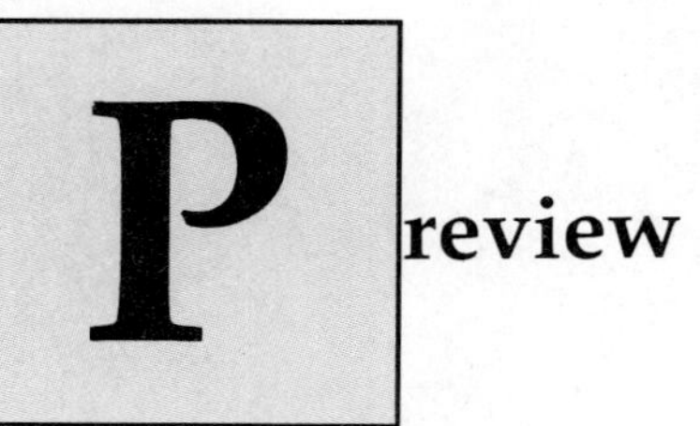

Memo to Nineveh: No More Mercy!

BOOK OF NAHUM

What a staggering change had taken place in this city, and all of it for the worse. Jonah the prophet would have been the first to notice. A great and glorious revival was going on when he last viewed the city from a nearby hill. In fact, the king himself had publicly repented, covered himself with sackcloth, and then sat down amidst ashes. His decree and testimony had been felt areawide, causing thousands to turn to God. And in great mercy the Lord had spared that wicked Gentile city of Nineveh!

But 150 years had come and gone since Jonah's preaching crusade. Its high and massive walls overflowed with bloodshed, dishonesty, witchcraft, immorality, pride, and materialism. But most tragic of all, unlike the generation Jonah preached to, there was now absolutely no desire to abandon sin and ask God for forgiveness. Thus, to Nahum the prophet was given the unpleasant task of pronouncing swift and terrible divine judgment on this great city, located on the banks of the Tigris River. In fact, this very river, as used by God, would play a vital role in the total destruction of Nineveh. Having rejected God's streams of mercy, the wicked citizens would now suffer His waters of judgment.

Overview

<table>
<tr><td>SCRIPTURE</td><td colspan="4">Book of Nahum</td></tr>
<tr><td>SUBJECT</td><td colspan="4">Ministry of Nahum</td></tr>
<tr><td rowspan="4">SPECIFICS</td><td colspan="4">The destruction of Nineveh</td></tr>
<tr><td>The why</td><td>The how</td><td colspan="2">The who</td></tr>
<tr><td>To protect Judah</td><td>The overflowing of the Tigris waters</td><td rowspan="2">God Himself</td><td>His patience was over</td></tr>
<tr><td>To punish Nineveh for its haughty heart and its bloody hands</td><td>The onslaught of the Babylonian warriors</td><td>His plagues would begin</td></tr>
<tr><td>SAINTS AND SINNERS</td><td colspan="4">Nahum</td></tr>
<tr><td rowspan="2">SENTENCE SUMMARIES</td><td>O.T. Verse</td><td colspan="3">"Except the LORD build the house, they labor in vain that build it; except the LORD keep the city, the watchman waketh but in vain" (Ps. 127:1).</td></tr>
<tr><td>N.T. Verse</td><td colspan="3">"Therefore shall her plagues come in one day: death, and mourning, and famine; and she shall be utterly burned with fire; for strong is the Lord God who judgeth her" (Rev. 18:8).</td></tr>
</table>

NAHUM

THE PATIENCE OF GOD

For over 500 years Nineveh and the Assyrians were feared as the terror of western Asia. But while God's patience is infinite in depth, it is not eternal in duration. The time for judgment would soon come.

"There is no healing of thy bruise, thy wound is grievous" (Nahum 3:19).

THE PRIDE OF SENNACHERIB

"There is one come out of thee, that imagineth evil against the LORD, a wicked counselor" (1:11).

It is generally agreed that the wicked counselor here was Sennacherib, the evil Assyrian king, who invaded Judah and surrounded Jerusalem in 701 B.C.

Though Sennacherib's armies had been smashed at Jerusalem's gates and the monarch himself murdered years before (see 2 Kings 19:35-37), the arrogant ruler seemed to symbolize the pride of Nineveh, and his name was therefore used here.

Sennacherib had made Nineveh a truly magnificent city, laying out its streets and squares, and built within a famous "palace without rival." The dimensions of this palace were fantastic, 600 by 630 feet. It comprised at least 80 rooms, many of which were lined with sculpture.

THE PROMISE TO JUDAH

"Behold upon the mountains the feet of him that bringeth good tidings, that publisheth peace! O Judah, keep thy solemn feasts, perform thy vows; for the wicked shall no more pass through thee; he is utterly cut off" (Nahum 1:15).

Judah would no longer need to fear this cruel nation.

THE PUNISHMENT OF NINEVEH

The certainty of this terrible punishment. Nahum compared Nineveh to Thebes (No-amon, see 3:8), that great capital of upper Egypt. It too boasted that no power on earth could subdue it. However, both Isaiah and Ezekiel predicted its destruction, which was fulfilled later by Sargon of Assyria in his campaign against Egypt. Now Nineveh's hour had come.

The sins causing this terrible punishment. Nineveh's sins included bloodshedding, dishonesty, witchcraft and immorality, and pride and materialism.

The description of this terrible punishment. The city would be emptied of its wealth. Her chariots were burned and she would be ridiculed by her enemies. Her warriors would be slain and the corpses heaped up in piles. The very location of the city would be forgotten.

The source of this terrible punishment—God Himself. "The LORD will take vengeance on His adversaries" (1:2).

" 'Behold, I am against thee,' saith the LORD of hosts" (2:13; 3:5).

God used two sources to accomplish His punishment on Assyria: the flooding of the Tigris River, and the allied forces of the Medes and Babylonians.

Nahum: the Prophet with a Magnificent Obsession

COMMENTS

Under Jonah's ministry some 100 to 150 years before Nahum, the Assyrian threat had been nullified by the mass conversion of the king and people. The generation of Assyria in Nahum's day reverted to the idolatrous ways of their ancestors before Jonah. Under Sennacherib they invaded Judah and laid siege to Jerusalem. It was only by God's supernatural intervention that the Assyrian threat was neutralized (cf. 2 Kings 19:35-36; 2 Chron. 32:21) or Judah would have suffered Israel's fate.

The prophecy of Nahum is dominated by a single subject: the doom of Nineveh, the capital of Assyria. Nahum's mission was particularly crucial in God's economy to comfort Judah. He pronounced God's judgment against Assyria assuring Judah that the day was coming when Assyria would no longer constitute a threat to their existence.

Nothing is known of Nahum beyond what can be gleaned about him in his prophecy. He identified himself simply as "Nahum the Elkoshite" (Nahum 1:1). Where Elkosh was located is not known. It is possible, though modern Jews don't put much stock in it, that it was renamed Capernaum (which literally means, "village of Nahum") in honor of its most famous citizen of the day. If that be the case, Nahum was born in Galilee. In the days of Israel's defection he, together with a large godly remnant, moved to Judah. In Jerusalem, so recently having experienced near-destruction under Sennacherib, king of Assyria, he responded to God's call to minister in behalf of Judah against Assyria.

In delivering his prophecy, Nahum wrote lyric poetry of the highest quality. Its poetic beauty stands in stark contrast to its severe tone, the most severe of any of the minor prophets. When God speaks harshly, He does so in beautiful language and style. Nahum reverses the normal prophetic order by beginning with a bright picture (cf. 1:7, 15) and ending with his magnificent obsession—the destruction of Nineveh/Assyria. So occupied was Nahum with his theme that he mentioned nothing of the sins of Israel or Judah, nothing of their coming judgment, and nothing of Judah's restoration.

Two passages from Nahum's prophecy are worthy of special comment. The first is 1:15, which is quoted by Paul in Romans 10:15. In Paul's day the Good News was the Good News of the Gospel. In Nahum's day the good news was word concerning Nineveh's doom and particularly concerning the death of Sennacherib. It was good news for Judah because their archenemy was dead and they would be able to observe their solemn feasts and perform their vows. The nature of this prophecy is elastic enough to include the lifting of Sennacherib's siege of Jerusalem in the days of Hezekiah (701 B.C.), as well as the good news of Sennacherib's death, and the destruction of Nineveh (612 B.C.), even though those events were 90 years apart.

The second passage is 2:3b-4 which has been thought by many to be a prophecy of the modern automobile. The chariot of the prophet's day was the most advanced and ominous weapon of warfare. To make it more ominous, the Assyrians attached sharp implements to the wheels so that they literally mowed down anyone who ventured too close. The idea of "torches" and "lightnings" may be a reference to the speed with which they moved or, better, the appearance that they had in the sunlight as they advanced with the sun reflecting off of the sharp blades protruding from their rotating wheels. To interpret these chariots as automobiles does violence to the prophecy and to the purpose of the prophet who was showing the ease with which the invading hordes and their military equipment would enter and move throughout Nineveh. The whole picture of Nineveh's destruction is the epitome of Nahum's magnificent obsession.

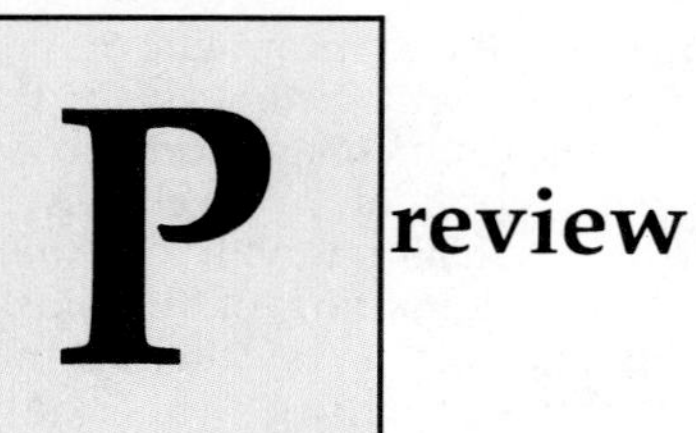

The Chosen City in the Hands of the Heathen

BOOK OF LAMENTATIONS

He sat there all alone, unmoving, and in great soul agony. Hot tears continually ran down his dirt-covered face, falling on the torn clothing he wore. How horrible to witness the burning buildings, including Solomon's temple, and to hear the laughs and curses of enemy soldiers. All this was bad enough. But far worse were the screams of women being ravished, men being killed, and children being led off into distant slavery. Those were the sights and sounds which would haunt him the rest of his days.

For years Jeremiah the prophet had warned Jerusalem of her sinful disease. But in spite of his weeping and warning, the patient had consistently ignored and reviled him. Now she was dead and he was there, attending her funeral. The bitter words of his former prophecy now struck him full force: *"The harvest is past, the summer is ended, and we are not saved"* (Jer. 8:20).

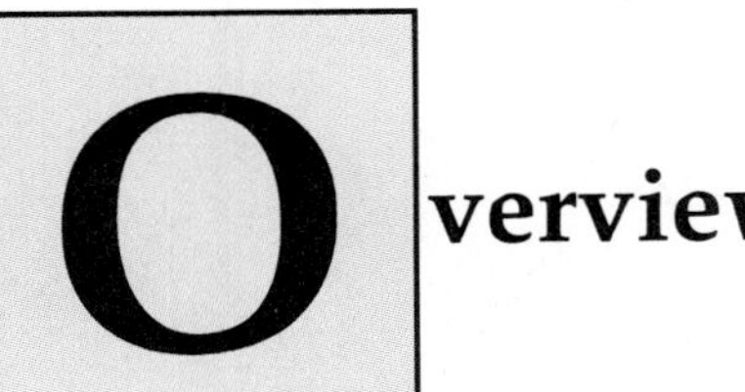

verview

<table>
<tr><td>SCRIPTURE</td><td colspan="4">Book of Lamentations</td></tr>
<tr><td>SUBJECT</td><td colspan="4">The sorrow over Jerusalem's destruction</td></tr>
<tr><td rowspan="3">SPECIFICS</td><td>The reasons for this destruction</td><td colspan="2">The results of this destruction</td><td>The reassurance in this destruction</td></tr>
<tr><td>God's fairness demanded it
The Northern Kingdom had previously been punished</td><td>Jeremiah's sufferings</td><td>From his friends
From his fears
From his flesh (doubt and despair)</td><td rowspan="2">Judah's afflictions would end (because) Jehovah's attributes were endless
1. His mercy
2. His compassion
3. His faithfulness</td></tr>
<tr><td>God's holiness demanded it
The Southern Kingdom had consistently refused to repent</td><td>Judah's sufferings</td><td>Religious—no more temple
Political—no more king
Personal—no more food</td></tr>
<tr><td>SAINTS AND SINNERS</td><td colspan="4">Jeremiah</td></tr>
<tr><td rowspan="2">SENTENCE SUMMARIES</td><td>O.T. Verse</td><td colspan="3">"His anger endureth but a moment; in His favor is life; weeping may endure for a night, but joy cometh in the morning" (Ps. 30:5).</td></tr>
<tr><td>N.T. Verse</td><td colspan="3">"God shall wipe away all tears from their eyes; and there shall be no more death, neither sorrow, nor crying, neither shall there be any more pain; for the former things are passed away" (Rev. 21:4).</td></tr>
</table>

L AMENTATIONS (DESTINATION SOUTHERN KINGDOM)

THE PROVOCATION AGAINST GOD

Around 1000 B.C. David had established his capital in Jerusalem. (See 2 Sam. 6.) Thus, God had blessed this beloved city for nearly 400 years. He had allowed the Northern Kingdom to be carried away by the Assyrians in 722 B.C. But Jerusalem had been spared for another 135 years. All this mercy and long-suffering, however, had been in vain, for Judah continued provoking the Holy One of Israel through constant sinning. The end had now come. Note the following verses of indictment: Lamentations 1:1, 3, 8-9, 17.

THE PUNISHMENT FROM GOD

He had destroyed every home in Judah. Every fortress and wall was broken. He bent His bow of judgment across the land. He allowed His own temple to fall as though it were a booth of leaves and branches in a garden. Judah's enemies were given full freedom to ridicule and destroy her citizens. Her people, old and young alike, choked the streets of Jerusalem with their lifeless bodies.

THE PROPHET OF GOD

The tears of Jeremiah fell like a spring rain over the destruction of Jerusalem and its suffering people.

The affliction of the prophet. All through Lamentations, Jeremiah expressed the agony of his soul. Jeremiah then related the sufferings he endured at the hands of his own countrymen even prior to the Babylonian invasion.

Sufferings caused by his own countrymen. *"Mine enemies chased me sore, like a bird, without cause. They have cut off my life in the dungeon, and cast a stone upon me. Waters flowed over mine head; then I said, 'I am cut off.' I called upon Thy name, O LORD, out of the low dungeon. Thou hast heard my voice: hide not Thine ear at my breathing, at my cry. Thou drewest near in the day that I called upon thee; Thou saidst, 'Fear not' " (3:52-57).*

Sufferings caused by the Babylonians. "Is it nothing to you, all ye that pass by? Behold, and see if there be any sorrow like unto my sorrow, which is done unto me, wherewith the LORD hath afflicted me in the day of His fierce anger. . . . For these things I weep; mine eye, mine eye runneth down with water, because the Comforter that should relieve my soul is far from me: my children are desolate, because the enemy prevailed" (1:12, 16).

"I am the man that hath seen affliction by the rod of His wrath. He hath led me, and brought me into darkness, but not into light. . . . He hath hedged me about, that I cannot get out; He hath made my chain heavy. Also when I cry and shout, He shutteth out my prayer. . . . He was unto me as a bear lying in wait, and as a lion in secret places" (3:1-2, 7-8, 10).

THE ASSURANCE OF THE PROPHET

In the midst of the terrible storm there shone a ray of glorious reassurance.

"This I recall to my mind, therefore have I hope. It is of the LORD's mercies that we are not consumed, because His compassions fail not. They are new every morning; great is Thy faithfulness. 'The LORD is my portion,' saith my soul; therefore will I hope in Him. The LORD is good unto them that wait for Him, to the soul that seeketh Him. It is good that a man should both hope and quietly wait for the salvation of the LORD. . . . for the LORD will not cast off forever; but though He cause grief, yet will He have compassion according to the multitude of His mercies. For He doth not afflict willingly nor grieve the children of men" (vv. 21-26, 31-33).

THE ADVICE OF THE PROPHET

"Let us search and try our ways, and turn again to the LORD. Let us lift up our heart with our hands unto God in the heavens" (vv. 40-41).

Death of the City of God

COMMENTS

In 586 B.C., Jerusalem was destroyed by the Babylonians. This was perhaps the most devastating event in the history of Israel. The fall of Jerusalem meant more than just the destruction of the nation's capital. The temple, where God had chosen to live with His people, was in Jerusalem (Deut. 16:16; Ps. 87). The desecration of the temple meant that God had given His people over to the enemy because of their sin.

The Book of Lamentations is a funeral song on the death of the city of God. Though no author is named in the book, both Jewish (Josephus) and Christian (Jerome) traditions have attributed authorship to Jeremiah. Here the "weeping prophet" mourns the death of the city. As Jeremiah's prophecy looked forward to the destruction of Jerusalem, so his poetry looks back in mourning to that awful event.

Jeremiah's composition consists of five elegies or songs of mourning, corresponding to each chapter. Dirge poetry was common in the ancient Near East. One of the most celebrated elegies of the ancient Near East was the Summerian lament over Ur. With the exception of chapter 5, Lamentations is alphabetical as well as poetical. This national funeral hymn was written as an acrostic in the first four chapters. In chapters 1, 2, and 4, each of the 22 verses begins with a new letter of the Hebrew alphabet, the first, *aleph,* then *beth, gimel,* etc. Chapter 3 uses a triplet acrostic with three verses to each Hebrew letter, making 66 in all. Psalm 119 is another good example of the acrostic in Hebrew poetry. Chapter 5 has 22 verses, but is a prayer and does not use the acrostic. The acrostic form would aid the memory in singing this death song for the city of God.

The Book of Lamentations was probably composed during the interval between the burning of Jerusalem and the departure of the remnant to Egypt (Jer. 39:2; 41:1, 18; 43:7). It is a description of the woes over the ruined city.

The first lament pictures the city as a widow. The city is personified and emphasizes its sorrow. Heathen nations have plundered and desecrated the holiest place—the temple. Judah is pictured as a winepress. The winepress is used in Scripture as a picture of divine judgment (Isa. 63:1-6; Rev. 14:19-20; 19:15).

In the second lament, God speaks. Judgment follows sin. God had not only delivered His people over to the enemy, but He also fought against them. The prophet's anguish of soul is seen in his metaphorical description of "my liver is poured upon the earth" (Lam. 2:11). The Hebrews regarded the liver as the seat of the emotions just as we regard the heart as the seat of the emotions. So terrible was the siege that the Jews resorted to cannibalism, eating their own children (v. 20).

In the third lament, the prophet speaks of the great sorrows of Jerusalem. Though all joy is gone, yet God remains faithful. This is evidenced by the very fact that a remnant is left.

The fourth lament contrasts the happy conditions of former days with the present devastation of the city. The "sons of Zion" had regarded themselves as gold, but now they are broken pieces of pottery (4:2). Jerusalem's sin is even greater than Sodom's sin and thus she will face greater punishment. Again, the prophet refers to the horrible crime of the women boiling and eating their own children (v. 10).

The final lament is a plea for mercy. The cry of the city is for God to regard her in her disgrace. They acknowledge that they have sinned as well as their fathers. One of the aftermaths of war is famine. Now the people have to risk their lives in order to find daily bread. The final prayer is for Jehovah to remember His people forever. Like the Prodigal Son, prodigal Israel will repent and God will restore and establish her forever.

THE PEOPLE OF GOD

The children's tongues stuck to the roofs of their mouths for thirst. The cream of Judah's youth were treated as earthenware pots. The rich and pampered were in the streets begging for bread. The mighty princes, once lean and tan, were now but skin and bones, and their faces black as soot. Tenderhearted women had cooked and eaten their own children. The false prophets and priests were blindly staggering through the streets, covered with blood. The king himself, Zedekiah, had been captured, blinded, and carried off into Captivity.

THE PRAYER TO GOD

That of remembrance. "Remember, O LORD, what is come upon us; consider, and behold our reproach" (5:1).

That of remembrance. "The crown is fallen from our head; woe unto us, that we have sinned!" (v. 16)

That of recognition. "Thou, O LORD, remainest forever, Thy throne from generation to generation" (v. 19).

That of renewal. "Turn Thou us unto thee, O LORD, and we shall be turned; renew our days as of old" (v. 21).

Babylonian Captivity

"If you can't do the time, then don't do the crime!" This seems to be the official in-house proverb among prisoners, used especially to taunt newcomers who often complain bitterly about their "unfair" incarcerations.

The Chaotic Kingdom Stage describes Israel's crime. The Captivity Stage records the time. The righteous Judge, however, does not "throw the book" at His guilty nation by imposing either the death sentence or life plus 99 years! Instead, He graciously limits confinement to 70 years. But then, wonder of wonders, He not only promises to be with His spiritual prisoners during that confinement, but to then fully restore them to their former homeland.

As one considers these facts it becomes evident that the real purpose for the Babylonian Captivity was more to purify than to punish.

A politician and a priest now become God's two chief spokesmen. Daniel and Ezekiel are used to promote, protect, and preserve those taken from Jerusalem to Babylon.

Their two books graphically describe those awesome events transpiring during those 70 years in exile. The time and the crime. As a result of those seven long decades, Israel learned its lesson. Never again would that nation be guilty of the crime of worshiping idols.

Preview

God's Faithfulness in a Foreign Land

DANIEL 1–3

They stood there silently, the three of them, the blaring music pounding in their ears, and in full view of the raging fire. What momentous events had transpired since they entered the political field over three years ago. It seemed the pressure had begun at the very start through an attempt by some state officials to force a secular lifestyle on them. God Himself, however, had rewarded their steadfastness, as clearly revealed on graduation day. The three stood at the top of their class, head and shoulders above all the rest. That was crisis number one.

The second crisis came about through a strange dream experienced by the king, resulting in a death penalty decree on all his political advisers, including these three young men. But once again God stepped in and revealed the secret of the dream to Daniel, their spiritual leader. He in turn explained it to the king who immediately rescinded the death decree.

Their former problems, however, seemed as nothing when compared to the one they now faced. There was nothing complicated about it. A very simple choice. Either bow down and worship a golden image at the sound of the music or be immediately thrown alive into a raging fire. Some choice. Bow down, or burn up. But Shadrach, Meshach, and Abednego displayed not the slightest concern. As the story turned out none was needed. Did they escape the fiery furnace. On the contrary, it was heated sevenfold and they were hurled down into its searing flames. Did they survive the fiery furnace? They not only survived but enjoyed intimate fellowship with a divine Comforter, the Lord Jesus Christ Himself, who actually ministered to them in that hellish heat. As they would later testify, that kind of fellowship was worth all the fires of hell.

Overview

<table>
<tr><td>SCRIPTURE</td><td colspan="6">Daniel 1–3</td></tr>
<tr><td>SUBJECT</td><td colspan="6">The faith and friends of Daniel</td></tr>
<tr><td rowspan="4">SPECIFICS</td><td colspan="4">His faith</td><td colspan="2">His friends</td></tr>
<tr><td rowspan="3">Daniel's political role</td><td>Chapter 1</td><td rowspan="3">Daniel's prophetical role</td><td>Chapter 2</td><td rowspan="2">They wouldn't bow</td><td>Chapter 3</td></tr>
<tr><td rowspan="2">His purpose

His proposal

His promotion</td><td>Nebuchad-nezzar:

The dream
The decree</td><td>The threats of the king

The testimony of the three</td></tr>
<tr><td>Daniel:

The information
The revelation</td><td>They wouldn't burn</td><td>Their safety from the fire

Their Saviour in the fire</td></tr>
<tr><td>SAINTS AND SINNERS</td><td colspan="6">Daniel, Nebuchadnezzar, Shadrach, Meshach, and Abednego</td></tr>
<tr><td rowspan="2">SENTENCE SUMMARIES</td><td>O.T. Verse</td><td colspan="5">"Cease from anger, and forsake wrath; fret not thyself in any wise to do evil" (Ps. 37:8).</td></tr>
<tr><td>N.T. Verse</td><td colspan="5">"Above all, taking the shield of faith, wherewith ye shall be able to quench all the fiery darts of the wicked" (Eph. 6:16).</td></tr>
</table>

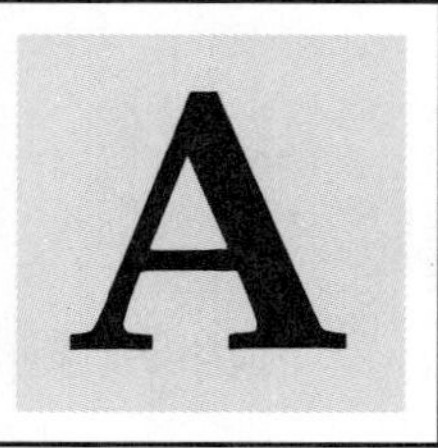

DIVINE DIET

THE RESOLUTION OF DANIEL

Daniel and his three friends, Shadrach, Meshach, and Abednego, along with other Hebrew youths, were selected by Nebuchadnezzar to prepare themselves for a life of political service. Daniel determined not to defile himself with food forbidden by Mosaic Law and perhaps even sacrificed to idols.

THE RECOMMENDATION OF DANIEL

He proposed a test, suggesting a 10-day diet of only vegetables and water. At the end of this short time, his superintendent could compare Daniel and his friends with the others who ate the king's rich food. The terms of this test were granted.

THE REWARDS OF DANIEL

At the hand of God. They were many times stronger at the end of the 10-day test. They were 10 times smarter at the end of the three-year training period.

At the hand of Nebuchadnezzar. Daniel was appointed to a political career.

STATUE AND A STONE

THE FRUSTRATION OF THE BABYLONIANS

Nebuchadnezzar had a terrifying nightmare and called his entire cabinet to relate and interpret his dream. Unable to do this, they were all condemned to death.

The frightened cabinet. "The Chaldeans answered before the king, and said, 'There is not a man upon the earth that can show the king's matter; therefore there is no king, lord, nor ruler, that asked such things at any magician, or astrologer, or Chaldean. And it is a rare thing that the king requireth, and there is none other that can show it before the king, except the gods, whose dwelling is not with flesh' " (Dan. 2:10-11).

The furious king. "For this cause the king was angry and very furious, and commanded to destroy all the wise men of Babylon" (v. 12).

THE REVELATION OF GOD

God revealed Nebuchadnezzar's dream to Daniel (who apparently was not present at the original demand of the king).

The faithfulness of God. "Then was the secret revealed unto Daniel in a night vision" (v. 19).

The thankfulness of Daniel. "Daniel answered and said, 'Blessed be the name of God forever and ever, for wisdom and might are His. And he changeth the times and the seasons; He removeth kings, and setteth up kings; He giveth wisdom unto the wise, and knowledge to them that know understanding. He revealeth the deep and secret things; He knoweth what is in the darkness, and the light dwelleth with Him. I thank Thee, and praise Thee, O Thou God of my fathers, who has given me wisdom and might, and hast made known unto me now what we desired of Thee: for Thou hast made known unto us the king's matter' " (vv. 20-23).

THE INTERPRETATION OF DANIEL

"Daniel answered in the presence of the king, and said, 'The secret which the king hath demanded cannot the wise men, the astrologers, the magicians, the soothsayers, show unto the king. But there is a God in heaven that revealeth secrets, and maketh known to the King Nebuchadnezzar what shall be in the latter days. Thy dream, and the visions of thy head upon thy bed, are these. . . . But as for me, this secret is not revealed to me for any wisdom that I have more

than any living, but for their sakes that shall make known the interpretation to the king, and that thou mightest know the thoughts of thy heart' " (vv. 27-28, 30).

A chronology of the dream—what did the king see? (vv. 31-35) He saw a huge and powerful statue of a man. It was made up of various materials. Its head was gold. Its breast and arms were silver. Its belly and thighs were brass. Its legs were iron and its feet part iron and clay.

This statue was then utterly pulverized into small powder by a special rock, supernaturally cut from a mountainside, which fell on it.

The rock then grew until it filled the entire earth (vv. 34-35).

A theology of the dream—what did this all mean? (vv. 36-45) The statue represented four Gentile world powers: the golden head was Babylon, the silver chest and arms were Persia, the brass belly and thighs were Greece, the iron legs and iron and clay feet were Rome.

In the days of the final world power the God of heaven will shatter all earthly kingdoms through His Rock (the Lord Jesus Christ) and set up an eternal kingdom (vv. 44-45).

The final Gentile power (Rome) will be revived during the Tribulation and will consist of 10 nations. This was implied, for the great prophecies concerning the fourth power were not fulfilled in the history of ancient Rome.

THE PROSTRATION OF NEBUCHADNEZZAR

The king bowed down to Daniel and commanded his people to offer sacrifices and burn sweet incense before him (v. 46). He acknowledged the God of Daniel as being *"God of gods" (v. 47)*. He elevated Daniel to the highest office in Babylon, as chief magistrate in the king's court (v. 48). Daniel then appointed Shadrach, Meshach, and Abednego to high offices (v. 49).

The Man God Uses

COMMENTS

When mighty Babylon swept into Judah and took captives, Daniel, Hananiah, Mishael, and Azariah were among the outstanding youths taken to be trained to serve in the court of Babylon. In spite of their favored treatment, Daniel and his friends were slaves. What chance does a slave have to amount to anything, especially when he is far-removed from his home and things he holds dear? The future was bleak and unpromising. And yet Daniel was to be mightily used of God. Had he not been among those captives and in the trying circumstances he probably would never have been heard of again. Consider the following characteristics that were true of Daniel which help us to understand why he was a man that God could use.

Daniel was a man of purpose (1:8). Though he was a captive and a slave, Daniel determined to do nothing that would compromise his beliefs and standards. As a slave, he had no rights and was in no position to determine what he would or would not do. Daniel came to the position that no matter what, he would not defile himself, even if it cost him his life. No price was too high and no benefits were great enough to deter him from his purpose.

Daniel was a man of courage (vv. 11-13). Not only did Daniel have a purpose, he let that purpose be known to his immediate superior in whose eyes God had given him favor. He took the initiative and suggested a plan whereby his purpose might be implemented and demonstrated to be not only to his benefit, but also to the benefit of his keeper and to the benefit of the king.

Daniel was a man of faith (2:16). When the matter of the king's demands, the Chaldeans' failure, and the pending death sentence came to his attention, Daniel did not falter. He confidently asserted in faith that he would show the king his dream and its interpretation. The king granted Daniel the privilege of trying and Daniel brought the matter to Hananiah, Mishael, and Azariah. Together in faith they sought God's revelation of the matter. God responded to Daniel's faith (v. 19).

Daniel was a man of praise and thanksgiving (vv. 20-23). When God revealed the dream and interpretation to Daniel, Daniel was prompt with thanksgiving and praise to Him.

Daniel was a man of action (v. 24). Having acted in faith and having been given the dream and its interpretation, Daniel went immediately to make the matter known to the king.

Daniel was a man of confidence (v. 25). Daniel was not intimidated by the mightiest king the world has ever seen. He was confident in his God and in the revelation that He had given him. He confidently stood before the king and declared both the dream and the interpretation.

Daniel was a man of integrity (vv. 27-30). Daniel did not try to be what he was not or to make a reputation for himself. He quickly and properly gave the credit to God and disowned any originality or special merit in the matter.

Daniel was a man of accuracy (vv. 31-35). Daniel presented the matter accurately as God had given it to him. He did not embellish or diminish the revelation in the least even though the message involved the demise of the ruler to whom he gave it.

Daniel was an unselfish man (v. 49). Most men would have taken the king's rewards and advancement gladly and forgotten their friends. Daniel was not such a man. His friends had shared the burden of faith and prayer with him. In his time of blessing he did not forget his friends who shared in his praise and exaltation.

A FIERY FURNACE

THE KING'S COMMAND

Nebuchadnezzar constructed a golden statue 90 feet high and 9 feet wide. This was set up in the Plain of Dura near Babylon. On dedication day at a given musical signal, all his officials were to bow down and worship the image. Failure to do so would result in a fiery death.

"And whoso falleth not down and worshipeth shall the same hour be cast into the midst of a burning fiery furnace" (3:6).

THE HEBREWS' STAND

Shadrach, Meshach, and Abednego refused to bow. This was brought to the attention of the king by some jealous Babylonians. Nebuchadnezzar offered them another chance. When they refused a second time, the three were bound and cast into a fiery furnace, heated seven times hotter than usual.

The concern of the king (vv. 13-15). Nebuchadnezzar did not want to lose these three capable public servants, so he offered them another chance.

"Now, if ye be ready . . . fall down and worship the image which I have made, well; but if ye worship not, ye shall be cast the same hour into the midst of a burning fiery furnace. And who is that God, that shall deliver you out of my hands?" (v. 15)

THE COURAGE OF THE THREE

"Shadrach, Meshach, and Abednego, answered and said to the king, 'O Nebuchadnezzar, we are not careful to answer thee in this matter. If it be so, our God whom we serve is able to deliver us from the burning fiery furnace, and He will deliver us out of thine hand, O king. But if not, be it known unto thee, O king, that we will not serve thy gods, nor worship the golden image which thou hast set up' " (vv. 16-18).

THE LORD'S OWN MAN

Peering into the furnace an amazed king saw a fourth figure.

The marvel. "Then Nebuchadnezzar the king was astonished, and rose up in haste, and spake, and said unto his counselors, 'Did not we cast three men bound into the midst of the fire?' They answered and said unto the king, 'True, O king' " (v. 24).

The miracle. "He answered and said, 'Lo, I see four men loose, walking in the midst of the fire, and they have no hurt; and the form of the fourth is like the Son of God' " (v. 25).

The three friends then walked out of the furnace unharmed with not even the smell of smoke on them.

Nebuchadnezzar issued a decree, making death the penalty for badmouthing the God of Israel.

Civil Disobedience

COMMENTS

The problem of having a government that is out of step with its constituents is not a new one at all. Hananiah, Mishael, and Azariah had that problem long before it was popular. They were captives in Babylon and had been elevated to prominence in the government by their association with Daniel (cf. 2:17, 49). Nebuchadnezzar had apparently forgotten the lesson he had learned from Daniel (cf. v. 47) for he made an image that was 90 feet high and 9 feet wide which he commanded all the people of the land to worship. To emphasize the seriousness of the command, the punishment for disobedience was to be unusually severe—incineration (3:6).

When the time came, the people gathered, the band played, and all the people did obeisance, as commanded—except for three: Hananiah, Mishael, and Azariah, who were identified by their Babylonian names as Shadrach, Meshach, and Abednego (v. 12). Because of his high regard for them, the king graciously offered them a second chance (vv. 14-15). They, however, refused to worship the king's image no matter what he might do. They were confident that God would deliver them out of the king's hand and unreasonable demand (v. 17). Even if He chose not to do so, they still would not worship the image (v. 18). The king's previous good nature turned to unreasonable rage as he commanded the furnace to be heated to seven times its normal temperature (v. 19). Shadrach, Meshach, and Abednego would pay the price for their civil disobedience; death in the fiery furnace. The flames of the furnace were so hot that the execution agents were themselves slain as they threw the men into the furnace (v. 22). Shadrach, Meshach, and Abednego fell into the furnace but the only things that burned on them were the ropes that the king's soldiers had put on them. The fire freed them from Chaldean bonds (vv. 23-25). They walked around in the furnace and were joined by a fourth Person who was "like the Son of God" (v. 25). No one was able to go into the furnace to bring Shadrach, Meshach, and Abednego out. They heeded the king's command to come out of the furnace and did not even have the smell of smoke on them nor was a single hair of their bodies singed (v. 27). The civil disobedience of Shadrach, Meshach, and Abednego stimulated the king's memory so that once again he gave credence to their God as he had done earlier with Daniel. The worship of Jehovah was made the official religion of the land and they were also promoted in their service of the government (vv. 29-30).

In modern days civil disobedience has been employed as a tool to change the government not because of obedience to Jehovah but in defiance of Him. Those who would advocate civil disobedience should consider Hananiah, Mishael, and Azariah. They were not trying to advance a cause or to gain a more favorable position for themselves but were devoted to Jehovah and wanted to be pleasing to Him. They did not question the king's right to punish them in any way he saw fit. There was no protest movement because the king adopted "cruel and inhumane punishment" against them. They recognized that the government had the right to punish them because they were in violation of the conduct that the government had prescribed. They took their punishment without resistance or remorse. In all probability they were certain that they would perish in the flames, but that made no difference; nor did they ask for an opportunity to change their minds once they found that the king intended that they should bow down to his image or certainly die. They did what they did out of a commitment to God; and God honored their faith. God used them to change their government and gave them a place of increased prominence in it.

review

The Control of God in the Hearts of Men

DANIEL 4–6

"We three kings of Orient are!" In this lesson there are three kings and they did live in the general vicinity of the Orient. Unlike John Hopkins' Christmas carol, however, they did not bear their gifts and traverse afar. Nor did they follow a star to a Jewish manger as a group of oriental kings would do six centuries later. But before the story ends, this trio learned much about that Hebrew Messiah who would later appear in Bethlehem. Nebuchadnezzar, the first king, learned that the Lord presides over the affairs of men. Belshazzar, the second king, discovered God punishes the sins of men, while Darius, the third king, found out He preserves His own.

He presides. Mighty Nebuchadnezzar was turned into the likes of a wild animal and restored to his throne by God.

He punishes. Wicked Belshazzar was weighed in the balance, found wanting, and executed in less than an hour's time by God.

He preserves. Powerless Darius watched in utter astonishment as Daniel walked out of a den of hungry lions, sustained by God.

Overview

<table>
<tr><td>SCRIPTURE</td><td colspan="6">Daniel 4–6</td></tr>
<tr><td>SUBJECT</td><td colspan="6">A tale of three kings</td></tr>
<tr><td rowspan="3">SPECIFICS</td><td colspan="2">Daniel and Nebuchadnezzar</td><td colspan="2">Daniel and Belshazzar</td><td colspan="2">Daniel and Darius</td></tr>
<tr><td>A demonstration of God's sovereignty</td><td>The haughtiness
The helplessness
The humbleness</td><td>A demonstration of God's sword</td><td>The sin at the table
The sign on the wall
The soldiers at the gate</td><td>A demonstration of God's salvation</td><td>The conspiracy of the enemies
The bravery of the prophet
The anxiety of the king
The sufficiency of the Lord</td></tr>
<tr><td colspan="2">He promotes</td><td colspan="2">He punishes</td><td colspan="2">He preserves</td></tr>
<tr><td>SAINTS AND SINNERS</td><td colspan="6">Daniel, Nebuchadnezzar, Belshazzar, Darius</td></tr>
<tr><td rowspan="2">SENTENCE SUMMARIES</td><td>O.T. Verse</td><td colspan="5">"Be wise, now therefore, O ye kings; be instructed, ye judges of the earth" (Ps. 2:10).</td></tr>
<tr><td>N.T. Verse</td><td colspan="5">"Who through faith subdued kingdoms, wrought righteousness, obtained promises, stopped the mouths of lions" (Heb. 11:33).</td></tr>
</table>

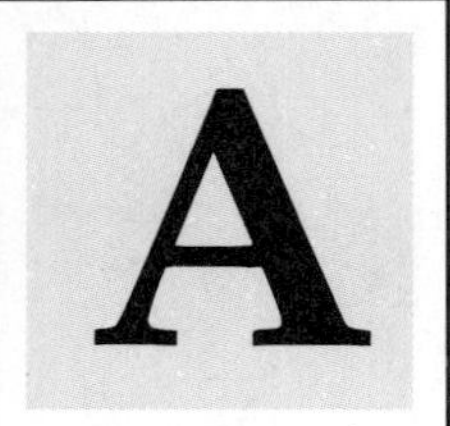

A TREE IN TURMOIL

THE TREE (NEBUCHADNEZZAR) CORRUPTED THROUGH VANITY

The prologue. "Nebuchadnezzar the king, unto all people, nations, and languages, that dwell in all the earth; Peace be multiplied unto you. I thought it good to show the signs and wonders that the high God hath wrought toward me. How great are His signs! And how mighty are His wonders! His kingdom is an everlasting kingdom, and His dominion is from generation to generation" (4:1-3).

The problem. "I Nebuchadnezzar was at rest in mine house, and flourishing in my palace. I saw a dream which made me afraid, and the thoughts upon my bed and the visions of my head troubled me. Therefore made I a decree to bring in all the wise men of Babylon before me, that they might make known unto me the interpretation of the dream. Then came in the magicians, the astrologers, the Chaldeans, and the soothsayers, and I told the dream before them; but they did not make known unto me the interpretation thereof" (vv. 4-7).

Nebuchadnezzar related his dream to Daniel. He saw a large and leafy tree increasing in size till it reached the heavens and was viewed by all. The wild animals and birds were shaded and sheltered by its leafy branches and the entire world was fed from its generous fruit supply (vv. 10-12).

Suddenly a heavenly figure appeared and ordered the tree cut down and its fruit scattered. Only the stump was to be left, banded with a chain of iron and brass. This felled tree represented a man who would be given the mind of an animal and remain in this pitiful condition for seven years (vv. 13-16).

This all was to be done so the entire world might *"know that the Most High ruleth in the kingdom of men, and giveth it to whomsoever he will, and setteth up over it the basest of men" (v. 17).*

Daniel revealed the dream to Nebuchadnezzar. The interpretation was so frightful that Daniel observed an hour of shocked silence (v. 19).

He then revealed the details. The tree indeed stood for a man, and that man was Nebuchadnezzar. The king would suffer a seven-year period of insanity for his pride. During this time, he would act and think like a wild animal. This affliction would only end when he realized that the powers that be are ordained by God. Daniel then begged the proud monarch to "break off thy sins," but all to no avail.

THE TREE (NEBUCHADNEZZAR) CORRECTED THROUGH INSANITY

The pride of Nebuchadnezzar. Twelve months after the dream the king was strolling on the roof of the royal palace in Babylon. We note his arrogant boast. *"Is not this great Babylon, that I have built for the house of the kingdom by the might of my power, and for the honor of my majesty?" (v. 30)*

The punishment of Nebuchadnezzar. Even while the king spoke his proud words, the judgment of God fell from heaven and he was driven from the palace (v. 31).

We note the sad results of his vanity. *"He was driven from men, and did eat grass as oxen, and his body was wet with the dew of heaven, till his hairs were grown like eagles' feathers, and his nails like birds' claws" (v. 33).*

The praise of Nebuchadnezzar. When he was restored his pride turned to praise. *"And at the end of the days I Nebuchadnezzar lifted up mine eyes unto heaven, and mine understanding returned unto me, and I blessed the Most High, and I praised and honored Him that liveth forever, whose dominion is an everlasting dominion, and His kingdom is from generation to generation.*

"And all the inhabitants of the earth are reputed as nothing; and He doeth according to His will in the army of heaven, and among the inhabitants of the earth; and none can stay His hand, or say unto Him, 'What doest thou?' . . .

"Now I Nebuchadnezzar praise and extol and honor the King of heaven, all whose works are truth, and His ways judgment; and those that walk in pride He is able to abase" (vv. 34-35, 37).

The Tale of Two Kings

COMMENTS

In Daniel 4 and 5 events relating to two of the most powerful kings ever to be on the face of the earth are related. By his own personal testimony, Nebuchadnezzar hadn't always believed in the greatness of God nor been obedient to Him. He recounted a dream which he had at the height of his career and in the midst of his plenty (4:4). His magicians, astrologers, and soothsayers, the Chaldeans, were not able to tell him the meaning of the dream (v. 7). Finally Daniel (known in Nebuchadnezzar's testimony by his Babylonian name, Belteshazzar) was brought to the king and told the details of the dream (vv. 9-18). Nebuchadnezzar had confidence in Daniel (v. 9, 18) for he had interpreted his dream before (cf. chap. 2).

Daniel sat in astonished silence for an hour when God revealed the interpretation of the dream to him. "My lord, the dream be to them that hate thee, and the interpretation thereof to thine enemies," said Daniel (4:19b). Such loyalty is amazing in view of the fact that it was this king who had caused Daniel and his people to be uprooted from their homeland and brought to pagan Babylon. In obedience to the king's prompting (v. 19a), Daniel faithfully gave the interpretation. The king was to be deposed, lose his sanity, be driven from human company, eat grass like an ox, and live out in the pasture for seven years (v. 25). He was assured, however, that he would recover his kingdom when he came to his senses and acknowledged the true and only God of heaven, Jehovah (v. 26).

In keeping with his position as a prophet, Daniel urged the king to repent of his sins if perchance God would change His mind (v. 27). Instead of humbling himself, he became more proud (v. 31). All that the interpretation had indicated befell Nebuchadnezzar one year later (vv. 28-29, 33). At the end of the seven years, King Nebuchadnezzar came to his senses and learned the lesson he should have learned seven years earlier (vv. 34-35)—it is God who is all; all kingdoms and lands belong to Him. Kings, even the basest king, have their kingdoms by virtue of God's permission (vv. 17, 25, 32). Nebuchadnezzar had thought that he was god and that there was no God. How gracious of God to stoop to bring this wicked and proud king to Himself.

In Belshazzar's case it was not "like father, like son." Belshazzar, who reigned in Nebuchadnezzar's stead, was a partaker of his father's pride, but not of his father's humility. He flaunted his greatness by commanding the golden and silver vessels (which Nebuchadnezzar had stolen from the temple in Jerusalem) be used by his guests at a huge state dinner (5:2-4). God sent a message of judgment to him in the form of the fingers of a man's hand which wrote the message on the wall of the banquet hall. None of the king's astrologers, Chaldeans, or soothsayers could interpret the message. As an incentive the king offered whoever could give the interpretation the third position in the kingdom (v. 7). Once again, Daniel was called on (vv. 12-13). Daniel refused the king's reward—it would be futile (v. 17)—and reminded Belshazzar of his knowledge of Nebuchadnezzar's experience and belief in the true God (vv. 18-22). In spite of this, Belshazzar had not humbled himself. Daniel again faithfully gave the interpretation of the writing even though it concerned the death of the king who had commanded the interpretation (vv. 25-28). Belshazzar made good on his promise (v. 29). That night, Belshazzar was killed (v. 30), Persia conquered Babylon, and a new king, Darius, reigned.

The tale of two kings concerns two kings who were both ruthless and proud. The difference between them was that one, Nebuchadnezzar, learned that God is everything and he was nothing. His kingdom was preserved and he was restored. The other, Belshazzar, refused to humble his heart and perished and his kingdom with him.

A HEAVENLY HAND

THE BALL

Belshazzar the king staged a huge dinner and drinking party and invited his top 1,000 officers to attend.

THE GALL

He ordered the gold and silver cups taken by his grandfather Nebuchadnezzar from the Jerusalem temple to be brought to this feast that he might drink wine from them and praise the Babylonian gods.

THE WALL

Suddenly he saw the fingers of a man's hand writing a mysterious message on the wall next to his table.

THE CALL

A terrified king turned to his astrologers for help and interpretation, but they could not assist him. At the suggestion of the queen, he called for Daniel, offering to make the great prophet third ruler in the kingdom if he could interpret the message. Daniel refused the offer, but interpreted the message.

The nature of this message. Mene, Mene—God has numbered your kingdom and finished it. *Tekel*—you are weighed in the balances, and found wanting. *Upharsin*—your kingdom is divided and given to the Medes and Persians.

The reason for this message. "O thou king, the Most High God gave Nebuchadnezzar thy father a kingdom, and majesty, and glory, and honor, and for the majesty that he gave him, all people, nations, and languages, trembled and feared before him; whom he would he slew; and whom he would he kept alive; and whom he would he set up; and whom he would he put down. But when his heart was lifted up, and his mind hardened in pride, he was deposed from his kingly throne, and they took his glory from him. And he was driven from the sons of men; and his heart was made like the beasts, and his dwelling was with the wild asses. They fed him with grass like oxen, and his body was wet with the dew of heaven; till he knew that the Most High God ruled in the kingdom of men, and that He appointeth over it whomsoever He will.

"And thou his son, O Belshazzar, hast not humbled thine heart, though thou knowest all this; but hast lifted up thyself against the Lord of heaven; and they have brought the vessels of His house before thee, and thou, and thy lords, thy wives, and thy concubines, have drunk wine in them; and thou hast praised the gods of silver, and gold, of brass, iron, wood, and stone, which see not, nor hear, nor know. And the God in whose hand thy breath is, and whose are all thy ways, hast thou not glorified" (5:18-23).

THE FALL

Belshazzar was slain that very night and the city was ruled by a 62-year-old Mede named Darius.

Same Song, Third Stanza

COMMENTS

Though he was a slave, Daniel survived the governments that enslaved him. When Babylon fell, Daniel survived, even though he had been promoted to the third highest in the kingdom (cf. 5:29). One of the most intelligent things that the new king, Darius, did was to preserve Daniel's life and make him first president in the newly reorganized government of Babylon. Daniel's prominence made his colleagues jealous and they sought some way to cause his downfall. There was nothing in Daniel's personal or professional life on which they could seize. The only fault they could find was with Daniel's God (6:5). With trickery the presidents got vain Darius to sign a decree outlawing appeal to any person or god except him.

The new law of the land did not deter Daniel from his regular practice of worship and prayer to his God. He had seen such efforts come and go before in his long life. He trusted his God and did what was right in His sight even though to do so was to place his own life in jeopardy (v. 10). Though Darius was the king of the land, his kingship was not as sovereign as Nebuchadnezzar's or Belshazzar's before him. Under a similar circumstance, Nebuchadnezzar or Belshazzar would simply have countermanded the law that they had put into effect. Darius, however, was weaker and recognized that the king had to be subject to the laws that he had made, even though his obedience would make him do something that he really did not want to do (v. 14).

The king had to keep his word. Daniel was thrown into the lions' den (v. 16) but Daniel was safer there than he was in the company of his colleagues. Darius did not sleep all night (v. 18). The next morning he was pleasantly surprised that Daniel was well and healthy (vv. 19-23). Daniel was brought up from the lions' den and Daniel's accusers were thrown in. The miracle of Daniel's preservation was demonstrated when they, their wives, and their children were devoured before they hit the bottom of the den (v. 24).

Having kept his own law, Darius was now able to make the needed revision. He made a decree officially recognizing Daniel's God, Jehovah, as the living God to be worshiped throughout the land (vv. 26-27). Having met the challenge, Daniel "prospered in the reign of Cyrus the Persian" (v. 28).

By now the scenario is familiar. This is the same song, the third stanza. Twice before similar things had happened under two other kings. With Nebuchadnezzar the narrative began with the proud king at the top of the world and Daniel and Daniel's God at the bottom of the heap. Nebuchadnezzar apparently had more opportunity to learn for Daniel interpreted his dream (chap. 2); Hananiah, Mishael, and Azariah were delivered from the fiery furnace (chap. 3); and he was removed from his kingdom, became like an animal, and was restored to his kingdom (chap. 4) when he finally learned that he was nothing and God was everything.

Belshazzar knew the history of Nebuchadnezzar, yet he failed to learn the lesson of Nebuchadnezzar. He appeared on the scene thinking himself to be over all (5:1-4). Belshazzar never came to repentance. His story comes to an end with his death, Daniel's promotion, and God's glory (v. 29).

Darius, while recognizing excellence in Daniel, lacked the courage to rescind his own law even though it was wrong. He thought that his law was greater than God. However, through the events recorded in chapter 6 Darius came to the realization that God is the only living and true God. By now one would think that man in general and kings in particular would get the message: God is sovereign. But alas, they don't. After Darius, kingdoms would rise and fall, but few would be the kings who would renounce "the divine right of kings" in favor of the right of the divine King.

HE LIONS AND THE LION-HEARTED

AN EVIL PLAN

The organization. Darius, the Mede, immediately set about to reorganize and consolidate this fantastic new kingdom called Babylon. He divided the kingdom into 129 provinces, each under a governor. These governors were accountable to three presidents, with Daniel being one of the three. Daniel, now over 80, was still blessed with so much skill and ability that Darius was considering elevating him over the other two presidents.

The orchestration. This so infuriated both the presidents and the governors that they plotted to take away his life. Being unable to see the slightest flaw in his secular life, they determined to trap him in his religious life.

Darius was tricked into signing a 30-day decree which said that all praying during that time was to be directed to the king himself.

A KNEELING MAN

The fearless prophet. Daniel learned of this and doubtless immediately saw through its clumsy effort to trap him. But the old warrior continued worshiping God as before. He kept his windows opened. He continued praying three times a day, in the morning, at noon, and in the evening. He knelt down. He faced Jerusalem.

The heartless plotters. Those vicious hunters who had set their trap now saw the prey inside and gleefully rushed to Darius to deliver the deathblow. Darius realized he had been had and desperately sought to find a loophole in the immutable law of the Medes and Persians, but all to no avail.

"Then the king, when he heard these words, was sore displeased with himself, and set his heart on Daniel to deliver him; and he labored till the going down of the sun to deliver him" (6:14).

Daniel was arrested and thrown into a den of hungry man-eating lions.

The sleepless potentate. After sealing the mouth of the den with his own signet ring, Darius returned to the royal palace and spent a sleepless and miserable night.

"Then the king went to his palace, and passed the night fasting; neither were instruments of music brought before him; and his sleep went from him" (v. 18).

At daybreak the next morning he rushed to the den, ordered the capstone removed, and called out in anguish: *"O Daniel, servant of the living God, is thy God, whom thou servest continually, able to deliver thee from the lions?" (v. 20)*

A HEAVENLY BAN

Daniel's response. Out of the blackness of the den of doom, there came a cheerful and clear voice: *"O king, live forever. My God hath sent His angel, and hath shut the lions' mouths, that they have not hurt me; forasmuch as before Him innocency was found in me; and also before thee, O king, have I done no hurt" (vv. 21-22).*

Darius' reaction. The king's reaction to all this was twofold; he was both glad and mad. He rejoiced at the salvation of Daniel and issued a decree ordering all the citizens of his kingdom to consider this almighty Judean God.

"I make a decree, that in every dominion of my kingdom men tremble and fear before the God of Daniel; for He is the living God, and steadfast forever, and His kingdom that which shall not be destroyed, and His dominion shall be even unto the end. He delivereth and rescueth, and He worketh signs and wonders in heaven and in earth, who hath delivered Daniel from the power of the lions" (vv. 26-27).

He took immediate vengeance on those who had tricked him in the first place and ordered them along with all their families thrown into this same den. Their bodies were instantly torn apart by the lions.

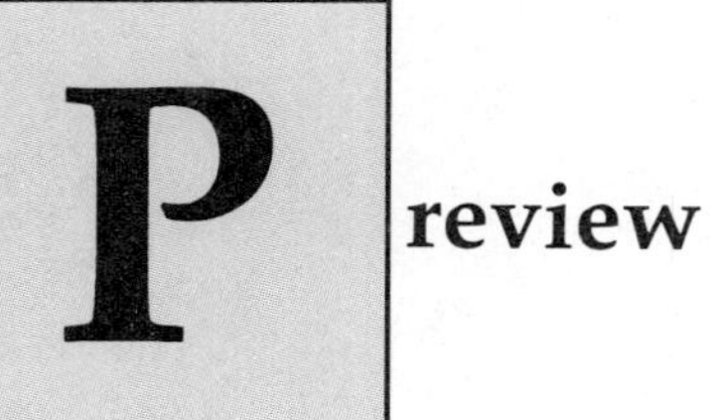

Thy Kingdom Come, Thy Will Be Done

DANIEL 7–9

A description of and the duration of Gentile kingdoms. A description of and the duration of God's kingdom. These subjects are explained and amplified in Daniel 7–9. It opens with a dream experienced by the prophet himself. In it he sees four horrible and bloodthirsty beasts, with the brutal characteristics of a lion, a bear, a leopard, and a one-horned hybrid monster with terrible teeth. In reality Daniel saw the same four godless kingdoms that Nebuchadnezzar had dreamed about in chapter 2. But the prophet was allowed to view them from an absolutely different perspective. Man may see his kingdoms as gleaming metals such as gold and silver, but God looks on them as wild and ravenous animals. Daniel also dreamed as did Nebuchadnezzar, of the glorious kingdom of God, ruled over by the blessed Son of God!

So much for the description. But what of the duration? In essence, God will allow Gentile world power to continue, reaching its high-water mark during the coming Great Tribulation when the apostate Antichrist will briefly rule the earth. But at the advent of heaven's King of kings and Lord of lords, godless kingdoms will be utterly and forever crushed, giving way to the eternal reign of the Lord Jesus Christ.

Overview

SCRIPTURE	Daniel 7–9
SUBJECT	Jews and Gentiles: God's final game plan

SPECIFICS

The who and how of the plan

Nations	Representatives	Symbols	Prophecies
Babylon	Nebuchadnezzar	Lion	To be defeated by Persia
Persia	Cyrus Darius III	Bear Ram	Cyrus to defeat Belshazzar Greece to defeat Persia
Greece	Alexander	Leopard/Goat	Alexander to defeat Darius
Syria Former Rome Future Rome	Antiochus Epiphanes Various Caesars Antichrist	Little horn Hybrid monster Little horn	Jews to suffer much Rome to defeat Greece Jews to suffer much
Final kingdom	Jesus Christ	Smiting stone	To rule over all kingdoms forever

The when of the plan

The prologue	Daniel and the Word of God Daniel and the God of the Word	The prophecy	Duration	Begin	End	Time periods		
			70 weeks or 490 years	445 B.C.	Armageddon	445 B.C. to 30 A.D. 483 years	Undisclosed Church Age	Great Tribulation 7 years

SAINTS AND SINNERS	Daniel, Gabriel, Alexander the Great, Darius III, Antichrist

SENTENCE SUMMARIES

O.T. Verses	"Behold, the nations are as a drop of a bucket, and are counted as the small dust of the balance; behold, He taketh up the isles as a very little thing. . . . But they that wait upon the LORD shall renew their strength; they shall mount up with wings as eagles; they shall run, and not be weary; and they shall walk, and not faint" (Isa. 40:15, 31).
N.T. Verse	"Then cometh the end, when He shall have delivered up the kingdom to God, even the Father; when He shall have put down all rule and all authority and power" (1 Cor. 15:24).

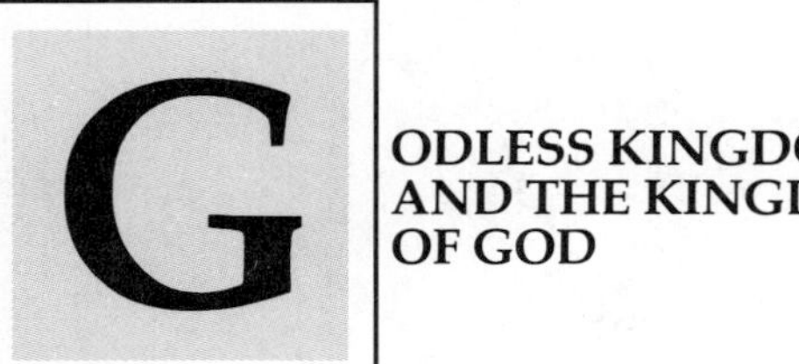

ODLESS KINGDOMS AND THE KINGDOM OF GOD

NEBUCHADNEZZAR, THE BABYLONIAN LION

Daniel, in a vision, saw a great storm on a mighty ocean with four winds blowing from every direction. Four great beasts came out of the ocean.

The first beast symbolized Nebuchadnezzar and Babylon. It was like a lion. It had eagle's wings. Those wings were plucked. See Daniel 4:33 (Nebuchadnezzar's wings), and 5:31 (Babylon's wings).

CYRUS, THE PERSIAN BEAR

This bear raised itself up on one side, probably referring to the stronger Persian part of the dual Medes and Persian alliance. It had three ribs in its mouth, a reference to Babylon, Egypt, and Lydia, three nations Persia had just conquered. It would devour much flesh. The Persian King Xerxes led a force of over 1½ million men and 300 ships into Greece alone.

ALEXANDER, THE GRECIAN LEOPARD

The third beast was like a leopard. Alexander traveled faster and conquered more land than any other man in all recorded history. It had four heads. After his untimely death at 32, his kingdom was divided among four of his generals.

LITTLE HORN, THE ROMAN MONSTER

This monster "retired" to its den in A.D. 476 for a while to hibernate. It will be awakened in the form of 10 nations during the Tribulation by the little horn, who is none other than the Antichrist! The Antichrist will defeat 3 of these 10 kingdoms (horns) in his rise to power. He will have a universal rule during the final three and one-half years of the Tribulation. He will shed blood on this earth in an unprecedented manner. He will wear out the saints of God. He will attempt to change seasons and laws. He will blaspheme God. He will be defeated at the coming of Christ and his body given over to the flames of hell.

JESUS CHRIST, THE KING OF KINGS

He will come in the clouds to claim His rightful earthly inheritance. *"I saw in the night visions and, behold, one like the Son of man came with the clouds of heaven, and came to the Ancient of Days, and they brought Him near before Him. And there was given Him dominion, and glory, and a kingdom, that all people, nations, and languages, should serve Him; His dominion is an everlasting dominion, which shall not pass away, and His kingdom that which shall not be destroyed. . . .*

"And the kingdom and dominion, and the greatness of the kingdom under the whole heaven, shall be given to the people of the saints of the Most High, whose kingdom is an everlasting kingdom, and all dominions shall serve and obey Him" (7:13-14, 27).

He was given His universal and eternal throne by His Father, the Ancient of Days.

"I beheld till the thrones were cast down, and the Ancient of Days did sit, whose garment was white as snow, and the hair of His head like the pure wool. His throne was like the fiery flame, and His wheels as burning fire. A fiery stream issued and came forth from before Him; thousand thousands ministered unto Him, and ten thousand times ten thousand stood before Him; the judgment was set, and the books were opened" (vv. 9-10).

Daniel saw a continuous river of fire gushing from the throne. Millions of angels stand and minister to the Ancient of Days and His Son. Hundreds of millions stood before Him ready to be judged and the books were opened.

THE HORNS OF THE HEATHEN

A TWO-HEADED RAM (PERSIA, AS REPRESENTED BY DARIUS III)

In this vision, Daniel saw himself in the fortress of Shushan (or Susa), a city some 230 miles east of Babylon and 100 miles north of the Persian Gulf. He saw a victorious ram coming from the east, and pushing its way westward, northward, and to the south. This, of course, represented the Persian conquests.

A ONE-HORNED GOAT (GREECE) AS REPRESENTED BY ALEXANDER THE GREAT)

Daniel then saw a goat from the west which rushed toward the ram, smashed it to the ground, and stomped it to pieces. Daniel then saw this powerful horn suddenly broken and its might divided fourfold. Alexander died in Babylon during a drunken orgy at the age of 32 in 323 B.C. His kingdom was then divided among his four leading generals.

TWO LITTLE-HORNED KINGS (SYRIA AND THE REVIVED ROMAN EMPIRE AS REPRESENTED BY ANTIOCHUS EPIPHANES AND THE ANTICHRIST)

We note that the Angel Gabriel interpreted all this to Daniel. This was the first mention of him in the Bible.

The historical little horn: Antiochus Epiphanes. He was a Syrian. He came to the throne in 175 B.C. and ruled until 164 B.C. He was anti-Semitic to the core. He assaulted Jerusalem, murdering over 40,000 in three days, and selling an equal number into cruel slavery. It is thought that he began his evil actions on September 6, 171 B.C. and ended them on December 25, 165 B.C. This would account for the 2,300 days of 8:14. Daniel became physically ill when he saw this terrible prophetic vision.

"And I Daniel fainted, and was sick certain days; afterward I rose up, and did the king's business; and I was astonished at the vision, but none understood it" (v. 27).

THE PROPHETICAL LITTLE HORN—THE ANTICHRIST

The future enemy of Israel will do all his forerunner did and much more. The following comparisons can be seen between the two. Both would conquer much and both would magnify themselves. Both would be masters of deceit and both would offer a false "peace program." Both would hate and persecute Israel. Both would profane the temple and both would be energized by Satan. Both would be active in the Middle East for about seven years. Both would speak against the Lord God and both would be utterly destroyed by God.

"He shall also stand up against the Prince of princes, but he shall be broken without hand" (v. 25).

The Times of the Gentiles in Parallel

COMMENTS

To get some idea of the problem that faced Daniel in communicating his revelation, try reading some early English literature by Chaucer. The gap between Chaucer and today is not nearly as great as the gap between Daniel's day and our day, but for most people it requires much more study to understand Chaucer's writings than it does Daniel's—and yet the subject matter communicated by Daniel is of infinitely greater importance than that communicated by Chaucer. What vehicle would be adequate to convey such important truth? The Holy Spirit chose parallel symbolism.

Daniel 2 and 7 contain the same basic material using different figures and giving increasing detail. Daniel 8 supplements Daniel 7, especially the second and third kingdoms. The vision of the great image of Daniel 2 primarily portrays the character of the four world kingdoms that are going to be predominate in the times of the Gentiles, which began with the carrying away of the nation Israel into the 70-year Babylonian Captivity and continues until the return of Jesus to the earth to set up His kingdom, or the Millennium.

The first world power was Babylon. In Daniel 2 this power is the head of gold (v. 38). The character of this kingdom was to be an absolute monarchy with absolute power. In Daniel 7 this kingdom is portrayed by the lion with eagle's wings whose wings were plucked and to whom was given the heart of a man. This showed the swiftness with which the armies of Babylon would be able to move, that its mobility would be curtailed, and its kings would come to recognize that God was sovereign and they were mere mortals.

The second world power was Medo-Persia. In Daniel 2, it is the silver chest and arms indicating a decay in power; the king would be subject to law (Dan. 6) and power would be shared between the Medes and Persians. This division in power is shown in Daniel 7 by the bear with one side raised up with three ribs in its mouth. It would have ferocious power and would devour much flesh (v. 5). The character is further amplified by the ram in Daniel 8. The two horns show the division of power and the higher horn, which came up last, represents the Persians who would gain dominance over the Medes.

The third world power was Greece. It is portrayed by the brass belly and thighs of the great image in Daniel 2. Its character is amplified by the four-winged and four-headed leopard of Daniel 7. It would move swiftly and be given dominion over all the world. The ram in Daniel 8 gives more details. The great horn between the eyes represented its strong leader, Alexander the Great, who at age 32 sat down and cried because there were no more worlds to conquer. He would be done away, his kingdom divided by four of his generals, three of whom were uprooted by the "little horn" who rose to preeminence, Antiochus Epiphanes.

The fourth kingdom was Rome. It was represented by the legs of iron in the great image of Daniel 2. It would be a strong kingdom, as is verified by its being represented by the "dreadful and terrible" great beast of Daniel 7 (v. 7). It had great iron teeth and stamped the residue with its feet. Ten horns were on the head of this beast and an eleventh "little horn" arose plucking up 3 of the original 10 horns. This ferocious beast had the eyes of a man and a mouth which could speak great and swelling words. This beast blasphemed God and turned his vengeance upon the saints.

The fifth kingdom is the kingdom of God which brings the times of the Gentiles to an end. In Daniel 2 the suddenness and force with which it will come is shown by the stone not cut out with man's hands coming, striking the image on the feet, and becoming a great mountain. In Daniel 7, Daniel saw the Ancient of Days (God) sit in judgment on all unbelievers (v. 10).

No wonder that Daniel was "troubled" by these visions (v. 28). No wonder that he "fainted" and did not understand the significance of all that he had seen. While we have the perspective of time and additional revelation that Daniel did not have, it is doubtful that we understand all the significance of what God has revealed. However, one thing is certain. The symbolism that God used to reveal His infinite truth to His finite servant is just as relevant today as it was in Daniel's day. We can appreciate the fact that part of Daniel's visions have been fulfilled in accurate detail (especially chap. 8). That which remains will be certainly fulfilled in just as great detail and accuracy. The day is yet coming when, "Jesus shall reign wherever the sun doth its successive journeys run!" Even so come, Lord Jesus.

THE SECRET OF SEVENTY SEVENS

DANIEL—THE PRAYER OF A PROPHET

Reading God's message. This is one of the greatest chapters in all the Bible. It has a double theme, that of prayer and prophecy. At this time Daniel was about 85. Daniel was reading from the Book of Jeremiah (the old prophet had probably become the official custodian of various Old Testament books after the destruction of the temple) and was reminded that God had determined Jerusalem must lie desolate for 70 years (see Jer. 25:11; 29:10).

Reading God's mercy. He then began an intense and prolonged prayer to God, concerning both his personal sins and those national sins of Israel which had caused the Captivity in the first place. His prayer was accompanied by fasting, sackcloth, and ashes. He reminded God of His covenants. He contrasted the grace and goodness of God with the immorality and idolatry of Israel.

Israel's immorality and idolatry. "We have . . . committed iniquity and have . . . rebelled" (Dan. 9:5).

"Yea, all Israel have transgressed Thy Law" (v. 11).

God's grace and goodness. "To the Lord our God belong mercies and forgiveness" (v. 9).

He mentioned Judah's kings. Two of them had been carried off into the Babylonian Captivity along with the Jewish people. He fully agreed that Judah had gotten just what she deserved and that God meant just what He said when He warned them about disobedience and punishment.

"And He hath confirmed His words, which He spake against us, and against our judges that judged us, by bringing upon us a great evil. For under the whole heaven hath not been done as hath been done upon Jerusalem. As it is written in the Law of Moses, all this evil is come upon us; yet we made not our prayer before the LORD our God, that we might turn from our iniquities, and understand Thy truth. Therefore hath the LORD watched upon the evil, and brought it upon us; for the LORD our God is righteous in all His works which He doeth; for we obeyed not His voice" (vv. 12-14).

He ended his prayer by throwing both himself and his people completely on the manifold grace of God.

"O my God, incline Thine ear, and hear; open Thine eyes, and behold our desolations, and the city which is called by Thy name. For we do not present our supplications before Thee for our righteousnesses, but for Thy great mercies. O Lord, hear; O Lord, forgive; O Lord, hearken and do; defer not, for Thine own sake, O my God: for Thy city and Thy people are called by Thy name" (9:18-19).

GABRIEL—THE PROPHECY OF AN ANGEL

Even while Daniel was praying, God sent Gabriel, a special angel, to both minister to him and explain the most important, the most amazing, and the most profound single prophecy in the entire Word of God.

"Seventy weeks are determined upon thy people and upon thy Holy City, to finish the transgression, and to make an end of sins, and to make reconciliation for iniquity, and to bring in everlasting righteousness, and to seal up the vision and prophecy, and to anoint the Most Holy. Know therefore and understand, that from the going forth of the commandment to restore and to build Jerusalem unto the Messiah the Prince shall be seven weeks, and threescore and two weeks; the street shall be built again, and the wall, even in troublous times. And after threescore and two weeks shall Messiah be cut off, but not for Himself; and the people of the prince that shall come shall destroy the city and the sanctuary; and the end thereof shall be with a flood, and unto the end of the war desolations are determined. And he shall confirm the covenant with many for one week; and in the midst of the week he shall cause the sacrifice and the oblation to cease, and for the overspreading of abominations he shall make it desolate, even until the consummation, and that determined shall be poured upon the desolate" (vv. 24-27).

We will consider this prophecy by asking and attempting to answer six key questions:

To whom does this prophecy refer? It refers to Israel. "Thy people" (v. 24).

What is meant by this term "70 weeks"?

The Hebrew word refers to 70 sevens of years, or a total of 490 years.

When was the 70-week period to begin? It was to begin with the command to rebuild Jerusalem's walls (v. 25).

What are the distinct time periods mentioned within the 70-week prophecy and what was to happen during each period?

The first period was seven weeks (49 years), from 445 B.C. to 396 B.C. The key events during this time were the building of the streets and walls of Jerusalem *"even in troublous times" (v. 25).*

The second period was 62 weeks (434 years), from 396 B.C. to A.D. 32. At the end of this second period, the Messiah was to be crucified.

The third period will be one week (seven years) from the Rapture till the Millennium. One-half week (three and one-half years), is the first half of the Tribulation. At the beginning of this period the Antichrist will break his pact with Israel and will begin his terrible bloodbath. At the end of the last week (and of the entire 70-week period), the true Messiah will come and establish His perfect Millennium.

Do the seventy weeks run continually? This is to say, is there a gap somewhere between these 490 years or do they run without pause until they are completed? Dispensational theology teaches that these "weeks" do not run continuously, but that there has been a gap or parenthesis of nearly 2,000 years between the sixty-ninth and seventieth weeks.

Does the Bible offer any other examples of time gaps in divine programs? It does indeed. At least three instances come to mind in which gaps of many centuries can be found in a single short program (Isa. 9:6-7; 61:1-2; Zech. 9:9-10).

As a final brief review of the 70 weeks, we may note that the six main accomplishments of the 70 weeks are to bring to an end all human transgressions and sins, especially those of the nation Israel, to make reconciliation for iniquity, to vindicate by fulfillment all true prophets and their prophecies, to provide the inability of the devil to rightfully rule this world, to destroy him and his chief henchman, the Antichrist, and to usher in the Millennium.

The three main time-periods of the 70 weeks (490 years) are: 49 years, or 7 weeks from 445 B.C. to 396 B.C.; 434 years, or 62 weeks from 396 B.C. to A.D. 32; a time-out period (which has already lasted almost 20 centuries), and the 7 years, or 1 week from the Rapture till the Millennium.

The two main individuals of the 70 weeks are Messiah—the Lord Jesus Christ, and the prince that shall come—the wicked Antichrist.

The Divine Mathematics

COMMENTS

Mathematics is a science, not an art. In art there is room for the artist's interpretation and manipulation of the various ingredients of his art. In science, there is no room for personal or creative interpretation; it is exact. 2 + 2 always equals 4; not 3½ or 4¼. So it is with God's divine mathematics. When God gives a precise measurement, that is exactly what He means; not one bit more or one bit less.

Daniel knew that God's revelation had said that the Babylonian Captivity would last 70 years for he had studied the prophecy of Jeremiah (Dan. 9:2; cf. Jer. 29:10). The thing that he did not know was whether it was to be measured from the carrying away of the first segment (when he was brought to Babylon) or with the third and final segment. Thus, he was certain of the length of the Captivity but was not certain of the exact time at which it was considered to have begun or the exact time at which it was to end (though it was 70 years whether it is figured from the taking of the first captives to the return of the first contingency or from the destruction of Solomon's temple to the dedication of Zerubbabel's temple). Daniel realized that the Captivity had come because of Israel's sins, thus he sought God's face in prayer and went about acting as a priest in Israel's stead confessing Israel's sins, seeking God's forgiveness, and Israel's restoration.

In response to Daniel's prayer of faith, God sent His Angel Gabriel to give Daniel some more divine mathematics. Gabriel revealed that 70 weeks (lit., 70 sevens) had been determined on Israel in which their sins would be completely done away, they would be reconciled to their God, and everlasting righteousness would be ushered in (Dan. 9:24). These 70 weeks paralleled and supplemented the revelation given to Daniel in his visions reported in Daniel 2, 7–8. To help Daniel (and us), Gabriel revealed that these 70 weeks are to be divided into two parts, the first being 69 weeks, divided into two segments of 49 and 434 years respectively. This would embrace a period of time from the decree to restore Jerusalem until the coming and cutting off of the Messiah. In other words, 49 years would lapse from the time Cyrus would issue the decree to rebuild Jerusalem until it would be rebuilt. Then 434 years after Jerusalem was rebuilt, the Messiah would come and would be cut off. The last year will be initiated when "the prince that shall come" (9:26) will execute a peace treaty guaranteeing Israel its sovereignty. At the end of that seventieth week, the Messiah's kingdom of everlasting righteousness would be established.

God's divine mathematics are precise. The decree to rebuild Jerusalem was issued by Artaxerxes in 445 B.C., Jerusalem was rebuilt 49 years later, in 396 B.C., thus the first segment indicated by Gabriel was right on schedule. In A.D. 32, Messiah was crucified; exactly 434 years after the rebuilding of Jerusalem. The apparent discrepancy in years is due to the change from the Jewish to the Gregorian calendar. Thus the second segment indicated by Gabriel was right on schedule. Sixty-nine of the 70 weeks have been realized precisely as predicted. But what of the third segment, the seventieth week? It begins with the signing of the defense pact between "the prince that shall come" (Antichrist, or the King of the West) and Israel. That act will accomplish two things: (1) the beginning of the seventieth week and (2) the positive identification of "the prince that shall come." Daniel's prophecy is silent about intervening events for they do not concern Israel, "thy people" (9:24). The fact that 69 of the 70 weeks have been fulfilled in detail and exactly on time indicates that the seventieth will likewise be fulfilled in God's time. In the meantime, we need to be busy "redeeming the time" and get the message of God's grace to as many people as we can.

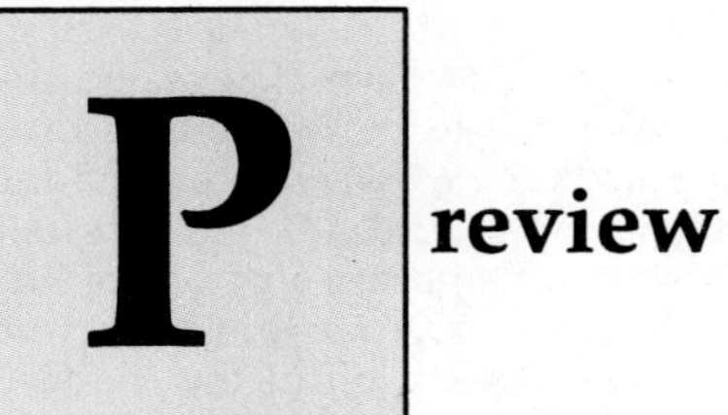

The Story Has a Happy Ending

DANIEL 10–12

Where in the Bible would you turn to find the most detailed account of the coming Antichrist? Or, where in the Bible would you turn to find one of the most dramatic accounts of angels, both hindering and helping God's people? The answer to each question can be located in Daniel 10–12.

Let's consider the first subject. What about this future satanic superman, known as the Antichrist? How does he come into power? When will he rule? How long will he rule? What terrible things will he do? Where will he establish his kingdom? Who will eventually destroy him? Daniel 11 deals with these questions.

And now the second subject. How do the elect angels help mankind and how do the evil angels hinder mankind? Daniel 10 and 12 clarify these matters for us. His final question to God is: *"O my Lord, what shall be the end of these things?"* God's final words to Daniel are: *"Go thy way, Daniel: for the words are closed up and sealed till the time of the end" (12:8-9).*

Do you know the staggering significance of these words? They mean that believers living today can understand more about the Book of Daniel than did the prophet himself. The reason? Because we live in (or near) "the time of the end."

Overview

<table>
<tr><td>SCRIPTURE</td><td colspan="5">Daniel 10–12</td></tr>
<tr><td>SUBJECT</td><td colspan="5">Tribulation and triumph: former and future</td></tr>
<tr><td rowspan="5">SPECIFICS</td><td colspan="2">Former</td><td colspan="3">Future</td></tr>
<tr><td rowspan="2">Tribulation</td><td rowspan="2">Daniel's prayer life was hindered by a hostile angel</td><td rowspan="2">Tribulation</td><td>The facts</td><td>Israel will be hindered by the Antichrist during the Great Tribulation</td></tr>
<tr><td>The foreshadows</td><td>Alexander is a type of Antichrist through his conquests
Antiochus is a type through his cruelty</td></tr>
<tr><td rowspan="2">Triumph</td><td rowspan="2">Daniel's prayer life was helped by a holy angel</td><td rowspan="2">Triumph</td><td>The facts</td><td>Israel will be helped by the archangel during the Great Tribulation</td></tr>
<tr><td>The friend</td><td>Michael</td></tr>
<tr><td>SAINTS AND SINNERS</td><td colspan="5">Daniel, an angel from God, Alexander the Great, Antiochus Epiphanes, Antichrist, Michael</td></tr>
<tr><td rowspan="2">SENTENCE SUMMARIES</td><td>O.T. Verse</td><td colspan="4">"So shall they fear the name of the LORD from the west, and His glory from the rising of the sun. When the enemy shall come in like a flood, the Spirit of the LORD shall lift up a standard against him" (Isa. 59:19).</td></tr>
<tr><td>N.T. Verse</td><td colspan="4">"We wrestle not against flesh and blood, but against principalities, against powers, against the rulers of the darkness of this world, against spiritual wickedness in high places" (Eph. 6:12).</td></tr>
</table>

THE CONFLICT ABOVE THE CLOUDS

A MAN IN MOURNING

Daniel had set aside a period of three weeks to be alone with God. During that time, he refrained from eating food, drinking wine, and anointing himself.

AN ANGEL IN ATTENDANCE

The description of the angel. *"Then I lifted up mine eyes, and looked, and behold a certain man clothed in linen, whose loins were girded with fine gold of Uphaz, his body also was like the beryl, and his face as the appearance of lightning, and his eyes as lamps of fire, and his arms and his feet like in color to polished brass, and the voice of his words like the voice of a multitude" (Dan. 10:5).*

Daniel immediately grew pale and weak with fright at such a dazzling sight. The men with Daniel were also in terror, though they did not actually see the vision as did Daniel.

The declaration of the angel. He had been hindered by the prince of Persia. Who was this prince? We quickly note that he was powerful—he singlehandedly blocked one of heaven's mightiest angels for 21 days. He was perverted—he withstood God's divinely appointed messenger. Thus, he must have been a high-ranking demon assigned by Satan to Persia to control the demonic activities in that kingdom.

He had been helped by the Archangel Michael. This angel then proceeded to comfort, reassure, strengthen, and instruct Daniel concerning the end times.

The determination of the angel. As he returned to God, the angel was aware that not only would he be once again confronted by the Persian demon, but also the demon of Greece. Apparently, Satan was throwing in new support by sending into battle his future appointee over the Grecian Empire. But the angel was confident, knowing he could again count on the help of Michael.

A CHRONOLOGY OF CHRISTLESS KINGS

ALEXANDER THE GREAT INCLUDING HIS PREDECESSORS AND SUCCESSORS

Four Persian kings would rule after Cyrus (who was ruling when Daniel wrote this) and the fourth would be the richest of all. This happened. After this, a mighty king ruled. This was Alexander the Great.

This king would suddenly die in his prime. His kingdom would not be given to his posterity, but would be divided by outsiders into four sections. This was what happened. Shortly after Alexander's death, Philip, his half-brother, Alexander II, his legitimate son, and Hercules, his illegitimate son, were all three murdered and Alexander's four generals took over.

ANTIOCHUS EPIPHANES

He was the youngest son of Antiochus the Great and was immediately classified as a vile (or contemptible) person by the Word of God. He was nicknamed "Epimanes" by those who knew him best, meaning "madman." He practiced deceit and pretended to be a second-century Robin Hood.

Antiochus had hoped to capture Egypt, but was stopped by the mighty Romans. He took out his insane rage on the city of Jerusalem.

"And arms shall stand on his part, and they shall pollute the sanctuary of strength, and shall take away the daily sacrifice, and they shall place the abomination that maketh desolate. . . . And they that understand among the people shall instruct many; yet they shall fall by the sword, and by flame, by captivity, and by spoil, many days" (11:31, 33).

He shall do everything according to his own selfish will. He shall magnify himself and malign God. The word "marvelous things" here in verse 36 is literally "astonishing, unbelievable." The Antichrist will scream out unbelievable blasphemies against God, insults no one else could ever think of, or would dare to say if they could.

He will be allowed by God to prosper (given full rope) during the Tribulation (the indignation), he will not regard "the gods of his fathers," he will not have the desire for (or of) women, and his god will be the god of fortresses. The Antichrist will spend all his resources on military programs.

In the latter days of the Tribulation, he shall be attacked by the king of the South (Egypt) and the king of the North (Russia, v. 40).

After the defeat of Russia, the Antichrist will occupy Palestine. Edom and Moab will not be occupied by him. After establishing control in Palestine, the Antichrist will march into Egypt and control that land. While he is in Egypt, he will hear alarming rumors from the East and the North. The exact nature of these rumors is uncertain, but he will quickly return and in great fury destroy many. Here again the identity of those who are destroyed cannot be dogmatically stated.

He apparently will deal successfully with the threat and establish his worldwide headquarters on Mount Zion. Here he will remain until his total destruction by the King of kings at the end of the Tribulation.

"And he shall plant the tabernacles of his palace between the seas in the glorious holy mountain; yet he shall come to his end, and none shall help him" (v. 45).

CLOSING CONDITIONS

THE MINISTRY OF MICHAEL

"And at that time shall Michael stand up, the great prince which standeth for the children of thy people; and there shall be a time of trouble, such as never was since there was a nation even to that same time; and at that time thy people shall be delivered, everyone that shall be found written in the book" (12:1).

Michael is Israel's guardian angel. He will help deliver Israel through the worst period of human history.

THE TWO RESURRECTIONS

"And many of them that sleep in the dust of the earth shall awake, some to everlasting life, and some to shame and everlasting contempt. And they that be wise shall shine as the brightness of the firmament; and they that turn many to righteousness as the stars forever and ever" (vv. 2-3).

The resurrection of those to eternal life will occur at the beginning of the Millennium and will include all Old Testament and martyred tribulational saints. (See Job 19:25-26; Ps. 49:15; Isa. 25:8; 26:19; Hosea 13:14; Heb. 11:35; Rev. 20:4, 6.) The reward of all righteous soul winners is mentioned in Daniel 12:3.

The resurrection of those to shame and everlasting contempt will transpire after the Millennium and will include all unsaved people who have ever lived (see Rev. 20:5). Our Lord summarizes these two resurrections in John 5:28-29.

THE TWO LAST-DAY PROPHECIES

There will be an increase of knowledge and an increase of speed.

THE THREE TIME PERIODS

Daniel saw two other angels who had been listening to this private prophecy conference the mighty angel was conducting for the old statesman. One of the two suddenly asked how long this terrible Tribulation period would last. Neither of these two angels had apparently overheard the details of the 70-week vision in Daniel 9:24-27.

The mighty angel informed them that the duration of this final horrible half of the Tribulation will last as long as it takes for the pride and power of the Jews to be broken, or three and one-half years.

1290 days. This period refers to the same as mentioned above, but includes an additional 30 days. Though we cannot be dogmatic, it would seem reasonable to conclude that an additional month will be needed here to carry out the sheep and goat judgment mentioned in Matthew 25:31-46.

1335 days. Here again a period of time is added, 45 days. What will be the need of these 45 days? It may be the time necessary for setting up the government machinery for carrying on the rule of Christ.

THE FOUR FINAL CONCLUSIONS

The mighty angel raises both hands into heaven as he attests to the veracity of all this. Many shall be cleansed (saved) during the Tribulation; this includes both Jews and Gentiles. The wicked, however, will continue their evil ways.

Daniel was to carefully preserve his writings but all its meaning would not be revealed to him until that glorious day when he stood alongside the righteous awaiting his inheritance.

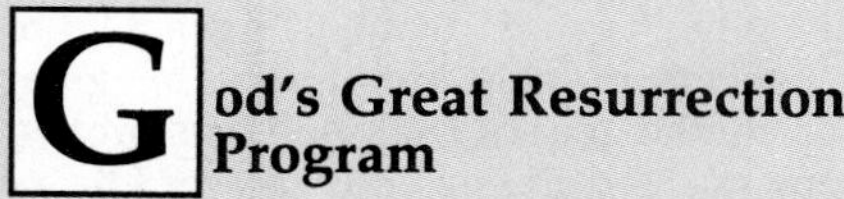

God's Great Resurrection Program

COMMENTS

If the prophecy of Daniel ended with Daniel 11:45 it would be wonderful, but incomplete. Chapter 12 continues the thought begun in chapters 10–11. After the briefest mention of a time of great trouble (the Great Tribulation) during which Michael, the archangel, will take Israel's part, and achieve their deliverance, the crowning jewel is added to Daniel's prophecy (12:1-2). The angel reveals to Daniel that there is going to be a great resurrection program. It will be in two parts: (1) some to everlasting life and (2) some to shame and everlasting contempt.

We must always realize in dealing with the prophecy of Daniel that it was given to a prophet of Israel and primarily concerns God's dealings as they relate to Israel. Therefore, the things in Daniel's prophecy do not relate to the church and its program at all. This is important because though the two resurrections mentioned in verse 2 appear in close juxtaposition to one another they pertain to Israel and are not to be confused with the Rapture of the church. The two events are actually separated by 1,000 years. The resurrection to life occurs at the beginning of the Millennium. At that time, all of the Old Testament saints will be raised from the dead. Abraham will realize all of the promises given him and will actually see the nation that God promised him on this earth (cf. Gen. 12:1-3). Moses will see that Israel has actually been given all of the land from the great river in Egypt to the great River Euphrates (cf. Deut. 30:1-8). David will see his Son, Jesus, reigning on his throne over his people (cf. 2 Sam. 7:12-16). Jeremiah will see the nation regathered, cleansed of its sins, and nationally regenerated (cf. Jer. 31:31-33). Every promise ever given to Israel or to any Old Testament saint will be completely and utterly fulfilled. What a glorious day the resurrection unto life will be for Israel and all the Old Testament saints who died having "received not the promise" (cf. Heb. 11:39).

Jesus mentioned these two resurrections in John 5:28-29. Paul gave us some supplementary revelation concerning the first resurrection in 1 Corinthians 15:22-23 and lets us know that the first resurrection actually consists of three parts: (1) the resurrection of Christ, (2) the resurrection and Rapture of the saints of the Church Age, and (3) the resurrection of the Old Testament saints. Only this last one is in view in Daniel's prophecy.

But what of the second resurrection? It will take place at the end of the Millennium and will involve all the unbelieving dead from Cain down to the last unbeliever to die. It is described in Revelation 20:11-15 in which those participating in this resurrection stand before God for the Great White Throne Judgment and "whosoever was not found written in the Book of Life was cast into the lake of fire" to be forever separated from God and His attributes.

Putting together this brief survey of what the Scripture teaches concerning these two resurrections we can see that it isn't a question of *whether* one is going to be raised from the dead; it is a question of *when*—the first resurrection, the resurrection to life, or the second resurrection, the resurrection to death. If one should be in doubt he can settle the question at any time he wishes. All one has to do is to believe in Jesus who loved him and gave Himself for him. For one who will do that, his sins will be forgiven and he will be given the righteousness of Christ. If he should die physically before Jesus comes in the air to receive His church to Himself, he will be a part of that Rapture unto life (cf. 1 Thes. 4:13-18).

Understandably, Daniel wondered about all of the things that he had learned. When he asked about them he was told that these words "are closed up and sealed till the time of the end' (Dan. 12:9). Those days are on us.

The Last Piece of the Puzzle

COMMENTS

One reason why it takes so long to assemble a jigsaw puzzle is because you have to put the first 999 pieces together so that you can find the last piece of the puzzle. When you find that last piece, you can sit back and enjoy the picture that with patience and perseverance you have put together.

In the previous revelations given him in chapters 2, 7–9, Daniel had been given pieces to the puzzle of God's future plan and program. Daniel set aside a three-week period to fast, pray, and seek to understand all the revelations that God had given to him. Unknown to Daniel, one piece of the puzzle was missing. God dispatched an angel to give Daniel the necessary interpretation and supplementary information. God's angel was waylaid by "the prince of Persia" (Satan's angel behind the kingdom of Persia). Only when Michael, the archangel, came, was the angel freed and able to complete his mission.

What was this message that occasioned such satanic resistance? It was the final piece of the puzzle to reveal to Daniel (and us) what we would need to know. The angel's message contained two pieces of information that Satan did not want Daniel to know: (1) that he was beloved of God (cf. 10:11, 19) and (2) the role that the forces of evil would play in the times of the Gentiles.

What did the angel reveal concerning the kingdom of Medo-Persia? The angel's message given in chapters 10–11 revealed that four Syrian kings would follow Darius the Mede and that the fourth one (Xerxes) would be the greatest and that he would stir up all against Greece (11:2).

What did the angel reveal concerning the kingdom of Greece? The angel's interpretation given in chapters 10 and 11 gave a lot of detail concerning this kingdom. The great horn on the he goat of chapter 8 was broken and four horns came up in its place. Out of the four horns came a little horn. The details of these four horns are amplified in the angel's interpretation in chapters 10 and 11. Alexander the Great's kingdom would be divided between his four generals. In the east Antiochus Epiphanes would arise having obtained his kingdom through flattery. It is further revealed that the kings of the North and South would be continually fighting each other.

What did the angel reveal about the end times (the Tribulation period)? The angel's interpretation given in chapters 10 and 11 emphasized the part that Antichrist will play during this period. He will be a king like Antiochus Epiphanes who will exalt and magnify himself. He will blaspheme God and will prosper until his time is fulfilled. He will not regard the God of his father and will not regard the desire of women (he will be a homosexual?), he will have great military might, will deal in strong fortresses, will honor those who follow him, and the kings of the North and South will come against him in the middle of the seventieth week.

The content of the angel's message, then, reveals in great detail the part that the forces of evil and those empowered by them are going to have in these events. Satan does not like to operate in the light. He wants his activities to be covert thus he did all in his power to keep these details from reaching God's man. However, in the warfare between the forces of God and the forces of Satan, there is no contest. God always is victorious and in control. Because of Daniel's determination to know God's truth; because of the angel's faithfulness; and because of Michael's intervention we know "the wiles of the devil" (cf. Eph. 6:10-11) and know that he is a defeated foe.

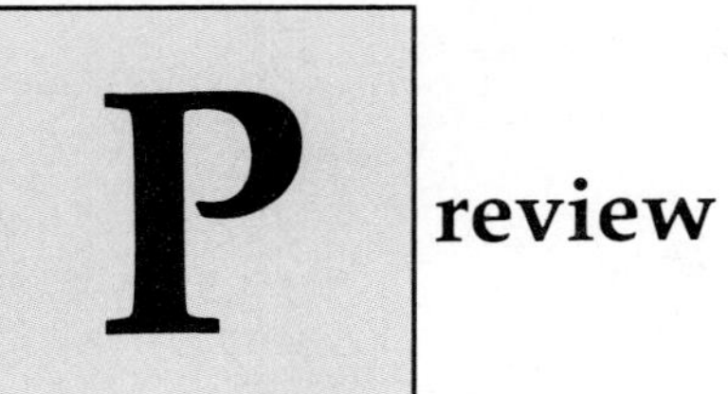

A Watchman on the Wall

EZEKIEL 1–24; 33

There could be absolutely no doubt about it whatever. This was the most impressive and unforgettable ordination service the world had ever known, or probably would ever know. To begin with, consider the special invited visitors. They consisted of heavenly angelic creatures known as the cherubim. These celestial beings arrived in whirlwind fashion, amidst bright coals of fire, rapidly rotating wheels of polished amber, traveling in groups of four at the speed of light. When all was ready, God Himself delivered "the charge" to the candidate, appointing him on the spot to be a watchman on the wall for Israel. Then the candidate was requested to eat the paper on which the ordination address was written. Finally, there was a blinding manifestation of the glory of God, orchestrated by the Spirit of God. Small wonder that the candidate, Ezekiel, was unable to speak for a long while afterward.

But why was Ezekiel afforded such glorious heavenly sights and sounds? Perhaps to compensate him, for later this prophet would be forced to witness and record the saddest moment in Israel's history, the removal of God's glory cloud from the temple and nation.

Overview

<table>
<tr><td>SCRIPTURE</td><td colspan="7">Ezekiel 1–24; 33</td></tr>
<tr><td>SUBJECT</td><td colspan="7">Ezekiel: the man and his message</td></tr>
<tr><td rowspan="5">SPECIFICS</td><td colspan="4">Ezekiel and Jehovah</td><td colspan="3">Ezekiel and Judah</td></tr>
<tr><td rowspan="4">His meeting with God</td><td colspan="2">The occasion</td><td>The onlookers</td><td rowspan="4">His mission for God</td><td rowspan="2">In Babylon</td><td>Warning</td></tr>
<tr><td colspan="2">To ordain Ezekiel as Israel's watchman on the wall</td><td>Four angelic creatures called the cherubim</td><td>Through pantomime
Through preaching
Through parables</td></tr>
<tr><td colspan="2">The order</td><td>The outcome</td><td rowspan="2">In Jerusalem</td><td>Witnessing</td></tr>
<tr><td>He encounters</td><td>God's Spirit
God's Scripture
God's splendor</td><td>For a while he could not speak</td><td>Jewish elders worshiping Satan
Jewish women worshiping Tammuz</td></tr>
<tr><td>SAINTS AND SINNERS</td><td colspan="7">Ezekiel, the cherubim, Ezekiel's wife</td></tr>
<tr><td rowspan="2">SENTENCE SUMMARIES</td><td colspan="2">O.T. Verse</td><td colspan="5">"Praise ye the LORD. Blessed is the man that feareth the LORD, that delighteth greatly in His commandments" (Ps. 112:1).</td></tr>
<tr><td colspan="2">N.T. Verse</td><td colspan="5">"Preach the Word; be instant in season, out of season; reprove, rebuke, exhort with all long-suffering and doctrine" (2 Tim. 4:2).</td></tr>
</table>

THE SANCTIFICATION OF THE MAN OF GOD— EZEKIEL

EZEKIEL SAW THE VISION OF THE LIVING CREATURES

These creatures were identified later as the cherubim. See Ezekiel 10:20.

Each cherubim had four faces. The face in front was as a man. The face on the right was as a lion. The face on the left was as an ox. The face in the back was as an eagle.

Each had two pairs of wings. One pair spread out from the middle of the back. The other pair was used to cover the body.

They had legs as of men, but cloven-like calves' feet, which shone like burnished brass.

They apparently traveled in groups of four and could move with the speed of light.

A whirling wheel, sparkling like a precious stone and full of eyes on its rim, stood next to each creature.

EZEKIEL HEARD THE VOICE OF THE LIVING GOD

He was to become a watchman for God. See chapters 18, 24.

"Son of man, I have made thee a watchman unto the house of Israel. Therefore hear the word at My mouth, and give them warning from Me. When I say unto the wicked, 'Thou shalt surely die'; and thou givest him not warning, nor speakest to warn the wicked from his wicked way, to save his life; the same wicked man shall die in his iniquity; but his blood will I require at thine hand. . . .

"Nevertheless if thou warn the righteous man, that the righteous sin not, and he doth not sin, he shall surely live, because he is warned; also thou hast delivered thy soul" (3:17-18, 21).

He was anointed by the Spirit of God. *"Then the Spirit took me up, and I heard behind me a voice of a great rushing, saying, 'Blessed be the glory of the LORD from His place.' . . . So the Spirit lifted me up, and took me away, and I went in bitterness, in the heat of my Spirit; but the hand of the LORD was strong upon me" (vv. 12, 14).*

He was to feed upon the Word of God. *"Moreover He said unto me, 'Son of man, eat that thou findest; eat this roll, and go speak unto the house of Israel.' So I opened my mouth, and He caused me to eat that roll. And He said unto me, 'Son of man, cause thy belly to eat, and fill thy bowels with this roll that I give thee.' Then did I eat it; and it was in my mouth as honey for sweetness" (vv. 1-3).*

He was allowed to see the glory of God. *"Then I arose, and went forth into the plain: and, behold, the glory of the LORD stood there, as the glory which I saw by the river of Chebar: and I fell on my face" (v. 23).*

For a while, Ezekiel would be unable to speak. *" 'And I will make thy tongue cleave to the roof of thy mouth, that thou shalt be dumb, and shalt not be to them a reprover; for they are a rebellious house. . . . In that day shall thy mouth be opened to him which is escaped, and thou shalt speak, and be no more dumb. And thou shalt be a sign unto them; and they shall know that I am the LORD.'*

"And it came to pass in the twelfth year of our Captivity, in the tenth month, in the fifth day of the month, that one that had escaped out of Jerusalem came unto me, saying, 'The city is smitten.' Now the hand of the LORD was upon me in the evening, afore he that was escaped came; and had opened my mouth, until he came to me in the morning; and my mouth was opened, and I was no more dumb" (v. 26; 24:27; 33:21-22).

THE DESOLATION OF THE CITY OF GOD—JERUSALEM

There were three distinct phases in the Babylonian Captivity and the siege of Jerusalem.

In 605 B.C. Daniel and other individuals of noble birth were carried away.

In 597 B.C. both King Jehoiachin and Ezekiel, along with many others, were taken into Babylon.

In 586 B.C., Judah's last king, Zedekiah, was carried away, the walls of Jerusalem were destroyed, and both temple and city were burned.

The events recorded here in Ezekiel 4–24 took place between the second and third phase. Apparently, there were false prophets, both in Jerusalem and in Babylon who

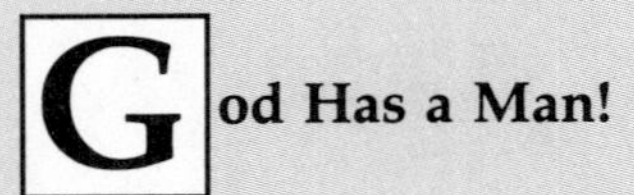

God Has a Man!

COMMENTS

God has a man or woman particularly suited for every job. It has always been and will continue to be so. Nowhere is this more graphically illustrated than in the case of the prophets of the Captivity Stage—Jeremiah, Ezekiel, and Daniel. Each was a man of God and to each God gave a specific task to accomplish. Jeremiah could not have done Ezekiel's job; Ezekiel could not have done Daniel's job; and Daniel could not have done Jeremiah's job. Each man was specially prepared by God and suited for the task to which God called him.

In the days of the Captivity, Jeremiah ministered in the land of Israel, while Ezekiel and Daniel ministered in Babylon. Jeremiah ministered to the "rejects" who were too poor, feeble, or old to be of any economic good to Nebuchadnezzar, so he left them behind in Israel to survive, if they could, or to perish—it made no difference to him. Ezekiel was taken captive in the second deportation along with King Jehoiachin, and ministered to the Israelites who were deported to Babylon. Daniel was taken captive in the first deportation and ministered in the Gentile courts of Nebuchadnezzar, Belshazzar, Darius, and Cyrus. God did not leave Himself without a witness whether among the Israelites left in Israel, or among the Israelites captive in Babylon, or in the court of the mightiest kings this world has ever seen. God is always intimately and actively involved in the affairs of this world whether among His people or among those who consider themselves to be the rulers of the world.

In the days of World War II, Hitler's Third Reich had great difficulties with two peoples: the Dutch and the Polish. Hitler's henchmen devised a fiendish plot which they thought would solve their problems. They reasoned that if they could uproot the populations of both nations and remove them from their familiar surroundings and homelands that their will to fight and resist would be broken. So they planned to exchange the populations. The population of Poland would be moved to Holland and the population of Holland would be moved to Poland. In the midst of the war, railroad rolling stock crucial to moving war materials could not be diverted for this task. Besides, such rebellious populations did not deserve such luxury. The exchange would take place by means of an overland forced march at the height of the winter. Many of the people would die on the way, but they were expendable. Their deaths would make the problem closer to solution.

Heinrich Himmler was second in command in the Third Reich. To him was entrusted the job of managing this cruel exchange of populations. Heinrich Himmler suffered from a "nervous stomach" during this time and employed the services of a naturopath whom he called "The Man with the Miracle Hands." The naturopath was a believer. In the course of his treatments of Himmler he learned of the fiendish plot to exchange the populations. The plot was repugnant to him. Little by little, he worked not only on Himmler's nervous stomach but on Himmler's seared conscience. Whether he succeeded with Himmler's stomach is not known. His success with Himmler's conscience is well known for the march was abandoned less than 24 hours before it was to have begun. The populations of Holland and Poland remained in their respective homelands for the duration of the war and continued to plague the Third Reich with their resistance until the war ended.

For every job, God has His man. The important thing is not what job one does or whether he is aware of what any other man of God is doing. The important thing is for God's man to do God's job in God's way.

brazenly assured the Jews that God would not dare destroy His own city, even though it had already suffered two bitter sieges. But Ezekiel knew otherwise, and he attempted through symbolic parables, dramatic acts, and messages to warn all that the Holy City would indeed suffer desolation and destruction.

EZEKIEL'S THIRTEEN SYMBOLIC ACTS

Drawing a map of Jerusalem with enemy camps around it. He drew a map of Jerusalem on a large flat tablet of soft clay, showing siege mounds being built against the city. He then added more details, portraying the enemy camps around it, and the placement of the battering rams. He finally placed an iron plate between the map and himself. This was to indicate the impenetrable wall of the Babylonian army, and also to show the impossibility of escape.

Laying a few hours a day for 390 days on his left side. He lay on his left side a few hours each day for 390 days to symbolize the iniquity of the Northern Kingdom. Each day was to represent a year.

Laying a few hours a day for 40 days on his right side. He then lay on his right side a few hours each day for 40 days to depict the iniquity of Judah, the Southern Kingdom. Again, each day was to represent a year.

Preparing a scant meal with mixed grains and baked over cow dung. He prepared bread made with mixed grains and baked it over dried cow dung which had been set afire. This was to indicate the scarcity of food in Jerusalem.

Shaving his head and beard. He shaved his head and beard with a sharp sword, and then divided the hair into three equal parts: one third he burned, one third he cut up with the sword, and one third he scattered to the wind.

All this was to indicate what was in store for Judah and Jerusalem. One third of her citizens died by fire in the Jerusalem siege. One third of her citizens fell by the sword, and the remaining third were scattered to the wind.

Stamping his feet and clapping his hands. He stamped his feet and clapped his hands to get their attention.

Digging an entrance through the city wall. He set some scant baggage outside his home. Then, in the evening he dug an entrance through the city wall. As he went through it carrying the baggage, he also covered his face. This was to vividly symbolize the following: the few articles of baggage represented the exiles hurriedly departing their homes, the entrance in the wall symbolized their desperation to leave the doomed city of Jerusalem, and the covered face depicted Zedekiah, Judah's last king, who was blinded by Nebuchadnezzar because of his rebellion and led captive into Babylon.

Trembling as he ate his food. "Moreover the word of the Lord *came to me saying, 'Son of man, eat thy bread with quaking, and drink thy water with trembling and with carefulness. And say unto the people of the land, "Thus saith the* Lord God *of the inhabitants of Jerusalem, and of the land of Israel; 'They shall eat their bread with carefulness, and drink their water with astonishment, that her land may be desolate from all that is therein, because of the violence of all them that dwell therein' " ' " (12:17-19).*

Weeping in public. "Sigh therefore, thou son of man, with the breaking of thy loins; and with bitterness sigh before their eyes. And it shall be, when they say unto thee, 'Wherefore sighest thou?' that thou shalt answer, 'For the tidings; because it cometh; and every heart shall melt, and all hands shall be feeble, and every spirit shall faint, and all knees shall be weak as water; behold, it cometh, and shall be brought to pass,' saith the Lord God*" (21:6-7).*

Slashing about a sword. "Thou therefore, son of man, prophesy, and smite thine hands together, and let the sword be doubled the third time, the sword of the slain. It is the sword of the great men that are slain, which entereth into their privy chambers" (v. 14).

Drawing a map of the Middle East with two routes on it. He drew a map of the Middle East and traced two routes for the king of Babylon to follow. One led to Jerusalem, and the other to Rabbath-Ammon. Both cities had rebelled against Nebuchadnezzar in 593 B.C. Ezekiel pictured the king here at the crossroads. Which city was destroyed first? The sad answer was immediately forthcoming.

"The king of Babylon stood at the parting of the way, at the head of the two ways, to use divination. He made his arrows bright, he consulted with images, he examined the liver. At his right hand was the divination for Jerusalem" (vv. 21-22).

Boiling a pot of water and baking it dry. He filled a pot of boiling water with the choicest meats and cooked it until the flesh fell off the bones. He then threw it all out and allowed the pot to bake itself dry to eliminate the scum and rust.

Remaining tearless at the funeral of his own wife. He was forbidden to express any outward sorrow over the sudden death of his beloved wife.

"So I spoke unto the people in the morning, and at even my wife died; and I did in the

morning as I was commanded" (24:18).

God ordered him not to mourn over the death of his wife to emphasize that He, the Lord, would not mourn over Jerusalem's death. It was especially significant to observe that she died the very day that Nebuchadnezzar began his third and final assault on Jerusalem.

EZEKIEL'S TWELVE JUDGMENT MESSAGES

Ezekiel's 12 judgment messages are found in 6:1-14; 7:1-27; 13:1-23; 14:1-11, 12-23; 18:1-32; 20:1-44, 45-49; 21:1-7; 22:1-16, 17-22, 23-31.

God had often held back His divine wrath in spite of Israel's brazen disobedience. *"But they rebelled against Me, and would not hearken unto Me; they did not every man cast away the abominations of their eyes, neither did they forsake the idols of Egypt. Then I said, 'I will pour out My fury upon them, to accomplish My anger against them in the midst of the land of Egypt.' But I wrought for My name's sake, that it should not be polluted before the heathen, among whom they were, in whose sight I made Myself known unto them, in bringing them forth out of the land of Egypt" (20:8-9).*

God took no joy in judging His people even at this desperate stage and again called for Judah's repentance. *" 'Cast away from you all your transgressions whereby ye have transgressed; and make you a new heart and a new spirit; for why will ye die, O house of Israel? For I have no pleasure in the death of him that dieth,' saith the Lord GOD. 'Wherefore turn yourselves, and live ye' " (18:31-32).*

But Judah would not listen and her hour of doom was now at hand.

Judah would then be destroyed not because of the sins of their fathers, but because of their own vile wickedness. *"The soul that sinneth, it shall die. The son shall not bear the iniquity of the father, neither shall the father bear the iniquity of the son. The righteousness of the righteous shall be upon him, and the wickedness of the wicked shall be upon him" (v. 20).*

Their prophets were wicked. " 'To wit, the prophets of Israel which prophesy concerning Jerusalem, and which see visions of peace for her, and there is no peace,' saith the Lord GOD. . . . 'There is a conspiracy of her prophets in the midst thereof, like a roaring lion ravening the prey; they have devoured souls; they have taken the treasure and precious things; they have made her many widows in the midst thereof' " (13:16; 22:25).

The princes were wicked. "Her princes in the midst thereof are like wolves ravening the prey, to shed blood, and to destroy souls, to get dishonest gain" (v. 27).

Their priests were wicked. "Her priests have violated My Law, and have profaned Mine holy things; they have put no difference between the holy and profane, neither have they shewed difference between the unclean and the clean, and have hid their eyes from My Sabbaths, and I am profaned among them" (v. 26).

Their women were wicked. Even the presence of such godly men as Noah, Daniel, and Job could not spare the city of Jerusalem. *" 'Though Noah, Daniel, and Job, were in it, as I live,' saith the Lord GOD, 'they shall deliver neither son nor daughter; they shall but deliver their own souls by their righteousness' " (14:20).*

Her armies would be absolutely helpless in defending her.

Her wealth could not purchase one additional minute of freedom. *"They shall cast their silver in the streets, and their gold shall be removed: their silver and their gold shall not be able to deliver them in the day of the wrath of the LORD. They shall not satisfy their souls, neither fill their bowels, because it is the stumbling block of their iniquity" (7:19).*

The Holy City of God had now become the Harlot City of Satan. God would, therefore, bring into Jerusalem the worst of nations and people to occupy their lands and homes. Judah's cities would be burned, her idols smashed, and her temple destroyed. Four great punishments would befall her citizens, that of war, famine, ferocious beasts, and plagues. A remnant, however, would survive to testify of God's holiness and hatred for sin.

EZEKIEL'S SIX PARABLES

A fruitless vine tree.

The adopted girl who became a harlot.

God's concern for Israel. God had found in a field an abandoned, despised, and dying baby girl. Her name was Israel. This was a reference to Israel's bondage to the Egyptians in the first few chapters of Exodus. (See especially Ex. 1:13-14; 2:23; 3:7.) God graciously adopted this ragged little girl and when she became of age, He entered into the sacred rite of marriage with her, and she legally became His elected wife. This, of course, all took place at Mount Sinai when God ratified His covenant with Israel. (See 19:5; also, compare Ezek. 16:9 with Ex. 19:14.)

After the marriage God dressed her in the most beautiful clothes, adorned her with the most costly jewels, and provided the finest

God Has a Language!

COMMENTS

Not only does God have a specific man to do a specific job, He also has a language in which His message is to be communicated. This is true whether the communication is between Himself and His prophet, or between His prophet and the people to whom the prophet has been sent.

In communicating His message to His Prophet Ezekiel, God used the language of a vision. These visions were of the cloud (1:4), the four cherubim (vv. 5-16), of the four wheels (vv. 15-21), and of the throne and rainbow (vv. 22-28). Taken in summary, the vision communicated to the prophet the glory of God and showed him that the coming judgment, righteousness, and discipline are all a part of the glory of God. The cloud represented God's judgment in the form of Babylon who would come into the land again. The cherubim and wheels showed the prophet that behind the events of earth there are the operations in heaven. The throne and the rainbow showed the prophet that Jehovah is supreme over all. The Person on the throne could well have been Jesus Christ who is the sovereign Ruler over all. In wrath He remembers mercy. In the end of His judgment there issues the triumph of His grace. God communicated again by means of a vision with His prophet in 3:22-27 to warn of the siege of Jerusalem; in 8:4-18 to warn of the destruction of Jerusalem and the temple; in chapters 10 and 11 to describe the departure of the glory cloud from Solomon's temple; and in 43:1-4 to tell of the glory of God filling the millennial temple.

Not only did God communicate with His prophet by visions, He communicated with him by voice and spoken language. In 2:1–3:3 God spoke to Ezekiel to give him a specific call (2:3); to call him to preach His Word (vv. 4, 7); and to call him to be obedient, courageous, steadfast, not rebellious, and to be filled with his message (v. 6–3:3).

The third way that God communicated with His prophet was by symbolic language (2:9–3:3). The prophet was shown a scroll which contained the message of God's judgment against Israel. He was commanded to eat this scroll and then to go and communicate its message to his people. God was showing His prophet that he must be full of His message and must communicate that message exactly. The scroll was "as honey for sweetness" in the prophet's mouth because even though it involved God's judgment, it embraced God's sovereign will which is perfect (cf. Rom. 12:2).

In communicating God's message to the people, God's prophet used the language of symbolic actions. Throughout the course of the prophecy (Ezek. 4–21) with 13 symbolic actions the prophet himself became the object lesson of God's relationship to Israel and the impending judgment that would fall if Israel did not repent.

Ezekiel also communicated God's message to his people with his voice, though those messages are not recorded in quoting what he said, but in quoting what he was commanded to say by the "Word of the LORD" (see, for instance, 13:1). The emphasis, then, was not on the prophet who delivered the message, but on God who was the source of the message. The message was certain not because of the prophet, but because of God who commissioned the message.

The Prophet Ezekiel and his prophecy demonstrate that God has a language and that that language is sufficient to communicate the message that He wants to have communicated, whether it is delivered directly to His prophet or through His prophet to His people. The language of God is always understood. He always uses just *the* language that will enable His message to be communicated in all of its purity and with all its authority. Language is not only God's tool, it is His creation and serves His purpose perfectly.

food available for His beloved. This occurred in Israel's history during the reigns of David and Solomon. (See 1 Sam. 8:11; 1 Kings 3:13; 10:4-7.)

Israel's contempt for God. But this little ex-orphan soon spurned all His love and faithfulness and became a common harlot of the streets. This intolerable action could not continue unpunished, for the beloved Husband was also the righteous Judge. He would, therefore, turn her over to her own murderous lovers to be abused and punished.

Her wickedness by this time had even surpassed that of her older sister (Samaria, the capital of the Northern Kingdom) and that of her younger sister (Sodom). (See Ezek. 16:46-50.) After He had chastened her, God would once again restore her to Himself, because of His love for her and His promise to Abraham.

The two eagles. The events mentioned in this parable narrated the international affairs of Judah, Babylon, and Egypt between 597 and 588 B.C. The figures involved are Jehoiachin, Zedekiah, and Nebuchadnezzar. For the recorded history of this period, see 2 Kings 24:8-20; 2 Chronicles 36:9-13; Jeremiah 37; 52:1-7.

The tender twig's growth. God Himself stated He would someday plant the finest and most tender twig of all on Israel's highest mountain. This twig would grow into a noble tree, blessing all who came near it by its fruit and shade.

The tender twig's glory. Through all this, the entire world would know the plan and power of God.

These verses without question introduce a messianic prophecy (see Isa. 2:2-4; Micah 4:1-4). The tender twig is the Messiah (see Isa. 11:1; 53:2; Jer. 23:5-6; Rev. 22:16) and the high mountain is Mount Zion (see Ps. 2:6).

The mother lioness and her cubs. A mother lioness had some cubs. One of her whelps grew up and learned to devour men. For this he was trapped and taken into Egypt.

Another of her cubs did the same thing. He also was captured and carried away into Babylon.

Some believed the mother lioness here was Hamutal, the wife of Josiah, and mother of three Judean kings. The first cub was Jehoahaz who was carried away into an Egyptian prison by Pharaoh Neco. The other cub was Zedekiah (Hamutal's youngest son). He was Judah's last king and was carried away by Nebuchadnezzar into Babylon.

The two harlot sisters' immorality. Two sisters began their sad history of prostitution by engaging in immorality with the Egyptians.

The sisters' identity. The names of these girls were Aholah and Aholibah and were identified as Samaria and Jerusalem. The word Aholah means "her tent" and may be a reference to the fact that God never approved of the false religion of Samaria (capital of the Northern Kingdom) as instituted by its first king, Jeroboam. Thus, "her tent" meant she had her own religion which did not include God. The word Aholibah means "my tent is in her," indicating perhaps that God's presence still dwelt in the Jerusalem temple in spite of Judah's sin. It was said here that both these girls became harlots because of their Egyptian immorality. This might have referred to the fact that both cities were impressed with the religious and political structures of Egypt.

Aholah then began illicit relations with Assyria. This happened under Northern king Menahem, who allied himself with Assyria.

Aholibah did the same thing with Babylon. King Hezekiah treated the Babylonian representatives almost as if they were gods (see 2 Kings 20:12-19; 2 Chron. 32:31).

God, therefore, determined to turn both these sisters over to the full brutality of their respective lovers.

The departure of Judah from the glory of God. Ezekiel was caught away in a vision from Babylon to Jerusalem. He saw 70 Israelite elders worshiping satanic images in the temple.

"So I went in and saw; and behold every form of creeping things, and abominable beasts, and all the idols of the house of Israel, portrayed upon the wall round about" (Ezek. 8:10).

He saw some Jewish women weeping for the false Babylonian god Tammuz. He saw 25 men with their backs to the temple, facing east and worshiping the sun. He then saw six angels marking certain unbelieving Jews for destruction and others for deliverance.

The departure of the glory of God from Judah. He viewed the glory cloud over the mercy seat and watched it move to stand over the door of the temple. From there it moved to the East Gate, and finally it hovered over Mount of Olives and disappeared.

"And the glory of the LORD went up from the midst of the city, and stood upon the mountain which is on the east side of the city" (11:23).

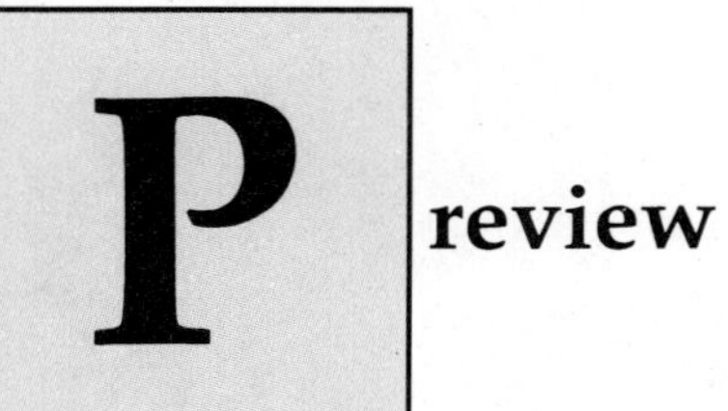

Israel's Enemies and God's Elect

EZEKIEL 25–32; 34–35

Isaiah had first written about these two things. Now Ezekiel is called on to do the same. Some of Isaiah's thoughts probably raced through Ezekiel's mind also. Could any two separate events be further removed in purpose and purity than these two? The first was historical, grievous, and characterized by self-will. The second was prophetic, glorious, and characterized by self-sacrifice. One had to do with a godless rebellion; the other will provide a godly reign. An angelic cherub instigated the former, while a divine shepherd will initiate the latter.

The historical tragedy? Lucifer's unsuccessful attempt to rule over the universal kingdom of God.

The prophetic triumph? Christ's successful reign over the universal kingdom of God.

The irony seen in all this is amazing. Lucifer began at the top, in Eden's beautiful Garden, enjoying vast wisdom and great beauty. Jesus began at the bottom, in Bethlehem's lowly manger, increasing in wisdom, and having no earthly beauty. And the results? The haughty in heart will be forever degraded in hell. But the humble in heart will be forever exalted in heaven.

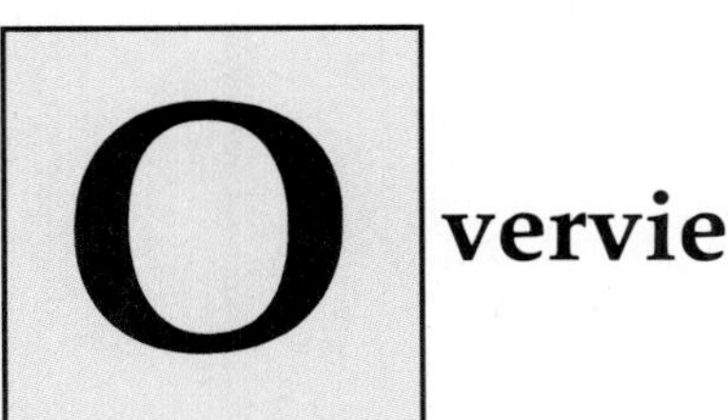

verview

<table>
<tr><td>SCRIPTURE</td><td colspan="4">Ezekiel 25–32; 34–35</td></tr>
<tr><td>SUBJECT</td><td colspan="4">The foes and friends of Judah</td></tr>
<tr><td rowspan="6">SPECIFICS</td><td colspan="3">Her current foes</td><td>Her coming friend</td></tr>
<tr><td>General</td><td colspan="2">Specific</td><td rowspan="5">His office: Jesus Christ, the all-caring Shepherd
His opposition: the many false shepherds
His omniscience: He knows all the needs of His flock
His omnipotence: He meets all the needs of His flock</td></tr>
<tr><td rowspan="4">Ammon
Moab
Edom
Philistia
Sidon</td><td rowspan="2">Tyre</td><td>How a city would fall</td></tr>
<tr><td>How a cherub once fell</td></tr>
<tr><td rowspan="2">Egypt</td><td>To be punished by the Babylonian king</td></tr>
<tr><td>To be punished by the King of kings</td></tr>
<tr><td>SAINTS AND SINNERS</td><td colspan="4">Ezekiel, prince of Tyre, King of Tyre</td></tr>
<tr><td rowspan="2">SENTENCE SUMMARIES</td><td>O.T. Verse</td><td colspan="3">"He shall feed His flock like a shepherd; He shall gather the lambs with His arm, and carry them in His bosom, and shall gently lead those that are with young" (Isa. 40:11).</td></tr>
<tr><td>N.T. Verses</td><td colspan="3">"The thief cometh not, but for to steal, and to kill, and to destroy. I am come that they might have life, and that they might have it more abundantly. I am the Good Shepherd; the Good Shepherd giveth His life for the sheep" (John 10:10-11).</td></tr>
</table>

THE CONDEMNATION OF THE ENEMIES OF GOD

AMMON

Their sin was the devilish glee they displayed over the destruction of the Jerusalem temple and the death of Judah's citizens.

MOAB

They had degraded Jehovah, looking on Him as just another national and tribal god.

EDOM

This nation had butchered helpless Jews during the Babylonian invasion.

PHILISTIA

Because the Philistines had acted with vengeance, God would execute judgment on them.

TYRE

The sin of Tyre. Tyre had rejoiced over the fall of Judah. The city was totally corrupted with gross materialism.

The ruler of Tyre. The ruler at the time Ezekiel wrote was Ithbaal II, who boasted he was as strong as a god and wiser than a Daniel.

The punishment of Tyre. Perhaps here it should be noted that Tyre was actually two cities, one on the coastline, some 60 miles northwest of Jerusalem, and the other on an island, a half mile out in the Mediterranean Sea. At the time of Ezekiel's prophecy, the Tyrians were in open revolt against Babylon. Various nations were to come up against Tyre like ocean waves. In spite of this strong watery protection, Ezekiel predicted her walls would be torn down, her very soil would be scrapped, making her as bare as a rock, and both cities would become a place for the spreading of fishing nets.

"Therefore thus saith the Lord God 'Behold, I am against thee, O Tyrus, and will cause many nations to come up against thee, as the sea causeth his waves to come up. And they shall destroy the walls of Tyrus, and break down her towers. I will also scrape her dust from her, and make her like the top of a rock. It shall be a place for the spreading of nets in the midst of the sea, for I have spoken it,' saith the Lord God, 'and it shall become a spoil to the nations' " (Ezek. 26:3-5).

The city would never again be inhabited. All this occurred later during the days of Alexander the Great exactly as Ezekiel had prophesied.

The sinister force behind Tyre. We have already noted, that in 28:1-10, Ezekiel described the pride of Ithbaal II who was ruler of Tyre at that time. But the prophet now moved beyond the earthly scene and described the creation and fall of a vile and vicious nonhuman creature. This fearful being was Satan himself, the real force behind the wickedness of Tyre.

The characteristics of this force. "Son of man, take up a lamentation upon the king of Tyrus, and say unto him, 'Thus saith the Lord God, "Thou sealest up the sum, full of wisdom, and perfect in beauty. Thou hast been in Eden the Garden of God; every precious stone was thy covering, the sardius, topaz, and the diamond, the beryl, the onyx, and the jasper, the sapphire, the emerald, and the carbuncle, and gold. The workmanship of thy tabrets and of thy pipes was prepared in thee in the day that thou wast created. Thou art the anointed cherub that covereth; and I have set thee so; thou wast upon the holy mountain of God; thou hast walked up and down in the midst of the stones of fire. Thou wast perfect in thy ways from the day that thou wast created, till iniquity was found in thee. By the multitude of thy merchandise they have filled the midst of thee with violence, and thou hast sinned. Therefore I will cast thee as profane out of the mountain of God, and I will destroy thee, O covering cherub, from the midst of the stones of fire. Thine heart was lifted up because of thy beauty, thou hast corrupted thy wisdom by reason of thy brightness. I will cast thee to the ground, I will lay thee before kings, that they may behold them" ' " (vv. 12-17).

The sum total of wisdom and beauty. The king of Tyre was the anointed cherub. He had been in Eden and was covered with precious stones.

SIDON

Because of her horrible influence, Sidon was likened to a pricking briar and a hurting thorn to the house of Israel. God would thus punish Sidon by sending an epidemic of disease and an army to destroy her. This occurred in 351 B.C., at which time the city was put to the torch by the Persians.

EGYPT

Her historical punishment (by Nebuchadnezzar). Egypt's sin, like that of so many other nations, was pride (2:6). Ezekiel, therefore, pronounced doom on Pharaoh, people, and even the animals. In chapter 31 Egypt was described as a mighty cedar of Lebanon, towering above all other trees. The birds nested in its branches, and animals gave birth under its shade. But soon the tree was corrupted by pride and God ordered the Babylonian wood choppers to hew it down.

Ezekiel informed us that Nebuchadnezzar conquered Egypt for its wealth in order to pay his soldiers after that long siege of Tyre. Egypt was to be desolate for 40 years. After the 40-year punishment period, Egypt would be restored somewhat, but would forever remain a minor kingdom, and Israel would never again depend on Egypt.

Her future punishment (by God). Though the name Nebuchadnezzar appears in this passage, it is thought the final fulfillment of the judgments mentioned here will transpire during the Tribulation. According to Daniel (11:40-43), Egypt will be destroyed during the Tribulation.

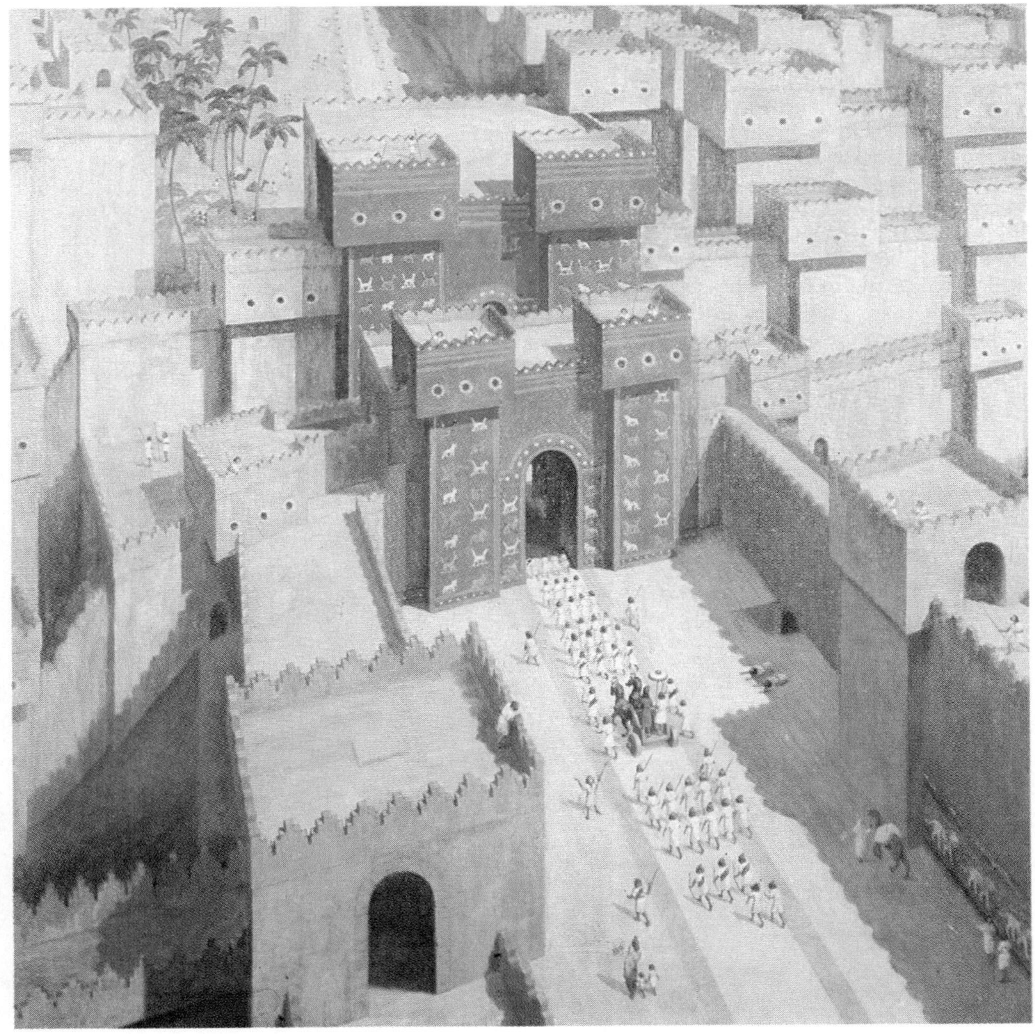

A painting of the famous Ishtar Gate of Babylon, leading into the city. In the upper right of the picture are the Hanging Gardens and beyond, the ziggurat, center of worship.

HE PRESENTATION OF THE SHEPHERD OF GOD— JESUS CHRIST

THE MANY FALSE SHEPHERDS

"Son of man, prophesy against the shepherds of Israel, prophesy, and say unto them, 'Thus saith the Lord GOD unto the shepherds, "Woe be to the shepherds of Israel that do feed themselves! Should not the shepherds feed the flocks?" ' . . .

"Thus saith the Lord GOD, 'Behold, I am against the shepherds; and I will require My flock at their hand, and cause them to cease from feeding the flock; neither shall the shepherds feed themselves anymore; for I will deliver My flock from their mouth, that they may not be meat for them" (Ezek. 34:2, 10).

They fed themselves instead of the flock. They had not taken care of the weak, nor tended the sick, nor bound up the broken bones, nor sought the lost. The sheep were then scattered having no shepherd. They had become prey to the wild animals. Therefore, the shepherds would be punished—their positions as shepherds would be removed; they would not be themselves fed by the Great Shepherd; and they would be judged and destroyed.

THE ONE TRUE SHEPHERD

"For thus saith the Lord GOD, 'Behold, I even I, will both search My sheep, and seek them out. As a shepherd seeketh out his flock in the day that he is among his sheep that are scattered; so will I seek out My sheep, and will deliver them out of all places where they have been scattered in the cloudy and dark day. . . .

" 'Thus shall they know that I the LORD their God am with them, and that they, even the house of Israel, are My people,' saith the Lord GOD" (vv. 11-12, 30).

He would search out the lost sheep and deliver them from their enemies. He would gather them from the mountains of Israel and give them rest in green pastures. He would put splints and bandages on their broken limbs and heal their sick. He would establish David as His trusted undershepherd. He would make an eternal pact with them and would guarantee their safety and place them in a perfect paradise.

The Worst Is Yet to Come

COMMENTS

In pronouncing judgment on the enemies of God, Ezekiel began with those who were related to Judah physically. Ammon and Moab were more distantly related to Judah having been born to Lot by each of his daughters. Edom is more closely related to Judah through Esau, Jacob's (Judah's immediate ancestor) brother. These enemies were judged because of the way they treated Judah during the time of its humiliation at the hands of Babylon. These enemies dwelt to the east and south of Judah. Philistia was a Gentile power to the west of Judah. God's judgment on them was to repay them for the vengeance they took against Judah and to bring them to the knowledge of Jehovah. Tyre and Sidon were the main cities of Judah's Gentile enemies to the north and west. They had exerted a corrupting moral influence on Judah. Egypt was Judah's principal Gentile enemy to the south. Thus Ezekiel pronounced judgment on all of Judah's enemies that surrounded her. Even though she was surrounded by enemies, Judah was safe and secure because Jehovah would protect her and take vengeance on those who hurt her. Later, Amos would use a similar technique to pronounce judgment on Judah's surrounding enemies (cf. Amos 1–6). Today, Israel is still surrounded by her enemies on whom God will ultimately bring judgment. Were it not for God's staying hand, Israel would be driven into the sea and would not be able to exist.

Ezekiel's prophecies against Tyre and Egypt are worthy of special note. They perfectly illustrate a feature of biblical prophecy known as "double fulfillment," or better, "partial fulfillment." Prophecy is God's revelation given to God's messenger, in this case Ezekiel, in a particular historical crisis. The prophecy is designed to meet that particular crisis but in some instances more is given than is applicable to the prophet's day. Because prophecy is God's revelation, frequently God will use the crisis in the prophet's day to speak not only to that crisis, but also to an even greater crisis which will occur long after the prophet has passed off of the scene. Such are the prophetic judgments against the prince of Tyre and the nation Egypt. Both of these were ominous enemies of Judah in Ezekiel's day. To the prophet God gave a message of judgment against the ruler of Tyre of that day and the Egyptian nation of that day. But there is an even more sinister power than that prince of Tyre and there is a more sinister Egypt than the Egypt of that day. God not only speaks to the immediate enemies but to the ultimate enemies as well. In the case of the prince of Tyre God delivers condemnation against the vile angelic character that is the power behind the prince of Tyre. Things are said of him that could not be true of the human prince of Tyre (Ezek. 28:12-19). Thus, part of the things spoken by the prophet were fulfilled in the destruction of Tyre by Alexander the Great, but the remainder will not be fulfilled until ultimately Satan, the evil force behind Tyre's wicked king, is defeated. This greater event is still future even to us today but will be as certainly fulfilled as was the earlier destruction.

In the case of Egypt, the nation of that day was punished by Nebuchadnezzar, king of Babylon. While Egypt was partially revived, the day is yet coming when an even greater Egypt will play a major role against Israel and will ultimately be completely destroyed (cf. Dan. 11:40-43). This day is yet future and is just as certain as the destruction of old.

In prophecies such as these, one is right to look not only at the partial fulfillment in the days of the prophet, but also at the partial fulfillment that is yet future. Only in taking a stance beyond the ultimate fulfillment and looking backward through history to the prophet's day, can one see that all of the details given to the prophet will be completely fulfilled.

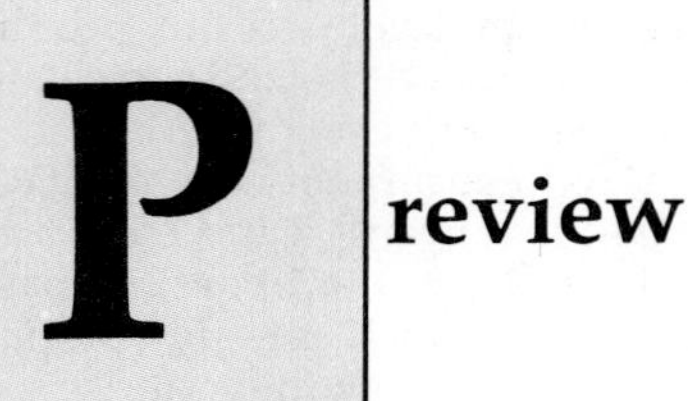

Preview

The Fall and Rise Versus the Rise and Fall

EZEKIEL 36–39

No other prophet before or after would ever see such a sight. Carried away by the Spirit of God, Ezekiel was set down in the midst of a valley utterly filled with human bones! He was then instructed to address those bleached bones, commanding them to heed God's Word. Then the miracle happened. The prophet could scarcely believe his eyes. By the untold thousands those brittle sticks of human structures arranged themselves into human skeletons. There they stood, a fleshless and lifeless army. But not for long.

The miracle was not over. In total fascination Ezekiel watched as they were all literally rebuilt from within. First, organs were attached to the bones, around which were wrapped muscles, flesh, and finally skin. Smooth skulls once again held eyes, projected ears, nose, and mouth.

This is what Ezekiel saw. But what did it all mean? In a nutshell, it depicted the resurrection and regeneration of the nation Israel.

The old black spiritual had it right. "Them bones goin' a rise again!"

Overview

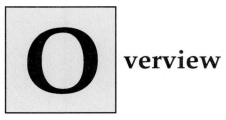

<table>
<tr><td>SCRIPTURE</td><td colspan="4">Ezekiel 36–39</td></tr>
<tr><td>SUBJECT</td><td colspan="4">Divine validation in two valleys</td></tr>
<tr><td rowspan="3">SPECIFICS</td><td colspan="2">Valley of dry bones</td><td colspan="2">Valley of Hamon</td></tr>
<tr><td rowspan="2">Validating God's faithfulness</td><td>Israel to be revived
Israel to be redeemed
Israel to be reunited
Israel to be restored</td><td rowspan="2">Validating God's furiousness</td><td>The confederacy
The conspiracy
The calamity
The carnage
The carnivorous
The cleaning up</td></tr>
<tr><td>The regathering of Israel</td><td>The renouncing of Russia</td></tr>
<tr><td>SAINTS AND SINNERS</td><td colspan="4">Ezekiel, Gog of Magog</td></tr>
<tr><td rowspan="2">SENTENCE SUMMARIES</td><td>O.T. Verse</td><td colspan="3">"The wicked shall be turned into hell, and all the nations that forget God" (Ps. 9:17).</td></tr>
<tr><td>N.T. Verses</td><td colspan="3">"For wheresoever the carcass is, there will the eagles be gathered together. . . . And He shall send His angels with a great sound of a trumpet, and they shall gather together His elect from the four winds, from one end of heaven to the other" (Matt. 24:28, 31).</td></tr>
</table>

HE RESTORATION OF THE NATION OF GOD—ISRAEL

"Therefore say, 'Thus saith the Lord God, "Although I have cast them far off among the heathen, and although I have scattered them among the countries, yet will I be to them as a little sanctuary in the countries where they shall come." '

"Therefore say, 'Thus saith the Lord God, "I will even gather you from the people, and assemble you out of the countries where ye have been scattered, and I will give you the land of Israel" ' " (Ezek. 11:16-17).

"Thus saith the Lord God, 'When I shall have gathered the house of Israel from the people among whom they are scattered, and shall be sanctified in them in the sight of the heathen, then shall they dwell in their land that I have given to My servant Jacob' " (28:25).

"For thus saith the Lord God, 'Behold, I, even I, will both search My sheep, and seek them out. As a shepherd seeketh out his flock in the day that he is among his sheep that are scattered; so will I seek out My sheep, and will deliver them out of all places where they have been scattered in the cloudy and dark day. And I will bring them out from the people, and gather them from the countries, and will bring them to their own land, and feed them upon the mountains of Israel by the river; and in all the inhabited places of the country' " (34:11-13).

"For I will take you from among the heathen, and gather you out of all countries, and will bring you into your own land" (36:24).

"And I will bring you out from the people, and will gather you out of the countries wherein ye are scattered, with a mighty hand, and with a stretched out arm, and with fury poured out" (20:34).

THE NECESSITY OF THIS RESTORATION

Israel had been previously driven from Palestine because of their sin. *"Wherefore I poured My fury upon them for the blood that they had shed upon the land, and for their idols wherewith they had polluted it. And I scattered them among the heathen, and they were dispersed through the countries, according to their way and according to their doings I judged them" (36:18-19).*

THE REASONS FOR THIS RESTORATION

The restoration would shame those Gentile nations which had sneered at Israel's tragedy and exonerate the great name of God. The rumor was being spread around that the God of Israel was unable (or unwilling) to protect and purify His own people.

"Therefore say unto the house of Israel, 'Thus saith the Lord God, "I do not this for your sakes, O house of Israel, but for Mine holy name's sake, which ye have profaned among the heathen, whither ye went. And I will sanctify My great name, which was profaned among the heathen, which ye have profaned in the midst of them; and the heathen shall know that I am the Lord," saith the Lord God, "when I shall be sanctified in you before their eyes. For I will take you from among the heathen, and gather you out of all countries, and will bring you into your own land. Then will I sprinkle clean water upon you, and ye shall be clean, from all your filthiness, and from all your idols, will I cleanse you" ' " (vv. 22-25).

THE VISION OF THIS RESTORATION

Ezekiel was commanded to prophesy over a valley filled with old dry human bones. There was a rattling noise from all across the valley and the bones of each body came together and attached as they had once been. After this, the muscles and flesh formed over the bones, and skin covered them. But the completed bodies had no breath. Ezekiel was then commanded to prophesy over them to give them breath. This he did.

"Then He said unto me, 'Son of man, these bones are the whole house of Israel. "Behold," they say, "Our bones are dried, and our hope is lost: we are cut off for our parts."

" 'Therefore prophesy and say unto them, "Thus saith the Lord God; 'Behold, O My people, I will open your graves, and cause you to come up out of your graves, and bring you into the land of Israel. And ye shall know that I am the Lord, when I have opened your graves, O

My people, and brought you up out of your graves' " ' " (37:11-13).

THE SYMBOL OF THIS RESTORATION

Ezekiel was to carve the following words on two wooden sticks. The first stick read: *"For Judah, and for the Children of Israel, his companions."* The second stick read: *"For Joseph, the stick of Ephraim, and for all the house of Israel, his companions."*

He was then to hold both sticks together in one hand, indicating the two kingdoms would someday be united again.

"And I will make them one nation in the land upon the mountains of Israel; and one king shall be king to them all; and they shall be no more two nations, neither shall they be divided into two kingdoms any more at all" (v. 22).

THE RESULTS OF THIS RESTORATION

To once again become God's people. "And ye shall dwell in the land that I gave to your fathers; and ye shall be My people, and I will be your God" (36:28).

"My tabernacle also shall be with them. Yea, I will be their God, and they shall be My people" (37:27).

To be sprinkled by clear water. This, of course, is an illusion to the Mosaic rite of purification (see Num. 19:17-19).

To possess the ministry of the indwelling Holy Spirit. "And I will put My Spirit within you, and cause you to walk in My statutes, and ye shall keep My judgments, and do them" (Ezek. 36:27).

" 'And shall put My Spirit in you, and ye shall live, and I shall place you in your own land. Then shall ye know that I the Lord have spoken it, and performed it,' saith the Lord" (37:14).

"And I will give them one heart, and I will put a new spirit within you; and I will take the stony heart out of their flesh, and will give them a heart of flesh" (11:19).

To be given new hearts and right desires. "A new heart also will I give you, and a new spirit will I put within you; and I will take away the stony heart out of your flesh, and I will give you a heart of flesh" (36:26).

To enjoy the blessings of the new temple. "Moreover I will make a covenant of peace with them; it shall be an everlasting covenant with them; and I will place them, and multiply them, and will set My sanctuary in the midst of them forevermore. My tabernacle also shall be with them. Yea, I will be their God, and they shall be My people. And the heathen shall know that I the Lord do sanctify Israel, when My sanctuary shall be in the midst of them forevermore" (37:26-28).

To be ruled over by David. "And David My servant shall be king over them; and they all shall have one shepherd. They shall also walk in My judgments, and observe My statutes, and do them. And they shall dwell in the land that I have given unto Jacob My servant, wherein your fathers have dwelt; and they shall dwell therein, even they, and their children, and their children's children forever. And My servant David shall be their prince forever" (vv. 24-25).

To be justified among the nations.

To have abundant crops. "And they shall say, 'This land that was desolate is become like the Garden of Eden; and the waste and desolate and ruined cities are become fenced, and are inhabited' " (36:35).

To repopulate the cities of Israel, especially Jerusalem.

To occupy the Holy Land forever.

A Case of Mistaken Identity

COMMENTS

When the sovereign nation of Israel came into existence in 1947 it was the cause of much rejoicing in the hearts of many Bible-believing Christians. They saw in the establishment of the nation Israel the fulfillment of the prophecies of Ezekiel 36 and 37. They felt that this was the beginning of God's literal fulfillment of His promise to make a great nation out of Abraham (Gen. 12:2-3) which has never been realized. Further, they saw the beginnings of the nation over which Jesus would reign when He returns to earth to set up His kingdom. All of this seemed certain proof that God was keeping and would ultimately fulfill all of His Word as promised to Abraham, Moses, David, and Jeremiah.

However well-intentioned such thoughts may be, they offer a classic example of a case of mistaken identity. The Israel that came into existence in 1947 is the Israel of today. But it is not the Israel over which Jesus will reign. Rather, it is the Israel of the Tribulation over which Antichrist will reign and is doomed to destruction. The Israel over which Jesus will reign, by contrast, will be established for 1,000 years (Rev. 20:1-7) and that reign will issue in Jesus' eternal reign (1 Cor. 15:24).

Lucifer was the highest created creature ot God's Creation. Sin was found in him when he determined that he would be like the Most High God and would demonstrate that he, not God, was truly God. Lucifer, now Satan, knew that it was God's plan to set up His kingdom on the earth and rule over it through His Messiah, Jesus. If he is to be God, Satan must do the works of God and even greater. This means that he must rule over all the world through his messiah. His attempt to unseat God involves the use of God's people, Israel. The Tribulation period will officially begin when he signs a peace pact guaranteeing to Israel its national sovereignty. In the middle of the Tribulation period he will defeat the kings of the North and South and will establish himself in the house of God showing himself off to be God (2 Thes. 2:4). He will turn against everyone and everything that does not recognize him to be God. While some Israelites will embrace him as their messiah because he seemingly guarantees them the promises made to Abraham, most of them will receive his fury and will be destroyed (cf. Matt. 24:15-22). The Israel of 1947, which is the Israel of today and will be the Israel of the Tribulation, will be virtually wiped out. The king of the East will come over into the land to do battle with the king of the West. It will be his desire to become "god" in the place of the king of the West. However, before they can do battle with one another, "the sign of the Son of man in heaven" will be given them (v. 30) and they will become confederates in the attempt to keep Jesus from returning to this earth to set up His kingdom. Their attempt will be futile for Jesus will slay them with the breath of His mouth (2 Thes. 2:8). He will send His angels to gather the nation Israel from the four corners of the earth (Matt. 24:31) and it will not take Him four decades to gather them; they will come instantaneously, will be regenerated (Jer. 31:31-33), and Jesus will reign over them for 1,000 years (Rev. 20:1-7). How is the Israel of 1947 related to the Israel of the Millennium? Physically, the Israel of the Tribulation will be the ones from whom the Israel of the Millennium will descend. Therefore, the Israel of 1947, the Israel of today, and the Israel of the Tribulation (which are all synonymous) is important to God's program and it is fitting for believers to accord Israel the respect due to those who are peculiarly the people of God.

THE DEMONSTRATION OF THE WRATH OF GOD—RUSSIA

In chapters 38–39, Ezekiel described for us an invasion into Palestine by a wicked nation north of Israel in the latter days.

"Son of man, set thy face against Gog, the land of Magog, the chief prince of Meshech and Tubal, and prophesy against him, and say, 'Thus saith the Lord God, "Behold I am against thee, O Gog, the chief prince of Meshech and Tubal" ' " (38:2-3).

The identity of the invaders. Where is the land of Magog? It seems almost certain that these verses in Ezekiel refer to the U.S.S.R.

The allies in the invasion. These are: Persia, Ethiopia, Libya, Gomer, Togarmah.

The reason for the invasion. "And thou shalt say, 'I will go up to the land of unwalled villages; I will go to them that are at rest, that dwell safely, all of them dwelling without walls, and having neither bars nor gates, to take a spoil, and to take a prey; to turn thine hand upon the desolate places that are now inhabited, and upon the people that are gathered out of the nations, which have gotten cattle and goods, that dwell in the midst of the land' " (vv. 11-12).

The destruction of the invaders. The nation Russia is totally defeated on the mountains of Israel. This smashing defeat is effected by the following events, caused by God Himself.

A mighty earthquake. "For in My jealousy and in the fire of My wrath have I spoken, surely in that day there shall be a great shaking in the land of Israel. So that the fishes of the sea, and fowls of the heaven, and the beasts of the field, and all creeping things that creep upon the earth, and all the men that are upon the face of the earth, shall shake at My presence, and the mountains shall be thrown down, and the steep places shall fall, and every wall shall fall to the ground" (vv. 19-20).

Mutiny among the Russian troops. " 'And I will call for a sword against him throughout all My mountains,' saith the Lord God. 'Every man's sword shall be against his brother' " (v. 21).

A plague among the troops. "And I will plead against him with pestilence and with blood; and I will rain upon him, and upon his bands, and upon the many people that are with him, and overflowing rain, and great hailstones, fire, and brimstone" (v. 22).

Floods, great hailstones, fire, and brimstone. "And I will send a fire on Magog, and among them that dwell carelessly in the isles; and they shall know that I am the Lord" (39:6).

THE RESULTS OF THE INVASION

Five-sixths (83%) of the Russian soldiers will be destroyed.

The first grisly feast of God will begin. "And, thou son of man, thus saith the Lord God; 'Speak unto every feathered fowl, and to every beast of the field, "Assemble yourselves, and come; gather yourselves on every side to My sacrifice that I do sacrifice for you, even a great sacrifice upon the mountains of Israel, that ye may eat flesh, and drink blood. Ye shall eat the flesh of the mighty, and drink the blood of the princes of the earth, of rams, of lambs, and of goats, of bullocks, all of them fatlings of Bashan" ' " (39:17-18).

A similar feast would seem to take place later, after the Battle of Armageddon.

The Communist threat will cease forever.

Seven months will be spent in burying the dead. "And seven months shall the house of Israel be burying of them, that they may cleanse the land" (v. 12).

Seven years will be spent in burning the weapons of war. "And they that dwell in the cities of Israel shall go forth, and shall set on fire and burn the weapons, both the shields and the bucklers, the bows and the arrows, and the handstaves, and the spears, and they shall burn them with fire seven years" (v. 9).

Israel in the Form of a Zombie

COMMENTS

Ezekiel 36–37 views the process of the restoration of the nation Israel to its land as a slow process in which the dry bones come together slowly as bone joins to bone. Once the skeleton is assembled, sinews connect them together and flesh comes on them, but "there was no breath in them" (37:8). This process began to be realized in 1947 when, for the first time since the Roman conquest under Titus in A.D. 70, the sovereign nation of Israel was established. Today, the skeleton is coming together and the sinews are beginning to bind it together. This process of gradual restoration will continue until the end of this age when the church will be removed from the earth. A short period of time will follow in which the rise of the king of the West over the western confederacy will be meteoric. He will sign a covenant with Israel which will guarantee them their national sovereignty. This will give rise to an increased emigration of Jews from their homelands (especially Russia and Europe) to Israel. At that time the skeleton will be clothed with skin but still the nation will have "no breath" in it. This is the condition of the nation all during the Tribulation period.

Ezekiel 38–39 shows what will happen to this Israel that is regathered, but without life. It will be violated once again as the king of the North (cf. 38:14-15) will encourage the king of the South (the directions are given with reference to Jerusalem) to come into the land. Together they will put a tremendous "pincer movement" on the land at a time when the nation is dwelling in peace because of the covenant signed by the king of the West (v. 11). This invasion will obligate the king of the West to honor his treaty so he will enter into a fierce battle with the kings of the North and South and will defeat them. With their demise, international Communism will be forever defeated. So great will be the casualties and refuse left from this warfare that it will take seven months to bury all of the dead (39:12) and seven years to burn all the war materials (v. 9). All of this time the nation Israel is a "zombie" from God's point of view. It will not live until God gives the breath of life (37:14). This will not be realized until Jesus returns to the earth to set up His kingdom at the end of the Tribulation period, some three and one half years later.

Some Bible students mistakenly identify this mid-Tribulation war with the Battle of Armageddon but the following observations can be made from Ezekiel 38 to indicate differently. (1) The warfare is said to take place in the "latter years," in distinction to the "last days," (v. 8). These are the latter years of Israel's existence and not the "last days" in which Israel will be glorified. (2) Israel is dwelling in its own land (v. 8). Their right to do so will be guaranteed by the covenant which the king of the West will sign with them. (3) Israel is at peace when this invasion takes place (v. 11). This peace is made possible by the covenant signed by the king of the West. At the time of the Battle of Armageddon, Israel will be in a state of turmoil being persecuted by the Beast. Indications from other prophetic teachings confirm the difference of these two events. (1) The covenant made by Antichrist is broken in the middle of the week (cf. Dan. 11:40-41) because of the invasion from the North. (2) Satan is cast out of heaven in the middle of the Tribulation and puts into motion a series of climactic events, beginning with the invasion of the kings of the North and South and concluded by the Battle of Armageddon. (3) Revelation 13:7 pictures the Antichrist as having worldwide power. He does not get this power till after the covenant he made with Israel is broken in the middle of the week. The two battles, then, are quite distinct but constitute the beginning and the ending of the darkest chapter of the history of the earth.

Preview

Joy to the World, the Lord Is Come

EZEKIEL 40–48

What fellowship and sharing must be enjoyed even at this moment in heaven among those saved who have departed this earth. Imagine the following conversation concerning the various earthly biblical buildings of God. Those participating in the discussion are Moses, Solomon, Peter, and Ezekiel.

MOSES: How well I still recall that splendid moment on Mount Sinai when the Lord instructed me to build a sanctuary that He might actually dwell among His people. What an assignment! Well, we all pitched in and a few months later the tabernacle was completed. What a day that was when God's Shekinah glory filled the entire building.

SOLOMON: I know how you felt, Moses. I'll never forget the thrill at the dedication of the first temple. My only regret was my father David could not be present. The glory of God also filled this temple, Moses, as it did your tabernacle.

PETER: Of course I had nothing to do with the building of Herod's temple, but we were all so proud of it. Often in fact we would go with the Master to the Mount of Olives and just stand there, admiring that beautiful edifice.

EZEKIEL *(perhaps with a smile)*: This is all well and good, brethren. But of course the tragedy in your accounts is that all three buildings were destroyed by Israel's enemies because of Israel's sin. Now, let me tell you about the final temple. First, it will be built by Christ Himself. Second, its glory will surpass the first three buildings combined. Third, it will never be destroyed by our enemies, but will stand in all its splendor during the entire Millennium—1,000 years.

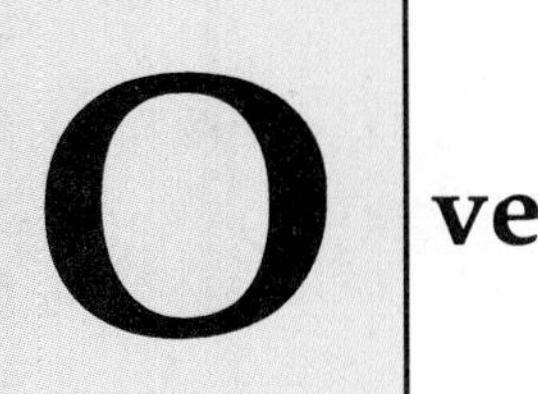

verview

<table>
<tr><td>SCRIPTURE</td><td colspan="6">Ezekiel 40–48</td></tr>
<tr><td>SUBJECT</td><td colspan="6">Israel's final and finest temple</td></tr>
<tr><td rowspan="5">SPECIFICS</td><td colspan="4">The when of the temple</td><td colspan="2">The where of the temple</td></tr>
<tr><td colspan="4">To be built at the beginning of the Millennium and last for 1,000 years</td><td>Standing over a river, on a mountain, overlooking the city of Jerusalem</td><td>The nature of the river
The glory of the city</td></tr>
<tr><td colspan="4">The who of the temple</td><td colspan="2">The why of the temple</td></tr>
<tr><td rowspan="2">Its priesthood</td><td rowspan="2">The descendants of Zadok</td><td rowspan="2">Its prince</td><td rowspan="2">Possibly a descendant of David—but not Christ</td><td>By its cloud</td><td>To serve as a center illustrating God's glory</td></tr>
<tr><td>By its sacrifices</td><td>To serve as a center illustrating God's holiness</td></tr>
<tr><td>SAINTS AND SINNERS</td><td colspan="6">Ezekiel, the prince in the millennial temple</td></tr>
<tr><td rowspan="2">SENTENCE SUMMARIES</td><td>O.T. Verse</td><td colspan="5">" 'The glory of this latter house shall be greater than of the former,' saith the LORD of hosts; 'and in this place will I give peace,' saith the LORD of hosts" (Hag. 2:9).</td></tr>
<tr><td>N.T. Verse</td><td colspan="5">"Him that overcometh will I make a pillar in the temple of My God, and he shall go no more out. And I will write upon him the name of My God, and the name of the city of My God, which is New Jerusalem, which cometh down out of heaven from My God. And I will write upon him My new name" (Rev. 3:12).</td></tr>
</table>

THE MANIFESTATION OF THE GLORY OF GOD— THE TEMPLE

ITS DIMENSIONS

ITS PURPOSE

To provide a dwelling place for the cloud of glory. "So the Spirit took me up, and brought me into the inner court; and, behold, the glory of the LORD *filled the house" (Ezek. 43:5).*

To provide a center for the King of glory. "And He said unto me, 'Son of man, the place of My throne, and the place of the soles of My feet, where I will dwell in the midst of the Children of Israel forever, and My holy name, shall the house of Israel no more defile, neither they, nor their kings, by their whoredom, nor by the carcasses of their kings in their high places' " (v. 7).

ITS PRIESTHOOD

The sons of Zadok will be the priests (40:46; 43:19; 44:15; 48:11). Zadok was the high priest in the days of King David.

ITS PRINCE

In his description of the temple, Ezekiel referred to a mysterious "prince" some 17 times. Whoever he is, he will occupy a very important role in the temple itself, apparently holding an intermediary place between the people and the priesthood. We are sure that he is not Christ, since he will prepare a sin offering for himself (45:22), and will be married and have sons (46:16). Some suggest that the prince is from the seed of King David, and that he will be to David what the false prophet will be to the Antichrist.

ITS UNIQUE FEATURES

Several articles and objects present in the temples of Moses, Solomon, and Herod will be absent from the millennial temple. There will be no veil. There will be no table of showbread. There will be no lampstands. There will be no ark of the covenant. The east gate will be closed. This gate, it has been suggested, will remain closed for the following reasons: This will be the gate by which the Lord Jesus Christ enters the temple. As a mark of honor to an Eastern king, no person could enter the gate by which he entered.

It was from the eastern gate that the glory of God departed for the last time in the Old Testament. By sealing the gate, God reminds all those within that His glory will never again depart from His people.

ITS SACRIFICES

As we have already seen, several pieces of furniture in the Old Testament temple will be missing in the millennial edifice. However, the brazen altar of sacrifice will again be present. There are at least four Old Testament prophecies which speak of animal sacrifices in the millennial temple: Isaiah 56:6-7; 60:6; Jeremiah 33:18; Zechariah 14:16-21. But why the need of these animal blood sacrifices during the Golden Age of the Millennium? They will function to remind all of the necessity of the new birth, as an object lesson of the costliness of salvation, as an example of the awfulness of sin, and as an illustration of the holiness of God.

ITS RIVER

The river's source is from beneath the temple. It flows eastward and then south through the desert and Jordan River to the Dead Sea where its sweet waters will purify that lifeless body of polluted water.

"Afterward He brought me again unto the door of the house; and, behold, waters issued out from under the threshold of the house eastward; for the forefront of the house stood toward the east, and the waters came down from under, from the right side of the house, at the south side of the altar" (47:1).

"Now when I had returned, behold, at the bank of the river were very many trees on the one side and on the other" (v. 7).

"And it shall come to pass, that everything

that liveth, which moveth, whithersoever the rivers shall come, shall live; and there shall be a very great multitude of fish, because these waters shall come thither; for they shall be healed; and everything shall live whither the river cometh'' (v. 9).

''And by the river upon the bank thereof, on this side and on that side, shall grow all trees for meat, whose leaf shall not fade, neither shall the fruit thereof be consumed. It shall bring forth new fruit according to his months, because their waters they issued out of the sanctuary; and the fruit thereof shall be for meat, and the leaf thereof for medicine'' (v. 12).

At first the river reached Ezekiel's ankles, then his knees, after this his waist, and finally he swam across its unknown depths (vv. 3-5).

ITS GLORY CLOUD

''Afterward He brought me to the gate, even the gate that looketh toward the east. And, behold, the glory of the God of Israel came from the way of the east; and His voice was like a noise of many waters; and the earth shined with His glory. And it was according to the appearance of the vision which I saw, even according to the vision that I saw when I came to destroy the city. And the visions were like the vision that I saw by the River Chebar; and I fell upon my face. And the glory of the LORD came into the house by the way of the gate whose prospect is toward the east. So the Spirit took me up, and brought me into the inner court; and, behold, the glory of the LORD filled the house'' (43:1-5).

ITS CITY

Jerusalem will become the worship center of the world and will occupy an elevated site. The city will be six miles in circumference. In the time of Christ the city was about four miles. There will be 12 gates in the city wall. Each will bear the name of one of the 12 tribes of Israel.

The city will be named ''Jehovah-Shammah,'' meaning ''The Lord Is There.''

Oh, What a Day That Will Be
COMMENTS

Oh, what a day that will be when the things prophesied in Ezekiel 40–48 become reality. The millennial temple (chaps. 40–42) will be constructed and it will be filled with the glory of God (chap. 43). A worship system similar to that of the Mosaic tabernacle will be instituted (chaps. 44–46) with one notable difference: whereas the worship of the Old Testament tabernacle and temple was predictive in looking forward to the Messiah to come, the worship of the millennial temple will be memorial in nature, looking backward to the time the Messiah came and His suffering for the sins of the world. All of this will take place in the millennial land (chaps. 47–48) that has been healed from the humiliations inflicted on it by the Adamic curse and the judgmental curses poured out on it during the Tribulation period. The renovated land will be divided among the tribes of Israel as in the days of the Judges with Joseph being given a double portion again.

For those captives of Israel in Ezekiel's day, it must have been a great encouragement to them to realize that there was coming a great day in which the temple would be rebuilt—a more glorious temple than Solomon's which they had seen destroyed. It must have been a great encouragement to the people of Ezekiel's day as they realized that there was coming a day when the temple worship would be resumed in much the same way that they had observed it when they were in their homeland. Now they were not able to worship Jehovah in that way, but the day was coming when that worship would be restored. It must have been a great comfort to the people wrenched out of their own land to realize that the day was coming when their tribes would be situated in a newly revitalized land never to be uprooted again.

As wonderful as Ezekiel's prophecy must have been to the people who first received it, it must be realized that they all died never having received the promise. The temple which Zerubbabel built when the captives returned did not even begin to match the splendor of Solomon's temple. The worship system restored did not differ from what they had observed before the Captivity because they still looked forward to Messiah to come. The land to which they returned was not healed and bore the marks of the ravishment it suffered. There was no visible manifestation of the glory of God about which Ezekiel had spoken. It is obvious that the restoration under Ezra and Nehemiah did not fulfill Ezekiel's prophecy. However, a greater day is coming when Jesus will return to the earth, call the nation Israel to Himself, and establish His reign over them. That is the day to which Ezekiel looks. Oh, what a day that will be. Putting with Ezekiel's prophecy bits of information gleaned from the rest of Scripture, Ezekiel does not begin to tell the half. The church, the bride of Christ, will come with Him when He returns to set up His kingdom. They will be residents of a "satellite city," the heavenly city, 1,000 miles square suspended above the earthly city, Jerusalem. The glorified saints will have access to the earth and will be visible testimony to the millennial people of what God can do with a sinner. Satan will be bound in the bottomless pit. The earth will be returned to Edenic conditions. All of the Old Testament and Tribulation saints will be raised from the dead and will be there to witness the fulfillment of all that God has promised to Abraham, Moses, David, and Jeremiah. All of His covenants will be completely fulfilled. Millennial residents will be able to talk to Abraham, David, Moses, and see what God can do with simple men who trust Him. But most important, Jesus Christ will be visibly present reigning on David's throne and speaking peace to the nations. Oh, what a day that will be. Even so come, Lord Jesus.

Return

If the truth were known, many Jewish exiles doubtless wondered whether their great Prophet Jeremiah really knew what he was talking about when he wrote those dramatic words just before the Babylonian Captivity: *"For thus saith the* L*ORD, 'That after 70 years be accomplished at Babylon, I will visit you, and perform My good word toward you, in causing you to return to this place' " (Jer. 29:10).*

Had Jeremiah heard God correctly? Should this amazing prophecy be taken literally? Now the truth was out. He had and it should.

The official Persian decree, issued by Cyrus the Great himself, which fulfilled Jeremiah's prediction read as follows: *"Now in the first year of Cyrus King of Persia, that the word of the* L*ORD by the mouth of Jeremiah might be fulfilled, the* L*ORD stirred up the spirit of Cyrus King of Persia, that he made a proclamation throughout all his kingdom, and put it also in writing, saying, 'Thus saith Cyrus King of Persia, "the LORD God of heaven hath given me all the kingdoms of the earth; and He that charged me to build Him a house at Jerusalem, which is in Judah.*

" ' "Who is there among you of all His people? His God be with him, and let him go up to Jerusalem, which is in Judah, and build the house of the LORD God of Israel, (He is the God,) which is in Jerusalem" ' " (Ezra 1:1-3).

The Return Stage in essence gives the account of what happened to the minority who decided to return and the majority who decided to remain. The actions of Zerubbabel, Joshua, Haggai, Zechariah, Ezra, and Nehemiah summarize the minority group. The actions of Esther and Mordecai summarize the majority group. Before the story ended, both groups found themselves in great conflict. The first faced bitter hostility, and the second, an outright holocaust. But in each case God's former promise concerning His people rang true: *"When thou passest through the waters, I will be with thee, and through the rivers, they shall not overflow thee; when thou walkest through the fire, thou shalt not be burned; neither shall the flame kindle upon thee" (Isa. 43:2).*

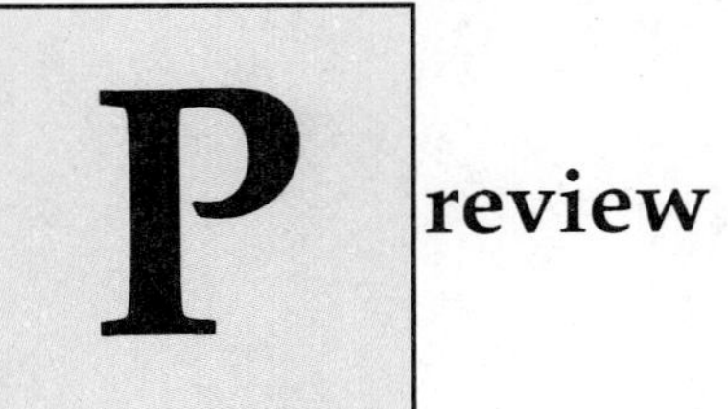

review

Rise Up, Return, and Rebuild

BOOK OF EZRA

Talk about getting behind in your payments. Israel in the sixth century B.C. would certainly have held the world's record. Here is their sad nonpayment story. After they settled in Canaan, the nation was commanded by God to allow the land to rest each seventh year. But Israel disobeyed this law. Nearly five centuries elapsed without their giving their land a rest. Thus, in 606 B.C. their divine Creditor stepped in and presented the bill, demanding full payment. It was a staggering debt, totaling 70 unobserved land rest-years. God used the 70-year Babylonian Captivity to pay off His peoples' debt.

But, 70 years later, in 536 B.C., the spiritual slate was wiped clean. Israel was free to return to its beloved land beyond the Jordan.

Overview

<table>
<tr><td>SCRIPTURE</td><td colspan="5">Book of Ezra</td></tr>
<tr><td>SUBJECT</td><td colspan="5">The first two returns from captivity to Jerusalem</td></tr>
<tr><td rowspan="5">SPECIFICS</td><td colspan="5">Twin trips to the Holy Land</td></tr>
<tr><td colspan="3">A historical account:
Ezra 1–6</td><td colspan="2">A biographical account:
Ezra 7–10</td></tr>
<tr><td rowspan="3">The return led by Zerubbabel</td><td>Pre-return circumstances</td><td>The decree of the ruler
The decision of the remnant</td><td rowspan="3">The return led by Ezra</td><td>Preparing in Persia</td></tr>
<tr><td>Post-return circumstances</td><td>Judah's enemies
Judah's edifice
Judah's exhorters Zechariah Haggai</td><td>Praying in Jerusalem</td></tr>
<tr><td colspan="2">Before Ezra's time:
events revealed to him</td><td>During Ezra's time:
events experienced by him</td></tr>
<tr><td>SAINTS AND SINNERS</td><td colspan="5">Cyrus, Zerubbabel, Joshua, Haggai, Zechariah, Ezra, Artaxerxes</td></tr>
<tr><td rowspan="2">SENTENCE SUMMARIES</td><td colspan="2">O.T. Verses</td><td colspan="3">"When the LORD turned again the captivity of Zion, we were like them that dream. Then was our mouth filled with laughter, and our tongue with singing; then said they among the heathen, 'The LORD hath done great things for them' " (Ps. 126:1-2).</td></tr>
<tr><td colspan="2">N.T. Verse</td><td colspan="3">"Study to show thyself approved unto God, a workman that needeth not to be ashamed, rightly dividing the Word of truth" (2 Tim. 2:15).</td></tr>
</table>

THE RETURN TO JERUSALEM UNDER ZERUBBABEL

THE KING, PROCLAIMING

The writing. God placed a desire in Cyrus' heart to issue his return decree. *"Thus saith Cyrus king of Persia, 'The LORD God of heaven hath given me all the kingdoms of the earth; and He hath charged me to build Him a house at Jerusalem, which is in Judah. Who is there among you of all His people? His God be with him, and let him go up to Jerusalem, which is in Judah, and build the house of the LORD God of Israel (He is the God), which is in Jerusalem' " (Ezra 1:2-3).*

The rising. A remnant of the Jews in Captivity (some 42,000, 2:64) responded to this decree, and began the trip to Jerusalem, carrying with them 5,400 golden and silver vessels Nebuchadnezzar had taken from the temple. They also took the Urim and Thummin (v. 63), 7,337 servants and 200 singers (v. 65), 736 horses and 245 mules (v. 66), 435 camels and 6,720 donkeys (v. 67), 1,100 pounds of gold, 5,000 pounds of silver, and 100 priestly garments (v. 69).

THE PEOPLE, RECLAIMING

The family trees of those who returned were carefully recorded for posterity. Especially to be noted was their leader, whose name was Zerubbabel, grandson of King Jehoiachin. The altar was built and the Mosaic sacrificial system was reinstituted, led by Jeshua (also called Joshua), grandson of Judah's last high priest before the Babylonian Captivity.

The altar was erected on the first day of the seventh month, which was the beginning of the Feast of Trumpets.

The Feast of Tabernacles (Booths) was then celebrated, from the fifteenth to the twenty-second of the seventh month.

In June of 535 B.C. a most unusual ceremony was held.

"And when the builders laid the foundation of the temple of the LORD, they set the priests in their apparel with trumpets, and the Levites the sons of Asaph with cymbals, to praise the LORD, after the ordinance of David king of Israel. And they sang together by course in praising and giving thanks unto the LORD; because He is good, for His mercy endureth forever toward Israel. And all the people shouted with a great shout, when they praised the LORD, because the foundation of the house of the LORD was laid.

"But many of the priests and Levites and chief of the fathers, who were ancient men, that had seen the first house, when the foundation of this house was laid before their eyes, wept with a loud voice; and many shouted aloud for joy, so that the people could not discern the noise of the shout of joy from the noise of the weeping of the people; for the people shouted with a loud shout, and the noise was heard afar off" (3:10-13).

THE DEVIL, DEFAMING

Satan tried his best to prevent the temple from going up.

*He tried accommodation: *"Now when the adversaries of Judah and Benjamin heard that the children of the Captivity builded the temple unto the LORD God of Israel, then they came to Zerubbabel, and to the chief of the fathers, and said unto them, 'Let us build with you, for we seek your God, as ye do; and we do sacrifice unto Him since the days of Esarhaddon king of Assur, which brought us up hither.'*

"But Zerubbabel, and Jeshua, and the rest of the chief of the fathers of Israel, said unto them, 'Ye have nothing to do with us to build a house unto our God; but we ourselves together will build unto the LORD God of Israel, as King Cyrus the king of Persia hath commanded us' " (4:1-3).

*He tried intimidation: *"Then the people of the land weakened the hands of the people of Judah, and troubled them in building" (v. 4).*

*He tried accusation: *"And hired counselors against them, to frustrate their purpose, all the days of Cyrus king of Persia, even until the reign of Darius king of Persia. And in the reign of Ahasuerus, in the beginning of his reign, wrote they unto him an accusation against the inhabitants of Judah and Jerusalem" (vv. 5-6).*

"This is the copy of the letter that they sent unto him, even unto Artaxerxes the king; 'Thy servants the men on this side the river, and at such a time. Be it known unto the king, that the Jews which came up from thee to us are come unto Jerusalem, building the rebellious and the

Problems in the Books of Ezra and Nehemiah

COMMENTS

The Books of Ezra and Nehemiah have, unfortunately, been assailed by critics as containing numerous internal contradictions and conflicts with external sources. However, there is a logical answer to all of these charges, and it is worthwhile to consider these solutions before we cast away the Word of God as unreliable. Since the two books were originally considered one book in the Hebrew Scriptures, they should be considered together as we deal with the problems.

(1) *The problem of the date of the second temple.* Both Ezra 5:1 and Haggai 2:18 date the laying of the temple's foundation during the ministry of Haggai or 520 B.C. This seems to contradict Ezra 1:2-5; 3:10; and 5:16 which point to the earlier date of 536 B.C. when Cyrus permitted the Jews to return in order to build the temple. Since the foundation could not have been laid twice, how can the two accounts be reconciled? The answer lies in recognizing that the foundation was laid in 536, but the work stopped immediately due to opposition and discouragement. It was not resumed until 520 when the foundation was most likely rededicated after such a long absence of work.

(2) *Dual lists of returnees in Ezra 2 and Nehemiah 7.* The fact that the latter list repeats almost verbatim the former list has caused some to charge that a confusion of sources has occurred. However, Nehemiah 7:5, 64 make it clear that Nehemiah was using the older list as a basis for genealogical application to his day.

(3) *The mention of Sheshbazzar and Zerubbabel.* At first glance, there seems to be some confusion as to who led the first return: in Ezra 1:8-11 Sheshbazzar is placed in charge of the work, but in 3:2 and 4:2 Zerubbabel is the overseer. We find out, however, from 1 Chronicles 3:17-18 that Zerubbabel was a nephew of Sheshbazzar (or Shenazar). This probably indicates that the older man died before the work was completed. In fact, Ezra 5:14-16 implies this.

(4) *Confusion of kings in Ezra 4.* It has been objected that this passage must have been written long after Ezra's time by a confused writer since it seems to mix up the order of the Persian monarchs, passing from Cyrus (539-530) to Xerxes (486-464) to Artaxerxes I (464-423), and then back to Darius I (522-486). Nevertheless, it is clear from Ezra 4:5 that the writer was familiar with the correct order. Also, it is obvious that the author's intention in chapter 4 is a topical survey of Judah's adversaries, not a chronological account.

(5) *Date of Ezra's return.* At least three passages have been viewed as testimonies to a late date for Ezra's return. (a) Ezra 9:9 mentions a city wall, but we know that the wall was not rebuilt until Nehemiah's time. (b) Ezra 10:1 states that a great congregation was present in Jerusalem, but Nehemiah 7:4 records that only a few people were present. (c) Ezra 10:6 observes that Johanan, son (or possibly grandson) of Eliashib, was the contemporary of Ezra, but from Nehemiah 3:1 we learn that Eliashib was Nehemiah's contemporary. To complicate matters further, the Elephantine Papyri mention a high priest named Johanan, a grandson of Eliashib, and who is dated somewhat later than Nehemiah. All of these objections may be answered. First, Ezra 4:12 shows that a wall of some kind was built during the reign of Artexerxes I and would have been known to Ezra. Nehemiah's wall came later and was a more extensive one. Second, the congregation in Ezra 10:1 was gathered from the environs of Jerusalem, whereas Nehemiah's reference is to actual dwellings. Third, Johanan was a common name, and it is not unreasonable to assume that the high priest named Johanan was a descendant of the man by the same name mentioned in Ezra. If they were the same, then certainly Ezra 10:6 would have mentioned the fact that Johanan was high priest. There is no good reason then not to date Ezra's return in the seventh year of Artaxerxes I (7:8), or about 458/457 B.C. Furthermore, there is no compelling reason to take this king to be Artaxerxes II, as some critics do, and thus force the date down to 398 B.C.

(6) *The mention of Jaddua in Nehemiah 12:11.* Josephus mentions that Jaddua was the high priest's name in the time of Alexander the Great in 330 B.C. Therefore, some argue that the Book of Nehemiah was written many years after the days of the historical person Nehemiah. However, it must be pointed out that Josephus' account makes a historical blunder in the same chapter by linking chronologically the fifth-century enemies of the Jews, Sanballat and Manasseh, with Jaddua. It seems that Josephus' sources were themselves confused at this point.

Though critics have set forth many problems in the Books of Ezra and Nehemiah, there are none to which a reasoned answer may not be given. The books may then be taken at face value as trustworthy accounts of the postexilic period.

bad city, and have set up the walls thereof, and joined the foundations. Be it known now unto the king, that, if this city be builded, and the walls set up again, then will they not pay toll, tribute, and custom, and so thou shalt endamage the revenue of the kings. Now because we have maintenance from the king's palace, and it was not meet for us to see the king's dishonor, therefore have we sent and certified the king; that search may be made in the book of the records of thy fathers; so shalt thou find in the book of the record, and know that this city is a rebellious city, and hurtful unto kings and provinces, and that they have moved sedition within the same of old time; for which cause was this city destroyed.

" 'We certify the king that, if this city be builded again, and the walls thereof set up, by this means thou shalt have no portion on this side the river' " (vv. 11-16).

THE LORD, SUSTAINING

In spite of all this, God was at work. Both Haggai and Zechariah began their comforting ministry at this time.

"Then the prophets, Haggai the prophet, and Zechariah the son of Iddo, prophesied unto the Jews that were in Judah and Jerusalem in the name of the God of Israel, even unto them. Then rose up Zerubbabel the son of Shealtiel, and Jeshua the son of Jozadak, and began to build the house of God which is at Jerusalem, and with them were the prophets of God helping them" (5:1-2).

After Judah's enemies had stopped the work on the temple for a while, it was continued and completed on March 12, 515 B.C.

The Jews wrote a letter to King Darius, requesting a search be made among the Persian records to validate their claim that King Cyrus had once issued the official permission to rebuild their temple. A search was made and the decree was discovered.

Darius then sent orders to not only allow the temple work to continue, but for the local Persian officials to help finance it. Note the penalty for disobeying this command:

"Also I have made a decree, that whosoever shall alter this word, let timber be pulled down from his house, and being set up, let him be hanged thereon; and let his house be made a dunghill for this. And the God that hath caused His name to dwell there destroy all kings and people, that shall put to their hand to alter and to destroy this house of God which is at Jerusalem. I Darius have made a decree; let it be done with speed" (6:11-12).

The completed temple was then dedicated. *"And the Children of Israel, the priests, and the Levites, and the rest of the children of the Captivity, kept the dedication of this house of God with joy" (v. 16).*

The Passover was observed on April 14, 515 B.C.

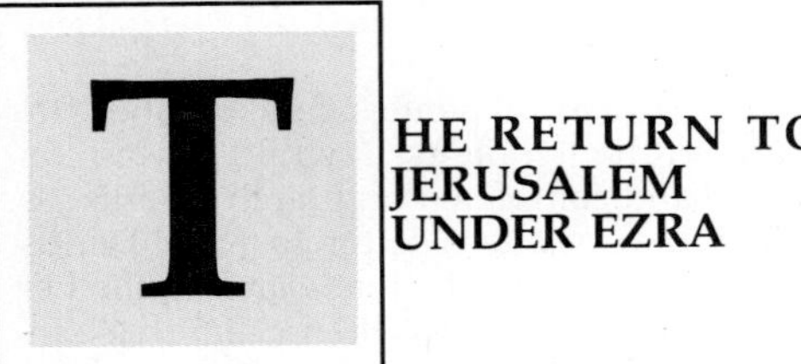

THE RETURN TO JERUSALEM UNDER EZRA

There is a period of some 60 years between chapters 6 and 7 of Ezra. During this time Ezra was born. Thus, the first part of his book is historical while the final part is biographical.

"This Ezra went up from Babylon; and he was a ready scribe in the Law of Moses, which the LORD God of Israel had given. And the king granted him all his request, according to the hand of the LORD his God upon him. . . .

"For Ezra had prepared his heart to seek the Law of the LORD, and to do it, and to teach in Israel statutes and judgments" (Ezra 7:6, 10).

THE COOPERATION FROM THE KING

Artaxerxes greatly aided this second return by issuing an official letter addressed to three parties.

To all Jews in Babylon, encouraging them to return. "I make a decree, that all they of the people of Israel, and of His priests and Levites, in my realm, which are minded of their own free will to go up to Jerusalem, go with thee" (v. 13).

To all Persian officials west of the Euphrates River to help with the return. "And I, even I Artaxerxes the king, do make a decree to all the treasurers which are beyond the river, that whatsoever Ezra the priest, the scribe of the Law of the God of heaven, shall require of you, it be done speedily" (v. 21).

They were to contribute to the upkeep of the temple. They were forbidden to impose tax on the temple.

To Ezra himself. " 'And thou, Ezra, after the wisdom of thy God, that is in thine hand, set magistrates and judges, which may judge all the people that are beyond the river, all such as know the laws of thy God; and teach ye them that know them not. And whosoever will not do the Law of thy God, and the law of the king, let judgment be executed speedily upon him, whether it be unto death, or to banishment, or to confiscation of goods, or to imprisonment.'

"Blessed be the LORD God of our fathers, which hath put such a thing as this in the king's heart, to beautify the house of the LORD which is in Jerusalem, and hath extended mercy unto me before the king's mighty princes. And I was strengthened as the hand of the LORD my God was upon me, and I gathered together out of Israel chief men to go up with me" (vv. 25-28).

THE PREPARATION FOR THE TRIP

Ezra left in March of 457 B.C. with approximately 5,000 people. They arrived in August of that year, carrying over 20 million dollars with them. A quick census taken enroute several days after leaving for Jerusalem revealed no Levites had joined the group. A special delegation sent back by Ezra convinced 40 Levites to go.

Ezra proclaimed a fast by the river Ahava. *"For I was ashamed to require of the king a band of soldiers and horsemen to help us against the enemy in the way, because we had spoken unto the king, saying, 'The hand of our God is upon all them for good that seek Him; but His power and His wrath is against all them that forsake him.' So we fasted and besought our God for this; and He was entreated of us" (8:22-23).*

THE SUPPLICATION OF THE SCRIBE

Ezra soon learned that the Jews already in the Holy City had compromised their testimony by practicing heathen customs and even marrying pagan women. The great Bible teacher immediately went into deep mourning and poured out his soul to God concerning this tragic situation.

His reaction to the bad news. "And when I heard this thing, I rent my garment and my mantle, and plucked off the hair of my head and of my beard, and sat down astonished. Then were assembled unto me everyone that trembled at the words of the God of Israel, because of the transgression of those that had been carried away; and I sat astonished until the evening sacrifice" (9:3-4).

His "knee" action to the bad news. "And at the evening sacrifice I arose up from my heaviness; and having rent my garment and my mantle, I fell upon my knees, and spread out my hands unto the LORD my God, and said, 'O my

Ezra: "A Ready Scribe"

COMMENTS

There is probably no better description of the man Ezra than that which is found in the text itself. "He was a ready scribe in the Law of Moses" (Ezra 7:6). Because Ezra was raised up by God at an important crossroads in the history of Israel, he helped shape the direction of Judaism. Even today he is regarded as a major figure of importance in the history of the Jews. His place in their history, therefore, deserves some special comment.

Our main sources of information about Ezra are the narratives of Ezra 7–10 and Nehemiah 8–10 and some accounts in the apocryphal books. From these passages we learn first that Ezra belonged to the priestly line, i.e., of the Zadokite family (Ezra 7:1-5). His priestly status is constantly reaffirmed in the text (vv. 11-12; 10:10, 16; Neh. 8:2, 9; 12:26). On the other hand, he is also described in a number of places as a scribe (Ezra 7:6, 11-12, 21; Neh. 8:9; 12:26). The duties of the priest as a mediator between God and men is well known to most Bible students, but the work of the scribe is less known and merits special consideration.

Since few people knew how to read and write in the ancient world, the office of the scribe was an important one in all ancient near Eastern cultures. The Hebrew word for scribe, *sōphēr,* has the meaning "to count, tell, or recount." This simple definition yields insight into the scribe's main duties. These included transcribing records or writing letters from dictation (Jer. 36:26), especially those of legal significance such as treaties or contracts (32:12). While there were public scribes, the most skilled scribes were no doubt pressed into service as "the king's scribes" (2 Chron. 24:11). The chief scribe achieved a status as a royal adviser or much like a secretary of state (1 Chron. 27:32). When Hezekiah sent representatives to bargain with the besieging Assyrians, Shebna the scribe was among them (1 Kings 18:18; 19:2; Isa. 36:3). Besides these duties, scribes were given tasks related to military matters such as compiling a census of those drafted for war (Jud. 5:14) or a list of the spoils captured (2 Kings 25:19; Jer. 52:25). Scribal involvement in the temple was limited, restricted, for example, to collecting revenues (2 Kings 12:10), though they could be actually resident in the temple (Jer. 36:10).

Though Shaphan the scribe read the newly found Law scroll to the king (2 Kings 22:8), it was left to Ezra to combine, for the first time, the roles of priest and scribe. Not only did he copy the Law but he preserved and interpreted it for the people (Neh. 8:1-8). The significance of Ezra's advancement is twofold: First, from this time forth the offices of priest and scribe became increasingly combined so that by the second century B.C., most scribes were also priests (see the apocryphal reference 1 Maccabees 7:12). Second, Ezra, in this new capacity was the forerunner of the class of religious scribes, or "lawyers" of Jesus' day, well known to readers of the Gospels.

Ezra emerges from the biblical text as an austere, authoritative figure. By his constant emphasis on the Law and its demands on the post-Exile community, he helped to usher in an era in which the Law had an influence and respect that shaped Judaism not only into the New Testament period but well beyond.

God, I am ashamed and blush to lift up my face to Thee, my God. For our iniquities are increased over our head, and our trespass is grown up unto the heavens. Since the days of our fathers have we been in a great trespass unto this day; and for our iniquities have we, our kings, and our priests, been delivered into the hand of the kings of the lands, to the sword, to Captivity, and to a spoil, and to confusion of face, as it is this day' '' (vv. 5-7).

He acknowledged the present sins of Israel, and the continuous grace of God. *''For we were bondmen; yet our God hath not forsaken us in our bondage, but hath extended mercy unto us in the sight of the kings of Persia, to give us a reviving, to set up the house of our God, and to repair the desolations thereof, and to give us a wall in Judah and in Jerusalem'' (v. 9).*

THE PURIFICATION OF THE PEOPLE

Soon conviction of sin settled down on the hearts of the leaders. *''Now when Ezra had prayed, and when he had confessed, weeping and casting himself down before the house of God, there assembled unto him out of Israel a very great congregation of men and women and children; for the people wept very sore'' (10:1).*

A proclamation went out throughout all Judah. *'' 'Now therefore let us make a covenant with our God to put away all the wives, and such as are born of them, according to the counsel of my lord, and of those that tremble at the commandment of our God; and let it be done according to the Law.' . . .*

''And they made proclamation throughout Judah and Jerusalem unto all the children of the Captivity, that they should gather themselves together unto Jerusalem. . . . Then all the men of Judah and Benjamin gathered themselves together unto Jerusalem within three days. It was the ninth month, on the twentieth day of the month; and all the people sat in the street of the house of God, trembling because of this matter, and for the great rain'' (vv. 3, 7, 9).

After hearing Ezra's sermon, the men agreed to dismiss their heathen wives. *''And Ezra the priest stood up, and said unto them, 'Ye have transgressed, and have taken strange wives, to increase the trespass of Israel. Now therefore make confession unto the LORD God of your fathers, and do His pleasure; and separate yourselves from the people of the land, and from the strange wives.'*

''Then all the congregation answered and said with a loud voice, 'As thou hast said, so must we do' '' (vv. 10-12).

Preview

Hitler Was Not the First to Try

BOOK OF ESTHER

The following question was asked of a group of Christian college students recently: "If you could choose to have lived your life during any period in human history, what generation would you select?" Here are some of the answers:

1. In the Garden of Eden with Adam and Eve
2. Before the great Flood
3. In Abraham's generation
4. During King David's time
5. When Christ walked this earth
6. When our country was founded, in 1776
7. At the turn of this present century

Would you have chosen any of these time periods? Well, according to the Book of Esther, in God's sight, unless you chose your own lifetime, you flunked the test. Actually, few periods in all Jewish history were darker than during the days of Esther. And the reason? A demon-possessed politician named Haman had attempted to carry out history's first holocaust, the utter extermination of all Jewish people. But did Esther despair and wish to be born in another era? She did not. On the contrary, she heeded the wonderful and wise words of her Uncle Mordecai, took the necessary action, and saved her people. His reminder to her is God's reminder to us today: *"Thou art come to the kingdom for such a time as this" (Es. 4:14).*

Overview

<table>
<tr><td>SCRIPTURE</td><td colspan="5">Book of Esther</td></tr>
<tr><td>SUBJECT</td><td colspan="5">History's first attempted holocaust</td></tr>
<tr><td rowspan="5">SPECIFICS</td><td colspan="5">The unseen hand of God</td></tr>
<tr><td colspan="3">As demonstrated by the rise of Esther and Mordecai</td><td colspan="2">As demonstrated by the ruin of Haman</td></tr>
<tr><td rowspan="2">The facts involved</td><td>Esther</td><td>Mordecai</td><td rowspan="2">Plotting</td><td rowspan="2">The holocaust</td></tr>
<tr><td>From a lowly maiden to the Queen of Persia</td><td>From a gatekeeper to the Prime Minister</td></tr>
<tr><td>The feast involved</td><td colspan="2">Feast of Purim</td><td>Perishing</td><td>The hanging</td></tr>
<tr><td>SAINTS AND SINNERS</td><td colspan="5">Ahasuerus (Xerxes), Vashti, Esther, Mordecai, Haman, Zeresh</td></tr>
<tr><td rowspan="2">SENTENCE SUMMARIES</td><td>O.T. Verse</td><td colspan="4">"Surely the wrath of man shall praise Thee; the remainder of wrath shalt Thou restrain" (Ps. 76:10).</td></tr>
<tr><td>N.T. Verse</td><td colspan="4">"We know that all things work together for good to them that love God, to them who are the called according to His purpose" (Rom. 8:28).</td></tr>
</table>

THE RISE OF ESTHER

THE REJECTION OF VASHTI

In the third year of his reign, the Persian monarch Ahasuerus (Xerxes) gave a fantastic feast which lasted 180 days. It was attended by thousands of his kingdom officials, coming from every one of the 127 provinces, stretching from India to Ethiopia.

During the final week of the feasting, the king called for his wife, Vashti, to come in and parade her beauty before some of his important, but half-drunk friends. The queen curtly refused to display herself in this cheap manner.

Burning with anger, the king acted on the advice of his friends and banished his wife forever from his presence, lest the other women of the kingdom get ideas from her insubordination.

THE SELECTION OF ESTHER

The contest. After his anger had cooled, the king regretted his hasty action, but was unable to change the strict Persian law even though he himself had decreed it. At the suggestion of his aides, he allowed an empire-wide beauty search to begin, with the winner of the contest to become his new wife.

The contestants. Among the beauties brought to the palace was a Jewish girl named Hadassah, also known as Esther. The beautiful young maiden had been raised by her older cousin, whose name was Mordecai, of the tribe of Benjamin.

Esther gained immediate favor with Hegai, who was in charge of the harem. However, at Mordecai's advice Esther did not reveal her Jewish identity at this time.

The contest lasted some four years, but after the king had seen all the available women, he wholeheartedly chose Esther to become his next queen.

"And the king loved Esther above all the women, and she obtained grace and favor in his sight more than all the virgins; so that he set the royal crown upon her head, and made her queen instead of Vashti" (Es. 2:17).

To celebrate this event, Ahasuerus threw another big party, and even went so far as to lower taxes in his province.

THE DETECTION OF MORDECAI

Mordecai, who had become a palace official, overheard a plot of two guards at the gate to assassinate Ahasuerus. He reported this to Queen Esther, who in turn informed the king. Both guards were executed, and this was duly recorded in the book of the history of King Ahasuerus' reign.

THE LIES OF HAMAN

Infernal servitude. Soon after Esther had become queen, Ahasuerus appointed as his prime minister a vicious politician named Haman, an unwitting servant of Satan himself.

The arrogant Haman soon learned that a Jew named Mordecai was refusing to bow before him, as had been commanded.

"And all the king's servants, that were in the king's gate, bowed, and reverenced Haman: for the king had so commanded concerning him. But Mordecai bowed not, nor did him reverence. . . . And when Haman saw that Mordecai bowed not, nor did him reverence, then was Haman full of wrath" (3:2, 5).

Haman hatched a plot to exterminate not only Mordecai, but every other Jew living in the Persian Empire. He approached the king with the following "recommendations."

That there was a *"certain people scattered abroad and dispersed among the people in all the provinces of thy kingdom, and their laws are diverse from all people; neither keep they the king's laws. Therefore, it is not for the king's profit to suffer them" (v. 8).*

He then planned to butcher them like cattle.

"If it please the king, let it be written that they may be destroyed: and I will pay 10,000 talents of silver to the hands of those that have the charge of the business, to bring it into the king's treasuries" (v. 9).

The careless and heartless king agreed to

this, without even checking the identity of this "certain people," to say nothing of their guilt.

"And the king took his ring from his hand, and gave it unto Haman the son of Hammedatha the Agagite, the Jews' enemy. And the king said unto Haman, 'The silver is given to thee, the people also, to do with them as it seemeth good to thee' " (vv. 10-11).

Royal riders were sent forth to announce this edict of execution which decreed that all Jews would be killed on February 28 of the following year—473 B.C.

"The posts went out, being hastened by the king's commandment, and the decree was given in Shushan the palace. And the king and Haman sat down to drink; but the city Shushan was perplexed" (v. 15).

Intestinal fortitude of Mordecai. After learning of the decree of death, Mordecai immediately identified with his people and went into deep mourning. Unaware of the new law, Esther learned of her cousin's sorrow and inquired concerning the reason behind it. Mordecai informed her and advised that she visit the king immediately. Esther pointed out to him that she had not been summoned to Xerxes' inner court for 30 days and to walk in uninvited would very possibly bring instant death. Mordecai answered with what is perhaps the key statement in the entire book.

"Then Mordecai commanded to answer Esther, 'Think not with thyself that thou shalt escape in the king's house, more than all the Jews. For if thou altogether holdest thy peace at this time, then shall there enlargement and deliverance arise to the Jews from another place; but thou and thy father's house shall be destroyed. And who knoweth whether thou art come to the kingdom for such a time as this?" (4:13-14)

Courage of Esther. Esther immediately ordered a three-day fast among the Jews, and determined that she would *"go in unto the king, which is not according to the law. And if I perish, I perish" (v. 16).* (See also Dan. 3:17-18.)

Three days later Esther entered the king's inner court, uninvited, but to her relief, she was warmly received.

"And it was so, when the king saw Esther the queen standing in the court, that she obtained favor in his sight. And the king held out to Esther the golden scepter that was in his hand. So Esther drew near, and touched the top of the scepter.

"Then said the king unto her, 'What wilt thou, Queen Esther? And what is thy request? It shall be even given thee to the half of the kingdom' " (Es. 5:2-3).

The queen did not reveal her request during her first banquet, but simply asked that both the king and Haman attend a second banquet she was preparing the next day. Ahasuerus quickly agreed. After attending this first banquet, the vain Haman was puffed up with pride. But when he saw Mordecai standing at the palace gate, still refusing to bow, he was furious. He related both his joy and frustration to Zeresh, his wife, and his friends at home.

"And Haman told them of the glory of his riches and the multitude of his children, and all the things wherein the king had promoted him, and how he had advanced him above the princes and servants of the king. Haman said moreover, 'Yea, Esther the queen did let no man come in with the king unto the banquet that she had prepared but myself; and tomorrow am I invited unto her also with the king. Yet all this availeth me nothing, so long as I see Mordecai the Jew sitting at the king's gate.'

"Then said Zeresh his wife and all his friends unto him, 'Let a gallows be made of 50 cubits high, and tomorrow speak thou unto the king that Mordecai be hanged thereon. Then go thou in merrily with the king unto the banquet.' And the thing pleased Haman; and he caused the gallows to be made" (vv. 11-14).

Esther: A Story of God's Providence

COMMENTS

Much has been made of the fact that the Book of Esther does not mention the name of God. This fact, along with the anonymity of the author, and the alleged bloodthirsty nationalism of the Jews described at the end of the book have caused many to doubt the canonicity of the book. These detractors range from first-century Jewish rabbis at Jamnia to Martin Luther in the sixteenth century. However, the book was rightly included in both the Jewish and Christian Scriptures. The canon of Origen (ca. A.D. 185-254), for example, included it. It was also part of the Hebrew canon which Jesus Himself endorsed (Luke 24:44).

There is, in fact, a very logical reason as to why the book does not mention the name of God: it relates the story of Jews who did not return to the Promised Land when given the opportunity to do so. The events of the book take place during the reign of Xerxes, or Ahasuerus, (486-464) over 50 years after Cyrus had issued a decree to allow the Jews to return to their land. Many had evidently become quite prosperous during the Exile and did not want to leave. Others no doubt dreaded the long journey to a land which most had not seen. As a result, they were content to stay out of the land of blessing.

In spite of the people's disobedience in remaining outside the land of God's blessing, He still protected them. As the story of God's protection of His erring children, the book constitutes the greatest testimony in the Scriptures to the providence of God. The doctrine of God's providence refers to His guidance that goes on behind the scenes. The Old Testament records many occasions of God's supernatural provisions, unexplainable deliverances, and phenomenal prophetic oracles. These, however, were not the usual, everyday occurrences. Otherwise, miracles would have been commonplace and ceased to be miracles. Rather, on most occasions God worked secretly behind the action guiding history toward His ends (cf. Deut. 29:29). In light of this reality the Book of Esther becomes the greatest biblical testimony to the providential workings of God—and in His care for a people who had refused to return to the land of blessing and promise.

It would be helpful to enumerate the ways God's providence is demonstrated in the book. First, Esther, a Jewess, is crowned queen after Vashti, the Persian queen, is deposed. In what amounted to a "Miss Persia" contest, Esther must have won the honor over hundreds of contestants from all over the realm. That a Jewess could be chosen for such an honor was certainly in the providence of God. There were, no doubt, many Persians who hated the Jews for their monotheism and for their maintenance of cultural distinctions. This fact is implied in Mordecai's counsel to Esther (Es. 2:20) as well as in Haman's hatred of the Jews (3:6).

Second, Mordecai just happened to be the one who overheard the plot on the king's life (2:21-23). The population of the Persian capital was quite large, but in the design of God this Jewish man was chosen as the one to be privy to the assassination plot. It was also providential that an administrative blunder resulted in no reward being paid at that time to Mordecai for his loyalty. However, it was dutifully recorded in the national chronicles to be revealed at a timely moment.

Third, Esther courageously (and successfully) approached the king when she had not been summoned. The Persian monarchs were quite ruthless in their application of the many grim and arbitrary laws. The king could easily have had Esther killed for violation of his royal privacy. However, as God moved behind the scenes, the king received her gladly and granted her request.

Fourth, when the king could not sleep, he had the chronicles read to him. Again, in God's providence, the particular passage which dealt with Mordecai's loyal report of the assassin's plot was read. As God would have it, Haman just happened to be waiting to speak to the king when the king decided to elevate Mordecai. Consequently, Mordecai was honored by the king and Haman was shamed.

Finally, Haman was hanged on the very gallows that he had prepared for Mordecai. It appears from 6:13-14 that Haman's wife and advisers were just about ready to suggest that Haman leave town, but before he could make a move, he was whisked away to the banquet which spelled his own doom.

Throughout the story it is quite evident that God is at work behind the action moving kings, queens, commoners, and chronicles to accomplish His goals. Though His name is not mentioned specifically, He is present and active. As a story of God's providence, the book is certainly an important testimony to God's silent, everyday working in the human arena.

THE PRIZE OF FAITH

The execution of a beast—Haman. Ahasuerus experienced insomnia and ordered the reading of some historical records, hoping perhaps that this dull material would put him to sleep. The reader, by "chance" just happened to begin reading at the place which related how Mordecai had once saved the king's life by exposing an assassination plot.

"And the king said, 'What honor and dignity hath been done to Mordecai for this?' Then said the king's servants that ministered unto him, 'There is nothing done for him' " (6:3).

At this exact moment, Haman had arrived at Ahasuerus' palace seeking the king's permission to hang Mordecai. The king, still determined to reward Mordecai (neither Ahasuerus nor Haman, of course, knew what the other was thinking), used Haman as a sounding board and inquired, *"What shall be done unto the man whom the king delighteth to honor?" (v. 6)*

The arrogant and self-centered Haman immediately thought Ahasuerus had him in mind and brazenly suggested the following: that the man to be honored be clothed in the king's own royal robes; that he be placed on Ahasuerus' personal horse; that he be allowed to wear the king's crown; and that the king's most noble prince lead this hero, seated on the horse, through the streets of the city, shouting his praises for all to hear (vv. 7-9).

The king quickly agreed to all this and then turned to Haman and ordered his wicked prime minister to perform all this for Mordecai!

"Then the king said to Haman, 'Make haste, and take the apparel and the horse, as thou hast said, and do even so to Mordecai the Jew, that sitteth at the king's gate; let nothing fail of all that thou hast spoken' " (v. 10).

Haman, totally dumbstruck, stumbled out to obey Xerxes' command and later hurried home, utterly humiliated. Even there he received no comfort.

"And Mordecai came again to the king's gate. But Haman hasted to his house mourning, and having his head covered. And Haman told Zeresh his wife and all his friends everything that had befallen him. Then said his wise men and Zeresh his wife unto him, 'If Mordecai be of the seed of the Jews, before whom thou hast begun to fall, thou shalt not prevail against him, but shalt surely fall before him' " (vv. 12-13).

While they yet spoke, he received the message to attend Esther's second banquet (v. 14).

"So the king and Haman came to banquet with Esther the queen. And the king said again unto Esther on the second day at the banquet of wine, 'What is thy petition, Queen Esther? And it shall be granted thee. And what is thy request? And it shall be performed, even to the half of the kingdom' " (7:1-2).

Esther warned the king that a plot was underway to slaughter both her and all her people. The king, filled with both astonishment and then anger, asked: *"Who is he, and where is he, who durst presume in his heart to do so?" (v. 5)*

Esther pointed to Haman and replied: *"The adversary and enemy is this wicked Haman" (v. 6).*

Ahasuerus, unable to speak because of his fury, walked outside into his palace garden for a moment. Filled with horrible fear, the cowardly Haman begged Esther to intercede to the king for him. In his terrible fright he accidentally fell on the couch where Esther was reclining.

At this point, Ahasuerus walked back in and viewed what he interpreted to be an attempted rape on the part of Haman. When he learned of the nearby gallows Haman had built for Mordecai, the king roared out in his wrath for Haman himself to be hanged that very night. The order was immediately carried out.

"So they hanged Haman on the gallows that he had prepared for Mordecai. Then was the king's wrath pacified" (v. 10).

After Haman's execution, Ahasuerus gave Esther Haman's estate and appointed Mordecai his new prime minister (8:1-2). Both now begged the king to reverse Haman's order. But the law of the Medes and Persians, once made, was immutable, and not even Ahasuerus himself could change it. He then did the next best thing. He ordered the Jews to defend themselves. Mordecai immediately sent copies of this new decree to all of the 127 provinces (vv. 3-14).

THE INSTITUTION OF A FEAST—PURIM

The Jews prepared themselves and were able to slaughter their enemies. *"Thus the Jews smote all their enemies with the stroke of the sword, and slaughter, and destruction, and did what they would unto those that hated them. . . . The 10 sons of Haman the son of Hammedatha, the enemy of the Jews, slew they; but on the spoil laid they not their hand" (9:5, 10).*

Mordecai and Esther then instituted a new memorial feast called Purim, to commemorate yearly their great salvation from Haman.

"And Mordecai wrote these things, and sent letters unto all the Jews that were in all the

provinces of the king Ahasuerus, both nigh and far, to establish this among them, that they should keep the fourteenth day of the month Adar, and the fifteenth day of the same, yearly. As the days wherein the Jews rested from their enemies, and the month which was turned unto them from sorrow to joy, and from mourning into a good day; that they should make them days of feasting and joy, and of sending portions one to another, and gifts to the poor. And the Jews undertook to do as they had begun, and as Mordecai had written unto them" (vv. 20-23).

"Wherefore they called these days Purim after the name of Pur. Therefore for all the words of this letter, and of that which they had seen concerning this matter, and which had come unto them" (v. 26).

Mordecai became a great and godly statesman, respected by both Jews and Gentiles for his abilities and actions.

"And Mordecai went out from the presence of the king in royal apparel of blue and white, and with a great crown of gold, and with a garment of fine linen and purple. And the city of Shushan rejoiced and was glad" (8:15).

"For Mordecai was great in the king's house, and his fame went out throughout all the provinces, for this man Mordecai waxed greater and greater" (9:4).

"And all the acts of his power and of his might, and the declaration of the greatness of Mordecai, whereunto the king advanced him, are they not written in the book of the chronicles of the kings of Media and Persia?

"For Mordecai the Jew was next unto King Ahasuerus, and great among the Jews, and accepted of the multitude of his brethren, seeking the wealth of his people, and speaking peace to all his seed" (10:2-3).

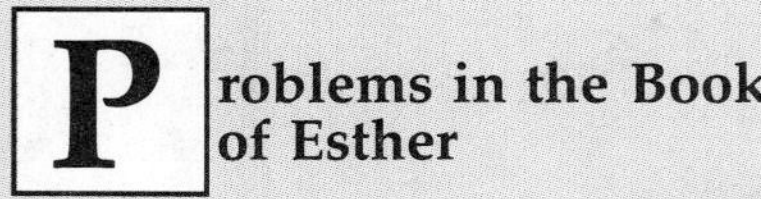

Problems in the Book of Esther

COMMENTS

A number of problems have been raised by critics regarding the Book of Esther. It is important that these issues be addressed and plausible solutions set forth. First, some have suggested that the entire book should be regarded as fiction. However, it is reasonable to assume from the descriptions in the book that the author had access to Persian records. Then too the events of the book could easily fit into the reign of Ahasuerus (486-464 B.C.). It is true that no record of the events of the Book of Esther exists in the Persian annals. Nevertheless, this is not an insurmountable problem since a majority of the chronicles have no doubt perished.

A second problem raised frequently centers simply on the identity of the king in the book. The name Ahasuerus is clearly a Hebrew name for a Persian king. But which king? A few scholars have identified the king as Artaxerxes II (404-359) but the majority have stayed with the long-held tradition that the king in question is Xerxes I (486-464). In favor of this latter identification is the fact that it easily answers to the unexplained gap between Ahasuerus' third year in 1:3 and his seventh year in 2:16. It is well known to historians that Xerxes was planning and executing his ill-fated invasion of Greece between 483 and 480 B.C.

A third problem is the identification of Ahasuerus' wife. The Greek historian Herodotus identifies Xerxes' wife as Amestris and, furthermore, states that the king was obligated to choose his wife from among seven noble families (cf. 1:14). However, it is easily proven historically that oriental despots often superseded custom on the basis of their own whim.

A fourth problem is, at first glance, a chronological problem: Esther 2:5-6 seems to describe Mordecai as having been captured during Nebuchadnezzar's second campaign against Jerusalem, i.e. in 597 B.C. By the time of Xerxes' reign, Mordecai would then have been over 120 years old. However, the word "who" in the statement "who had been carried into exile" can easily refer to Kish, Mordecai's great grandfather. Indeed, the name Kish is the nearest antecedent.

A final problem revolves around the issue of the Jews' destination. Would the king really have listened to Haman? And why would Haman have fixed a date for the massacre so far in advance? In answer to the first point, history is replete with examples of wars begun by wounded pride, slighted feelings, and false reports. Also, Haman was a favorite of the king and he deceptively represented the Jews as traitors. As far as the second point is concerned, the text of the book clearly indicates that Haman was a superstitious man, often depending on lots to indicate "lucky" days (3:7).

In summary, the book is a true story as it stands, and there is no problem within it to which an adequate explanation cannot be given.

Preview

Original Mission: To Build Up a Wall for God

NEHEMIAH 1–5

To tell the truth, he felt a bit sore. First there had been that long trip across the desert. Then, during the previous night, he had ridden around the area. Unusual activity for a professional politician. Now, in the light of the rising sun, he could fully view the ruins. What he saw was not encouraging, to say the least. Enemy soldiers and the ravages of time had utterly devastated all that had once stood tall and strong in the beloved city. He realized God called different men to different tasks. Moses was commissioned to lead, David to rule, and men like Amos to reform. But his assignment was unique.

Dismounting somewhat stiffly from his horse, the rider entered a room filled with men he had personally summoned. The rider was Nehemiah, the city was Jerusalem, the ruins were its walls, and the assembled men were key Jewish leaders. But what was the reason for all this? In the words of Nehemiah himself: *"Then I told them of the hand of my God which was good upon me, as also the king's words that he had spoken unto me. And they said, 'Let us rise up and build.' So they strengthened their hands for this good work" (Neh. 2:18).*

Overview

<table>
<tr><td>SCRIPTURE</td><td colspan="4">Nehemiah 1–5</td></tr>
<tr><td>SUBJECT</td><td colspan="4">The building of Nehemiah's wall</td></tr>
<tr><td rowspan="3">SPECIFICS</td><td colspan="4">The what, where, why, and who of the wall</td></tr>
<tr><td>The what</td><td>A fallen wall
to be rebuilt
with the gates</td><td>The where</td><td>Around the city
of Jerusalem</td></tr>
<tr><td>The why</td><td>For protection
For separation</td><td>The who</td><td>Nehemiah
His energy
His enemies
His endurance
His example
His efficiency</td></tr>
<tr><td>SAINTS AND SINNERS</td><td colspan="4">Nehemiah, Artaxerxes, Sanballat, Tobiah, Geshem</td></tr>
<tr><td rowspan="2">SENTENCE SUMMARIES</td><td>O.T. Verse</td><td colspan="3">"Do good in Thy good pleasure unto Zion; build Thou the walls of Jerusalem" (Ps. 51:18).</td></tr>
<tr><td>N.T. Verse</td><td colspan="3">"Therefore, my beloved brethren, be ye steadfast, unmovable, always abounding in the work of the Lord, forasmuch as ye know that your labor is not in vain in the Lord" (1 Cor. 15:58).</td></tr>
</table>

EHEMIAH

THE NEWS CONCERNING THE WALL

Learning. In December of 446 B.C. Nehemiah learned from a returning Jew named Hanani (who was his own brother—see Neh. 1:2; 7:2) of the pitiful state of Jerusalem. The report broke his heart.

"And they said unto me, 'The remnant that are left of the Captivity there in the province are in great affliction and reproach; the wall of Jerusalem also is broken down, and the gates thereof are burned with fire' " (1:3).

Lamenting. After hearing this, Nehemiah began a time of confession and intercession.

"And it came to pass, when I heard these words, that I sat down and wept, and mourned certain days, and fasted, and prayed before the God of heaven" (v. 4).

He identified with his people Israel and their sin. *"Let Thine ear now be attentive, and Thine eyes open, that Thou mayest hear the prayer of Thy servant, which I pray before Thee now, day and night, for the Children of Israel, which we have sinned against Thee. Both I and my father's house have sinned" (v. 6).*

He acknowledged the righteousness of God in punishing His people (v. 7) and reminded God of His promise to regather His people (vv. 8-10). He asked God to soften the heart of the king (v. 11).

THE REQUEST TO BUILD THE WALL

In April of 445 B.C., after a prayer period of four months, Nehemiah asked the king to *"send me unto Judah, unto the city of my fathers' sepulchers, that I may build it" (2:5).* Artaxerxes agreed and gave Nehemiah the necessary assistance.

THE NECESSITY FOR THE WALL

Soon after reaching Jerusalem, Nehemiah made a secret midnight ride around the city itself. The next morning he assembled Judah's leaders and shared with them the burden of his heart.

"Then said I unto them, 'Ye see the distress that we are in, how Jerusalem lieth waste, and the gates thereof are burned with fire. Come, and let us build up the wall of Jerusalem, that we be no more a reproach.' Then I told them of the hand of my God which was good upon me; as also the king's words that he has spoken unto me. And they said, 'Let us rise up and build.' So they strengthened their hands for this good work" (vv. 17-18).

It may be concluded that there were at least two compelling reasons for building the wall. It was necessary for protection, to keep the outsiders out, and to protect against sneak attacks. (See 7:1-3.) It was necessary for separation, to keep the insiders in. It would cut down the growing worldliness of the Jews who had been associating freely with the surrounding pagan people.

THE GATES IN THE WALL

The various gates mentioned here are in themselves a beautiful picture summary of the Christian life.

The sheep gate (Neh. 3:1). This speaks of the Cross. See John 10:11.

The fish gate (Neh. 3:3). This speaks of evangelism. See Matthew 4:19.

The old gate (Neh. 3:6). This speaks of our old nature. See Romans 6:1-23.

The valley gate (Neh. 3:13). This speaks of sufferings and testing. See 2 Corinthians 1:3-5.

The dung gate (Neh. 3:14). This speaks of the works of the flesh. See Galatians 5:16-21.

The fountain gate (Neh. 3:15). This speaks of the Holy Spirit. See John 7:37-39.

The water gate (Neh. 3:26). This speaks of the Word of God. See John 4:10-14.

The horse gate (Neh. 3:29). This speaks of the believer's warfare. See Ephesians 6:10-17.

The east gate (Neh. 3:29). This speaks of the return of Christ. See Ezekiel 43:1-2.

The Niphkad gate (Neh. 3:31). This was thought to be the judgment gate and therefore speaks of the Judgment Seat of Christ. See 1 Corinthians 3:9-15; 2 Corinthians 5:10.

THE OPPOSITION TO THE WALL

"When Sanballat the Horonite, and Tobiah the servant, the Ammonite, heard of it, it grieved them exceedingly that there was come a man to seek the welfare of the Children of Israel" (Neh. 2:10).

A work for God will always be met by both human and Satanic opposition. These combined forces did their perverted best to halt the wall-building. Many methods were employed to accomplish this.

Ridicule. "But when Sanballat the Horonite, and Tobiah the servant, the Ammonite, and Geshem the Arabian, heard it, they laughed us to scorn, and despised us, and said, 'What is this thing that ye do? Will ye rebel against the king?' " (v. 19)

"But it came to pass, that when Sanballat heard that we builded the wall, he was wroth, and took great indignation, and mocked the Jews. And he spake before his brethren and the army of Samaria, and said, 'What do these feeble Jews? Will they fortify themselves? Will they sacrifice? Will they make an end in a day? Will they revive the stones out of the heaps of the rubbish which are burned?'

"Now Tobiah the Ammonite was by him, and he said, 'Even that which they build, if a fox go up, he shall even break down their stone wall' " (4:1-3).

Discouragement. "And Judah said, 'The strength of the bearers of burdens is decayed, and there is much rubbish; so that we are not able to build the wall' " (v. 10).

Conspiracy. "And conspired all of them together to come and to fight against Jerusalem, and to hinder it" (v. 8).

"And our adversaries said, 'They shall not know, neither see, till we come in the midst among them, and slay them, and cause the work to cease' " (v. 11).

Laziness. "And next unto them the Tekoites repaired; but their nobles put not their necks to the work of their Lord" (3:5).

Internal strife. Some of the more well-to-do Jews were guilty of extortion toward their less-fortunate countrymen.

Compromise. "That Sanballat and Geshem sent unto me, saying, 'Come, let us meet together in some one of the villages in the plain of Ono.' But they thought to do me mischief.

"And I sent messengers unto them, saying, 'I am doing a great work, so that I cannot come down. Why should the work cease, whilst I leave it, and come down to you?'

"Yet they sent unto me four times after this sort; and I answered them after the same manner" (6:2-4).

Slander. Sanballat spread vicious rumors that Nehemiah was actually plotting to become king and revolt against Persia.

Treachery. Shemaiah claimed to have a special revelation about a plot against Nehemiah's life and suggested that the holy place in the temple would be the only safe place for Nehemiah. But the suggestion unmasked Shemaiah's treachery, since only the priests could enter the holy place (Num. 18:7). If Nehemiah had done so, his testimony would have been ruined.

Outright fear. "For they all made us afraid, saying, 'Their hands shall be weakened from the work, that it be not done.'

" 'Now therefore, O God, strengthen my hands' " (Neh. 6:9).

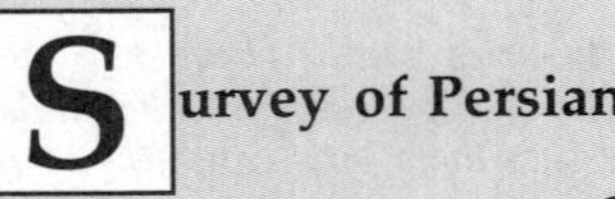

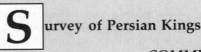

Survey of Persian Kings

COMMENTS

The mention of Artaxerxes in Nehemiah 2:1 makes a fitting occasion to survey here the kings of the Persian Empire. Though mentioned only briefly in the biblical text, much is known about these kings from extra-biblical literature, including the Persian records themselves. Not every Persian king is mentioned in the Bible, but all are included here for the sake of completeness.

Cyrus II ("the Great") (539-530) came to the throne of the tiny Elamite province of Anshan about 559 B.C. With ambitions of worldwide conquest he soon added the province of Parsua (Persia) to his rule. By 550 B.C., with the help of a rebellion in the Median army, he had conquered Astyages and assumed his title, "King of the Medes."

With amazing rapidity he extended his holdings westward and northward. The next major kingdom to fall was that of Lydia, ruled by Croesus and famous for its wealth. In 549 he marched through Assyria and added it to his domain. For a number of years he threatened Babylon, but it was not until October 12, 539 that he entered Babylon as conqueror. According to the Greek historian Herodotus, Cyrus was able to conquer the city by diverting the river and entering the city via the riverbed. From Daniel 5:30 we must conclude that Belshazzar, the Babylonian co-regent, was slain in a palace skirmish. On October 29 Cyrus entered the city and was welcomed by the people as a liberator because they hated the policies of the co-rulers, Belshazzar and Nabonidus. The latter had tried to escape but was captured, though later Cyrus graciously gave him parole. We are particularly well-informed about the capture of Babylon, having both Persian and Babylonian accounts which agree remarkably. At this point, Cyrus could truly be considered the ruler of a world empire.

The biblical picture of Cyrus as a benevolent ruler in allowing the Jews to return to their land (Ezra 1:1-4) is borne out by his own inscriptions. Unlike many of his Assyrian and Babylonian predecessors, Cyrus did not engage in wholesale massacres and desecration of conquered shrines. Rather, he allowed local peoples to have their own worship and to some extent their own governments. Quite significant for Bible students is Isaiah's prophecy, delivered over 150 years earlier, that Cyrus would release the Jews (Isa. 44:28; 45:1).

Cambyses II (530-522), son of Cyrus, had ruled as a co-regent with his father and succeeded him at Cyrus' death. Though not mentioned in the Scriptures, it was evidently during his reign that the rebuilding of the temple stopped (Ezra 4). Cambyses is remembered for having conquered Egypt and even sacking the capital at Memphis. When he heard reports of conspiracy at home, Cambyses began the long trek back to Persia, but died on the way.

Darius I (522-486), son of Hystaspes, succeeded Cambyses, but only after putting down two usurpers to the throne. Darius attempted what every Persian monarch had dreamed of: the conquest of Greece. Though he easily conquered Thrace and Macedonia, he was defeated at Marathon in Greece (490) and forced to return home. Under Darius the Jews were permitted to finish the temple (516), especially after the preaching of Haggai and Zechariah (Ezra 5:1; Hag. 1:1; Zech. 1:1). All four of Haggai's messages are dated to specific days during Darius' reign.

Xerxes I (486-464), or, as he is known in the Book of Esther, Ahasuerus, was the son of Darius by Atossa, a daughter of Cyrus. He tried, as his father had done, to conquer Greece. He first defeated the Spartans at Thermopylae (480) and even occupied and sacked Athens. However, at Salamis the Persian fleet was routed and during the next year the army was devastated at the Battle of Platea (479).

Xerxes carried on an active building program at Persepolis and many remains are standing today. It is known that he was assassinated by one of his own guards.

According to Herodotus, Xerxes' wife was named Amestria, not Esther, but Herodotus' reference seems to apply to Xerxes' old age. Esther may have died or Amestria may have been added as another (younger) wife who became better known in secular history.

Artaxerxes I (464-423), son of Xerxes, was also called Longimanus because his right hand was longer than his left. Under his rule Persian power declined significantly, and he found himself busy putting down numerous revolts. In his seventh year (457) he permitted a group of Jews to return to Palestine under Ezra (Ezra 7–10). In his twentieth year (444) he allowed Nehemiah, his cupbearer, also to return for the expressed purpose of rebuilding the walls of Jerusalem (Neh. 1–2). The prophecy of Malachi was delivered during his rule (432).

The biblical records are silent during the final 92 years of the Persian Empire. This period witnessed six kings on the throne:

Xerxes II (432 for 45 days), Darius II (423-404), Artaxerxes II (409-359), Artaxerxes III (359-338), Arses (338-335), and Darius III (335-331). Though not mentioned by name, the defeat of Darius III at Gaugemala by Alexander the Great in 331 was prophesied by Daniel (Dan. 8:3-7).

The Importance of Walls in the Ancient World

COMMENTS

The concern of Nehemiah in rebuilding the walls of Jerusalem seems quite strange to most modern readers. Once the strategic importance of walls is discerned, however, the puzzlement vanishes. To begin with, most cities were built on mounds or high places for protection. Jerusalem is no exception to this rule. This alone, however, did not provide adequate protection. A wall had to be erected around the entire city to provide the fullest possible protection in that day. Thus, almost every city excavated by archeologists had a wall around it.

The earliest walls were made of whatever was available—stone, unbaked mud, unfinished wood, etc. By the second millennium B.C., however, Palestinian walls included stone footings or foundations, dressed wood, mud-bricks, and stones. Furthermore, these rough, massive walls were smoothed over by plaster on the outside and some even contained rooms within them. The building of walls thus became an important skill in the ancient world as it came to represent the chief means of a city's defense. Walls were so strong that cities (with adequate stores of food) could hold out against enemies for years. Tyre in Phoenicia, for example, held Nebuchadnezzar's army off for 13 years.

Once an adequate wall was erected, the most important feature of defense became the establishment of defensible city gates. This explains Nehemiah's concern for the gates as well as the wall. Since enemies usually attacked the gate (and often succeeded at this point), the gates were further protected by the establishment of towers on either side. These could accommodate a greater number of defenders at this point of weakness. In large cities, the gates were often wide enough for two-lane chariot traffic, and multiple gates were frequently constructed, as in Nehemiah's case. In regard to multiple gates, however, it must be observed that most of these would be classified as "secondary" gates and would be constructed no doubt only as wide as necessary for their purpose. Some were probably no wider than a loaded donkey. The larger gates were held by huge piers and reinforced by additional piers on the inside. The smaller gates were turned on pivots below and above.

When walls and gates are seen in this light, the accomplishment of Nehemiah stands out as the more remarkable. Though he began his career as a civil servant (we would say "white-collar worker"), he was not too proud to work manually nor too reticent to tackle an unfamiliar task. To his courage and perseverance, the Jews of his day were much indebted.

THE BUILDER OF THE WALL

Nehemiah set an unselfish example for all the people. During his entire 12-year ministry as governor, Nehemiah took no salary. He in fact paid for the food consumed by 150 of his helpers. He worked hard on the wall himself. He loaned money to needy Jews without interest. He displayed total confidence in God.

"And I looked, and rose up, and said unto the nobles, and to the rulers, and to the rest of the people, 'Be not ye afraid of them. Remember the Lord, which is great and terrible, and fight for your brethren, your sons, and your daughters, your wives, and your houses' " (Neh. 4:14).

"Then he said unto them, 'Go your way, eat the fat, and drink the sweet, and send portions unto them for whom nothing is prepared; for this day is holy unto our Lord. Neither be ye sorry; for the joy of the L*ORD* *is your strength' "* (8:10).

He refused to compromise. "Then answered I them, and said unto them, 'The God of heaven, He will prosper us; therefore we His servants will arise and build; but ye have no portion, nor right, nor memorial, in Jerusalem' " (2:20).

He prayed. "Nevertheless we made our prayer unto our God, and set a watch against them day and night, because of them" (4:9).

"For they all made us afraid, saying, 'Their hands shall be weakened from the work, that it be not done.' Now therefore, O God, strengthen my hands" (6:9).

He contended for the faith. "And it came to pass from that time forth, that the half of my servants wrought in the work, and the other half of them held both the spears, the shields, and the bows, and the habergeons; and the rulers were behind all the house of Judah. They which builded on the wall, and they that bare burdens, with those that laded, everyone with one of his hands wrought in the work, and with the other hand held a weapon. For the builders, every one had his sword girded by his side, and so builded. And he that sounded the trumpet was by me. . . .

"So neither I nor my brethren, nor my servants, nor the men of guard which followed me, none of us put off our clothes, saving that everyone put them off for washing" (4:16-18, 23).

He remained steadfast. "And I sent messengers unto them, saying, 'I am doing a great work, so that I cannot come down. Why should the work cease, whilst I leave it, and come down to you?' " (6:3)

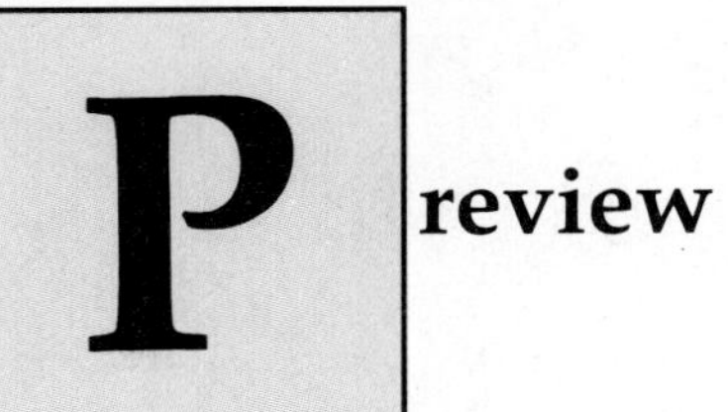

Ultimate Mission: To Build Up the People of God

NEHEMIAH 6–13

Two historical Watergates! One was connected with tragedy, the other with triumph. Here are the details. The Watergate of tragedy: On June 17, 1972, five men were arrested for breaking into the offices of the Democratic National Committee in the Watergate office complex in Washington, D.C. This seemingly petty theft event would grow in importance until it finally forced the resignation of an American President.

The Watergate of triumph: On September 25, 445 B.C., thousands of grateful Jews stood by the newly rebuilt water gate in Jerusalem to hear the public reading of God's Word by Ezra the prophet. Among the multitude was Nehemiah who doubtless stood with blistered hands and grateful heart. In just 52 days this man of faith had rebuilt the fallen walls of the beloved city.

Two historical Watergates. One was marked by corruption; the other, by celebration.

Overview

<table>
<tr><td>SCRIPTURE</td><td colspan="3">Nehemiah 6–13</td></tr>
<tr><td>SUBJECT</td><td colspan="3">The blessings of Nehemiah's wall</td></tr>
<tr><td rowspan="5">SPECIFICS</td><td colspan="3">Events following the completed wall</td></tr>
<tr><td>The priests of God</td><td colspan="2">The people of God</td></tr>
<tr><td>Explaining the Word of the Lord
Exalting the Lord of the Word</td><td colspan="2">Celebrating a feast
Signing a covenant
Separating from sin
Singing with joy</td></tr>
<tr><td>The place of God</td><td colspan="2">The prophet of God</td></tr>
<tr><td>Lots were cast to bring one tenth of the country's population into Jerusalem</td><td>Nehemiah</td><td>Rebuking certain priests for compromising
Rebuking certain people for compromising</td></tr>
<tr><td>SAINTS AND SINNERS</td><td colspan="3">Nehemiah, Ezra, Eliashib</td></tr>
<tr><td rowspan="2">SENTENCE SUMMARIES</td><td>O.T. Verse</td><td colspan="2">"The LORD doth build up Jerusalem; He gathereth together the outcasts of Israel" (Ps. 147:2).</td></tr>
<tr><td>N.T. Verses</td><td colspan="2">"Wherefore I take you to record this day, that I am pure from the blood of all men. . . . I have coveted no man's silver, or gold, or apparel. Yea, ye yourselves know, that these hands have ministered unto my necessities, and to them that were with me" (Acts 20:26, 33-34).</td></tr>
</table>

NEHEMIAH'S WALL

BLESSINGS OF THE COMPLETED WALL

In spite of all the persecution and hardships, Nehemiah had the wall up and completed in early September, just 52 days after they had begun.

"So the wall was finished in the twenty and fifth day of the month Elul, in fifty and two days. And it came to pass, that when all our enemies heard thereof, and all the heathen that were about us saw these things, they were much cast down in their own eyes: for they perceived that this work was wrought of our God" (Neh. 6:15-16).

It resulted in many blessings, including: the reading of the Word of God. *"And all the people gathered themselves together as one man into the street that was before the water gate; and they spake unto Ezra the scribe to bring the Book of the Law of Moses, which the LORD had commanded to Israel. And Ezra the priest brought the Law before the congregation both of men and women, and all that could hear with understanding, upon the first day of the seventh month" (8:1-2).*

Ezra stood and read it for six hours. He stood on a specially built wooden podium. Various teachers of the Law helped the crowd to understand what was being read. *"So they read in the Book in the Law of God distinctly, and gave the sense, and caused them to understand the reading" (v. 8).*

The Feast of Tabernacles was restored. *"And they found written in the Law which the LORD had commanded by Moses, that the Children of Israel should dwell in booths in the feast of the seventh month. . . . And all the congregation of them that were come again out of the Captivity made booths, and sat under the booths. For since the days of Jeshua the son of Nun unto that day had not the Children of Israel done so. And there was very great gladness" (vv. 14, 17).*

Israel's history was recited in prayer. In this remarkable public prayer, the Levites summarized the history of Israel from Abraham to Moses (9:6-8), from Moses to Joshua (vv. 9-23), from Joshua to the Judges (vv. 24-25), from the Judges to the Captivity (vv. 26-30), and from the Captivity to Nehemiah's time (vv. 31-37).

The God of Israel is the Creator. "Thou, even Thou, art LORD alone; Thou hast made heaven, the heaven of heavens, with all their host, the earth, and all things that are therein, the seas, and all that is therein, and Thou preservest them all; and the host of heaven worshipeth Thee" (v. 6).

He is a Communicator. "Thou camest down also upon Mount Sinai, and spakest with them from heaven, and gavest them right judgments, and true laws, good statutes, and commandments" (v. 13).

The leadership of God was mentioned. "Moreover Thou leddest them in the day by a cloudy pillar; and in the night by a pillar of fire, to give them light in the way wherein they should go" (v. 12).

God is a Sustainer. "And gavest them bread from heaven for their hunger, and broughtest forth water for them out of the rock for their thirst, and promisedst them that they should go in to possess the land which Thou hadst sworn to give them. . . . Yea, 40 years didst Thou sustain them in the wilderness, so that they lacked nothing; their clothes waxed not old, and their feet swelled not" (vv. 15, 21).

God is the Forgiver of sins. "But they and our fathers dealt proudly, and hardened their necks, and hearkened not to Thy commandments, and refused to obey, neither were mindful of Thy wonders that Thou didst among them; but hardened their necks, and in their rebellion appointed a captain to return to their bondage. But Thou art a God ready to pardon, gracious and merciful, slow to anger, and of great kindness, and forsookest them not" (vv. 16-17).

God is an Instructor. "Thou gavest also Thy good spirit to instruct them, and withheldest not Thy manna from their mouth, and gavest them water for their thirst. . . . Yet many years didst Thou forbear them, and testifiedst against them by Thy Spirit in Thy prophets; yet would they not give ear. Therefore gavest Thou them into the hand of the people of the lands" (vv. 20, 30).

THE RATIFICATION OF A SPECIAL COVENANT

"And because of all this we make a sure covenant, and write it; and our princes, Levites, and priests, seal unto it" (v. 38).

The Israelites promised that they would not marry the heathen, they would keep the Sabbath and holy days free from commercial activity, they would observe the Sabbatical Year, and they would support the temple.

THE REPOPULATION OF THE CITY OF DAVID

Lots were cast to bring one tenth of the country's population into Jerusalem.

THE RENUNCIATION OF SINS

Of ungodly alliances. "And the seed of Israel separated themselves from all strangers, and stood and confessed their sins, and the iniquities of their fathers. . . . Now it came to pass, when they had heard the Law, that they separated from Israel all the mixed multitude" (9:2; 13:3).

Of untithed money. "Then brought all Judah the tithe of the corn and the new wine and the oil unto the treasuries" (v. 12).

Of unlawful Sabbath work. "And if the people of the land bring ware or any victuals on the Sabbath Day to sell, that we would not buy it of them on the Sabbath, or on the holy days: and that we would leave the seventh year, and the exaction of every debt" (10:31).

Of unequal marriages. "And that we would not give our daughters unto the people of the land, nor take their daughters for our sons" (v. 30).

Of unauthorized usage of the temple. Nehemiah's fantastic zeal and fearless actions helped bring into being all this repentance over sin.

He had gone back to Persia for a while (13:6), but when he returned he discovered several very disquieting things. Eliashib, the temple high priest, had actually converted a storage room into a beautiful guest room for (of all people) Israel's enemy Tobiah. Eliashib was the grandson of Joshua the high priest. Nehemiah ordered Tobiah to leave and threw out all his belongings from the room. He then had to regather the temple choir which had dissolved during his absence.

His zeal simply knew no limits, as the following account brings out. *"In those days also saw I Jews that had married wives of Ashdod, of Ammon, and of Moab; and their children spoke half in the speech of Ashdod, and could not speak in the Jews' language, but according to the language of each people. And I contended with them, and cursed them, and smote certain of them, and plucked off their hair, and made them swear by God, saying, 'Ye shall not give your daughters unto their sons, nor take their daughters unto your sons, or for yourselves' " (vv. 23-25).*

His last recorded act was to excommunicate Joiada (the very son of Eliashib, the high priest) because of his unlawful marriage to Sanballat's daughter.

THE REJOICING OF ALL THE REMNANT

When God's work is done in God's way, joy will follow. Note the various references to this.

The thanksgiving from within. The people sent presents to each other and ate festive meals. *"And all the people went their way to eat, and to drink, and to send portions, and to make great mirth, because they had understood the words that were declared unto them" (8:12).*

"And at the dedication of the wall of Jerusalem they sought the Levites out of all their places, to bring them to Jerusalem, to keep the dedication with gladness, both with thanksgivings, and with singing, with cymbals, psalteries, and with harps" (12:27).

Nehemiah divided the people into two groups. Each walked in opposite directions on the completed wall singing their songs of praise to God.

"Then I brought up the princes of Judah upon the wall, and appointed two great companies of them that gave thanks, whereof one went on the right hand upon the wall toward the dung gate. . . . And the other company of them that gave thanks went over against them, and I after them, and the half of the people upon the wall, from beyond the tower of the furnaces even unto the board wall" (vv. 31, 38).

Ezra led a special corps of trumpet-playing priests.

The testimony from without. The result of all this was that the joy of Jerusalem was heard even from afar off. *"Also that day they offered great sacrifices, and rejoiced; for God had made them rejoice with great joy. The wives also and the children rejoiced; so that the joy of Jerusalem was heard even afar off" (v. 43).*

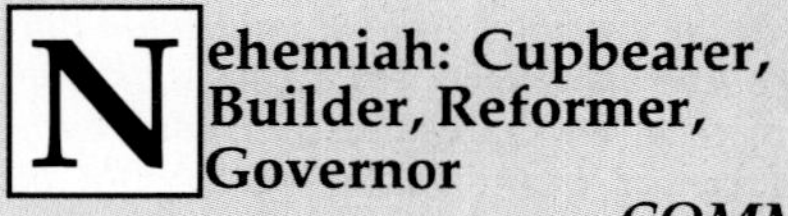

Nehemiah: Cupbearer, Builder, Reformer, Governor

COMMENTS

Our only knowledge of Nehemiah is found in the book named after him. Fortunately the book is rich with information that reveals his solid character and unceasing, godly zeal. As the title of this comment suggests, his life may be summed up under his four key roles in life. First, as cupbearer he held an important position in the Persian government. The office of cupbearer was widely established in the ancient Near East. The Egyptian "butler" in the Joseph narrative was actually a cupbearer (Gen. 40:1). In Egypt cupbearers tasted the king's wine and are sometimes depicted on tomb-paintings in the act of serving wine. Solomon also included cupbearers as part of his extensive retinue (1 Kings 10:5; 2 Chron. 9:4). Both Canaanite and Assyrian reliefs picture the role of the cupbearer. Due to his close association with the king, the cupbearer often became the king's favorite confidant, sometimes even wielding political power. The dignity and importance of the office is demonstrated by the fact that Nehemiah was even permitted to approach the king while the queen was present (Neh. 2:6). The king's subsequent, favorable response to Nehemiah's request indicates that he had won the king's trust and support.

Nehemiah's role as builder began with a serious concern about God's people. It seems clear from his grief for the desolation of Jerusalem and from his concern for God's laws that he must have been brought up by godly parents who ingrained within him the theology and values of God's people. This is the only adequate explanation to account for his fasting and prayer to God and his courage in approaching the king for his support. After receiving the king's permission and appointment as governor, he immediately set out for Jerusalem with the king's letters in hand. In God's providence the king not only granted permission for the rebuilding, but even contributed royal building supplies.

The presence of the wall to the Jews was crucial. Every ancient city was walled for protection. An unwalled city was an open invitation to attack, robbery, looting, etc. Then too at this point, the Persian government was quite weak and unable to ensure protection to all of its colonies. It was imperative in Nehemiah's mind that the wall be rebuilt. It is highly unlikely that Nehemiah had had any experience in building walls, but he tackled the task because he was the only one who was concerned enough to undertake it. His success as a builder is therefore quite remarkable. In spite of both external and internal opposition, he and his workmen completed the wall in just 52 days. According to archeologists some of Nehemiah's wall has been uncovered and can be seen south of the present-day walls in Jerusalem.

As a reformer, Nehemiah displayed an unusual zeal for wholehearted conformity to the commands of the Law. His reforms began with a six-hour reading of the Law (8:1-8). The people stood during the entire exposition. Next, the Feast of Tabernacles was restored (vv. 13-18). This feast had been commanded by Moses to be observed forever by the Jews as a reminder that God had taken care of them in the wilderness when they lived in "tabernacles" or "booths." Subsequently, the people also listened carefully as the Levites recited as a prayer, the history of Israel and God's care for His people through the ages (9:6-38). As such, this prayer linked the present Jews with their glorious past and was an encouragement and motivation to live up to their spiritual heritage. Finally, a special covenant in which the people promised obedience to the Law was instituted (v. 38; 10:1-29). Nehemiah not only demanded a response but even listed the names of those who sealed the covenant (vv. 1-27).

Nehemiah's second visit to Jerusalem revealed an even greater sense of outrage at unrighteousness. From 13:6 we find out that he had returned to Persia around 432 B.C. for a visit. After receiving permission from the king, he returned to the land, only to find gross abuses of the Law that included the following: a lack of separation from ungodly aliens (v. 3), an enemy named Tobiah actually resident in the temple (vv. 4-8), unpaid tithes (vv. 10-12), Sabbath work (vv. 15-22), spiritually mixed marriages (vv. 23-25), and defilement of the priesthood (vv. 28-30). Nehemiah took it on himself to correct these abuses by the most drastic measures, from kicking out Tobiah (v. 8) to pulling out the hair of offenders (v. 25). Few men in the Bible display such zeal for God's laws. It was probably at this time that the Book of Malachi was written, since it deals with many of the same abuses.

Finally, Nehemiah's rule as governor was unquestionably exemplary. He did not eat "the bread of the governor" (5:14), i.e., he did not take the salary normally given to the governor since it was paid solely by taxes exacted from the people; he worked as hard as anyone on the wall (v. 16); he personally supported many of the workers (vv. 17-18); and he lent money without interest and shamed other leaders into doing the same (v. 10). It is not known when Nehemiah died but it is certain that he was no longer governor in 407 B.C. At that time, according to an Aramaic letter written from Elephantine to the priests at Jerusalem, Bagoas held the position as governor. In any case, Nehemiah did rule for at least 12 years (5:14).

Nehemiah is one of the most courageous and zealous leaders in the pages of Scripture. Through his two great concerns, rebuilding the wall and conforming to the Law, he appears as a warm but exacting character who demanded as much of himself as of others.

Preview

The King Is Coming. He Did! The King Is Coming. He Will!

BOOK OF ZECHARIAH

What a night it had been! Little did Zechariah the prophet realize as the sun set, that before it rose again he would receive 10 visions from God. And what weighty prophecies they were, dealing with Jerusalem, judgment, evil, righteousness, and the building of the second temple. In fact, during one vision he was actually transported into the heavenlies and with utter amazement viewed a deadly confrontation between Satan and Christ concerning Joshua, the high priest in Zechariah's time.

But this momentous night was in reality a warmup for the visions which would later follow. And the nature of those prophecies? In a word, they all concerned Jesus. The prophet was allowed to see His triumphal entry, crucifixion, and glorious second coming, touching down on the Mount of Olives. Finally, in a breathtaking climax, Zechariah described the Saviour's victory over Satan at Armageddon, and His millennial rule over all the earth.

Overview

<table>
<tr><td>SCRIPTURE</td><td colspan="7">Book of Zechariah</td></tr>
<tr><td>SUBJECT</td><td colspan="7">A servant of God and the Son of God</td></tr>
<tr><td rowspan="7">SPECIFICS</td><td colspan="5">His ten visions</td><td colspan="2">His two visitations</td></tr>
<tr><td rowspan="6">Zechariah, the servant</td><td colspan="4">Illustrating five truths</td><td rowspan="6">Jesus Christ, the Son</td><td>First coming</td></tr>
<tr><td colspan="2">Jerusalem</td><td colspan="2">Judgment</td><td rowspan="2">His colt
His cross</td></tr>
<tr><td colspan="2">God's concern & reign as illustrated by Red horse, measuring line, crowning of Joshua</td><td colspan="2">Four horns
Four artisans
Flying scroll
Four chariots</td></tr>
<tr><td>Salvation</td><td colspan="2">Witnessing</td><td>Wickedness</td><td>Second coming</td></tr>
<tr><td>Clothing of Joshua</td><td colspan="2">Two olive trees</td><td>Woman in the ephah</td><td rowspan="2">To defeat the Antichrist
To deliver Jerusalem
The waters from God
The worship of God</td></tr>
<tr><td colspan="4"></td></tr>
<tr><td>SAINTS AND SINNERS</td><td colspan="7">Zechariah</td></tr>
<tr><td rowspan="2">SENTENCE SUMMARIES</td><td colspan="2">O.T. Verse</td><td colspan="5">"The scepter shall not depart from Judah, nor a lawgiver from between his feet, until Shiloh come; and unto Him shall the gathering of the people be" (Gen. 49:10).</td></tr>
<tr><td colspan="2">N.T. Verse</td><td colspan="5">"Beginning at Moses and all the prophets, He expounded unto them in all the Scriptures the things concerning Himself" (Luke 24:27).</td></tr>
</table>

Z ECHARIAH

THE VISIONS OF THE PROPHET

Zechariah received 10 visions, all apparently during the same night.

The rider on the red horse. Zechariah saw a heavenly Rider on a red horse, surrounded by other riders, all mounted also on various-colored horses. This special Rider on the red horse is probably Christ. The other riders are angels who had been sent by God to *"walk to and fro through the earth" (Zech. 1:10).* The Angel of the Lord (Jesus) then prayed over the troubled state of Jerusalem and was reassured by the Father that *"the LORD shall yet comfort Zion, and shall yet choose Jerusalem" (v. 17).*

The question by the Son. "Then the Angel of the LORD answered and said, 'O LORD of hosts, how long wilt Thou not have mercy on Jerusalem and on the cities of Judah, against which Thou hast had indignation these threescore and ten years?' " (v. 12)

The answer by the Father. "Therefore thus saith the LORD: 'I am returned to Jerusalem with mercies; My house shall be built in it,' saith the LORD of hosts, 'and a line shall be stretched forth upon Jerusalem' " (v. 16).

The four horns. Zechariah saw four animal horns and was told they represented the four world powers that had scattered Judah, Israel, and Jerusalem. These powers are probably Assyria, Egypt, Babylon, and Medo-Persia.

The four artisans. An artisan is a worker in wood, stone, or metal. These may refer to the four judgments spoken by both Ezekiel (Ezek. 14:21) and John (Rev. 6:1-8). These judgments are war, famine, wild animals, and pestilence.

The purpose of the artisans was this: *"These are come to fray them, to cast out the horns of the Gentiles, which lifted up their horn over the land of Judah to scatter it" (Zech. 1:21).*

This will happen during the Great Tribulation. See especially Revelation 6:15-17.

The man with a measuring line. Zechariah saw a man carrying a measuring stick in his hand enroute to measure Jerusalem. He was assured of thrilling facts concerning the millennial Jerusalem. Jerusalem would someday be so full of people that some would have to live outside its city walls, yet would dwell in perfect safety. God Himself would be a wall of fire protecting them. He would be the glory of the city.

" 'Sing and rejoice, O daughter of Zion. For, lo, I come, and I will dwell in the midst of thee,' saith the LORD. 'And many nations shall be joined to the LORD in that day, and shall be My people; and I will dwell in the midst of thee; and thou shalt know that the LORD of hosts hath sent Me unto thee. And the LORD shall inherit Judah His portion in the Holy Land, and shall choose Jerusalem again' " (2:10-12).

The one who harmed them, touched the apple of His eye (see also Deut. 32:10; Ps. 17:8).

Palestine is referred to as "the Holy Land" in verse 12. This is the only place in Scripture where it is called by this name.

THE CLOTHING OF JOSHUA, THE HIGH PRIEST

"And he showed me Joshua the high priest standing before the Angel of the LORD, and Satan standing at his right hand to resist him. And the LORD said unto Satan, 'The LORD rebuke thee, O Satan; even the LORD that hath chosen Jerusalem rebuke thee. Is not this a brand plucked out of the fire?' Now Joshua was clothed with filthy garments, and stood before the Angel.

"And He answered and spake unto those that stood before Him, saying, 'Take away the filthy garments from him.' And unto him He said, 'Behold, I have caused thine iniquity to pass from thee, and I will clothe thee with change of raiment' " (3:1-4).

This is undoubtedly the greatest single chapter on the subject of salvation in all the Old Testament. In this vision Zechariah saw Joshua, the high priest, dressed in filthy clothing, and standing before God in heaven. He was being accused by Satan because of this soiled clothing. Christ, however, rebuked Satan, removed Joshua's dirty clothing, and dressed him in clean apparel. Joshua then was challenged to serve God with his whole heart. He was promised that someday God's Branch would appear to cleanse the land of its sin. The following facts concerning salvation are brought out here.

The enemy of salvation. Satan (v. 1).

The Person of salvation. He is, of course, the Saviour.

His names. The Branch (v. 8), the Cornerstone (v. 9).

His ministry. To clothe all believers in robes of righteousness, to make intercession for the believer against Satan's lies, and to bring in and rule over the Millennium.

The purpose of salvation. These verses may be paraphrased as follows: *"If you will walk in My ways and keep My charge, you [Joshua] shall not only have the honor of judging My house, and keeping My courts, but when your work on earth is done, you shall be transplanted to higher service in heaven, and have places to walk among these pure angelic beings who stand by Me hearkening unto the voice of My Word" (v. 7).*

(See also Ps. 103:21; Eph. 2:4-10.)

THE GOLDEN LAMPSTAND AND THE TEN OLIVE TREES

Here Zechariah saw a seven-branched golden lampstand, supplied by a reservoir of olive oil. On either side of the lampstand was a carved olive tree. A lampstand in the Bible represents God's witnesses in this world. The olive oil, is, of course, a symbol of the Holy Spirit. (See Luke 4:18; Acts 10:38; Heb. 1:9; 1 John 2:20.)

We note the words of God here in Zechariah 4:6 at this point: *" 'Not by might, nor by power, but by My Spirit,' saith the LORD of hosts."*

The context here means that the unfinished temple will be completed by the power of the Holy Spirit.

"The hands of Zerubbabel have laid the foundation of this house; his hands shall also finish it; and thou shalt know that the LORD of hosts hath sent me unto you" (v. 9).

The olive trees refer to two famous teams:
*The historical team of Zerubbabel and Joshua: *"Then said he, 'These are the two anointed ones, that stand by the Lord of the whole earth' " (v. 14).*

*The prophetical team of Elijah and Moses (See Rev. 11.): *"And I will give power unto My two witnesses, and they shall prophesy a thousand two hundred and threescore days, clothed in sackcloth. These are the two olive trees, and the two candlesticks standing before the God of the earth" (Rev. 11:3-4).*

Some believe Elijah and Moses are the two witnesses mentioned in Revelation 11.

THE FLYING SCROLL

Zechariah saw a flying scroll, 15 feet wide and 30 feet long. This represented the words of God's curse going out over the entire land of Israel.

The scope of this judgment. Though only two of the original commandments are mentioned here, that of swearing (the third), and stealing (the eighth), they nevertheless covered the entire moral code of God.

The accused at this judgment. All unsaved Israelites throughout history.

The time of this judgment. After the Tribulation and just prior to the Millennium.

The penalty of this judgment. It will apparently include both physical and spiritual death.

THE WOMAN IN THE EPHAH

The prophet viewed a flying bushel basket (ephah) covered by a heavy lead top piece. When the lid was lifted, he saw a woman inside. He was then told that the woman inside represented sin and wickedness. Often in the Bible iniquity is symbolized by a woman. The heavy lead cover probably symbolized the restraining power of God over evil. The destination is said to be Babylon where it (evil and wickedness) would *"be established, and set there upon her own base" (5:11).* Thus, this is where it officially began and where it will end (Rev. 18).

THE FOUR CHARIOTS

Zechariah saw four chariots driven by four heavenly spirits proceeding from two brass mountains. Each chariot was pulled by a different colored team of horses. These colors were red, white, black, and gray. The various symbols here would seem to be as follows: the two brass mountains speak of God's judgment; and the angelic-driven chariots represent God's agents to effect various judgments on Gentile nations.

THE CROWNING OF JOSHUA

Zechariah was told that three Jewish exiles would soon return to Jerusalem from Babylon, carrying gifts of silver and gold from the remnant there. Zechariah was instructed to make a golden crown from these gifts and place it on Joshua, explaining to him that he (Joshua) would then represent the future Branch of Israel, the Messiah Himself. This blessed Messiah would someday function

Christ in Zechariah 1–8

COMMENTS

While most Christians are aware of the great messianic prophecies in Isaiah, few are cognizant of the fact that Zechariah is rich with predictions of Christ as well—of both His first and second comings. Before these passages are considered, it should be noted that the Old Testament prophets often merged the first and second comings of Christ since they did not distinguish them clearly (cf. Isa. 61:1-2 with Luke 4:17-21). Therefore, in Zechariah there is not strict chronological order. It is as though the prophets were looking at two distant mountain peaks, not realizing that there was a great valley between them, the Church Age. The prophets then describe both comings of Christ without clearly separating them and, at the same time, completely pass over the Church Age.

Zechariah 1:8 The "Man riding upon a red horse" is probably the preincarnate Christ. The red color speaks of His blood-bought redemption of believers or perhaps of His victorious battle at His second coming (Rev. 19:11).

Zechariah 2:1 The "Man with a measuring line" in all likelihood represents Christ as the Surveyor of the New Jerusalem over which He will rule during the Millennium.

Zechariah 2:5-13 "[I] will be the glory. . . I will dwell in the midst of thee," etc. are prophecies of Christ's rule over Israel during the Millennium. His glory will fill the land.

Zechariah 3:1-2 The "Angel of the LORD" in verse 1 is identified as the LORD Himself in verse 2. This proves that the Angel of Jehovah in the Old Testament, the preincarnate Christ, is God. The verse speaks of His role as Intercessor for believers (Rom. 8:34; Heb. 7:25).

Zechariah 3:8 "My Servant the Branch" is a messianic title given here to Christ as representative of His redemptive work at His first coming (Isa. 42:1; 53:1-10; Phil. 2:6-8).

Zechariah 3:9 The "Stone" depicts the Messiah at His second advent when the nation of Israel will be converted (12:10). The "graving" or carving on the stone may represent His wounds received at His first coming.

Zechariah 4:2 The golden candlestick may well represent Christ as our Light (Matt. 5:14; John 8:12). The gold may represent His deity, the seven lamps the fullness of His testimony, and the seven pipes the abundance of His power (Rev. 1:4).

Zechariah 4:12 While the two branches represent God's two witnesses, the two golden pipes represent the two offices of King and Priest united in Christ.

Zechariah 4:14 "The Lord of the whole earth" is a messianic title to be applied to Christ at His second coming (Rev. 19:16).

Zechariah 5:3 Enforcement of the curse on the scroll is a representation of the Messiah's iron rule during the Millennium (Ps. 2:9; Rev. 2:27; 12:5; 19:15).

Zechariah 6:1-8 While not an explicit vision of the Messiah, the four chariots represent the judgments that will fall on the Gentile nations prior to the Second Coming.

Zechariah 6:9-15 The crowning of Joshua is highly significant. Joshua, the high priest, receives a crown which is the normal symbol of kingship. He then becomes a type of Christ, the perfect King-Priest. Furthermore, as Messiah and King-Priest, Christ will build the millennial temple (vv. 12-13), bring Jew and Gentile into harmony (v. 13), and demand unquestioned obedience (v. 15).

Zechariah 8:1-8 The present partial restoration of the Jews to their land is taken by the prophet as only a precursor of a glorious future millennial restoration which will be complete. It will include Christ's return (v. 3), His permanent presence (v. 3), the glorification of Jerusalem, His capital (vv. 3-5), and the manifestation of His power (v. 7).

Zechariah 8:18-23 Fasts will give way to feasts when Christ's kingdom is established.

both as Priest and King. He would also build the temple of God.

"And speak unto him, saying, 'Thus speaketh the Lord *of hosts, saying, "Behold the Man whose name is The BRANCH: and He shall grow up out of His place, and He shall build the temple of the* Lord. *Even He shall build the temple of the* Lord *. . . and He shall be a Priest upon His throne; and the counsel of peace shall be between them both"* ' " *(Zech. 6:12-13).*

Zechariah was told that the three returning exiles represented many others who would someday come from distant lands back to Palestine.

"And they that are far off shall come and build in the temple of the Lord, *and ye shall know that the* Lord *of hosts hath sent Me unto you. And this shall come to pass, if ye will diligently obey the voice of the* Lord *your God" (v. 15; see also Isa. 56:6-8).*

THE VANITIES OF THE PEOPLE

A group of Jews had come to Jerusalem from Bethel to ask the priests there if they could set aside their traditional custom of fasting and mourning each year during the month of August.

The full question was: Now that the temple is being rebuilt, is it necessary to keep that fast [in August] which commemorated the burning of the first temple by Nebuchadnezzar in 586 B.C.?

God told them through the priests that it did not really make much difference what they did, for their hearts were insincere. He admonished them to be honest in their dealings with their God and their neighbors. Besides, some of their fast days were man-made and not God-appointed.

He promised that, because of His grace, their fast days would someday be feast days, and their sorrow turned into singing.

"Thus saith the Lord, *'I am returned unto Zion, and will dwell in the midst of Jerusalem; and Jerusalem shall be called a city of truth; and the mountain of the* Lord *of hosts the holy mountain.'*

"Thus saith the Lord *of hosts, 'There shall yet old men and old women dwell in the streets of Jerusalem, and every man with his staff in his hand for every age. And the streets of the city shall be full of boys and girls playing in the streets thereof.' . . .*

"Thus saith the Lord *of hosts, 'Behold, I will save My people from the east country, and from the west country. And I will bring them, and they shall dwell in the midst of Jerusalem. And they shall be My people, and I will be their God, in truth and in righteousness. . . . And it shall come to pass, that as ye were a curse among the heathen, O house of Judah, and house of Israel, so will I save you, and ye shall be a blessing. Fear not, but let your hands be strong. . . .*

" 'Yea, many people and strong nations shall come to seek the Lord *of hosts in Jerusalem, and to pray before the* Lord.*' Thus saith the* Lord *of hosts, 'In those days it shall come to pass, that 10 men shall take hold of all languages of the nations, even shall take hold of the skirt of him that is a Jew, saying, "We will go with you: for we have heard that God is with you"* ' " *(Zech. 8:3-5, 7-8, 13, 22-23).*

THE VICTORIES OF THE GREEKS AND JEWS

Here the prophet describes two future battles. One would occur around 334 B.C., and the other around 165 B.C. The first was the success of Alexander the Great over Tyre, and the second was the success of the Maccabean Jews over the Syrians.

THE VISITATIONS OF THE PRINCE

The first coming of the Prince. He came to feed the flock as His Father had instructed Him to do. The false shepherds of Israel, however, rejected Him. He, thus, broke one of His two staffs and set Israel aside for a while. He finished His ministry by the Triumphal Entry into Jerusalem.

"Rejoice greatly, O daughter of Zion; shout, O daughter of Jerusalem; behold, thy King cometh unto thee; He is just, and having salvation; lowly, and riding upon an ass, and upon a colt, the foal of an ass" (9:9).

He was sold for 30 pieces of silver, the price of a slave which had been gored by an ox. This price, contemptuously given, was then cast aside with additional contempt, for the word "cast" used here is a gesture of disgust. He then broke His second staff, signifying perhaps the destruction of Jerusalem by Titus in A.D. 70. He was finally crucified.

The second coming of the Prince. Because the false shepherds rejected their Good Shepherd at His first coming, Israel will be given over for a while to the cruel Antichrist shepherd just prior to the second appearing of their Glorious Shepherd.

"For, lo, I will raise up a Shepherd in the land, which shall not visit those that be cut off, neither shall seek the young one, nor heal that that is broken, nor feed that that standeth still; but he shall eat the flesh of the fat, and tear their claws in pieces" (11:16).

Two out of three will die in this horrible

hrist in Zechariah 9–12

COMMENTS

Zechariah 9:9 The first advent of Christ is given a special sign: He will come to His people riding a young donkey. This passage is referred to in all four Gospels (Matt. 21:4-5; Mark 11:7; Luke 19:29-35; John 12:14-15).

Zechariah 9:10–10:1 The second advent of Christ is described. It is a time when He will establish peace (9:10), and He will deliver and bless His people (v. 16–10:1).

Zechariah 10:4 Messiah is described as a cornerstone, tent peg, battle bow, and ruler, all of which speak of His second coming in its various aspects. The cornerstone is the main part of a building's foundation; Christ will be the focal point of the kingdom of God on earth. The tent peg provides stability for the tent; Christ will be the stabilizing force for the world. The battle bow symbolizes victory over opposition; Christ will be the victor and no one will be able to stay His hand. The ruler was, in the ancient world, the one to whom all subjects answered; Christ will be the sovereign to whom all men must give account.

Zechariah 10:5-12 Christ will be present with His people at the Second Advent, guaranteeing their deliverance and restoration. The passage speaks of a supernatural regathering of Israel (v. 10) and a spiritual regeneration of her people (v. 12).

Zechariah 11:4-14 The rejection of Christ, the Good Shepherd, at His first coming is depicted. The breaking of the rods (vv. 7-8) symbolizes His temporary rejection of Israel after His own rejection (vv. 9-10) was accomplished by a payment of "30 pieces of silver" (v. 12; Matt. 27:3-10). Zechariah 11:13 was fulfilled when, after Judas had hanged himself, the chief priests bought the potter's field (Matt. 27:9–10; Jer. 32:6-9).

Zechariah 11:15-17 While rejecting the Good Shepherd, the people accept a bad shepherd, the Antichrist. His doom is certain, however, in light of the "woe" that is pronounced on him.

Zechariah 12:1-9 Jerusalem will be surrounded but delivered by her Lord, a reference again to the Second Coming.

Zechariah 12:11-14 There will be a great national conversion at the return of Christ. All of the passages which speak of national regeneration will be fulfilled at this time.

Zechariah 13:1 The fountain opened for Israel's cleansing refers to Christ's work on the cross. Flowing sources of water were scarce in ancient Palestine. The ever-flowing, cleansing fountain, a much-desired water supply, forms a perfect picture of spiritual cleansing from the dirtiness of sin.

Zechariah 13:6-7 The cleanser from idolatry is Christ who is described in His death (v. 7a) and in His deity (v. 7b).

Zechariah 14:3 Christ will intervene with deliverance when Jerusalem is besieged for the last time at the end of the Tribulation.

Zechariah 14:4-7 The time of the second advent of Christ is vividly described: its place, the Mount of Olives; its effect, a massive earthquake; its participants, Christ, His angels and saints; and its purpose, to deliver His people and eradicate their enemies.

Zechariah 14:9-11 Christ will reign during the Millennium as the absolute Monarch of the world, with Jerusalem as His capital. There will be one King, one government, one religion, and one unified land.

There can be little question that these prophecies must have a tremendous bearing on any attempts to describe the work of Christ, either past or future. It is to our shame as Christians that we have so often neglected this rich picture of our Lord in His suffering and triumph.

purge. " 'And it shall come to pass, that in all the land,' saith the LORD, 'two parts therein shall be cut off and die, but the third shall be left therein' " (13:8).

However, the one third shall be saved. *"And I will bring the third part through the fire, and will refine them as silver is refined, and will try them as gold is tried. They shall call on My name, and I will hear them. I will say, 'It is My people'; and they shall say, 'The LORD is my God' " (v. 9).*

The bereavement of Israel. When He comes again, Israel will finally recognize Him and mourn over their heinous national crime of rexicide, the killing of one's own king.

"And they shall look upon Me whom they have pierced, and they shall mourn for Him, as one mourneth for his only son" (12:10; see also vv. 12-14).

The Battle of Armageddon. Jerusalem will be surrounded and occupied by the Antichrist. *"Behold, I will make Jerusalem a cup of trembling unto all the people round about, when they shall be in the siege both against Judah and against Jerusalem. And in that day will I make Jerusalem a burdensome stone for all people. All that burden themselves with it shall be cut in pieces, though all the people of the earth be gathered together against it" (vv. 2-3).*

"For I will gather all nations against Jerusalem to battle; and the city shall be taken, and the houses rifled, and the women ravished; and half of the city shall go forth into captivity, and the residue of the people shall not be cut off from the city" (14:2).

Christ will touch down on the Mount of Olives to personally lead the battle against His enemies. *"Then shall the LORD go forth, and fight against those nations, as when He fought in the day of battle. And His feet shall stand in that day upon the Mount of Olives, which is before Jerusalem on the east, and the Mount of Olives shall cleave in the midst thereof toward the east and toward the west, and there shall be a very great valley; and half of the mountain shall remove toward the north, and half of it toward the south" (vv. 3-4).*

He will smite them with a divine plague. *" 'In that day,' saith the LORD, 'I will smite every horse with astonishment, and his rider with madness. And I will open Mine eyes upon the house of Judah, and will smite every horse of the people with blindness' " (12:4).*

"And this shall be the plague wherewith the LORD will smite all the people that have fought against Jerusalem. Their flesh shall consume away while they stand upon their feet, and their eyes shall consume away in their holes, and their tongue shall consume away in their mouth" (14:12).

"And it shall come to pass in that day, that I will seek to destroy all the nations that come against Jerusalem" (12:9).

The Bow of victory. This Bow is, of course, the Son of God. We are assured of His deity because of the Father's statement in 13:7: *" 'The Man who is My fellow,' saith the LORD of hosts."* This is literally translated, *"The Man who is My equal."* From the bow of God this avenging Arrow comes to earth.

The blessings of God. Israel will be gathered. *"And I will strengthen the house of Judah, and I will save the house of Joseph, and I will bring them again to place them; for I have mercy upon them. And they shall be as though I had not cast them off; for I am the LORD their God, and will hear them. . . . I will hiss for them, and gather them; for I have redeemed them; and they shall increase as they have increased" (10:6, 8).*

God Himself will become Jerusalem's Defender. *"In that day shall the LORD defend the inhabitants of Jerusalem; and he that is feeble among them at that day shall be as David; and the house of David shall be as God, as the Angel of the LORD before them" (12:8).*

Israel will be purified. *"In that day there shall be a fountain opened to the house of David and to the inhabitants of Jerusalem for sin and for uncleanness" (13:1).*

Christ Himself will rule. *"And the LORD shall be King over all the earth. In that day shall there be one LORD, and His name one" (14:9).*

All nations will worship Him. *"And it shall come to pass, that everyone that is left of all the nations which came against Jerusalem shall even go up from year to year to worship the King, the LORD of hosts, and to keep the Feast of Tabernacles" (v. 16).*

Living waters will flow from the Mediterranean to the Dead Sea. *"And it shall be in that day, that living waters shall go out from Jerusalem; half of them toward the former sea, and half of them toward the hinder sea; in summer and in winter shall it be" (v. 8).*

Every object will be holy. *"In that day shall there be upon the bells of the horses, HOLINESS UNTO THE LORD: and the pots in the LORD's house shall be like the bowls before the altar. Yea, every pot in Jerusalem and in Judah shall be holiness unto the LORD of hosts; and all they that sacrifice shall come and take of them, and seethe therein. And in that day there shall be no more the Canaanite in the house of the LORD of hosts" (vv. 20-21).*

The Deliverance of Jerusalem at the Second Coming

COMMENTS

There is an important passage in Zechariah which speaks at some length of the deliverance of Jerusalem at the time of Christ's return to the earth (12:1-9). It is worthy of additional comment because Jerusalem is the scene of the final battle, the Battle of Armageddon. It is, therefore, crucial to see how far the Lord intends to protect His people. This passage provides, as no other does, an insight into the Lord's commitment to Jerusalem's deliverance. In this passage, the prophet describes Jerusalem and her victory over her enemies under several vivid figures. First, Jerusalem is compared to a cup that all the nations will be forced to drink (v. 2). The cup is used throughout Scripture as a symbol of judgment (and sometimes of blessing) which will befall a man or nation (Ps. 75:8; Isa. 51:17, 22, etc.). The picture is that of a cup of wine that someone is being forced to drink against their will. Occasionally when this figure of speech is used, it is added that the recipient will have to drink it down to the very dregs, an amplified description of the severity of the judgment (Ps. 75:8). The contents of the cup represent the Lord's judgment, and the forced consumption of them the inevitable reception of that judgment.

A second illustration compares Jerusalem to an immovable rock which the nations will unwisely try to move (Zech. 12:3). It is as though God gives the enemies of Jerusalem an incurable hernia. The nations will strain themselves into irreversible injury and destruction by attacking Jerusalem.

A third image of judgment on Jerusalem's enemies is found in the promise that the Lord will cause their horses to go blind and their cavalry men to be seized with madness (vv. 4-5). It is a clear picture of the fact that the nations' weapons will be rendered ineffective.

In the fourth illustration, Jerusalem is compared to a torch or firepot (v. 6). Their enemies are compared to sheaves of dried grain which are highly flammable. The Lord will light the torch, toss it into those sheaves, and it will consume them.

Finally, after using illustrations that show the ultimate destruction of Jerusalem's enemies, the prophet concludes the section with a promise of divine protection for Jerusalem's inhabitants (vv. 7-9). The Lord promises to shield His people so that the weakest, an infant or elderly person, will be as mighty as David, the great warrior.

One cannot read this passage without sensing the undying love that God has for the Holy City of Jerusalem. Though He has allowed it to suffer through the centuries, for His own mysterious purposes, He will not allow her to be obliterated by her enemies. In the final battle, He will be there to protect and deliver. Christians today should exhibit a similar devotion to Jerusalem, and we are in fact commanded to pray for the peace of this city (Ps. 122:6).

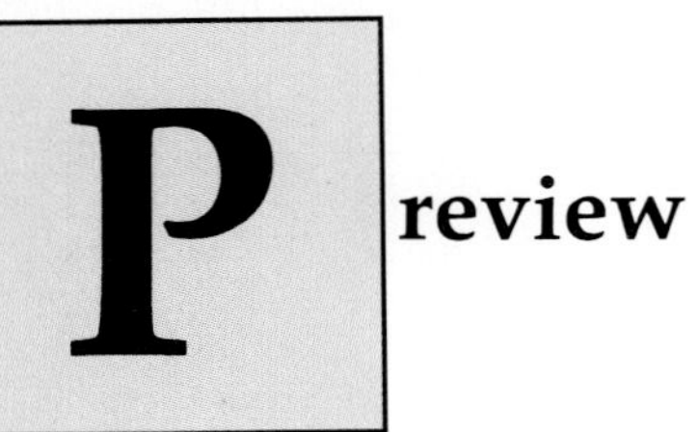

review

Final Facts on the First Phase: End of the Old Testament

BOOKS OF HAGGAI AND MALACHI

"For God so loved the world that He didn't send a Committee." Most could probably agree that this little proverb is both amusing and accurate. On many occasions, of course, committees are vital to progress. But for the most part, in His dealings with the world, God has bypassed committees and used individual leaders. In fact, the team concept seems to have been a divine favorite. We read of Moses and Joshua, Elijah and Elisha, Ezra and Nehemiah. Following the Babylonian Captivity return, God appointed yet another team, that of Zechariah and Haggai, to instruct and encourage the people in building the second temple. In a real sense these two men, especially Haggai, served as God's spiritual cheerleaders along this line.

Where does all this leave us? In a phrase, at the very end. After over 4,000 years of human history, recorded in 38 inspired books, we arrive at Malachi, the final pre-Bethlehem message from Almighty God to finite man.

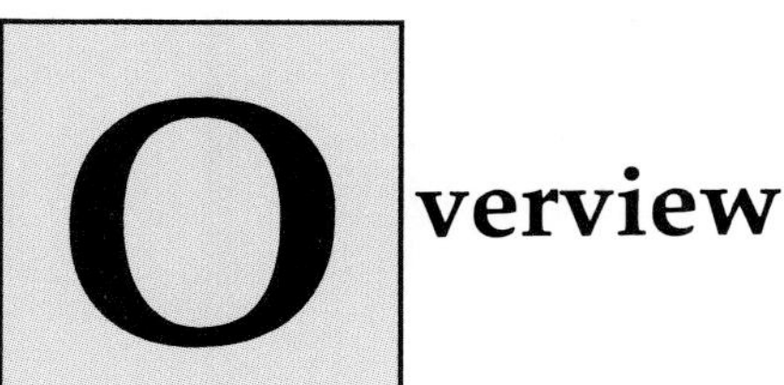

verview

<table>
<tr><td>SCRIPTURE</td><td colspan="4">Books of Haggai and Malachi</td></tr>
<tr><td>SUBJECT</td><td colspan="4">Ministries of Haggai and Malachi</td></tr>
<tr><td rowspan="5">SPECIFICS</td><td colspan="4">A final building and a final book</td></tr>
<tr><td colspan="2">Final Old Testament building</td><td colspan="2">Final Old Testament book</td></tr>
<tr><td rowspan="3">Book of Haggai</td><td>A tale of 3 temples</td><td rowspan="3">Book of Malachi</td><td>A tale of tenderness</td></tr>
<tr><td>First Old Testament temple: had been built by Solomon
Final Old Testament temple: needed to be built by Judah
Future temple: will be built by Christ</td><td>The love of God: Declared
Disbelieved
Demonstrated</td></tr>
<tr><td>The house of God</td><td>The heart of God</td></tr>
<tr><td>SAINTS AND SINNERS</td><td colspan="4">Haggai, Malachi</td></tr>
<tr><td rowspan="2">SENTENCE SUMMARIES</td><td>O.T. Verse</td><td colspan="3">"The LORD gave the Word; great was the company of those that published it" (Ps. 68:11).</td></tr>
<tr><td>N.T. Verses</td><td colspan="3">"Think not that I am come to destroy the Law or the Prophets; I am not come to destroy, but to fulfill. For verily I say unto you, 'Till heaven and earth pass, one jot or one tittle shall in no wise pass from the Law, till all be fulfilled' " (Matt. 5:17-18).</td></tr>
</table>

AGGAI

A September message, directed to the hands of the people. It said, "Perform." The people had about given up concerning the building of their temple. After 15 years it remained unfinished. Their lame excuse was, *"The time is not come, the time that the Lord's house be built" (Hag.1:2).* Because of this carelessness, God could not and would not bless them with either spiritual or financial prosperity.

"Is it time for you, O ye, to dwell in your ceiled houses, and this house lie waste? Now therefore thus saith the LORD of hosts, 'Consider your ways. Ye have sown much, and bring in little, ye eat, but ye have not enough; ye drink, but ye are not filled with drink; ye clothe you, but there is none warm; and he that earneth wages earneth wages to put it into a bag with holes' " (vv. 4-6).

God's advice to them was therefore to *" 'go up to the mountain, and bring wood, and build the house; and I will take pleasure in it, and I will be glorified,' saith the LORD" (v. 8).*

The spirits of Zerubbabel (the governor) and Joshua (the high priest) were then stirred up by the Lord. This godly pair thus led the people to finish building the temple. *"And the LORD stirred up the spirit of Zerubbabel the son of Shealtiel, governor of Judah, and the spirit of Joshua the son of Josedech, the high priest, and the spirit of all the remnant of the people; and they came and did work in the house of the LORD of hosts, their God" (v. 14).*

An October message, directed to the hearts of the people. It said, "Patience!" *"Who is left among you that saw this house in her first glory? And how do ye see it now? Is it not in your eyes in comparison of it as nothing? . . .*

"For thus saith the LORD of hosts, 'Yet once, it is a little while, and I will shake the heavens, and the earth, and the sea, and the dry land; and I will shake all nations, and the desire of all nations shall come; and I will fill this house with glory,' saith the LORD of hosts. . . . 'The glory of this latter house shall be greater than of the former,' saith the LORD of hosts, 'and in this place will I give peace,' saith the LORD of hosts" (2:3, 6-7, 9).

In spite of the insignificant temple they had just built, as we have already seen (Ezra 3:8-13), there was weeping as well as joy at the dedication of the temple during Zerubbabel's time as some of the old men remembered the glories of Solomon's temple. The new temple was far inferior to that temple in size and cost. However, Haggai attempted to encourage even the old men as he spoke of the magnificent millennial temple that would someday be built (Hag. 2:9).

A December message, directed to the head of the people. It said, "Ponder!" There were facts Haggai desired that the people ponder over. God asked Judah to answer two questions: If one of you is carrying a holy sacrifice in his robes, and happens to brush against some bread, or wine, or meat, will it too become holy? The answer, of course, was, No, holiness does not pass to other things that way.

If someone touches a dead person, and so becomes ceremonially impure, and then brushes against something, does it become contaminated? Here the answer was yes! The point God was making here is that whatever righteousness the nation Israel might have once possessed was not automatically transferred on them at this time. But their own unrighteousness was affecting both them and their children.

God promised them that because of their decision to finish the temple, He would bless them from that day on, even before the structure was completed. Someday God would destroy all those Gentile nations which had afflicted Israel throughout the years.

"I will shake the heavens and the earth; and I will overthrow the throne of kingdoms, and I will destroy the strength of the kingdoms of the heathen; and I will overthrow the chariots, and those that ride in them; and the horses and their riders shall come down, everyone by the sword of his brother" (vv. 21-22; see also Heb. 12:26; Rev. 16:18-20).

" 'In that day,' saith the LORD of hosts, 'will I take thee, O Zerubbabel, My servant . . . and will make thee as a signet; for I have chosen thee' " (Hag. 2:23).

Some believe that Zerubbabel will be God's prime minister during the Millennium.

Haggai and Malachi: A Stirring Exhortation and a Loving Rebuke

COMMENTS

There are many contrasts between Haggai and Malachi. Haggai's four messages are all dated; the date of Malachi's prophecy is a matter of controversy, though correlation with the Book of Nehemiah would suggest a date of 432 B.C. Haggai dealt with a single theme, the rebuilding of the temple and its glorification; Malachi preached on a number of abuses in his society and also predicted the forerunner to the Messiah. Haggai's messages might be called exhortations; Malachi's are loving rebukes. Though the two prophets contrast greatly in their approaches, each was God's man preaching God's messages for his day.

Haggai's four messages are the most precisely dated in the Old Testament. It is known that the Jews adopted the Babylonian system of chronology during the Exile. Since all of Haggai's sermons are pegged to specific days in Darius' reign, we can date them accurately to within one day, all during 520 B.C.: August 29, October 17, and two messages on December 18.

In the first message (1:1-15) there are three specific people addressed: Zerubbabel, the civil leader; Joshua, the religious leader; and the people in general. The heart of the message was directed toward the people's excuse: "The time is not come . . . that the LORD's house should be built" (v. 2). Fifteen years had passed since the foundation of the temple had been laid. The people had been busy building their own houses; God's house had been forgotten. Haggai also reminded the people that God had placed a curse on them until they put their priorities in right order (vv. 5-6). Surprisingly enough, the people obeyed and began the work (v. 12).

The second message (2:1-9) was one of encouragement. There were evidently a few who remembered the Solomonic temple which had been destroyed 66 years earlier. They were tempted to live in the past and compare the present, smaller temple unfavorably with the past, glorious Solomonic temple (cf. Ezra 3:8-13). In this message God exhorted the builders not to make such discouraging comparisons and also promised that He would glorify the temple in His timing, i.e., during the Millennium (Hag. 2:6-9).

The third message (vv. 10-19) was one in which the prophet emphasized the theme that obedience brings blessing. Two questions were addressed to the priests in order to drive home this reality: first, holiness cannot be transmitted (v. 12); second, defilement can be transmitted (v. 13). The application of the two points is simple: (1) Israel's calling as a holy nation (Ex. 19:6) did not transfer holiness to their actions. (2) Their defilement, caused by misplaced priorities, had made everything they undertook unclean. Haggai 2:15-19 cites specific examples of how God judged them for their sin and blessed them for their obedience.

The fourth message (vv. 20-23) was addressed to an individual, Zerubbabel. There are two key promises in the message: Gentile nations will be overthrown (vv. 20-22) and the Davidic kingdom (2 Sam. 7:16) will be established (Hag. 2:23). Some scholars say Zerubbabel will personally fulfill this prophecy; others say that he is only a type of Messiah. In any case, it is a reference to the glorious kingdom to be established in the Millennium.

Malachi's prophecy is not organized around specific messages. Therefore, the best way to study the Book of Malachi is by looking at its three key themes: the love of God, the sins of the people, and the coming of the Day of the Lord. First, God's love was demonstrated in His election of Jacob (Mal. 1:2-3). It is important to remember that "to love" in the Old Testament means "to choose for intimate fellowship" and "to hate" means "to reject from intimate fellowship." God chose Jacob, the ancestor of the Israelites, for His own special purposes. This demonstrated His love for them.

The second theme, the current sins of the people, was explained fully and takes up most of the book. A special teaching device of Malachi was the question and answer approach. At least eight times in the book he employed a question and answer to isolate what the people were thinking. The questions of the people or priests were always permeated with pretended innocence (cf. v. 6) which Malachi easily showed to be false. In spite of the people's grievous sins, the book always has the tone of the appeal of a loving father.

Finally, the book closes with an ominous note: the certainty of the Day of the Lord (3:1; 4). It will be a day of judgment for sinners (v. 1) but a day of exaltation for the righteous (vv. 2-3). The Lord also promises a forerunner to the Messiah who will come in the power of Elijah (3:1; 4:5-6). It is significant that this prophecy, the last in the Old Testament revelation, is fulfilled in the person of John the Baptist, the first person with whom two of the four Gospels open (Mark 1:2; Luke 1:17).

ALACHI

THE LOVE OF GOD STATED

In the second verse of his book, Malachi listed the first of six rather flippant questions the carnal Israelites had required of God. Each question was the result of a previous clear statement from God. Question: In what way hast Thou loved us?

Answer: I have demonstrated this love by choosing as My special servants Jacob and his descendants instead of Esau and his descendants.

Question: In what way have we despised Thy name?

Answer: You have despised My name by refusing to give Me the honor a son would give to his father and that of a servant to his master.

Question: In what way have we polluted Thee?

Answer: You offer Me defiled food and blemished animals.

Question: In what way have we wearied Thee?

Answer: You have wearied Me by not only trying to make evil good, but by implying that I delight in evil because I do not dispense immediate justice.

Question: How have we robbed Thee?

Answer: You have robbed Me in unpaid tithes.

Question: What have we spoken so much against Thee?

Answer: You have spoken against Me in saying it is vain to serve Me unless I bless you with immediate prosperity.

THE LOVE OF GOD SCORNED

By the prophets. They cheated the Lord through their shabby offerings. They had offered lame and sick animals to God. These cheap sacrifices were refused by the Lord who challenged them if they dared to *"offer it now unto thy governor; will he be pleased with thee, or accept thy person?" (Mal. 1:8)*

They had not offered the proper honor and respect to God that a child should give to his father, a servant should render to his master, or a citizen should pay to his king.

" 'For the priest's lips should keep knowledge, and they should seek the Law at his mouth, for he is the messenger of the LORD of hosts. But ye are departed out of the way; ye have caused many to stumble at the Law; ye have corrupted the covenant of Levi,' saith the LORD of hosts. 'Therefore have I also made you contemptible and base before all the people, according as ye have not kept My ways, but have been partial in the Law' " (2:7-9).

"Have we not all one father? Hath not one God created us? Why do we deal treacherously every man against his brother, by profaning the covenant of our fathers?" (v. 10)

"Judah hath dealt treacherously, and an abomination is committed in Israel and in Jerusalem; for Judah hath profaned the holiness of the LORD which He loved, and hath married the daughter of a strange god" (v. 11).

"Yet, ye say, 'Wherefore?' Because the LORD hath been witness between thee and the wife of thy youth, against whom thou hast dealt treacherously; yet is she thy companion, and the wife of thy covenant" (v. 14).

" 'Will a man rob God? Yet ye have robbed Me.' But ye say, 'Wherein have we robbed Thee?' 'In tithes and offerings. Ye are cursed with a curse, for ye have robbed Me, even this whole nation. Bring ye all the tithes into the storehouse, that there may be meat in Mine house, and prove Me now herewith,' saith the LORD of hosts, 'if I will not open you the windows of heaven, and pour you out a blessing, that there shall not be room enough to receive it' " (3:8-10).

"Ye have said, 'It is vain to serve God, and what profit is it that we have kept His ordinance, and that we have walked mournfully before the LORD of hosts?' " (v. 14)

THE LOVE OF GOD SHOWN

By remembering His own saints. "Then they that feared the LORD spake often one to another; and the LORD hearkened, and heard it, and a book of remembrance was written before Him from them that feared the LORD, and that thought upon His name.

" 'And they shall be Mine,' saith the LORD of hosts, 'in that day when I make up My jewels; and I will spare them, as a man spareth his own son that serveth him' " (vv. 16-17).

By sending His own Son. His first coming was introduced by John the Baptist. *" 'Behold, I will send My messenger, and he shall prepare the way before Me: and the Lord, whom ye seek, shall suddenly come to His temple, even the messenger of the covenant, whom ye delight in. Behold, he shall come,' saith the* LORD *of hosts" (v. 1).*

His second coming will be introduced by Elijah the prophet. *"Behold, I will send you Elijah the prophet before the coming of the great and dreadful Day of the* LORD. *And He shall turn the heart of the fathers to the children, and the heart of the children to their fathers, lest I come and smite the earth with a curse" (4:5-6).*

Elijah, thus, will be awarded the privilege of preparing this cruel, corrupt, and cursed old world for its greatest, grandest, and most glorious moment—the visible appearance of the King of kings and Lord of lords.

He will come to punish the Gentiles. *" 'For, behold, the day cometh, that shall burn as an oven; and all the proud, yea, and all that do wickedly, shall be stubble. And the day that cometh shall burn them up,' saith the* LORD *of hosts, 'that it shall leave them neither root nor branch' " (v. 1).*

He will come to purify Israel. *"But who may abide the day of His coming? And who shall stand when He appeareth? For He is like a refiner's fire, and like fullers' soap. And He shall sit as a refiner and purifier of silver; and He shall purify the sons of Levi, and purge them as gold and silver, that they may offer unto the* LORD *an offering in righteousness. Then shall the offering of Judah and Jerusalem be pleasant unto the* LORD, *as in the days of old, and as in former years" (3:2-4).*

"But unto you that fear My name shall the Sun of righteousness arise with healing in His wings; and ye shall go forth, and grow up as calves of the stall" (4:2).

" 'And all nations shall call you blessed. For ye shall be a delightsome land,' saith the LORD *of hosts" (3:12).*

He shall come to publish His great name. *" 'For from the rising of the sun even unto the going down of the same My name shall be great among the Gentiles; and in every place incense shall be offered unto My name, and a pure offering. For My name shall be great among the heathen,' saith the* LORD *of hosts" (1:11).*

Malachi's Prophecy of Elijah

COMMENTS

Two key prophecies in Malachi have intrigued Bible students since the time of the apostles: the prophecy of a messenger in 3:1 and the prophecy of Elijah in 4:5-6. Fortunately, both of these passages are quoted in the New Testament by Jesus and applied to John the Baptist. Malachi 3:1 is quoted in Matthew 11:10; Malachi 4:5-6 is referred to in Matthew 17:9-13; Mark 9:9-13; and Luke 1:17. The passage in Luke is an angelic announcement to Zechariah predicting that his son, John, would minister in the spirit of Elijah. Certainly this is meant to refer to Malachi's prophecy. The later words of Jesus to His disciples, however, close the case on the identity of the revived Elijah. Jesus plainly stated that Elijah had already come and His disciples knew that He spoke of John the Baptist (Matt. 17:9-13; Mark 9:9-13).

In what sense then was John the Baptist a messenger? A messenger is simply one who delivers a pronouncement on behalf of another. John's role, therefore, was to deliver the message that the Messiah was coming. This was precisely how John viewed his ministry. He denied being the Messiah but claimed that his role was that of a herald calling to men to prepare for the Lord's coming (John 1:19-24). His role was simply to point men to Jesus (v. 29).

In what sense did John come in the power and spirit of Elijah? Just as Elijah spoke authoritatively for God, so did John. Just as Elijah was able to capture the hearts of the people, so did John. While he was not a literal reincarnation of Elijah, John did come in his spirit and for similar purposes.

One problem remains: in Matthew 11:14 Jesus seems to hedge on the idea of identifying John as Elijah. Here Jesus is only willing to say that John is Elijah if the Jews will accept him as such. The solution to this problem is found in realizing that John's role as Elijah was not fulfilled, just as John's preaching (and Jesus' also) of the nearness of the kingdom was not fulfilled. If the Jews had accepted Jesus as Messiah, then John's role as Elijah would have been completed and his messages on the approaching kingdom of God would have been fulfilled. Nevertheless, the Jews did not accept Jesus as Messiah, the kingdom was not set up, and the Elijah prophecy was left unfulfilled. It may await fulfillment in another messenger, perhaps in the Tribulation. On the other hand, one way to view it, possibly, is as completely fulfilled in John but with a long gap (i.e., the Church Age) between that fulfillment and the coming of the Day of the Lord which he proclaimed.

Regardless of which view one takes, there can be little doubt that God held this prophecy of Elijah's return in great significance. It is the last prophetic oracle of the Old Testament and the first of the New (Mark 1:1-8). As such it stands as a clear reminder not only of the unity of the Testaments, but especially of the divine stamp of approval on John's role as forerunner to God's Anointed One.

INDEX

A

B

C

D

E

F

G

H

K

L

M

N

O

P

R

S

T

U

V

W

Z